Lecture Notes in Computer Science   12651

Advanced Research in Computing and Software Science

Subline of Lecture Notes in Computer Science

More information about this subseries at http://www.springer.com/series/7407

Jan Friso Groote · Kim Guldstrand Larsen (Eds.)

Tools and Algorithms for the Construction and Analysis of Systems

27th International Conference, TACAS 2021
Held as Part of the European Joint Conferences
on Theory and Practice of Software, ETAPS 2021
Luxembourg City, Luxembourg, March 27 – April 1, 2021
Proceedings, Part I

 Springer

Editors
Jan Friso Groote
Eindhoven University of Technology
Eindhoven, The Netherlands

Kim Guldstrand Larsen
Aalborg University
Aalborg East, Denmark

ISSN 0302-9743   ISSN 1611-3349   (electronic)
Lecture Notes in Computer Science
ISBN 978-3-030-72015-5   ISBN 978-3-030-72016-2   (eBook)
https://doi.org/10.1007/978-3-030-72016-2

LNCS Sublibrary: SL1 – Theoretical Computer Science and General Issues

This Springer imprint is published by the registered company Springer Nature Switzerland AG
The registered company address is: Gewerbestrasse 11, 6330 Cham, Switzerland

ETAPS Foreword

Welcome to the 24th ETAPS! ETAPS 2021 was originally planned to take place in Luxembourg in its beautiful capital Luxembourg City. Because of the Covid-19 pandemic, this was changed to an online event.

ETAPS 2021 was the 24th instance of the European Joint Conferences on Theory and Practice of Software. ETAPS is an annual federated conference established in 1998, and consists of four conferences: ESOP, FASE, FoSSaCS, and TACAS. Each conference has its own Program Committee (PC) and its own Steering Committee (SC). The conferences cover various aspects of software systems, ranging from theoretical computer science to foundations of programming languages, analysis tools, and formal approaches to software engineering. Organising these conferences in a coherent, highly synchronised conference programme enables researchers to participate in an exciting event, having the possibility to meet many colleagues working in different directions in the field, and to easily attend talks of different conferences. On the weekend before the main conference, numerous satellite workshops take place that attract many researchers from all over the globe.

ETAPS 2021 received 260 submissions in total, 115 of which were accepted, yielding an overall acceptance rate of 44.2%. I thank all the authors for their interest in ETAPS, all the reviewers for their reviewing efforts, the PC members for their contributions, and in particular the PC (co-)chairs for their hard work in running this entire intensive process. Last but not least, my congratulations to all authors of the accepted papers!

ETAPS 2021 featured the unifying invited speakers Scott Smolka (Stony Brook University) and Jane Hillston (University of Edinburgh) and the conference-specific invited speakers Işil Dillig (University of Texas at Austin) for ESOP and Willem Visser (Stellenbosch University) for FASE. Inivited tutorials were provided by Erika Ábrahám (RWTH Aachen University) on analysis of hybrid systems and Madhusudan Parthasararathy (University of Illinois at Urbana-Champaign) on combining machine learning and formal methods.

ETAPS 2021 was originally supposed to take place in Luxembourg City, Luxembourg organized by the SnT - Interdisciplinary Centre for Security, Reliability and Trust, University of Luxembourg. University of Luxembourg was founded in 2003. The university is one of the best and most international young universities with 6,700 students from 129 countries and 1,331 academics from all over the globe. The local organisation team consisted of Peter Y.A. Ryan (general chair), Peter B. Roenne (organisation chair), Joaquin Garcia-Alfaro (workshop chair), Magali Martin (event manager), David Mestel (publicity chair), and Alfredo Rial (local proceedings chair).

ETAPS 2021 was further supported by the following associations and societies: ETAPS e.V., EATCS (European Association for Theoretical Computer Science), EAPLS (European Association for Programming Languages and Systems), and EASST (European Association of Software Science and Technology).

The ETAPS Steering Committee consists of an Executive Board, and representatives of the individual ETAPS conferences, as well as representatives of EATCS, EAPLS, and EASST. The Executive Board consists of Holger Hermanns (Saarbrücken), Marieke Huisman (Twente, chair), Jan Kofron (Prague), Barbara König (Duisburg), Gerald Lüttgen (Bamberg), Caterina Urban (INRIA), Tarmo Uustalu (Reykjavik and Tallinn), and Lenore Zuck (Chicago).

Other members of the steering committee are: Patricia Bouyer (Paris), Einar Broch Johnsen (Oslo), Dana Fisman (Be'er Sheva), Jan Friso Groote (Eindhoven), Esther Guerra (Madrid), Reiko Heckel (Leicester), Joost-Pieter Katoen (Aachen and Twente), Stefan Kiefer (Oxford), Fabrice Kordon (Paris), Jan Křetínský (Munich), Kim G. Larsen (Aalborg), Tiziana Margaria (Limerick), Andrew M. Pitts (Cambridge), Grigore Roşu (Illinois), Peter Ryan (Luxembourg), Don Sannella (Edinburgh), Lutz Schröder (Erlangen), Ilya Sergey (Singapore), Mariëlle Stoelinga (Twente), Gabriele Taentzer (Marburg), Christine Tasson (Paris), Peter Thiemann (Freiburg), Jan Vitek (Prague), Anton Wijs (Eindhoven), Manuel Wimmer (Linz), and Nobuko Yoshida (London).

I'd like to take this opportunity to thank all the authors, attendees, organizers of the satellite workshops, and Springer-Verlag GmbH for their support. I hope you all enjoyed ETAPS 2021.

Finally, a big thanks to Peter, Peter, Magali and their local organisation team for all their enormous efforts to make ETAPS a fantastic online event. I hope there will be a next opportunity to host ETAPS in Luxembourg.

February 2021

Marieke Huisman
ETAPS SC Chair
ETAPS e.V. President

Preface

TACAS 2021 was the 27th edition of the International Conference on Tools and Algorithms for the Construction and Analysis of Systems conference series. TACAS 2021 was part of the 24th European Joint Conferences on Theory and Practice of Software (ETAPS 2021), which although originally planned to take place in Luxembourg City, was held as an online event on March 27 to April 1 due the the COVID-19 pandemic.

TACAS is a forum for researchers, developers, and users interested in rigorously based tools and algorithms for the construction and analysis of systems. The conference aims to bridge the gaps between different communities with this common interest and to support them in their quest to improve the utility, reliability, flexibility, and efficiency of tools and algorithms for building computer-controlled systems. There were four types of submissions for TACAS:

- Research papers advancing the theoretical foundations for the construction and analysis of systems.
- Case study papers with an emphasis on a real-world setting.
- Regular tool papers presenting a new tool, a new tool component, or novel extensions to an existing tool and requiring an artifact submission.
- Tool demonstration papers focusing on the usage aspects of tools, also subject to the artifact submission requirement.

This year 141 papers were submitted to TACAS, consisting of 90 research papers, 29 regular tool papers, 16 tool demo papers, and 6 case study papers. Authors were allowed to submit up to four papers. Each paper was reviewed by three Program Committee (PC) members, who made extensive use of subreviewers.

Similarly to previous years, it was possible to submit an artifact alongside a paper, which was mandatory for regular tool and tool demo papers. An artifact might consist of a tool, models, proofs, or other data required for validation of the results of the paper. The Artifact Evaluation Committee (AEC) was tasked with reviewing the artifacts, based on their documentation, ease of use, and, most importantly, whether the results presented in the corresponding paper could be accurately reproduced. Most of the evaluation was carried out using a standardised virtual machine to ensure consistency of the results, except for those artifacts that had special hardware requirements.

The evaluation consisted of two rounds. The first round was carried out in parallel with the work of the PC. The judgment of the AEC was communicated to the PC and weighed in their discussion. The second round took place after paper acceptance notifications were sent out; authors of accepted research papers who did not submit an artifact in the first round could submit their artifact here. In total, 72 artifacts were submitted (63 in the first round and 9 in the second), of which 57 were accepted and 15 rejected. This corresponds to an acceptance rate of 79 percent. Papers with an accepted artifact include a badge on the first page.

Selected authors were requested to provide a rebuttal for both papers and artifacts in case a review gave rise to questions. In total 166 rebuttals were provided. Using the review reports and rebuttals the Programme and the Artifact Evaluation Committees extensively discussed the papers and artifacts and ultimately decided to accept 32 research papers, 7 tool papers, 6 tool demos, and 2 case studies.

Besides the regular conference papers, this two-volume proceedings also contains 8 short papers that describe the participating verification systems and a competition report presenting the results of the 10th SV-COMP, the competition on automatic software verifiers for C and Java programs. These papers were reviewed by a separate program committee (PC); each of the papers was assessed by at least three reviewers. A total of 30 verification systems with developers from 11 countries entered the systematic comparative evaluation, including four submissions from industry. Two sessions in the TACAS program were reserved for the presentation of the results: (1) a summary by the competition chair and of the participating tools by the developer teams in the first session, and (2) an open community meeting in the second session.

March/April 2021

Jan Friso Groote
Kim Guldstrand Larsen
Frédéric Lang
Thierry Lecomte
Thomas Neele
Peter Gjøl Jensen
Dirk Beyer
Alfredo Rial

Organization

Program Committee (TACAS)

Christel Baier	TU Dresden, Germany
Dirk Beyer	LMU Munich, Germany
Armin Biere	Johannes Kepler University Linz, Austria
Valentina Castiglioni	Reykjavik University, Iceland
Alessandro Cimatti	Fondazione Bruno Kessler, Italy
Rance Cleaveland	University of Maryland, USA
Pedro R. D'Argenio	Universidad Nacional de Córdoba - CONICET, Argentina
Yuxin Deng	East China Normal University, China
Carla Ferreira	Universidade NOVA de Lisboa, Portugal
Goran Frehse	ENSTA Paris, France
Susanne Graf	Université Grenoble Alpes/CNRS/VERIMAG, France
Jan Friso Groote (Chair)	Eindhoven University of Technology, Netherlands
Orna Grumberg	Technion - Israel Institute of Technology, Israel
Kim Guldstrand Larsen (Chair)	Aalborg University, Denmark
Klaus Havelund	Jet Propulsion Laboratory, USA
Holger Hermanns	Saarland University, Germany
Peter Höfner	Australian National University, Australia
Hossein Hojjat	Rochester Institute of Technology, USA
Falk Howar	TU Dortmund, Germany
David N. Jansen	Institute of Software, Chinese Academy of Sciences, China
Marcin Jurdziński	The University of Warwick, Great Britain
Joost-Pieter Katoen	RWTH Aachen/Universiteit Twente, Germany/Netherlands
Jeroen J. A. Keiren	Eindhoven University of Technology, Netherlands
Sophia Knight	University of Minnesota, USA
Laura Kovács	Vienna University of Technology, Austria
Jan Křetínský	Technical University of Munich, Germany
Alfons Laarman	Leiden University, Netherlands
Frédéric Lang	Inria Grenoble - Rhône-Alpes/CONVECS, France
Thierry Lecomte	ClearSy Systems Engineering, France
Xinxin Liu	Institute of Software, Chinese Academy of Sciences, China
Mieke Massink	CNR-ISTI, Italy
Radu Mateescu	Inria, France
Jun Pang	University of Luxembourg, Luxembourg

Dave Parker	University of Birmingham, Great Britain
Jaco van de Pol	Aarhus University, Denmark
Natasha Sharygina	Università della Svizzera Italiana, Switzerland
Jan Strejček	Masaryk University, Czech Republic
Antti Valmari	University of Jyväskylä, Finland
Björn Victor	Uppsala University, Sweden
Sarah Winkler	Free University of Bozen-Bolzano, Italy

Artifact Evaluation Committee – AEC

Elvio Gilberto Amparore	University of Turin, Italy
Haniel Barbosa	Universidade Federal de Minas Gerais, France
František Blahoudek	University of Texas at Austin, USA
Olav Bunte	Eindhoven University of Technology, Netherlands
Damien Busatto-Gaston	Université Libre de Bruxelles, Belgium
Nathalie Cauchi	University of Oxford, Great Britain
Jesús Mauricio Chimento	KTH, Sweden
Joshua Dawes	University of Luxembourg, Luxembourg
Mathias Fleury	Johannes Kepler University Linz, Austria
Daniel J. Fremont	University of California, Santa Cruz, USA
Manuel Gieseking	University of Oldenburg, Germany
Peter Gjøl Jensen (Chair)	Aalborg University, Denmark
Kush Grover	Technical University of Munich, Germany
Hans-Dieter Hiep	CWI, Netherlands
Daniela Kaufmann	Johannes Kepler University Linz, Austria
Mitja Kulczynski	Kiel University, Germany
Alfons Laarman	Leiden University, Netherlands
Luca Laurenti	University of Oxford, Great Britain
Maurice Laveaux	Eindhoven University of Technology, Netherlands
Yong Li	Institute of Software, Chinese Academy of Sciences, China
Debasmita Lohar	Max Planck Institute for Software Systems, Germany
Viktor Malík	Brno University of Technology, Czech Republic
Joshua Moerman	RWTH Aachen University, Germany
Stefanie Mohr	Technische Universität München, Germany
Marco Muñiz	Aalborg University, Denmark
Thomas Neele (Chair)	Royal Holloway University of London, Great Britain
Wytse Oortwijn	University of Twente, Netherlands
Elizabeth Polgreen	University of Edinburgh, Great Britain
José Proenca	CISTER-ISEP and HASLab-INESC TEC, Portugal
Etienne Renault	LRDE, France
Alceste Scalas	Technical University of Denmark, Denmark
Morten Konggaard Schou	Aalborg University, Denmark
Veronika Šoková	Brno University of Technology, Czech Republic
Yoni Zohar	Stanford University, USA

Program Committee and Jury – SV-COMP

Pavel Andrianov (CPALockator)	ISP RAS, Russia
Philipp Berger (NITWIT)	RWTH Aachen, Germany
Dirk Beyer (Chair)	LMU Munich, Germany
Marek Chalupa (Symbiotic)	Masaryk University, Brno, Czech Republic
Lucas Cordeiro (ESBMC-kind)	University of Manchester, Great Britain
Priyanka Darke (VeriAbs)	Tata Consultancy Services, India
Daniel Dietsch (UTaipan)	University of Freiburg, Germany
Gidon Ernst (Korn)	LMU Munich, Germany
Ákos Hajdu (Gazer-Theta)	BME, Hungary
Matthias Heizmann (UAutomizer)	University of Freiburg, Germany
Hossein Hojjat (JayHorn)	Rochester Institute of Technology, USA
Stephan Holzner (CPA-Seq)	LMU Munich, Germany
Falk Howar (JDart)	TU Dortmund, Germany
Soha Hussein (Java Ranger)	University of Minnesota, USA
Omar Inverso (Lazy-CSeq)	Gran Sasso Science Institute, Italy
Saurabh Joshi (Pinaka)	IIT Hyderabad, India
Dominik Klumpp (UKojak)	University of Freiburg, Germany
Henrich Lauko (DIVINE)	Masaryk University, Brno, Czech Republic
Viktor Malík (2LS)	Brno University of Technology, Czech Republic
Felipe R. Monteiro (ESBMC-incr)	Amazon Web Services, USA
Vadim Mutilin (CPA-BAM-BnB)	ISP RAS, Russia
Hernán Ponce de León (Dartagnan)	Bundeswehr University Munich, Germany
Zvonimir Rakamaric (SMACK)	University of Utah, USA
Cedric Richter (PeSCo)	Paderborn University, Germany
Simmo Saan (rGoblint)	University of Tartu, Estonia
Peter Schrammel (JBMC)	University of Sussex/Diffblue, Great Britain
Martin Spiessl (Frama-C)	LMU Munich, Germany
Michael Tautschnig (CBMC)	Amazon Web Services, USA

Steering Committee

Dirk Beyer	LMU Munich, Germany
Rance Cleaveland	University of Maryland, USA
Holger Hermanns	Saarland University, Germany

Joost-Pieter Katoen (Chair)   RWTH Aachen/Universiteit Twente,
                                Germany/Netherlands
Kim Guldstrand Larsen   Aalborg University, Denmark
Bernhard Steffen   Technische Universität Dortmund, Germany

Additional Reviewers

Abate, Carmine
Achilleos, Antonis
Akshay, S.
Andriushchenko, Roman
André, Étienne
Asadi, Sepideh
Ashok, Pranav
Azeem, Muqsit
Bannister, Callum
Barnett, Lee
Basile, Davide
Batz, Kevin
Baumgartner, Peter
Becchi, Anna
ter Beek, Maurice H.
Bendík, Jaroslav
Bensalem, Saddek
van der Berg, Freark
Berg, Jeremias
Berger, Philipp
Bernardo, Marco
Biewer, Sebastian
Bischopink, Christopher
Blicha, Martin
Bønneland, Frederik M.
Bouvier, Pierre
Bozzano, Marco
Brellmann, David
Broccia, Giovanna
Budde, Carlos E.
Bursuc, Sergiu
Cassel, Sofia
Castro, Pablo
Chalupa, Marek
Chen, Mingshuai
Chiang, James
Ciancia, Vincenzo
Ciesielski, Maciej

Clement, Bradley
Coenen, Norine
Cubuktepe, Murat
Degiovanni, Renzo
Demasi, Ramiro
Dierl, Simon
Dixon, Alex
van Dijk, Tom
Donatelli, Susanna
Dongol, Brijesh
Edera, Alejandro
Eisentraut, Julia
Emmi, Michael
Evangelidis, Alexandros
Fedotov, Alexander
Fedyukovich, Grigory
Fehnker, Ansgar
Feng, Weizhi
Ferreira, Francisco
Fleury, Mathias
Freiberger, Felix
Frenkel, Hadar
Friedberger, Karlheinz
Fränzle, Martin
Funke, Florian
Gallá, Francesco
Garavel, Hubert
Geatti, Luca
Gengelbach, Arve
Goodloe, Alwyn
Goorden, Martijn
Goudsmid, Ohad
Griggio, Alberto
Groce, Alex
Grover, Kush
Hafidi, Yousra
Hallé, Sylvain
Hecking-Harbusch, Jesko

Heizmann, Matthias
Holzner, Stephan
Holík, Lukáš
Hyvärinen, Antti
Irfan, Ahmed
Javed, Omar
Jensen, Mathias Claus
Jonas, Martin
Junges, Sebastian
Käfer, Nikolai
Kanav, Sudeep
Kapus, Timotej
Kauffman, Sean
Khamespanah, Ehsan
Kheireddine, Anissa
Kiviriga, Andrej
Klauck, Michaela
Kobayashi, Naoki
Köhl, Maximilian Alexander
Kozachinskiy, Alexander
Kutsia, Temur
Lahkim Bennani, Ismail
Lammich, Peter
Lang, Frédéric
Lanotte, Ruggero
Latella, Diego
Laurenti, Luca
Ledent, Philippe
Lehtinen, Karoliina
Lemberger, Thomas
Li, Jianlin
Li, Qin
Li, Xie
Li, Xin
Lin, Shaokai
Lion, Benjamin
Liu, Jiaxiang
Liu, Wanwei
Loreti, Michele
Magnago, Enrico
Major, Juraj
Marché, Claude
Mariegaard, Anders
Marsso, Lina
Mauritz, Malte
McClurg, Jedidiah

Meggendorfer, Tobias
Metzger, Niklas
Meyer, Roland
Micheli, Andrea
Mittelmann, Munyque
Mizera, Andrzej
Moerman, Joshua
Mohr, Stefanie
Mora, Federico
Mover, Sergio
Mues, Malte
Muller, Lucie
Muroor-Nadumane, Ajay
Möhle, Sibylle
Neele, Thomas
Noll, Thomas
Norman, Gethin
Otoni, Rodrigo
Parys, Paweł
Pattinson, Dirk
Pavela, Jiří
Pena, Lucas
Pinault, Laureline
Piribauer, Jakob
Pirogov, Anton
Pommellet, Adrien
Quatmann, Tim
Rappoport, Omer
Raskin, Jean-François
Rothenberg, Bat-Chen
Rouquette, Nicolas
Rümmer, Philipp
S., Krishna
Šafránek, David
Sankaranarayanan, Sriram
Schallau, Till
Schupp, Stefan
Serwe, Wendelin
Shafiei, Nastaran
Shi, Xiaomu
Síč, Juraj
Sickert, Salomon
Singh, Gagandeep
Slivovsky, Friedrich
Sølvsten, Steffan
Song, Fu

Spel, Jip
Srivathsan, B.
Stankovic, Miroslav
Stock, Gregory
Strejček, Jan
Su, Cui
Suda, Martin
Sun, Jun
Svozil, Alexander
Tian, Chun
Tibo, Alessandro
Tini, Simone
Tonetta, Stefano
Trtík, Marek
Turrini, Andrea

Vandin, Andrea
Weber, Tjark
Weininger, Maximilian
Wendler, Philipp
Wolf, Karsten
Wolovick, Nicolás
Wu, Zhilin
Xu, Ming
Yang, Pengfei
Yang, Xiaoxiao
Zhan, Naijun
Zhang, Min
Zhang, Wenbo
Zhang, Wenhui
Zhao, Hengjun

Contents – Part I

Timed Systems

Neural Networks

Analysis of Network Communication

Contents – Part II

Tool Papers

Tool Demo Papers

Game Theory

A Game for Linear-time–Branching-time Spectroscopy

Benjamin Bisping[✉] and Uwe Nestmann

Technische Universität Berlin, Berlin, Germany
{benjamin.bisping,uwe.nestmann}@tu-berlin.de

Abstract We introduce a generalization of the bisimulation game that can be employed to find all relevant distinguishing Hennessy–Milner logic formulas for two compared finite-state processes. By measuring the use of expressive powers, we adapt the formula generation to just yield formulas belonging to the coarsest distinguishing behavioral preorders/equivalences from the linear-time–branching-time spectrum. The induced algorithm can determine the best fit of (in)equivalences for a pair of processes.

Keywords: Process equivalence spectrum · Distinguishing formulas · Bisimulation games.

1 Introduction

Have you ever looked at two system models and wondered what would be the finest notions of behavioral equivalence to equate them—or, conversely: the coarsest ones to distinguish them? We run into this situation often when analyzing models and, especially, when devising examples for teaching. We then find ourselves fiddling around with whiteboards and various tools, each implementing different equivalence checkers. Would it not be nice to *decide all equivalences at once*?

Example 1. Consider the following CCS process $P_1 = a.(b + c) + a.d$. It describes a machine that can be activated (a) and then either is in a state where one can choose from b and c or where it can only be deactivated again (d). P_1 shares a lot of properties with $P_2 = a.(b + d) + a.(c + d)$. For example, they have the same traces (and the same completed traces). Thus, they are (completed) trace equivalent.

But they also have differences. For instance, P_1 has a run where it executes a and then cannot do d, while P_2 does not have such a run. Hence, they are *not failure equivalent*. Moreover, P_1 may perform a and then choose from b and c, and P_2 cannot. This renders the two processes also *not simulation equivalent*. Failure equivalence and simulation equivalence are incomparable—that is, neither one follows from the other one. *Both* are coarsest ways of telling the processes apart. Other inequivalences, like bisimulation inequivalence, are implied by both.

In the following, we present a uniform game-based way of finding the most fitting notions of (in)equivalence for process pairs like in Ex. 1.

J. F. Groote and K. G. Larsen (Eds.): TACAS 2021, LNCS 12651, pp. 3–19, 2021.
https://doi.org/10.1007/978-3-030-72016-2_1

Our approach is based on the fact that notions of process equivalence can be characterized by two-player games. The defender's winning region in the game corresponds to pairs of equivalent states, and the attacker's winning strategies correspond to distinguishing formulas of Hennessy–Milner logic (HML).

Each notion of equivalence in van Glabbeek's famous linear-time–branching-time spectrum [10] can be characterized by a subset of HML with specific distinguishing power. Some of the notions are incomparable. So, often a process pair that is equivalent with respect to one equivalence, is distinguished by a set of slightly coarser or incomparable equivalences, without any one of them alone being *the* coarsest way to distinguish the pair. As with the spectrum of light where a mix of wave lengths shows to us as a color, there is a "mix" of distinguishing capabilities involved in establishing whether a specific equivalence is finest. Our algorithm is meant to analyze what is in the mix.

Contributions. This paper makes the following contributions:

- We introduce a *special bisimulation game* that neatly characterizes the distinguishing formulas of HML for pairs of states in finite transition systems (Subsection 3.1 and 3.2).
- We show how to *enumerate the relevant distinguishing formulas* using the attacker's winning region (Subsection 3.3).
- We give a way of constructing a *finite set of distinguishing formulas guaranteed to contain observations of the weakest possible observation languages*, which can be seen as a "spectroscopy" of the differences between two processes (Subsection 3.4).
- We present a small *web tool that is able to run the algorithm on finite-state processes* and output a visual representation of the game (Section 4). We also report on the distinctions it finds for all the finitary examples from the report version of the linear-time–branching-time spectrum [12].

We frame the contributions by a roundtrip through the basics of HML, games and the spectrum (Section 2), a discussion of related work (Section 5), and concluding remarks on future lines of research (Section 6).

2   Preliminaries: HML, Games, and the Spectrum

We use the concepts of transition systems, games, observations, and notions of equivalence, largely due to the wake of Hennessy and Milner's seminal paper [14].

2.1   Transition Systems and Hennessy–Milner Logic

Labeled transition systems capture a discrete world view, where there is a current state and a branching structure of possible state changes to future states.

Definition 1 (Labeled transition system). *A labeled transition system is a tuple $\mathcal{S} = (\mathcal{P}, \Sigma, \rightarrow)$ where $\mathcal{P}$ is the set of states, Σ is the set of actions, and $\rightarrow \subseteq \mathcal{P} \times \Sigma \times \mathcal{P}$ is the transition relation.*

Hennessy–Milner logic [14] describes finite *observations* (or "tests") that one can perform on such a system.

Definition 2 (Hennessy–Milner logic). *Given an alphabet Σ, the syntax of Hennessy–Milner logic formulas, $\mathsf{HML}[\Sigma]$, is inductively defined as follows:*

Observations *If $\varphi \in \mathsf{HML}[\Sigma]$ and $a \in \Sigma$, then $\langle a \rangle \varphi \in \mathsf{HML}[\Sigma]$.*
Conjunctions *If $\varphi_i \in \mathsf{HML}[\Sigma]$ for all i from an index set I, then $\bigwedge_{i \in I} \varphi_i \in \mathsf{HML}[\Sigma]$.*
Negations *If $\varphi \in \mathsf{HML}[\Sigma]$, then $\neg \varphi \in \mathsf{HML}[\Sigma]$.*

We often just write $\bigwedge\{\varphi_0, \varphi_1, ...\}$ for $\bigwedge_{i \in I} \varphi_i$. T denotes $\bigwedge \emptyset$, the nil-element of the syntax tree, and $\langle a \rangle$ is a short-hand for $\langle a \rangle \mathsf{T}$. Let us also implicitly assume that formulas are flattened in the sense that conjunctions do not contain other conjunctions as immediate subformulas. We will sometimes talk about the syntax tree height of a formula and consider the height of T to equal 0.

Intuitively, $\langle a \rangle \varphi$ means that one can observe a system transition labeled by a and then continue to make observation(s) φ. Conjunction and negation work as known from propositional logic. We will provide a common game semantics for HML in the following subsection.

2.2   Games Semantics of HML

Let us fix some notions for *Gale-Stewart-style reachability games* where the defender wins all infinite plays.

Definition 3 (Games). *A simple reachability game $\mathcal{G}[g_0] = (G, G_d, \rightarrowtail, g_0)$ consists of*

- *a set of* game positions G, *partitioned into*
  - *a set of* defender positions $G_d \subseteq G$
  - *and* attacker positions $G_a := G \setminus G_d$,
- *a graph of* game moves $\rightarrowtail \subseteq G \times G$, *and*
- *an* initial position $g_0 \in G$.

Definition 4 (Plays and wins). *We call the paths $g_0 g_1 ... \in G^\infty$ with $g_i \rightarrowtail g_{i+1}$ plays of $\mathcal{G}[g_0]$. The defender wins infinite plays. If a finite play $g_0 ... g_n \nrightarrow$ is stuck, the stuck player loses: The defender wins if $g_n \in G_a$, and the attacker wins if $g_n \in G_d$.*

Definition 5 (Strategies and winning strategies). *A (positional, nondeterministic) strategy is a subset of the moves, $F \subseteq \rightarrowtail$. If (fairly) picking elements of strategy F ensures a player to win, F is called a winning strategy for this player. The player with a winning strategy for $\mathcal{G}[g_0]$ is said to win $\mathcal{G}[g_0]$.*

Definition 6 (Winning regions). *The set $W_a \subseteq G$ of all positions g where the attacker wins $\mathcal{G}[g]$ is called the attacker winning region (defender winning region W_d analogous).*

All Gale-Stewart-style reachability games are *determined*, that is, $W_a \cup W_d = G$. The winning regions of finite simple reachability games can be computed in linear time of the number of game moves (cf. [13]). This is why the spectroscopy game of this paper can easily be used in algorithms. It derives from the following game.

Definition 7 (HML game). *For a transition system* $\mathcal{S} = (\mathcal{P}, \Sigma, \to)$, *the* HML *game* $\mathcal{G}^{\mathcal{S}}_{\mathsf{HML}}[g_0] = (G, G_d, \rightarrowtail, g_0)$ *is played on* $G = \mathcal{P} \times \mathsf{HML}[\Sigma]$, *where the defender controls observations and negated conjunctions, that is* $(p, \langle a \rangle \varphi) \in G_d$ *and* $(p, \neg \bigwedge_{i \in I} \varphi_i) \in G_d$ *(for all* φ, p, I), *and the attacker controls the rest. There are five kinds of moves:*

- $(p, \langle a \rangle \varphi) \ \rightarrowtail \ (p', \varphi) \quad$ *if* $p \xrightarrow{a} p'$,
- $(p, \neg \langle a \rangle \varphi) \ \rightarrowtail \ (p', \neg \varphi) \quad$ *if* $p \xrightarrow{a} p'$,
- $(p, \bigwedge_{i \in I} \varphi_i) \ \rightarrowtail \ (p, \varphi_i) \quad$ *with* $i \in I$,
- $(p, \neg \bigwedge_{i \in I} \varphi_i) \ \rightarrowtail \ (p, \neg \varphi_i) \quad$ *with* $i \in I$, *and*
- $(p, \neg \neg \varphi) \ \rightarrowtail \ (p, \varphi)$.

Like in other logical games in the Ehrenfeucht–Fraïssé tradition, the attacker plays the conjunctions and universal quantifiers, whereas the defender plays the disjunctions and existential quantifiers. For instance, $(p, \langle a \rangle \varphi)$ is declared as defender position, since $\langle a \rangle \varphi$ is meant to become true precisely if *there exists* a state p' reachable $p \xrightarrow{a} p'$ where φ is true.

As every move strictly reduces the height of the formula, the game must be finite-depth (and cycle-free), and, for image-finite systems and formulas, also finite. It is determined and the following semantics is total.

Definition 8 (HML semantics). *For a transition system* $\mathcal{S} = (\mathcal{P}, \Sigma, \to)$, *the semantics of* HML *is given by defining that* φ *is true at* p *in* $\mathcal{S}$, *written* $[\![\varphi]\!]^{\mathcal{S}}_p$, *iff the defender wins* $\mathcal{G}^{\mathcal{S}}_{\mathsf{HML}}[(p, \varphi)]$.

Example 2. Continuing Ex. 1, $[\![\langle a \rangle \neg \langle d \rangle \mathsf{T}]\!]^{\mathsf{CCS}}_{\mathsf{P}_2}$ is false: No matter whether the defender plays to $(b + d, \neg \langle d \rangle \mathsf{T})$ or to $(c + d, \neg \langle d \rangle \mathsf{T})$, the attacker wins by moving to the stuck defender position $(\mathbf{0}, \neg \mathsf{T})$. (Recall that T is the empty conjunction and that $\mathbf{0}$ is the completed process!)

2.3 The Spectrum of Behavioral Equivalences

Definition 9 (**Distinguishing formula**). *A formula* φ *distinguishes state* p *from* q *iff* $[\![\varphi]\!]_p$ *is true and* $[\![\varphi]\!]_q$ *is not.*[1]

Example 3. $\langle a \rangle \neg \langle d \rangle \mathsf{T}$ distinguishes P_1 from P_2 in Ex. 1 (but not the other way around). $\langle a \rangle \bigwedge \{\langle b \rangle \mathsf{T}, \langle d \rangle \mathsf{T}\}$ distinguishes P_2 from P_1.

Definition 10 (**Observational preorders and equivalences**). *A set of observations,* $\mathcal{O}_X \subseteq \mathsf{HML}[\Sigma]$, *preorders two states* p, q, *written* $p \sqsubseteq_X q$, *iff no formula* $\varphi \in \mathcal{O}_X$ *distinguishes* p *from* q. *If* $p \sqsubseteq_X q$ *and* $q \sqsubseteq_X p$, *then the two are* X-equivalent, *written* $p \equiv_X q$.

---

[1] In the following, we usually leave the transition system $\mathcal{S}$ implicit.

Definition 11 (Linear-time–branching-time languages [12]). *The linear-time–branching-time spectrum is a lattice of observation languages (and of entailed process preorders and equivalences). Every observation language $\mathcal{O}_X$ can perform trace observations, that is, $\mathsf{T} \in \mathcal{O}_X$ and, if $\varphi \in \mathcal{O}_X$, then $\langle a \rangle \varphi \in \mathcal{O}_X$. At the more linear-time side of the spectrum we have:*

- *trace observations $\mathcal{O}_T$: Just trace observations,*
- *failure observations $\mathcal{O}_F$: $\bigwedge_{i \in I} \neg \langle a_i \rangle \in \mathcal{O}_F$,*
- *readiness observations $\mathcal{O}_R$: $\bigwedge_{i \in I} \varphi_i \in \mathcal{O}_R$ with each φ_i of form $\neg \langle a_i \rangle$ or $\langle a_i \rangle$,*
- *failure trace observations $\mathcal{O}_{FT}$: $\bigwedge_{i \in I} \varphi_i \in \mathcal{O}_{FT}$ with $\varphi_0 \in \mathcal{O}_{FT}$ and, for $i > 0$, $\varphi_i = \neg \langle a_i \rangle$,*
- *ready trace observations $\mathcal{O}_{RT}$: $\bigwedge_{i \in I} \varphi_i \in \mathcal{O}_{RT}$ with $\varphi_0 \in \mathcal{O}_{RT}$ and, for $i > 0$, φ_i of form $\neg \langle a_i \rangle$ or $\langle a_i \rangle$,*
- *impossible futures $\mathcal{O}_{IF}$: $\bigwedge_{i \in I} \neg \varphi_i \in \mathcal{O}_{IF}$ with all $\varphi_i \in \mathcal{O}_T$, and*
- *possible futures $\mathcal{O}_{PF}$: $\bigwedge_{i \in I} \varphi_i \in \mathcal{O}_{PF}$ with all $\varphi_i \in \{\neg \psi_i, \psi_i\}$ and $\psi_i \in \mathcal{O}_T$.[2]*

At the more branching-time side, we have simulation observations. Every simulation observation language $\mathcal{O}_{XS}$, has full conjunctive capacity, that is, if $\varphi_i \in \mathcal{O}_{XS}$ for all $i \in I$, then $\bigwedge_{i \in I} \varphi_i \in \mathcal{O}_{XS}$.

- *simulation observations $\mathcal{O}_{1S}$: Just simulation (and trace) observations,*
- *n-nested simulation observations $\mathcal{O}_{nS}$: $\neg \varphi \in \mathcal{O}_{nS}$ with $\varphi \in \mathcal{O}_{(n-1)S}$,*
- *ready simulation observations $\mathcal{O}_{RS}$: $\neg \langle a \rangle \in \mathcal{O}_{RS}$, and*
- *bisimulation observations $\mathcal{O}_B$: The same as $\mathcal{O}_{\infty S}$, which is exactly $\mathsf{HML}[\Sigma]$.*

The observation languages of the spectrum differ in how many of the syntactic features of HML one will encounter when descending into a formula's syntax tree. We will come back to this in Subsection 3.4.

Note that we consider $\bigwedge \{\varphi\}$ to be an alias for φ. With this aliasing, all the listed observation languages are *closed* in the sense that all subformulas of an observation are themselves part of that language. They thus are *inductive* in the sense that all observations must be built from observations of the same language with lower syntax tree height.

3   Distinguishing Formula Games

This section introduces our main contribution: the spectroscopy game (Def. 13), and how to build all interesting distinguishing HML formulas from its winning region (Def. 14). To justify our construction and to prove that we indeed find distinguishing formulas (Thm. 1), let us first examine the formula preorder game (Def. 12), which is closer to the problem whether formulas are (non-)distinguishing.

---

[2] Like Kučera and Esparza [17], who studied the properties of "good" observation languages, we glimpse over completed trace, completed simulation and possible worlds observations here, because these observations need a special exhaustive $\bigwedge_{a \in \Sigma} \varphi$. While it could be provided for with additional operators, it would add another case in each of the upcoming definitions and would break the closure property of observation languages, without giving much in return.

3.1   The Formula Preorder Game

Def. 10 entails a straightforward way of turning the problem whether a set of observations $\mathcal{O} \subseteq \mathcal{O}_X$ preorders two states p, q into a game: Have the attacker pick a supposedly distinguishing formula $\varphi \in \mathcal{O}$, and then have the defender choose whether to play the HML game (Def. 7) for $[\![\neg\varphi]\!]_p$ or for $[\![\varphi]\!]_q$. This direct route will yield infinite games for infinite $\mathcal{O}$—and all the languages from Def. 11 are infinite!

To bypass the infinity issue, we will introduce a variation of this game *where the attacker gradually chooses their attacking formula*. In particular, this means that the attacker now decides which observations to play. In return, the defender does not need to pick a side in the beginning and may postpone the decision where (on the right-hand side) an observation leads. Postponing decisions here means that the defender may play non-deterministically, moving to multiple states at once. The mechanics are analogous to the standard powerset construction when transforming non-deterministic finite automata into deterministic ones.

Definition 12 (Formula preorder game). *For a transition system $\mathcal{S} = (\mathcal{P}, \Sigma, \rightarrow)$ and a set of observations $\mathcal{O}_X$, the formula preorder game $\mathcal{G}_X^{\mathcal{S}}[g_0] = (G, G_d, \rightarrowtail, g_0)$ consists of*

- *attacker positions $(p, Q, \mathcal{O})_a \in G_a$ with $p \in \mathcal{P}$, $Q \in 2^{\mathcal{P}}$, and $\mathcal{O} \subseteq \mathcal{O}_X$,*
- *defender conjunction positions $(p, Q, \mathcal{O})_d^{\wedge} \in G_d$ where the defender has to answer to conjunction challenges, and*
- *defender negation positions $(p, Q, \mathcal{O})_d^{\neg} \in G_d$ where the defender has to answer to negation challenges,*

and five kinds of moves

- *observation moves* $(p, Q, \mathcal{O})_a \;\rightarrowtail\; (p', Q', \mathcal{O}')_a$
  if $p \xrightarrow{a} p'$ with $Q' = \{q' \mid \exists q \in Q.\, q \xrightarrow{a} q'\}$ and $\mathcal{O}' = \{\varphi \mid \langle a \rangle \varphi \in \mathcal{O}\}$,
- *conjunct challenges* $(p, Q, \mathcal{O})_a \;\rightarrowtail\; (p, Q, \{\varphi_i \mid i \in I\})_d^{\wedge}$
  if $\bigwedge_{i \in I} \varphi_i \in \mathcal{O}$,
- *conjunct answers* $(p, Q, \mathcal{O})_d^{\wedge} \;\rightarrowtail\; (p, \{q\}, \mathcal{O})_a$
  if $q \in Q$,
- *negation challenges* $(p, Q, \mathcal{O})_a \;\rightarrowtail\; (p, Q, \{\varphi\})_d^{\neg}$
  if $\neg\varphi \in \mathcal{O}$, and
- *negation answers* $(p, Q, \mathcal{O})_d^{\neg} \;\rightarrowtail\; (q, \{p\}, \mathcal{O})_a$
  if $q \in Q$.

The formula preorder game precisely characterizes whether an observation language is distinguishing:

Lemma 1. *For a closed observation language $\mathcal{O}_X$, the formula preorder game $\mathcal{G}_X^{\mathcal{S}}[(p, Q, \mathcal{O})_a]$ with $\mathcal{O} \subseteq \mathcal{O}_X$ is won by the defender precisely if, for every observation $\varphi \in \mathcal{O}$ with $[\![\varphi]\!]_p$, there is a $q \in Q$ such that $[\![\varphi]\!]_q$.*

Proof (Sketch). By induction over the height of formulas in $\mathcal{O}_X$ with arbitrary p and Q, and strengthening the induction predicate to not only consider φ but also partial conjunctions $\bigwedge \mathcal{O}''$ with $\mathcal{O}'' \subseteq \mathcal{O}'$ whenever $\varphi = \bigwedge \mathcal{O}'$. To prove the right-to-left direction, exploiting the determinacy of the game is convenient.

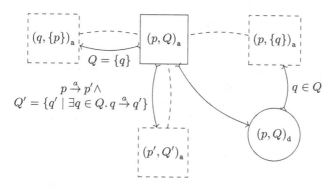

Figure 1. Schematic spectroscopy game $\mathcal{G}_{\triangle}$ of Def. 13. Boxes stand for attacker positions, circles for defender positions, arrows for moves. From the dashed boxes, the moves are analogous to the ones of the connected solid positions.

3.2   The Spectroscopy Game

Let us now remove the formulas from the formula game (Def. 12). The idea is to look at the game for the whole of HML, called $\mathcal{G}_B$. Only attack moves in the formula game change the current set of observations, and they are completely guided by the context-free grammar of HML (Def. 2). Therefore, we can[3] assume $\mathcal{O}$ to equal HML$[\Sigma]$ in every reachable position of $\mathcal{G}_B$. Effectively, $\mathcal{O}$ can be canceled out of the game, without losing any information. We call the remaining game the "spectroscopy game." Figure 1 gives a graphical representation.

Definition 13 (Spectroscopy game). *For a transition system* $\mathcal{S} = (\mathcal{P}, \Sigma, \rightarrow)$, *the L-labeled spectroscopy game* $\mathcal{G}_{\triangle}^{\mathcal{S}}[g_0] = (G, G_d, \stackrel{\cdot}{\rightarrowtail}, g_0)$ *with* $L = \{\neg, \wedge, *, \langle a \rangle\}$ *consists of*

- *attacker positions* $(p, Q)_a \in G_a$ *with* $p \in \mathcal{P}$, $Q \in 2^{\mathcal{P}}$,
- *defender positions* $(p, Q)_d \in G_d$ *where the defender has to answer to conjunction challenges,*

and four kinds of moves:

- *observation moves* $(p, Q)_a \stackrel{\langle a \rangle}{\rightarrowtail} (p', \{q' \mid \exists q \in Q.\, q \stackrel{a}{\rightarrow} q'\})_a$ *if* $p \stackrel{a}{\rightarrow} p'$
- *conjunct challenges* $(p, Q)_a \stackrel{\wedge}{\rightarrowtail} (p, Q)_d$,
- *conjunct answers* $(p, Q)_d \stackrel{*}{\rightarrowtail} (p, \{q\})_a$ *if* $q \in Q$, *and*
- *negation moves* $(p, \{q\})_a \stackrel{\neg}{\rightarrowtail} (q, \{p\})_a$.

We have already introduced two tricks in this definition to ease formula reconstruction in the next subsection. (1) The attack moves are labeled with the

---

[3] To be precise: Finite conjunctions may only lead to *arbitrarily large* subsets of HML$[\Sigma]$. If the attacker has a way of winning by playing a conjunction, we can as well approximate this move as playing $\bigwedge$HML.

syntactic constructs from which they originate. This does not change expressive power. (2) Negation moves are restricted to situations where $Q = \{q\}$. After all, winning attacker strategies will pay attention to only playing a negation after minimizing the odds of being put on a bad position, anyways.

Note that, like in the formula game with arbitrary-depth formulas, the attacker could force infinite plays by cycling through conjunction moves (and also negation moves). However, they will not do this, as infinite plays are won by the defender.

Lemma 2. *The spectroscopy game* $\mathcal{G}_\triangle[(p, \{q\})_a]$ *is won by the defender precisely if p and q are bisimilar.*

This fact is a corollary of the well-known Hennessy–Milner theorem (HML characterizes bisimilarity), given that $\mathcal{G}_\triangle$ is constructed as a simplification of $\mathcal{G}_B$.

Comparing $\mathcal{G}_\triangle$ to the standard bisimulation game from the literature (with symmetry moves, see e.g. [3]), we can easily transfer attacker strategies from there. In the standard game, the attacker will play $(p, q) \rightarrowtail (a, p', q)$ with $p \xrightarrow{a} p'$ and the defender has to answer by $(a, p', q) \rightarrowtail (p', q')$ with $q \xrightarrow{a} q'$. In the spectroscopy game, the attacker can enforce analogous moves by playing $(p, \{q\})_a \overset{\langle a \rangle}{\rightarrowtail} (p', Q')_a \overset{\wedge}{\rightarrowtail} (p', Q')_d$, which will make the defender pick $(p', Q')_d \overset{*}{\rightarrowtail} (p', \{q'\})_a$.

The opposite direction of transfer is not so easy, as the attacker has more ways of winning in $\mathcal{G}_\triangle$. But this asymmetry is precisely why we have to use the spectroscopy game instead of the standard bisimulation game if we want to learn about, for example, interesting failure-trace attacks.

Due to the subset construction over $\mathcal{P}$, the game size clearly is exponential in the size of the state space. Going exponential is necessary, as we want to also characterize weaker preorders like the trace preorder, where exponential $\mathcal{P}$-subset or Σ^*-word constructions cannot be circumvented. However, for moderate real-world systems, such constructions will not necessarily show their full exponential blow-up (cf. [6]).

For concrete implementations, the subset construction also means that the costs of storing game nodes and of comparing two nodes is linear in the state space size. Complexity-wise this factor is dominated by the overall exponentialities.

3.3   Building Distinguishing Formulas from Attacker Strategies

Definition 14 (Strategy formulas). *Given an attacker strategy* $F \subseteq (G_a \times L \times G)$ *for the spectroscopy game* $\mathcal{G}_\triangle$, *the set of* strategy formulas, $\mathsf{Strat}_F(g_a)$, *is inductively defined by:*

- *If* $\varphi \in \mathsf{Strat}_F(g_a')$ *and* $(g_a, \langle b \rangle, g_a') \in F$, *then* $\langle b \rangle \varphi \in \mathsf{Strat}_F(g_a)$,
- *if* $\varphi \in \mathsf{Strat}_F(g_a')$ *and* $(g_a, \neg, g_a') \in F$, *then* $\neg \varphi \in \mathsf{Strat}_F(g_a)$, *and*
- *if* $\varphi_{g_a'} \in \mathsf{Strat}_F(g_a')$ *for all* $g_a' \in I = \{g_a' \mid g_d \overset{*}{\rightarrowtail}_\triangle g_a'\}$, *and* $(g_a, \wedge, g_d) \in F$, *then* $\bigwedge_{g_a' \in I} \varphi_{g_a'} \in \mathsf{Strat}_F(g_a)$.

Example 4. The attacks $(P_1, \{P_2\})_a \overset{\langle a \rangle}{\rightarrowtail} (b+c, \{b+d, c+d\})_a \overset{\wedge}{\rightarrowtail} \overset{*}{\rightarrowtail} \overset{\neg}{\rightarrowtail} \overset{\langle d \rangle}{\rightarrowtail} (0, \emptyset)_a \overset{\wedge}{\rightarrowtail}$ give rise to the formula $\langle a \rangle \bigwedge \{\neg \langle d \rangle \mathsf{T}\}$, which can be written as $\langle a \rangle \neg \langle d \rangle$.

Definition 15 (Winning strategy graph). *Given the attacker winning region* W_a *and a starting position* $g_0 \in W_a$, *the* attacker winning strategy graph F_a *is the subset of the* $\rightarrowtail$-*graph that can be visited from* g_0 *when following all* $\rightarrowtail$-*edges unless they lead out of* W_a.

This graph can be cyclic. However, if the attacker plays inside their winning region according to F_a, they will always have paths to their final winning positions. So even though the attacker could loop (and thus lose), they can always end the game and *win* in the sense of Def. 5.

Theorem 1. *If* W_a *is the attacker winning region of the spectroscopy game* $\mathcal{G}_\triangle$, *every* $\varphi \in \mathsf{Strat}_{F_a}((p, \{q\})_\mathsf{a})$ *distinguishes* p *from* q.

Proof. Due to Lem. 1, it suffices to show that $\varphi \in \mathsf{Strat}_{F_a}((p, Q)_\mathsf{a})$ implies that the attacker wins $\mathcal{G}_B[(p, Q, \{\varphi\})]$. We proceed by induction on the structure of Strat_{F_a} with arbitrary p, Q.

- Assume $\varphi \in \mathsf{Strat}_{F_a}((p', Q')_\mathsf{a})$ and $((p, Q)_\mathsf{a}, \langle b \rangle, (p', Q')_\mathsf{a}) \in F_a$. By induction hypothesis, the attacker wins $\mathcal{G}_B[(p', Q', \{\varphi\})]$. By moving there, the attacker also wins $\mathcal{G}_B[(p, Q, \{\langle b \rangle \varphi)\}]$, which must be a valid move as F_a is a strategy for $\mathcal{G}_\triangle$.
- Assume $\varphi \in \mathsf{Strat}_{F_a}((p', Q')_\mathsf{a})$ and $((p, Q)_\mathsf{a}, \neg, (p', Q')_\mathsf{a}) \in F_a$. By induction hypothesis, the attacker wins $\mathcal{G}_B[(p', Q', \{\varphi\})]$. By the construction of $\mathcal{G}_\triangle$, $Q = \{p'\}$. So the attacker can win $\mathcal{G}_B[(p, Q, \{\neg\varphi\})]$ by moving to this position (with the defender having no choice when picking from Q).
- Assume $\varphi_{g'_a} \in \mathsf{Strat}_{F_a}(g'_a)$ for all $g'_a = (p', \{q'\})_\mathsf{a} \in I = \{g'_a \mid g_d \overset{*}{\rightarrowtail}_\triangle g'_a\}$, and $((p, Q)_\mathsf{a}, \wedge, g_d) \in F_a$. Due to the construction of $\mathcal{G}_\triangle$, $Q = \{q' \mid (p', \{q'\})_\mathsf{a} \in I\}$ and $p' = p$. By induction hypothesis, the attacker wins all $\mathcal{G}_B[(p', \{q'\}, \{\varphi_{g'_a}\})]$ and, as they can always focus on consuming just one formula, also all $\mathcal{G}_B[(p, \{q'\}, \{\varphi_{g''_a} \mid g''_a \in I\})]$. This matches all the positions the defender can move to after $(p, Q, \{\varphi_{g''_a} \mid g''_a \in I\})_\mathsf{d}$. Moving there, the attacker wins $\mathcal{G}_B[(p, Q, \{\bigwedge_{g'_a \in I} \varphi_{g'_a}\})]$.

Note that the theorem is only one-way, as every distinguishing formula can neutrally be extended by saying that some additional clause that is true for *both* processes does hold. Def. 14 will not find such bloated formulas.

Due to cycles in the game graph, Strat_{F_a} will usually yield infinitely many formulas. But we can become finite by injecting some way of discarding long formulas that unfold negation cycles or recursions of the underlying transition system. The next section will discuss how to do this without discarding the formulas that are interesting from the point of view of the spectrum.

3.4   Retrieving Cheapest Distinguishing Formulas

In our quest for the coarsest behavioral preorders (or equivalences) distinguishing two states, we actually are only interested in the ones that are part of the *smallest observation languages* from the spectrum (Def. 11). We can think of the amount of HML-expressiveness used by a formula as its *price*.

Let us look at the price structure of the spectrum from Def. 11. Table 1 gives an overview of how many syntactic HML-features the observation languages may use at most. (If formulas use fewer, they still are considered part of that observation language.) So, we are talking *budgets*, in the price analogy.

Conjunctions: How often may one run into a conjunction when descending down the syntax tree. Negations in the beginning or following an observation are counted as implicit conjunctions.

Positive deep branches: How many positive deep branches may appear in each conjunction? We call subformulas of the form $\langle a \rangle$ or $\neg\langle a \rangle$ *flat branches*, and the others *deep branches*.

Positive flat branches: How many positive flat branches may appear in each conjunction?[4]

Negations: How many negations may be visited when descending?

Negations height: How high can the syntax trees under each negation be?

We say that a formula φ_1 *dominates* φ_2 if φ_1 has lower or equal values than φ_2 in each dimension of the metrics with at least one entry strictly lower. Let us note the following facts:

---

[4] There is a special case for failure-traces where 1 positive flat branch may be counted as deep, if there are no other deep branches. Hence the * in Table 1.

Table 1. Dimensions of observation expressiveness.

Observations	Conjunctions	Positive deep br.	Positive flat br.	Negations	Negation height
trace $\mathcal{O}_T$	0	0	0	0	0
failure $\mathcal{O}_F$	1	0	0	1	1
readiness $\mathcal{O}_R$	1	0	∞	1	1
failure-trace $\mathcal{O}_{FT}$	∞	1	0*	1	1
ready-trace $\mathcal{O}_{RT}$	∞	1	∞	1	1
impossible-future $\mathcal{O}_{IF}$	1	0	0	1	∞
possible-future $\mathcal{O}_{PF}$	1	∞	∞	1	∞
ready-simulation $\mathcal{O}_{RS}$	∞	∞	∞	1	1
$(n{+}1)$-nested-simulation $\mathcal{O}_{(n+1)S}$	∞	∞	∞	n	∞
bisimulation $\mathcal{O}_B$	∞	∞	∞	∞	∞

```
 1  def game_spectroscopy(S, p_0, q_0):
 2      G_△^S = (G, G_a, ↣) := construct_spectroscopy_game(S)
 3      W_a := compute_winning_region(G_△^S)
 4      if (p_0, {q_0})_a ∈ W_a :
 5          F_a := winning_graph(G_△^S, W_a, (p_0, {q_0})_a)
 6          strats[] := ∅
 7          todo := [(p_0, {q_0})_a]
 8          while todo ≠ []:
 9              g := todo.dequeue()
10              sg := strats[g]
11              if sg = undefined :
12                  strats[sg] := ∅
13              gg' := {g' | (g, ·, g') ∈ F_a ∧ strats(g') = undefined}
14              if gg' = ∅ :
15                  sg' = nonDominatedOrIF(Strat'_{F_a, strats}(g))
16                  if sg ≠ sg' :
17                      strats(g) := sg'
18                      todo.enqueueEachEnd({g* | (g*, ·, g) ∈ F_a ∧ g* ∉ todo})
19              else:
20                  todo.enqueueEachFront(gg')
21          return strats((p_0, {q_0})_a)
22      else:
23          R := {(p, q) | (p, {q})_a ∈ G_a \ W_a}
24          return R
```

Algorithm 1: Spectroscopy procedure.

1. When formulas are constructed recursively, like the strategy formulas in Def. 14, they can only contribute to dominating (i.e. more expensive) or equivalently valued formulas with respect to the metrics.
2. Formulas can be incomparable. For example, $\langle a \rangle \bigwedge \{\langle b \rangle, \langle c \rangle\}$ and $\langle a \rangle \neg \langle a \rangle$, corresponding to coordinates (1,0,2,0,0) and (1,0,0,1,1), are incomparable.
3. A locally more expensive formula may pay off as part of a bigger global formula. For example, if two states are distinguished by $\neg \langle a \rangle$ and $\langle b \rangle$, the dominated formula $\neg \langle a \rangle$ may later be handy to construct a (comparably cheap) failure formula.

These observations justify our algorithm to prune all formulas from the set $\text{Strat}_{F_a}(g)$ that are dominated with respect to the metrics by any other formula in this set, unless they are *impossible trace futures* of the form $\neg \langle a_1 \rangle \langle a_2 \rangle$.... We moreover add formula height in terms of observations as a dimension in the metric, which leads to loop unfoldings being dominated by the shorter paths.

Algorithm 1 shows all the elements in concert. It constructs the spectroscopy game $G_△^S$ (Def. 13) and computes its attacker winning strategy graph F_a (Def. 15). If the attacker cannot win, the algorithm returns a bisimulation relation. Otherwise, it constructs the distinguishing formulas: It keeps a map strats of strategy formulas that have been found so far and a list of game positions todo that have

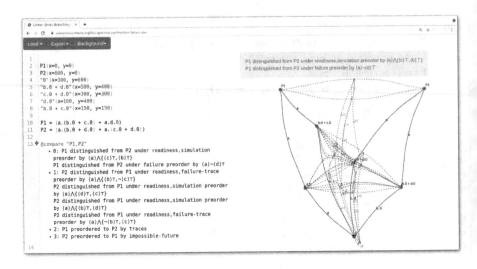

Figure 2. Screenshot of a linear-time–branching-time spectroscopy of the processes from Ex. 1.

to be updated. In every round, we take a game position g from todo. If some of its successors have not been visited yet, we add them to the top of the work list. Otherwise we call $\mathsf{Strat}'_{F_a,\mathrm{strats}}(\mathbf{g})$ to compute distinguishing formulas using the follow-up formulas *found so far* strats. This function mostly corresponds to Def. 14 with the twist, that partial follow-ups are used instead of recursion, and that the construction for conjunctions is split onto attacker *and* defender positions. Of the found formulas, we keep only the non-dominated ones and impossible future traces. If the result changes strats(g), we enqueue each game predecessor to propagate the update there.

The algorithm structure is mostly usual fixed point machinery. It terminates because, for each state in a finite transition system, there must be a bound on the distinguishing mechanisms necessary with respect to our metrics, and Strat' will only generate finitely many formulas under this bound. Keeping the impossible future formulas unbounded is alright, because they have to be constructed from trace formulas, which are subject to the bound.

4   A Webtool for Equivalence Spectroscopy

We have implemented the game and the generation of minimal distinguishing formulas in the "Linear-time–Branching-time Spectroscope", a Scala.js program that can be run in the browser on https://concurrency-theory.org/ltbt-spectroscope/.

The tool (screenshot in Fig. 2) consists of a text editor to input basic CCS-style processes and a view of the transition system graph. When queried to compare two processes, the tool yields the cheapest distinguishing HML-formulas it can find for both directions. Moreover, it displays the attacker-winning part of the spectroscopy game overlayed over the transition system. The latter can also enlighten matters, at least for small and comparably deterministic transition systems. From the found formulas, the tool can also infer the finest fitting preorders for pairs of processes (Fig. 3).

To "benchmark" the quality of the distinguishing formulas, we have run the algorithm on all the finitary counterexample processes from the report version of "The Linear-time–Branching-time Spectrum" [12]. Table 2 reports the output of our tool, on how to distinguish certain processes. The results match the (in)equivalences given in [12]. In some cases, the tool finds slightly better ways of distinction using impossible futures equivalence, which was not known at the time of the original paper. All the computed formulas are quite elegant / minimal.

For each of the examples (from papers) we have considered, the browser's capacities sufficed to run the algorithm in 30 to 250 milliseconds. This does not mean that one should expect the algorithm to work for systems with thousands of states. There, the exponentialities of game and formula construction would hit. However, such big instances would usually stem from preexisting models where one would very much hope for the designers to already know under which semantics to interpret their model. The practical applications of our browser tool are more on the research side: When devising compiler optimizations, encodings, or distributed algorithms, it can be very handy to fully grasp the equivalence structure of isolated instances. The Linear-time–Branching-time Spectroscope supports this process.

Table 2. Formulas found by our implementation for some interesting processes from [12].

p	q	Cheapest distinguishing formulas found	From
P1	P2	$\langle a\rangle\bigwedge\{\langle c\rangle, \langle b\rangle\} \in \mathcal{O}_R \cap \mathcal{O}_S,$ $\langle a\rangle\neg\langle d\rangle \in \mathcal{O}_F$	Ex. 1
$a.b + a$	$a.b$	$\langle a\rangle\neg\langle b\rangle \in \mathcal{O}_F$	p. 13
$a.b + a.(b + c)$	$a.(b + c)$	$\langle a\rangle\neg\langle c\rangle \in \mathcal{O}_F$	p. 16
$a.(b + c.d) +$ $a.(f + c.e)$	$a.(b + c.e) +$ $a.(f + c.d)$	$\langle a\rangle\bigwedge\{\langle c\rangle\langle d\rangle, \langle b\rangle\} \in \mathcal{O}_{RT} \cap \mathcal{O}_{PF} \cap \mathcal{O}_S,$ $\langle a\rangle\bigwedge\{\langle c\rangle\langle d\rangle, \neg\langle f\rangle\} \in \mathcal{O}_{FT} \cap \mathcal{O}_{PF},$ $\langle a\rangle\bigwedge\{\neg\langle b\rangle, \neg\langle c\rangle\langle d\rangle\} \in \mathcal{O}_{IF}$ (+3 variants)	p. 21
$a.b+a.(b+c)+a.c$	$a.b + a.c$	$\langle a\rangle\bigwedge\{\langle c\rangle, \langle b\rangle\} \in \mathcal{O}_R \cap \mathcal{O}_S$	p. 24
$a.(b+a.(b+c.d) +$ $a.c.e) + a.(a.c.d +$ $a.(c.e + b))$	$a.(a.(b + c.d) +$ $a.c.e) + a.(a.c.d +$ $a.(c.e + b) + b)$	$\langle a\rangle\bigwedge\{\langle b\rangle, \langle a\rangle\bigwedge\{\langle c\rangle\langle d\rangle, \langle b\rangle\}\} \in \mathcal{O}_{RT} \cap \mathcal{O}_S,$ $\langle a\rangle\bigwedge\{\neg\langle b\rangle, \langle a\rangle\bigwedge\{\langle c\rangle\langle d\rangle, \neg\langle b\rangle\}\} \in \mathcal{O}_{FT}$	p. 27
$a.(b.c + b.d)$	$a.b.c + a.b.d$	$\langle a\rangle\bigwedge\{\langle b\rangle\langle c\rangle, \langle b\rangle\langle d\rangle\} \in \mathcal{O}_{PF} \cap \mathcal{O}_S$	p. 31
$a.b.c+a.(b.c+b.d)$	$a.(b.c + b.d)$	$\langle a\rangle\neg\langle b\rangle\langle d\rangle \in \mathcal{O}_{IF}$	p. 34
$a.b+a+a.c$	$a.b+a.(b+c)+a.c$	$\langle a\rangle\bigwedge\{\neg\langle b\rangle, \neg\langle c\rangle\} \in \mathcal{O}_F$	p. 38
$a.b.c + a.(b.c + b)$	$a.(b.c + b)$	$\langle a\rangle\neg\langle b\rangle\neg\langle c\rangle \in \mathcal{O}_B$	p. 42

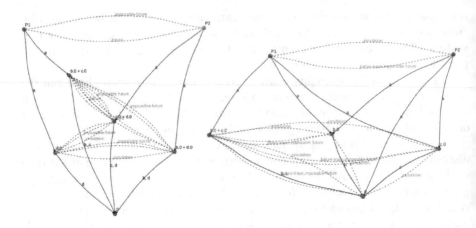

Figure 3. Tool output of finest preorders for transition systems. (Left: Ex. 1; right: $a.b + a.(b + c) + a.c$ vs. $a.b + a + a.c$.

5   Related Work and Alternatives

The game and the algorithm presented fill a blank spot in between the following previous directions of work:

Distinguishing formulas in general. Cleaveland [5] showed how to restore (non-minimal) distinguishing formulas for bisimulation equivalence from the execution of a bisimilarity checker based on the splitting of blocks. There, it has been named as possible future work to extend the construction to other notions of the spectrum. We are not aware of any place where this has previously been done completely. But there are related islands like the encoding between CTL and failure traces by Bruda and Zhang [7]. There is also more recent work like Jasper et. al [15] extending to the generation of characteristic invariant formulas for bisimulation classes. Previous algorithms for bisimulation in-equivalence tend to generate formulas that alternate $\langle a \rangle$ and $[b]$ observations while pushing negation to the innermost level. Such formulas can not as easily be linked to the spectrum as ours.

Game-characterizations of the spectrum. After Shukla et al. [18] had shown how to characterize many notions of equivalence by HORNSAT games, Chen and Deng [4] presented a hierarchy of games characterizing all the equivalences of the linear-time–branching-time spectrum. The games from [4] cannot be applied as easily as ours in algorithms because they allow word moves and thus are infinite already for finite transition systems with cycles. Constructing distinguishing formulas from attacker strategies of these games would be less convenient than in our solution. Their parametric approach is comparable to fixing maximal price budgets *ex ante*. Our on-the-fly picking of minimal prices is more flexible.

Using game-characterizations for distinguishing formulas. There is recent work by Mika-Michalski et al. [16] on constructing distinguishing formulas using games in a more abstract coalgebraic setting focussed on the absence of bisimulation. The game and formula generation there, however, cannot easily be adapted for our purpose of performing a *spectroscopy* also for weaker notions.

Alternatives. One can also find the finest notion of equivalence between two states by *gradually minimizing* the transition system with ever coarser equivalences from bisimulation to trace equivalence until the states are conflated (possibly also trying branches). Within a big tool suite of highly optimized algorithms this should be quite efficient. We preferred the game approach, because it can uniformly be extended to the whole spectrum and also has the big upside of explaining the in-equivalences by distinguishing formulas.

An avenue of optimization for our approach, we have already tried, is to run the formula search on a *directed acyclic subgraph* of the winning strategy graph. For our purpose of finding most fitting equivalences, DAG-ification may preclude the algorithm from finding the right formulas. On the other hand, if one is mainly interested in a short distinguishing formula for instance, one can speed up the process with DAG-ification by the order of remaining game rounds.

6   Conclusion

In this paper, we have established a convenient way of finding distinguishing formulas that use a minimal amount of expressiveness.

System analysis tools can employ the algorithm to tell their users in more detail *how equivalent* two process models are. While the generic approach is costly, instantiations to more specific, symbolic, compositional, on-the-fly or depth-bounded settings may enable wider applications. There are also some algorithmic tricks (like building the concrete formulas only after having found the price bounds and heuristics in handling the game graph) we have not explored in this paper.

So far, we have only looked at *strong* notions of equivalence [10]. We plan to verify the game in Isabelle/HOL and to extend our algorithm, so it also deals with *weak* notions of equivalence [11]. These equivalences abstract over τ-actions representing "internal activity" and correspond to observation languages with a special temporal $\langle\epsilon\rangle$-observation (cf. [9]). This would generalize work on weak game characterizations such as de Frutos-Escrig et al.'s [8] and our own [2,3]. The vision is to arrive at *one* certifying algorithm that can yield finest equivalences and cheapest distinguishing formulas as witnesses for the whole discrete spectrum.

On a different note, our group is also working on an educational computer game about process equivalences.[5] The (theoretical) game of this paper can likely

---

[5] A prototype featuring equivalences between strong bisimulation and coupled simulation (result of Dominik Peacock's bachelor thesis) can be played on https://www.concurrency-theory.org/rvg-game/.

be adapted to go in the other direction: from formulas to distinguished transition systems. It may thereby synthesize levels for the (computer) game. So, in the end, all this might actually contribute to actual people having actual fun.

Acknowledgments. We are thankful to members of our research group (especially Kim Völlinger), participants of our course Modelle Dynamischer Systeme, and the anonymous reviewers for lots of helpful comments.

Data availability. The source code git repository of our implementation can be accessed via https://concurrency-theory.org/ltbt-spectroscope/code/. Code to reproduce the results presented in this paper is available on Zenodo [1].

References

1. Bisping, B.: Linear-time–branching-time spectroscope: TACAS 2021 edition (2021). https://doi.org/10.5281/zenodo.4475878, archived on Zenodo
2. Bisping, B., Nestmann, U.: Computing coupled similarity. In: Proceedings of TACAS. pp. 244–261. LNCS, Springer (2019). https://doi.org/10.1007/978-3-030-17462-0_14
3. Bisping, B., Nestmann, U., Peters, K.: Coupled similarity: the first 32 years. Acta Informatica **57**(3-5), 439–463 (2020). https://doi.org/10.1007/s00236-019-00356-4
4. Chen, X., Deng, Y.: Game characterizations of process equivalences. In: Ramalingam, G. (ed.) Programming Languages and Systems. pp. 107–121. Springer Berlin Heidelberg, Berlin, Heidelberg (2008). https://doi.org/10.1007/978-3-540-89330-1_8
5. Cleaveland, R.: On automatically explaining bisimulation inequivalence. In: Clarke, E.M., Kurshan, R.P. (eds.) Computer-Aided Verification. pp. 364–372. Springer Berlin Heidelberg, Berlin, Heidelberg (1991). https://doi.org/10.1007/BFb0023750
6. Cleaveland, R., Hennessy, M.: Testing equivalence as a bisimulation equivalence. Formal Aspects of Computing **5**(1), 1–20 (1993). https://doi.org/10.1007/BF01211314
7. D. Bruda, S., Zhang, Z.: Model checking is refinement – from computation tree logic to failure trace testing. In: Proceedings of the 5th International Conference on Software and Data Technologies - Volume 2: ICSOFT,. pp. 173–178. INSTICC, SciTePress (2010). https://doi.org/10.5220/0003006801730178
8. de Frutos-Escrig, D., Keiren, J.J.A., Willemse, T.A.C.: Games for bisimulations and abstraction. Logical Methods in Computer Science **13**(4) (Nov 2017). https://doi.org/10.23638/LMCS-13(4:15)2017
9. Gazda, M., Fokkink, W., Massaro, V.: Congruence from the operator's point of view: Syntactic requirements on modal characterizations. Acta Informatica **57**(3-5), 329–351 (10 2020). https://doi.org/10.1007/s00236-019-00355-5
10. van Glabbeek, R.J.: The linear time–branching time spectrum. In: International Conference on Concurrency Theory. pp. 278–297. Springer (1990). https://doi.org/10.1007/BFb0039066
11. van Glabbeek, R.J.: The linear time–branching time spectrum II. In: International Conference on Concurrency Theory. pp. 66–81. Springer (1993). https://doi.org/10.1007/3-540-57208-2_6
12. van Glabbeek, R.J.: The linear time–branching time spectrum I – the semantics of concrete, sequential processes. In: Handbook of Process Algebra. pp. 3–99. Elsevier, Amsterdam (2001). https://doi.org/10.1016/B978-044482830-9/50019-9

13. Grädel, E.: Finite model theory and descriptive complexity. In: Grädel, E., Kolaitis, P., Libkin, L., Marx, M., Spencer, J., Vardi, M., Venema, Y., Weinstein, S. (eds.) Finite Model Theory and Its Applications, pp. 125–230. Texts in Theoretical Computer Science. An EATCS Series, Springer Berlin Heidelberg (2007). https://doi.org/10.1007/3-540-68804-8_3

14. Hennessy, M., Milner, R.: On observing nondeterminism and concurrency. In: de Bakker, J., van Leeuwen, J. (eds.) Automata, Languages and Programming. pp. 299–309. Springer Berlin Heidelberg, Berlin, Heidelberg (1980). https://doi.org/10.1007/3-540-10003-2_79

15. Jasper, M., Schlüter, M., Steffen, B.: Characteristic invariants in Hennessy–Milner logic. Acta Informatica pp. 671–687 (2020). https://doi.org/10.1007/s00236-020-00376-5

16. König, B., Mika-Michalski, C., Schröder, L.: Explaining non-bisimilarity in a coalgebraic approach: Games and distinguishing formulas. In: Petrişan, D., Rot, J. (eds.) Coalgebraic Methods in Computer Science. pp. 133–154. Springer International Publishing, Cham (2020). https://doi.org/10.1007/978-3-030-57201-3_8

17. Kučera, A., Esparza, J.: A logical viewpoint on process-algebraic quotients. In: Flum, J., Rodriguez-Artalejo, M. (eds.) Computer Science Logic. pp. 499–514. Springer Berlin Heidelberg, Berlin, Heidelberg (1999). https://doi.org/10.1007/3-540-48168-0_35

18. Shukla, S.K., Hunt, H.B., Rosenkrantz, D.J.: HORNSAT, model checking, verification and games (1995). https://doi.org/10.1007/3-540-61474-5_61

On Satisficing in Quantitative Games

Suguman Bansal[1] ✉, Krishnendu Chatterjee[2], and Moshe Y. Vardi[3]

[1] University of Pennsylvania, Philadelphia, USA suguman@seas.upenn.edu
[2] IST Austria, Klosterneuburg, Austria, krishnendu.chatterjee@ist.ac.at
[3] Rice University, Houston, USA vardi@cs.rice.edu

Abstract. Several problems in planning and reactive synthesis can be reduced to the analysis of two-player quantitative graph games. *Optimization* is one form of analysis. We argue that in many cases it may be better to replace the optimization problem with the *satisficing problem*, where instead of searching for optimal solutions, the goal is to search for solutions that adhere to a given threshold bound.
This work defines and investigates the satisficing problem on a two-player graph game with the discounted-sum cost model. We show that while the satisficing problem can be solved using numerical methods just like the optimization problem, this approach does not render compelling benefits over optimization. When the discount factor is, however, an integer, we present another approach to satisficing, which is purely based on automata methods. We show that this approach is algorithmically more performant – both theoretically and empirically – and demonstrates the broader applicability of satisficing over optimization.

1 Introduction

Quantitative properties of systems are increasingly being explored in automated reasoning [4,14,16,20,21,26]. In decision-making domains such as planning and reactive synthesis, quantitative properties have been deployed to describe *soft constraints* such as quality measures [11], cost and resources [18,22], rewards [31], and the like. Since these constraints are soft, it suffices to generate solutions that are *good enough* w.r.t. the quantitative property.

Existing approaches on the analysis of quantitative properties have, however, primarily focused on *optimization* of these constraints, i.e., to generate optimal solutions. We argue that there may be disadvantages to searching for optimal solutions, where *good enough* ones may suffice. First, optimization may be more expensive than searching for good-enough solutions. Second, optimization restricts the search-space of possible solutions, and thus could limit the broader applicability of the resulting solutions. For instance, to generate solutions that operate *within* battery life, it is too restrictive to search for solutions with *minimal* battery consumption. Besides, solutions with minimal battery consumption may be limited in their applicability, since they may not satisfy other goals, such as desirable temporal tasks.

To this end, this work focuses on directly searching for good-enough solutions. We propose an alternate form of analysis of quantitative properties in

J. F. Groote and K. G. Larsen (Eds.): TACAS 2021, LNCS 12651, pp. 20–37, 2021.
https://doi.org/10.1007/978-3-030-72016-2_2

which the objective is to search for a solution that adheres to *a given thresh-old bound*, possibly derived from a physical constraint such as battery life. We call this the *satisficing problem*, a term popularized by H.A.Simon in economics to mean *satisfy and suffice*, implying a search for good-enough solutions [1]. Through theoretical and empirical investigation, we make the case that satis-ficing is algorithmically more performant than optimization and, further, that satisficing solutions may have broader applicability than optimal solutions.

This work formulates and investigates the satisficing problem on two-player, finite-state games with the discounted-sum (DS) cost model, which is a standard cost-model in decision-making domains [24,25,28]. In these games, players take turns to pass a token along the *transition relation* between the states. As the token is pushed around, the play accumulates costs along the transitions using the DS cost model. The players are assumed to have opposing objectives: one player maximizes the cost, while the other player minimizes it. We define the satisficing problem as follows: *Given a threshold value $v \in \mathbb{Q}$, does there exist a strategy for the minimizing (or maximizing) player that ensures the cost of all resulting plays is strictly or non-strictly lower (or greater) than the threshold v?*

Clearly, the satisficing problem is decidable since the optimization prob-lem on these quantitative games is known to be solvable in pseudo-polynomial time [17,23,32]. To design an algorithm for satisficing, we first adapt the cele-brated value-iteration (VI) based algorithm for optimization [32] (§ 3). We show, however, that this algorithm, called VISatisfice, displays the same complexity as optimization and hence renders no complexity-theoretic advantage. To obtain worst-case complexity, we perform a thorough worst-case analysis of VI for op-timization. It is interesting that a thorough analysis of VI for optimization had hitherto been absent from the literature, despite the popularity of VI. To ad-dress this gap, we first prove that VI should be executed for $\Theta(|V|)$ iterations to compute the optimal value, where V and E refer to the sets of states and transitions in the quantitative game. Next, to compute the overall complexity, we take into account the cost of arithmetic operations as well, since they appear in abundance in VI. We demonstrate an orders-of-magnitude difference between the complexity of VI under different cost-models of arithmetic. For instance, for integer discount factors, we show that VI is $\mathcal{O}(|V| \cdot |E|)$ and $\mathcal{O}(|V|^2 \cdot |E|)$ under the unit-cost and bit-cost models of arithmetic, respectively. Clearly, this shows that VI for optimization, and hence VISatisfice, does not scale to large quantitative games.

We then present a purely automata-based approach for satisficing (§ 4). While this approach applies to integer discount factors only, it solves satisficing in $\mathcal{O}(|V| + |E|)$ time. This shows that there is a fundamental separation in com-plexity between satisficing and VI-based optimization, as even the lower bound on the number of iterations in VI is higher. In this approach, the satisficing prob-lem is reduced to solving a safety or reachability game. Our core observation is that the criteria to fulfil satisficing with respect to threshold value $v \in \mathbb{Q}$ can be expressed as membership in an automaton that accepts a weight sequence A iff $DS(A, d) \mathrel{R} v$ holds, where $d > 1$ is the discount factor and $\mathrm{R} \in \{\le, \ge, <, >\}$. In existing literature, such automata are called *comparator automata* (comparators, in short) when the threshold value $v = 0$ [6,7]. They are known to have a compact safety or co-safety automaton representation [9,19], which could be used to reduce the satisficing problem with zero threshold value. To solve satisficing for arbitrary threshold values $v \in Q$, we extend existing results on comparators to permit arbitrary but fixed threshold values $v \in \mathbb{Q}$. An empirical comparison between the performance of VISatisfice, VI for optimization, and automata-based solution for satisficing shows that the latter outperforms the others in efficiency, scalability, and robustness.

In addition to improved algorithmic performance, we demonstrate that satisficing solutions have broader applicability than optimal ones (§ 5). We examine this with respect to their ability to extend to temporal goals. That is, the problem is to find optimal/satisficing solutions that also satisfy a given temporal goal. Prior results have shown this to not be possible with optimal solutions [13]. In contrast, we show satisficing extends to temporal goals when the discount factor is an integer. This occurs because both satisficing and satisfaction of temporal goals are solved via automata-based techniques, which can be easily integrated.

In summary, this work contributes to showing that satisficing has algorithmic and applicability advantages over optimization in (deterministic) quantitative games. In particular, we have shown that the automata-based approach for satisficing have advantages over approaches in numerical methods like value-iteration. This gives yet another evidence in favor of automata-based quantitative reasoning and opens up several compelling directions for future work.

2   Preliminaries

2.1   Two-player graph games

Reachability and safety games. Both *reachability* and *safety games* are defined over the structure $G = (V = V_0 \uplus V_1, v_{\text{init}}, E, \mathcal{F})$ [30]. It consists of a directed graph (V, E), and a partition (V_0, V_1) of its states V. State v_{init} is the *initial state* of the game. The set of successors of state v is designated by vE. For convenience, we assume that every state has at least one outgoing edge, i.e, $vE \neq \emptyset$ for all $v \in V$. $\mathcal{F} \subseteq V$ is a non-empty set of states. $\mathcal{F}$ is referred to as *accepting* and *rejecting* states in reachability and safety games, respectively.

A *play* of a game involves two players, denoted by P_0 and P_1, to create an infinite path by moving a token along the transitions as follows: At the beginning, the token is at the initial state. If the current position v belongs to V_i, then P_i chooses the successor state from vE. Formally, a play $\rho = v_0 v_1 v_2 \ldots$ is an infinite sequence of states such that the first state $v_0 = v_{\text{init}}$, and each pair of successive states is a transition, i.e., $(v_k, v_{k+1}) \in E$ for all $k \geq 0$. A play is *winning for player P_1* in a reachability game if it visits an accepting state, and *winning for player P_0* otherwise. The opposite holds in safety games, i.e., a play is winning for player P_1 if it does not visit any rejecting state, and winning for P_0 otherwise.

A *strategy* for a player is a recipe that guides the player on which state to go next to based on the history of the play. A *strategy is winning for a player P_i* if for all strategies of the opponent player P_{1-i}, the resulting plays are winning for P_i. To *solve* a graph game means to determine whether there exists a winning strategy for player P_1. Reachability and safety games are solved in $\mathcal{O}(|V|+|E|)$.

Quantitative graph games. A *quantitative graph game* (or quantitative game, in short) is defined over a structure $G = (V = V_0 \uplus V_1, v_{\mathsf{init}}, E, \gamma)$. V, V_0, V_1, v_{init}, E, plays and strategies are defined as earlier. Each transition of the game is associated with a *cost* determined by the *cost function* $\gamma : E \to \mathbb{Z}$. The *cost sequence* of a play ρ is the sequence of costs $w_0 w_1 w_2 \ldots$ such that $w_k = \gamma((v_k, v_{k+1}))$ for all $i \geq 0$. Given a discount factor $d > 1$, the *cost of play* ρ, denoted $wt(\rho)$, is the discounted sum of its cost sequence, i.e., $wt(\rho) = DS(\rho, d) = w_0 + \frac{w_1}{d} + \frac{w_2}{d^2} + \ldots$.

2.2   Automata and formal languages

Büchi automata. A *Büchi automaton* is a tuple $\mathcal{A} = (S, \Sigma, \delta, s_{\mathcal{I}}, \mathcal{F})$, where S is a finite set of *states*, Σ is a finite *input alphabet*, $\delta \subseteq (S \times \Sigma \times S)$ is the *transition relation*, state $s_{\mathcal{I}} \in S$ is the *initial state*, and $\mathcal{F} \subseteq S$ is the set of *accepting states* [30]. A Büchi automaton is *deterministic* if for all states s and inputs a, $|\{s'|(s, a, s') \in \delta$ for some $s'\}| \leq 1$. For a word $w = w_0 w_1 \cdots \in \Sigma^\omega$, a *run* ρ of w is a sequence of states $s_0 s_1 \ldots$ s.t. $s_0 = s_{\mathcal{I}}$, and $\tau_i = (s_i, w_i, s_{i+1}) \in \delta$ for all i. Let $inf(\rho)$ denote the set of states that occur infinitely often in run ρ. A run ρ is an *accepting run* if $inf(\rho) \cap \mathcal{F} \neq \emptyset$. A word w is an accepting word if it has an accepting run. The language of Büchi automaton $\mathcal{A}$ is the set of all words accepted by $\mathcal{A}$. Languages accepted by Büchi automata are called ω-*regular*.

Safety and co-safety languages. Let $\mathcal{L} \subseteq \Sigma^\omega$ be a language over alphabet Σ. A finite word $w \in \Sigma^*$ is a *bad prefix* for $\mathcal{L}$ if for all infinite words $y \in \Sigma^\omega$, $x \cdot y \notin \mathcal{L}$. A language $\mathcal{L}$ is a *safety language* if every word $w \notin \mathcal{L}$ has a bad prefix for $\mathcal{L}$ [3]. A *co-safety language* is the complement of a safety language [19]. Safety and co-safety languages that are ω-regular are represented by specialized Büchi automata called *safety* and *co-safety automata*, respectively.

Comparison language and comparator automata. Given integer bound $\mu > 0$, discount factor $d > 1$, and relation $\mathsf{R} \in \{<, >, \leq, \geq, =, \neq\}$ the *comparison language with upper bound* μ, *relation* R, *discount factor* d is the language of words over the alphabet $\Sigma = \{-\mu, \ldots, \mu\}$ that accepts $A \in \Sigma^\omega$ iff $DS(A, d) \mathsf{R} 0$ holds [5,9]. The *comparator automata with upper bound* μ, *relation* R, *discount factor* d is the automaton that accepts the corresponding comparison language [6]. Depending on R, these languages are safety or co-safety [9]. A comparison language is said to be ω-*regular* if its automaton is a Büchi automaton. Comparison languages are ω-regular iff the discount factor is an integer [7].

3   Satisficing via Optimization

This section shows that there are no complexity-theoretic benefits to solving the satisficing problem via algorithms for the optimization problem.

§ 3.1 formally defines the satisficing problem and reviews the celebrated value-iteration (VI) algorithm for optimization by Zwick and Patterson (ZP). While ZP *claim without proof* that the algorithm runs in pseudo-polynomial time [32], its worst-case analysis is absent from literature. This section presents a detailed account of the said analysis, and exposes the dependence of VI's worst-case complexity on the discount factor $d > 1$ and the cost-model for arithmetic operations i.e. unit-cost or bit-cost model. The analysis is split into two parts: First, § 3.2 shows it is sufficient to terminate after a finite-number of iterations. Next, § 3.3 accounts for the cost of arithmetic operations per iteration to compute VI's worst-case complexity under unit- and bit-cost cost models of arithmetic Finally, § 3.4 presents and analyzes our VI-based algorithm for satisficing VISatisfice.

3.1   Satisficing and Optimization

Definition 1 (Satisficing problem). *Given a quantitative graph game G and a threshold value $v \in \mathbb{Q}$, the* satisficing problem *is to determine whether the minimizing (or maximizing) player has a strategy that ensures the cost of all resulting plays is strictly or non-strictly lower (or greater) than the threshold v.*

The satisficing problem can clealy be solved by solving the *optimization problem*. The optimal cost of a quantitative game is that value such that the maximizing and minimizing players can guarantee that the cost of plays is at least and at most the optimal value, respectively.

Definition 2 (Optimization problem). *Given a quantitative graph game G, the* optimization problem *is to compute the optimal cost from all possible plays from the game, under the assumption that the players have opposing objectives to maximize and minimize the cost of plays, respectively.*

Seminal work by Zwick and Patterson showed the optimization problem is solved by the value-iteration algorithm presented here [32]. Essentially, the algorithm plays a min-max game between the two players. Let $wt_k(v)$ denote the optimal cost of a k-length game that begins in state $v \in V$. Then $wt_k(v)$ can be computed using the following equations: The optimal cost of a 1-length game beginning in state $v \in V$ is $\max\{\gamma(v, w)|(v, w) \in E\}$ if $v \in V_0$ and $\min\{\gamma(v, w)|(v, w) \in E\}$ if $v \in V_1$. Given the optimal-cost of a k-length game, the optimal cost of a $(k + 1)$-length game is computed as follows:

$$wt_{k+1}(v) = \begin{cases} max\{\gamma(v, w) + \frac{1}{d} \cdot wt_k(w)|(v, w) \in E\} & \text{if } v \in V_0 \\ min\{\gamma(v, w) + \frac{1}{d} \cdot wt_k(w)|(v, w) \in E\} & \text{if } v \in V_1 \end{cases}$$

Let W be the optimal cost. Then, $W = \lim_{k \to \infty} wt_k(v_{\text{init}})$. [27,32].

3.2   VI: Number of iterations

The VI algorithm described above terminates at *infinitum*. To compute the algorithms' worst-case complexity, we establish a linear bound on the number of iterations that is sufficient to compute the optimal cost. We also establish a matching lower bound, showing that our analysis is tight.

Upper bound on number of iterations. The upper bound computation utilizes one key result from existing literature: There exist memoryless strategies for both players such that the cost of the resulting play is the optimal cost [27]. Then, there must exists an optimal play in the form of a *simple lasso* in the quantitative game, where a *lasso* is a play represented as $v_0 v_1 \ldots v_n (s_0 s_2 \ldots s_m)^\omega$. We call the initial segment $v_0 v_1 \ldots v_n$ its *head*, and the cycle segment $s_0 s_1 \ldots s_m$ its *loop*. A lasso is *simple* if each state in $\{v_0 \ldots v_n, s_0, \ldots s_m\}$ is distinct. We begin our proof by assigning constraints on the optimal cost using the simple lasso structure of an optimal play (Corollary 1 and Corollary 2).

Let $l = a_0 \ldots a_n (b_0 \ldots b_m)^\omega$ be the cost sequence of a lasso such that $l_1 = a_0 \ldots a_n$ and $l_2 = b_0 \ldots b_m$ are the cost sequences of the head and the loop, respectively. Then the following can be said about $DS(l_1 \cdot l_2^\omega, d)$,

Lemma 1. *Let $l = l_1 \cdot (l_2)^\omega$ represent an integer cost sequence of a lasso, where l_1 and l_2 are the cost sequences of the head and loop of the lasso. Let $d = \frac{p}{q}$ be the discount factor. Then, $DS(l, d)$ is a rational number with denominator at most $(p^{|l_2|} - q^{|l_2|}) \cdot (p^{|l_1|})$.*

Lemma 1 is proven by unrolling $DS(l_1 \cdot l_2^\omega, d)$. Then, the first constraint on the optimal cost is as follows:

Corollary 1. *Let $G = (V, v_{\mathsf{init}}, E, \gamma)$ be a quantitative graph game. Let $d = \frac{p}{q}$ be the discount factor. Then the optimal cost of the game is a rational number with denominator at most $(p^{|V|} - q^{|V|}) \cdot (p^{|V|})$*

Proof. Recall, there exists a simple lasso that computes the optimal cost. Since a simple lasso is of $|V|$-length at most, the length of its head and loop are at most $|V|$ each. So, the expression from Lemma 1 simplifies to $(p^{|V|} - q^{|V|}) \cdot (p^{|V|})$. $\square$

The second constraint has to do with the minimum non-zero difference between the cost of simple lassos:

Corollary 2. *Let $G = (V, v_{\mathsf{init}}, E, \gamma)$ be a quantitative graph game. Let $d = \frac{p}{q}$ be the discount factor. Then the minimal non-zero difference between the cost of simple lassos is a rational with denominator at most $(p^{(|V|)} - q^{(|V|)})^2 \cdot (p^{(2 \cdot |V|)})$.*

Proof. Given two rational numbers with denominator at most a, an upper bound on the denominator of minimal non-zero difference of these two rational numbers is a^2. Then, using the result from Corollary 1, we immediately obtain that the minimal non-zero difference between the cost of two lassos is a rational number with denominator at most $(p^{(|V|)} - q^{(|V|)})^2 \cdot (p^{(2 \cdot |V|)})$. $\square$

For notational convenience, let $\mathsf{bound}_\mathsf{w} = (p^{|V|} - q^{|V|}) \cdot (p^{|V|})$ and $\mathsf{bound}_\mathsf{diff} = (p^{(|V|)} - q^{(|V|)})^2 \cdot (p^{(2 \cdot |V|)})$. Wlog, $|V| > 1$. Since, $\frac{1}{\mathsf{bound}_\mathsf{diff}} < \frac{1}{\mathsf{bound}_\mathsf{w}}$, there is at most one rational number with denominator $\mathsf{bound}_\mathsf{w}$ or less in any interval of size $\frac{1}{\mathsf{bound}_\mathsf{diff}}$. Thus, if we can identify an interval of size less than $\frac{1}{\mathsf{bound}_\mathsf{diff}}$ around the optimal cost, then due to Corollary 1, the optimal cost will be the unique rational number with denominator $\mathsf{bound}_\mathsf{w}$ or less in this interval.

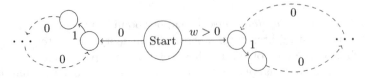

Fig. 1. Sketch of game graph which requires $\Omega(|V|)$ iterations

Thus, the final question is to identify a small enough interval (of size $\frac{1}{\text{bound}_{\text{diff}}}$ or less) such that the optimal cost lies within it. To find an interval around the optimal cost, we use a finite-horizon approximation of the optimal cost:

Lemma 2. *Let W be the optimal cost in quantitative game G. Let $\mu > 0$ be the maximum of absolute value of cost on transitions in G. Then, for all $k \in \mathbb{N}$,*

$$wt_k(v_{\text{init}}) - \frac{1}{d^{k-1}} \cdot \frac{\mu}{d-1} \le W \le wt_k(v_{\text{init}}) + \frac{1}{d^{k-1}} \cdot \frac{\mu}{d-1}$$

Proof. Since W is the limit of $wt_k(v_{\text{init}})$ as $k \to \infty$, W must lie in between the minimum and maximum cost possible if the k-length game is extended to an infinite-length game. The minimum possible extension would be when the k-length game is extended by iterations in which the cost incurred in each round is $-\mu$. Therefore, the minimum possible value is $wt_k(v_{\text{init}}) - \frac{1}{d^{k-1}} \cdot \frac{\mu}{d-1}$. Similarly, the maximum possible value is $wt_k(v_{\text{init}}) + \frac{1}{d^{k-1}} \cdot \frac{\mu}{d-1}$. $\qquad\square$

Now that we have an interval around the optimal cost, we can compute the number of iterations of VI required to make it smaller than $1/\text{bound}_{\text{diff}}$.

Theorem 1. *Let $G = (V, v_{\text{init}}, E, \gamma)$ be a quantitative graph game. Let $\mu > 0$ be the maximum of absolute value of costs along transitions. The number of iterations required by the value-iteration algorithm is*

1. $\mathcal{O}(|V|)$ *when discount factor $d \ge 2$,*
2. $\mathcal{O}\left(\frac{\log(\mu)}{d-1} + |V|\right)$ *when discount factor $1 < d < 2$.*

Proof (Sketch). As discussed in Corollary 1-2 and Lemma 2, the optimal cost is the unique rational number with denominator $\frac{1}{\text{bound}_W}$ or less within the interval $\left(wt_k(v_{\text{init}}) - \frac{1}{d^{k-1}} \cdot \frac{\mu}{d-1}, wt_k(v_{\text{init}}) + \frac{1}{d^{k-1}} \cdot \frac{\mu}{d-1}\right)$ for a large enough $k > 0$ such that the interval's size is less than $\frac{1}{\text{bound}_{\text{diff}}}$. Thus, our task is to determine the value of $k > 0$ such that $2 \cdot \frac{\mu}{d-1 \cdot d^{k-1}} \le \frac{1}{\text{bound}_{\text{diff}}}$ holds. The case $d \ge 2$ is easy to simplify. The case $1 < d < 2$ involves approximations of logarithms of small values. $\qquad\square$

Lower bound on number of iterations of VI. We establish a matching lower bound of $\Omega(|V|)$ iterations to show that our analysis is tight.

Consider the sketch of a quantitative game in Fig 1. Let all states belong to the maximizing player. Hence, the optimization problem reduces to searching for a *path* with optimal cost. Now let the loop on the right-hand side (RHS) be larger than the loop on the left-hand side (LHS). For carefully chosen values of

w and lengths of the loops, one can show that the path for optimal cost of a k-length game is along the RHS loop when k is small, but along the LHS loop when k is large. This way, the correct maximal value can be obtained only at a large value for k. Hence the VI algorithm runs for at least enough iterations that the optimal path will be in the LHS loop. By meticulous reverse engineering of the size of both loops and the value of w, one can guarantee that $k = \Omega(|V|)$.

3.3 Worst-case complexity analysis of VI for optimization

Finally, we complete the worst-case complexity analysis of VI for optimization. We account for the the cost of arithmetic operations since they appear in abundance in VI. We demonstrate that there are orders-of-magnitude of difference in complexity under different models of arithmetic, namely unit-cost and bit-cost.

Unit-cost model. Under the unit-cost model of arithmetic, all arithmetic operations are assumed to take constant time.

Theorem 2. *Let $G = (V, v_{\mathrm{init}}, E, \gamma)$ be a quantitative graph game. Let $\mu > 0$ be the maximum of absolute value of costs along transitions. The worst-case complexity of the optimization problem under unit-cost model of arithmetic is*

1. $\mathcal{O}(|V| \cdot |E|)$ *when discount factor $d \geq 2$,*
2. $\mathcal{O}\left(\frac{\log(\mu) \cdot |E|}{d-1} + |V| \cdot |E|\right)$ *when discount factor $1 < d < 2$.*

Proof. Each iteration takes $\mathcal{O}(E)$ cost since every transition is visited once. Thus, the complexity is $\mathcal{O}(|E|)$ multiplied by the number of iterations (Theorem 1). $\square$

Bit-cost model. Under the bit-cost model, the cost of arithmetic operations depends on the size of the numerical values. Integers are represented in their bit-wise representation. Rational numbers $\frac{r}{s}$ are represented as a tuple of the bit-wise representation of integers r and s. For two integers of length n and m, the cost of their addition and multiplication is $O(m+n)$ and $O(m \cdot n)$, respectively.

Theorem 3. *Let $G = (V, v_{\mathrm{init}}, E, \gamma)$ be a quantitative graph game. Let $\mu > 0$ be the maximum of absolute value of costs along transitions. Let $d = \frac{p}{q} > 1$ be the discount factor. The worst-case complexity of the optimization problem under the bit-cost model of arithmetic is*

1. $\mathcal{O}(|V|^2 \cdot |E| \cdot \log p \cdot \max\{\log \mu, \log p\})$ *when $d \geq 2$,*
2. $\mathcal{O}\left(\left(\frac{\log(\mu)}{d-1} + |V|\right)^2 \cdot |E| \cdot \log p \cdot \max\{\log \mu, \log p\}\right)$ *when $1 < d < 2$.*

Proof (Sketch). Since arithmetic operations incur a cost and the length of representation of intermediate costs increases linearly in each iteration, we can show that the cost of conducting the j-th iteration is $\mathcal{O}(|E| \cdot j \cdot \log \mu \cdot \log p)$. Their summation will return the given expressions. $\square$

Remarks on integer discount factor. Our analysis shows that when the discount factor is an integer ($d \geq 2$), VI requires $\Theta(|V|)$ iterations. Its worst-case complexity is, therefore, $\mathcal{O}(|V| \cdot |E|)$ and $\mathcal{O}(|V|^2 \cdot |E|)$ under the unit-cost and bit-cost models for arithmetic, respectively. From a practical point of view, the bit-cost model is more relevant since implementations of VI will use multi-precision libraries to avoid floating-point errors. While one may argue that the upper bounds in Theorem 3 could be tightened, they would not improve significantly due to the $\Omega(|V|)$ lower bound on number of iterations.

3.4   Satisficing via value-iteration

We present our first algorithm for the satisficing problem. It is an adaptation of VI. However, we see that it does not fare better than VI for optimization.

VI-based algorithm for satisficing is described as follows: Perform VI for optimization. Terminate as soon as one of these occurs: (a). VI completes as many iterations from Theorem 1, or (b). The threshold value falls outside the interval defined in Lemma 2. Either way, one can tell how the threshold value relates to the optimal cost to solve satisficing. Clearly, (a) needs as many iterations as optimization; (b) does not reduce the number of iterations since it is inversely proportional to the distance between optimal cost and threshold value:

Theorem 4. *Let $G = (V, v_{\text{init}}, E, \gamma)$ be a quantitative graph game with optimal cost W. Let $v \in \mathbb{Q}$ be the threshold value. Then number of iterations taken by a VI-based algorithm for the satisficing problem is $\min\{O(|V|), \log \frac{\mu}{|W|-v}\}$ if $d \geq 2$ and $\min\{\mathcal{O}\left(\frac{\log(\mu)}{d-1} + |V|\right), \log \frac{\mu}{|W|-v}\}$ if $1 < d < 2$.*

Observe that this bound is tight since the lower bounds from optimization apply here as well. The worst-case complexity can be completed using similar computations from § 3.3. Since, the number of iterations is identical to Theorem 1, the worst-case complexity will be identical to Theorem 2 and Theorem 3, showing no theoretical improvement. However, its implementations may terminate soon for threshold values far from the optimal but it will retain worst-case behavior for ones closer to the optimal. The catch is since the optimal cost is unknown apriori, this leads to a highly variable and *non-robust* performance.

4   Satisficing via Comparators

Our second algorithm for satisficing is purely based on automata-methods. While this approach operates with integer discount factors only, it runs linearly in the size of the quantitative game. This is lower than the number of iterations required by VI, let alone the worst-case complexities of VI. This approach reduces satisficing to solving a safety or reachability game using comparator automata.

The intuition is as follows: Given threshold value $v \in \mathbb{Q}$ and relation R, let the satisficing problem be to ensure cost of plays relates to v by R. Then, a play ρ is *winning for satisficing with v and* R if its cost sequence A satisfies $DS(A, d)$ R

v, where $d > 1$ is the discount factor. When d is an integer and $v = 0$, this simply checks if A is in the safety/co-safety comparator, hence yielding the reduction.

The caveat is the above applies to $v = 0$ only. To overcome this, we extend the theory of comparators to permit arbitrary threshold values $v \in \mathbb{Q}$. We find that results from $v = 0$ transcend to $v \in \mathbb{Q}$, and offer compact comparator constructions (§ 4.1). These new comparators are then used to reduce satisficing to develop an efficient and scalable algorithm (§ 4.2). Finally, to procure a well-rounded view of its performance, we conduct an empirical evaluation where we see this comparator-based approach outperform the VI approaches § 4.3.

4.1 Foundations of comparator automata with threshold $v \in \mathbb{Q}$

This section extends the existing literature on comparators with threshold value $v = 0$ [6,5,9] to permit non-zero thresholds. The properties we investigate are of safety/co-safety and ω-regularity. We begin with formal definitions:

Definition 3 (Comparison language with threshold $v \in \mathbb{Q}$). *For an integer upper bound $\mu > 0$, discount factor $d > 1$, equality or inequality relation $\mathsf{R} \in \{<, >, \leq, \geq, =, \neq\}$, and a threshold value $v \in \mathbb{Q}$ the comparison language with upper bound μ, relation R, discount factor d and threshold value v is a language of infinite words over the alphabet $\Sigma = \{-\mu, \ldots, \mu\}$ that accepts $A \in \Sigma^\omega$ iff $DS(A, d) \mathsf{R} v$ holds.*

Definition 4 (Comparator automata with threshold $v \in \mathbb{Q}$). *For an integer upper bound $\mu > 0$, discount factor $d > 1$, equality or inequality relation $\mathsf{R} \in \{<, >, \leq, \geq, =, \neq\}$, and a threshold value $v \in \mathbb{Q}$ the comparator automata with upper bound μ, relation R, discount factor d and threshold value v is an automaton that accepts the DS comparison language with upper bound μ, relation R, discount factor d and threshold value v.*

Safety and co-safety of comparison languages. The primary observation is that to determine if $DS(A, d) \mathsf{R} v$ holds, it should be sufficient to examine finite-length prefixes of A since weights later on get heavily discounted. Thus,

Theorem 5. *Let $\mu > 1$ be the integer upper bound. For arbitrary discount factor $d > 1$ and threshold value $v \in \mathbb{Q}$*

1. *Comparison languages are safety languages for relations $\mathsf{R} \in \{\leq, \geq, =\}$.*
2. *Comparison language are co-safety languages for relations $\mathsf{R} \in \{<, >, \neq\}$.*

Proof. The proof is identical to that for threshold value $v = 0$ from [9]. □

Regularity of comparison languages. Prior work on threshold value $v = 0$ shows that a comparator is ω-regular iff the discount factor is an integer [7]. We show the same result for arbitrary threshold values $v \in \mathbb{Q}$.

First of all, trivially, comparators with arbitrary threshold value are not ω-regular for non-integer discount factors, since that already holds when $v = 0$.

The rest of this section proves ω-regularity with arbitrary threshold values for integer discount factors. But first, let us introduce some notations: Since $v \in \mathbb{Q}$, w.l.o.g. we assume that the it has an n-length representation $v = v[0]v[1] \ldots v[m](v[m+1]v[m+2] \ldots v[n])^\omega$. By abuse of notation, we denote both the expression $v[0]v[1] \ldots v[m](v[m+1]v[m+2] \ldots v[n])^\omega$ and the value $DS(v[0]v[1] \ldots v[m](v[m+1]v[m+2] \ldots v[n])^\omega, d)$ by v.

We will construct a Büchi automaton for the comparison language $\mathcal{L}_\leq$ for relation $\leq$, threshold value $v \in \mathbb{Q}$ and an integer discount factor. This is sufficient to prove ω-regularity for all relations since Büchi automata are closed.

From safety/co-safety of comparison languages, we argue it is sufficient to examine the discounted-sum of finite-length weight sequences to know if their infinite extensions will be in $\mathcal{L}_\leq$. For instance, if the discounted-sum of a finite-length weight-sequence W is *very large*, W could be a bad-prefix of $\mathcal{L}_\leq$. Similarly, if the discounted-sum of a finite-length weight-sequence W is *very small* then for all of its infinite-length bounded extensions Y, $DS(W \cdot Y, d) \leq v$. Thus, a mathematical characterization of *very large* and *very small* would formalize a criterion for membership of sequences in $\mathcal{L}_\leq$ based on their finite-prefixes.

To this end, we use the concept of a *recoverable gap* (or gap value), which is a measure of distance of the discounted-sum of a finite-sequence from 0 [12]. The recoverable gap of a finite weight-sequences W with discount factor d, denoted $\mathsf{gap}(W, d)$, is defined as follows: If $W = \varepsilon$ (the empty sequence), $\mathsf{gap}(\varepsilon, d) = 0$, and $\mathsf{gap}(W, d) = d^{|W|-1} \cdot DS(W, d)$ otherwise. Then, Lemma 3 formalizes *very large* and *very small* in Item 1 and Item 2, respectively, w.r.t. recoverable gaps. As for notation, given a sequence A, let $A[\ldots i]$ denote its i-length prefix:

Lemma 3. *Let $\mu > 0$ be the integer upper bound, $d > 1$ be the discount factor. Let $v \in \mathbb{Q}$ be the threshold value s.t. $v = v[0] \ldots v[m](v[m+1] \ldots v[n])^\omega$. Let W be a non-empty, bounded, finite-length weight-sequence.*

1. $\mathsf{gap}(W - v[\cdots |W|], d) > \frac{1}{d} \cdot DS(v[|W| \cdots], d) + \frac{\mu}{d-1}$. *iff for all infinite-length, bounded extensions Y, $DS(W \cdot Y, d) > v$*
2. $\mathsf{gap}(W - v[\cdots |W|], d) \leq \frac{1}{d} \cdot DS(v[|W| \cdots], d) - \frac{\mu}{d-1}$ *iff For all infinite-length, bounded extensions Y, $DS(W \cdot Y, d) \leq v$*

Proof. We present proof of one direction of Item 1. The others follow similarly. Let W be s.t for every infinite-length, bounded Y, $DS(W \cdot Y, d) > v$ holds. Then $DS(W, d) + \frac{1}{d^{|W|}} \cdot DS(Y, d) \geq DS(v[\cdots |W|] \cdot v[|W| \cdots], d)$ implies $DS(W, d) - DS(v[\cdots |W|], d) > \frac{1}{d^{|W|}} \cdot (DS(v[|W| \cdots], d) - DS(Y, d))$ implies $\mathsf{gap}(W - v[\cdots |W|], d) > \frac{1}{d}(DS(v[|W| \cdots], d) + \frac{\mu \cdot d}{d-1})$. $\square$

This segues into the state-space of the Büchi automaton. We define the state space so that state s represents the gap value s. The idea is that all finite-length weight sequences with gap value s will terminate in state s. To assign transition between these states, we observe that gap value is defined inductively as follows: $\mathsf{gap}(\varepsilon, d) = 0$ and $\mathsf{gap}(W \cdot w, d) = d \cdot \mathsf{gap}(W, d) + w$, where $w \in \{-\mu, \ldots, \mu\}$. Thus there is a transition from state s to state t on $a \in \{-\mu, \ldots, \mu\}$ if $t = d \cdot s + a$. Since $\mathsf{gap}(\varepsilon, d) = 0$, state 0 is assigned to be the initial state.

The issue with this construction is it has infinite states. To limit that, we use Lemma 3. Since Item 1 is a necessary and sufficient criteria for bad prefixes of safety language $\mathcal{L}_\leq$, all states with value larger than Item 1 are fused into one non-accepting sink. For the same reason, all states with gap value less than Item 1 are accepting states. Due to Item 2, all states with value less than Item 2 are fused into one accepting sink. Finally, since d is an integer, gap values are integral. Thus, there are only finitely many states between Item 2 and Item 1.

Theorem 6. *Let $\mu > 0$ be an integer upper bound, $d > 1$ an integer discount factor, R an equality or inequality relation, and $v \in \mathbb{Q}$ the threshold value with an n-length representation given by $v = v[0]v[1]\ldots v[m](v[m+1]v[m+2]\ldots v[n])^\omega$.*

1. *The DS comparator automata for μ, d, R, v is ω-regular iff d is an integer.*
2. *For integer discount factors, the DS comparator is a safety or co-safety automaton with $\mathcal{O}(\frac{\mu \cdot n}{d-1})$ states.*

Proof. To prove Item 1 we present the construction of an ω-regular comparator automaton for integer upper bound $\mu > 0$, integer discount factor $d > 1$, inequality relation $\leq$, and threshold value $v \in \mathbb{Q}$ s.t. $v = v[0]v[1]\ldots v[m](v[m+1]v[m+2]\ldots v[n])^\omega$. , denoted by $\mathcal{A} = (S, s_I, \Sigma, \delta, \mathcal{F})$ where:

For $i \in \{0, \ldots, n\}$, let $\mathsf{U}_i = \frac{1}{d} \cdot DS(v[i\cdots], d) + \frac{\mu}{d-1}$ (Lemma 3, Item 1)
For $i \in \{0, \ldots, n\}$, let $\mathsf{L}_i = \frac{1}{d} \cdot DS(v[i\cdots], d) - \frac{\mu}{d-1}$ (Lemma 3, Item 2)

- $S = \bigcup_{i=0}^n S_i \cup \{\mathsf{bad}, \mathsf{veryGood}\}$ where $S_i = \{(s,i)|s \in \{\lfloor \mathsf{L}_i \rfloor + 1, \ldots, \lfloor \mathsf{U}_i \rfloor\}\}$
- Initial state $s_I = (0, 0)$, Accepting states $\mathcal{F} = S \setminus \{\mathsf{bad}\}$
- Alphabet $\Sigma = \{-\mu, -\mu + 1, \ldots, \mu - 1, \mu\}$
- Transition function $\delta \subseteq S \times \Sigma \to S$ where $(s, a, t) \in \delta$ then:
    1. If $s \in \{\mathsf{bad}, \mathsf{veryGood}\}$, then $t = s$ for all $a \in \Sigma$
    2. If s is of the form (p, i), and $a \in \Sigma$
        (a) If $d \cdot p + a - v[i] > \lfloor \mathsf{U}_i \rfloor$, then $t = \mathsf{bad}$
        (b) If $d \cdot p + a - v[i] \leq \lfloor \mathsf{L}_i \rfloor$, then $t = \mathsf{veryGood}$
        (c) If $\lfloor \mathsf{L}_i \rfloor < d \cdot p + a - v[i] \leq \lfloor \mathsf{U}_i \rfloor$,
            i. If $i == n$, then $t = (d \cdot p + a - v[i], m + 1)$
            ii. Else, $t = (d \cdot p + a - v[i], i + 1)$

We skip proof of correctness as it follows from the above discussion. Observe, $\mathcal{A}$ is deterministic. It is a safety automaton as all non-accepting states are sinks.

To prove Item 2, observe that since the comparator for $\leq$ is a deterministic safety automaton, the comparator for $>$ is obtained by simply flipping the accepting and non-accepting states. This is a co-safety automaton of the same size. One can argue similarly for the remaining relations. □

4.2 Satisficing via safety and reachability games

This section describes our comparator-based linear-time algorithm for satisficing for integer discount factors.

As described earlier, given discount factor $d > 1$, a play is winning for satis-ficing with threshold value $v \in \mathbb{Q}$ and relation R if its cost sequence A satisfies $DS(A, d)$ R v. We now know from Theorem 6, that the winning condition for plays can be expressed as a safety or co-safety automaton for any $v \in \mathbb{Q}$ as long as the discount factor is an integer. Therefore, a *synchronized product* of the quantitative game with the safety or co-safety comparator denoting the winning condition completes the reduction to a safety or reachability game, respectively.

Theorem 7. *Let $G = (V, v_{\text{init}}, E, \gamma)$ be a quantitative game, $d > 1$ the integer discount factor, R the equality or inequality relation, and $v \in \mathbb{Q}$ the threshold value with an n-length representation. Let $\mu > 0$ be the maximum of absolute values of costs along transitions in G. Then,*

1. *The satisficing problem reduces to solving a safety game if $R \in \{\leq, \geq\}$*
2. *The satisficing problem reduces to solving a reachability game if $R \in \{<, >\}$*
3. *The satisficing problem is solved in $\mathcal{O}((|V| + |E|) \cdot \mu \cdot n)$ time.*

Proof. The first two points use a standard synchronized product argument on the following formal reduction [15]: Let $G = (V = V_0 \uplus V_1, v_{\text{init}}, E, \gamma)$ be a quantitative game, $d > 1$ the integer discount factor, R the equality or inequality relation, and $v \in \mathbb{Q}$ the threshold value with an n-length representation. Let $\mu > 0$ be the maximum of absolute values of costs along transitions in G. Then, the first step is to construct the safety/co-safety comparator $\mathcal{A} = (S, s_I, \Sigma, \delta, \mathcal{F})$ for μ, d, R and v. The next is to synchronize the product of G and $\mathcal{A}$ over weights to construct the game $\mathsf{GA} = (W = W_0 \cup W_1, s_0 \times \text{init}, \delta_W, \mathcal{F}_W)$, where

- $W = V \times S$. In particular, $W_0 = V_0 \times S$ and $W_1 = V_1 \times S$. Since V_0 and V_1 are disjoint, W_0 and W_1 are disjoint too.
- Let $s_0 \times \text{init}$ be the initial state of GA.
- Transition relation $\delta_W = W \times W$ is defined such that transition $((v, s), (v', s'))$ $\in \delta_W$ synchronizes between transitions $(v, v') \in \delta$ and $(s, a, s') \in \delta_C$ if $a = \gamma((v, v'))$ is the cost of transition in G.
- $\mathcal{F}_W = V \times \mathcal{F}$. The game is a safety game if the comparator is a safety au-tomaton and a reachability game if the comparator is a co-safety automaton.

We need the size of GA to analyze the worst-case complexity. Clearly, GA consists of $\mathcal{O}(|V| \cdot \mu \cdot n)$ states. To establish the number of transitions in GA, observe that every state (v, s) in GA has the same number of outgoing edges as state v in G because the comparator $\mathcal{A}$ is deterministic. Since GA has $\mathcal{O}(\mu \cdot n)$ copies of every state $v \in G$, there are a total of $\mathcal{O}(|E| \cdot \mu \cdot n)$ transitions in GA. Since GA is either a safety or a reachability game, it is solved in linear-time to its size. Thus, the overall complexity is $\mathcal{O}((|V| + |E|) \cdot \mu \cdot n)$.   □

With respect to the value μ, the VI-based solutions are logarithmic in the worst case, while comparator-based solution is linear due to the size of the com-parator. From a practical perspective, this may not be a limitation since weights along transitions can be scaled down. The parameter that cannot be altered is the size of the quantitative game. With respect to that, the comparator-based

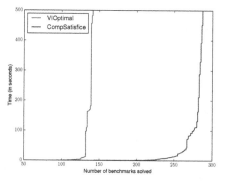
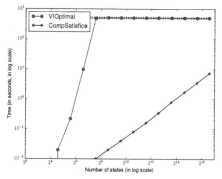

Fig. 2. Cactus plot. $\mu = 5, v = 3$. Total benchmarks = 291

Fig. 3. Single counter scalable benchmark. $\mu = 5, v = 3$. Timeout = 500s.

solution displays clear superiority. Finally, the comparator-based solution is affected by n, length of the representation of the threshold value while the VI-based solution does not. It is natural to assume that the value of n is small.

4.3 Implementation and Empirical Evaluation

The goal of the empirical analysis is to determine whether the practical performance of these algorithms resonate with our theoretical discoveries.

For an apples-to-apples comparison, we implement three algorithms: (a) VIOptimal: Optimization via value-iteration, (b)VISatisfice: Satisficing via value-iteration, and (c). CompSatisfice: Satisficing via comparators. All tools have been implemented in C++. To avoid floating-point errors in VIOptimal and VISatisfice, the tools invoke the open-source GMP (GNU Multi-Precision) [2]. Since all arithmetic operations in CompSatisfice are integral only, it does not use GMP.

To avoid completely randomized benchmarks, we create ~290 benchmarks from LTL$_f$ benchmark suite [29]. The state-of-the-art LTL$_f$-to-automaton tool Lisa [8] is used to convert LTL$_f$ to (non-quantitative) graph games. Weights are randomly assigned to transitions. The number of states in our benchmarks range from 3 to 50000+. Discount factor $d = 2$, threshold $v \in [0 - 10]$. Experiments were run on 8 CPU cores at 2.4GHz, 16GB RAM on a 64-bit Linux machine.

Observations and Inferences Overall, we see that VISatisfice is efficient and scalable, and exhibits steady and predictable performance.

CompSatisfice *outperforms* VIOptimal in both runtime and number of benchmarks solved, as shown in Fig 2. It is crucial to note that all benchmarks solved by VIOptimal had fewer than 200 states. In contrast, CompSatisfice solves much larger benchmarks with 3-50000+ number of states.

To test scalability, we compared both tools on a set of scalable benchmarks. For integer parameter $i > 0$, the i-th scalable benchmark has $3 \cdot 2^i$ states. Fig 3

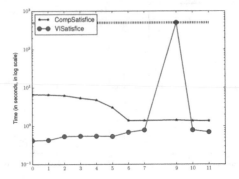

Fig. 4. Robustness. Fix benchmark, vary v. $\mu = 5$. Timeout $= 500$s.

plots number-of-states to runtime in log-log scale. Therefore, the slope of the straight line will indicate the degree of polynomial (in practice). It shows us that CompSatisfice exhibits linear behavior (slope ~1), whereas VIOptimal is much more expensive (slope >> 1) even in practice.

CompSatisfice *is more robust than* VISatisfice. We compare CompSatisfice and VISatisfice as the threshold value changes. This experiment is chosen due to Theorem 4 which proves that VISatisfice is non-robust. As shown in Fig 4, the variance in performance of VISatisfice is very high. The appearance of peak close to the optimal value is an empirical demonstration of Theorem 4. On that other hand, CompSatisfice stays steady in performance owning to its low complexity.

5   Adding Temporally Extended Goals

Having witnessed algorithmic improvements of comparator-based satisficing over VI-based algorithms, we now shift focus to the question of applicability. While this section examines this with respect to the ability to extend to temporal goals, this discussion highlights a core strength of comparator-based reasoning in satisficing and shows its promise in a broader variety of problems.

The problem of extending optimal/satisficing solutions with a temporal goal is to determine whether there exists an optimal/satisficing solution that also satisfies a given temporal goal. Formally, given a quantitative game G, a labeling function $\mathcal{L} : V \to 2^{AP}$ which assigns states V of G to atomic propositions from the set AP, and a temporal goal φ over AP, we say a *play* $\rho = v_0 v_1 \ldots$ *satisfies* φ if its proposition sequence given by $\mathcal{L}(v_0)\mathcal{L}(v_1)\ldots$ satisfies the formula φ. Then to solve *optimization/satisficing with a temporal goal* is to determine if there exists a solutions that is optimal/satisficing and also satisfies the temporal goal along resulting plays. Prior work has proven that the optimization problem cannot be extended to temporal goals [13] unless the temporal goals are very simple safety properties [10,31]. In contrast, our comparator-based solution for satisficing can naturally be extended to temporal goals, in fact to all ω-regular properties, owing to its automata-based underpinnings, as shown below:

Theorem 8. *Let G a quantitative game with state set V, $\mathcal{L} : V \rightarrow 2^{AP}$ be a labeling function over set of atomic propositions AP, and φ be a temporal goal over AP and $\mathcal{A}_\varphi$ be its equivalent deterministic parity automaton. Let $d > 1$ be an integer discount factor, μ be the maximum of the absolute values of costs along transitions, and $v \in Q$ be the threshold value with an n-length representation. Then, solving satisficing with temporal goals reduces to solving a parity game of size linear in $|V|$, μ, n and $|\mathcal{A}_\varphi|$.*

Proof. The reduction involves two steps of synchronized products. The first reduces the satisficing problem to a safety/reachability game while preserving the labelling function. The second synchronization product is between the safety/reachability game with the DPA $\mathcal{A}_\varphi$. These will synchronize on the atomic propositions in the labeling function and DPA transitions, respectively. Therefore, resulting parity game will be linear in $|V|$, μ and n, and $|\mathcal{A}_\varphi|$.   □

Broadly speaking, our ability to solve satisficing via automata-based methods is a key feature as it propels a seamless integration of quantitative properties (threshold bounds) with qualitative properties, as both are grounded in automata-based methods. VI-based solutions are inhibited to do so since numerical methods are known to not combine well with automata-based methods which are so prominent with qualitative reasoning [5,20]. This key feature could be exploited in several other problems to show further benefits of comparator-based satisficing over optimization and VI-based methods.

6   Concluding remarks

This work introduces the satisficing problem for quantitative games with the discounted-sum cost model. When the discount factor is an integer, we present a comparator-based solution for satisficing, which exhibits algorithmic improvements – better worst-case complexity and efficient, scalable, and robust performance – as well as broader applicability over traditional solutions based on numerical approaches for satisficing and optimization. Other technical contributions include the presentation of the missing proof of value-iteration for optimization and the extension of comparator automata to enable direct comparison to arbitrary threshold values as opposed to zero threshold value only.

An undercurrent of our comparator-based approach for satisficing is that it offers an automata-based replacement to traditional numerical methods. By doing so, it paves a way to combine quantitative and qualitative reasoning without compromising on theoretical guarantees or even performance. This motivates tackling more challenging problems in this area, such as more complex environments, variability in information availability, and their combinations.

Acknowledgements. We thank anonymous reviewers for valuable inputs. This work is supported in part by NSF grant 2030859 to the CRA for the CIFellows Project, NSF grants IIS-1527668, CCF-1704883, IIS-1830549, the ERC CoG 863818 (ForM-SMArt), and an award from the Maryland Procurement Office.

References

1. Satisficing. https://en.wikipedia.org/wiki/Satisficing.
2. GMP. https://gmplib.org/.
3. B. Alpern and F. B. Schneider. Recognizing safety and liveness. *Distributed computing*, 2(3):117–126, 1987.
4. C. Baier. Probabilistic model checking. In *Dependable Software Systems Engineering*, pages 1–23. 2016.
5. S. Bansal, S. Chaudhuri, and M. Y. Vardi. Automata vs linear-programming discounted-sum inclusion. In *Proc. of International Conference on Computer-Aided Verification (CAV)*, 2018.
6. S. Bansal, S. Chaudhuri, and M. Y. Vardi. Comparator automata in quantitative verification. In *Proc. of International Conference on Foundations of Software Science and Computation Structures (FoSSaCS)*, 2018.
7. S. Bansal, S. Chaudhuri, and M. Y. Vardi. Comparator automata in quantitative verification (full version). *CoRR*, abs/1812.06569, 2018.
8. S. Bansal, Y. Li, L. Tabajara, and M. Y. Vardi. Hybrid compositional reasoning for reactive synthesis from finite-horizon specifications. In *Proc. of AAAI*, 2020.
9. S. Bansal and M. Y. Vardi. Safety and co-safety comparator automata for discounted-sum inclusion. In *Proc. of International Conference on Computer-Aided Verification (CAV)*, 2019.
10. J. Bernet, D. Janin, and I. Walukiewicz. Permissive strategies: from parity games to safety games. *RAIRO-Theoretical Informatics and Applications-Informatique Théorique et Applications*, 36(3):261–275, 2002.
11. R. Bloem, K. Chatterjee, T. Henzinger, and B. Jobstmann. Better quality in synthesis through quantitative objectives. In *Proc. of CAV*, pages 140–156. Springer, 2009.
12. U. Boker and T. A. Henzinger. Exact and approximate determinization of discounted-sum automata. *LMCS*, 10(1), 2014.
13. K. Chatterjee, T. A. Henzinger, J. Otop, and Y. Velner. Quantitative fair simulation games. *Information and Computation*, 254:143–166, 2017.
14. D. Clark, S. Hunt, and P. Malacaria. A static analysis for quantifying information flow in a simple imperative language. *Journal of Computer Security*, 15(3):321–371, 2007.
15. T. Colcombet and N. Fijalkow. Universal graphs and good for games automata: New tools for infinite duration games. In *Proc. of FSTTCS*, pages 1–26. Springer, 2019.
16. B. Finkbeiner, C. Hahn, and H. Torfah. Model checking quantitative hyperproperties. In *Proc. of CAV*, pages 144–163. Springer, 2018.
17. T. D. Hansen, P. B. Miltersen, and U. Zwick. Strategy iteration is strongly polynomial for 2-player turn-based stochastic games with a constant discount factor. *Journal of the ACM*, 60, 2013.
18. K. He, M. Lahijanian, L. Kavraki, and M. Vardi. Reactive synthesis for finite tasks under resource constraints. In *Intelligent Robots and Systems (IROS), 2017 IEEE/RSJ International Conference on*, pages 5326–5332. IEEE, 2017.
19. O. Kupferman and M. Y. Vardi. Model checking of safety properties. In *Proc. of CAV*, pages 172–183. Springer, 1999.
20. M. Kwiatkowska. Quantitative verification: Models, techniques and tools. In *Proc. 6th joint meeting of the European Software Engineering Conference and the ACM SIGSOFT Symposium on the Foundations of Software Engineering (ESEC/FSE)*, pages 449–458. ACM Press, September 2007.

21. M. Kwiatkowska, G. Norman, and D. Parker. Advances and challenges of probabilistic model checking. In *2010 48th Annual Allerton Conference on Communication, Control, and Computing (Allerton)*, pages 1691–1698. IEEE, 2010.
22. M. Lahijanian, S. Almagor, D. Fried, L. Kavraki, and M. Vardi. This time the robot settles for a cost: A quantitative approach to temporal logic planning with partial satisfaction. In *AAAI*, pages 3664–3671, 2015.
23. M. L. Littman. *Algorithms for sequential decision making*. Brown University Providence, RI, 1996.
24. M. Osborne and A. Rubinstein. *A course in game theory*. MIT press, 1994.
25. M. Puterman. Markov decision processes. *Handbooks in operations research and management science*, 2:331–434, 1990.
26. S. A. Seshia, A. Desai, T. Dreossi, D. J. Fremont, S. Ghosh, E. Kim, S. Shivakumar, M. Vazquez-Chanlatte, and X. Yue. Formal specification for deep neural networks. In *Proc. of ATVA*, pages 20–34. Springer, 2018.
27. L. S. Shapley. Stochastic games. *Proceedings of the National Academy of Sciences of the United States of America*, 39(10):1095, 1953.
28. R. Sutton and A. Barto. *Introduction to reinforcement learning*, volume 135. MIT press Cambridge, 1998.
29. L. M. Tabajara and M. Y. Vardi. Partitioning techniques in LTLf synthesis. In *IJCAI*, pages 5599–5606. AAAI Press, 2019.
30. W. Thomas, T. Wilke, et al. *Automata, logics, and infinite games: A guide to current research*, volume 2500. Springer Science & Business Media, 2002.
31. M. Wen, R. Ehlers, and U. Topcu. Correct-by-synthesis reinforcement learning with temporal logic constraints. In *2015 IEEE/RSJ International Conference on Intelligent Robots and Systems (IROS)*, pages 4983–4990. IEEE, 2015.
32. U. Zwick and M. Paterson. The complexity of mean payoff games on graphs. *Theoretical Computer Science*, 158(1):343–359, 1996.

Quasipolynomial Computation
of Nested Fixpoints

Daniel Hausmann (✉) and Lutz Schröder (✉) *

Friedrich-Alexander-Universität Erlangen-Nürnberg, Erlangen, Germany
{daniel.hausmann,lutz.schroeder}@fau.de

Abstract. It is well-known that the winning region of a parity game with n nodes and k priorities can be computed as a k-nested fixpoint of a suitable function; straightforward computation of this nested fixpoint requires $\mathcal{O}(n^{\frac{k}{2}})$ iterations of the function. Calude et al.'s recent quasipolynomial-time parity game solving algorithm essentially shows how to compute the same fixpoint in only quasipolynomially many iterations by reducing parity games to quasipolynomially sized safety games. Universal graphs have been used to modularize this transformation of parity games to equivalent safety games that are obtained by combining the original game with a universal graph. We show that this approach naturally generalizes to the computation of solutions of systems of *any* fixpoint equations over finite lattices; hence, the solution of fixpoint equation systems can be computed by quasipolynomially many iterations of the equations. We present applications to modal fixpoint logics and games beyond relational semantics. For instance, the model checking problems for the energy μ-calculus, finite latticed μ-calculi, and the graded and the (two-valued) probabilistic μ-calculus – with numbers coded in binary – can be solved via nested fixpoints of functions that differ substantially from the function for parity games but still can be computed in quasipolynomial time; our result hence implies that model checking for these μ-calculi is in QP. Moreover, we improve the exponent in known exponential bounds on satisfiability checking.

Keywords: Fixpoint theory, model checking, satisfiability checking, parity games, energy games, μ-calculus

1 Introduction

Fixpoints are pervasive in computer science, governing large portions of recursion theory, concurrency theory, logic, and game theory. One famous example are parity games, which are central, e.g., to networks and infinite processes [5], tree automata [43], and μ-calculus model checking [17]. Winning regions in parity games can be expressed as nested fixpoints of particular set functions (e.g. [8,16]). In recent breakthrough work on the solution of parity games in quasipolynomial

---

* Work forms part of the DFG-funded project CoMoC (SCHR 1118/15-1, MI 717/7-1).

J. F. Groote and K. G. Larsen (Eds.): TACAS 2021, LNCS 12651, pp. 38–56, 2021.
https://doi.org/10.1007/978-3-030-72016-2_3

time, Calude et al. [9] essentially show how to compute this particular fixpoint in quasipolynomial time, that is, in time $2^{\mathcal{O}((\log n)^c)}$ for some constant c. Subsequently, it has been shown [13,14,28] that universal graphs (that is, even graphs into which every even graph of a certain size embeds by a graph morphism) can be used to transform parity games to equivalent safety games obtained by pairing the original game with a universal graph; the size of these safety games is determined by the size of the employed universal graphs and it has been shown [13,14] that there are universal graphs of quasipolynomial size. This yields a uniform algorithm for solving parity games to which all currently known quasipolynomial algorithms for parity games have been shown to instantiate using appropriately defined universal graphs [13,14].

Briefly, our contribution in the present work is to show that the method of using universal graphs to solve parity games generalizes to the computation of nested fixpoints of arbitrary functions over finite lattices. That is, given functions $f_i : \mathcal{P}(U)^{k+1} \to \mathcal{P}(U)$, $0 \leq i \leq k$ on a finite lattice U, we give an algorithm that uses universal graphs to compute the solutions of systems of equations

$$X_i =_{\eta_i} f_i(X_0, \ldots, X_k) \qquad 0 \leq i \leq k$$

where $\eta_i = \mathsf{GFP}$ (greatest fixpoint) or $\eta_i = \mathsf{LFP}$ (least fixpoint). Since there are universal graphs of quasipolynomial size, the algorithm requires only quasipolynomially many iterations of the functions f_i and hence runs in quasipolynomial time, provided that all f_i are computable in quasipolynomial time. While it seems plausible that this time bound may also be obtained by translating equation systems to equivalent standard parity games by emulating Turing machines to encode the functions f_i as Boolean circuits (leading to many additional states but avoiding exponential blowup during the process), we emphasize that the main point of our result is not so much the ensuing time bound but rather the insight that universal graphs and hence many algorithms for parity games can be used on a much more general level which yields a precise (and relatively low) quasipolynomial bound on the number of function calls that are required to obtain solutions of fixpoint equation systems.

In more detail, the method of Calude et al. can be described as annotating nodes of a parity game with histories of quasipolynomial size and then solving this annotated game, but with a safety winning condition instead of the much more involved parity winning condition. It has been shown that these histories can be seen as nodes in universal graphs, in a more general reduction of parity games to safety games in which nodes from the parity game are annotated with nodes from a universal graph. This method has also been described as pairing *separating automata* with safety games [14]. It has been shown [13,14] that there are exponentially sized universal graphs (essentially yielding the basis for e.g. the fixpoint iteration algorithm [8] or the small progress measures algorithm [27]) and quasipolynomially sized universal graphs (corresponding, e.g., to the succinct progress measure algorithm [28], or to the recent quasipolynomial variant of Zielonka's algorithm [38]).

Hasuo et al. [22], and more generally, Baldan et al. [4] show that nested fixpoints in highly general settings can be computed by a technique based on progress measures, implicitly using exponentially sized universal graphs, obtaining an exponential bound on the number of iterations. Our technique is based on showing that one can make explicit use of universal graphs, correspondingly obtaining a quasipolynomial upper bound on the number of iterations. In both cases, computation of the nested fixpoint is reduced to a single (least or greatest depending on exact formulation) fixpoint of a function that extends the given set function to keep track of the exponential and quasipolynomial histories, respectively, in analogy to the previous reduction of parity games to safety games. Our central result can then be phrased as saying that the method of transforming parity conditions to safety conditions using universal graphs generalizes from solving parity games to solving systems of equations that use arbitrary functions over finite lattices. We use *fixpoint games* [4, 42] to obtain the crucial result that the solutions of equation systems have history-free witnesses, in analogy to history-freeness of winning strategies in parity games. These fixpoint games have exponential size but we show how to extract *polynomial-size* witnesses for winning strategies of Eloise, and use these witnesses to show that any node won by Eloise is also won in the safety game obtained by a universal graph. For the backwards direction, we show that a witness for satisfaction of the safety condition regarding the universal graph induces a winning strategy in the fixpoint game. This proves that universal graphs can be used to compute nested fixpoints of arbitrary functions over finite lattices and hence yields the quasipolynomial upper bound for computation of nested fixpoints. Moreover, we present a progress measure algorithm that uses the nodes of a quasipolynomial universal graph to measure progress and that can be used to efficiently compute nested fixpoints of arbitrary functions over finite lattices.

As an immediate application of these results, we improve known deterministic algorithms for solving *energy parity games* [10], that is, parity games in which edges have additional integer weights and for which the winning condition is a combined parity condition and a (quantitative) positivity condition on the sum of the accumulated weights. Our results also show that the model checking problem for the associated *energy μ-calculus* [2] is in QP. In a similar fashion, we obtain quasipolynomial algorithms for model checking in latticed μ-calculi [7] in which the truth values of formulae are computed over arbitrary finite lattices, and for solving associated latticed parity games [30].

Furthermore, our results improve generic upper complexity bounds on model checking and satisfiability checking in the *coalgebraic μ-calculus* [12], which serves as a generic framework for fixpoint logics beyond relational semantics. Well-known instances of the coalgebraic μ-calculus include the alternating-time μ-calculus [1], the graded μ-calculus [32], the (two-valued) probabilistic μ-calculus [12, 34], and the monotone μ-calculus [18] (the ambient fixpoint logic of concurrent dynamic logic CPDL [39] and Parikh's game logic [37]). This level of generality is achieved by abstracting system types as set functors and systems as coalgebras for the given functor following the paradigm of universal coalgebra [40]. It was previously shown [24] that the model checking problem for coalgebraic μ-calculi reduces to the computation of a nested fixpoint. This fixpoint may be seen as a coalgebraic generalization of a parity game winning region but can be literally phrased in terms of small standard parity games (implying quasipolynomial run time) only in restricted cases. Our results show that the relevant nested fixpoint can be computed in quasipolynomial time in all cases of interest. Notably, we thus obtain as new specific upper bounds that even under binary coding of numbers, the model checking problems of both the graded μ-calculus and the probabilistic μ-calculus are in QP, even when the syntax is extended to allow for (monotone) polynomial inequalities.

Similarly, the satisfiability problem of the coalgebraic μ-calculus has been reduced to a computation of a nested fixpoint [25], and our present results imply a marked improvement in the exponent of the associated exponential time bound. Specifically, the nesting depth of the relevant fixpoint is exponentially smaller than the basis of the lattice. Our results imply that this fixpoint is computable in polynomial time so that the complexity of satisfiability checking in coalgebraic μ-calculi drops from $2^{\mathcal{O}(n^2 k^2 \log n)}$ to $2^{\mathcal{O}(nk \log n)}$ for formulae of size n and with alternation depth k.

Related Work The quasipolynomial bound on parity game solving has in the meantime been realized by a number of alternative algorithms. For instance, Jurdzinski and Lazic [28] use succinct progress measures to improve to quasilinear (instead of quasipolynomial) space; Fearnley et al. [19] similarly achieve quasilinear space. Lehtinen [33] and Boker and Lehtinen [6] present a quasipolynomial algorithm using register games. Parys [38] improves Zielonka's algorithm [43] to run in quasipolynomial time. In particular the last algorithm is of interest as an additional candidate for generalization to nested fixpoints, due to the known good performance of Zielonka's algorithm in practice. Daviaud et al. [15] generalize quasipolynomial-time parity game solving by providing a pseudo-quasipolynomial algorithm for mean-payoff parity games. On the other hand, Czerwinski et al. [14] give a quasipolynomial lower bound on universal trees, implying a barrier for prospective polynomial-time parity game solving algorithms. Chatterjee et al. [11] describe a quasipolynomial time set-based symbolic algorithm for parity game solving that is parametric in a *lift* function that determines how ranks of nodes depend on the ranks of their successors, and thereby unifies the complexity and correctness analysis of various parity game algorithms. Although part of the parity game structure is encapsulated in a set operator *CPre*, the development is tied to standard parity games, e.g. in the definition of the *best* function, which picks minimal or maximal ranks of successors depending on whether a node belongs to Abelard or Eloise.

Early work on the computation of unrestricted nested fixpoints has shown that greatest fixpoints require less effort in the fixpoint iteration algorithm, which can hence be optimized to compute nested fixpoints with just $\mathcal{O}(n^{\frac{k}{2}})$ calls of the functions at hand [35,41], improving the previously known (straightforward) bound $\mathcal{O}(n^k)$; here, n denotes the size of the basis of the lattice and k the number of fixpoint operators. Recent progress in the field has established the above-mentioned approaches using progress measures [22] and fixpoint games [4] in general settings, both with a view to applications in coalgebraic model checking like in the present paper. In comparison to the present work, the respective bounds on the required number of function iterations in the above unrestricted approaches all are exponential.

A preprint of our present results, specifically the quasipolynomial upper bound on function iteration in fixpoint computation, has been available as an arXiv preprint for some time [23]. Subsequent to this preprint, Arnold, Niwinski and Parys [3] have improved the actual run time by reducing the overhead incurred per iteration (and they give a form of quasipolynomial lower bound for universal-tree-based algorithms), working (like [23]) in the less general setting of directly nested fixpoints over powerset lattices; we show in Section 6 how such an improvement can be incorporated also in our lattice-based algorithm.

2   Notation and Preliminaries

Let U and V be sets, and let $R \subseteq U \times U$ be a binary relation on U. For $u \in U$, we then put $R(u) := \{v \in U \mid (u,v) \in R\}$. We put $[k] = \{0, \ldots, k\}$ for $k \in \mathbb{N}$. *Labelled graphs* $G = (W, R)$ consist of a set W together with a relation $R \subseteq W \times A \times W$ where A is some set of labels; typically, we use $A = [k]$ for some $k \in \mathbb{N}$. An R-*path* in a labelled graph is a finite or infinite sequence $v_0, a_0, v_1, a_1, v_2 \ldots$ (ending in a node from W if finite) such that $(v_i, a_i, v_{i+1}) \in R$ for all i. For $v \in W$ and $a \in A$, we put $R_a(v) = \{w \in W \mid (v,a,w) \in R\}$ and sometimes write $|G|$ to refer to $|W|$. As usual, we write U^* and U^ω for the sets of finite sequences or infinite sequences, respectively, of elements of U. The *domain* $\mathrm{dom}(f)$ of a partial function $f : U \rightharpoonup V$ is the set of elements on which f is defined. As usual, the *(forward) image* of $A' \subseteq A$ under a function $f : A \to B$ is $f[A'] = \{b \in B \mid \exists a \in A'. f(a) = b\}$ and the *preimage* $f^{-1}[B']$ of $B' \subseteq B$ under f is defined by $f^{-1}[B'] = \{a \in A \mid \exists b \in B'. f(a) = b\}$. *Projections* $\pi_j : A_1 \times \ldots \times A_m \to A_j$ for $1 \le j \le m$ are given by $\pi_i(a_1, \ldots, a_m) = a_j$. We often regard (finite) sequences $\tau = u_0, u_1, \ldots \in U^* \cup U^\omega$ of elements of U as partial functions of type $\mathbb{N} \rightharpoonup U$ and then write $\tau(i)$ to denote the element u_i, for $i \in \mathrm{dom}(\tau)$. For $\tau \in U^* \cup U^\omega$, we define the set $\mathrm{Inf}(\tau) = \{u \in U \mid \forall i \ge 0. \exists j > i. \tau(j) = u\}$ of elements that occur infinitely often in τ (so $\mathrm{Inf}(\tau) = \emptyset$ for $\tau \in U^*$). An infinite R-path $v_0, p_0, v_1, p_1, \ldots$ in a labelled graph $G = (W, R)$ with labels from $[k]$ is *even* if $\max(\mathrm{Inf}(p_0, p_1, \ldots))$ is even, and G is *even* if every infinite R-path in G is even. We write $\mathcal{P}(U)$ for the powerset of U, and U^m for the m-fold Cartesian product $U \times \cdots \times U$.

Finite Lattices and Fixpoints A *finite lattice* $(L, \sqsubseteq)$ (often written just as L) consists of a non-empty finite set L together with a partial order $\sqsubseteq$ on L, such that there is, for all subsets $X \subseteq L$, a join $\bigsqcup X$ and a meet $\bigsqcap X$. The least and greatest elements of L are defined as $\top = \bigsqcup \emptyset$ and element $\top = \bigsqcap \emptyset$, respectively. A set $B_L \subseteq L$ such that $l = \bigsqcup \{b \in B_L \mid b \sqsubseteq l\}$ is a *basis* of L. Given a finite lattice L, a function $g : L^k \to L$ is *monotone* if $g(V_1, \ldots, V_k) \sqsubseteq g(W_1, \ldots, W_k)$ whenever $V_i \sqsubseteq W_i$ for all $1 \le i \le k$. For monotone $f : L \to L$, we put

$$\mathrm{GFP}\, f = \bigsqcup \{V \sqsubseteq L \mid V \sqsubseteq f(V)\} \qquad \mathrm{LFP}\, f = \bigsqcap \{V \sqsubseteq L \mid f(V) \sqsubseteq V\},$$

which, by the Knaster-Tarski fixpoint theorem, are the greatest and the least fixpoint of f, respectively. Furthermore, we define $f^0(V) = V$ and $f^{m+1}(V) = f(f^m(V))$ for $m \geq 0$, $V \sqsubseteq L$; since L is finite, we have $\mathsf{GFP}\, f = f^n(\top)$ and $\mathsf{LFP}\, f = f^n(\bot)$ by Kleene's fixpoint theorem. Given a finite set U and a natural number n, $(n^U, \sqsubseteq)$ is a finite lattice, where $n^U = \{f : U \to [n-1]\}$ denotes the function space from U to $[n-1]$ and $f \sqsubseteq g$ if and only if for all $u \in U$, $f(u) \leq g(u)$. For $n = 2$, we obtain the powerset lattice $(2^U, \subseteq)$, also denoted by $\mathcal{P}(U)$, with least and greatest elements $\emptyset$ and U, respectively, and basis $\{\{u\} \mid u \in U\}$.

Parity games A *parity game* (V, E, Ω) consists of a set of *nodes* V, a left-total relation $E \subseteq V \times V$ of *moves* encoding the rules of the game, and a *priority function* $\Omega : V \to \mathbb{N}$, which assigns *priorities* $\Omega(v) \in \mathbb{N}$ to nodes $v \in V$. Moreover, each node belongs to exactly one of the two players Eloise or Abelard, where we denote the set of Eloise's nodes by $V_\exists$ and that of Abelard's nodes by $V_\forall$. A *play* $\rho \in V^\omega$ is an infinite sequence of nodes that follows the rules of the game, that is, such that for all $i \geq 0$, we have $(\rho(i), \rho(i+1)) \in E$. We say that an infinite play $\rho = v_0, v_1, \ldots$ is *even* if the largest priority that occurs infinitely often in it (i.e. $\max(\mathsf{Inf}(\Omega \circ \rho))$) is even, and *odd* otherwise, and call this property the *parity* of ρ. Player Eloise *wins* exactly the even plays and player Abelard *wins* all other plays. A *(history-free)* Eloise-*strategy* $s : V_\exists \rightharpoonup V$ is a partial function that assigns single moves $s(x)$ to Eloise-nodes $x \in \mathsf{dom}(s)$. Given an Eloise-strategy s, a play ρ is an *s-play* if for all $i \in \mathsf{dom}(\rho)$ such that $\rho(i) \in V_\exists$, we have $\rho(i+1) = s(\rho(i))$. An Eloise-strategy *wins* a node $v \in V$ if Eloise wins all s-plays that start at v. We have a dual notion of Abelard-strategies; *solving* a parity game consists in computing the *winning regions* $\mathsf{win}_\exists$ and $\mathsf{win}_\forall$ of the two players, that is, the sets of states that they respectively win by some strategy.

It is known that solving parity games is in $\mathsf{NP} \cap \mathsf{coNP}$ (and, more specifically, in $\mathsf{UP} \cap \mathsf{co\text{-}UP}$). Recently it has also been shown [9] that for parity games with n nodes and k priorities, $\mathsf{win}_\exists$ and $\mathsf{win}_\forall$ can be computed in quasipolynomial time $\mathcal{O}(n^{\log k + 6})$. Another crucial property of parity games is that they are *history-free determined* [21], that is, that every node in a parity game is won by exactly one of the two players and then there is a history-free strategy for the respective player that wins the node.

3   Systems of Fixpoint Equations

We now introduce our central notion, that is, systems of fixpoint equations over a finite lattice. Throughout, we fix a finite lattice $(L, \sqsubseteq)$ and a basis B_L of L such that $\bot \notin B_L$, and $k + 1$ monotone functions $f_i : L^{k+1} \to L$, $0 \leq i \leq k$.

Definition 3.1. A *system of equations* consists of $k + 1$ equations of the form

$$X_i =_{\eta_i} f_i(X_0, \ldots, X_k)$$

where $\eta_i \in \{\mathsf{LFP}, \mathsf{GFP}\}$, briefly referred to as f. For a partial valuation $\sigma : [k] \rightharpoonup L$, we inductively define

$$[\![X_i]\!]^\sigma = \eta_i X_i . f_i^\sigma ,$$

where the function f_i^σ is given by

$$f_i^\sigma(A) = f_i([\![X_0]\!]^{\sigma'}, \ldots, [\![X_{i-1}]\!]^{\sigma'}, A, \mathsf{ev}(\sigma', i+1), \ldots, \mathsf{ev}(\sigma', k))$$

for $A \in L$, where $(\sigma[i \mapsto A])(j) = \sigma(j)$ for $j \neq i$ and $(\sigma[i \mapsto A])(i) = A$, $\sigma' = \sigma[i \mapsto A]$ and where $\mathsf{ev}(\sigma, j) = \sigma(j)$ if $j \in \mathsf{dom}(\sigma)$ and $\mathsf{ev}(\sigma, j) = [\![X_j]\!]^\sigma$ otherwise (the latter clause handles *free variables*). Then, the *solution* of the system of equations is $[\![X_k]\!]^\epsilon$ where $\epsilon : [k] \rightharpoonup L$ denotes the empty valuation (i.e. $\mathsf{dom}(\epsilon) = \emptyset$). Similarly, we can obtain solutions for the other components as $[\![X_i]\!]^\epsilon$ for $0 \leq i < k$; we drop the valuation index if no confusion arises, and sometimes write $[\![X_i]\!]_f$ to make the equation system f explicit. We denote by E^{f_0} the solution $[\![X_k]\!]$ for the *canonical system of equations* of the particular shape

$$X_i =_{\eta_i} X_{i-1} \qquad\qquad X_0 =_{\mathsf{GFP}} f_0(X_0, \ldots, X_k),$$

where $0 < i \leq k$, $\eta_i = \mathsf{LFP}$ for odd i and $\eta_i = \mathsf{GFP}$ for even i.

Example 3.2. (1) *Parity games and the modal μ-calculus:* Let (V, E, Ω) be a parity game with priorities 0 to k, take $L = \mathcal{P}(V)$, and consider the canonical system of fixpoint equations $\mathsf{E}^{f_\exists}$ for the function $f_\exists \colon \mathcal{P}(V)^{k+1} \to \mathcal{P}(V)$ given by

$$f_\exists(V_0, \ldots, V_k) = \{v \in V_\exists \mid E(v) \cap V_{\Omega(v)} \neq \emptyset\} \cup \{v \in V_\forall \mid E(v) \subseteq V_{\Omega(v)},\}$$

for $(V_0, \ldots, V_k) \in \mathcal{P}(V)^{k+1}$. It is well known that $\mathsf{win}_\exists = \mathsf{E}^{f_\exists}$, i.e. parity games can be solved by solving fixpoint equation systems. Intuitively, $v \in f_\exists(V_0, \ldots, V_k)$ iff Eloise can enforce that some node in $V_{\Omega(v)}$ is reached in the next step. The nested fixpoint expressed by $\mathsf{E}^{f_\exists}$ (in which least (greatest) fixpoints correspond to odd (even) priorities) is constructed in such a way that Eloise only has to rely infinitely often on an argument V_i for odd i if she can also ensure that some argument V_j for $j > i$ is used infinitely often.

Model checking for the *modal μ-calculus* [29] and solving parity games are linear-time equivalent problems. Formulae of the μ-calculus are evaluated over Kripke frames (U, R) with set of states U and transition relation R. Formulae ϕ of the μ-calculus can be directly represented as equation systems over the lattice $\mathcal{P}(U)$ by recursively translating ϕ to equations, mapping subformulae $\mu X_i . \psi(X_0, \ldots, X_k)$ and $\nu X_j . \psi(X_0, \ldots, X_k)$ to equations

$$X_i =_\mu \psi(X_0, \ldots, X_k) \qquad\qquad X_j =_\nu \chi(X_0, \ldots, X_k),$$

and interpreting the modalities $\Diamond$ and $\Box$ by functions

$$f_\Diamond(X) = \{u \in U \mid R(u) \cap X \neq \emptyset\} \qquad f_\Box(X) = \{u \in U \mid R(u) \subseteq X\}$$

The solution of the resulting system of equations then is the truth set of the formula ϕ, that is, model checking for the model μ-calculus reduces to solving fixpoint equation systems. Furthermore, satisfiability checking for the modal μ-calculus can be reduced to solving so-called *satisfiability games* [20], that is, parity games that are played over the set of states of a determinized parity automaton. These satisfiability games can be expressed as systems of fixpoint equations, where the functions track transitions in the determinized automaton.

(2) *Energy parity games and the energy μ-calculus:* Energy parity games [10] are two-player games played over weighted game arenas (V, E, w, Ω), where $w : E \to \mathbb{Z}$ assigns integer weights to edges. The winning condition is the combination of a parity condition with a (quantitative) positivity condition on the sum of the accumulated weights. It has been shown [2, 10], that $b = n \cdot d \cdot W$ is a sufficient upper bound on energy level accumulations in energy parity games with n nodes, k priorities and maximum absolute weight W. We define a function $f_\exists^e : ((b+1)^V)^{k+1} \to (b+1)^V$ over the finite lattice $(b+1)^V$ (whose elements are functions from V to the set $\{0, \ldots, b+1\}$) by putting

$$(f_\exists^e(V_0, \ldots, V_k))(v) = \begin{cases} \min(\mathsf{en}(v, V_{\Omega(v)})) & \text{if } v \in V_\exists \\ \max(\mathsf{en}(v, V_{\Omega(v)})) & \text{if } v \in V_\forall, \end{cases}$$

for $(V_0, \ldots, V_k) \in ((b+1)^V)^{k+1}$ and $v \in V$, using $\mathsf{en}(v, \sigma)$ as abbreviation for

$$\mathsf{en}(v, \sigma) = \{n \in \{0, \ldots, b\} \mid \exists u \in E(v). n = \max\{0, \sigma(u) - w(v, u)\}\} \cup$$
$$\{b + 1 \mid \exists u \in E(v). \sigma(u) - w(v, u) > b \text{ or } \sigma(u) > b\},$$

where $\sigma : V \to \{0, \ldots, b+1\}$. Then it follows from the results of [2] that player Eloise wins a node v in the energy parity game with minimal initial credit $c < b+1$ if $(\mathsf{E}^{f_\exists^e})(v) = c$, that is, if the solution of the canonical equation system over $f_\exists^e$ maps v to a value c that is at most b.

The *energy μ-calculus* [2] is the fixpoint logic that corresponds to energy parity games. Its formulae are evaluated over *weighted game structures* and involve operators $\Diamond_E \phi$ and $\Box_E \phi$ that are evaluated depending on the energy function $\llbracket \phi \rrbracket : V \to \{0, \ldots, b+1\}$ that is obtained by first evaluating the argument formula ϕ. The semantics of the diamond operator then is an energy function that assigns, to each state v, the least energy value $c \in \{0, \ldots, b+1\}$ such that there is a move from v to some node u such that the credit c suffices to take the move from v to u and retain an energy level of at least $\llbracket \phi \rrbracket(u)$. Formulae can be translated to equation systems over the finite lattice $(b+1)^V$, where the functions for modal operators are defined according to their semantics as presented in [2]. Solving these equation systems then amounts to model checking energy μ-calculus formulae over weighted game structures.

(3) *Latticed μ-calculi:* In latticed μ-calculi [7], formulae are evaluated over complete lattices L rather than the powerset lattice; for finite lattices L, formulae of latticed μ-calculi hence can be translated to fixpoint equation systems over L, so that model checking reduces to solving equation systems. An associated latticed

variant of games has been introduced in [30] and for finite lattices L, solving latticed parity games over L reduces to solving equation systems over L.

(4) *The coalgebraic μ-calculus and coalgebraic parity games:* The coalgebraic μ-calculus [12] supports generalized modal branching types by using *predicate liftings* to interpret formulae over T-coalgebras, that is, over structures whose transition type is specified by an endofunctor T on the category of sets. For instance the functors $T = \mathcal{P}$, $T = \mathcal{D}$ and $T = \mathcal{G}$ map sets X to their powerset $\mathcal{P}(X)$, the set of probability distributions $\mathcal{D}(X) = \{f : X \to [0,\ldots,1]\}$ over X, and to the set of multisets $\mathcal{G}(X) = \{f : X \to \mathbb{N}\}$ over X, respectively. The corresponding T-coalgebras then are Kripke frames (for $T = \mathcal{P}$), Markov chains (for $T = \mathcal{D}$) and graded transition systems (for $T = \mathcal{G}$), respectively. Instances of the coalgebraic μ-calculus comprise, e.g. the two-valued probabilistic μ-calculus [12,34] with modalities $\Diamond_p \phi$ for $p \in [0,\ldots,1]$, expressing 'the next state satisfies ϕ with probability more than p'; the graded μ-calculus [32] with modalities $\Diamond_g \phi$ for $g \in \mathbb{N}$, expressing 'there are more than ϕ successor states that satisfy ϕ'; or the alternating-time μ-calculus [1] that is interpreted over concurrent game frames and uses modalities $\langle D \rangle \phi$ for finite $D \subseteq \mathbb{N}$ (encoding a *coalition*) that express that 'coalition D has a joint strategy to enforce ϕ'.

It has been shown in previous work [24] that model checking for coalgebraic μ-calculi against coalgebras with state space U reduces to solving a canonical fixpoint equation system over the powerset lattice $\mathcal{P}(U)$, where the involved function interprets modal operators using predicate liftings, as described in [12,24]. This canonical equation system can alternatively be seen as the winning region of Eloise in *coalgebraic parity games*, a highly general variant of parity games where the game structure is a coalgebra and nodes are annotated with modalities. Examples include *two-valued probabilistic parity games* and *graded parity games* in which nodes and edges are annotated with probabilities or grades, respectively. In order to win a node v, player Eloise then has to have a strategy that picks a *set* of moves to nodes that in turn are *all* won by Eloise, and such that the joint probability (joint grade) of the picked moves is greater than the probability (grade) that is assigned to v. It is known that solving coalgebraic parity games reduces to solving fixpoint equation systems [24].

Furthermore, the satisfiability problem of the coalgebraic μ-calculus has been reduced to solving canonical fixpoint equations systems over lattices $\mathcal{P}(U)$, where U is the state set of a determinized parity automaton and where the innermost equation checks for joint one-step satisfiability of sets of coalgebraic modalities [25]. By interpreting coalgebraic formulae over finite lattices d^U rather than over powerset lattices, one obtains the *finite-valued coalgebraic μ-calculus* (with values $\{0,\ldots,d\}$), which has the *finite-valued probabilistic μ-calculus* (e.g. [36]) as an instance. Model checking for the finite-valued probabilistic μ-calculus hence reduces to solving equation systems over the finite lattice $d^{|U|}$, where $\{0,\ldots,d\}$ encodes a finite set of probabilities.

4   Fixpoint Games and History-free Witnesses

We instantiate the existing notion of fixpoint games [4, 42], which characterize solutions of equation systems, to our setting (that is, to finite lattices), and then use these games as a technical tool to establish our crucial notion of history-freeness for systems of fixpoint equations.

Definition 4.1 (Fixpoint games). Let $X_i =_{\eta_i} f_i(X_0, \ldots, X_k)$, $0 \leq i \leq k$, be a system of fixpoint equations. The associated *fixpoint game* is a parity game (V, E, Ω) with set of nodes $V = (B_L \times [k]) \cup L^{k+1}$, where nodes from $B_L \times [k]$ belong to player Eloise and nodes from L^{k+1} belong to player Abelard. For nodes $(u, i) \in B_L \times [k]$, we put

$$E(u, i) = \{(U_0, \ldots, U_k) \in L^{k+1} \mid u \sqsubseteq f_i(U_0, \ldots, U_k)\},$$

and for nodes $(U_0, \ldots, U_k) \in L^{k+1}$, we put

$$E(U_0, \ldots, U_k) = \{(u, i) \in B_L \times [k] \mid u \sqsubseteq U_i\}.$$

The *alternation depth* $\mathsf{ad}(i)$ of an equation $X_i =_{\eta_i} f_i(X_0, \ldots, X_1)$ is defined as ad_i^μ if $\eta_i = \mu$ and as ad_i^ν if $\eta_i = \nu$, where ad_i^μ, ad_i^ν are recursively defined by

$$\mathsf{ad}_i^\mu = \begin{cases} \mathsf{ad}_{i-1}^\mu & i > 0, \eta_{i-1} = \mu \\ \mathsf{ad}_{i-1}^\nu + 1 & i > 0, \eta_{i-1} = \nu \\ 1 & i = 0 \end{cases} \qquad \mathsf{ad}_i^\nu = \begin{cases} \mathsf{ad}_{i-1}^\mu + 1 & i > 0, \eta_{i-1} = \mu \\ \mathsf{ad}_{i-1}^\nu & i > 0, \eta_{i-1} = \nu \\ 0 & i = 0 \end{cases}$$

for $0 \leq i \leq k$. The priority function $\Omega : V \to [\mathsf{ad}(k)]$ then is defined by $\Omega(u, i) = \mathsf{ad}(i)$ and $\Omega(U_0, \ldots, U_k) = 0$.

Remark 4.2. In [4], an alternative priority function $\Omega' : V \to [2k + 1]$ with

$$\Omega'(u, i) = \begin{cases} 2i & \text{if } \eta_i = \mathsf{GFP} \\ 2i + 1 & \text{if } \eta_i = \mathsf{LFP} \end{cases}$$

and $\Omega'(U_0, \ldots, U_k) = 0$ is used. Since $\mathsf{ad}(i)$ is even if and only if η_i is even, and moreover $\mathsf{ad}(i) \leq \mathsf{ad}(j)$ for $i \leq j$, and $i < j$ whenever $\mathsf{ad}(i) < \mathsf{ad}(j)$, it is easy to see that Ω and Ω' in fact assign identical parities to all plays. In the following, we will use the more economic parity function Ω so that fixpoint games have only $d := \mathsf{ad}(k) \leq k$ priorities.

We import the associated characterization theorem [4, Theorem 4.8]:

Theorem 4.3 ([4]). *We have $u \sqsubseteq [\![X_i]\!]_f$ if and only if Eloise wins the node (u, i) in the fixpoint game for the given system f of equations.*

Remark 4.4. While this shows that parity game solving can be used to solve equation systems, the size of fixpoint games is exponential in $|B_L|$, so they do not directly yield a quasipolynomial algorithm for solving equation systems.

Next we define our notion of history-freeness for systems of fixpoint equations.

Definition 4.5 (History-free witness). A *history-free witness* for $u \sqsubseteq [\![X_i]\!]_f$ is an even labelled graph (W, R) with labels from $[d]$ such that $W \subseteq B_L \times [d]$, $(u, i) \in W$, and for all $(v, p) \in W$, we have $v \sqsubseteq f_p(U_0, \ldots, U_k)$ where $U_j = \bigsqcup \pi_1[R_{\mathsf{ad}(j)}(v, p)]$ for $0 \leq j \leq k$, noting that $R_{\mathsf{ad}(j)}(v, p) \subseteq W$ so that $\pi_1[R_{\mathsf{ad}(j)}(v, p)] \subseteq B_L$ and $U_j \in L$.

In analogy to history-free strategies for parity games, history-free witnesses assign tuples $(R_1(v, p), \ldots, R_d(v, p))$ of sets $R_j(v, p) \subseteq W$ to pairs $(v, p) \in W$ without relying on a history of previously visited pairs. We have $|W| \leq (d+1)|B_L|$ and $|R| \leq (d+1)|W|^2$, that is, the size of history-free witnesses is polynomial in $|B_L|$. Crucially, history-free witnesses always exist:

Lemma 4.6. *For all $u \in B_L$ and $i \in [k]$, we have*

$$u \sqsubseteq [\![X_i]\!]_f \text{ if and only if there is a history-free witness for } u \sqsubseteq [\![X_i]\!]_f.$$

Proof. In one direction, we have $u \sqsubseteq [\![X_i]\!]_f$ so that Eloise wins the node (u, i) in the according fixpoint game by Lemma 4.3. Let s be a corresponding *history-free* winning strategy (such strategies always exists, see e.g. [21]). We inductively construct a witness for $u \sqsubseteq [\![X_i]\!]_f$, starting at (u, i). When at $(v, p) \in B_L \times [k]$ with $s(v, p) = (U_0, \ldots, U_k)$, we put $R_i(v, p) = \bigcup_{j|\mathsf{ad}(j)=i}(U_j \times \{j\})$ for $0 \leq i \leq d$ and hence have $\mathsf{ad}(j) = i$ for all $((v, p), i, (u, j)) \in R$. Since s is a winning strategy, the resulting graph (W, R) is a history-free witness for $u \sqsubseteq [\![X_i]\!]_f$ by construction; in particular, (W, R) is even. For the converse direction, the witness for $u \sqsubseteq [\![X_i]\!]_f$ directly yields a winning Eloise-strategy for the node (u, i) in the associated fixpoint game. This implies $u \sqsubseteq [\![X_i]\!]_f$ by Lemma 4.3. $\qquad\square$

5 Solving Equation Systems using Universal Graphs

We go on to prove our main result. To this end, we fix a system f of fixpoint equations $f_i : L^{k+1} \to L$, $0 \leq i \leq k$, and put $n := |B_L|$ and $d := \mathsf{ad}(k)$ for the remainder of the paper.

Definition 5.1 (Universal graphs [13, 14]). Let $G = (W, R)$ and $G' = (W', R')$ be labelled graphs with labels from $[d]$. A *homomorphism of labelled graphs* from G to G' is a function $\Phi : W \to W'$ such that for all $(v, p, w) \in R$, we have $(\Phi(v), p, \Phi(w)) \in R'$. An $(n, d+1)$-*universal graph* S is an even graph with labels from $[d]$ such that for all even graphs G with labels from $[d]$ and with $|G| \leq n$, there is a homomorphism from G to S.

We fix an $(n(d+1), (d+1))$-universal graph $S = (Z, K)$, noting that there are $(n(d+1), (d+1))$-universal graphs (obtained from universal trees) of size quasipolynomial in n and d [14]. We now combine the system f with the universal graph S to turn the parity conditions associated to general systems of fixpoint equations into a safety condition, associated to a single greatest fixpoint equation.

Definition 5.2 (Chained-product fixpoint). We define a function

$$g \colon \mathcal{P}(B_L \times [k] \times Z) \to \mathcal{P}(B_L \times [k] \times Z)$$
$$U \qquad \mapsto \{(v, p, q) \in B_L \times [k] \times Z \mid v \sqsubseteq f_p(P_0^{U,q}, \ldots, P_k^{U,q})\}$$

where

$$P_i^{U,q} = \bigsqcup \{u \in B_L \mid \exists s \in K_{\mathsf{ad}(i)}(q). (u, i, s) \in U\}.$$

We refer to $Y_0 =_{\mathsf{GFP}} g(Y_0)$ as the *chained-product fixpoint (equation)* of f and S.

We now show our central result: apart from the annotation with states from the universal graph, the chained-product fixpoint g is the solution of the system f.

Theorem 5.3. *For all $u \in B_L$ and $0 \le i \le k$, we have*

$$u \sqsubseteq [\![X_i]\!]_f \text{ if and only if there is } q \in Z \text{ such that } (u, i, q) \in [\![Y_0]\!]_g.$$

Proof. For the forward direction, let $u \sqsubseteq [\![X_i]\!]_f$. By Lemma 4.6, there is a history-free witness $G = (W, R)$ for $u \sqsubseteq [\![X_i]\!]_f$. Since S is a $(n(d+1), d+1)$-universal graph and since G is a witness and hence an even labelled graph of suitable size $|G| \le n(d+1)$, there is a graph homomorphism Φ from G to S. Starting at $(u, i, \Phi(u, i), 0)$, we inductively construct a witness for containment of $(u, i, \Phi(u, i))$ in $[\![Y_0]\!]_g$. When at $(v_1, p_1, \Phi(v_1, p_1), 0)$ with $(v_1, p_1) \in W$, we put

$$R'_0(v_1, p_1, \Phi(v_1, p_1), 0) = \{(v_2, p_2, \Phi(v_2, p_2), 0) \in B_L \times [d] \times Z \times [0] \mid$$
$$(v_2, p_2) \in R_{\mathsf{ad}(p_2)}(v_1, p_1), \Phi(v_2, p_2) \in K_{\mathsf{ad}(p_2)}(\Phi(v_1, p_1))\}$$

and continue the inductive construction with all these $(v_2, p_2, \Phi(v_2, p_2), 0)$, having $(v_2, p_2) \in W$. The resulting structure $G' = (W', R')$ indeed is a witness for containment of (u, i, q) in $[\![Y_0]\!]_g$: G' is even by construction. Moreover, we need to show that for $(v_1, p_1, \Phi(v_1, p_1), 0) \in W'$, we have $(v_1, p_1, \Phi(v_1, p_1), 0) \in g(\pi_1[R'_0(v_1, p_1, \Phi(v_1, p_1), 0)])$, i.e. $v_1 \sqsubseteq f_{p_1}(P_0^{U, \Phi(v_1, p_1)}, \ldots, P_k^{U, \Phi(v_1, p_1)})$ where $U = \pi_1[R'_0(v_1, p_1, \Phi(v_1, p_1), 0)]$. Since G is a witness and $(v_1, p_1) \in W$ by construction of W', we have $v_1 \sqsubseteq f_{p_1}(U_0, \ldots, U_k)$ where $U_j = \bigsqcup(\pi_j[R_{\mathsf{ad}(i)}(v_1, p_1)])$. By monotonicity of f_{p_1}, it thus suffices to show that $U_j \sqsubseteq P_j^{U, \Phi(v_1, p_1)}$ for $0 \le j \le k$; by definition of $P_j^{U, \Phi(v_1, p_1)}$ this follows if

$$\pi_1[R_{\mathsf{ad}(j)}(v_1, p_1)] \subseteq \{u \in B_L \mid \exists s \in K_{\mathsf{ad}(j)}(\Phi(v_1, p_1)). (u, j, s) \in W\},$$

where $W = \pi_1[R'_0(v_1, p_1, q_1, 0)]$. So let $w \in B_L$ such that $w \in \pi_1[R_{\mathsf{ad}(j)}(v_1, p_1)]$. Since R is a witness that is constructed as in the proof of Lemma 4.6, we have $i = \mathsf{ad}(i')$ for all $((v', p'), i, (w', i')) \in R$. Thus $(w, j) \in R_{\mathsf{ad}(j)}(v_1, p_1)$ for some j such that $\mathsf{ad}(j) = i$, that is, $((v_1, p_1), \mathsf{ad}(j), (w, j)) \in R$, hence $(\Phi(v_1, p_1), \mathsf{ad}(j), \Phi(w, j)) \in K$ because Φ is a graph homomorphism. By definition of R'_0 we have $(w, j, \Phi(w, j), 0) \in R'_0(v_1, p_1, \Phi(v_1, p_1), 0)$ so that $(w, j, \Phi(w, j)) \in \pi_1[R'_0(v_1, p_1, \Phi(v_1, p_1), 0)]$. We are done since $\Phi(w, j) \in K_{\mathsf{ad}(j)}(\Phi(v_1, p_1))$.

For the converse implication, let $(u_0, p_0, q_0) \in [\![Y_0]\!]_g$ for some $q_0 \in Z$. Let $G = (W, R)$ be a history-free witness for this fact. By Lemma 4.3, it suffices to provide a strategy in the fixpoint game for the system f with which Eloise wins the node (u_0, p_0). We inductively construct a *history-dependent* strategy s as follows: For $i \geq 0$, we abbreviate $U_i = R_0(u_i, p_i, q_i, 0)$. We put $s(u_0, p_0) = (P_0^{U_0, q_0}, \ldots, P_k^{U_0, q_0})$. For the inductive step, let

$$\tau = (u_0, p_0), (P_0^{U_0, q_0}, \ldots, P_k^{U_0, q_0}), \ldots, (P_0^{U_{n-1}, q_{n-1}}, \ldots, P_k^{U_{n-1}, q_{n-1}}), (u_n, p_n)$$

be a partial play of the fixpoint game that follows the strategy that has been constructed so far. Then we have an R-path $(u_0, p_0, q_0, 0), (u_1, p_1, q_1, 0), \ldots, (u_n, p_n, q_n, 0)$, where, for $0 \leq i < n$, we have $(q_i, p_{i+1}, q_{i+1}) \in K$ since $u_{i+1} \sqsubseteq P_{p_{i+1}}^{U_i, q_i}$ by the inductive construction. Put $s(\tau) = (P_0^{U_n, q_n}, \ldots, P_k^{U_n, q_n})$. Since G is a witness, the strategy uses only moves that are available to Eloise (i.e. ones with $u_n \sqsubseteq f_{p_n}(s(\tau))$). Also, s is a winning strategy as can be seen by looking at the K-paths that are induced by complete plays τ that follow s, as described (for partial plays) above. Since S is a universal graph and hence even, every such K-path is even and the sequence of priorities in τ is just the sequence of priorities of one of these K-paths. $\square$

Remark 5.4. Since the set $[\![Y_0]\!]_g$ is the greatest fixpoint of g, it can be computed by simple approximation from above, that is, as $g^m(B_L \times [k] \times Z)$ where $m = |B_L \times [k] \times Z|$. However, each iteration of the function g may require up to $|Z|$ evaluations of an equation. In the next section, we will show how this additional iteration factor in the computation of $[\![Y_0]\!]_g$ can be avoided.

6   A Progress Measure Algorithm

We next introduce a lifting algorithm that computes the set $[\![Y_0]\!]_g$ efficiently, following the paradigm of the progress measure approach for parity games (e.g. [27,28]). Our progress measures will map pairs $(u, i) \in B_L \times [k]$ to nodes in a universal graph that is equipped with a simulation order, that is, a total order that is suitable for measuring progress.

Definition 6.1 (Simulation order). For natural numbers i, i', we put $i \succeq i'$ if and only if either i is even and $i = i'$, or both i and i' are odd and $i \geq i'$. A total order $\leq$ on Z is a *simulation order* if for all $q, q' \in Z$,

$$q \leq q' \text{ implies that for all } 0 \leq i \leq k \text{ and } s \in K_i(q), \text{ there are}$$
$$i' \succeq i \text{ and } s' \in K_{i'}(q') \text{ such that } s \leq s'.$$

Lemma 6.2. *There is an $(n(d+1), d+1)$-universal graph (Z, K) of size quasipolynomial in n and d, and over which a simulation order $\leq$ exists.*

Proof (Sketch). It has been shown [14, Theorem 2.2] (originally, in different terminology, [28]) that there are (l, h)-*universal trees* (a concept similar to, but slightly more concrete than universal graphs) with set of leaves T such that $|T| \leq 2l\binom{\log l + h + 1}{h}$. Leaves in universal trees are identified by *navigation paths*, that is, sequences of branching directions, so that the leaves are linearly ordered by the lexicographic order $\leq$ on navigation paths (which orders leafs from the left to the right). As described in [13], one can obtain a universal graph (T, K) over T in which transitions $(q, i, q') \in K$ for odd i (the crucial case) move to the left, that is, q' is a leaf that is to the left of q in the universal tree (so that $q' < q$), ensuring universality. As it turns out, the lexicographic ordering on T is a simulation order. Adapting this construction to our setting, we put $l = n(d+1)$ and $h = d+1$ and obtain a $(n(d+1), d+1)$-universal graph (along with a simulation order $\leq$) of size at most $2n(d+1)\binom{\log(n(d+1)) + d + 2}{d+1}$ which is quasipolynomial in n and d. □

We fix an $(n(d+1), d+1)$-universal graph (Z, K) and a simulation order $\leq$ on Z for the remainder of the paper (these exist by the above lemma).

Definition 6.3 (Progress measure, lifting function). We let $q_{\min} \in Z$ denote the least node w.r.t. $\leq$ and fix a distinguished top element $\star \notin Z$, and extend $\geq$ to $Z \cup \{\star\}$ by putting $\star \geq q$ for all $q \in Z$. A *measure* is a map $\mu: B_L \times [k] \to Z \cup \{\star\}$, i.e. assigns nodes in the universal graph or $\star$ to pairs $(v, p) \in B_L \times [k]$. A measure μ is a *progress measure* if whenever $\mu(v, p) \neq \star$, then $v \sqsubseteq f_p(U_0^{\mu, q}, \ldots, U_k^{\mu, q})$ where $q = \mu(v, p)$ and

$$U_i^{\mu, q} = \bigsqcup \{u \in B_L \mid \exists s \in K_{\mathsf{ad}(i)}(q). \, \mu(u, i) \leq s\}.$$

We define a function $\mathsf{Lift} : (B_L \times [k] \to Z \cup \{\star\}) \to (B_L \times [k] \to Z \cup \{\star\})$ on measures by

$$(\mathsf{Lift}(\mu))(v, p) = \min\{q \in Z \mid v \sqsubseteq f_p(U_0^{\mu, q}, \ldots, U_k^{\mu, q})\}$$

where $\min(Z')$ denotes the least element of Z' w.r.t. $\leq$, for $\emptyset \neq Z' \subseteq Z$; also we put $\min(\emptyset) = \star$.

The lifting algorithm then starts with the least measure $\mathsf{m_{min}}$ that maps all pairs $(v, p) \in B_L \times [k]$ to the minimal node (i.e. $\mathsf{m_{min}}(v, p) = q_{\min}$) and repeatedly updates the current measure using Lift until the measure stabilizes.

Lifting algorithm

(1) Initialize: Put $\mu := \mathsf{m_{min}}$.

(2) If $\mathsf{Lift}(\mu) \neq \mu$, then put $\mu := \mathsf{Lift}(\mu)$ and go to 2. Otherwise go to 3.

(3) Return the set $\mathbb{E} = \{(v, p) \in B_L \times [k] \mid \mu(v, p) \neq \star\}$.

Lemma 6.4 (Correctness). *For all $v \in B_L$ and $0 \leq p \leq k$, we have*

$$(v, p) \in \mathbb{E} \text{ if and only if } v \in [\![X_p]\!]_f.$$

Proof (Sketch). Let μ denote the progress measure that the algorithm computes. For one direction of the proof, let $(v, p) \in \mathbb{E}$. By Lemma 4.6 it suffices to construct a witness for $v \in [\![X_p]\!]_f$. We extract such a witness $(\mathbb{E}, R)$ from the progress measure μ, relying on the properties of the simulation order $\leq$ that is used to measure the progress of μ to ensure that any infinite sequence of measures that μ assigns to some R-path induces an infinite (and hence even) path in the employed universal graph. This shows that $(\mathbb{E}, R)$ indeed is an even graph and hence a witness. For the converse direction, let $v \in [\![X_p]\!]_f$ so that there is, by Theorem 5.3, some $q \in Z$ such that $(v, p, q) \in [\![Y_0]\!]_g$. For (u, i) such that there is $q' \in Z$ such that $(u, i, q') \in [\![Y_0]\!]_g$, let $q_{(u,i)} \in Z$ denote the minimal such node w.r.t. $\leq$. It now suffices that $\mu(u, i) \leq q_{(u,i)}$ for all such (u, i), which is shown by induction on the number of iterations of the lifting algorithm. $\qquad \square$

Corollary 6.5. *Solutions of systems of fixpoint equations can be computed with quasipolynomially many evaluations of equations.*

Proof. Given an $(n(d+1), d+1)$-universal graph (Z, K) and a simulation order on Z, the lifting algorithm terminates and returns the solution of f after at most $n(d+1) \cdot |Z|$ many iterations. This is the case since each iteration (except the final iteration) increases the measure for at least one of the $n(d+1)$ nodes and the measure of each node can be increased at most $|Z|$ times. Using the universal graph and the simulation order from the proof of Lemma 6.2, we have $|Z| \leq 2n(d+1)\binom{\log(n(d+1))+d+2}{d+1}$ so that the algorithm terminates after at most $2(n(d+1))^2\binom{\log(n(d+1))+d+2}{d+1} \in \mathcal{O}((n(d+1))^{\log(d+1)})$ iterations of the function Lift. Each iteration can be implemented to run with at most $n(d+1)$ evaluations of an equation. $\qquad \square$

Corollary 6.6. *The number of function calls required for the solution of systems of fixpoint equations with $d \leq \log n$ is bounded by a polynomial in n and d.*

Proof. Following the insight of Theorem 2.8 in [9], Theorem 2.2. in [14] implies that if $d < \log n$, then there is an $(n(d+1), d+1)$-universal tree of size polynomial in n and d. In the same way as in the proof of Lemma 6.2, one obtains a universal graph of polynomial size and a simulation order on it. $\qquad \square$

Example 6.7. Applying Corollary 6.5 and Corollary 6.6 to Example 3.2, we obtain the following results:

(1) The model checking problems for the energy μ-calculus and finite latticed μ-calculi are in QP. For energy parity games with sufficient upper bound b on energy level accumulations, we obtain a progress measure algorithm that terminates after a number of iterations that is quasipolynomial in b.

(2) Under mild assumptions on the modalities (see [24]), the model checking problem for the coalgebraic μ-calculus is in QP; in particular, this yields QP model checking algorithms for the graded μ-calculus and the two-valued probabilistic μ-calculus (equivalently: QP progress measure algorithms for solving graded and two-valued probabilistic parity games).

(3) Under mild assumptions on the modalities (see [25]), we obtain a novel upper bound $2^{\mathcal{O}(nd\log n)}$ for the satisfiability problems of coalgebraic μ-calculi, in particular including the monotone μ-calculus, the alternating-time μ-calculus, the graded μ-calculus and the (two-valued) probabilistic μ-calculus, even when the latter two are extended with (monotone) polynomial inequalities. This improves on the best previous bounds in all cases.

7 Conclusion

We have shown how to use universal graphs to compute solutions of systems of fixpoint equations $X_i = \eta_i. f_i(X_0, \ldots, X_k)$ (with the η_i marking least or greatest fixpoints) that use functions $f_i : L^{k+1} \to L$ (over a finite lattice L with basis B_L) and involve up to $k + 1$-fold nesting of fixpoints. Our progress measure algorithm needs quasipolynomially many evaluations of equations, and runs in time $\mathcal{O}(q \cdot t(f))$, where q is a quasipolynomial in $|B_L|$ and the alternation depth of the equation system, and where $t(f)$ is an upper bound on the time it takes to compute f_i for all i.

As a consequence of our results, the upper time bounds for the evaluation of various general parity conditions improve. Example domains beyond solving parity games to which our algorithm can be instantiated comprise model checking for latticed μ-calculi and solving latticed parity games [7, 30], solving energy parity games and model checking for the energy μ-calculus [2, 10], and model checking and satisfiability checking for the coalgebraic μ-calculus [12]. The resulting model checking algorithms for latticed μ-calculi and the energy μ-calculus run in time quasipolynomial in the provided basis of the respective lattice. In terms of concrete instances of the coalgebraic μ-calculus, we obtain, e.g., quasipolynomial-time model checking for the graded [32] and the probabilistic μ-calculus [12, 34] as new results (corresponding results for, e.g., the alternating-time μ-calculus [1] and the monotone μ-calculus [18] follow as well but have already been obtained in our previous work [24]), as well as improved upper bounds for satisfiability checking in the graded μ-calculus, the probabilistic μ-calculus, the monotone μ-calculus, and the alternating-time μ-calculus. We foresee further applications, e.g. in the computation of fair bisimulations and fair equivalence [26, 31] beyond relational systems, e.g. for probabilistic systems.

As in the case of parity games, a natural open question that remains is whether solutions of fixpoint equations can be computed in polynomial time (which would of course imply that parity games can be solved in polynomial time). A more immediate perspective for further investigation is to generalize the recent quasipolynomial variant [38] of Zielonka's algorithm [43] for solving parity games to solving systems of fixpoint equations, with a view to improving efficiency in practice.

References

1. Alur, R., Henzinger, T., Kupferman, O.: Alternating-time temporal logic. J. ACM **49**, 672–713 (2002), https://doi.org/10.1145/585265.585270

2. Amram, G., Maoz, S., Pistiner, O., Ringert, J.O.: Energy mu-calculus: Symbolic fixed-point algorithms for omega-regular energy games. CoRR **abs/2005.00641** (2020), https://arxiv.org/abs/2005.00641
3. Arnold, A., Niwinski, D., Parys, P.: A quasi-polynomial black-box algorithm for fixed point evaluation. In: Computer Science Logic, CSL 2021. LIPIcs, vol. 183, pp. 9:1–9:23. Schloss Dagstuhl – Leibniz-Zentrum für Informatik (2021), https://doi.org/10.4230/LIPIcs.CSL.2021.9
4. Baldan, P., König, B., Mika-Michalski, C., Padoan, T.: Fixpoint games on continuous lattices. In: Principles of Programming Languages, POPL 2021. Proceedings of the ACM on Programming Languages, vol. 3, pp. 26:1–26:29. ACM (2019), https://doi.org/10.1145/3290339
5. Bodlaender, H., Dinneen, M., Khoussainov, B.: On game-theoretic models of networks. In: Algorithms and Computation, ISAAC 2001. LNCS, vol. 2223, pp. 550–561. Springer (2001), https://doi.org/10.1007/3-540-45678-3_47
6. Boker, U., Lehtinen, K.: On the way to alternating weak automata. In: Foundations of Software Technology and Theoretical Computer Science, FSTTCS 2018. LIPIcs, vol. 122, pp. 21:1–21:22. Schloss Dagstuhl – Leibniz-Zentrum für Informatik (2018), https://doi.org/10.4230/LIPIcs.FSTTCS.2018.21
7. Bruns, G., Godefroid, P.: Model checking with multi-valued logics. In: Automata, Languages and Programming, ICALP 2004. LNCS, vol. 3142, pp. 281–293. Springer (2004), https://doi.org/10.1007/978-3-540-27836-8_26
8. Bruse, F., Falk, M., Lange, M.: The fixpoint-iteration algorithm for parity games. In: Games, Automata, Logics and Formal Verification, GandALF 2014. EPTCS, vol. 161, pp. 116–130. Open Publishing Association (2014), https://doi.org/10.4204/EPTCS.161.12
9. Calude, C., Jain, S., Khoussainov, B., Li, W., Stephan, F.: Deciding parity games in quasipolynomial time. In: Theory of Computing, STOC 2017. pp. 252–263. ACM (2017), https://doi.org/10.1145/3055399.3055409
10. Chatterjee, K., Doyen, L.: Energy parity games. Theor. Comput. Sci. **458**, 49–60 (2012). https://doi.org/10.1016/j.tcs.2012.07.038
11. Chatterjee, K., Dvorák, W., Henzinger, M., Svozil, A.: Quasipolynomial set-based symbolic algorithms for parity games. In: Logic for Programming, Artificial Intelligence and Reasoning, LPAR 2018. EPiC, vol. 57, pp. 233–253. EasyChair (2018), https://doi.org/10.29007/5z5k
12. Cîrstea, C., Kupke, C., Pattinson, D.: EXPTIME tableaux for the coalgebraic μ-calculus. Log. Meth. Comput. Sci. **7** (2011), https://doi.org/10.2168/LMCS-7(3:3)2011
13. Colcombet, T., Fijalkow, N.: Universal graphs and good for games automata: New tools for infinite duration games. In: Foundations of Software Science and Computation Structures, FOSSACS 2019. LNCS, vol. 11425, pp. 1–26. Springer (2019), https://doi.org/10.1007/978-3-030-17127-8_1
14. Czerwinski, W., Daviaud, L., Fijalkow, N., Jurdzinski, M., Lazic, R., Parys, P.: Universal trees grow inside separating automata: Quasi-polynomial lower bounds for parity games. In: Symposium on Discrete Algorithms, SODA 2019. pp. 2333–2349. SIAM (2019), https://doi.org/10.1137/1.9781611975482.142
15. Daviaud, L., Jurdzinski, M., Lazic, R.: A pseudo-quasi-polynomial algorithm for mean-payoff parity games. In: Logic in Computer Science, LICS 2018. pp. 325–334. ACM (2018), https://doi.org/10.1145/3209108.3209162
16. Dawar, A., Grädel, E.: The descriptive complexity of parity games. In: Computer Science Logic, CSL 2008. LNCS, vol. 5213, pp. 354–368. Springer (2008), https://doi.org/10.1007/978-3-540-87531-4_26

17. Emerson, E.A., Jutla, C., Sistla, A.P.: On model checking for the μ-calculus and its fragments. Theor. Comput. Sci. **258**, 491–522 (2001), https://doi.org/10.1016/S0304-3975(00)00034-7

18. Enqvist, S., Seifan, F., Venema, Y.: Monadic second-order logic and bisimulation invariance for coalgebras. In: Logic in Computer Science, LICS 2015. pp. 353–365. IEEE (2015), https://doi.org/10.1109/LICS.2015.41

19. Fearnley, J., Jain, S., de Keijzer, B., Schewe, S., Stephan, F., Wojtczak, D.: An ordered approach to solving parity games in quasi-polynomial time and quasi-linear space. STTT **21**(3), 325–349 (2019), https://doi.org/10.1007/s10009-019-00509-3

20. Friedmann, O., Lange, M.: Deciding the unguarded modal μ-calculus. J. Appl. Non-Classical Log. **23**, 353–371 (2013), https://doi.org/10.1080/11663081.2013.861181

21. Grädel, E., Thomas, W., Wilke, T. (eds.): Automata, Logics, and Infinite Games: A Guide to Current Research, LNCS, vol. 2500. Springer (2002), https://doi.org/10.1007/3-540-36387-4

22. Hasuo, I., Shimizu, S., Cîrstea, C.: Lattice-theoretic progress measures and coalgebraic model checking. In: Principles of Programming Languages, POPL 2016. pp. 718–732. ACM (2016), https://doi.org/10.1145/2837614.2837673

23. Hausmann, D., Schröder, L.: Computing nested fixpoints in quasipolynomial time. CoRR **abs/1907.07020** (2019), http://arxiv.org/abs/1907.07020

24. Hausmann, D., Schröder, L.: Game-based local model checking for the coalgebraic μ-calculus. In: Concurrency Theory, CONCUR 2019. LIPIcs, vol. 140, pp. 35:1–35:16. Schloss Dagstuhl–Leibniz-Zentrum fuer Informatik (2019), https://doi.org/10.4230/LIPIcs.CONCUR.2019.35

25. Hausmann, D., Schröder, L.: Optimal satisfiability checking for arithmetic μ-calculi. In: Foundations of Software Science and Computation Structures, FOS-SACS 2019. LNCS, vol. 11425, pp. 277–294. Springer (2019), https://doi.org/10.1007/978-3-030-17127-8_16

26. Henzinger, T., Rajamani, S.: Fair bisimulation. In: Tools and Algorithms for Construction and Analysis of Systems, TACAS 2000. LNCS, vol. 1785, pp. 299–314. Springer (2000), https://doi.org/10.1007/3-540-46419-0_21

27. Jurdziński, M.: Small progress measures for solving parity games. In: Symposium on Theoretical Aspects of Computer Science, STACS 2000. LNCS, vol. 1770, pp. 290–301. Springer (2000), https://doi.org/10.1007/3-540-46541-3_24

28. Jurdzinski, M., Lazic, R.: Succinct progress measures for solving parity games. In: Logic in Computer Science, LICS 2017. pp. 1–9. IEEE Computer Society (2017), https://doi.org/10.1109/LICS.2017.8005092

29. Kozen, D.: Results on the propositional μ-calculus. Theor. Comput. Sci. **27**, 333–354 (1983), https://doi.org/10.1016/0304-3975(82)90125-6

30. Kupferman, O., Lustig, Y.: Latticed simulation relations and games. In: Automated Technology for Verification and Analysis, ATVA 2007. LNCS, vol. 4762, pp. 316–330. Springer (2007), https://doi.org/10.1007/978-3-540-75596-8_23

31. Kupferman, O., Piterman, N., Vardi, M.: Fair equivalence relations. In: Verification: Theory and Practice. LNCS, vol. 2772, pp. 702–732. Springer (2003), https://doi.org/10.1007/978-3-540-39910-0_30

32. Kupferman, O., Sattler, U., Vardi, M.: The complexity of the graded μ-calculus. In: Automated Deduction, CADE 2002. LNCS, vol. 2392, pp. 423–437. Springer (2002), https://doi.org/10.1007/3-540-45620-1_34

33. Lehtinen, K.: A modal μ perspective on solving parity games in quasi-polynomial time. In: Logic in Computer Science, LICS 2018. pp. 639–648. ACM (2018), https://doi.org/10.1145/3209108.3209115

34. Liu, W., Song, L., Wang, J., Zhang, L.: A simple probabilistic extension of modal mu-calculus. In: International Joint Conference on Artificial Intelligence, IJCAI 2015. pp. 882–888. AAAI Press (2015), http://ijcai.org/proceedings/2015

35. Long, D.E., Browne, A., Clarke, E.M., Jha, S., Marrero, W.R.: An improved algorithm for the evaluation of fixpoint expressions. In: Computer Aided Verification, CAV 1994. LNCS, vol. 818, pp. 338–350. Springer (1994), https://doi.org/10.1007/3-540-58179-0_66

36. Mio, M.: On the equivalence of game and denotational semantics for the probabilistic μ-calculus. Log. Methods Comput. Sci. **8** (2012), https://doi.org/10.2168/LMCS-8(2:7)2012

37. Parikh, R.: The logic of games and its applications. Ann. Discr. Math. **24**, 111–140 (1985), https://doi.org/10.1016/S0304-0208(08)73078-0

38. Parys, P.: Parity games: Zielonka's algorithm in quasi-polynomial time. In: Mathematical Foundations of Computer Science, MFCS 2019. LIPIcs, vol. 138, pp. 10:1–10:13. Schloss Dagstuhl – Leibniz-Zentrum für Informatik (2019), https://doi.org/10.4230/LIPIcs.MFCS.2019.10

39. Peleg, D.: Concurrent dynamic logic. J. ACM **34**, 450–479 (1987), https://doi.org/10.1145/23005.23008

40. Rutten, J.: Universal coalgebra: A theory of systems. Theor. Comput. Sci. **249**, 3–80 (2000), https://doi.org/10.1016/S0304-3975(00)00056-6

41. Seidl, H.: Fast and Simple Nested Fixpoints. Inf. Process. Lett. **59**, 303–308 (1996), https://doi.org/10.1016/0020-0190(96)00130-5

42. Venema, Y.: Lectures on the modal μ-calculus. Lecture notes, Institute for Logic, Language and Computation, Universiteit van Amsterdam (2008), https://staff.fnwi.uva.nl/y.venema/teaching/ml/notes/20201212-mu.pdf

43. Zielonka, W.: Infinite games on finitely coloured graphs with applications to automata on infinite trees. Theor. Comput. Sci. **200**(1-2), 135–183 (1998), https://doi.org/10.1016/S0304-3975(98)00009-7

SMT Verification

A Flexible Proof Format for SAT Solver-Elaborator Communication

Seulkee Baek (✉) *, Mario Carneiro *, and Marijn J.H. Heule**

Carnegie Mellon University, Pittsburgh, PA, United States
{seulkeeb,mcarneir,mheule}@andrew.cmu.edu

Abstract. We introduce FRAT, a new proof format for unsatisfiable SAT problems, and its associated toolchain. Compared to DRAT, the FRAT format allows solvers to include more information in proofs to reduce the computational cost of subsequent elaboration to LRAT. The format is easy to parse forward and backward, and it is extensible to future proof methods. The provision of optional proof steps allows SAT solver developers to balance implementation effort against elaboration time, with little to no overhead on solver time. We benchmark our FRAT toolchain against a comparable DRAT toolchain and confirm >84% median reduction in elaboration time and >94% median decrease in peak memory usage.

Keywords: Satisfiability · Proof format · DRAT · LRAT · FRAT.

1 Introduction

The *Boolean satsifiability problem* is the problem of determining, for a given Boolean formula consisting of Boolean variables and connectives, whether there exists a variable assignment under which the formula evaluates to true. Boolean satisfiability (SAT) is interesting in part because there are surprisingly diverse types of problems that can be encoded as Boolean formulas and solved efficiently by checking their satisfiability. *SAT solvers*, programs that automatically solve SAT problems, have been successfully applied to a wide range of areas, including hardware verification [2], planning [14], and combinatorics [12].

The performance of SAT solvers has taken great strides in recent years, and modern solvers can often solve problems involving millions of variables and clauses, which would have been unthinkable a mere 20 years ago [15]. But this improvement comes at the cost of significant increase in the code complexity of SAT solvers, which makes it difficult to either assume their correctness on faith, or certify their program correctness directly. As a result, the ability of SAT solvers to produce independently verifiable certificates has become a pressing necessity. Since there is an obvious certificate format (the satisfying boolean assignment) for satisfiable problems, the real challenge in proof-producing SAT

---

* Partially supported by AFOSR grant FA9550-18-1-0120
** Supported by the National Science Foundation under grant CCF-2010951

J. F. Groote and K. G. Larsen (Eds.): TACAS 2021, LNCS 12651, pp. 59–75, 2021.
https://doi.org/10.1007/978-3-030-72016-2_4

solving is in devising a compact proof format for unsatisfiable problems, and developing a toolchain that efficiently produces and verifies it.

The current de facto standard proof format for unsatisfiable SAT problems is DRAT [10]. The format, as well as its predecessor DRUP, were designed with a strong focus on quick adaptation by the community, emphasizing easy proof emission, practically zero overhead, and reasonable validation speed [11]. The DRAT format has become the only supported proof format in SAT Competition and Races since 2014 due to entrants losing interest in alternatives.

DRAT is a *clausal* proof format [6], which means that a DRAT proof consists of a sequence of instructions for adding and deleting clauses. It is helpful to think of a DRAT proof as a program for modifying the 'active multiset' of clauses: the initial active multiset is the clauses of the input problem, and this multiset grows and shrinks over time as the program is executed step by step. The invariant throughout program execution is that the active multiset at any point of time is *at least as satisfiable* as the initial active multiset. This invariant holds trivially in the beginning and after a deletion; it is also preserved by addition steps by either RUP or RAT, which we explain shortly. The last step of a DRAT proof is the addition of the empty clause, which ensures the unsatisfiability of the final active multiset, and hence that of the initial active multiset, i.e. the input problem.

Every addition step in DRAT is either a *reverse unit propagation* (RUP) step [6] or a *resolution asymmetric tautology* (RAT) [13] step. A clause C has the property AT (asymmetric tautology) with respect to a formula F if $F, \overline{C} \vdash_1 \bot$, which is to say, there is a proof of the empty clause by unit propagation using F and the negated literals in C. A RUP step that adds C to the active multiset F is valid if C has property AT with respect to F. A clause $l \vee C$ has property RAT with respect to F if for every clause $\overline{l} \vee D \in F$, the clause $C \vee D$ has property AT with respect to F. In this case, C is not logically entailed by F, but F and $F \wedge C$ are equisatisfiable, and a RAT step will add C to the active multiset if C has property RAT with respect to F. (See [10] for more about the justification for this proof system.)

DRAT has a number of advantages over formats based on more traditional proof calculi, such as resolution or analytic tableaux. For SAT solvers, DRAT proofs are easier to emit because CNF clauses are the native data structures that the solvers store and manipulate internally. Whenever a solver obtains a new clause, the clause can be simply streamed out to a proof file without any further modification. Also, DRAT proofs are more compact than resolution proofs, as the latter can become infeasibly large for some classes of SAT problems [7].

There is, however, room for further improvement in the DRAT format due to the information loss incurred by DRAT proofs. Consider, for instance, the SAT problem and proofs shown in Figure 1. The left column is the input problem in the DIMACS format, the center column is its DRAT proof, and the right column is the equivalent proof in the LRAT format, which can be thought of as an enriched version of DRAT with more information. The numbers before the first zero on lines without a "d" represent literals: positive numbers denote positive literals, while negative numbers denote negative literals. The first clause of the input formula is $(x_1 \vee x_2 \vee \overline{x}_3)$, or equivalently 1 2 -3 0 in DIMACS.

The first lines of both DRAT and LRAT proofs are RUP steps for adding the clause $(x_1 \vee x_2)$, written 1 2 0. When an LRAT checker verifies this step, it is informed of the IDs of active clauses (the trailing numbers 1 6 3) relevant for unit propagation, in the exact order they should be used. Therefore, the LRAT checker only has to visit the first, sixth, and third clauses and confirm that, starting with unit literals $\overline{x}_1, \overline{x}_2$, they yield the new unit literals $\overline{x}_3, x_4, \bot$. In contrast, a DRAT checker verifying the same step must add the literals $\overline{x}_1, \overline{x}_2$ to the active multiset (in this case, the eight initial clauses) and carry out a blind unit propagation with the whole resulting multiset until contradiction. This omission of RUP information in DRAT proofs introduces significant overheads in proof verification. Although the exact figures vary from problem to problem, checking a DRAT proof typically takes approximately twice as long as solving the original problem, whereas the verification time for an LRAT proof is negligible compared to its solution time. This additional cost of checking DRAT proofs also represents a lost opportunity: when a SAT solver emits a RUP step, it knows exactly how the new clause was obtained, and this knowledge can (in theory) be turned into an LRAT-style RUP annotation, which can cut down verification costs significantly if conveyed to the verifier.

For the DRAT format, a design choice was made not to include such information since demanding explicit proofs for all steps turned out to be impractical. Although it is *theoretically* possible to always glean the correct RUP annotation from the solver state, computing this information can be intricate and costly for some types of inferences (e.g. conflict-clause minimization [22]), making it harder to support proof logging [25]. Reducing such overheads is particularly important for solving satisfiable formulas, as proofs are superfluous for them and the penalty for maintaining such proofs should be minimized. We should note, however, that proof elaboration need not be an all-or-nothing business; if it is infeasible to demand 100% elaborated proofs, we can still ask solvers to fill in as many gaps as it is convenient for them to do so, which would still be a considerable improvement over handling all of it from the verifier side.

Inclusion of final clauses is another potential area for improvement over the DRAT format. A DRAT proof typically includes many addition steps that do not ultimately contribute to the derivation of the empty clause. This is unavoidable in the proof emission phase, since a SAT solver cannot know in advance whether a given clause will be ultimately useful, and must stream out the clause before it can find out. All such steps, however, should be dropped in the postprocessing phase in order to compress proofs and speed up verification. The most straightforward way of doing this is processing the proof in reverse order [6]: when processing a clause C_{k+1}, identify all the clauses used to derive C_{k+1}, mark them as 'used', and move on to clause C_k. For each clause, process it if it is marked as used, and skip it otherwise. The only caveat of this method is that the postprocessor needs to know which clauses were present at the very end of the proof, since there is no way to identify which clauses were used to derive the

```
     DIMACS              DRAT                    LRAT

   p cnf 4 8                1 2 0        9 1 2 0        1 6 3 0
    1  2 -3 0      d   1 -3 2 0          9                d 1 0
   -1 -2  3 0                1 3 0       10 1 3 0       9 8 6 0
    2  3 -4 0      d     1 4 3 0         10               d 6 0
   -2 -3  4 0                1 0         11    1 0      10 9 4 8 0
   -1 -3 -4 0      d       1 3 0         11             d 10
    1  3  4 0      d       1 2 0                        9
   -1  2  4 0      d 1 -4 -2 0                            8 0
    1 -2 -4 0                2 0         12    2 0      11 7 5 3 0
                  d    -1 4 2 0          12             d 7
                  d   2 -4 3 0                            3 0
                            0           13     0 11 12 2 4 5 0
```

Fig. 1. DRAT and LRAT proofs of a SAT problem. All whitespace and alignment is not significant; we have aligned lines of the DRAT proof with the corresponding LRAT lines (d steps in LRAT may correspond to multiple DRAT d steps).

empty clause otherwise. Although it is possible to enumerate the final clauses by a preliminary forward pass through a DRAT proof, this is clearly unnecessary work since SAT solvers know exactly which clauses are present at the end, and it is desirable to put this information in the proof in the first place.

2   The FRAT format

To address the above issues, we introduce FRAT, a new proof format designed to allow fine-grained communication between SAT solvers and elaborators. The main differences between FRAT and DRAT are:

(1) optional annotation of RUP steps,
(2) inclusion of final clauses, and
(3) identification of clauses by unique IDs.

We've already explained the rationale for (1) and (2); (3) is necessary for concise references to clauses in deletions and RUP step annotations. More specifically, a FRAT proof consists of the following six types of proof steps:

o: An original step; a clause from the input file. The purpose of these lines is to name the clauses from the input with identifiers; they are not required to come in the same order as the file, they are not required to be numbered in order, and not all steps in the input need appear here. Proof may also progress (with a and d steps) before all o steps are added.

a, l: An addition step, and an optional LRAT-style unit propagation proof of the step. The proof, if provided, is a sequence of clauses in the current formula in the order that they become unit. For solver flexibility, they are allowed to come out of order, but the elaborator is optimized for the case where they are correctly ordered. For a RAT step, the negative numbers in the proof refer to the clauses in the active set that contain the negated pivot literal, followed by the unit propagation proof of the resolvent. See [3] for more details on the LRAT checking algorithm.

d: A deletion step for deleting the clause with the given ID from the formula. The literals given must match the literals in the corresponding addition step up to permutation.

r: A relocation step. The syntax is r ⟨ids⟩ 0, where ⟨ids⟩ has the form s_0, t_0, ..., s_k, t_k and must consist of an even number of clause IDs. It indicates that the active clause with ID s_i is re-labeled and now has ID t_i, for each $0 \leq i \leq k$. (This is used for solvers that use pointer identity for clauses, but also do garbage collection to decrease memory fragmentation.)

f: A finalization step. These steps come at the end of a proof, and provide the list of all active clauses at the end of the proof. The clauses may come in any order, but every step that has been added and not deleted must be present. (For best results, clauses should be finalized in roughly reverse order of when they were added.)

(Our modified version of CADICAL also outputs a seventh kind of step, t ⟨todo_id⟩ 0, to collect statistics on code paths that produce a steps without proofs. See Section 3 for how this information is used.)

Figure 1 is an example from [3], which includes a SAT problem in DIMACS format, and the proofs of its unsatisfiability in DRAT and LRAT formats. It shows how proofs are produced and elaborated via the DRAT toolchain. Figure 2 shows the corresponding problem and proofs for the FRAT toolchain. Notice how the FRAT proof is more verbose than its DRAT counterpart and includes all the hints for addition steps, which are reused in the subsequent LRAT proof.

Binary FRAT The files shown in Figure 2 are in the text version of the FRAT format, but for efficiency reasons solvers may also wish to use a binary encoding. The binary FRAT format is exactly the same in structure, but the integers are encoded using the same variable-length integer encoding used in binary DRAT [9]. Unsigned numbers are encoded in 7-bit little endian, with the high bit set on each byte except the last. That is, the number

$$n = x_0 + 2^7 x_1 + \cdots + 2^{7k} x_k$$

(with each $x_i < 2^7$) is encoded as

$$1x_0\ 1x_1\ \ldots\ 0x_k.$$

Signed numbers are encoded by mapping $n \geq 0$ to $f(n) := 2n$ and $-n$ (with $n > 0$) to $f(n) := 2n + 1$, and then using the unsigned encoding. (Incidentally, the mapping f is not surjective, as it misses 1. But it is used by other formats so we have decided not to change it.)

```
                         FRAT
  o  1               1 2 -3 0    |  f  1      1 2 -3 0
  o  2              -1 -2 3 0     |  f  2     -2 -1 3 0
  o  3               2 3 -4 0     |  f  3      2 3 -4 0
  o  4              -2 -3 4 0     |  f  4     -2 -3 4 0
  o  5              -1 -3 -4 0    |  f  5    -1 -3 -4 0
  o  6               1 3 4 0      |  f  6      1 3 4 0
  o  7              -1 2 4 0      |  f  7     -1 2 4 0
  o  8               1 -2 -4 0    |  f  8    1 -2 -4 0
  a  9 -3 -4 0 1     5 1 8 0      |  f  9     -3 -4 0
  a 10    -4 0 1     9 3 2 8 0    |  f 10       -4 0
  a 11     3 0                    |  f 11        3 0
  a 12    -2 0                    |  f 12       -2 0
  a 13     1 0 1    12 11 1 0     |  f 13        1 0
  a 14     0 1 13 12 10 7 0       |  f 14          0

                         LRAT
   9 -3 -4 0          5 1 8 0
   9                  d 5 0
  10    -4 0          9 3 2 8 0
  10                  d 8 3 9 0
  11     3 0          10 6 7 2 0
  11                  d 2 6 0
  12    -2 0          11 10 4 0
  12                  d 4 0
  13     1 0          12 11 1 0
  13                  d 1 11 0
  14      0 13 12 10 7 0
```

Fig. 2. FRAT and LRAT proofs of a SAT problem. To illustrate that proofs are optional, we have omitted the proofs of steps 11 and 12 in this example. The steps must still be legal RAT steps but the elaborator will derive the proof rather than the solver.

2.1 Flexibility and extensibility

The purpose of the FRAT format is for solvers to be able to quickly write down what they are doing while they are doing it, with the elaborator stage "picking up the pieces" and preparing the proof for consumption by simpler mechanisms such as certified LRAT checkers. As such, it is important that we are able to concisely represent all manner of proof methods used by modern SAT solvers.

The high level syntax of a FRAT file is quite simple: A sequence of "segments", each of which begins with a character, followed by zero or more nonzero numbers, followed by a 0. In the binary version, each segment similarly begins with a printable character, followed by zero or more nonzero bytes, followed by a zero byte. (Note that continuation bytes in an unsigned number encoding are always nonzero.) This means that it is possible to jump into a FRAT file and find segment boundaries by searching for a nearby zero byte.

$$\langle proof \rangle \leftarrow \langle line \rangle^*$$
$$\langle line \rangle \leftarrow \langle orig \rangle \mid \langle add \rangle \mid \langle del \rangle \mid \langle final \rangle \mid \langle reloc \rangle$$
$$\langle add \rangle \leftarrow \langle add\_seg \rangle \mid \langle add\_seg \rangle \langle hint \rangle$$
$$\langle orig \rangle \leftarrow \text{o} \; \langle id \rangle \; \langle literal \rangle^* \; 0$$
$$\langle add\_seg \rangle \leftarrow \text{a} \; \langle id \rangle \; \langle literal \rangle^* \; 0$$
$$\langle del \rangle \leftarrow \text{d} \; \langle id \rangle \; \langle literal \rangle^* \; 0$$
$$\langle final \rangle \leftarrow \text{f} \; \langle id \rangle \; \langle literal \rangle^* \; 0$$
$$\langle reloc \rangle \leftarrow \text{r} \; (\langle id \rangle \; \langle id \rangle)^* \; 0$$
$$\langle hint \rangle \leftarrow \text{l} \; (\langle id \rangle \mid -\langle id \rangle)^* \; 0$$
$$\langle id \rangle \leftarrow \langle pos \rangle$$
$$\langle literal \rangle \leftarrow \langle pos \rangle \mid \langle neg \rangle$$
$$\langle neg \rangle \leftarrow -\langle pos \rangle$$
$$\langle pos \rangle \leftarrow [\text{1-9}] \; [\text{0-9}]^*$$

Fig. 3. Context-free grammar for the FRAT format.

text	a	9	-3	-4	0	1	5	1	8	0
binary	61	09	07	09	00	6C	0A	02	10	00

Fig. 4. Comparison of binary and text formats for a step. Note that the step ID 9 uses the unsigned encoding, but literals and LRAT style proof steps use signed encoding.

This is in contrast to binary LRAT, in which add steps are encoded as a $\langle id \rangle \langle literal \rangle^* 0 \; (\pm\langle id \rangle)^* \; 0$, because a random zero byte could either be the end of a segment or the middle of an add step. Since 0x61, the ASCII representation of a, is also a valid step ID (encoding the signed number -48), in a sequence such as (a $\langle nonzero \rangle^* \; 0)^*$, the literals and the steps cannot be locally disambiguated.

The local disambiguation property is important for our FRAT elaborator, because it means that we can efficiently parse FRAT files generated by solvers *backward*, reading the segments in reverse order so that we can perform backward checking in a single pass.

DRAT is based on adding clauses that are RAT with respect to the active formula. It is quite versatile and sufficient for most common cases, covering CDCL steps, hyper-resolution, unit propagation, blocked clause elimination and many other techniques. However, we recognize that not all methods can be cast into this format, or are too expensive to translate into this proof system. In this work we define only six segment characters (a, d, f, l, o, r), that suffice to cover methods used by SAT solvers targeting DRAT. However, the format is forward-compatible with new kinds of proof steps, that can be indicated with different characters.

For example, CRYPTOMINISAT [21] is a SAT solver that also supports XOR clause extraction and reasoning, and can derive new XOR clauses using proof techniques such as Gaussian elimination. Encoding this in DRAT is quite complicated: The XOR clauses must be Tseitin transformed into CNF, and Gaussian elimination requires a long resolution proof. Participants in SAT competitions therefore turn this reasoning method off as producing the DRAT proofs is either too difficult or the performance gains are canceled out by the overhead.

FRAT resolves this impasse by allowing the solver to express itself with minimal encoding overhead. A hypothetical extension to FRAT would add new segment characters to allow adding and deleting XOR clauses, and a new proof method for proof by linear algebra on these clauses. The FRAT elaborator would be extended to support the new step kinds, and it could either perform the expensive translation into DRAT at that stage (only doing the work when it is known to be needed for the final proof), or it could pass the new methods on to some XLRAT backend format that understands these steps natively. Since the extension is backward compatible, it can be done without impacting any other FRAT-producing solvers.

3   FRAT-producing solvers

The FRAT proof format is designed to allow conversion of DRAT-producing solvers into FRAT-producing solvers at minimal cost, both in terms of implementation effort and impact on runtime efficiency. In order to show the feasibility of such conversions, we chose two popular SAT solvers, CADICAL[1] and MINISAT[2], to modify as case studies. The solvers were chosen to demonstrate two different aspects of feasibility: since MINISAT forms the basis of the majority of modern SAT solvers, an implementation using MINISAT shows that the format is widely applicable, and provides code which developers can easily incorporate into a large number of existing solvers. CADICAL, on the other hand, is a cutting-edge modern solver which employs a wide range of sophisticated optimizations. A successful conversion of CADICAL shows that the technology is scalable, and is not limited to simpler toy examples.

As mentioned in Section 2, the main solver modifications required for FRAT production are inclusions of clause IDs, finalization steps, and LRAT proof traces. The provision of IDs requires some non-trivial modification as many solvers, including CADICAL and MINISAT, do not natively keep track of clause IDs, and DRAT proofs use literal lists up to permutation for clause identity. In CADICAL, we added IDs to all clauses, leading to 8 bytes overhead per clause. Additionally, unit clauses are tracked separately, and ensuring proper ID tracking for unit clauses resulted in some added code complexity. In MINISAT, we achieved 0 byte overhead by using the pointer value of clauses as their ID, with unit clauses having computed IDs based on the literal. This requires the use of relocation steps during garbage collection. The output of finalization steps requires identifying

---

[1] https://github.com/digama0/cadical

[2] https://github.com/digama0/minisat

the active set from the solver state, which can be subtle depending on the solver architecture, but is otherwise a trivial task assuming knowledge of the solver.

LRAT trace production is the heart of the work, and requires the solver to justify each addition step. This modification is relatively easier to apply to MINI-SAT, as it only adds clauses in a few places, and already tracks the "reasons" for each literal in the current assignment, which makes the proof trace straightforward. In contrast, CADICAL has over 30 ways to add clauses; in addition to the main CDCL loop, there are various in-processing and optimization passes that can create new clauses.

To accommodate this complexity, we leverage the flexibility of the FRAT format which allows optional hints to focus on the most common clause addition steps, to reap the majority of runtime advantage with only a few changes. The FRAT elaborator falls back on the standard elaboration-by-unit propagation when proofs are not provided, so future work can add more proofs to CADICAL without any changes to the toolchain.

To maximize the efficacy of the modification, we used a simple method to find places to add proofs. In the first pass, we added support for clause ID tracking and finalization, and changing the output format to FRAT syntax. Since CADICAL was already producing DRAT proofs, we can easily identify the addition and removal steps and replace them with a and d steps. Once this is done, CADICAL is producing valid FRAT files which can pass through the elaborator and get LRAT results, but it will be quite slow since the FRAT elaborator is essentially acting as a less-optimized version of DRAT-trim at this point.

We then find all code paths that lead to an a step being emitted, and add an extra call to output a step of the form t $\langle todo\_id \rangle$ 0, where $\langle todo\_id \rangle$ is some unique identifier of this position in the code. The FRAT elaborator is configured to ignore these steps, so they have no effect, but by running the solver on benchmarks we can count how many t steps of each kind appear, and so see which code paths are hottest.

The basic idea is that elaborating a step that has a proof is much faster than elaborating a step that doesn't, but the distribution of code paths leading to add steps is highly skewed, so adding proofs to to the top 3 or 4 paths already decreases the elaboration time by over 70%. At the time of writing, about one third of CADICAL code paths are covered, and median elaboration time is about 15% that of DRAT-trim (see Section 5). (This is despite the fact that our elaborator could stand to improve on low level optimizations, and runs about twice as slow as DRAT-trim when no proofs are provided.)

4   Elaboration

The main tasks of the FRAT-to-LRAT elaborator[3] are provision of missing RUP step hints, elimination of irrelevant clause additions, and re-labeling clauses with new IDs. These tasks are performed in two separate 'passes' over files, writing

---

[3] The elaborator used for this paper can be found at https://github.com/digama0/frat/tree/tacas.

Algorithm 1 First pass (elaboration): FRAT to elaborated reversed FRAT

1: **function** ELABORATE(*cert*)
2:     $F \leftarrow \emptyset$, *revcert* $\leftarrow$ []   ▷ F is a map ID $\rightarrow$ clause with a **bool** marking
3:     **for** *step* in reverse(*cert*) **do**
4:         **case** *step* **of**
5:             o$(i, C) \Rightarrow$
6:                 $C' \leftarrow F$.remove(i); **assert** $C' \simeq C$
7:                 **if** C'.marked **then** *revcert* $\leftarrow$ *revcert*, o(i, C)
8:             a$(i, C, proof^?) \Rightarrow$
9:                 $C' \leftarrow F$.remove(i); **assert** $C' \simeq C$
10:                **if** C'.marked **then**
11:                    *steps'* $\leftarrow$ **case** *proof$^?$* **of**
12:                        $\varepsilon \Rightarrow$ PROVERAT(F, C)
13:                        l(*steps*) $\Rightarrow$ CHECKHINT($F, C, steps$)
14:                    **for** j in $\{j \mid \pm j \in steps'\}$ **do**
15:                        **if** $\neg F_j$.marked **then**
16:                            F_j.marked $\leftarrow$ **true**
17:                            *revcert* $\leftarrow$ *revcert*, d$(step, F_j)$
18:                    *revcert* $\leftarrow$ *revcert*, a$(i, C, l(steps'))$
19:            d$(i, C) \Rightarrow F$.insert(i, C, marked: **false**)
20:            f$(i, C) \Rightarrow F$.insert(i, C, marked: $C = \bot$)
21:            r$(R) \Rightarrow$
22:                $R' \leftarrow \{(s, t) \in R \mid \exists x.(t, x) \in F\}$
23:                $F \leftarrow F - \{(t, F_t) \mid (s, t) \in R'\} + \{(s, F_t) \mid (s, t) \in R'\}$
24:                *revcert* $\leftarrow$ *revcert*, r(R')
25:     **return** *revcert*

---

and reading directly to disk (so the entire proof is never in memory at once). In the first pass, the elaborator reads the FRAT file and produces a temporary file (which may be stored on disk or in memory depending on configuration). The temporary file is essentially the original FRAT file with the steps put in reverse order, while satisfying the following additional conditions:

- All a steps have annotations.
- Every clause introduced by an o, a, or r step ultimately contributes to the proof of $\bot$. Note that we consider an r step as using an old clause with the old ID and introducing a new clause with the new ID.
- There are no f steps.

Algorithm 1 shows the pseudocode of the first pass, ELABORATE(*cert*). Here, *cert* is the FRAT proof obtained from the SAT solver, and the pass works by iterating over its steps in reverse order, producing the temporary file *revcert*. The map F maintains the active formula as a map with unique IDs for each clause (double inserts and removes to F are always error conditions), and the effect of each step is replayed backwards to reconstruct the solver's state at the point each step was produced.

Algorithm 2 Second pass (renumbering): elaborated reversed FRAT to LRAT

1: **function** RENUMBER(F_{orig}, $revcert$)
2:      $M \leftarrow \emptyset$, $k \leftarrow |F_{\text{orig}}|$, $lrat \leftarrow []$ ▷ M is a map ID → ID
3:      **for** $step$ **in** reverse($revcert$) **do**
4:          **case** $step$ **of**
5:              $\mathsf{o}(i, C) \Rightarrow$ find j such that $C \simeq (F_{\text{orig}})_j$; M.insert(i, j)
6:              $\mathsf{a}(i, C, \mathsf{l}(steps)) \Rightarrow$
7:                  $k \leftarrow k + 1$; M.insert(i, k)
8:                  $lrat \leftarrow lrat, \mathsf{add}(k, C, [\pm M_i \mid \pm i \in steps])$
9:                  **if** $C = \bot$ **then return** $lrat$
10:             $\mathsf{d}(i, C) \Rightarrow lrat \leftarrow lrat, \mathsf{del}(k, M.\text{remove}(i))$
11:             $\mathsf{r}(R) \Rightarrow M \leftarrow M - \{(s, M_s) \mid (s, t) \in R\} + \{(t, M_s) \mid (s, t) \in R\}$
12:      **assert false**   ▷ no proof of $\bot$ found

- All d or f clauses are immediately inserted to F, but (with the exception of the empty clause) are marked as not necessarily required for the proof, and the d step is deferred until just before its first use (or rather, just after the last use).
- PROVERAT(F, C), not given here, checks that C has property RAT with respect to F, and produces a step list in LRAT format (where positive numbers are clause references in a unit propagation proof, and negative numbers are used in RAT steps, indicating the clauses to resolve against).
- CHECKHINT($F, C, steps$) does the same thing, but it has been given a candidate proof, $steps$. It will check that $steps$ is a valid proof, and if so, returns it, but the steps in the unit propagation proof may be out of order (in which case they are reordered to LRAT conformity), and if the given proof is not salvageable, it falls back on PROVERAT(F, C) to construct the proof.

In the second pass, RENUMBER(F_{orig}, $revcert$) reads the input DIMACS file and the temporary file from the first pass, and produces the final result in LRAT format. Not much checking happens in this pass, but we ensure that the o steps in the FRAT file actually appear (up to permutation) in the input. The state that is maintained in this pass is a list of all active clause IDs, and the corresponding list of LRAT IDs (in which original steps are always numbered sequentially in the file, and add/delete steps use a monotonic counter that is incremented on each addition step).

The resulting LRAT file can then be verified by any of the verified LRAT checkers [26] (and our toolchain also includes a built-in LRAT checker for verification).

The 2-pass algorithm is used in order to optimize memory usage. The result of the first pass is streamed out so that the intermediate elaboration result does not have to be stored in memory simultaneously. Once the temporary file is streamed out, we need at least one more pass to reverse it (even if the labels did not need renumbering) since its steps are in reverse order.

5   Test results

We performed benchmarks comparing our FRAT toolchain (modified CaDiCaL + FRAT-to-LRAT elaborator written in Rust) against the DRAT toolchain (standard CaDiCaL + DRAT-trim) and measured their execution times, output file sizes, and peak memory usages while solving SAT instances in the DIMACS format and producing their LRAT proofs. All tests were performed on Amazon EC2 r5a.xlarge instances, running Ubuntu Server 20.04 LTS on 2.5 GHz AMD EPYC 7000 processors with 32 GB RAM and 512 GB SSD.

The instances used in the benchmark were chosen by selecting all 97 instances for which default-mode CaDiCaL returned 'UNSAT' in the 2019 SAT Race results. One of these instances was excluded because DRAT-trim exhausted the available 32GB memory and failed during elaboration. Although this instance was not used for comparisons below, we note that it offers further evidence of the FRAT toolchain's efficient use of memory, since the FRAT-to-LRAT elaboration of this instance succeeded on the same system. The remaining 96 instances were used for performance comparison of the two toolchains. [4]

Figures 5 and 6 show the time and memory measurements from the benchmark. We can see from Figure 5 that the FRAT toolchain is significantly faster than DRAT toolchain. Although the modified CaDiCaL tends to be slightly (6%) slower than standard CaDiCaL, that overhead is more than compensated by a median 84% decrease in elaboration time (the sum over all instances are 1700.47 s in the DRAT toolchain vs. 381.70 s in the FRAT toolchain, so the average is down by 77%). If we include the time of the respective solvers, the FRAT + modified CaDiCaL toolchain takes 53.6% of the DRAT + CaDiCaL toolchain on median. The difference in the toolchains' time budgets is clear: the DRAT toolchain spends 42% of its time in solving and 58% in elaboration, while FRAT spends 85% on solving and only 15% on elaboration.

Figure 6 shows a dramatic difference in peak memory usage between the FRAT and DRAT toolchains. On median, the FRAT toolchain used only 5.4% as much peak memory as DRAT. (The average is 318.62 MB, which is 11.98% that of the DRAT toolchain's 2659.07 MB, but this is dominated by the really large instances. The maximum memory usage was 2.99 GB for FRAT and 21.5 GB for DRAT, but one instance exhausted the available 32 GB in DRAT and is not included in this figure.) This result is in agreement with our initial expectations: the FRAT toolchain's 2-pass elaboration method allows it to limit the number of clauses held in memory to the size of the active set used by the solver, whereas the DRAT toolchain loads all clauses in a DRAT file into memory at once during elaboration. This difference suggests that the FRAT toolchain can be used to verify instances that would otherwise require more memory than the system limit on the DRAT toolchain.

There were no noticeable differences in the sizes or verification times of LRAT proofs produced by the two toolchains. On average, LRAT proofs produced by

---

[4] A CSV of detailed benchmark results can be found at https://github.com/digama0/ frat/blob/tacas/benchmark/benchmark-results.csv.

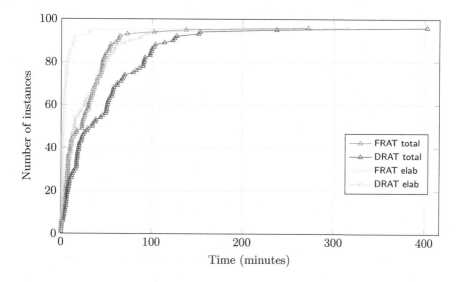

Fig. 5. FRAT vs. DRAT time comparison. The datapoints of 'FRAT total' and 'DRAT total' show the number of instances that each toolchain could generate LRAT proofs for within the given time limit. The datapoints of 'FRAT elab' and 'DRAT elab' show the number of instances whose intermediate format proof files (FRAT or DRAT) could be elaborated to LRAT within the given time limit.

the FRAT toolchain were 1.873% smaller and 3.314% faster[5] to check than those from the DRAT toolchain.

One minor downside of the FRAT toolchain is that it requires the storage of a temporary file during elaboration, but we do not expect this to be a problem in practice since the temporary file is typically much smaller than either the FRAT or LRAT file. In our test cases, the average temporary file size was 28.68% and 47.60% that of FRAT and LRAT files, respectively. In addition, users can run the elaborator with the -m option to bypass temporary files and write the temporary data to memory instead, which further improves performance but foregoes the memory conservation that comes with 2-pass elaboration.

The CADICAL modification is only a prototype, and some of its weaknesses show in the data. The general pattern we observed is that on problems for which the predicted CADICAL code paths were taken, the generated files have a large number of hints and the elaboration time is negligible (the "FRAT elab" line in fig. 5); but on problems which make use of the more unusual in-processing operations, many steps with no hints are given to the elaborator, and performance becomes comparable to DRAT-trim. For solver developers, this means that there

---

[5] One instance was omitted from the LRAT verification time comparison due to what seems to be a bug in the standard LRAT checker included in DRAT-trim. Detailed information regarding this instance can be found at https://github.com/digama0/frat/blob/tacas/benchmark/README.md.

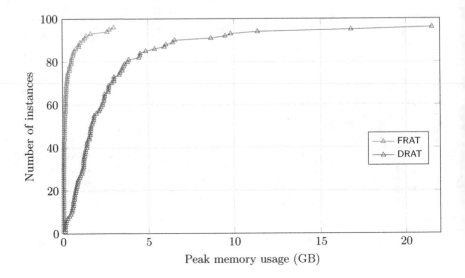

Fig. 6. FRAT vs. DRAT peak memory usage comparison. Each datapoint shows the number of instances that each toolchain could successfully generate LRAT proofs for within the given peak memory usage limit.

is a very direct relationship between proof annotation effort and mean solution + elaboration time. Currently, elaboration of FRAT files with no annotations (the worst-case scenario for the FRAT toolchain) typically takes slightly more than twice as long as elaboration of DRAT files with DRAT-trim, likely due to missing optimizations from DRAT-trim that could be incorporated, but this only underscores the effectiveness of adding hints to the format.

6   Related works

As already mentioned, the FRAT format is most closely related to the DRAT format [8], which it seeks to replace as an intermediate output format for SAT solvers. It is also dependent on the LRAT format and related tools [3], as the FRAT toolchain targets LRAT as the final output format.

The GRAT format [16] and toolchain also aims to improve elaboration of SAT unsatisfiability proofs, but takes a different approach from that of FRAT. It retains DRAT as the intermediate format, but uses parallel processing and targets a new final format with more information than LRAT in order to improve overall performance. GRAT also comes with its own verified checker [17].

Specifying and verifying the program correctness of SAT solvers (sometimes called the *autarkic* method, as opposed to the proof-producing *skeptical* method) is a radically different approach to ensuring the correctness of SAT solvers. There have been various efforts to verify nontrivial SAT solvers [18,20,19,4,5]. Although these solvers have become significantly faster, they cannot compete with the (unverified) state-of-the-art solvers. It is also difficult to maintain and modify certified solvers. Proving the correctness of nontrivial SAT solvers can provide new insights about key invariants underlying the used techniques [5].

Generally speaking, devising proof formats for automated reasoning tools and augmenting the tools with proof output capability is an active research area. Notable examples outside SAT solving include the LFSC format for SMT solving [23] and the TSTP format for classical first-order ATPs [24]. In particular, the recent work on the VERIT SMT solver [1] is motivated by similar rationales as that for the FRAT toolchain; the key insight is that a proof production pipeline is often easier to optimize on the solver side than on the elaborator side, as the former has direct access to many types of useful information.

7 Conclusion

The test results show that the FRAT format and toolchain made significant performance gains relative to their DRAT equivalents in both elaboration time and memory usage. We take this as confirmation of our initial conjectures that (1) there is a large amount of useful and easily extracted information in SAT solvers that is left untapped by DRAT proofs, and (2) the use of streaming verification is the key to verifying very large proofs that cannot be held in memory at once.

The practical ramification is that, provided that solvers produce well-annotated FRAT proofs, the elaborator is no longer a bottleneck in the pipeline. Typically, when DRAT-trim hangs it does so either by taking excessive time, or by attempting to read in an entire proof file at once and exhausting memory (the so-called "uncheckable" proofs that can be produced but not verified). But FRAT-to-LRAT elaboration is typically faster than FRAT production, and the memory consumption of the FRAT-to-LRAT elaborator at any given point is proportional to the memory used by the solver at the same point in the proof. Since LRAT verification is already efficient, the only remaining limiting factor is essentially the time and memory usage of the solver itself.

In addition to performance, the other main consideration in the design of the FRAT format and toolchain was flexibility of use and extension. The encoding of FRAT files allows them to be read and parsed both backward and forward, and the format can be modified to include more advanced inferences, as we have discussed in the example of XOR steps. The optional 1 steps allow SAT solvers to decide precisely when they will provide explicit proofs, thereby promoting a workable compromise between implementation complexity and runtime efficiency. SAT solver developers can begin using the format by producing the most bare-bones FRAT proofs with no annotations (essentially DRAT proofs with metadata for original/final clauses) and gradually work toward providing more complete hints. We hope that this combination of efficiency and flexibility will motivate performance-minded SAT solver developers to adopt the format and support more robust proof production, which is presently only an afterthought in most SAT solvers.

References

1. Barbosa, H., Blanchette, J.C., Fleury, M., Fontaine, P.: Scalable fine-grained proofs for formula processing. Journal of Automated Reasoning pp. 1–26 (2019)
2. Biere, A., Cimatti, A., Clarke, E.M., Fujita, M., Zhu, Y.: Symbolic model checking using SAT procedures instead of BDDs. In: Proceedings 1999 Design Automation Conference (Cat. No. 99CH36361). pp. 317–320. IEEE (1999)
3. Cruz-Filipe, L., Heule, M.J.H., Hunt, W.A., Kaufmann, M., Schneider-Kamp, P.: Efficient certified RAT verification. In: International Conference on Automated Deduction. pp. 220–236. Springer (2017)
4. Fleury, M.: Optimizing a verified SAT solver. In: Badger, J.M., Rozier, K.Y. (eds.) NFM. LNCS, vol. 11460, pp. 148–165. Springer (2019)
5. Fleury, M., Blanchette, J.C., Lammich, P.: A verified SAT solver with watched literals using imperative HOL. In: Andronick, J., Felty, A.P. (eds.) CPP. pp. 158–171. ACM (2018)
6. Goldberg, E., Novikov, Y.: Verification of proofs of unsatisfiability for CNF formulas. In: Proceedings of the conference on Design, Automation and Test in Europe-Volume 1. p. 10886. IEEE Computer Society (2003)
7. Haken, A.: The intractability of resolution. Theoretical Computer Science **39**, 297–308 (1985)
8. Heule, M.J.H.: The DRAT format and DRAT-trim checker. arXiv preprint arXiv:1610.06229 (2016)
9. Heule, M.J.H., Biere, A.: Clausal proof compression. In: International Workshop on the Implementation of Logics (2015)
10. Heule, M.J.H., Hunt, W.A., Wetzler, N.: Verifying refutations with extended resolution. In: International Conference on Automated Deduction. pp. 345–359. Springer (2013)
11. Heule, M.J.H., Hunt, W.A., Wetzler, N.: Bridging the gap between easy generation and efficient verification of unsatisfiability proofs. Softw. Test. Verif. Reliab. **24**(8), 593–607 (Sep 2014)
12. Heule, M.J.H., Kullmann, O., Marek, V.W.: Solving and verifying the boolean pythagorean triples problem via cube-and-conquer. In: International Conference on Theory and Applications of Satisfiability Testing. pp. 228–245. Springer (2016)
13. Järvisalo, M., Heule, M.J.H., Biere, A.: Inprocessing rules. In: Gramlich, B., Miller, D., Sattler, U. (eds.) IJCAR. LNCS, vol. 7364, pp. 355–370. Springer (2012)
14. Kautz, H., Selman, B.: Pushing the envelope: Planning, propositional logic, and stochastic search. In: Proceedings of the National Conference on Artificial Intelligence. pp. 1194–1201 (1996)
15. Knuth, D.E.: The Art of Computer Programming, Volume 4, Fascicle 6: Satisfiability. Addison-Wesley Professional (2015)
16. Lammich, P.: The GRAT tool chain. In: International Conference on Theory and Applications of Satisfiability Testing. pp. 457–463. Springer (2017)
17. Lammich, P.: Efficient verified (un) SAT certificate checking. Journal of Automated Reasoning pp. 1–20 (2019)
18. Marić, F.: Formal verification of a modern SAT solver by shallow embedding into Isabelle/HOL. Theoretical Computer Science **411**(50), 4333–4356 (2010)
19. Oe, D., Stump, A., Oliver, C., Clancy, K.: versat: A verified modern SAT solver. In: International Workshop on Verification, Model Checking, and Abstract Interpretation. pp. 363–378. Springer (2012)

20. Shankar, N., Vaucher, M.: The mechanical verification of a dpll-based satisfiability solver. Electronic Notes in Theoretical Computer Science **269**, 3 – 17 (2011), proceedings of the Fifth Logical and Semantic Frameworks, with Applications Workshop (LSFA 2010)
21. Soos, M., Nohl, K., Castelluccia, C.: Extending SAT solvers to cryptographic problems. In: Kullmann, O. (ed.) Theory and Applications of Satisfiability Testing - SAT 2009, 12th International Conference, SAT 2009, Swansea, UK, June 30 - July 3, 2009. Proceedings. Lecture Notes in Computer Science, vol. 5584, pp. 244–257. Springer (2009)
22. Sörensson, N., Biere, A.: Minimizing learned clauses. In: Kullmann, O. (ed.) Theory and Applications of Satisfiability Testing - SAT 2009. pp. 237–243. Springer Berlin Heidelberg, Berlin, Heidelberg (2009)
23. Stump, A., Oe, D., Reynolds, A., Hadarean, L., Tinelli, C.: SMT proof checking using a logical framework. Formal Methods in System Design **42**(1), 91–118 (2013)
24. Sutcliffe, G., Zimmer, J., Schulz, S.: Tstp data-exchange formats for automated theorem proving tools. Distributed Constraint Problem Solving and Reasoning in Multi-Agent Systems **112**, 201–215 (2004)
25. Van Gelder, A.: Improved conflict-clause minimization leads to improved propositional proof traces. In: Proceedings of the 12th International Conference on Theory and Applications of Satisfiability Testing. p. 141–146. SAT '09, Springer-Verlag, Berlin, Heidelberg (2009)
26. Wetzler, N., Heule, M.J.H., Hunt, W.A.: Mechanical verification of SAT refutations with extended resolution. In: International Conference on Interactive Theorem Proving. pp. 229–244. Springer (2013)

Generating Extended Resolution Proofs
with a BDD-Based SAT Solver

Randal E. Bryant (✉) and Marijn J. H. Heule*

Computer Science Department
Carnegie Mellon University, Pittsburgh, PA, United States
{Randy.Bryant, mheule}@cs.cmu.edu

Abstract. In 2006, Biere, Jussila, and Sinz made the key observation that the underlying logic behind algorithms for constructing Reduced, Ordered Binary Decision Diagrams (BDDs) can be encoded as steps in a proof in the *extended resolution* logical framework. Through this, a BDD-based Boolean satisfiability (SAT) solver can generate a checkable proof of unsatisfiability. Such proofs indicate that the formula is truly unsatisfiable without requiring the user to trust the BDD package or the SAT solver built on top of it.

We extend their work to enable arbitrary existential quantification of the formula variables, a critical capability for BDD-based SAT solvers. We demonstrate the utility of this approach by applying a prototype solver to obtain polynomially sized proofs on benchmarks for the mutilated chessboard and pigeonhole problems—ones that are very challenging for search-based SAT solvers.

Keywords: extended resolution, binary decision diagrams, mutilated chessboard, pigeonhole problem

1 Introduction

When a Boolean satisfiability (SAT) solver returns a purported solution to a Boolean formula, its validity can easily be checked by making sure that the solution indeed satisfies the formula. When the formula is unsatisfiable, on the other hand, having the solver simply declare this to be the case requires the user to have faith in the solver, a complex piece of software that could well be flawed. Indeed, modern solvers employ a number of sophisticated techniques to reduce the search space. If one of those techniques is invalid or incorrectly implemented, the solver may overlook actual solutions and label a formula as unsatisfiable, even when it is not.

With SAT solvers providing the foundation for a number of different real-world tasks, this "false negative" outcome could have unacceptable consequences. For example, when used as part of a formal verification system, the usual strategy is to encode some undesired property of the system as a formula. The SAT solver is then used to determine whether some operation of the system could lead to this undesirable property. Having the solver declare the formula to be unsatisfiable is an indication that the undesirable behavior cannot occur, but only if the formula is truly unsatisfiable.

---

* Supported by the National Science Foundation under grant CCF-2010951

J. F. Groote and K. G. Larsen (Eds.): TACAS 2021, LNCS 12651, pp. 76–93, 2021.
https://doi.org/10.1007/978-3-030-72016-2_5

Rather than requiring users to place their trust in a complex software system, a *proof-generating* solver constructs a proof that the formula is indeed unsatisfiable. The proof has a form that can readily be checked by a simple proof checker. Initial work of checking unsatisfiability results was based on resolution proofs, but modern checkers are based on stronger proof systems [16,33]. The checker provides an independent validation that the formula is indeed unsatisfiable. The checker can even be simple enough to be formally verified [9,23,29]. Such a capability has become an essential feature for modern SAT solvers.

In their 2006 papers [21,28], Jussila, Sinz and Biere made the key observation that the underlying logic behind algorithms for constructing Reduced, Ordered Binary Decision Diagrams (BDDs) [4] can be encoded as steps in a proof in the *extended resolution* logical framework [30]. Through this, a BDD-based Boolean satisfiability solver can generate checkable proofs of unsatisfiability for a set of clauses. Such proofs indicate that the formula is truly unsatisfiable without requiring the user to trust the BDD package or the SAT solver built on top of it.

In this paper, we refine these ideas to enable a full-featured, BDD-based SAT solver. Chief among these is the ability to perform existential quantification on arbitrary variables. (Jussila, Sinz, and Biere [21] extended their original work [28] to allow existential quantification, but only for the root variable of a BDD.) In addition, we allow greater flexibility in the choice of variable ordering and the order in which conjunction and quantification operations are performed. This combination allows a wide range of strategies for creating a sequence of BDD operations that, starting with a set of input clauses, yield the BDD representation of the constant function **0**, indicating that the formula is unsatisfiable. Using the extended-resolution proof framework, these operations can generate a proof showing that the original set of clauses logically implies the empty clause, providing a checkable proof that the formula is unsatisfiable.

As the experimental results demonstrate, our refinements enable a proof-generating BDD-based SAT solver to achieve polynomial performance on several classic "hard" problems [1,15]. Since the performance of a proof-generating SAT solver affects not only the runtime of the program, but also the length of the proofs generated, achieving polynomial performance is an important step forward. Our results for these benchmarks rely on a novel approach to ordering the conjunction and quantification operations, inspired by symbolic model checking [7].

This paper is structured as follows. First, it provides a brief introduction to the resolution and extended resolution logical frameworks and to BDDs. Then we show how a BDD-based SAT solver can generate proofs by augmenting algorithms for computing the conjunction of two functions represented as BDDs, and for checking that one function logically implies another. We then describe our prototype implementation and evaluate its performance on several classic problems. We conclude with some general observations and suggestions for further work.

2 Preliminaries

Given a Boolean formula over a set of variables $\{x_1, x_2, \ldots, x_n\}$, a SAT solver attempts to find an assignment to these variables that will satisfy the formula, or it declares that the formula is unsatisfiable. As is standard practice, we use the term *literal* to refer to either a variable or its complement. Most SAT solvers use Boolean formulas expressed in *conjunctive normal form*, where the formula consists of a set of *clauses*, each consisting of a set of literals. Each clause is a disjunction: if an assignment sets any of its literals to true, the clause is considered to be satisfied. The overall formula is a conjunction: a satisfying assignment must satisfy all of the clauses.

We write $\top$ to denote both tautology and logical truth, and $\bot$ to represent both an empty clause and logical falsehood. When writing clauses, we omit disjunction symbols and use overlines to denote negation, writing $\bar{u} \vee v \vee \bar{w}$ as $\bar{u} v \bar{w}$.

2.1 (Extended) Resolution Proofs

Robinson [26] observed that a single inference rule could form the basis for a refutation theorem-proving technique for first-order logic. Here, we consider its specialization to propositional logic. For clauses of the form $C \vee x$, and $\bar{x} \vee D$, the resolution rule derives the new clause $C \vee D$. This inference is written with a notation showing the required conditions above a horizontal line, and the resulting inference (the *resolvent*) below:

$$\frac{C \vee x \qquad \bar{x} \vee D}{C \vee D}$$

Resolution provides a mechanism for proving that a set of clauses is unsatisfiable. Suppose the input consists of m clauses. A resolution proof is given as a *trace* consisting of a series of *steps* S, where each step s_i consists of a clause C_i and a (possibly empty) list of antecedents A_i, where each antecedent is the index of one of the previous steps. The first set of steps, denoted S_m, consists of the input clauses without any antecedents. Each successive step then consists of a clause and a set of antecedents, such that the clause can be derived from the clauses in the antecedents by one or more resolution steps. It follows by transitivity that for each step s_i, with $i > m$, clause C_i is logically implied by the input clauses, written $S_m \vdash C_i$. If, through a series of steps, we can reach a step s_t where C_t is the empty clause, then the trace provides a proof that $S_m \vdash \bot$, i.e., the set of input clauses is not satisfiable.

Tseitin [30] introduced the extended-resolution proof framework in 1966. It allows the addition of new *extension* variables to a resolution proof in a manner that preserves the integrity of the proof. In particular, in introducing variable e, there must be an accompaning set of clauses that encode $e \leftrightarrow F$, where F is a formula over variables (both original and extension) that were introduced earlier. These are referred to as the *defining clauses* for extension variable e. Variable e then provides a shorthand notation by which F can be referenced multiple times. Doing so can reduce the size of a clausal representation of a problem by an exponential factor.

An extension variable e is introduced into the proof by including its defining clauses in the list of clauses being generated. The proof checker must ensure that these added clauses do not artificially restrict the set of satisfying solutions. The checker can do this by making sure that the defining clauses are *blocked* with respect to variable e [22]. That is, for each defining clause C containing literal e and each defining clause D containing literal $\bar{e}$, there must be some literal l in C such that its complement $\bar{l}$ is in D. As a result, resolving clauses C and D will yield a tautology.

Tseitin transformations are commonly used to encode a logic circuit or formula as a set of clauses without requiring the formulas to be "flattened" into a conjunctive normal form over the circuit inputs or formula variables. These introduced variables are called *Tseitin variables* and are considered to be part of the input formula. An extended resolution proof takes this concept further by introducing additional variables as part of the proof. Some problems for which the minimum resolution proof must be of exponential size can be expressed with polynomial-sized proofs in extended resolution [8].

To validate the proofs, we use a clausal proof system, known as Resolution Asymmetric Tautology (RAT), that generalizes extended resolution [32]. RAT is used in industry and to validate the results of the SAT competitions [18]. There are various fast and formally-verified RAT proof checkers [10,23,29].

Clausal proofs also allow the removal of clauses. In our use, we delete clauses when the program can determine that they will not be referenced as antecedents for any succeeding clauses. As the experimental results of Section 4 demonstrate, deleting clauses that are no longer needed can substantially reduce the number of clauses the checker must track while processing a proof.

2.2 Binary Decision Diagrams

Reduced, Ordered Binary Decision Diagrams (which we refer to as simply "BDDs") provide a canonical form for representing Boolean functions, and an associated set of algorithms for constructing them and testing their properties. A number of tutorials have been published [2,5,6]. providing a background on BDDs and their algorithms.

With BDDs, functions are defined over a set of variables $X = \{x_1, x_2, \ldots, x_n\}$. We let L_1 and L_0 denote the two leaf nodes, representing the constant functions **1** and **0**, respectively. Each nonterminal node u has an associated variable $\mathsf{Var}(u)$ and children $\mathsf{Hi}(u)$, indicating the case where the node variable has value 1, and $\mathsf{Lo}(u)$, indicating the case where the node variable has value 0.

Nodes are stored in a *unique table*, indexed by the key $\langle \mathsf{Var}(u), \mathsf{Hi}(u), \mathsf{Lo}(u) \rangle$, so that isomorphic nodes are never created. The nodes are shared across all of the generated BDDs [24]. In presenting algorithms, we assume a function GETNODE(x, u_1, u_0) that checks the unique table for a node with variable x and children u_1 and u_0. It either returns the node stored there, or it creates a new node and enters it into the table. With this table, we can guarantee that the subgraphs with root nodes u and v represent the same Boolean function if and only if $u = v$. We can therefore identify Boolean functions with their BDD root nodes.

BDD packages support multiple operations for constructing and testing the properties of Boolean functions represented by BDDs. A number of these are based on the *Apply* algorithm [4]. Given BDDs u and v representing functions f and g, respectively, and a Boolean operation (e.g., AND), the algorithm generates the BDD representation w of the operation applied to those functions (e.g., $f \wedge g$.) For each operation, the program maintains an *operation cache* indexed by the argument nodes u and v, mapping to the result node w. With this cache, the worst case number of recursive steps required by the algorithm is bounded by the product of the sizes (in nodes) of the arguments.

We use the term APPLYAND to refer to the Apply algorithm for Boolean operation $\wedge$ and APPLYOR to refer to the Apply algorithm for Boolean operation $\vee$.

3   Proof Generation During BDD Construction

In our formulation, every newly created BDD node u is assigned an extension variable. (As notation, we use the same name for the node and for its extension variable.) We then extend the Apply algorithm to generate proofs based on the recursive structure of the BDD operations.

Let S_m denote the set of input clauses. Our goal is to generate a proof that $S_m \vdash \perp$, i.e., there is no satisfying assignment for these clauses. Our BDD-based approach generates a sequence of BDDs with root nodes $u_1, u_2, \ldots, u_t$, where $u_t = L_0$, based on a combination of the following operations. (The exact sequencing of operations is determined by the *evaluation mechanism*, as is described in Section 4.)

1. For input clause C_i generate its BDD representation u_i using a series of APPLYOR operations.
2. For roots u_j and u_k, generate the BDD representation of their conjunction $u_l = u_j \wedge u_k$ using the APPLYAND operation.
3. For root u_j and some set of variables $Y \subseteq X$, perform existential quantification: $u_k = \exists Y\, u_j$.

Although the existential quantification operation is not mandatory for a BDD-based SAT solver, it can greatly improve its performance [13]. It is the BDD counterpart to Davis-Putnam variable elimination on clauses [11]. As the notation indicates, there are often multiple variables that can be eliminated simultaneously. Although the operation can cause a BDD to increase in size, it generally causes a reduction. Our experimental results demonstrate the importance of this operation.

As these operations proceed, we simultaneously generate a set of proof steps. The details of each step are given later in the presentation. For each BDD generated, we maintain the proof invariant that its root node u_j satisfies $S_m \vdash u_j$.

1. Following the generation of the BDD u_i for clause C_i, we also generate a proof that $C_i \vdash u_i$. This is described in Section 3.1.
2. Justifying the conjunctions requires two parts:
   (a) Using a modified version of the APPLYAND algorithm we follow the structure of its recursive calls to generate a proof that the algorithm preserves implication: $u_j \wedge u_k \to u_l$. This is described in Section 3.2.
   (b) This implication can be combined with the earlier proofs that $S_m \vdash u_j$ and $S_m \vdash u_k$ to prove $S_m \vdash u_l$.
3. Justifying the quantification also requires two parts:
   (a) Following the generation of u_k via existential quantification, we perform a separate check that $u_j \to u_k$. This check uses a proof-generating version of the Apply algorithm for implication testing that we refer to as PROVEIMPLICATION. This is described in Section 3.3.
   (b) This implication can be combined with the earlier proof that $S_m \vdash u_j$ to prove $S_m \vdash u_k$.

As case 3(a) states, we do not attempt to track the detailed logic underlying the quantification operation. Instead, we run a separate check that the quantification preserves implication. As is the case with many BDD packages, our implementation can perform existential quantification of an arbitrary set of variables in a single pass over the argument BDD. A single implication test suffices for the entire quantification.

Sinz and Biere's formulation of proof generation by a BDD-based SAT solver [28] introduces special extension variables n_1 and n_0 to represent the BDD leaves L_1 and L_0. Their proof then includes unit clauses n_1 and $\overline{n}_0$ to force these variables to be set to 1 and 0, respectively. This formulation greatly reduces the number of special cases to consider in the proof-generating version of the APPLYAND operation, but it complicates the generation of resolution proofs for the implication test. Instead, we directly associate leaves L_1 and L_0 with $\top$ and $\bot$, respectively.

The n variables in the input clauses all have associated BDD variables. The proof then introduces an extension variable every time a new BDD node is created. In the following presentation, we use the node name (e.g., u) to indicate the associated extension variable. In the actual implementation, the extension variable identifier (an integer) is stored as one of the fields in the node representation.

When creating a new node, the GETNODE function adds (up to) four defining clauses for the associated extension variable. For node u with variable $\mathsf{Var}(u) = x$, $\mathsf{Hi}(u) = u_1$, and $\mathsf{Lo}(u) = u_0$, the clauses are:

Notation	Formula	Clause
$\mathsf{HD}(u)$	$x \rightarrow (u \rightarrow u_1)$	$\overline{x}\,\overline{u}\,u_1$
$\mathsf{LD}(u)$	$\overline{x} \rightarrow (u \rightarrow u_0)$	$x\,\overline{u}\,u_0$
$\mathsf{HU}(u)$	$x \rightarrow (u_1 \rightarrow u)$	$\overline{x}\,\overline{u}_1\,u$
$\mathsf{LU}(u)$	$\overline{x} \rightarrow (u_0 \rightarrow u)$	$x\,\overline{u}_0\,u$

The names for these clauses combine an indication of whether they correspond to variable x being 1 (H) or 0 (L) and whether they form an implication from the node down to its child (D) or from the child up to its parent (U). When either node u_0 or u_1 is a leaf node, some of these clauses degenerate to tautologies. Such clauses are omitted from the proof. Each clause is numbered according to its position in the sequence of clauses comprising the proof. These defining clauses encode the assertion $u \leftrightarrow ITE(x, u_1, u_0)$, where ITE denotes the *if-then-else* operation, defined as $ITE(x, y, z) = (x \wedge y) \vee (\overline{x} \wedge z)$. As can be seen, the defining clauses are blocked with respect to extension variable u.

3.1 Generating BDD Representations of Clauses

The BDD representation u of a clause C is generated by using the APPLYOR operation on the BDD representations of its literals. This BDD has a simple, linear structure with one node for each literal. Each successive node has a branch to leaf node L_1 when the literal is true and to the next node in the chain when the literal is false. The proof that $C \vdash u$ is based on this linear structure, employing the upward defining clauses HU and LU for the nodes in the chain [28].

3.2 The APPLYAND Operation

The key idea in generating proofs for the AND operation is to follow the recursive structure of the Apply algorithm. We do this by integrating proof generation into the

Terminal Cases	
Case	Result
$u = v$	$(u, \top)$
$u = L_0$	$(L_0, \top)$
$v = L_0$	$(L_0, \top)$
$u = L_1$	$(v, \top)$
$v = L_1$	$(u, \top)$

```
APPLYANDRECUR(u, v)
    J ⟵ {}
    x ⟵ min(Var(u), Var(v))
    if x = Var(u):
        u₁, u₀ ⟵ Hi(u), Lo(u)
        J ⟵ J ∪ {HD(u), LD(u)}
    else:    u₁, u₀ ⟵ u, u
    if x = Var(v):
        v₁, v₀ ⟵ Hi(v), Lo(v)
        J ⟵ J ∪ {HD(v), LD(v)}
    else:    v₁, v₀ ⟵ v, v
    w₁, s₁ ⟵ APPLYAND(u₁, v₁)
    w₀, s₀ ⟵ APPLYAND(u₀, v₀)
    J ⟵ J ∪ {s₁, s₀}
    if w₁ = w₀:
        w ⟵ w₁
    else:
        w ⟵ GETNODE(x, w₁, w₀)
        J ⟵ J ∪ {HU(w), LU(w)}
    s ⟵ JUSTIFYAND(⟨u, v, w⟩, J)
    AndCache(⟨u, v⟩) ⟵ (w, s)
    return (w, s)
```

Fig. 1. Terminal cases and recursive step of APPLYAND operation, modified for proof generation. Each call returns both a node and a proof step.

APPLYAND procedure. The overall control flow is identical to the standard version, except the function returns both a BDD node w and a step number s. For arguments u and v, the generated step s has clause $\overline{u}\,\overline{v}\,w$ along with antecedents defining a resolution proof of the implication $u \wedge v \rightarrow w$. We refer to this as the *justification* for the operation. The operation cache is modified to hold both the returned node and the justifying step number as values.

Figure 1 shows the main components of the implementation. When the two arguments are equal or one of the leaves is a terminal node, then the recursion terminates (left). These cases have tautologies as their justification. Failing a terminal case, the code checks in the operation cache for matching arguments u and v, returning the cached result if found.

Failing the terminal case tests and the cache lookup, the program proceeds as shown in the procedure APPLYANDRECUR (right). Here, the procedure branches on the variable x that is the minimum of the two root variables. The procedure accumulates a set of steps J to be used in the implication proof. These include the two steps (possibly tautologies) from the two recursive calls. At the end, it invokes a function JUSTIFYAND to generate the required proof. It stores both the result node w and the proof step s in the operation cache, and it provides these values as the return values.

Proof Generation for the General Case. Proving the nodes generated by APPLYAND satisfy the implication property proceeds by inducting on the structure of the argument

$$
\begin{array}{cccccc}
 & & \text{WHU} & \text{ANDH} & \text{ANDL} & \text{WLU} \\
 & \text{UHD} & \overline{x}\,\overline{w}_1\,w & \overline{u}_1\,\overline{v}_1\,w_1 & \overline{u}_0\,\overline{v}_0\,w_0 & x\,\overline{w}_0\,w & \text{ULD} \\
\text{VHD} & \overline{x}\,\overline{u}\,u_1 & & \overline{x}\,\overline{u}_1\,\overline{v}_1\,w & x\,\overline{u}_0\,\overline{v}_0\,w & & x\,\overline{u}\,u_0 & \text{VLD} \\
\overline{x}\,\overline{v}\,v_1 & & \overline{x}\,\overline{u}\,\overline{v}_1\,w & & & x\,\overline{u}\,\overline{v}_0\,w & & x\,\overline{v}\,v_0 \\
 & \overline{x}\,\overline{u}\,\overline{v}\,w & & & & & x\,\overline{u}\,\overline{v}\,w \\
 & & & \overline{u}\,\overline{v}\,w
\end{array}
$$

Fig. 2. Resolution proof for general step of the APPLYAND operation

and result BDDs. That is, it can assume that the results w_1 and w_0 of the recursive calls to arguments u_1 and v_1 and to u_0 and v_0 satisfy the implications $u_1 \wedge v_1 \to w_1$ and $u_0 \wedge v_0 \to w_0$, and that these calls generated proof steps s_1 and s_0 justifying these implications. Figure 2 shows the structure of the resolution proof for the general case, where none of the equalities hold and the recursive calls do not yield tautologies. The proof relies on the following clauses as antecedents, arising from the recursive calls and from the defining clauses for nodes u, v, and w:

Term	Formula	Clause	Term	Formula	Clause
ANDH	$u_1 \wedge v_1 \to w_1$	$\overline{u}_1\,\overline{v}_1\,w_1$	ANDL	$u_0 \wedge v_0 \to w_0$	$\overline{u}_0\,\overline{v}_0\,w_0$
WHU	$x \to (w_1 \to w)$	$\overline{x}\,\overline{w}_1\,w$	WLU	$\overline{x} \to (w_0 \to w)$	$x\,\overline{w}_0\,w$
UHD	$x \to (u \to u_1)$	$\overline{x}\,\overline{u}\,u_1$	ULD	$\overline{x} \to (u \to u_0)$	$x\,\overline{u}\,u_0$
VHD	$x \to (v \to v_1)$	$\overline{x}\,\overline{v}\,v_1$	VLD	$\overline{x} \to (v \to v_0)$	$x\,\overline{v}\,v_0$

Along the left, the clauses cover the case of $x = 1$, first resolving clause ANDH and WHU, then resolving the result first with clause UHD and then clause VHD. A similar progression occurs along the right covering the case of $x = 0$. The two chains are then merged by resolving on variable x to yield the final implication. As this figure illustrates, a total of seven resolution steps are required. These can be merged into two linear resolution chains, and so the proof generator produces at most two clauses per APPLYAND operation.

Proof Generation for Special Cases. The proof structure shown in Figure 2 only holds for the most general form of the recursion. However, there are many special cases, such as when the recursive calls yield tautologous results, when some of the child nodes are equal, and when the two recursive calls return the same node.

Our method for handling both the general and special cases relies on the V-shaped structure of the proofs, as is illustrated in Figure 2. That is, there are two linear chains, one along the left and one along the right consisting of some subsequence of the following clauses:

$$A_H = \text{ANDH, WHU, UHD, VHD}$$
$$A_L = \text{ANDL, WLU, ULD, VLD}$$

These will be proper subsequences when some of the clauses are not included in the set J in APPLYAND (Figure 1), or they are tautologies. In addition, some of the clauses may be extraneous and therefore must not occur as antecedents.

Rather than trying to enumerate the special cases, we found it better to create a general-purpose linear chain resolver that handles all of the cases in a uniform way. This resolver is called on the each of the clause sequences A_H and A_L. It proceeds through a sequence of clauses, discarding any tautologies and any clauses that do not resolve with the result so far. It then emits the proof clauses with the selected antecedents.

3.3 Testing Implication

Terminal Cases	
Case	Result
$u = v$	$\top$
$u = L_0$	$\top$
$v = L_1$	$\top$
$u = L_1, v \neq L_1$	Error
$v = L_0, u \neq L_0$	Error

PROVEIMPLICATIONRECUR(u, v)
  $J \longleftarrow \{\}$
  $x \longleftarrow \min(\mathsf{Var}(u), \mathsf{Var}(v))$
  if $x = \mathsf{Var}(u)$:
      $u_1, u_0 \longleftarrow \mathsf{Hi}(u), \mathsf{Lo}(u)$
      $J \longleftarrow J \cup \{\mathsf{HD}(u), \mathsf{LD}(u)\}$
  else: $u_1, u_0 \longleftarrow u, u$
  if $x = \mathsf{Var}(v)$:
      $v_1, v_0 \longleftarrow \mathsf{Hi}(v), \mathsf{Lo}(v)$
      $J \longleftarrow J \cup \{\mathsf{HU}(v), \mathsf{LU}(v)\}$
  else: $v_1, v_0 \longleftarrow v, v$
  $s_1 \longleftarrow$ PROVEIMPLICATION(u_1, v_1)
  $s_0 \longleftarrow$ PROVEIMPLICATION(u_0, v_0)
  $J \longleftarrow J \cup \{s_1, s_0\}$
  $s \longleftarrow$ JUSTIFYIMPLICATION($\langle u, v \rangle, J$)
  $ImplyCache(\langle u, v \rangle) \longleftarrow s$
  return s

Fig. 3. Terminal cases and recursive step of PROVEIMPLICATION operation

When the existential quantification operation applied to node u generates node v, the program generates a proof that $u \to v$, by calling procedure PROVEIMPLICATION with u and v as arguments. This procedure has the same recursive structure as the Apply algorithm, except that it does not generate any new nodes. It only returns the step number for a proof of the clause $\overline{u}\,v$. It uses an operation cache, but only to hold proof step numbers. Figure 3 shows the terminal cases for this procedure, as well as the recursion that occurs when neither a terminal case applies nor are the arguments found in the operation cache. A failure of the implication test indicates an error in the solver, and so it signals a fatal error if the implication does not hold.

Each recursive step accumulates up to six proof steps as the set J to be used in the implication proof:

Term	Formula	Clause		Term	Formula	Clause
IMH	$u_1 \to v_1$	$\overline{u}_1 v_1$		IML	$u_0 \to v_0$	$\overline{u}_0 v_0$
UHD	$x \to (u \to u_1)$	$\overline{x}\,\overline{u}\,u_1$		ULD	$\overline{x} \to (u \to u_0)$	$x\,\overline{u}\,u_0$
VHU	$x \to (v_1 \to v)$	$\overline{x}\,\overline{v}_1 v$		VLU	$\overline{x} \to (v_0 \to v)$	$x\,\overline{v}_0 v$

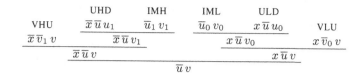

Fig. 4. Resolution proof for general step of the PROVEIMPLICATION operation

The resolution proof for the general case is shown in Figure 4. It has a similar structure to the proof for the APPLYAND operation, with two linear chains combined by a resolution on variable x. Our same general-purpose linear chain resolver can handle both the general case and the many special cases that arise.

4   Experimental Results

We implemented the proof-generating, SAT solver PGBDD (for Proof-Generating BDD). It is written entirely in Python and consists of around 2000 lines of code, including a BDD package, support for generating extended-resolution proofs, and the overall SAT solver framework.[1]

Although slow, it can handle large enough benchmarks to provide useful insights into the potential for a BDD-based SAT solver to generate proofs of challenging problems, especially when quantification is supported. It generates proofs in the LRAT format [9].

Our BDD package supports mark-and-sweep garbage collection. It starts the marking using the root nodes for all active terms in the sequence of root nodes $u_1, u_2, \ldots$. Following the marking phase, it traverses the unique table and eliminates the unmarked nodes. It also traverses the operation caches and eliminates any entries for which one of the argument nodes or the result node is unmarked. When a node is deleted, the solver can also direct the proof checker to delete its defining clauses. Similarly, when an entry is deleted from the operation cache, the solver can direct the proof checker to delete those clauses added while generating the justification for the entry.

In addition to the input CNF file, the program can accept a variable-ordering file, mapping the input variables in the CNF to their levels in the BDD.

The solver supports three different evaluation mechanisms:

Linear: Form the conjunction of the clauses, according to their order in the input file. No quantification is performed. This matches the operation described in [28].

Bucket Elimination: Place the BDDs representing the clauses into buckets according to the level of their topmost variable. Then process the buckets from lowest to highest. While a bucket has more than one element, repeatedly remove two elements, form their conjunction, and place the result in the bucket designated by the topmost variable. Once the bucket has a single element, existentially quantify the topmost

---

[1] The solver, along with code for generating and testing a set of benchmarks, is available at https://github.com/rebryant/pgbdd-artifact.

variable and place the result in the appropriate bucket [12]. This matches the operation described in [21].

Scheduled: Perform operations as specified by a scheduling file. This file contains a sequence of lines, each providing a command in a simple, stack-based notation:

c $c_1, \ldots, c_k$	Generate and push the BDDs for the specified clauses.
a m	Pop and conjoin the top m elements. Push the result.
q $v_1, \ldots, v_k$	Quantify the top element by the specified variables.

In generating benchmarks, we wrote programs to generate the CNF files, the variable orderings, and the schedules in a unified framework.

For all of our benchmarks we report the total number of clauses in the proof, including the input clauses, the defining clauses for the extension variables (up to four per BDD node generated) and the derived clauses (one per input clause and up to two per result inserted into either *AndCache* or *ImplyCache*.)

We compare the performance of our BDD-based SAT solver with that of KISSAT, the winner of the 2020 SAT competition [3], representing the state of the art in search-based SAT solvers.

4.1   Mutilated Chessboard

The mutilated chessboard problem considers an $n \times n$ chessboard, with the corners on the upper left and the lower right removed. It attempts to tile the board with dominos, with each domino covering two squares. Since the two removed squares had the same color, and each domino covers one white and one black square, no tiling is possible. This problem has been well studied in the context of resolution proofs, for which it can be shown that any proof must be of exponential size [1].

A standard CNF encoding involves defining Boolean variables to represent the boundaries between adjacent squares, set to 1 when a domino spans the two squares, and set to 0 otherwise. The clauses then encode an Exactly1 constraint for each square, requiring each square to share a domino with exactly one of its neighbors. We label the variables representing a horizontal boundary between a square and the one below as $y_{i,j}$, with $1 \le i < n$ and $1 \le j \le n$. The variables representing the vertical boundaries are labeled $x_{i,j}$, with $1 \le i \le n$ and $1 \le j < n$. With a mutilated chessboard, we have $y_{1,1} = x_{1,1} = y_{n-1,n} = x_{n,n-1} = 0$.

As the log-log plot in Figure 5 shows, PGBDD has exponential performance when using linear conjunction or bucket elimination. Indeed, KISSAT outperforms PGBDD when operating in these modes. However, KISSAT can also be seen to have exponential performance—to reach $n = 22$, it generates a proof with over 136 million clauses.

On the other hand, another approach, inspired by symbolic model checking [7] yields polynomial performance. It is based on the following observation: when processing the columns from left to right, the only information required to place dominos in column j is the identity of those rows i for which a domino crosses horizontally from $j - 1$ to j. This information is encoded in the values of $x_{i,j-1}$ for $1 \le i \le n$.

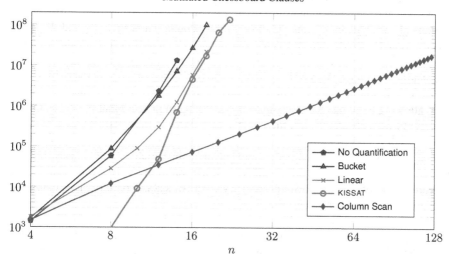

Fig. 5. Total number of clauses in proofs of $n \times n$ mutilated chess boards. The proofs using the column scanning approach grow as $n^{2.69}$.

Let us group the variables into columns, with X_j denoting variables $x_{1,j}, \ldots, x_{n,j}$, and Y_j denoting variables $y_{1,j}, \ldots, y_{n-1,j}$. Scanning the board from left to right, consider X_j to encode the "state" of processing after completing column j. As the scanning process reaches column j, there is a *characteristic function* $\sigma_{j-1}(X_{j-1})$ describing the set of allowed crossings of horizontally-oriented dominos from column $j - 1$ into column j. No other information about the configuration of the board to the left is required. The characteristic function after column j can then be computed as:

$$\sigma_j(X_j) = \exists X_{j-1} \left[\sigma_{j-1}(X_{j-1}) \wedge \exists Y_j \, T_j(X_{j-1}, Y_j, X_j) \right] \tag{1}$$

where $T_j(X_{j-1}, Y_j, X_j)$ is a "transition relation" consisting of the conjunction of the Exactly1 constraints for column j. From this, we can existentially quantify the variables Y_j to obtain a BDD encoding all compatible combinations of the variables X_{j-1} and X_j. By conjuncting this with the characteristic function for column $j - 1$ and existentially quantifying the variables X_{j-1}, we obtain the characteristic function for column j. With a mutilated chessboard, we generate leaf node L_0 in attempting the final conjunction. Note that Equation (1) does not represent a reformulation of the mutilated chessboard problem. It simply defines a way to schedule the conjunction and quantification operations over the input clauses and variables.

In our experiments, we found that this scanning reaches a fixed point after processing $n/2$ columns. That is, from that column onward, the characteristic functions become identical, except for a renaming of variables. This indicates that the set of all possible horizontal configurations stabilizes halfway across the board. Moreover, the BDD representations of the states grow as $O(n^2)$. For $n = 124$, the largest has just 3,969 nodes.

One important rule-of-thumb in symbolic model checking is that the successive values of the next-state variables must be adjacent in the variable ordering. Furthermore, the vertical variables in Y_j must be close to their counterparts in X_{j-1} and X_j. Both objectives can be achieved by ordering the variables row-wise, interleaving the variables $x_{i,j}$ and $y_{i,j}$, ordering first by row index i and then by column index j. This requires the quantification operations of Equation 1 to be performed on non-root variables.

Figure 5 shows that the "column-scanning" approach yields performance scaling as $n^{2.69}$, allowing us to handle cases up to $n = 124$. Keep in mind that the problem size here should be measured as n^2, the number of squares in the board. Thus, a problem instance with $n = 124$ is over 31 times larger than one with $n = 22$ (the upper limit reached by KISSAT), in terms of the number of input variables and clauses. Indeed, the case of $n = 22$ is straightforward for PGBDD, requiring only a few seconds and generating a proof with 161,694 clauses.[2] By contrast, KISSAT requires 12.6 hours and generates over 136 million clauses.

The plot labeled "No Quantification" demonstrates the importance of including existential quantification in solving this problem. These data were generated by using the same schedule as with column scanning, but with all quantification operations omitted. As can be seen, this approach could not scale beyond $n = 14$.

Most attempts to generate propositional proofs of the mutilated chessboard have exponential performance. No solver in the 2018 SAT competition could handle the instance with $n = 20$. Heule, Kiesl, and Biere [19] devised a problem-specific approach that could generate proofs up to $n = 50$ by exploiting special symmetries in the problem, using a set of rewriting rules to dramatically reduce the search space. Our approach also exploits symmetries in the problem, but by exploiting a way to compactly encode the set of possible configurations between successive columns. Other than these two, we know of no other approach for generating polynomially-sized propositional proofs for the problem.

4.2 Pigeonhole Problem

The pigeonhole problem is one of the most studied problems in propositional reasoning. Given a set of n holes and a set of $n+1$ pigeons, it asks whether there is an assignment of pigeons to holes such that 1) every pigeon is in some hole, and 2) every hole contains at most one pigeon. The answer is no, of course, but any resolution proof for this must be of exponential length [15]. Groote and Zantema have shown that any BDD-based proof of the principle that only uses the Apply algorithm must be of exponential size [14]. On the other hand, Cook constructed an extended resolution proof of size $O(n^4)$, in part to demonstrate the expressive power of extended resolution [8].

We consider two encodings of the problem. Both are based on a set of variables $p_{i,j}$ for $1 \leq i \leq n$ and $1 \leq j \leq n + 1$, with the interpretation that pigeon j is assigned to hole i. Encoding the property that each pigeon j is assigned to some hole can be expressed as a single clause:

$$Pigeon_j = \bigvee_{i=1}^{n} p_{i,j}$$

---

[2] All times reported here were measured on a 3 GHz Intel i7-9700 CPU with 16GB of memory.

Pigeonhole Clauses

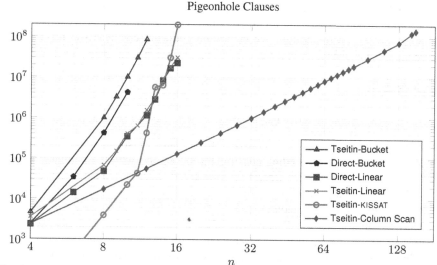

Fig. 6. Total number of clauses in proofs of pigeonhole problem for n holes. Using a direct encoding led to exponential performance, but using a Tseitin encoding and column scanning gives proofs that grow as $n^{3.03}$.

Encoding the property that each hole i contains at most one pigeon can be done in two different ways. A *direct* encoding simply states that for any pair of pigeons j and k, at least one of them must not be in hole i:

$$Direct_i = \bigwedge_{j=1}^{n+1} \bigwedge_{k=j+1}^{n+1} \overline{p}_{i,j} \vee \overline{p}_{i,k}$$

This encoding requires $\Theta(n^2)$ clauses for each hole, yielding a total CNF size of $\Theta(n^3)$.

A second, *Tseitin* encoding introduces Tseitin variables to track which holes are occupied, starting with pigeon 1 and working upward. We use an encoding published by Sinz [27] that uses Tseitin variables $s_{i,j}$ for $1 \leq i \leq n$ and $1 \leq j \leq n$, where $s_{i,j}$ equals 1 if a pigeon j' occupies hole i for some $j' \leq j$. It requires $3n - 1$ clauses and n Tseitin variables per hole, yielding an overall CNF size of $\Theta(n^2)$.

As is illustrated by the log-log plots of Figure 6, this choice of encoding not only affects the CNF size, it dramatically affects the size of the proofs generated by PGBDD. With a direct encoding, we could not find any combination of evaluation strategy or variable ordering that could go beyond $n = 16$. Similarly, the Tseitin encoding did not help when using linear evaluation or bucket elimination. Indeed, we see KISSAT, using the Tseitin encoding, matching or exceeding our program for these cases, but all of these have exponential performance. (KISSAT could only reach $n = 15$ when using a direct encoding.)

On the other hand, the column scanning approach used for the mutilated checkerboard can also be applied to the pigeonhole problem when the Tseitin encoding is used. Consider an array with hole i represented by row i and pigeon j represented by column j. Let S_j represent the Tseitin variables $s_{i,j}$ for $1 \leq i \leq n$. The "state" is then encoded in these Tseitin variables. In processing pigeon j, we can assume that the possible combinations of values of Tseitin variables S_{j-1} is encoded by a characteristic function $\sigma_{j-1}(S_{j-1})$. In addition, we incorporate into this characteristic function the requirement that each pigeon k, for $1 \leq k \leq j-1$ is assigned to some hole. Letting P_j denote the variables $p_{i,j}$ for $1 \leq i \leq n$, the characteristic function at column j can then be expressed as:

$$\sigma_j(S_j) = \exists S_{j-1} \left[\sigma_{j-1}(S_{j-1}) \wedge \exists P_j \, T_j(S_{j-1}, P_j, S_j) \right] \tag{2}$$

where the "transition relation" T_j consists of the clauses associated with the Tseitin variables, plus the clause encoding constraint $Pigeon_j$. As with the mutilated chessboard, having a proper variable ordering is critical to the success of a column scanning approach. We interleave the ordering of the variables $p_{i,j}$ and $s_{i,j}$, ordering them first by i (holes) and then by j (pigeons.)

Figure 6 demonstrates the effectiveness of the column-scanning approach. We were able to handle instances up to $n = 150$, and with an overall performance trend of $n^{3.03}$. Our achieved performance therefore improves on Cook's bound of $O(n^4)$. A SAT-solving method developed by Heule, Kiesl, Seidl, and Biere can generate short proofs of multiple encodings of pigeon hole formulas, including the direct encoding [20]. These proofs are similar to ours after transforming them into the same proof format and the size is also $O(n^3)$ [17].

Unlike with the mutilated chessboard, the scanning does not reach a fixed point. Instead, the BDDs start very small, because they must encode the locations of only a small number of occupied holes. They reach their maximum size at pigeon $n/2$, as the number of combinations for occupied and unoccupied holes reaches its maximum. Then the BDD sizes drop off as the encoding needs to track the positions of a decreasing number of unoccupied holes. Fortunately, all of these BDDs grow quadratically with n, reaching a maximum of 5,702 nodes for $n = 150$.

4.3 Evaluation

Overall, our results demonstrate the potential for generating small proofs of unsatisfiability using BDDs. We have achieved polynomial performance for problems for which search-based SAT solvers have exponential performance.

Other studies have compared BDDs to search-based SAT on a variety of benchmark problems. Several of these observed exponential performance for BDD-based solvers for problems for which we have obtained polynomial performance. Uribe and Stickel [31] ran experiments with the mutilated chessboard problem, but they did not do any variable quantification. Pan and Vardi [25] applied a variety of scheduling and variable ordering strategies for the mutilated chessboard and pigeonhole problems. Although they were able to get better performance than with a search-based SAT solver, they still observed exponential scaling. Obtaining polynomial performance for these problems requires more problem-specific approaches than the ones they considered.

Table 1 provides some performance data for the largest instances solved for the two benchmark problems. A first observation is that these problems are very large, with tens of thousands of input variables and clauses.

Table 1. Summary data for the largest problems solved

Instance	Chessboard Chess-124	Pigeonhole Pigeon-Tseitin-150
Input variables	30,500	45,150
Total BDD nodes	3,409,112	17,861,833
Maximum live nodes	198,967	225,446
Input clauses	106,136	67,501
Defining clauses	12,127,031	62,585,397
Derived clauses	5,348,303	81,019,084
Maximum live clauses	751,944	1,297,039
SAT time (secs)	5,366	5,206
Checking time (secs)	30	240

The total number of BDD nodes indicates the total number generated by the function GETNODE, and for which extension variables are created. These are numbered in the millions, and far exceed the number of input variables. On the other hand, the maximum number of live nodes shows the effectiveness of garbage collection—at any given point in the program, at most 6% of the total number of nodes must be stored in the unique table and tracked in the operation caches. Garbage collection also keeps the number of clauses that must be tracked by the proof checker below 5% of the total number of clauses. The elapsed time for the SAT solver ranges up to 1.5 hours. We believe, however, that an implementation in a more performant language would reduce these times greatly. The checking times are shown for an LRAT proof checker written in the C programming language. The proofs have also been checked with a formally verified proof checker based on the HOL theorem prover [29].

5   Conclusion

Biere, Sinz, and Jussila [21,28] made the critical link between BDDs and extended resolution proofs. We have shown that adding the ability to perform arbitrary existential quantification can greatly increase the performance of a proof-generating, BDD-based SAT solver.

Generating proofs for the two benchmarks problems required special insights into their structure and then crafting evaluation mechanisms to exploit their properties. We believe, however, that the column scanning approach we employed could be generalized and made more automatic.

The ability to generate correctness proofs in a BDD-based SAT solver invites us to consider generating proofs for other tasks to which BDDs are applied, including QBF solving, model checking, and model counting. Perhaps a proof of unsatisfiability could provide a useful building block for constructing correctness proofs for these other tasks.

References

1. Alekhnovich, M.: Mutilated chessboard problem is exponentially hard for resolution. Theoretical Computer Science **310**(1-3), 513–525 (Jan 2004)
2. Andersen, H.R.: An introduction to binary decision diagrams. Tech. rep., Technical University of Denmark (October 1997)
3. Biere, A., Fazekas, K., Fleury, M., Heisinger, M.: CaDiCaL, Kissat, Paracooba, Plingeling, and Treengeling entering the SAT competition 2020 (2020), unpublished
4. Bryant, R.E.: Graph-based algorithms for Boolean function manipulation. IEEE Trans. Computers **35**(8), 677–691 (1986)
5. Bryant, R.E.: Symbolic Boolean manipulation with ordered binary decision diagrams. ACM Computing Surveys **24**(3), 293–318 (September 1992)
6. Bryant, R.E.: Binary decision diagrams. In: Clarke, E.M., Henzinger, T.A., Veith, H., Bloem, R. (eds.) Handbook of Model Checking, pp. 191–217. Springer (2018)
7. Burch, J.R., Clarke, E.M., McMillan, K.L., Dill, D.L., Hwang, L.J.: Symbolic model checking: 10^{20} states and beyond. Information and Computation **98**(2), 142–170 (1992)
8. Cook, S.A.: A short proof of the pigeon hole principle using extended resolution. SIGACT News **8**(4), 28–32 (Oct 1976)
9. Cruz-Filipe, L., Heule, M.J.H., Hunt, W.A., Kaufmann, M., Schneider-Kamp, P.: Efficient certified RAT verification. In: Automated Deduction (CADE). LNCS, vol. 10395, pp. 220–236 (2017)
10. Cruz-Filipe, L., Marques-Silva, J., Schneider-Kamp, P.: Efficient certified resolution proof checking. In: Tools and Algorithms for the Construction and Analysis of Systems (TACAS). LNCS, vol. 10205, pp. 118–135 (2017)
11. Davis, M., Putnam, H.: A computing procedure for quantification theory. J.ACM **7**(3), 201–215 (1960)
12. Dechter, R.: Bucket elimination: A unifying framework for reasoning. Artificial Intelligence **113**(1–2), 41–85 (1999)
13. Franco, J., Kouril, M., Schlipf, J., Ward, J., Weaver, S., Dransfield, M., Vanfleet, W.M.: SBSAT: a state-based, BDD-based satisfiability solver. In: Theory and Applications of Satisfiability Testing (SAT). LNCS, vol. 2919, pp. 398–410 (2004)
14. Groote, J.F., Zantema, H.: Resolution and binary decision diagrams cannot simulate each other polynomially. Discrete Applied Mathematics **130**(2), 157–171 (2003)
15. Haken, A.: The intractability of resolution. Theoretical Computer Science **39**, 297–308 (1985)
16. Heule, M.J.H., Biere, A.: Proofs for satisfiability problems. In: All about Proofs, Proofs for All (APPA), Math. Logic and Foundations, vol. 55. College Pub. (2015)
17. Heule, M.J.H., Biere, A.: What a difference a variable makes. In: Tools and Algorithms for the Construction and Analysis of Systems (TACAS). LNCS, vol. 10806, pp. 75–92 (2018)
18. Heule, M.J.H., Hunt, W.A., Kaufmann, M., Wetzler, N.D.: Efficient, verified checking of propositional proofs. In: Interactive Theorem Proving. LNCS, vol. 10499, pp. 269–284 (2017)
19. Heule, M.J.H., Kiesl, B., Biere, A.: Clausal proofs of mutilated chessboards. In: NASA Formal Methods. LNCS, vol. 11460, pp. 204–210 (2019)
20. Heule, M.J.H., Kiesl, B., Seidl, M., Biere, A.: PRuning through satisfaction. In: Haifa Verification Conference (HVC). LNCS, vol. 10629, pp. 179–194 (2017)
21. Jussila, T., Sinz, C., Biere, A.: Extended resolution proofs for symbolic SAT solving with quantification. In: Theory and Applications of Satisfiability Testing (SAT). LNCS, vol. 4121, pp. 54–60 (2006)

22. Kullmann, O.: On a generalization of extended resolution. Discrete Applied Mathematics **96-97**, 149–176 (1999)
23. Lammich, P.: Efficient verified (UN)SAT certificate checking. Journal of Automated Reasoning **64**, 513–532 (2020)
24. Minato, S.I., Ishiura, N., Yajima, S.: Shared binary decision diagrams with attributed edges for efficient Boolean function manipulation. In: 27th ACM/IEEE Design Automation Conference. pp. 52–57 (June 1990)
25. Pan, G., Vardi, M.Y.: Search vs. symbolic techniques in satisfiability solving. In: Theory and Applications of Satisfiability Testing (SAT). LNCS, vol. 3542, pp. 235–250 (2005)
26. Robinson, J.A.: A machine-oriented logic based on the resolution principle. J.ACM **12**(1), 23–41 (January 1965)
27. Sinz, C.: Towards an optimal CNF encoding of Boolean cardinality constraints. In: Principles and Practice of Constraint Programming (CP). LNCS, vol. 3709, pp. 827–831 (2005)
28. Sinz, C., Biere, A.: Extended resolution proofs for conjoining BDDs. In: Computer Science Symposium in Russia (CSR). LNCS, vol. 3967, pp. 600–611 (2006)
29. Tan, Y.K., Heule, M.J.H., Myreen, M.O.: cake_lpr: Verified propagation redundancy checking in CakeML. In: Tools and Algorithms for the Construction and Analysis of Systems (TACAS) (2021)
30. Tseitin, G.S.: On the complexity of derivation in propositional calculus. In: Automation of Reasoning: 2: Classical Papers on Computational Logic 1967–1970. pp. 466–483. Springer (1983)
31. Uribe, T.E., Stickel, M.E.: Ordered binary decision diagrams and the Davis-Putnam procedure. In: Constraints in Computational Logics. LNCS, vol. 845, pp. 34–49 (1994)
32. Wetzler, N.D., Heule, M.J.H., Hunt Jr., W.A.: DRAT-trim: Efficient checking and trimming using expressive clausal proofs. In: Theory and Applications of Satisfiability Testing (SAT). LNCS, vol. 8561, pp. 422–429 (2014)
33. Zhang, L., Malik, S.: Validating SAT solvers using an independent resolution-based checker: Practical implementations and other applications. In: Design, Automation and Test in Europe (DATE) Volume 1. p. 10880. IEEE Computer Society (2003)

Bounded Model Checking for Hyperproperties*

Tzu-Han Hsu[1], César Sánchez[2], and ✉Borzoo Bonakdarpour[1]

[1] Michigan State University, East Lansing, MI, USA, {tzuhan,borzoo}@msu.edu
[2] IMDEA Software Institute, Madrid, Spain, cesar.sanchez@imdea.org

Abstract. This paper introduces a bounded model checking (BMC) algorithm for *hyperproperties* expressed in HyperLTL, which — to the best of our knowledge — is the first such algorithm. Just as the classic BMC technique for LTL primarily aims at finding bugs, our approach also targets identifying counterexamples. BMC for LTL is reduced to SAT solving, because LTL describes a property via inspecting individual traces. Our BMC approach naturally reduces to QBF solving, as Hyper-LTL allows explicit and simultaneous quantification over multiple traces. We report on successful and efficient model checking, implemented in our tool called HyperQube, of a rich set of experiments on a variety of case studies, including security, concurrent data structures, path planning for robots, and mutation testing.

1 Introduction

Hyperproperties [10] have been shown to be a powerful framework for specifying and reasoning about important classes of requirements that were not possible with trace-based languages such as the classic temporal logics. Examples include information-flow security, consistency models in concurrent computing [6], and robustness models in cyber-physical systems [5,35]. The temporal logic Hyper-LTL [9] extends LTL by allowing explicit and simultaneous quantification over execution traces, describing the property of multiple traces. For example, the security policy *observational determinism* can be specified by the following HyperLTL formula: $\forall \pi_A.\forall \pi_B.(o_{\pi_A} \leftrightarrow o_{\pi_B}) \mathcal{W} \neg(i_{\pi_A} \leftrightarrow i_{\pi_B})$ which stipulates that every pair of traces π_A and π_B have to agree on the value of the (public) output o as long as they agree on the value of the (secret) input i, where '$\mathcal{W}$' denotes the weak until operator.

There has been a recent surge of model checking techniques for HyperLTL specifications [9,12,22,24]. These approaches employ various techniques (e.g., alternating automata, model counting, strategy synthesis, etc) to verify hyper-properties. However, they generally fall short in proposing a general push-button method to deal with identifying bugs with respect to HyperLTL formulas involving quantifier alternation. Indeed, quantifier alternation has been shown to generally elevate the complexity class of model checking HyperLTL specifications in

---

* This work was funded in part by the United States NSF SaTC Award 2100989, the Madrid Regional Government under project "S2018/TCS-4339 (BLOQUES-CM)", and by Spanish National Project "BOSCO (PGC2018-102210-B-100)".

© The Author(s) 2021
J. F. Groote and K. G. Larsen (Eds.): TACAS 2021, LNCS 12651, pp. 94–112, 2021.
https://doi.org/10.1007/978-3-030-72016-2_6

different shapes of models [2,9]. For example, consider the simple Kripke structure K in Fig. 1 and HyperLTL formulas $\varphi_1 = \forall \pi_A. \forall \pi_B. \Box(p_{\pi_A} \leftrightarrow p_{\pi_B})$ and $\varphi_2 = \forall \pi_A.\exists \pi_B.\Diamond\Box(p_{\pi_A} \nleftrightarrow p_{\pi_B})$. Proving that $K \not\models \varphi_1$ (where traces for π_A and π_B are taken from K) can be reduced to building the self-composition of K and applying standard LTL model checking, resulting in worst-case complexity $|K|^2$ in the size of the system. On the contrary, proving that $K \models \varphi_2$ is not as straightforward. In the worst case, this requires a subset generation to encode the existential quantifier within the Kripke structure, resulting in $|K| \cdot 2^{|K|}$ blow up. In addition, the quantification is over traces rather than states, adding to the complexity of reasoning.

Following the great success of bounded model checking (BMC) for LTL specifications [8], in this paper, we propose a BMC algorithm for HyperLTL. To the best of our knowledge this is the first such algorithm. Just as BMC for LTL is reduced to SAT solving to search for a counterex-

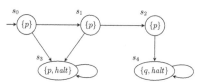

Fig. 1: A Kripke structure.

ample trace whose length is bounded by some integer k, we reduce BMC for HyperLTL to QBF solving to be able to deal with quantified counterexample traces in the input model. More formally, given a HyperLTL formula, e.g., $\varphi = \forall \pi_A.\exists \pi_B.\psi$, and a family of Kripke structures $\mathcal{K} = (K_A, K_B)$ (one per trace variable), the reduction involves three main components. First, the transition relation of K_π (for every π) is represented by a Boolean encoding $[\![K_\pi]\!]$. Secondly, the inner LTL subformula ψ is translated to a Boolean representation $[\![\psi]\!]$ in a similar fashion to the BMC unrolling technique for LTL. This way, the QBF encoding for a bound $k \geq 0$ roughly appears as:

$$[\![\mathcal{K}, \neg\varphi]\!]_k = \exists \overline{x_A}.\forall \overline{x_B}.[\![K_A]\!]_k \wedge \big([\![K_B]\!]_k \rightarrow [\![\neg\psi]\!]_k\big) \tag{1}$$

where the vector of Boolean variables $\overline{x_A}$ (respectively, $\overline{x_B}$) are used to represent the states and propositions of K_A (resp. K_B) for steps from 0 to k. Formulas $[\![K_A]\!]_k$ and $[\![K_B]\!]_k$ are the unrollings K_A (using $\overline{x_A}$) and K_B (using $\overline{x_B}$), and $[\![\neg\psi]\!]$ (that uses both $\overline{x_A}$ and $\overline{x_B}$) is the fixpoint Boolean encoding of $\neg\psi$. The proposed technique in this paper does not incorporate a loop condition, as implementing such a condition for multiple traces is not straightforward. This, of course, comes at the cost of lack of a completeness result.

While our QBF encoding is a natural generalization of BMC for HyperLTL, the first contribution of this paper is a more refined view of how to interpret the behavior of the formula beyond the unrolling depth k. Consider LTL formula $\forall \pi.\Box p_\pi$. BMC for LTL attempts to find a counterexample by unrolling the model and check for satisfiability of $\exists \pi.\Diamond \neg p_\pi$ up-to bound k. Now consider LTL formula $\forall \pi.\Diamond p_\pi$ whose negation is $\exists \pi.\Box \neg p_\pi$. In the classic BMC, due to its *pessimistic* handling of $\Box$, the unsatisfiability of the formula cannot be established in the finite unrolling (handling these formulas requires either a looping condition or to reach the diameter of the system). This is because $\Box \neg p_\pi$ is not *sometimes finitely satisfiable* (SFS), in the terminology introduced by Havelund and Peled [27], meaning that not all satisfying traces of $\square p_\pi$ have a finite prefix that witness the satisfiability.

We propose a method that allows to interpret a wide range of outcomes of the QBF solver and relate these to the original model checking decision problem. To this end, we propose the following semantics for BMC for HyperLTL:

- *Pessimistic* semantics (like in LTL BMC) under which pending eventualities are considered to be unfulfilled. This semantics works for SFS temporal formulas and paves the way for bug hunting.
- *Optimistic* semantics considers the dual case, where pending eventualities are assumed to be fulfilled at the end of the trace. This semantics works for *sometimes finitely refutable* (SFR) formulas, and allows us to interpret unsatisfiability of QBF as proof of correctness even with bounded traces.
- *Halting* variants of the optimistic and pessimistic semantics, which allow sound and complete decision on a verdict for terminating models.

We have fully implemented our technique in the tool HyperQube. Our experimental evaluation includes a rich set of case studies, such as information-flow security, linearizability in concurrent data structures, path planning in robotic applications, and mutation testing. Our evaluation shows that our technique is effective and efficient in identifying bugs in several prominent examples. We also show that our QBF-based approach is certainly more efficient than a brute-force SAT-based approach, where universal and existential quantifiers are eliminated by combinatorial expansion to conjunctions and disjunctions. We also show that in some cases our approach can also be used as a tool for synthesis. Indeed, a witness to an existential quantifier in a HyperLTL formula is an execution path that satisfies the formula. For example, our experiments on path planning for robots showcase this feature of HyperQube.

In summary, the contributions of this paper are as follows. We (1) propose a QBF-based BMC approach for verification and falsification of HyperLTL specifications; (2) introduce complementary semantics that allow proving and disproving formulas, given a finite set of finite traces, and (3) rigorously analyze the performance of our technique by case studies from different areas of computing.

2   Preliminaries

2.1   Kripke Structures

Let AP be a finite set of *atomic propositions* and $\Sigma = 2^{\mathsf{AP}}$ be the *alphabet*. A *letter* is an element of Σ. A *trace* $t \in \Sigma^\omega$ over alphabet Σ is an infinite sequence of letters: $t = t(0)t(1)t(2)\cdots$

Definition 1. *A* Kripke structure *is a tuple* $K = \langle S, S_{init}, \delta, L \rangle$, *where*

- *S is a finite set of states;*
- *$S_{init} \subseteq S$ is the set of* initial *states;*
- *$\delta \subseteq S \times S$ is a transition relation, and*
- *$L : S \to \Sigma$ is a labeling function on the states of K.*

We require that for each $s \in S$, there exists $s' \in S$, such that $(s, s') \in \delta$.

Fig. 1 shows a Kripke structure, where $S_{init} = \{s_0\}$, $L(s_0) = \{p\}$, $L(s_4) = \{q, halt\}$, etc. The *size* of the Kripke structure is the number of its states. A *loop* in K is a finite sequence $s(0)s(1) \cdots s(n)$, such that $(s(i), s(i+1)) \in \delta$, for all $0 \le i < n$, and $(s(n), s(0)) \in \delta$. We call a Kripke frame *acyclic*, if the only loops are self-loops on otherwise terminal states, i.e., on states that have no other outgoing transition. Since Definition 1 does not allow terminal states, we only consider acyclic Kripke structures with such added self-loops. We also label such states by atomic proposition *halt*.

A *path* of a Kripke structure is an infinite sequence of states $s(0)s(1) \cdots \in S^\omega$, such that $s(0) \in S_{init}$, and $(s(i), s(i+1)) \in \delta$, for all $i \ge 0$. A trace of a Kripke structure is a trace $t(0)t(1)t(2) \cdots \in \Sigma^\omega$, such that there exists a path $s(0)s(1) \cdots \in S^\omega$ with $t(i) = L(s(i))$ for all $i \ge 0$. We denote by $Traces(K, s)$ the set of all traces of K with paths that start in state $s \in S$, and use $Traces(K)$ as a shorthand for $\bigcup_{s \in S_{init}} Traces(K, s)$.

2.2   The Temporal Logic HyperLTL

Syntax. HyperLTL [9] is an extension of the linear-time temporal logic (LTL) for hyperproperties. The syntax of HyperLTL formulas is defined inductively by the following grammar:

$$\varphi ::= \exists \pi . \varphi \mid \forall \pi . \varphi \mid \phi$$
$$\phi ::= \text{true} \mid a_\pi \mid \neg \phi \mid \phi \vee \phi \mid \phi \wedge \phi \mid \phi \, \mathcal{U} \, \phi \mid \phi \, \mathcal{R} \, \phi \mid \bigcirc \phi$$

where $a \in \text{AP}$ is an atomic proposition and π is a *trace variable* from an infinite supply of variables $\mathcal{V}$. The Boolean connectives $\neg$, $\vee$, and $\wedge$ have the usual meaning, $\mathcal{U}$ is the temporal *until* operator, $\mathcal{R}$ is the temporal *release* operator, and $\bigcirc$ is the temporal *next* operator. We also consider other derived Boolean connectives, such as $\rightarrow$, and $\leftrightarrow$, and the derived temporal operators *eventually* $\Diamond \varphi \equiv \text{true} \, \mathcal{U} \, \varphi$ and *globally* $\Box \varphi \equiv \neg \Diamond \neg \varphi$. Even though the set of operators presented is not minimal, we have introduced this set to uniform the treatment with the variants in Section 3. The quantified formulas $\exists \pi$ and $\forall \pi$ are read as "along some trace π" and "along all traces π", respectively. A formula is *closed* (i.e., a *sentence*) if all trace variables used in the formula are quantified. We assume, without loss of generality, that no variable is quantified twice. We use $Vars(\varphi)$ for the set of path variables used in formula φ.

Semantics. An interpretation $\mathcal{T} = \langle T_\pi \rangle_{\pi \in Vars(\varphi)}$ of a formula φ consists of a tuple of sets of traces, with one set T_π per trace variable π in $Vars(\varphi)$, denoting the set of traces assigned to π. Note that we allow quantifiers to range over different models. We will use this feature in the verification of hyperproperties such as linearizability, where different quantifiers are associated with different sets of executions (in this case one for the concurrent implementation and one for the sequential implementation). That is, each set of traces comes from a Kripke structure and we use $\mathcal{K} = \langle K_\pi \rangle_{\pi \in Vars(\varphi)}$ to denote a *family* of Kripke structures, so $T_\pi = Traces(K_\pi)$ is the traces that π can range over, which comes from K_π. Abusing notation, we write $\mathcal{T} = Traces(\mathcal{K})$. Note that picking a single K and letting $K_\pi = K$ for all π is a particular case, which leads to the original semantics of HyperLTL [9].

Our semantics of HyperLTL is defined with respect to a trace assignment, which is a partial map $\Pi\colon Vars(\varphi) \rightharpoonup \Sigma^\omega$. The assignment with the empty domain is denoted by $\Pi_\emptyset$. Given a trace assignment Π, a trace variable π, and a concrete trace $t \in \Sigma^\omega$, we denote by $\Pi[\pi \to t]$ the assignment that coincides with Π everywhere but at π, which is mapped to trace t. The satisfaction of a HyperLTL formula φ is a binary relation $\models$ that associates a formula to the models $(\mathcal{T}, \Pi, i)$ where $i \in \mathbb{Z}_{\geq 0}$ is a pointer that indicates the current evaluating position. The semantics is defined as follows:

$$
\begin{array}{llll}
(\mathcal{T}, \Pi, 0) \models \exists\pi.\,\psi & \text{iff} & \text{there is a } t \in T_\pi, \text{ such that } (\mathcal{T}, \Pi[\pi \to t], 0) \models \psi, \\
(\mathcal{T}, \Pi, 0) \models \forall\pi.\,\psi & \text{iff} & \text{for all } t \in T_\pi, \text{ such that } (\mathcal{T}, \Pi[\pi \to t], 0) \models \psi, \\
(\mathcal{T}, \Pi, i) \models \text{true} \\
(\mathcal{T}, \Pi, i) \models a_\pi & \text{iff} & a \in \Pi(\pi)(i), \\
(\mathcal{T}, \Pi, i) \models \neg\psi & \text{iff} & (\mathcal{T}, \Pi, i) \not\models \psi, \\
(\mathcal{T}, \Pi, i) \models \psi_1 \vee \psi_2 & \text{iff} & (\mathcal{T}, \Pi, i) \models \psi_1 \text{ or } (\mathcal{T}, \Pi, i) \models \psi_2, \\
(\mathcal{T}, \Pi, i) \models \psi_1 \wedge \psi_2 & \text{iff} & (\mathcal{T}, \Pi, i) \models \psi_1 \text{ and } (\mathcal{T}, \Pi, i) \models \psi_2, \\
(\mathcal{T}, \Pi, i) \models \bigcirc\psi & \text{iff} & (\mathcal{T}, \Pi, i+1) \models \psi, \\
(\mathcal{T}, \Pi, i) \models \psi_1 \,\mathcal{U}\, \psi_2 & \text{iff} & \text{there is a } j \geq i \text{ for which } (\mathcal{T}, \Pi, j) \models \psi_2 \text{ and} \\
& & \quad \text{for all } k \in [i, j), (\mathcal{T}, \Pi, k) \models \psi_1, \\
(\mathcal{T}, \Pi, i) \models \psi_1 \,\mathcal{R}\, \psi_2 & \text{iff} & \text{either for all } j \geq i, (\mathcal{T}, \Pi, j) \models \psi_2, \text{ or,} \\
& & \quad \text{for some } j \geq i, (\mathcal{T}, \Pi, j) \models \psi_1 \text{ and} \\
& & \quad \text{for all } k \in [i, j] : (\mathcal{T}, \Pi, k) \models \psi_2.
\end{array}
$$

This semantics is slightly different from the definition in [9], but equivalent (see [30]). We say that an interpretation $\mathcal{T}$ satisfies a sentence φ, denoted by $\mathcal{T} \models \varphi$, if $(\mathcal{T}, \Pi_\emptyset, 0) \models \varphi$. We say that a family of Kripke structures $\mathcal{K}$ satisfies a sentence φ, denoted by $\mathcal{K} \models \varphi$, if $\langle Traces(K_\pi) \rangle_{\pi \in Vars(\varphi)} \models \varphi$. When the same Kripke structure K is used for all path variables we write $K \models \varphi$. For example, the Kripke structure in Fig. 1 satisfies HyperLTL formula $\varphi = \forall\pi_A.\exists\pi_B.\Diamond\Box(p_{\pi_A} \not\leftrightarrow p_{\pi_B})$.

3 Bounded Semantics for HyperLTL

We introduce now the bounded semantics of HyperLTL, used in Section 4 to generate queries to a QBF solver to aid solving the model checking problem.

3.1 Bounded Semantics

We assume the HyperLTL formula is closed and of the form $\mathcal{Q}_A\pi_A.\mathcal{Q}_B\pi_B \ldots \mathcal{Q}_Z\pi_Z.\psi$, where $\mathcal{Q} \in \{\forall, \exists\}$ and it has been converted into negation-normal form (NNF) so that the negation symbol only appears in front of atomic propositions, e.g., $\neg a_{\pi_A}$. Without loss of generality and for the sake of clarity from other numerical indices, we use roman alphabet as indices of trace variables. Thus, we assume that $Vars(\varphi) \subseteq \{\pi_A, \pi_B, \ldots, \pi_Z\}$. The main idea of BMC is to perform incremental exploration of the state space of the systems by unrolling the systems and the formula up-to a bound. Let $k \geq 0$ be the unrolling *bound* and let $\mathcal{T} = \langle T_A \ldots T_Z \rangle$ be a tuple of sets of traces, one per trace variable. We start by defining a satisfaction relation between HyperLTL formulas for a bounded exploration k and models $(\mathcal{T}, \Pi, i)$, where $\mathcal{T}$ is the tuple of set of traces, Π is a trace assignment mapping (as defined in Section 2), and $i \in \mathbb{Z}_{\geq 0}$ that points to the position of traces. We will define different finite satisfaction relations for general models (for $* = pes, opt, hpes, hopt$):

- $\models_k^*$, the common satisfaction relation among all semantics,
- $\models_k^{pes}$, called *pessimistic* semantics,
- $\models_k^{opt}$, called *optimistic* semantics, and
- $\models_k^{hpes}$ and $\models_k^{hopt}$, variants of $\models_k^{pes}$ and $\models_k^{opt}$ for Kripke structures that encode termination of traces (modeled as self-loops to provide infinite traces).

All these semantics coincide in the interpretation of quantifiers, Boolean connectives, and temporal operators up-to instant $k-1$, but differ in their assumptions about unseen future events after the bound of observation k.

Quantifiers. The satisfaction relation for the quantifiers is the following:

$$(\mathcal{T}, \Pi, 0) \models_k^* \exists \pi. \ \psi \quad \text{iff} \quad \text{there is a } t \in T_\pi : (\mathcal{T}, \Pi[\pi \to t], 0) \models_k^* \psi, \tag{1}$$
$$(\mathcal{T}, \Pi, 0) \models_k^* \forall \pi. \ \psi \quad \text{iff} \quad \text{for all} \quad t \in T_\pi : (\mathcal{T}, \Pi[\pi \to t], 0) \models_k^* \psi. \tag{2}$$

Boolean operators. For every $i \leq k$, we have:

$$(\mathcal{T}, \Pi, i) \models_k^* \text{true}, \tag{3}$$
$$(\mathcal{T}, \Pi, i) \models_k^* a_\pi \quad \text{iff} \quad a \in \Pi(\pi)(i), \tag{4}$$
$$(\mathcal{T}, \Pi, i) \models_k^* \neg a_\pi \quad \text{iff} \quad a \notin \Pi(\pi)(i), \tag{5}$$
$$(\mathcal{T}, \Pi, i) \models_k^* \psi_1 \vee \psi_2 \quad \text{iff} \quad (\mathcal{T}, \Pi, i) \models_k^* \psi_1 \text{ or } (\mathcal{T}, \Pi, i) \models_k^* \psi_2, \tag{6}$$
$$(\mathcal{T}, \Pi, i) \models_k^* \psi_1 \wedge \psi_2 \quad \text{iff} \quad (\mathcal{T}, \Pi, i) \models_k^* \psi_1 \text{ and } (\mathcal{T}, \Pi, i) \models_k^* \psi_2. \tag{7}$$

Temporal connectives. The case where $(i < k)$ is common between the optimistic and pessimistic semantics:

$$(\mathcal{T}, \Pi, i) \models_k^* \bigcirc \psi \quad \text{iff} \quad (\mathcal{T}, \Pi, i+1) \models_k^* \psi, \tag{8}$$
$$(\mathcal{T}, \Pi, i) \models_k^* \psi_1 \mathcal{U} \psi_2 \quad \text{iff} \quad (\mathcal{T}, \Pi, i) \models_k^* \psi_2, \text{ or}$$
$$(\mathcal{T}, \Pi, i) \models_k^* \psi_1 \text{ and } (\mathcal{T}, \Pi, i+1) \models_k^* \psi_1 \mathcal{U} \psi_2, \tag{9}$$
$$(\mathcal{T}, \Pi, i) \models_k^* \psi_1 \mathcal{R} \psi_2 \quad \text{iff} \quad (\mathcal{T}, \Pi, i) \models_k^* \psi_2, \text{ and}$$
$$(\mathcal{T}, \Pi, i) \models_k^* \psi_1 \text{ or } (\mathcal{T}, \Pi, i+1) \models_k^* \psi_1 \mathcal{R} \psi_2. \tag{10}$$

For $(i = k)$, in the pessimistic semantics the eventualities (including $\bigcirc$) are assumed to never be fulfilled in the future, so the current instant k is the last chance:

$$\begin{aligned}
(\mathcal{T},\Pi,i) \models_k^{pes} \bigcirc\psi & \quad\text{iff}\quad \text{never happens,} & (P_1)\\
(\mathcal{T},\Pi,i) \models_k^{pes} \psi_1\,\mathcal{U}\,\psi_2 & \quad\text{iff}\quad (\mathcal{T},\Pi,i) \models_k^{pes} \psi_2, & (P_2)\\
(\mathcal{T},\Pi,i) \models_k^{pes} \psi_1\,\mathcal{R}\,\psi_2 & \quad\text{iff}\quad (\mathcal{T},\Pi,i) \models_k^{pes} \psi_1 \wedge \psi_2. & (P_3)
\end{aligned}$$

On the other hand, in the optimistic semantics the eventualities are assumed to be fulfilled in the future:

$$\begin{aligned}
(\mathcal{T},\Pi,i) \models_k^{opt} \bigcirc\psi & \quad\text{iff}\quad \text{always happens,} & (O_1)\\
(\mathcal{T},\Pi,i) \models_k^{opt} \psi_1\,\mathcal{U}\,\psi_2 & \quad\text{iff}\quad (\mathcal{T},\Pi,i) \models_k^{opt} \psi_1 \vee \psi_2, & (O_2)\\
(\mathcal{T},\Pi,i) \models_k^{opt} \psi_1\,\mathcal{R}\,\psi_2 & \quad\text{iff}\quad (\mathcal{T},\Pi,i) \models_k^{opt} \psi_2. & (O_3)
\end{aligned}$$

To capture the halting semantics, we use the predicate *halt* that is true if the state corresponds to a halting state (self-loop), and define $halted \overset{\text{def}}{=} \bigwedge_{\pi\,Vars(\varphi)} halt_\pi$ which holds whenever all traces have halted (and their final state will be repeated ad infinitum). Then, the halted semantics of the temporal case for $i = k$ in the pessimistic case consider the halting case to infer the actual value of the temporal operators on the (now fully known) trace:

$$\begin{aligned}
(\mathcal{T},\Pi,i) \models_k^{hpes} \bigcirc\psi & \quad\text{iff}\quad (\mathcal{T},\Pi,i) \models_k^{*} halted \text{ and } (\mathcal{T},\Pi,i) \models_k^{hpes} \psi & (HP_1)\\
(\mathcal{T},\Pi,i) \models_k^{hpes} \psi_1\,\mathcal{U}\,\psi_2 & \quad\text{iff}\quad (\mathcal{T},\Pi,i) \models_k^{hpes} \psi_2 & (HP_2)\\
(\mathcal{T},\Pi,i) \models_k^{hpes} \psi_1\,\mathcal{R}\,\psi_2 & \quad\text{iff}\quad (\mathcal{T},\Pi,i) \models_k^{hpes} \psi_1 \wedge \psi_2, \text{ or} & \\
& \quad\phantom{\text{iff}}\quad (\mathcal{T},\Pi,i) \models_k^{*} halted \text{ and } (\mathcal{T},\Pi,i) \models_k^{hpes} \psi_2 & (HP_3)
\end{aligned}$$

Dually, in the halting optimistic case:

$$\begin{aligned}
(\mathcal{T},\Pi,i) \models_k^{hopt} \bigcirc\psi & \quad\text{iff}\quad (\mathcal{T},\Pi,i) \not\models_k^{*} halted \text{ or } (\mathcal{T},\Pi,i) \models_k^{hopt} \psi & (HO_1)\\
(\mathcal{T},\Pi,i) \models_k^{hopt} \psi_1\,\mathcal{U}\,\psi_2 & \quad\text{iff}\quad (\mathcal{T},\Pi,i) \models_k^{hopt} \psi_2, \text{ or} & \\
& \quad\phantom{\text{iff}}\quad (\mathcal{T},\Pi,i) \not\models_k^{*} halted \text{ and } (\mathcal{T},\Pi,i) \models_k^{hopt} \psi_1 & (HO_2)\\
(\mathcal{T},\Pi,i) \models_k^{hopt} \psi_1\,\mathcal{R}\,\psi_2 & \quad\text{iff}\quad (\mathcal{T},\Pi,i) \models_k^{hpes} \psi_2 & (HO_3)
\end{aligned}$$

Complete semantics. We are now ready to define the four semantics:

- Pessimistic semantics: $\models_k^{pes}$ use rules (1)-(10) and (P_1)-(P_3).
- Optimistic semantics: $\models_k^{opt}$ use rules (1)-(10) and (O_1)-(O_3).
- Halting pessimistic semantics: $\models_k^{hpes}$ use rules (1)-(10) and (HP_1)-(HP_3).
- Halting optimistic semantics: $\models_k^{hopt}$ use rules (1)-(10) and (HO_1)-(HO_3).

3.2   The Logical Relation between Different Semantics

Observe that the pessimistic semantics is the semantics in the traditional BMC for LTL. In the pessimistic semantics a formula is declared false unless it is witnessed to be true within the bound explored. In other words, formulas can only get "truer" with more information obtained by a longer unrolling. Dually, the optimistic semantics considers a formula true unless there is evidence within the bounded exploration on the contrary. Therefore, formulas only get "falser" with further unrolling. For example, formula $\Box p$ always evaluates to false in the pessimistic semantics. In the optimistic semantics, it evaluates to true up-to bound

k if p holds in all states of the trace up-to and including k. However, if the formula evaluates to false at some point before k, then it evaluates to false for all $j \geq k$. The following lemma formalizes this intuition in HyperLTL.

Lemma 1. *Let* $k \leq j$. *Then,*
1. *If* $(\mathcal{T}, \Pi, 0) \models_k^{pes} \varphi$, *then* $(\mathcal{T}, \Pi, 0) \models_j^{pes} \varphi$.
2. *If* $(\mathcal{T}, \Pi, 0) \not\models_k^{opt} \varphi$, *then* $(\mathcal{T}, \Pi, 0) \not\models_j^{opt} \varphi$.
3. *If* $(\mathcal{T}, \Pi, 0) \models_k^{hpes} \varphi$, *then* $(\mathcal{T}, \Pi, 0) \models_j^{hpes} \varphi$.
4. *If* $(\mathcal{T}, \Pi, 0) \not\models_k^{hopt} \varphi$, *then* $(\mathcal{T}, \Pi, 0) \not\models_j^{hopt} \varphi$.

In turn, the verdict obtained from the exploration up-to k can (in some cases) be used to infer the verdict of the model checking problem. As in classical BMC, if the pessimistic semantics find a model, then it is indeed a model. Dually, if our optimistic semantics fail to find a model, then there is no model. The next lemma formally captures this intuition.

Lemma 2 (Infinite inference). *The following hold for every* k,
1. *If* $(\mathcal{T}, \Pi, 0) \models_k^{pes} \varphi$, *then* $(\mathcal{T}, \Pi, 0) \models \varphi$.
2. *If* $(\mathcal{T}, \Pi, 0) \not\models_k^{opt} \varphi$, *then* $(\mathcal{T}, \Pi, 0) \not\models \varphi$.
3. *If* $(\mathcal{T}, \Pi, 0) \models_k^{hpes} \varphi$, *then* $(\mathcal{T}, \Pi, 0) \models \varphi$.
4. *If* $(\mathcal{T}, \Pi, 0) \not\models_k^{hopt} \varphi$, *then* $(\mathcal{T}, \Pi, 0) \not\models \varphi$.

Example 1. Consider the Kripke structure in Fig. 1, bound $k = 3$, and formula $\varphi_1 = \forall \pi_A. \exists \pi_B. ((p_{\pi_A} \not\leftrightarrow p_{\pi_B}) \mathcal{R} \neg q_{\pi_A})$. It is easy to see that instantiating π_A with trace $s_0 s_1 s_2 s_4$ falsifies φ_1 in the pessimistic semantics. By Lemma 2, this counterexample shows that the Kripke structure is a model of $\neg \varphi_1$ in the infinite semantics as well. That is, $K \models_3^{pes} \neg \varphi_1$ and, hence, $K \models \neg \varphi_1$, so $K \not\models \varphi_1$.

Consider again the same Kripke structure, bound $k = 3$, and formula $\varphi_2 = \forall \pi_A. \exists \pi_B. \Diamond (p_{\pi_A} \leftrightarrow q_{\pi_B})$. To disprove φ_2, we need to find a trace π_A such that for all other π_B, proposition q in π_B always disagrees with p in π_A. It is straightforward to observe that such a trace π_A does not exist. By Lemma 2, proving the formula is not satisfiable up-to bound 3 in the optimistic semantics implies that K is not a model of $\neg \varphi_2$ in the infinite semantics. That is, $K \not\models_3^{opt} \neg \varphi_2$ implies $K \not\models \neg \varphi_2$. Hence, we conclude $K \models \varphi_2$.

Consider again the same Kripke structure which has two terminating states, s_3 and s_4, labeled by atomic proposition *halt* with only a self-loop. Let $k = 3$, and $\varphi_3 = \forall \pi_A. \exists \pi_B. (\neg q_{\pi_B} \mathcal{U} \neg p_{\pi_A})$. Instantiating π_A by trace $s_0 s_1 s_3$, which is of the form $\{p\}^{\omega}$ satisfies $\neg \varphi_3$. By Lemma 2, the fulfillment of formula implies that in infinite semantics it will be fulfilled as well. That is, $K \models_3^{hpes} \neg \varphi_3$ implies $K \models \neg \varphi_3$. Hence, $K \not\models \varphi_3$.

Consider again the same Kripke structure with halting states and formula $\varphi_4 = \forall \pi_A. \exists \pi_B. \Diamond \Box (p_{\pi_A} \not\leftrightarrow p_{\pi_B})$. A counterexample is an instantiation of π_A such that for all π_B, both traces will always eventually agree on p. Trace $s_0 s_1 s_2 s_4$, which is of the form $\{p\}\{p\}\{p\}\{q, halt\}^{\omega}$ with $k = 3$. This trace never agrees with a trace that ends in state s_3 (which is of the form $\{p\}^{\omega}$) and vice versa. By Lemma 2, the absence of counterexample up-to bound 3 in the halting optimistic semantics implies that K is not a model of $\neg\varphi_4$ in the infinite semantics. That is, $K \not\models_3^{hopt} \neg\varphi_4$ implies $K \not\models \neg\varphi_4$. Hence, we conclude $K \models \varphi_4$.   □

4   Reducing BMC to QBF Solving

Given a family of Kripke structures $\mathcal{K}$, a HyperLTL formula φ, and bound $k \geq 0$, our goal is to construct a QBF formula $[\![\mathcal{K}, \varphi]\!]_k$ whose satisfiability can be used to infer whether or not $\mathcal{K} \models \varphi$.

In the following paragraphs, we first describe how to encode the model and the formula, and then how to combine the two to generate the QBF query. We will illustrate the constructions using formula φ_1 in Example 1 in Section 3, whose negation is $\exists\pi_A.\forall\pi_B.\neg\psi$ with $\neg\psi = (p_{\pi_A} \leftrightarrow p_{\pi_B}) \mathcal{U} q_{\pi_A}$.

Encoding the models. The unrolling of the transition relation of a Kripke structure $K_A = \langle S, S_{init}, \delta, L \rangle$ up to bound k is analogous to the BMC encoding for LTL [8]. First, note that the state space S can be encoded with a (logarithmic) number of bits in $|S|$. We introduce additional variables $n_0, n_1, \ldots$ to encode the state of the Kripke structure and use $\mathsf{AP}^* = \mathsf{AP} \cup \{n_0, n_1, \ldots\}$ for the extended alphabet that includes the encoding of S. In this manner, the set of initial states of a Kripke structure is a Boolean formula over AP^*. For example, for the Kripke structure K_A in Fig. 1 the set of initial states (in this case $S_{init} = \{s_0\}$) corresponds to the following Boolean formula:

$$I_A := (\neg n_0 \wedge \neg n_1 \wedge \neg n_2) \wedge p \wedge \neg q \wedge \neg halt$$

assuming that $(\neg n_0 \wedge \neg n_1 \wedge \neg n_2)$ represents state s_0 (we need three bits to encode five states.) Similarly, R_A is a binary relation that encodes the transition relation δ of K_A (representing the relation between a state and its successor). The encoding into QBF works by introducing fresh Boolean variables (a new copy of AP^* for each Kripke structure K_A and position), and then producing a Boolean formula that encodes the unrolling up-to k. We use x_A^i for the set of fresh copies of the variables AP^* of K_A corresponding to position $i \in [0, k]$. Therefore, there are $k|x_A| = k|\mathsf{AP}_A^*|$ Boolean variables to represent the unrolling of K_A. We use $I_A(x)$ for the Boolean formula (using variables from x) that encodes the initial states, and $R_A(x, x')$ (for two copies of the variables x and x') for the Boolean formula whether x' encodes a successor states of x. For example, for $k = 3$, we unroll the transition relation up-to 3 as follows,

$$[\![K_A]\!]_3 = I_A(x_A^0) \wedge R_A(x_A^0, x_A^1) \wedge R(x_A^1, x_A^2) \wedge R(x_A^2, x_A^3)$$

which is the Boolean formula representing valid traces of length 4, using four copies of the variables AP_A^* that represent the Kripke structure K_A.

Encoding the inner LTL formula. The idea of the construction of the inner LTL formula is analogous to standard BMC as well, except for the choice of different semantics described in Section 3. In particular, we introduce the following inductive construction and define four different unrollings for a given k: $[\![\cdot]\!]_{i,k}^{pes}$, $[\![\cdot]\!]_{i,k}^{opt}$, $[\![\cdot]\!]_{i,k}^{hpes}$, and $[\![\cdot]\!]_{i,k}^{hopt}$.

- **Inductive Case**: Since the semantics only differ on the temporal operators at the end of the unrolling, the inductive case is common to all unrollings and we use $[\![\cdot]\!]_{i,k}^*$ to mean any of the choices of semantic (for $* = pes, opt, hpes, hopt$). For all $i \leq k$:

$$
\begin{aligned}
[\![p_\pi]\!]_{i,k}^* &:= p_\pi^i \\
[\![\neg p_\pi]\!]_{i,k}^* &:= \neg p_\pi^i \\
[\![\psi_1 \vee \psi_2]\!]_{i,k}^* &:= [\![\psi_1]\!]_{i,k}^* \vee [\![\psi_2]\!]_{i,k}^* \\
[\![\psi_1 \wedge \psi_2]\!]_{i,k}^* &:= [\![\psi_1]\!]_{i,k}^* \wedge [\![\psi_2]\!]_{i,k}^* \\
[\![\psi_1 \, \mathcal{U} \, \psi_2]\!]_{i,k}^* &:= [\![\psi_2]\!]_{i,k}^* \vee \left([\![\psi_1]\!]_{i,k}^* \wedge [\![\psi_1 \, \mathcal{U} \, \psi_2]\!]_{i+1,k}^* \right) \\
[\![\psi_1 \, \mathcal{R} \, \psi_2]\!]_{i,k}^* &:= [\![\psi_2]\!]_{i,k}^* \wedge \left([\![\psi_1]\!]_{i,k}^* \vee [\![\psi_1 \, \mathcal{R} \, \psi_2]\!]_{i+1,k}^* \right) \\
[\![\bigcirc \psi]\!]_{i,k}^* &:= [\![\psi]\!]_{i+1,k}^*
\end{aligned}
$$

Note that, for a given path variable π_A, the atom $p_{\pi_A}^i$ that results from $[\![p_{\pi_A}]\!]_{i,k}^*$ is one of the Boolean variables in x_A^i.

- For the **base case**, the formula generated is different depending on the intended semantics:

$$[\![\psi]\!]_{k+1,k}^{pes} := \mathsf{false} \qquad\qquad [\![\psi]\!]_{k+1,k}^{opt} := \mathsf{true}$$
$$[\![\psi]\!]_{k+1,k}^{hpes} := [\![halted]\!]_{k,k}^{hpes} \wedge [\![\psi]\!]_{k,k}^{hpes} \qquad [\![\psi]\!]_{k+1,k}^{hopt} := [\![halted]\!]_{k,k}^{hopt} \to [\![\psi]\!]_{k,k}^{hopt}$$

Note that the base case defines the value to be assumed for the formula after the end k of the unrolling, which is spawned in the temporal operators in the inductive case at k. The pessimistic semantics assume the formula to be false, and the optimistic semantics assume the formula to be true. The halting cases consider the case at which the traces have halted (using in this case the evaluation at k) and using the unhalting choice otherwise.

Example 2. Consider again the formula $\neg\psi = (p_{\pi_A} \leftrightarrow p_{\pi_B}) \, \mathcal{U} \, q_{\pi_A}$. Using the pessimistic semantics $[\![\neg\psi]\!]_{0,3}^{pes}$ with three steps is

$$q_{\pi_A}^0 \vee \left((p_{\pi_A}^0 \leftrightarrow p_{\pi_B}^0) \wedge \left(q_{\pi_A}^1 \vee \left((p_{\pi_A}^1 \leftrightarrow p_{\pi_B}^1) \wedge \left(q_{\pi_A}^2 \vee (p_{\pi_A}^2 \leftrightarrow p_{\pi_B}^2) \wedge q_{\pi_A}^3 \right) \right) \right) \right).$$

In this encoding, the collection x_A^2, contains all variables of AP^* of K_A (that is $\{p_{\pi_A}^2, q_{\pi_A}^2, \ldots\}$) connecting to the corresponding valuation for p_{π_A} in the trace of K_A at step 2 in the unrolling of K_A. In other words, the formula $[\![\neg\psi]\!]_{0,3}^{pes}$ uses variables from $x_A^0, x_A^1, x_A^2, x_A^3$ and $x_B^0, x_B^1, x_B^2, x_B^3$ (that is, from $\overline{x_A}$ and $\overline{x_B}$). □

Combining the encodings. Now, let φ be a HyperLTL formula of the form $\varphi = \mathbb{Q}_A \pi_A . \mathbb{Q}_B \pi_B . \ldots . \mathbb{Q}_Z \pi_Z . \psi$ and $\mathcal{K} = \langle K_A, K_B, \ldots, K_Z \rangle$. Combining all the components, the encoding of the HyperLTL BMC problem in QBF is the following (for $* = pes, opt, hpes, hopt$):

$$[\![\mathcal{K}, \varphi]\!]_k^* = \mathbb{Q}_A \overline{x_A} . \mathbb{Q}_B \overline{x_B} \cdots . \mathbb{Q}_Z \overline{x_Z} \left([\![K_A]\!]_k \circ_A [\![K_B]\!]_k \circ_B \cdots [\![K_Z]\!]_k \circ_Z [\![\psi]\!]_{0,k}^* \right)$$

where $[\![\psi]\!]_{0,k}^*$ is the choice of semantics, $\circ_j = \wedge$ if $\mathbb{Q}_j = \exists$, and $\circ_j = \to$ if $\mathbb{Q}_j = \forall$, for $j \in Vars(\varphi)$.

Example 3. Consider again Example 2. To combine the model description with the encoding of the HyperLTL formula, we use two identical copies of the given Kripke structure to represent different paths π_A and π_B on the model, denoted as K_A and K_B. The final resulting formula is:

$$\llbracket K, \neg \varphi \rrbracket_3 := \exists \overline{x_A}.\forall \overline{x_B}.(\llbracket K_A \rrbracket_3 \wedge (\llbracket K_B \rrbracket_3 \rightarrow \llbracket \neg \varphi \rrbracket_{0,3}^{pes}))$$

The sequence of assignments $(\neg n_2, \neg n_1, \neg n_0, p, \neg q, \neg halt)^0$ $(\neg n_2, \neg n_1, n_0, p, \neg q, \neg halt)^1$ $(\neg n_2, n_1, \neg n_0, p, \neg q, \neg halt)^2$ $(n_2, \neg n_1, \neg n_0, \neg p, q, halt)^3$ on K_A, corresponding to the path $s_0 s_1 s_2 s_4$, satisfies $\llbracket \neg \varphi \rrbracket_{0,3}^{pes}$ for all traces on K_B. The satisfaction result shows that $\llbracket K, \neg \varphi \rrbracket_3^{pes}$ is true, indicating that a witness of violation is found. Theorem 1, by a successful detection of a counterexample witness, and the use of the pessimistic semantics, allows to conclude that $K \not\models \varphi$. □

The main result of this section is Theorem 1 that connects the output of the solver to the original model checking problem. We first show an auxiliary lemma.

Lemma 3. *Let φ be a closed HyperLTL formula and $\mathcal{T} = \text{Traces}(\mathcal{K})$ be an interpretation. For $* = pes, opt, hpes, hopt$, it holds that*

$$\llbracket \mathcal{K}, \varphi \rrbracket_k^* \text{ is satisfiable if and only if } (\mathcal{T}, \Pi_\emptyset, 0) \models_k^* \varphi.$$

Proof (sketch). The proof proceeds in two steps. First, let ψ be the largest quantifier-free sub-formula of φ. Then, every tuple of traces of length k (one for each π) is in one-to-one correspondence with the collection of variables p_π^i, that satisfies that the tuple is a model of ψ (in the choice semantics) if and only if the corresponding assignment makes $\llbracket \psi \rrbracket_0^*$. Then, the second part shows inductively in the stack of quantifiers that each subformula obtained by adding a quantifier is satisfiable if and only if the semantics hold. □

Lemma 3, together with Lemma 2, allows to infer the outcome of the model checking problem from satisfying (or unsatisfying) instances of QBF queries, summarized in the following theorem.

Theorem 1. *Let φ be a HyperLTL formula. Then,*
1. *For $* = pes, hpes$, if $\llbracket K, \neg\varphi \rrbracket_k^*$ is satisfiable, then $K \not\models \varphi$.*
2. *For $* = opt, hopt$, if $\llbracket K, \neg\varphi \rrbracket_k^*$ is unsatisfiable, then $K \models \varphi$.*

Table 1 illustrates what Theorem 1 allows to soundly conclude from the output of the QBF solver about the model checking problem of formulas from Example 1 in Section 3.

5   Evaluation and Case Studies

We now evaluate our approach by a rich set of case studies on information-flow security, concurrent data structures, path planning for robots, and mutation testing. In this section, we will refer to each property in HyperLTL as in Table 2.

Formula	Bound	Semantics		
		pessimistic	*optimistic*	*halting*
φ_1	$k = 2$	UNSAT (inconclusive)	SAT (inconclusive)	UNSAT (inconclusive)
	$k = 3$	SAT (*counterexample*)	SAT (inconclusive)	UNSAT (inconclusive)
φ_2	$k = 2$	UNSAT (inconclusive)	SAT (inconclusive)	UNSAT (inconclusive)
	$k = 3$	UNSAT (inconclusive)	UNSAT (*proved*)	UNSAT (inconclusive)
φ_3	$k = 2$	UNSAT (inconclusive)	UNSAT (inconclusive)	non-halted (inconclusive)
	$k = 3$	UNSAT (inconclusive)	UNSAT (inconclusive)	halted (*counterexample*)
φ_4	$k = 2$	UNSAT (inconclusive)	UNSAT (inconclusive)	non-halted (inconclusive)
	$k = 3$	UNSAT (inconclusive)	UNSAT (inconclusive)	halted (*proved*)

Table 1: Comparison of Properties with Different Semantics

We have implemented the technique described in Section 4 in our tool HyperQube. Given a transition relation, the tool automatically unfolds it up to $k \geq 0$ by a home-grown procedure written in Ocaml, called genqbf. Given the choice of the semantics (pessimistic, optimistic, and halting variants) the unfolded transition relation is combined with the QBF encoding of the input HyperLTL formula to form a complete QBF instance which is then fed to the QBF solver QuAbS [28]. All experiments in this section are run on an iMac desktop with Intel i7 CPU @3.4 GHz and 32 GB of RAM. A full description of the systems and formulas used can be accessed in the longer version of this paper [30].

Case Study 1: Symmetry in Lamport's Bakery algorithm [12]. Symmetry states that no specific process has special privileges in terms of a faster access to the critical section (see different symmetry formulas in Table 2). In these formulas, each process P_n has a program counter denoted by $pc(P_n)$, *select* indicates which process is selected to process next, *pause* if both processes are not selected, sym_break is which process is selected after a tie, and $\mathsf{sym}(select_{\pi_A}, select_{\pi_B})$ indicates if two traces are selecting two opposite processes. The Bakery algorithm does not satisfy symmetry (i.e. φ_{sym_1}), because when two or more processes are trying to enter the critical section with the same ticket number, the algorithm always gives priority to the process with the smaller process ID. HyperQube returns SAT using the pessimistic semantics, indicating that there exists a counterexample in the form of a falsifying witness to π_A in formula φ_{sym_1}. Table 3 includes our result on other symmetry formulas presented in Table 2.

Case Study 2: Linearizability in SNARK [14]. SNARK implements a concurrent double-ended queue using double-compare-and-swap (DCAS) and a doubly linked-list that stores values in each node. *Linearizability* [29] requires that any *history* of execution of a concurrent data structure (i.e., sequence of *invocation* and *response* by different threads) matches some sequential order of invocations and responses (see formula φ_{lin} in Table 2). SNARK is known to have two linearizability bugs and HyperQube returns SAT using the pessimistic semantics, identifying both bugs as two counterexamples. The bugs we identified are precisely the same as the ones reported in [14].

Property	Property in HyperLTL
Symmetry	$\varphi_{S1} = \forall \pi_A. \forall \pi_B. (\neg sym(select_{\pi_A}, select_{\pi_B}) \vee \neg(pause_{\pi_A} = pause_{\pi_B})) \mathcal{R}$ $((pc(P_0)_{\pi_A} = pc(P_1)_{\pi_B}) \wedge (pc(P_1)_{\pi_A} = pc(P_0)_{\pi_B}))$
	$\varphi_{S2} = \forall \pi_A. \forall \pi_B. (\neg sym(select_{\pi_A}, select_{\pi_B}) \vee \neg(pause_{\pi_A} = pause_{\pi_B}) \vee$ $\neg(select_{\pi_A} < 3) \vee \neg(select_{\pi_B} < 3)) \mathcal{R}$ $((pc(P_0)_{\pi_A} = pc(P_1)_{\pi_B}) \wedge (pc(P_1)_{\pi_A} = pc(P_0)_{\pi_B}))$
	$\varphi_{S3} = \forall \pi_A. \forall \pi_B. (\neg sym(select_{\pi_A}, select_{\pi_B}) \vee \neg(pause_{\pi_A} = pause_{\pi_B}) \vee$ $\neg(select_{\pi_A} < 3) \vee \neg(select_{\pi_B} < 3) \vee$ $\neg sym(sym\_break_{\pi_A}, sym\_break_{\pi_B})) \mathcal{R}$ $((pc(P_0)_{\pi_A} = pc(P_1)_{\pi_B}) \wedge (pc(P_1)_{\pi_A} = pc(P_0)_{\pi_B}))$
	$\varphi_{sym_1} = \forall \pi_A. \exists \pi_B. \square sym(select_{\pi_A}, select_{\pi_B}) \wedge (pause_{\pi_A} = pause_{\pi_B}) \wedge$ $(pc(P_0)_{\pi_A} = pc(P_1)_{\pi_B}) \wedge (pc(P_1)_{\pi_A} = pc(P_0)_{\pi_B})$
	$\varphi_{sym_2} = \forall \pi_A. \exists \pi_B. \square sym(select_{\pi_A}, select_{\pi_B}) \wedge (pause_{\pi_A} = pause_{\pi_B}) \wedge$ $(select_{\pi_A} < 3) \wedge (select_{\pi_B} < 3) \wedge$ $(pc(P_0)_{\pi_A} = pc(P_1)_{\pi_B}) \wedge (pc(P_1)_{\pi_A} = pc(P_0)_{\pi_B})$
Linearizability	$\varphi_{lin} = \forall \pi_A. \exists \pi_B. \square(history_{\pi_A} \leftrightarrow history_{\pi_B})$
NI	$\varphi_{NI} = \forall \pi_A. \exists \pi_B. (PIN_{\pi_A} \neq PIN_{\pi_B}) \wedge ((\neg halt_{\pi_A} \vee \neg halt_{\pi_B})$ $\mathcal{U} ((halt_{\pi_A} \wedge halt_{\pi_B}) \wedge (Result_{\pi_A} = Result_{\pi_B})))$
Fairness	$\varphi_{fair} = \exists \pi_A. \forall \pi_B. (\lozenge m_{\pi_A}) \wedge (\lozenge NRR_{\pi_A}) \wedge (\lozenge NRO_{\pi_A}) \wedge$ $((\square \bigwedge_{act \in Act_P} act_{\pi_A} \leftrightarrow act_{\pi_B}) \rightarrow ((\lozenge NRR_{\pi_B}) \leftrightarrow (\lozenge NRO_{\pi_B}))) \wedge$ $((\square \bigwedge_{act \in Act_Q} act_{\pi_A} \leftrightarrow act_{\pi_B}) \rightarrow ((\lozenge NRR_{\pi_B}) \leftrightarrow (\lozenge NRO_{\pi_B})))$
Path Planning	$\varphi_{sp} = \exists \pi_A. \forall \pi_B. (\neg goal_{\pi_B} \mathcal{U} goal_{\pi_A})$
	$\varphi_{rb} = \exists \pi_A. \forall \pi_B. (strategy_{\pi_B} \leftrightarrow strategy_{\pi_A}) \mathcal{U} (goal_{\pi_A} \wedge goal_{\pi_B})$
Mutant	$\varphi_{mut} = \exists \pi_A. \forall \pi_B (mut_{\pi_A} \wedge \neg mut_{\pi_B}) \wedge ((in_{\pi_A} \leftrightarrow in_{\pi_B}) \mathcal{U} (out_{\pi_A} \not\leftrightarrow out_{\pi_B}))$

Table 2: Hyperproperties investigated in case studies.

Case Study 3: Non-interference in multi-threaded Programs. *Non-interference* [25] states that low-security variables are independent from the high-security variables, thus preserving secure information flow. We consider the concurrent program example in [32], where *PIN* is high security input and *Result* is low security output. HyperQube returns SAT in the halting pessimistic semantics, indicating that there is a trace that we can detect the difference of a high-variable by observing a low variable, that is, violating non-interference. We also verified the correctness of a fix to this algorithm, proposed in [32] as well. HyperQube uses the UNSAT results from the solver (with halting optimistic semantics) to infer the absence of violation, that is, verification of *non-interference*.

Case Study 4: Fairness in non-repudiation protocols. A *non-repudiation* protocol ensures that a receiver obtains a receipt from the sender, called *non-repudiation of origin* (*NRO*), and the sender ends up having an evidence, named *non-repudiation of receipt* (*NRR*), through a trusted third party. A non-repudiation protocol is *fair* if both *NRR* and *NRO* are either received or not received by the parties (see formula φ_{fair} in Table 2). We verified two different protocols from [31], namely, $T_{incorrect}$ that chooses not to send out *NRR* after receiving *NRO*, and a correct implementation $T_{correct}$ which is fair. For $T_{correct}$

(respectively, $T_{incorrect}$), HyperQube returns UNSAT in the halting optimistic semantics (respectively, SAT in the halting pessimistic semantics), which indicates that the protocol satisfies (respectively, violates) fairness.

Case Study 5: Path planning for robots. We have used HyperQube beyond verification, to synthesize strategies for robotic planning [34]. Here, we focus on producing a strategy that satisfies two control requirements for a robot to reach a goal in a grid. First, the robot should take the *shortest path* (see formula φ_{sp} in Table 2). Fig. 2 shows a 10×10 grid, where the red, green, and black cells are initial, goal, and blocked cells, respectively. HyperQube returns SAT and the synthesized path is shown by the blue arrows. We also used HyperQube to solve the *path robustness* problem, meaning that starting from an arbitrary initial state, a robot reaches the goal by following a single strategy (see formula φ_{rb} in Table 2). Again, HyperQube returns SAT for the grid shown in Fig. 3.

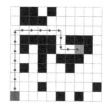

Fig. 2: Shortest Path

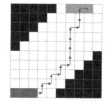

Fig. 3: Robust path

Case Study 6: Mutation testing. We adopted the model from [15] and apply the original formula that describes a good test mutant together with the model (see formula φ_{mut} in Table 2). HyperQube returns SAT, indicating successful finding of a qualified mutant. We note that in [15] the authors were not able to generate test cases via φ_{mut}, as the model checker MCHyper is not able to handle quantifier alternation in pushbutton fashion.

Results and analysis. Table 3 summarizes our results including running times, the bounded semantics applied, the output of the QBF solver, and the resulting infinite inference conclusion using Theorem 1. As can be seen, our case studies range over model checking of different fragments of HyperLTL. It is important to note that HyperQube run time consists of generating a QBF formula by genqbf and then checking its satisfiability by QuAbS. It is remarkable that in some cases, QBF formula generation takes longer than checking its satisfiability. The models in our experiments also have different sizes. The most complex case study is arguably the SNARK algorithm, where we identify both bugs in the algorithm in 472 and 1497 seconds. In cases 5.1 – 6.2, we also demonstrate the ability of HyperQube to solve synthesis problems by leveraging the existential quantifier in a HyperLTL formula.

Finally, we elaborate more on scalability of the path planning problem for robots. This problem was first studied in [34], where the authors reduce the problem to SMT solving using Z3 [13] and by eliminating the trace quantifiers through a combinatorial enumeration of conjunctions and disjunctions. Table 4 compares our approach with the brute-force technique employed in [34] for different grid sizes. Our QBF-based approach clearly outperforms the solution in [34], in some cases by an order of magnitude.

#	Model K	Formula	bound k	|AP*|	QBF	semantics	genqbf [s]	QuAbS [s]	Total [s]	
0.1	Bakery.3proc	φ_{S1}	7	27	SAT	pes	0.44	0.04	**0.48**	✗
0.2	Bakery.3proc	φ_{S2}	12	27	SAT	pes	1.31	0.15	**1.46**	✗
0.3	Bakery.3proc	φ_{S3}	20	27	UNSAT	opt	2.86	4.87	**7.73**	✓
1.1	Bakery.3proc	φ_{sym1}	10	27	SAT	pes	0.86	0.11	**0.97**	✗
1.2	Bakery.3proc	φ_{sym2}	10	27	SAT	pes	0.76	0.17	**0.93**	✗
1.3	Bakery.5proc	φ_{sym1}	10	45	SAT	pes	23.57	1.08	**24.65**	✗
1.4	Bakery.5proc	φ_{sym2}	10	45	SAT	pes	29.92	1.43	**31.35**	✗
2.1	SNARK-bug1	φ_{lin}	26	160	SAT	pes	88.42	383.60	**472.02**	✗
2.2	SNARK-bug2	φ_{lin}	40	160	SAT	pes	718.09	779.76	**1497.85**	✗
3.1	3-Thread$_{incorrect}$	φ_{NI}	57	31	SAT	h-pes	19.56	46.66	**66.22**	✗
3.2	3-Thread$_{correct}$	φ_{NI}	57	31	UNSAT	h-opt	23.91	33.54	**57.45**	✓
4.1	$NRP : T_{incorrect}$	φ_{fair}	15	15	SAT	h-pes	0.10	0.27	**0.37**	✗
4.2	$NRP : T_{correct}$	φ_{fair}	15	15	UNSAT	h-opt	0.08	0.12	**0.20**	✓
5.1	Shortest Path									
5.2	Initial State Robustness			(see Table 4)						synthesis
6.1	Mutant	φ_{mut}	8	6	SAT	h-pes	1.40	0.35	**1.75**	

Table 3: Performance of HyperQube, where column *case#* identifies the artifact, ✓ denotes satisfaction, and ✗ denotes violation of the formula. AP* is the set of Boolean variables encoding K.

Formula	grid size	bound k	|AP*|	HyperQube				[34]		
				genqbf [s]	QuAbS [s]	Total [s]		gensmt [s]	Z3 [s]	Total[s]
φ_{sp}	10^2	20	12	1.30	0.57	**1.87**		8.31	0.33	**8.64**
	20^2	40	14	4.53	12.16	**16.69**		124.66	6.41	**131.06**
	40^2	80	16	36.04	35.75	**71.79**		1093.12	72.99	**1166.11**
	60^2	120	16	105.82	120.84	**226.66**		4360.75	532.11	**4892.86**
φ_{rb}	10^2	20	12	1.40	0.35	**1.75**		11.14	0.45	**11.59**
	20^2	40	14	15.92	15.32	**31.14**		49.59	2.67	**52.26**
	40^2	80	16	63.16	20.13	**83.29**		216.16	19.81	**235.97**

Table 4: Path planning for robots and comparison to [34]. All cases use the halting pessimistic semantics and QBF solver returns SAT, meaning successful path synthesis.

6   Related Work

There has been a lot of recent progress in automatically verifying [12,22–24] and monitoring [1,6,7,20,21,26,33] HyperLTL specifications. HyperLTL is also supported by a growing set of tools, including the model checker MCHyper [12,24], the satisfiability checkers EAHyper [19] and MGHyper [17], and the runtime monitoring tool RVHyper [20]. The complexity of *model checking* for HyperLTL for tree-shaped, acyclic, and general graphs was rigorously investigated in [2]. The first algorithms for model checking HyperLTL and HyperCTL* using alternating automata were introduced in [24]. These techniques, however, were not able to deal in practice with alternating HyperLTL formulas in a fully automated fashion. We also note that previous approaches that reduce model checking HyperLTL—typically of formulas without quantifier alternations—to model checking LTL can use BMC in the LTL model checking phase. However, this is a different approach than the one presented here, as these approaches simply instruct the model checker to use a BMC *after* the problem has been fully reduced to an LTL model checking problem while we avoid this translation. These algorithms were then extended to deal with hyperliveness and alternating formulas in [12] by finding a winning strategy in $\forall\exists$ games. In this paper, we take an alternative approach by reducing the model checking problem to QBF solving, which is arguably more effective for finding bugs (in case a finite witness exists).

The *satisfiability* problem for HyperLTL is shown to be undecidable in general but decidable for the $\exists^*\forall^*$ fragment and for any fragment that includes a $\forall\exists$ quantifier alternation [16]. The hierarchy of hyperlogics beyond HyperLTL were studied in [11]. The synthesis problem for HyperLTL has been studied in [3] in the form of *program repair*, in [4] in the form of *controller synthesis*, and in [18] for the general case.

7   Conclusion and Future Work

We introduced the first bounded model checking (BMC) technique for verification of hyperproperties expressed in HyperLTL. To this end, we proposed four different semantics that ensure the soundness of inferring the outcome of the model checking problem. To handle trace quantification in HyperLTL, we reduced the BMC problem to checking satisfiability of quantified Boolean formulas (QBF). This is analogous to the reduction of BMC for LTL to the simple propositional satisfiability problem. We have introduced different classes of semantics, beyond the pessimistic semantics common in LTL model checking, namely *optimistic* semantics that allow to infer full verification by observing only a finite prefix and *halting* variations of these semantics that additionally exploit the termination of the execution, when available. Through a rich set of case studies, we demonstrated the effectiveness and efficiency of our approach in verification of information-flow properties, linearizability in concurrent data structures, path planning in robotics, and fairness in non-repudiation protocols.

As for future work, our first step is to solve the loop condition problem. This is necessary to establish completeness conditions for BMC and can help cover even more examples efficiently. The application of QBF-based techniques in the framework of abstraction/refinement is another unexplored area. Success of BMC for hyperproperties inherently depends on effectiveness of QBF solvers. Even though QBF solving is not as mature as SAT/SMT solving techniques, recent breakthroughs on QBF have enabled the construction of our tool HyperQube, and more progress in QBF solving will improve its efficiency.

References

1. Shreya Agrawal and Borzoo Bonakdarpour. Runtime verification of k-safety hyperproperties in HyperLTL. In *Proc. of the 29th IEEE Computer Security Foundations Symposium (CSF'16)*, pages 239–252. IEEE, 2016.
2. Borzoo Bonakdarpour and Bernd Finkbeiner. The complexity of monitoring hyperproperties. In *Proc. of the IEEE 31st Computer Security Foundations Symposium (CSF'18)*, pages 162–174. IEEE, 2018.
3. Borzoo Bonakdarpour and Bernd Finkbeiner. Program repair for hyperproperties. In *Proc. of the 17th Symposium on Automated Technology for Verification and Analysis (ATVA'19)*, volume 11781 of *LNCS*, pages 423–441. Springer, 2019.
4. Borzoo Bonakdarpour and Bernd Finkbeiner. Controller synthesis for hyperproperties. In *Proc. of the 33rd IEEE Computer Security Foundations Symposium (CSF'20)*, pages 366–379. IEEE, 2020.
5. Borzoo Bonakdarpour, Pavithra Prabhakar, and César Sánchez. Model checking timed hyperproperties in discrete-time systems. In *Proc. of the 12th NASA Formal Methods Symposium (NFM'20)*, volume 12229 of *LNCS*, pages 311–328. Springer, 2020.
6. Borzoo Bonakdarpour, César Sánchez, and Gerardo Schneider. Monitoring hyperproperties by combining static analysis and runtime verification. In *Proc. of the 8th Int'l Symposium on Leveraging Applications of Formal Methods, Verification and Validation (ISoLA'18), Part II*, volume 11245 of *LNCS*, pages 8–27. Springer, 2018.
7. Noel Brett, Umair Siddique, and Borzoo Bonakdarpour. Rewriting-based runtime verification for alternation-free HyperLTL. In *Proc. of the 23rd Int'l Conf. on Tools and Algorithms for the Construction and Analysis of Systems (TACAS'17), Part II*, volume 10206 of *LNCS*, pages 77–93. Springer, 2017.
8. Edmund M. Clarke, Armin Biere, Richard Raimi, and Yunshan Zhu. Bounded model checking using satisfiability solving. *Formal Methods in System Design*, 19(1):7–34, 2001.
9. Michael R. Clarkson, Bernd Finkbeiner, Masoud Koleini, Kristopher K. Micinski, Markus N. Rabe, and César Sánchez. Temporal logics for hyperproperties. In *Proc. of the 3rd Int'l Conf. on Principles of Security and Trust (POST'14)*, volume 8414 of *LNCS*, pages 265–284. Springer, 2014.
10. Michael R. Clarkson and Fred B. Schneider. Hyperproperties. *Journal of Computer Security*, 18(6):1157–1210, 2010.
11. Norine Coenen, Bernd Finkbeiner, Cristopher Hahn, and Jana Hofmann. The hierarchy of hyperlogics. In *Proc. of the 34th Annual ACM/IEEE Symposium on Logic in Computer Science (LICS'19)*, pages 1–13. IEEE, 2019.
12. Norine Coenen, Bernd Finkbeiner, César Sánchez, and Leander Tentrup. Verifying hyperliveness. In *Proc. of the 31st Int'l Conf. on Computer Aided Verification (CAV'19), Part I*, volume 11561 of *LNCS*, pages 121–139. Springer, 2019.
13. Leonardo de Moura and Nikolaj Bjorner. Z3 – a tutorial. Technical report, Microsoft, 2012.
14. Simon Doherty, David Detlefs, Lindsay Groves, Christine H. Flood, Victor Luchangco, Paul Alan Martin, Mark Moir, Nir Shavit, and Guy L. Steele Jr. DCAS is not a silver bullet for nonblocking algorithm design. In *Proc. of the 16th Annual ACM Symposium on Parallelism in Algorithms and Architectures (SPAA'04)*, pages 216–224. ACM, 2004.

15. Andreas Fellner, Mitra Tabaei Befrouei, and Georg Weissenbacher. Mutation testing with hyperproperties. In *Proc. of the 17th Int'l Conf. on Software Engineering and Formal Methods (SEFM'19)*, volume 11724 of *LNCS*, pages 203–221. Springer, 2019.

16. Bernd Finkbeiner and Cristopher Hahn. Deciding hyperproperties. In *Proc. of the 27th Int'l Conf. on Concurrency Theory (CONCUR'16)*, volume 59 of *LIPIcs*, pages 13:1–13:14. Schloss Dagstuhl - Leibniz-Zentrum für Informatik, 2016.

17. Bernd Finkbeiner, Cristopher Hahn, and Tobias Hans. MGHyper: Checking satisfiability of HyperLTL formulas beyond the $\exists^*\forall^*$ fragment. In *Proc. of the 16th Int'l Symposium on Automated Technology for Verification and Analysis (ATVA'18)*, volume 11138 of *LNCS*, pages 521–527. Springer, 2018.

18. Bernd Finkbeiner, Cristopher Hahn, Philip Lukert, Marvin Stenger, and Leander Tentrup. Synthesis from hyperproperties. *Acta Informatica*, 57(1-2):137–163, 2020.

19. Bernd Finkbeiner, Cristopher Hahn, and Marvin Stenger. Eahyper: Satisfiability, implication, and equivalence checking of hyperproperties. In *Proc. of the 29th Int'l Conf. on Computer Aided Verification (CAV'17), Part II*, volume 10427 of *LNCS*, pages 564–570. Springer, 2017.

20. Bernd Finkbeiner, Cristopher Hahn, Marvin Stenger, and Leander Tentrup. RVHyper: A runtime verification tool for temporal hyperproperties. In *Proc. of the 24th Int'l Conf. on Tools and Algorithms for the Construction and Analysis of Systems (TACAS'18), Part II*, volume 10806 of *LNCS*, pages 194–200. Springer, 2018.

21. Bernd Finkbeiner, Cristopher Hahn, Marvin Stenger, and Leander Tentrup. Monitoring hyperproperties. *Formal Methods in System Design*, 54(3):336–363, 2019.

22. Bernd Finkbeiner, Cristopher Hahn, and Hazem Torfah. Model checking quantitative hyperproperties. In *Proc. of the 30th Int'l Conf. on Computer Aided Verification (CAV'18), Part I*, volume 10981 of *LNCS*, pages 144–163. Springer, 2018.

23. Bernd Finkbeiner, Christian Müller, Helmut Seidl, and Eugene Zalinescu. Verifying security policies in multi-agent workflows with loops. In *Proc. of the 15th ACM Conf. on Computer and Communications Security (CCS'17)*, pages 633–645. ACM, 2017.

24. Bernd Finkbeiner, Markus N. Rabe, and César Sánchez. Algorithms for model checking HyperLTL and HyperCTL*. In *Proc. of the 27th Int'l Conf. on Computer Aided Verification (CAV'15), Part I*, volume 9206 of *LNCS*, pages 30–48. Springer, 2015.

25. Joseph A. Goguen and José Meseguer. Security policies and security models. In *1982 IEEE Symposium on Security and Privacy*, pages 11–20. IEEE Computer Society, 1982.

26. Cristopher Hahn, Marvin Stenger, and Leander Tentrup. Constraint-based monitoring of hyperproperties. In *Proc. of the 25th Int'l Conf. on Tools and Algorithms for the Construction and Analysis of Systems (TACAS'19)*, volume 11428 of *LNCS*, pages 115–131. Springer, 2019.

27. Klaus Havelund and Doron Peled. Runtime verification: From propositional to first-order temporal logic. In *Proc. of the 18th Int'l Conf. on Runtime Verification (RV'18)*, volume 11237 of *LNCS*, pages 90–112. Springer, 2018.

28. Jesko Hecking-Harbusch and Leander Tentrup. Solving QBF by abstraction. In *Proc. of the 9th Int'l Symposium on Games, Automata, Logics and Formal Verification (GandALF'18)*, volume 277 of *EPTCS*, pages 88–102, 2018.

29. Maurice Herlihy and Jeannette M. Wing. Linearizability: A correctness condition for concurrent objects. *ACM Transactions on Programming Languages and Systems*, 12(3):463–492, 1990.

30. Tzu-Han Hsu, César Sánchez, and Borzoo Bonakdarpour. Bounded model checking for hyperproperties. *CoRR*, abs/2009.08907, 2020.
31. Wojciech Jamroga, Sjouke Mauw, and Matthijs Melissen. Fairness in non-repudiation protocols. In *Proc. of the 7th Int'l Workshop on Security and Trust Management (STM'11)*, volume 7170 of *LNCS*, pages 122–139. Springer, 2011.
32. Geoffrey Smith and Dennis M. Volpano. Secure information flow in a multi-threaded imperative language. In *Proc. of the 25th ACM Symposium on Principles of Programming Languages (POPL'98)*, pages 355–364. ACM, 1998.
33. Sandro Stucki, César Sánchez, Gerardo Schneider, and Borzoo Bonakdarpour. Graybox monitoring of hyperproperties. In *Proc. of the 23rd Int'l Symposium on Formal Methods (FM'19)*, volume 11800 of *LNCS*, pages 406–424. Springer, 2019.
34. Yu Wang, Siddharta Nalluri, and Miroslav Pajic. Hyperproperties for robotics: Planning via HyperLTL. In *2020 IEEE Int'l Conf. on Robotics and Automation (ICRA'20)*, pages 8011–8017. IEEE, 2020.
35. Yu Wang, Mojtaba Zarei, Borzoo Bonakdarpour, and Miroslav Pajic. Statistical verification of hyperproperties for cyber-physical systems. *ACM Transactions on Embedded Computing systems*, 18(5s):92:1–92:23, 2019.

Counterexample-Guided Prophecy for Model Checking Modulo the Theory of Arrays

Makai Mann[1]([⊠]) , Ahmed Irfan[1] , Alberto Griggio[2] ,
Oded Padon[1,3], and Clark Barrett[1]

[1] Stanford University, Stanford, USA {makaim,irfan,barrett}@cs.stanford.edu
[2] Fondazione Bruno Kessler, Trento, Italy griggio@fbk.eu
[3] VMware Research, Palo Alto, USA oded.padon@gmail.com

Abstract. We develop a framework for model checking infinite-state systems by automatically augmenting them with auxiliary variables, enabling quantifier-free induction proofs for systems that would otherwise require quantified invariants. We combine this mechanism with a counterexample-guided abstraction refinement scheme for the theory of arrays. Our framework can thus, in many cases, reduce inductive reasoning with quantifiers and arrays to quantifier-free and array-free reasoning. We evaluate the approach on a wide set of benchmarks from the literature. The results show that our implementation often outperforms state-of-the-art tools, demonstrating its practical potential.

1 Introduction

Model checking is a widely-used and highly-effective technique for automated property checking. While model checking finite-state systems is a well-established technique for hardware and software systems, model checking infinite-state systems is more challenging. One challenge, for example, is that proving properties by induction over infinite-state systems often requires the use of universally quantified invariants. While some automated reasoning tools can reason about quantified formulas, such reasoning is typically not very robust. Furthermore, just discovering these quantified invariants remains very challenging.

Previous work (e.g., [52]) has shown that prophecy variables can sometimes play the same role as universally quantified variables, making it possible to transform a system that would require quantified reasoning into one that does not. However, to the best of our knowledge, there has been no automatic method for applying such transformations. In this paper, we introduce a technique we call *counterexample-guided prophecy*. During the refinement step of an abstraction-refinement loop, our technique automatically introduces prophecy variables, which both help with the refinement step and may also reduce the need for quantified reasoning. We demonstrate the technique in the context of model checking for infinite-state systems with arrays, a domain which is known for requiring quantified reasoning. We show how a standard abstraction for arrays can be augmented with counterexample-guided prophecy to obtain an algorithm that reduces the model checking problem to quantifier-free, array-free reasoning.

J. F. Groote and K. G. Larsen (Eds.): TACAS 2021, LNCS 12651, pp. 113–132, 2021.
https://doi.org/10.1007/978-3-030-72016-2_7

The paper makes the following contributions: i) we introduce an algorithm called **Prophecize** which uses history and prophecy variables to target a specific term at a specific time step of an execution, producing a new transition system that can effectively reason universally about that term; ii) we develop an automatic abstraction-refinement procedure for arrays, which leverages the **Prophecize** algorithm during the refinement step, and show that it is sound and produces no false positives; iii) we develop a prototype implementation of our technique; and iv) we evaluate our technique on four sets of model checking benchmarks containing arrays and show that our implementation outperforms state-of-the-art tools on a majority of the benchmark sets.

2   Background

We assume the standard many-sorted first-order logical setting with the usual notions of signature, term, formula, and interpretation. A *theory* is a pair $\mathcal{T} = (\Sigma, \mathbf{I})$ where Σ is a signature and $\mathbf{I}$ is a class of Σ-interpretations, the *models* of T. A Σ-formula φ is *satisfiable* (resp., *unsatisfiable*) in $\mathcal{T}$ if it is satisfied by some (resp., no) interpretation in $\mathbf{I}$. Given an interpretation $\mathcal{M}$, a variable assignment s over a set of variables X is a mapping that assigns each variable $x \in X$ of sort σ to an element of $\sigma^{\mathcal{M}}$, denoted x^s. We write $\mathcal{M}[s]$ for the interpretation that is equivalent to $\mathcal{M}$ except that each variable $x \in X$ is mapped to x^s. Let x be a variable, t a term, and ϕ a formula. We denote with $\phi\{x \mapsto t\}$ the formula obtained by replacing every free occurrence of x in ϕ with t. We extend this notation to sets of variables and terms in the usual way. If f and g are two functions, we write $f \circ g$ to mean functional composition, i.e., $f \circ g(x) = f(g(x))$.

Let $\mathcal{T}_A$ be the standard theory of arrays [50] with extensionality, extended with constant arrays. Concretely, we assume sorts for arrays, indices, and elements, and function symbols *read*, *write*, and *constarr*. Here and below, we use a and b to refer to arrays, i and j to refer to array indices, and e and c to refer to array elements, where c is also restricted to be an interpreted constant. The theory contains the class of all interpretations satisfying the following axioms:

$$\begin{aligned}\forall a, i, j, e.\; i = j &\implies read(write(a, j, e), i) = e \;\wedge \\ i \neq j &\implies read(write(a, j, e), i) = read(a, i)\end{aligned} \tag{write}$$

$$\forall a, b.\; (\forall i.\; read(a, i) = read(b, i)) \implies a = b \tag{ext}$$

$$\forall i.\; read(constarr(c), i) = c \tag{const}$$

Symbolic Transition Systems and Model Checking. For generality, assume a background theory $\mathcal{T}$ with signature Σ. We will assume that all terms and formulas are Σ-terms and Σ-formulas, that entailment is entailment modulo $\mathcal{T}$, and interpretations are $\mathcal{T}$-interpretations. A symbolic transition system (STS) $\mathcal{S}$ is a tuple $\mathcal{S} := \langle X, I, T \rangle$, where X is a finite set of state variables, $I(X)$ is a formula denoting the initial states of the system, and $T(X, X')$ is a formula expressing a transition relation. Here, X' is the set obtained by replacing each variable $x \in X$ with a new variable x' of the same sort. Let $prime(x) = x'$ be the bijection corresponding to this replacement. We say that a variable x is *frozen* if $T \models x' = x$. When the state variables are obvious, we will often drop X.

A state s of $\mathcal{S}$ is a variable assignment over X. An *execution* of $\mathcal{S}$ of length k is a pair $\langle \mathcal{M}, \pi \rangle$, where $\mathcal{M}$ is an interpretation and $\pi := s_0, s_1, \ldots, s_{k-1}$ is a *path* of length k, a sequence of states such that $\mathcal{M}[s_0] \models I(X)$ and $\mathcal{M}[s_i][s_{i+1} \circ prime^{-1}] \models T(X, X')$ for all $0 \leq i < k - 1$. When reasoning about paths, it is often convenient to have multiple copies of the state variables X. We use $X@n$ to denote the set of variables obtained by replacing each variable $x \in X$ with a new variable called $x@n$ of the same sort. We refer to these as *timed* variables. A state s is *reachable* in $\mathcal{S}$ if it appears in a path of some execution of $\mathcal{S}$. We say that a formula $P(X)$ is an *invariant* of $\mathcal{S}$, denoted by $\mathcal{S} \models P(X)$, if $P(X)$ is satisfied in every reachable state of $\mathcal{S}$ (i.e., for every execution $\langle \mathcal{M}, \pi \rangle$, $\mathcal{M}[s] \models P(X)$ for each s in π). The *invariant checking problem* is, given $\mathcal{S}$ and $P(X)$, to determine if $\mathcal{S} \models P(X)$. A *counterexample* is an execution $\langle \mathcal{M}, \pi \rangle$ of $\mathcal{S}$ of length k such that $\mathcal{M}[s_{k-1}] \not\models P(X)$. If $I(X) \models \phi(X)$ and $\phi(X) \wedge T(X, X') \models \phi(X')$, then $\phi(X)$ is an *inductive* invariant. Every inductive invariant is an invariant (by induction over path length). In this paper we focus on model checking problems where I, T and P are quantifier-free. However, a *quantified inductive invariant* might still be necessary to prove a property of the system.

Bounded Model Checking (BMC) is a bug-finding technique which attempts to find a counterexample for a property, $P(X)$, of length k for some finite k [9]. A single BMC query at bound k for an invariant property uses a constraint solver to check the satisfiability of the following formula: $BMC(\mathcal{S}, P, k) := I(X@0) \wedge (\bigwedge_{i=0}^{k-1} T(X@i, X@(i+1))) \wedge \neg P(X@k)$. If the query is satisfiable, there is a bug.

Counterexample-Guided Abstraction Refinement (CEGAR). CEGAR is a general technique in which a difficult conjecture is tackled iteratively [44]. Algorithm 1 shows a simple CEGAR loop for checking an invariant P for an STS $\mathcal{S}$. It is parameterized by three functions. The **Abstract** function produces an initial abstraction of the problem. It must satisfy the contract that if $\langle \widehat{S}, \widehat{P} \rangle = $ **Abstract**$(\mathcal{S}, P)$, then $\widehat{S} \models \widehat{P} \implies \mathcal{S} \models P$. The next function is the **Prove** function. This can be any (unbounded) model-checking algorithm that can return counterexamples. It checks whether a given property P is an invariant of a given STS $\mathcal{S}$. If it is, it returns with *proven* set to true. Otherwise, it returns a bound k at which a counterexample exists. The final function is **Refine**. It takes the abstracted STS and property together with a bound k at which a known counterexample for the abstract STS exists. Its job is to refine the abstraction until there is no longer a counterexample of size k. If it succeeds, it returns the new STS and property. It fails if there is an actual counterexample of size k for the concrete system. In this case, it sets the return value *refined* to false.

Auxiliary variables. We finish this section with relevant background on *auxiliary* variables, a crucial part of the refinement step described in Sec. 4. Auxiliary variables are new variables added to the system which do not influence its behavior (i.e., the reduct to the old set of variables of any reachable state in the new system is a reachable state in the old system), but may assist in proofs. There are two main categories of auxiliary variables we consider: *history* and

---

Algorithm 1 STS-CEGAR($\mathcal{S} := \langle X, I, T \rangle, P$)

1: $\langle \langle \widehat{X}, \widehat{I}, \widehat{T} \rangle, \widehat{P} \rangle \leftarrow$ **Abstract**$(\mathcal{S}, P)$
2: **while** true **do**
3:     $\langle k, proven \rangle \leftarrow$ **Prove**$(\langle \widehat{X}, \widehat{I}, \widehat{T} \rangle, \widehat{P})$ // try to prove
4:     **if** *proven* **then return** true   // property proved
5:     $\langle \langle \widehat{X}, \widehat{I}, \widehat{T} \rangle, \widehat{P}, refined \rangle \leftarrow$ **Refine**$(\langle \widehat{X}, \widehat{I}, \widehat{T} \rangle, \widehat{P}, k)$ // try to refine
6:     **if** ¬*refined* **then return** false   // found counterexample
7: **end while**

---

prophecy. History variables, also known as *ghost state*, preserve a value, making its past value available in future states. Prophecy variables are the dual of history variables and provide a way to refer to a value that occurs in a future state. Abadi and Lamport formally characterized soundness conditions for the introduction of history and prophecy variables [1]. Here, we consider a simple, structured form of history variables.

Definition 1. *Let* $\mathcal{S} = \langle X, I, T \rangle$ *be an STS, t a term whose free variables are in X, and $n > 0$, then* **Delay**$(\mathcal{S}, t, n)$ *returns a new STS and variable* $\langle \langle X^h, I^h, T^h \rangle, h_t^n \rangle$, *where* $X^h = X \uplus \{h_t^1, \ldots, h_t^n\}$, $I^h = I$, *and* $T^h = T \cup \{h_t^{1'} = t\} \cup \bigcup_{i=2}^{n} \{h_t^{i'} = h_t^{i-1}\}$.

The **Delay** operator makes the current value of a term t available for the next n states in a path. This is accomplished by adding n new history variables and creating an assignment chain that passes the value to the next history variable at each state. Thus, h_t^k contains the value that t had k states ago. The initial value of each history variable is unconstrained.

Theorem 1. *Let* $\mathcal{S} = \langle X, I, T \rangle$ *be an STS, P a property, and* **Delay**$(\mathcal{S}, v, n) = \langle \mathcal{S}^h, h_v^n \rangle$. *Then* $\mathcal{S} \models P$ *iff* $\mathcal{S}^h \models P$.

We refer to [1] for a general proof which subsumes Theorem 1. In contrast to the general approach for history variables, we use a version of prophecy that only requires a single frozen variable. The motivation for this is that a frozen variable can be used in place of a universal quantifier, as the following theorem adapted from [52] shows.

Theorem 2. *Let* $\mathcal{S} = \langle X, I, T \rangle$ *be an STS, x a variable in formula $P(X)$, and v a fresh variable (i.e., not in X or X'). Let* $\mathcal{S}^p = \langle X \cup \{v\}, I, T \cup \{v' = v\} \rangle$. *Then* $\mathcal{S} \models \forall x. P(X)$ *iff* $\mathcal{S}^p \models P(X)\{x \mapsto v\}$.

Theorem 2 shows that a universally quantified variable in an invariant can be replaced with a fresh symbol in a process similar to skolemization. The intuition is as follows. The frozen variable has the same value in all states, but it is uninitialized by I. Thus, for each path in $\mathcal{S}$, there is a corresponding path (i.e., identical except at v) in $\mathcal{S}^p$ for *every* possible value of v. This proliferation of paths plays the same role as the quantified variable in P. We mention here one more theorem from [52]. This one allows us to *introduce* a universal quantifier.

Algorithm 2 Prophecize($\langle X, I, T \rangle, P(X), t, n$)

1: **if** n = 0 **then**
2:     **return** $\langle\langle X \uplus \{p_t\}, I, T \cup \{p'_t = p_t\}\rangle, p_t = t \implies P(X), p_t\rangle$
3: **else**
4:     $\langle\langle X^h, I^h, T^h\rangle, h^n_t\rangle := \textbf{Delay}(\langle X, I, T\rangle, t, n)$
5:     **return** $\langle\langle X^h \uplus \{p^n_t\}, I, T \cup \{p^{n'}_t = p^n_t\}\rangle, p_t = h^n_t \implies P(X), p^n_t\rangle$
6: **end if**

Theorem 3. *Let $\mathcal{S} = \langle X, I, T \rangle$ be an STS, $P(X)$ a formula, and t a term. Then, $\mathcal{S} \models P(X)$ iff $\mathcal{S} \models \forall y.(y = t \implies P(X))$, where y is not free in $P(X)$.*

Theorems 2 and 3 are special cases of Theorems 3 and 4 of [52]. The original theorems handle the more general case where $P(X)$ can be a temporal formula.

3 Using Auxiliary Variables to Assist Induction

We can use Theorem 3 followed by Theorem 2 to introduce frozen prophecy variables that predict the value of a term t when the property P is being checked. We refer to t as the prophecy *target* and the process as *universal* prophecy. If we also use **Delay**, we can target a term at some finite number of steps *before* the property is checked. This is captured by Algorithm 2, which takes a transition system, property $P(X)$, term t, and $n \geq 0$. If $n = 0$, it introduces a universal prophecy variable for t. Otherwise, it first introduces history variables for t and then applies universal prophecy to the delayed t. In either case it returns the augmented system, augmented property, and the prophecy variable.

We will use the STS shown in Fig. 1(a) as a running example throughout the paper (it is inspired by the hardware example from [10]). We assume the background theory $\mathcal{T}$ includes integer arithmetic and arrays of integers indexed by integers. The variables in this STS include an array and four integer variables, representing the read index, write index, read data, and write data, respectively. The system starts with an array of all zeros. At every step, if the write data is less than 200, it writes that data to the array at the write index. Otherwise, the array stays the same. Additionally, the read data is updated with the current value of a at i_r. This effectively introduces a one-step delay between when the value is read from a and when the value is present in d_r. The property is that $d_r < 200$. This property is clearly true, but it is not straightforward to prove with standard model checking techniques because it is not inductive. Note that it is also not k-inductive for any k [59]. The primary issue is that it does not constrain the value of a at all, so in an inductive proof, the value of a could be anything in the induction hypothesis.

One way to prove the property is to strengthen it with the quantified invariant: $\forall i. read(a, i) < 200$. Remarkably, observe that by augmenting the system using **Prophecize**, it is possible to prove the property using only a *quantifier-free* invariant. In this case, the relevant prophecy target is the value of i_r one

$$I := a = constarr(0) \wedge d_r < 200$$
$$T := a' = ite(d_w < 200,$$
$$write(a, i_w, d_w), a) \wedge$$
$$d'_r = read(a, i_r)$$
$$P := d_r < 200$$

$$I := a = constarr(0) \wedge d_r < 200$$
$$T := a' = ite(d_w < 200,$$
$$write(a, i_w, d_w), a) \wedge$$
$$d'_r = read(a, i_r) \wedge {p^{1}_{i_r}}' = p^1_{i_r} \wedge {h^{1}_{i_r}}' = i_r$$
$$P := p^1_{i_r} = h^1_{i_r} \implies d_r < 200$$

(a)   (b)

Fig. 1: (a) Running example. (b) Running example with prophecy variable.

step before checking the property. We run **Prophecize**($\langle X, I, T \rangle, P, i_r, 1$) and it returns the system and property shown in Fig. 1(b), along with the prophecy variable $p^1_{i_r}$. This augmented system has a simple, quantifier-free invariant which can be used to strengthen the property, making it inductive: $read(a, p_{i_r}) < 200$. This formula holds in the initial state because of the constant array, and if we start in a state where it holds, it still holds after a transition.

Notice that the invariant learned over the prophecy variable has the same form as the original quantified invariant. However, we have instantiated that universal quantifier with a fresh, frozen prophecy variable. Intuitively, the prophecy variable captures a proof by contradiction: assume the property does not hold, consider the value of i_r one step before the first failure of the property, and then use this value to show the property holds. This example shows that auxiliary variables can be used to transform an STS without a quantifier-free inductive invariant into an STS with one. However, it is not yet clear how to identify good targets for history and prophecy variables. In the next section, we show how this can be done as part of an abstraction refinement scheme for symbolic transition systems over the theory of arrays.

4   Abstraction Refinement for Arrays

We now introduce our main contribution. Given a background theory $\mathcal{T}_B$ and a model checking algorithm for STS's over $\mathcal{T}_B$, we use an instantiation of the CEGAR loop in Algorithm 1 to check properties of STS's over the theory that combines $\mathcal{T}_B$ and the theory of arrays, $\mathcal{T}_A$. The key idea is to abstract all array operators and then add array lemmas as needed during refinement.

Abstract and Prove. We use a standard abstraction for the theory of arrays, which we denote **Abstract-Arrays**. Every array sort is replaced with an uninterpreted sort, and the array variables are abstracted accordingly. Each constant array is replaced by a fresh abstract array variable, which is then constrained to be frozen (because constant arrays do not change over time). Additionally, we replace the *read* and *write* array operations with uninterpreted functions. Note that if the system contains multiple array sorts, we need to introduce a separate read and write function for each uninterpreted abstract array sort. Using uninterpreted sorts and functions for abstracting arrays is a common technique in Satisfiability Modulo Theories [7] (SMT) solvers [32]. Intuitively, our initial abstraction starts with *memoryless* arrays. We then incrementally refine the arrays'

$$\widehat{I} := \widehat{a} = \widehat{constarr0} \wedge d_r < 200$$
$$\widehat{T} := \widehat{a}' = ite(d_w < 200, \widehat{write}(\widehat{a}, i_w, d_w), \widehat{a}) \wedge$$
$$d_r' = \widehat{read}(\widehat{a}, i_r) \wedge \widehat{constarr0}' = \widehat{constarr0}$$
$$\widehat{P} := d_r < 200$$

Fig. 2: Result of calling **Abstract** on the example from Fig. 1(a)

memory as needed. Fig. 2 shows the result of running **Abstract-Arrays** on the example from Fig. 1(a). **Prove** can be instantiated with any (unbounded) model checker that can accept expressions over the background theory $\mathcal{T}_B$ combined with the theory of uninterpreted functions. In particular, due to our abstraction, the model checker does not need to support the theory of arrays.

Refine. Here, we explain the refinement approach for our array abstraction. At a high level, we solve a BMC problem over the abstract STS at bound k. We then look for violations of array axioms in the returned counterexample, and instantiate each violated axiom (this is essentially the same as the lazy array axiom instantiation approach used in SMT solvers [13,14,17,27]). We then *lift* these axioms to the STS-level by modifying the STS. It is this step that may require introducing auxiliary variables. The details are shown in Algorithm 3.

We start by computing a set $\mathcal{I}$ of index terms with *ComputeIndices* – this set is used in the lazy axiom instantiation step below. We add to $\mathcal{I}$ every term that appears in a $\widehat{read}$ or $\widehat{write}$ operation in $BMC(\widehat{S}, \widehat{P}, k)$. We also add a witness index for every array equality - the witness corresponds to a skolemized existential variable in the contrapositive of axiom (ext). For soundness, we must add an extra variable λ_σ for each index sort σ and constrain it to be different from all the other index variables of the same sort (this is based on the approach in [13]). Intuitively, this variable represents an arbitrary index different from those mentioned in the STS. We assume that the index sorts are from an infinite domain so that a distinct element is guaranteed. For simplicity of presentation, we also assume from now on that there is only a single index sort (e.g. integers). Otherwise, $\mathcal{I}$ must be partitioned by sort. For the abstract STS in Fig. 2, with $k = 1$, the index set would be $\mathcal{I} := \{i_r@0, i_w@0, w_0@0, w_1@0, \lambda_{Int}@0, i_r@1, i_w@1, w_0@1, w_1@1, \lambda_{Int}@1\}$, where w_0 and w_1 are witness indices.

After computing indices, the algorithm enters the main loop. We first check the $BMC(\widehat{S}, \widehat{P}, k)$ query. The result ρ is either a counterexample, or the distinguished value $\bot$, indicating that the query is unsatisfiable. If it is the latter, then we return the refined STS and property, as the property now holds on the STS up to bound k. Otherwise, we continue. The next step (line 5) is to find violations of array axioms in the execution ρ based on the index set $\mathcal{I}$.

CheckArrayAxioms takes two arguments, a counterexample and an index set, and returns instantiated array axioms that do not hold over the counterexample. This works as follows. We first look for occurrences of $\widehat{write}$ in the BMC formula.

Algorithm 3 Refine-Arrays ($\widehat{S} := \langle \widehat{X}, \widehat{I}, \widehat{T} \rangle, \widehat{P}, k$)

1: $\mathcal{I} \leftarrow ComputeIndices(\widehat{S}, \widehat{P}, k)$
2: **loop**
3:    $\rho \leftarrow \mathrm{BMC}(\widehat{S}, \widehat{P}, k)$
4:    **if** $\rho = \bot$ **then return** $\langle \langle \widehat{X}, \widehat{I}, \widehat{T} \rangle, \widehat{P}, true \rangle$ // Property holds up to bound k
5:    $\langle ca, nca \rangle \leftarrow CheckArrayAxioms(\rho, \mathcal{I})$
6:    **if** $ca = \emptyset \wedge nca = \emptyset$ **then return** $\langle \langle \widehat{X}, \widehat{I}, \widehat{T} \rangle, \widehat{P}, false \rangle$ // True counterexample
7:    // Go through non-consecutive array axiom instantiations
8:    **for** $\langle ax, i@n_i \rangle \in nca$ **do**
9:       **let** $n_{min} := min(\tau(ax) \setminus \{n_i\})$
10:       $\langle \langle X^p, I^p, T^p \rangle, P^p, p_i^{k-n_i} \rangle \leftarrow$ **Prophecize**$(\langle \widehat{X}, \widehat{I}, \widehat{T} \rangle, \widehat{P}, i, k - n_i)$
11:       $ax_c \leftarrow ax\{i@n_i \mapsto p_i^{k-n_i}@n_{min}\}$
12:       $ca \leftarrow ca \uplus \{ax_c@n_{min}\}$ // add consecutive version of axiom
13:       $\mathcal{I} \leftarrow \mathcal{I} \uplus \{p_i^{k-n_i}@0, \ldots, p_i^{k-n_i}@k\}$
14:       $\widehat{X} \leftarrow X^p; \widehat{I} \leftarrow I^p; \widehat{T} \leftarrow T^p; \widehat{P} \leftarrow P^p$
15:    **end for**
16:    // Go through consecutive array axiom instantiations
17:    **for** $ax \in ca$ **do**
18:       **let** $n_{min} := min(\tau(ax))$, $n_{max} := max(\tau(ax))$
19:       $assert(n_{max} = n_{min} \vee n_{max} = n_{min} + 1)$
20:       **if** $k = 0$ **then**
21:          $\widehat{I} \leftarrow \widehat{I} \wedge ax\{X@n_{min} \mapsto X\}$
22:       **else if** $n_{min} = n_{max}$ **then**
23:          $\widehat{T} \leftarrow \widehat{T} \wedge ax\{X@n_{min} \mapsto X\} \wedge ax\{X@n_{min} \mapsto X'\}$
24:       **else**
25:          $\widehat{T} \leftarrow \widehat{T} \wedge ax\{X@n_{min} \mapsto X\}\{X@(n_{min} + 1) \mapsto X'\}$
26:       **end if**
27:    **end for**
28: **end loop**

For each such occurrence, we instantiate the (write) axiom so that the $\widehat{write}$ term in the axiom matches the term in the formula (i.e., we use the $\widehat{write}$ term as a trigger). This instantiates all quantified variables except for i. We then instantiate i once for each variable in the index set. We evaluate each of the instantiated axioms using the values from the counterexample and keep those instantiations that reduce to false. We do the same thing for the (const) axiom, using each constant array term in the BMC formula as a trigger. Finally, for each array equality $a@m = b@n$ in the BMC formula, we check an instantiation of the contrapositive of (ext): $a@m \neq b@n \rightarrow read(a@m, w_i@n) \neq read(b@n, w_i@n)$. We add instantiated formulas that do not hold in ρ to the set of violated axioms.

CheckArrayAxioms sorts the collected axiom instantiations into two sets based on which timed variables they contain. The *consecutive* set contains formulas with timed variables whose timing differs by at most one; whereas the timed variables in the formulas contained in the *non-consecutive* set may differ by more. Formally, let τ be a function which takes a single timed variable and returns its time (e.g., $\tau(i@2) = 2$). We lift this to formulas by having $\tau(\phi)$ return the set of all time-steps for variables in ϕ. A formula ϕ is *consecutive* iff $max(\tau(\phi)) - min(\tau(\phi)) \leq 1$. Note that instantiations of (ext) are consecutive by construction. Additionally, because constant arrays have the same value in all time steps, we can always choose a representative time step for instantiations of (const) that results in a consecutive formula. However, instantiations of (write) may be non-consecutive, because the variable from the index set may be from a time step that is different from that of the trigger term. *CheckArrayAxioms* returns the pair $\langle ca, nca \rangle$, where ca is a set of consecutive axiom instantiations and nca is a set of pairs – each of which contains a non-consecutive axiom instantiation and the index-set variable that was used to create that instantiation.

At line 6, we check if the returned sets are empty. If so, then there are no array axiom violations and ρ is a concrete counterexample. In this case, the system, property, and *false* are returned. Otherwise, we process the two sets. In lines 8-15, we process the non-consecutive formulas. Given a non-consecutive formula ax together with its index-set variable $i@n_i$, we first compute the minimum time-step of the axiom's other variables, n_{min}. We then use the **Prophecize** method to create a prophecy variable $p_i^{k-n_i}$, that is effectively a way to refer to $i@n_i$ at time-step n_{min} (line 10). This allows us to create a consecutive formula ax_c that is semantically equivalent to ax (line 11). This new consecutive formula is added to ca in line 12, and in line 13 the introduced prophecy variables (one for each time-step) are added to the index set. Then, line 14 updates the abstraction.

At line 17, we are left with a set of consecutive formulas to process. For each consecutive formula ax, we compute the minimum and maximum time-step of its variables (line 18), which must differ by no more than 1 (line 19). There are three cases to consider: i) when $k = 0$, the counterexample consists of only the initial state—we thus refine the initial state by adding the untimed version of ax to $\widehat{I}$ (line 21); ii) if ax contains only variables from a single time step, then we add the untimed version of ax as a constraint for both X and X', ensuring that it will hold in every state (line 23); iii) finally, if ax contains variables from two adjacent time steps, we can translate this directly into a transition formula to be added to $\widehat{T}$ (line 25). The loop then repeats with the newly refined STS.

Example. Consider again the example from Fig. 2, and suppose **Refine-Arrays** is called on $\widehat{S}$ and $\widehat{P}$ with $k = 3$. At this unrolling, one possible abstract counterexample violates the following nonconsecutive axiom instantiation:

$$(i_r@2 = i_w@0 \implies \widehat{read}(\widehat{write}(\widehat{a@0}, i_w@0, d_w@0), i_r@2) = d_w@0) \;\wedge$$
$$(i_r@2 \neq i_w@0 \implies \widehat{read}(\widehat{write}(\widehat{a@0}, i_w@0, d_w@0), i_r@2) = \widehat{read}(\widehat{a@0}, i_r@2))$$

Calling **Prophecize**$(\widehat{S}, \widehat{P}, i_r, 1)$ returns the new STS $\langle\langle \widehat{X} \uplus \{h_{i_r}^1, p_{i_r}^1\}, \widehat{I}, \widehat{T} \wedge h_{i_r}^{1'} = i_r \wedge p_{i_r}^{1'} = p_{i_r}^1\rangle$ and the new property $p_{i_r}^1 = h_{i_r}^1 \implies d_r < 200$. The history variable $h_{i_r}^1$ makes the previous value of i_r available at each time-step, and the prophecy variable $p_{i_r}^1$ mimics a universally quantified variable. We substitute $p_{i_r}^1@0$ for $i_r@2$ to obtain a consecutive formula. Its untimed version (and a primed version) is added to the transition relation.

We stress that processing nonconsecutive axioms using **Prophecize** is how we automatically discover the universal prophecy variable $p_{i_r}^1$, and it is exactly the universal prophecy variable that was needed in Sec. 3 to prove correctness of the running example. An alternative approach could avoid nonconsecutive axioms using Craig interpolants [26] so that only consecutive axioms are found [15]. However, quantifier-free interpolants are not guaranteed to exist for the standard theory of arrays, and the auxiliary variables found using nonconsecutive axioms are needed to improve the chances of finding a quantifier-free inductive invariant.

It is important to have enough prophecy variables to assist in constructing inductive invariants. We found that we could often obtain a larger, richer set of prophecy variables by weakening our array abstraction. We do this by replacing equality between arrays by an uninterpreted predicate, and also checking the congruence axiom, the converse of (ext). Since more axioms are checked, there are more opportunities to introduce auxiliary variables. We call this *weak* abstraction (**WA**) as opposed to *strong* abstraction (**SA**), which uses regular equality between abstract arrays and guarantees congruence through UF axioms.

On the other hand, an excessive number of unnecessary auxiliary variables could overwhelm the **Prove** step. Thus, an improvement not shown in Algorithm 3 is to check consecutive axioms first and only add nonconsecutive ones when necessary. This is the motivation behind the custom array solver implementation *CheckArrayAxioms* based on [13]. In principle, we could have used an SMT solver to find array axioms, but it would give no preference to consecutive axioms. Similarly, we could overwhelm the algorithm with unnecessary consecutive axioms. *CheckArrayAxioms* can still produce hundreds or even thousands of (consecutive) axiom instantiations. Once these are lifted to the transition system, some may be redundant. To mitigate this issue, when the BMC check returns $\perp$ and we are about to return (line 4), we keep only axioms that appear in the unsat core of the BMC formula [22].

Correctness. We now state two important correctness theorems. Note that here and below, proofs are omitted due to space constraints. An extended version with proofs is available at: https://arxiv.org/abs/2101.06825.

Theorem 4. *Algorithm 1, instantiated with* **Abstract-Arrays**, *a model-checker* **Prove** *as described above, and* **Refine-Arrays** *is sound.*

Theorem 5. *If Algorithm 1, instantiated with* **Abstract-Arrays**, **Prove** *as described above, and* **Refine-Arrays**, *returns false, there is a concrete counterexample of length k in the concrete transition system.*

5   Expressiveness and Limitations

We now address the expressiveness of counterexample-guided prophecy with regard to the introduction of auxiliary variables. For simplicity, we ignore the array abstraction, relying on the correctness theorems. An inductive invariant using auxiliary variables can be converted to one without auxiliary variables by first universally quantifying over the prophecy variables, then existentially quantifying over the history variables. The details are captured by this theorem:

Theorem 6. *Let $S := \langle X, I, T \rangle$ be an STS, and $P(X)$ be a property such that $S \models P(X)$. Let H be the set of history variables, and $\mathcal{P}$ be the set of prophecy variables introduced by* **Refine-Arrays.** *Let $\tilde{S} := \langle X \cup H \cup \mathcal{P}, I, \tilde{T} \rangle$ and $\tilde{P} := (\bigwedge_{p \in \mathcal{P}} p = \tilde{t}(p)) \implies P(X)$ be the system and property with auxiliary variables. The function $\tilde{t}$ maps prophecy variables to their target term from* **Prophecize.** *If $Inv(X, H, \mathcal{P})$ is an inductive invariant for $\tilde{S}$ and entails $\tilde{P}$, then $\exists H \forall \mathcal{P} Inv(X, H, \mathcal{P})$ is an inductive invariant for S and entails P, where $\exists H$ and $\forall \mathcal{P}$ bind each variable in the set with the corresponding quantifier.*

Although the invariants found using counterexample-guided prophecy correspond to $\exists \forall$ invariants over the unmodified system, we must acknowledge that the existential power is very weak. The existential quantifier is only used to remove history variables. While history variables can certainly be employed for existential power in an invariant [55], these specific history variables are introduced solely to target a term for prophecy and only save a term for some fixed, finite number of steps. Thus, we do not expect to gain much existential power in finding invariants on practical problems. This use of history and prophecy variables can be thought of as quantifier instantiation at the model checking level, where the instantiation semantically uses a term appearing in an execution of the system. Consequently, our technique performs well on systems where there is only a small number of instantiations needed over terms that are not too distant in time from a potential property violation that must be disproved (i.e., not many history variables are required). This appears to be a common situation for invariant-finding benchmarks, as we show empirically in Sec. 6.

Limitations. If our CEGAR loop terminates, it either terminates with a proof or with a true counterexample. However, it is possible that the procedure may not terminate. In particular, while we can always refine the abstraction for a given bound k, there is no guarantee that this will eventually result in a refinement that rules out all spurious counterexamples (of any length).

This failure mode occurs, for instance, when no finite number of instantiations can capture all the relevant indices of the array. Consider an example system with $I := a = constarr(0)$, $T := a' = write(a, i_0, read(a, i_1) + 1)$, and $P := read(a, i_r) \geq 0$. The array a is initialized with 0 at every index, and at every step, a is updated at a single index by reading from an arbitrary index of a and adding 1 to the result. Note that the index variables are unconstrained: they can range over the integers freely at each time step. Then, the property is that every element of a is positive. This property clearly holds because of a quantified invariant maintained by the system: $\forall i \, . \, read(a, i) \geq 0$.

However, the initial abstraction is a memoryless array which can easily violate the property by returning negative values from reads. Since the array is updated in each step at an arbitrary index based on a read from another arbitrary index, no finite number of prophecy variables can capture all the relevant indices. It will successively rule out longer finite spurious counterexamples, but will never be refined enough to prove the property unboundedly. We believe that this limitation can be addressed in future work, perhaps by adapting techniques from [52]. However, it is not yet clear how to automate that process. Note that an even simpler system which does not add 1 in the update would already be problematic; however, for that case, it is straightforward to extend our algorithm to have it learn that the array does not change.

A related, but less fundamental issue is that the index set might not contain the best choice of targets for prophecy. While the index set *is* sufficient for ruling out bounded counterexamples, it is possible there is a better target for universal prophecy that does not appear in the index set. However, based on the evaluation in Sec. 6, it appears that the index set does work well in practice.

6   Experiments

Implementation. In this section, we evaluate a prototype implementation of counterexample-guided prophecy, which instantiates **Prove** with ic3ia [34] (downloaded Apr 27, 2020), an open-source C++ implementation of IC3 via Implicit Predicate Abstraction (IC3IA) [20], which is itself a CEGAR loop that uses implicit predicate abstraction to perform IC3 [12] on infinite-state systems and uses interpolants to find new predicates. ic3ia uses MathSAT [21] (version 5.6.3) as the backend SMT solver and interpolant producer. We call our prototype prophic3 [48]. In our implementation, we also include a simple abstraction-refinement wrapper which abstracts large constant integers and refines them with the actual values if that fails. This is especially useful for dealing with software benchmarks with large constant loop bounds. Otherwise, the system might need to be unrolled to a very large bound to reach an abstract counterexample.

Setup. We evaluate our tool against three state-of-the-art tools for inferring universally quantified invariants over linear arithmetic and arrays: freqhorn, quic3, and gspacer. All these tools are Constrained Horn Clause (CHC) solvers built on Z3 [54]. The algorithm implemented in freqhorn [28] is a *syntax-guided synthesis* [4] approach for inferring universally quantified invariants over arrays [29]. quic3 is built on Spacer [40], the default CHC engine in Z3, and extends IC3 over linear arithmetic and arrays to allow universally quantified frames (frames are candidates for inductive invariants maintained by the IC3 algorithm). It also maintains a set of quantifier instantiations which are provided to the underlying SMT solver. quic3 was recently incorporated into Z3. We used Z3 version 4.8.9 with parameters suggested by the quic3 authors.[4] Finally, gspacer is an extension of Spacer which adds three new inference rules for improving local generalizations with global guidance. While this last technique does not specifically target universally quantified invariants, it can be used along with the quic3 options in Spacer and potentially executes a much different search. The gspacer

---

[4] `fp.spacer.q3.use_qgen=true fp.spacer.ground_pobs=false`
  `fp.spacer.mbqi=false fp.spacer.use_euf_gen=true`

group	freqhorn (81)	quic3 (42)	vizel (32)		chc-comp (501)		tool total	
prophic3	**67**/4	**42**/0	**20**/3	1	43/159	59	172/166	60
prophic3-SA	62/4	37/0	19/3	1	36/**160**	67	154/**167**	68
freqhorn	65/4	0/0	0/1	0	5/46	1	70/51	1
quic3	55/4	34/0	15/4	1	**74**/137	75	**178**/145	76
gspacer	35/5	27/0	18/4	1	66/138	**94**	146/147	**95**
ic3ia	0/4	0/0	0/3	1	0/158	59	0/165	60
spacer	0/5	0/0	0/4	1	0/134	77	0/143	78

Fig. 3: Experimental results. The safe results are reported as $\# Q / \# QF$. The second column per group shows unsafe results, the first two groups had only safe benchmarks.

submission [43] won the arrays category in CHC-COMP 2020 [58]. We also include ic3ia and the default configuration of Spacer in our results, neither of which can produce universally quantified invariants. Our default configuration of prophic3 uses weak abstraction, but we also include a version running strong abstraction (prophic3-SA) in our experiments. We chose to build our prototype on ic3ia instead of Spacer, in part because we needed uninterpreted functions for our array abstraction, and Spacer does not handle them in a straightforward way, due to the semantics of CHC [11].

We compare these solvers on four benchmark sets: i) *freqhorn* - benchmarks from the freqhorn paper [29]; ii) *quic3* - benchmarks from the quic3 paper [37] (these were C programs from SV-COMP [8] that were modified to require universally quantified invariants); iii) *vizel* - additional benchmarks provided to us by the authors of [37]; and iv) *chc-comp-2020* - the array category benchmarks of CHC-COMP 2020 [57]. Additionally, we sort the benchmarks into three categories: 1) Q - safe benchmarks solved by some tool supporting quantified invariants but none of the solvers that do not; 2) QF - those solved by at least one of the tools that do not support quantified invariants, plus any unsafe benchmarks; and 3) U - unsolved benchmarks. Because not all of the benchmark sets were guaranteed to require quantifiers, this is an approximation of which benchmarks required quantified reasoning to prove safe.

Both prophic3 and ic3ia take a transition system and property specified in the Verification Modulo Theories (VMT) format [23], which is a transition system format built on SMT-LIB [6]. All other solvers read the CHC format. We translated benchmark sets i and iv from CHC to VMT using the *horn2vmt* program which is distributed with ic3ia. For benchmark sets ii and iii, we started with the C programs and generated both VMT and CHC using *Kratos2* (an updated version of *Kratos* [19]). We ran all experiments on a 3.5GHz Intel Xeon E5-2637 v4 CPU with a timeout of 2 hours and a memory limit of 32Gb. An artifact for reproducing these results is publicly available [49,38].

Results. The results are shown in Fig. 3. We first observe that prophic3 solves the most benchmarks in each of the first three sets, both overall and in category Q. The quic3 (and most of the freqhorn) benchmarks require quantified invariants; thus, ic3ia and Spacer cannot solve any of them. On solved instances in the Q category, prophic3 introduced an average of 1.2 prophecy variables and a median of 1. This makes sense because, upon inspection, most benchmarks only require one quantifier and we are careful to only introduce prophecy variables when needed. On benchmarks it cannot solve, `ic3ia` either times out or fails to compute an interpolant. This is expected because quantifier-free interpolants are not guaranteed over the standard theory of arrays. Even without arrays, it is also possible for `prophic3` to fail to compute an interpolant, because MathSAT's interpolation procedure is incomplete for combinations with non-convex theories such as integers. However, this was rarely observed in practice.

We also observe that `prophic3-SA` solves fewer benchmarks in the first three sets. However, it is faster on commonly solved instances. This makes sense because it needs to check fewer axioms (it uses built-in equality and thus does not check equality axioms). We suspect that it solves fewer benchmarks in the first three sets because it was unable to find the right prophecy variable. For example, for the `standard_find_true-unreach-call_ground` benchmark in the *quic3* set, a prophecy variable is needed to find a quantifier-free invariant. However, because of the stronger reasoning power of **SA**, the system can be sufficiently refined without introducing auxiliary variables. `ic3ia` is then unable to prove the property on the resulting system without the prophecy variable, instead timing out. Interestingly, notice that `prophic3-SA` solves the most benchmarks in the QF category overall, suggesting that there are practical performance benefits of the CEGAR approach even when quantified reasoning is not needed.

There was one discrepancy on the CHC-COMP 2020 benchmarks: `gspacer` disagrees with `quic3`, Spacer, and `prophic3` on *chc-LIA-lin-arrays_381*. This is the same discrepancy mentioned in the CHC-COMP 2020 report [58]. `prophic3` proved this benchmark safe without introducing any auxiliary variables and we used both CVC4 [5] and MathSAT to verify that the solution was indeed an inductive invariant for the concrete system. We are confident that this benchmark is safe and thus do not count it as a solved instance for `gspacer`.

Some of the tools are sensitive to the encoding. Since it is syntax-guided, `freqhorn` is sensitive to the encoding syntax. The freqhorn benchmarks were hand-written to be syntactically simple, an encoding which is also good for `prophic3`. However, `prophic3` can be sensitive to other encodings. For example, the quic3 benchmarks are also included in the *chc-comp-2020* set, but translated by SeaHorn [35] instead of *Kratos2*. `prophic3` does much worse on the SeaHorn encoding (6 vs 42). We stress that the CHC solvers performed similarly on both encodings, so we did not compare against disadvantaged solvers. In fact, `quic3` and `freqhorn` solved exactly the same number in both translations. However, `gspacer` solved fewer using the *Kratos2* encoding (27 vs 34). Importantly, `prophic3` on the *Kratos2* encoding solved more benchmarks than any other tool and encoding pair.

There are two main reasons why `prophic3` fails on the SeaHorn encodings. First, due to the LLVM-based encoding, some of the SeaHorn translations have index sets which are insufficient for finding the right prophecy variable. This has to do with the memory encoding and the way that fresh variables and guards are used. SeaHorn also splits memories into ranges which is problematic for our technique. Second, the SeaHorn translation is optimized for CHC, not for transition systems. For example, it introduces many new variables, and the argument order between different predicates may not match. In the transition system, this essentially has the effect of interchanging the values of variables between each loop. SeaHorn has options that address some of these issues, and these helped prophic3 solve more benchmarks, but none of these options produce encodings that work as well as the *Kratos2* encodings. The difference between good CHC and transition system encodings could also explain the overall difference in performance on *chc-comp-2020* benchmarks, most of which were translated by SeaHorn. Both of these issues are practical, not fundamental, and we believe they can be resolved with additional engineering effort.

7   Related Work

There are two important related approaches for abstracting arrays in horn clauses [53] and memories in hardware [10]. Both make a similar observation that arrays can be abstracted by modifying the property to maintain values at only a finite set of symbolic indices. We differ from the former by using a refinement loop that automatically adjusts the precision and targets relevant indices. The latter is also a refinement loop that adjusts precision, but differs in the domain and the refinement approach, which uses a multiplexer tree. We differ from both approaches in our use of array axioms to find and add auxiliary variables.

A similar lazy array axiom instantiation technique is proposed in [15]. However, their technique utilizes interpolants for finding violated axioms and cannot infer universally quantified invariants. The work of [18] also uses lazy axiom-based refinement, abstracting non-linear arithmetic with uninterpreted functions. We differ in the domain and the use of auxiliary variables. In [55], prophecy variables defined by temporal logic formulas are used for liveness and temporal proofs, with the primary goal of increasing the power of a temporal proof system. In contrast, we use prophecy variables here for a different purpose, and we also find them automatically. The work of [24] includes an approach for synthesizing auxiliary variables for modular verification of concurrent programs. Our approach differs significantly in the domain and details.

There is a substantial body of work on automated quantified invariant generation for arrays using first-order theorem provers [42,16,41,51]. These include extensions to saturation-based theorem proving to analyze specific kinds of predicates, and an extension to paramodulation-based theorem proving to produce universally quantified interpolants. In [46], the authors propose an abstract interpretation approach to synthesize universally quantified array invariants. Our method also uses abstraction, but in a CEGAR framework.

Two other notable approaches capable of proving properties over arrays that require invariants with alternating quantifiers are [30,56]. The former proposes *trace logic* for extending first-order theorem provers to software verification, and the latter takes a *counterexample-guided inductive synthesis* approach. Our approach takes a model checking perspective and differs significantly in the details.

While these approaches are more general, we compared against state-of-the-art tools that focus specifically on universally quantified invariants.

MCMT [31,33,25] and its derivatives [2,3] are backward-reachability algorithms for proving properties over "array-based systems," which are typically used to model parameterized protocols. These approaches target syntactically restricted *functional* transition systems with universally quantified properties, whereas our approach targets general transition systems. Two other approaches for solving parameterized systems modeled with arrays are [36] and [47]. The former iteratively fixes the number of expected universal quantifiers, then eagerly instantiates them and encodes the invariant search to nonlinear CHC. The latter first uses a finite-state model checker to discover an inductive invariant for a specific parameterization and then applies a heuristic generalization process. We differ from all these techniques in domain and the use of auxiliary variables. Due to the limitations explained in Sec. 5, we do not expect our approach to work well for parameterized protocol verification without improvements.

In [45], heuristics are proposed for finding predicates with free indices that can be universally quantified in a predicate abstraction-based inductive invariant search. Our approach is counterexample-guided and does not utilize predicate abstraction directly (although IC3IA does). The authors of [39] propose a technique for Java programs that associates heap memory with the program location where it was allocated and generates CHC verification conditions. This enables the discovery of invariants over all heap memory allocated at that location, which implicitly provides quantified invariants. This is similar to our approach in that it gives quantification power without explicitly using quantifiers and in that their encoding removes arrays. However, we differ in that we focus on transition systems and utilize a different paradigm to obtain this implicit quantification.

8   Conclusion

We presented a novel approach for model checking transition systems containing arrays. We observed that history and prophecy variables can be extremely useful for reducing quantified invariants to quantifier-free invariants. We demonstrated that an initially weak abstraction in our CEGAR loop can help us to *automatically* introduce relevant auxiliary variables. Finally, we evaluated our approach on four sets of interesting array-manipulating benchmarks. In future work, we hope to improve performance, explore a tighter integration with the underlying model checker, address the limitations described in Sec. 5, and investigate applications of counterexample-guided prophecy to other theories.

Acknowledgments. This work was supported by the National Science Foundation Graduate Research Fellowship Program under Grant No. DGE-1656518. Any opinions, findings, and conclusions or recommendations expressed in this material are those of the author(s) and do not necessarily reflect the views of the National Science Foundation. Additional support was provided by DARPA, under grant No. FA8650-18-2-7854. We thank these sponsors for their support. We would also like to thank Alessandro Cimatti for his invaluable feedback on the initial ideas of this paper.

References

1. Abadi, M., Lamport, L.: The existence of refinement mappings. In: Proceedings of the 3rd Annual Symposium on Logic in Computer Science. pp. 165–175 (July 1988), https://www.microsoft.com/en-us/research/publication/the-existence-of-refinement-mappings/, IICS 1988 Test of Time Award
2. Alberti, F., Bruttomesso, R., Ghilardi, S., Ranise, S., Sharygina, N.: SAFARI: smt-based abstraction for arrays with interpolants. In: CAV. Lecture Notes in Computer Science, vol. 7358, pp. 679–685. Springer (2012)
3. Alberti, F., Ghilardi, S., Sharygina, N.: Booster: An acceleration-based verification framework for array programs. In: ATVA. Lecture Notes in Computer Science, vol. 8837, pp. 18–23. Springer (2014)
4. Alur, R., Bodík, R., Dallal, E., Fisman, D., Garg, P., Juniwal, G., Kress-Gazit, H., Madhusudan, P., Martin, M.M.K., Raghothaman, M., Saha, S., Seshia, S.A., Singh, R., Solar-Lezama, A., Torlak, E., Udupa, A.: Syntax-guided synthesis. In: Dependable Software Systems Engineering, NATO Science for Peace and Security Series, D: Information and Communication Security, vol. 40, pp. 1–25. IOS Press (2015)
5. Barrett, C., Conway, C.L., Deters, M., Hadarean, L., Jovanović, D., King, T., Reynolds, A., Tinelli, C.: CVC4. In: Gopalakrishnan, G., Qadeer, S. (eds.) Proceedings of the 23rd International Conference on Computer Aided Verification (CAV '11). Lecture Notes in Computer Science, vol. 6806, pp. 171–177. Springer (Jul 2011), http://www.cs.stanford.edu/~barrett/pubs/BCD+11.pdf, snowbird, Utah
6. Barrett, C., Fontaine, P., Tinelli, C.: The Satisfiability Modulo Theories Library (SMT-LIB). www.SMT-LIB.org (2016)
7. Barrett, C.W., Tinelli, C.: Satisfiability modulo theories. In: Handbook of Model Checking, pp. 305–343. Springer (2018)
8. Beyer, D.: Software verification with validation of results - (report on SV-COMP 2017). In: TACAS (2). Lecture Notes in Computer Science, vol. 10206, pp. 331–349 (2017)
9. Biere, A., Cimatti, A., Clarke, E., Zhu, Y.: Symbolic model checking without bdds. In: Cleaveland, W.R. (ed.) Tools and Algorithms for the Construction and Analysis of Systems. pp. 193–207. Springer Berlin Heidelberg, Berlin, Heidelberg (1999)
10. Bjesse, P.: Word-level sequential memory abstraction for model checking. In: 2008 Formal Methods in Computer Aided Design. pp. 1–9 (Nov 2008). https://doi.org/10.1109/FMCAD.2008.ECP.20
11. Bjørner, N., Gurfinkel, A., McMillan, K.L., Rybalchenko, A.: Horn clause solvers for program verification. In: Fields of Logic and Computation II. Lecture Notes in Computer Science, vol. 9300, pp. 24–51. Springer (2015)
12. Bradley, A.R.: Sat-based model checking without unrolling. In: VMCAI. Lecture Notes in Computer Science, vol. 6538, pp. 70–87. Springer (2011)
13. Bradley, A.R., Manna, Z., Sipma, H.B.: What's decidable about arrays? In: Emerson, E.A., Namjoshi, K.S. (eds.) Verification, Model Checking, and Abstract Interpretation. pp. 427–442. Springer Berlin Heidelberg, Berlin, Heidelberg (2006)
14. Brummayer, R., Biere, A.: Lemmas on demand for the extensional theory of arrays. In: Proceedings of the Joint Workshops of the 6th International Workshop on Satisfiability Modulo Theories and 1st International Workshop on Bit-Precise Reasoning. p. 6–11. SMT '08/BPR '08, Association for Computing Machinery, New York, NY, USA (2008). https://doi.org/10.1145/1512464.1512467, https://doi.org/10.1145/1512464.1512467

15. Bueno, D., Cox, A., Sakallah, K.: Euficient reachability for software with arrays. In: Formal Methods in Computer Aided Design (2020)

16. Chen, Y., Kovács, L., Robillard, S.: Theory-specific reasoning about loops with arrays using vampire. In: Vampire@IJCAR. EPiC Series in Computing, vol. 44, pp. 16–32. EasyChair (2016)

17. Christ, J., Hoenicke, J.: Weakly equivalent arrays. In: Lutz, C., Ranise, S. (eds.) Frontiers of Combining Systems. pp. 119–134. Springer International Publishing, Cham (2015)

18. Cimatti, A., Griggio, A., Irfan, A., Roveri, M., Sebastiani, R.: Incremental linearization for satisfiability and verification modulo nonlinear arithmetic and transcendental functions. ACM Trans. Comput. Log. 19(3), 19:1–19:52 (2018)

19. Cimatti, A., Griggio, A., Micheli, A., Narasamdya, I., Roveri, M.: Kratos - A software model checker for systemc. In: CAV. Lecture Notes in Computer Science, vol. 6806, pp. 310–316. Springer (2011)

20. Cimatti, A., Griggio, A., Mover, S., Tonetta, S.: Infinite-state invariant checking with IC3 and predicate abstraction. Formal Methods in System Design 49(3), 190–218 (2016)

21. Cimatti, A., Griggio, A., Schaafsma, B., Sebastiani, R.: The MathSAT5 SMT Solver. In: Piterman, N., Smolka, S. (eds.) Proceedings of TACAS. LNCS, vol. 7795. Springer (2013)

22. Cimatti, A., Griggio, A., Sebastiani, R.: Computing small unsatisfiable cores in satisfiability modulo theories. J. Artif. Intell. Res. 40, 701–728 (2011)

23. Cimatti, A., Roveri, M., Griggio, A., Irfan, A.: Verification Modulo Theories. http://www.vmt-lib.org (2011)

24. Cohen, A., Namjoshi, K.S.: Local proofs for global safety properties. Formal Methods Syst. Des. 34(2), 104–125 (2009)

25. Conchon, S., Goel, A., Krstic, S., Majumdar, R., Roux, M.: Far-cubicle - A new reachability algorithm for cubicle. In: FMCAD. pp. 172–175. IEEE (2017)

26. Craig, W.: Linear reasoning. A new form of the herbrand-gentzen theorem. J. Symb. Log. 22(3), 250–268 (1957)

27. de Moura, L., Bjørner, N.: Generalized, efficient array decision procedures. In: 2009 Formal Methods in Computer-Aided Design. pp. 45–52 (Nov 2009). https://doi.org/10.1109/FMCAD.2009.5351142

28. Fedyukovich, G.: Freqhorn implementation, https://github.com/grigoryfedyukovich/aeval/commit/f5cc11808c1b73886a4e7d5a71daeffb45470b9a

29. Fedyukovich, G., Prabhu, S., Madhukar, K., Gupta, A.: Quantified invariants via syntax-guided synthesis. In: CAV (1). Lecture Notes in Computer Science, vol. 11561, pp. 259–277. Springer (2019)

30. Georgiou, P., Gleiss, B., Kovács, L.: Trace logic for inductive loop reasoning. In: Formal Methods in Computer Aided Design (2020)

31. Ghilardi, S., Ranise, S.: MCMT: A model checker modulo theories. In: Giesl, J., Hähnle, R. (eds.) Automated Reasoning. pp. 22–29. Springer Berlin Heidelberg, Berlin, Heidelberg (2010)

32. Goel, A., Krstić, S., Fuchs, A.: Deciding array formulas with frugal axiom instantiation. In: Proceedings of the Joint Workshops of the 6th International Workshop on Satisfiability Modulo Theories and 1st International Workshop on Bit-Precise Reasoning. p. 12–17. SMT '08/BPR '08, Association for Computing Machinery, New York, NY, USA (2008). https://doi.org/10.1145/1512464.1512468, https://doi.org/10.1145/1512464.1512468

33. Goel, A., Krstic, S., Leslie, R., Tuttle, M.R.: Smt-based system verification with DVF. In: SMT@IJCAR. EPiC Series in Computing, vol. 20, pp. 32–43. EasyChair (2012)
34. Griggio, A.: Open-source ic3 modulo theories with implicit predicate abstraction. https://es-static.fbk.eu/people/griggio/ic3ia/index.html (Accessed 2020), https://es-static.fbk.eu/people/griggio/ic3ia/index.html
35. Gurfinkel, A., Kahsai, T., Komuravelli, A., Navas, J.A.: The seahorn verification framework. In: CAV (1). Lecture Notes in Computer Science, vol. 9206, pp. 343–361. Springer (2015)
36. Gurfinkel, A., Shoham, S., Meshman, Y.: Smt-based verification of parameterized systems. In: SIGSOFT FSE. pp. 338–348. ACM (2016)
37. Gurfinkel, A., Shoham, S., Vizel, Y.: Quantifiers on demand. In: Lahiri, S.K., Wang, C. (eds.) Automated Technology for Verification and Analysis. pp. 248–266. Springer International Publishing, Cham (2018)
38. Hyberts, S.H., Jensen, P.G., Neele, T.: Tacas 21 artifact evaluation vm - ubuntu 20.04 lts (Sep 2020). https://doi.org/10.5281/zenodo.4041464
39. Kahsai, T., Kersten, R., Rümmer, P., Schäf, M.: Quantified heap invariants for object-oriented programs. In: LPAR. EPiC Series in Computing, vol. 46, pp. 368–384. EasyChair (2017)
40. Komuravelli, A., Gurfinkel, A., Chaki, S.: Smt-based model checking for recursive programs. In: Biere, A., Bloem, R. (eds.) Computer Aided Verification. pp. 17–34. Springer International Publishing, Cham (2014)
41. Kovács, L., Voronkov, A.: Finding loop invariants for programs over arrays using a theorem prover. In: FASE. Lecture Notes in Computer Science, vol. 5503, pp. 470–485. Springer (2009)
42. Kovács, L., Voronkov, A.: First-order theorem proving and vampire. In: CAV. Lecture Notes in Computer Science, vol. 8044, pp. 1–35. Springer (2013)
43. Krishnan, H.G.V., Gurfinkel, A.: Spacer CHC-COMP 2020 Submission (2020), https://www.starexec.org/starexec/secure/details/configuration.jsp?id=350966
44. Kroening, D., Groce, A., Clarke, E.M.: Counterexample guided abstraction refinement via program execution. In: ICFEM. Lecture Notes in Computer Science, vol. 3308, pp. 224–238. Springer (2004)
45. Lahiri, S.K., Bryant, R.E.: Indexed predicate discovery for unbounded system verification. In: CAV. Lecture Notes in Computer Science, vol. 3114, pp. 135–147. Springer (2004)
46. Li, B., Tang, Z., Zhai, J., Zhao, J.: Automatic invariant synthesis for arrays in simple programs. In: 2016 IEEE International Conference on Software Quality, Reliability and Security (QRS). pp. 108–119 (Aug 2016). https://doi.org/10.1109/QRS.2016.23
47. Ma, H., Goel, A., Jeannin, J., Kapritsos, M., Kasikci, B., Sakallah, K.A.: I4: incremental inference of inductive invariants for verification of distributed protocols. In: SOSP. pp. 370–384. ACM (2019)
48. Mann, M., Irfan, A.: Prophic3 prototype, https://github.com/makaimann/prophic3/commit/497e2fbfb813bcf0a2c3bcb5b55ad47b2a678611
49. Mann, M., Irfan, A., Griggio, A., Padon, O., Barrett, C.: FigShare Artifact for Counterexample Guided Prophecy for Model Checking Modulo the Theory of Arrays, https://doi.org/10.6084/m9.figshare.13619096
50. Mccarthy, J.: Towards a mathematical science of computation. In: In IFIP Congress. pp. 21–28. North-Holland (1962)

51. McMillan, K.L.: Quantified invariant generation using an interpolating saturation prover. In: Ramakrishnan, C.R., Rehof, J. (eds.) Tools and Algorithms for the Construction and Analysis of Systems. pp. 413–427. Springer Berlin Heidelberg, Berlin, Heidelberg (2008)

52. McMillan, K.L.: Eager abstraction for symbolic model checking. In: Chockler, H., Weissenbacher, G. (eds.) Computer Aided Verification. pp. 191–208. Springer International Publishing, Cham (2018)

53. Monniaux, D., Gonnord, L.: Cell morphing: From array programs to array-free horn clauses. In: SAS. Lecture Notes in Computer Science, vol. 9837, pp. 361–382. Springer (2016)

54. de Moura, L., Bjørner, N.: Z3: An efficient smt solver. In: Ramakrishnan, C.R., Rehof, J. (eds.) Tools and Algorithms for the Construction and Analysis of Systems. pp. 337–340. Springer Berlin Heidelberg, Berlin, Heidelberg (2008)

55. Padon, O., Hoenicke, J., McMillan, K.L., Podelski, A., Sagiv, M., Shoham, S.: Temporal prophecy for proving temporal properties of infinite-state systems. In: 2018 Formal Methods in Computer Aided Design, FMCAD 2018, Austin, TX, USA, October 30 - November 2, 2018. pp. 1–11 (2018). https://doi.org/10.23919/FMCAD.2018.8603008, https://doi.org/10.23919/FMCAD.2018.8603008

56. Polgreen, E., Seshia, S.A.: Synrg: Syntax guided synthesis of invariants with alternating quantifiers. CoRR **abs/2007.10519** (2020)

57. Rümmer, P.: CHC COMP 2020. https://chc-comp.github.io/ (2020)

58. Rümmer, P.: Competition Report: CHC-COMP-20 (2020), https://arxiv.org/abs/2008.02939

59. Sheeran, M., Singh, S., Stålmarck, G.: Checking safety properties using induction and a sat-solver. In: FMCAD. Lecture Notes in Computer Science, vol. 1954, pp. 108–125. Springer (2000)

SAT Solving with GPU Accelerated Inprocessing

Muhammad Osama (✉)[1] * ⓘ, Anton Wijs[1] † ⓘ, and Armin Biere[2] ‡ ⓘ

[1] Eindhoven University of Technology, Eindhoven, The Netherlands
[2] Johannes Kepler University, Linz, Austria

o.m.m.muhammad@tue.nl   a.j.wijs@tue.nl   biere@jku.at

Abstract. Since 2013, the leading SAT solvers in the SAT competition all use inprocessing, which unlike preprocessing, interleaves search with simplifications. However, applying inprocessing frequently can still be a bottle neck, i.e., for hard or large formulas. In this work, we introduce the first attempt to parallelize inprocessing on GPU architectures. As memory is a scarce resource in GPUs, we present new space-efficient data structures and devise a data-parallel garbage collector. It runs in parallel on the GPU to reduce memory consumption and improves memory access locality. Our new parallel variable elimination algorithm is twice as fast as previous work. In experiments our new solver PARAFROST solves many benchmarks faster on the GPU than its sequential counterparts.

Keywords: Satisfiability · Variable Elimination · Eager Redundancy Elimination · Parallel SAT Inprocessing · Parallel Garbage Collection · GPU.

1 Introduction

During the past decade, SAT solving has been used extensively in many applications, such as combinational equivalence checking [27], automatic test pattern generation [33, 40], automatic theorem proving [14], and symbolic model checking [7, 13]. Simplifying SAT problems prior to solving them has proven its effectiveness in modern conflict-driven clause learning (CDCL) SAT solvers [5, 6, 17], particularly when applied on real-world applications relevant to software and hardware verification [16, 20, 22, 24].

Since 2013, simplification techniques [8, 16, 19, 21, 41] are also used periodically *during* SAT solving, which is known as *inprocessing* [3–6, 23]. Applying inprocessing iteratively to large problems can be a performance bottleneck in SAT solving procedure, or even increase the size of the formula, negatively impacting the solving time.

Graphics processors (GPUs) have become attractive for general-purpose computing with the availability of the Compute Unified Device Architecture (CUDA) programming model. CUDA is widely used to accelerate applications that are computationally intensive w.r.t. data processing. For instance, we have applied GPUs to accelerate explicit-state model checking [11, 43], bisimilarity checking [42], the reconstruction of

---

* This work is part of the GEARS project with project number TOP2.16.044, which is (partly) financed by the Netherlands Organisation for Scientific Research (NWO).
† We gratefully acknowledge the support of NVIDIA Corporation with the donation of the GeForce Titan RTX used for this research.
‡ Partially funded by the LIT AI Lab.

genetic networks [12], wind turbine emulation [30], metaheuristic SAT solving [44], and SAT-based test generation [33]. Recently, we introduced SIGmA [34, 35] as the first SAT simplification preprocessor to exploit GPUs.

Contributions. Embedding GPU inprocessing in a SAT solver is highly non-trivial and has never been attempted before, according to the best of our knowledge. Efficient data structures are needed that allow parallel processing, and that support efficient adding and removing of clauses. For this purpose, we contribute the following:

1. We propose a new dynamically expanded data structure for clauses supporting both 32-bit [17] and 64-bit references with a minimum of 20 bytes per clause.
2. A new parallel garbage collector is presented, tailored for GPU inprocessing.
3. Our new parallel variable elimination algorithm is twice as fast as [34] and together with other improvements yields much higher performance and robustness.
4. Our parallel inprocessing is deterministic (i.e., results are reproducible).

In addition, we propose a new preprocessing technique targeted towards data-parallel execution, called *Eager Redundancy Elimination* (ERE), which is applicable on both original and learnt clauses. All contributions have been implemented in our solver PARAFROST and benchmarked on a larger set than considered previously in [34], using 493 application problems. We discuss the potential performance gain of the GPU inprocessing and its impact on SAT solving, compared to a sequential version of our solver as well as CADICAL [6], a state-of-the-art solver developed by the last author.

2 Preliminaries

All SAT formulas in this paper are in conjunctive normal form (CNF). A CNF formula is a conjunction of m clauses $\bigwedge_{i=1}^{m} C_i$, where each clause C_i is a disjunction of k literals $\bigvee_{j=1}^{k} \ell_j$, and a literal is a Boolean variable x or its complement $\neg x$, which we refer to as $\bar{x}$. We represent clauses by sets of literals, i.e., $\{\ell_1, \ldots, \ell_k\}$ represents the formula $\ell_1 \vee \ldots \vee \ell_k$, and a SAT formula by a set of clauses, i.e., $\{C_1, \ldots, C_m\}$ represents the formula $C_1 \wedge \ldots \wedge C_m$. With $\mathcal{S}_\ell$, we refer to the set of clauses containing literal ℓ, i.e., $\mathcal{S}_\ell = \{C \in \mathcal{S} \mid \ell \in C\}$. If for a variable x, we have either $\mathcal{S}_x = \emptyset$ or $\mathcal{S}_{\bar{x}} = \emptyset$ (but not both), then the literal $\bar{x}$ or x, respectively, is called a *pure literal*. A clause C is a *tautology* iff there exists a variable x with $\{x, \bar{x}\} \subseteq C$, and C is *unit* iff $|C| = 1$.

In this paper we integrate GPU-accelerated inprocessing and CDCL [28, 32, 36]. One important aspect of CDCL is to learn from previous assignments to prune the search space and make better decisions in the future. This learning process involves the periodic adding of new *learnt* clauses to the input formula while CDCL is running.

In this paper, clauses are either considered to be LEARNT or ORIGINAL (*redundant* and *irredundant* in [23] and in the SAT solver CADICAL [6]). A LEARNT clause is added to the formula by the CDCL clause learning process, and an ORIGINAL clause is part of the formula from the very start. Furthermore, each assignment is associated with a *decision level* that acts as a time stamp, to monitor the order in which assignments are performed. The first assignment is made at decision level one.

Variable Elimination (VE). Variables can be removed from clauses by either applying the *resolution rule* or *substitution* (also known as gate equivalence reasoning) [16, 23].

Concerning the former, we represent application of the resolution rule w.r.t. some variable x using a *resolving operator* $\otimes_x$ on clauses C_1 and C_2. The result of applying the rule is called the *resolvent* [41]. It is defined as $C_1 \otimes_x C_2 = C_1 \cup C_2 \setminus \{x, \bar{x}\}$, and can be applied iff $x \in C_1$, $\bar{x} \in C_2$. The $\otimes_x$ operator can be extended to resolve sets of clauses w.r.t. variable x. For a formula $\mathcal{S}$, let $\mathcal{L} \subset \mathcal{S}$ be the set of learnt clauses when we apply the resolution rule. The set of new resolvents is then defined as $R_x(\mathcal{S}) = \{C_1 \otimes_x C_2 \mid C_1 \in \mathcal{S}_x \setminus \mathcal{L} \wedge C_2 \in \mathcal{S}_{\bar{x}} \setminus \mathcal{L} \wedge \neg\exists y.\{y, \bar{y}\} \subseteq C_1 \otimes_x C_2\}$. Notice that the learnt clauses can be ignored [23] (i.e., in practice, it is not effective to apply resolution on learnt clauses). The last condition avoids that a resolvent should not be a tautology. After eliminating variable x in $\mathcal{S}$, the resulting formula $\mathcal{S}'$ is defined as $\mathcal{S}' = R_x(\mathcal{S}) \cup (\mathcal{S} \setminus (\mathcal{S}_x \cup \mathcal{S}_{\bar{x}}))$, i.e., the new resolvents are combined with the original and learnt clauses that do not reference x.

Substitution detects patterns encoding logical gates, and substitutes the involved variables with their gate-equivalent counterparts. Previously [34], we only considered AND gates. In the current work, we add support for *Inverter*, *If-Then-Else* and *XOR* gate extractions. For all logical gates, substitution can be performed by resolving non-gate clauses (i.e., clauses not contributing to the gate itself) with gate clauses [23].

For instance, the first three clauses in the formula $\{\{x, \bar{a}, \bar{b}\}, \{\bar{x}, a\}, \{\bar{x}, b\}, \{x, c\}\}$ together encode a logical AND-gate, hence the final clause can be resolved with the second and the third clauses, producing the simplified formula $\{\{a, c\}, \{b, c\}\}$. Combining gate equivalence reasoning with the resolution rule tends to result in smaller formulas compared to only applying the resolution rule [16, 23, 37].

Subsumption elimination. SUB performs *self-subsuming resolution* followed by *subsumption elimination* [16]. The former can be applied on clauses C_1, C_2 iff for some variable x, we have $C_1 = C_1' \cup \{x\}$, $C_2 = C_2' \cup \{\bar{x}\}$, and $C_2' \subseteq C_1'$. In that case, x can be removed from C_1. The latter is applied on clauses C_1, C_2 with $C_2 \subseteq C_1$. In that case, C_1 is redundant and can be removed. If C_2 is a LEARNT clause, it must be considered as ORIGINAL in the future, to prevent deleting it during learnt clause reduction, a procedure which attempts to reduce the number of learnt clauses [6, 23]. For instance, consider the formula $\mathcal{S} = \{\{a, b, c\}, \{\bar{a}, b\}, \{b, c, d\}\}$. The first clause is self-subsumed by the second clause w.r.t. variable a and can be strengthened to $\{b, c\}$ which in turn subsumes the last clause $\{b, c, d\}$. The latter clause is then removed from $\mathcal{S}$ and the simplified formula becomes $\{\{b, c\}, \{\bar{a}, b\}\}$.

Blocked clause elimination. BCE [25] can remove clauses for which variable elimination always results in tautologies. Consider the formula $\{\{a, b, c\}, \{\bar{a}, \bar{b}\}, \{\bar{a}, \bar{c}\}\}$. All three literals a, b and c are blocking the first clause, since resolving a produces the tautologies $\{\{b, c, \bar{b}\}, \{b, c, \bar{c}\}\}$, resolving b produces $\{\bar{a}, a, c\}$, and resolving c produces $\{\bar{a}, a, b\}$. Hence the blocked clause $\{a, b, c\}$ can be removed from $\mathcal{S}$. Again, as for VE, only original clauses are considered.

Eager Redundancy Elimination. ERE is a new elimination technique that we propose, which repeats the following until a fixpoint has been reached: for a given formula $\mathcal{S}$ and clauses $C_1 \in \mathcal{S}, C_2 \in \mathcal{S}$ with $x \in C_1$ and $\bar{x} \in C_2$ for some variable x, if there exists a clause $C \in \mathcal{S}$ for which $C \equiv C_1 \otimes_x C_2$, then let $\mathcal{S} := \mathcal{S} \setminus \{C\}$. In this work, we restrict removing C to the condition (C_1 is LEARNT $\vee$ C_2 is LEARNT) $\implies$ C is LEARNT.

If the condition holds, C is called a *redundancy* and can be removed without altering the original satisfiability. For example, consider $S = \{\{a, \bar{c}\}, \{c, b\}, \{\bar{d}, \bar{c}\}, \{b, a\}, \{a, d\}\}$. Resolving the first two clauses gives the resolvent $\{a, b\}$ which is equivalent to the fourth clause in S. Also, resolving the third clause with the last clause yields $\{a, \bar{c}\}$ which is equivalent to the first clause in S. ERE can remove either $\{a, \bar{c}\}$ or $\{a, b\}$ but not both. Note that this method is entirely different from *Asymmetric Tautology Elimination* in [21]. The latter requires adding so-called hidden literals to all clauses to check which is a hidden tautology. ERE can operate on learnt clauses and does not require literals addition, making it more effective and adequate to data parallelism.

3   GPU Memory and Data Structures

GPU Architecture. Since 2007, NVIDIA has been developing a parallel computing platform called CUDA [31] that allows developers to use GPU resources for general purpose processing. A GPU contains multiple streaming multiprocessors (SMs), each SM consisting of an array of streaming processors (SPs). Every SM can execute multiple threads grouped together in 32-thread scheduling units called *warps*.

A GPU computation can be launched in a program by the *host* (CPU side of a program) by calling a GPU function called a *kernel*, which is executed by the *device* (GPU side of a program). When a kernel is called, it is specified how many threads need to execute it. These threads are partitioned into thread *blocks* of up to 1,024 threads (or 32 warps). Each block is assigned to an SM. All threads together form a *grid*. A hardware warp scheduler evenly distributes the launched blocks to the available SMs. Concerning the memory hierarchy, a GPU has multiple types of memory:

- *Global memory* with high bandwidth but also high latency is accessible by both GPU threads and CPU threads and thus acts as interface between CPU and GPU.
- *Constant memory* is read-only for all GPU threads. It has a lower latency than global memory, and can be used to store any pre-defined constants.
- *Shared memory* is on-chip memory shared by the threads in a block. Each SM has its own shared memory. It is much smaller in size than global and constant memory (in the order of tens of kilobytes), but has a much lower latency. It can be used to efficiently communicate data between threads in a block.
- *Registers* are used for on-chip storage of thread-local data. It is very small, but provides the fastest memory.

To hide the latency of global memory, ensuring that the threads perform *coalesced accesses* is one of the best practices. When the threads in a warp try to access a consecutive block of 32-bit words, their accesses are combined into a single (coalesced) memory access. Uncoalesced memory accesses can, for instance, be caused by data sparsity or misalignment. Furthermore, we use *unified memory* [31] to store the main data structures that need to be regularly accessed by both the CPU and the GPU. Unified memory creates a pool of managed memory that is shared between the CPU and GPU. This pool is accessible to both sides using the same addresses. Regarding atomicity, a GPU can run *atomic* instructions on both global and shared memory. Such an instruction performs a *read-modify-write* memory operation on one 32-bit or 64-bit word.

```
class SCLAUSE {                          class CNF {
    char state, flag;                        struct {
    char added, used;                            uint32* memory;
    int size, lbd;                               uint64 size, cap;
    uint32 sig;                              } clauses;
    union {                                  struct {
        uint32 literals[1];                      uint64* memory;
    };                                           uint32 size, cap;
}                                            } references;
                                         }
        (a) container for a clause              (b) container for a formula
```

Fig. 1: Data structures to store a SAT formula on a GPU

Data Structures. To efficiently implement inprocessing techniques for GPU architectures, we designed a new data structure from scratch to count the number of learnt clauses, and store other relevant clause information, while keeping the memory consumption as low as possible. Fig. 1 shows the proposed structures to store a clause (denoted by SCLAUSE) and the SAT formula represented in CNF form (denoted by CNF). The state member in Fig. 1a stores the current *clause state*. A clause is either ORIGINAL, LEARNT (see Section 2) or DELETED. A GPU thread is not allowed to deallocate memory, however, a clause can be set to DELETED and freed later during garbage collection. The members added and flag mark the clause for being resolvent (when applying the resolution rule) and contributing to a gate (for substitution), respectively. The lbd entry denotes the *literal block distance* (LBD), i.e., the number of decision levels contributing to a conflict [2]. The used counter is used to keep track of how long a LEARNT clause should be used before it gets deleted during database reduction [6,38]. Both used and lbd can be altered via clause *strengthening* [6] in SUB.

The signature (sig) of a clause is computed by hashing its literals to a 32-bit value [16]. It is used to quickly compare clauses. The first literal in a clause is preallocated and stored in the fixed array literals[1]. As has been done for the MINISAT solver, we adapted the union structure to allow dynamically expanding the literals array. This is accepted by NVIDIA's compiler (NVCC). In our previous work [34], we stored a pointer in each clause referencing the first literal, with the literals being in a separate array. This consumes 8 bytes of the clause space. However, SCLAUSE only needs 4 bytes for the literals array, resulting in the clause occupying 20 bytes in total, including the extra information of the learnt clause, compared to 24 bytes in our previous work.

As implemented in MINISAT, we use the clauses field in CNF (Fig. 1b) to store the raw bytes of SCLAUSE instances with any extra literals in 4-byte buckets with 64-bit reference support. The cap variable indicates the total memory capacity available for the storage of clauses, and size reflects the current size of the list of clauses. We always have size ≤ cap. The references field is used to directly access the clauses by saving for each clause a reference to their first bucket. The mechanism for storing references works in the same way as for clauses.

In addition, in a similar way, an *occurrence table* structure, denoted by OT, is created which has a raw pointer to store the 64-bit clause references for each literal in the formula and a member structure OL. The creation of an OL instance is done in parallel on the GPU for each literal using atomic instructions. For each clause C, a thread is launched to insert the occurrences of C's literals in the associated lists.

Initially, we pre-allocate unified memory for clauses and references which is in size twice as large as the input formula, to guarantee enough space for the original and learnt clauses. This amount is guaranteed to be enough as we enforce that the number of resolvents never exceeds the number of ORIGINAL clauses. The OT memory is real-located dynamically if needed after each variable elimination. Furthermore, we check the amount of free available GPU memory before allocation is done. If no memory is available, the inprocessing step is skipped and the solving continues on the CPU.

4 Parallel Garbage Collection

Modern sequential SAT solvers implement a *garbage collection* (GC) algorithm to reduce memory consumption and maintain data locality [2, 6, 17].

Since GPU global memory is a scarce resource and coalesced accesses are essential to hide the latency of global memory (see Section 2), we decided to develop an efficient and parallel GC algorithm for the GPU without adding overhead to the GPU computations.

Fig. 2 demonstrates the proposed approach for a simple SAT formula $S = \{\{a, \bar{b}, c\}, \{a, b, \bar{c}\}, \{d, \bar{b}\}, \{\bar{d}, b\}\}$, in which $\{a, b, \bar{c}\}$ is to be deleted. The figure shows, in addition, how the references and clauses lists in Fig. 1b are updated for the given formula. The reference for each clause C is calculated based on the sum of the sizes (in buckets) of all clauses preceding C in the list of clauses. For example, the first clause (C_1) requires $\alpha + (k - 1) = 5 + 2 = 7$ buckets, where the constant α is the number of buckets needed to store SCLAUSE, in our case 20 bytes / 4 bytes, and k is the clause size in terms of the number of literals. Given the number of buckets needed for C_1, the next clause (C_2) must be stored starting from position 7

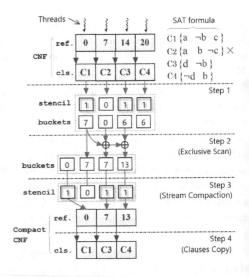

Fig. 2: An example of parallel GC on a GPU

in the list of clauses. This position plus the size of C_2 determines in a similar way the starting position for C_3, and so on.

The first step towards compacting the CNF instance when C_2 is to be deleted is to compute a *stencil* and a list of corresponding clause sizes in terms of numbers of buckets. In this step, each clause C_i is inspected by a different thread that writes a '0'

Algorithm 1: Parallel Garbage Collection

Input : __global__ $\mathcal{S}_{in}$, stencil, buckets, __constant__ α, __shared__ shCls, shLits
Output: numCls, numLits

1   numCls, numLits ← COUNTSURVIVED($\mathcal{S}_{in}$);
2   $\mathcal{S}_{out}$ ← ALLOCATE(numCls, numLits);
3   stencil, buckets ← COMPUTESTENCIL($\mathcal{S}_{in}$);
4   buckets ← EXCLUSIVESCAN(buckets);
5   references($\mathcal{S}_{out}$) ← COMPACTREFS(buckets, stencil);
6   COPYCLAUSES($\mathcal{S}_{out}$, $\mathcal{S}_{in}$, buckets, stencil);

7   **kernel** COUNTSURVIVED ($\mathcal{S}_{in}$):
8   *register* rCls ← 0, rLits ← 0;
9   **for all** $i \in [\![0, |\mathcal{S}_{in}|]\!]$ **in parallel**
10   *register* C ← $\mathcal{S}_{in}[i]$;
11   **if** $state(C) \neq DELETED$ **then**
12   rCls ← rCls + 1, rLits ← rLits + |C|;
13   **if** tid < $|\mathcal{S}_{in}|$ **then**
14   shCls[tid] = rCls, shLits[tid] = rLits;
15   **else**
16   shCls[tid] = 0, shLits[tid] = 0;
17   SYNCTHREADS();
18   **for** $b : blockDim/2, b/2 \rightarrow 1$ **do**   // b will be blockDim/2, (blockDim/2)/2, ..., 1
19   **if** tid < b **then**
20   shCls[tid] ← shCls[tid] + shCls[tid + b], shLits[tid] ← shLits[tid] + shLits[tid + b];
21   SYNCTHREADS();
22   **if** tid = 0 **then**
23   ATOMICADD(numCls, shCls[tid]), ATOMICADD(numLits, shLits[tid]);
24   **kernel** COMPUTESTENCIL ($\mathcal{S}_{in}$):
25   **for all** $i \in [\![0, |\mathcal{S}_{in}|]\!]$ **in parallel**
26   *register* C ← $\mathcal{S}_{in}[i]$;
27   **if** $state(C) = DELETED$ **then**
28   stencil[i] ← 0, buckets[i] ← 0;
29   **else**
30   stencil[i] ← 1, buckets[i] ← $\alpha + (|C| - 1)$;
31   **kernel** COPYCLAUSES ($\mathcal{S}_{out}$, $\mathcal{S}_{in}$, buckets, stencil):
32   **for all** $i \in [\![0, |\mathcal{S}_{in}|]\!]$ **in parallel**
33   **if** stencil[i] **then**
34   *register* & C_{dest} ← (SCLAUSE &)(clauses($\mathcal{S}_{out}$) + buckets[i]);
35   C_{dest} ← $\mathcal{S}_{in}[i]$;

---

at position i of a list named stencil if the clause must be deleted, and a '1' otherwise. The size of stencil is equal to the number of clauses. In a list of the same size called buckets, the thread writes at position i '0' if the clause will be deleted, and otherwise the size of the clause in terms of the number of buckets.

At step 2, a parallel *exclusive-segmented scan* operation is applied on the buckets array to compute the new references. In this scan, the value stored at position i, masked by the corresponding stencil, is the sum of the values stored at positions 0 up to, but not including, i. An optimised GPU implementation of this operation is available via the CUDA CUB library [29], which transforms a list of size n in $\log(n)$ iterations. In the example, this results in C_3 being assigned reference 7, thereby replacing C_2.

At step 3, the stencil list is used to update references in parallel, which are be kept together in consecutive positions. The standard DeviceSelect::Flagged function of the CUB library can be used for this, which uses stream compaction [10]. Finally, the actual clauses are copied to their new locations in clauses.

Alg. 1 describes in detail the GPU implementation of the parallel GC. As input, Alg. 1 requires a SAT formula $\mathcal{S}_{in}$ as an instance of CNF. The constant α is kept in

GPU constant memory for fast access. The highlighted lines in grey are executed on GPU. To begin GC, we count the number of clauses and literals in the S_{in} formula after simplification has been applied (line 1). The counting is done via the parallel reduction kernel COUNTSURVIVED, listed at lines 7-23. In kernels, we use two conventions. First of all, with *tid*, we refer to the *block-local* ID of the executing thread. By using this ID, we can achieve that different threads in the same block work on different data, as for instance at lines 13-16. Second of all, we use so-called *grid-stride loops* to process data elements in parallel. An example of this starts at line 9. The statement **for all** $i \in [\![0, N]\!]$ **in parallel** expresses that all natural numbers in the range $[0, N)$ must be considered in the loop, and that this is done in parallel by having each executing thread start with element *tid*, i.e., $i = tid$, and before starting each additional iteration through the loop, the thread adds to i the total number of threads on the GPU. If the updated i is smaller than N, the next iteration is performed with this updated i. Otherwise, the thread exits the loop. A grid-stride loop ensures that when the range of numbers to consider is larger than the number of threads, all numbers are still processed.

The values *rCls* and *rLits* at line 8 will hold the current number of clauses and literals, respectively, counted by the executing thread. The **register** keyword indicates that the variables are stored in the thread-local register memory. Within the loop at lines 9-12, the counters *rCls*, *rLits* are updated incrementally if the clause at position i in clauses is not deleted. Once a thread has checked all its assigned clauses, it stores the counter values in the (block-local) shared memory arrays (*shCls*, *shLits*) at lines 13-14.

A non-participating thread simply writes zeros (line 16). Next, all threads in the block are synchronised by the SYNCTHREADS call. The loop at lines 18-21 performs the actual parallel reduction to accumulate the number of non-deleted clauses and literals in shared memory within thread blocks. In the **for** loop, b is initially set to the number of threads in the block (*blockDim*), and in each iteration, this value is divided by 2 until it is equal to 1 (note that blocks always consist of a power of two number of threads).

The total number of clauses and threads is in the end stored by thread 0, and this thread adds those numbers using atomic instructions to the globally stored counters *numCls* and *numLits* at line 23, resulting in the final output. In the procedure described here, we prevent having each thread perform atomic instructions on the global memory, by which we avoid a potential performance bottleneck. The computed numbers are used to allocate enough memory for the output formula at line 2 on the CPU side.

The kernel COMPUTESTENCIL, called at line 3, is responsible for checking clause states and computing the number of buckets for each clause. The COMPUTESTENCIL kernel is given at lines 24-30. If a clause C is set to DELETED (line 27), the corresponding entries in stencil and buckets are cleared at line 28, otherwise the stencil entry is set to 1 and the buckets entry is updated with the number of clause buckets.

The EXCLUSIVESCAN routine at line 4 calculates the new references to store the remaining clauses based on the collected buckets. For that, we use the exclusive scan method offered by the CUB library. The COMPACTREFS routine called at line 5 groups the *valid* references, i.e., those flagged by stencil, into consecutive values and stores them in references(S_{out}), which refers to the references field of the output formula S_{out}. Finally, copying clause contents (literals, state, etc.) is done in the COPY-CLAUSES kernel, called at line 6. This kernel is described at lines 31-35. If a clause in

S_{in} is flagged by `stencil` via thread i, then a new SCLAUSE reference is created in clauses(S_{out}), which refers to the `clauses` field in S_{out}, offset by `buckets[i]`.

The GC mechanism described above resulted from experimenting with several less efficient mechanisms first. In the first attempt, two atomic additions per thread were performed for each clause, one to move the non-deleted clause buckets and the other for moving the corresponding reference. However, the excessive use of atomics resulted in a performance bottleneck and produced a different simplified formula on each run, that is, the order in which the new clauses were stored depended on the outcome of the atomic instructions. The second attempt was to maintain stability by moving the GC to the host side. However, accessing unified memory on the host side results in a performance penalty, as it implicitly results in copying data to the host side.

5   Parallel Inprocessing Procedure

To exploit parallelism in simplifications, each elimination method is applied on multiple variables simultaneously. Doing so is non-trivial, since variables may *depend* on each other; two variables x and y are dependent iff there exists a clause C with $(x \in C \vee \bar{x} \in C) \wedge (y \in C \vee \bar{y} \in C)$. If both x and y were to be processed for simplification, two threads might manipulate C at the same time. To guarantee soundness of the parallel simplifications, we apply our *least constrained variable elections* algorithm (LCVE) [34] prior to simplification. It is responsible for electing a set of mutually independent variables (candidates) from a set of authorised candidates. The remaining variables relying on the elected ones are frozen. These notions are defined by Defs. 1-4.

Definition 1 (Authorised candidates). *Given a CNF formula S, we call A the set of* authorised candidates: $A = \{x \mid 1 \leq h[x] \leq \mu \vee 1 \leq h[\bar{x}] \leq \mu\}$, *where*

- h *is a histogram array ($h[x]$ is the number of occurrences of x in S).*
- μ *denotes a given maximum number of occurrences allowed for both x and its negation $\bar{x}$, representing the cut-off point for the LCVE algorithm.*

Definition 2 (Candidate Dependency Relation). *We call a relation $D : A \times A$ a* candidate dependency relation *iff $\forall x, y \in A$, $x \mathcal{D} y$ implies that $\exists C \in S.(x \in C \vee \bar{x} \in C) \wedge (y \in C \vee \bar{y} \in C)$*

Definition 3 (Elected candidates). *Given a set of authorised candidates A, we call a* set $\varphi \subseteq A$ a set of *elected candidates iff $\forall x, y \in \varphi. \neg(x \mathcal{D} y)$*

Definition 4 (Frozen candidates). *Given the sets A and φ, the set of* frozen candidates *$F \subseteq A$ is defined as $F = \{x \mid x \in A \wedge \exists y \in \varphi. x \mathcal{D} y\}$*

A top-level description of GPU parallel inprocessing is shown in Alg. 2. The blue-colored lines highlight new contributions of the current work compared to our preprocessing algorithm presented in [34]. As input, it takes the current formula S_h from the solver (executed on the host) and copies it to the device global memory as S_d (line 1).

Initially, before simplification, we compute the clause signatures and order variables via concurrent streams at lines 2-3. A stream is a sequence of instructions that are executed in issue-order on the GPU [31]. The use of concurrent streams allows the running

---

Algorithm 2: Parallel Inprocessing

Input : $\mathcal{S}_h$, μ, phases

1. $\mathcal{S}_d \leftarrow$ COPYTODEVICE $(\mathcal{S}_h)$;
2. CALCSIGNATURES $(\mathcal{S}_d, stream0)$;
3. $\mathcal{A} \leftarrow$ ORDERVARIABLES $(\mathcal{S}_d, stream1)$;
4. **while** $p : 0 \rightarrow phases$ **do**
5.   SYNCALL ( );   // Synchronize all streams
6. $\mathcal{T} \leftarrow$ CREATEOT $(\mathcal{S}_d)$;
7.   PROPAGATE $(\mathcal{U}_h, \mathcal{S}_d, \mathcal{T})$;
8. $\varphi \leftarrow$ LCVE $(\mathcal{S}_d, \mathcal{T}, \mathcal{A}, \mu)$;
9.   **if** $p = phases$ **then**
10.   ERE $(\mathcal{S}_d, \mathcal{T}, \varphi)$;
11.   break;
12.   SORTOT $(\mathcal{T}, \varphi, \text{LISTKEY})$;
13. $\mathcal{U}_d \leftarrow$ ELIMINATE $(\mathcal{S}_d, \mathcal{T}, \varphi)$;   // Applies VE, SUB, and BCE
14. $\mathcal{U}_h \leftarrow$ COPYTOHOSTASYNC $(\mathcal{U}_d, stream1)$;
15.   COLLECT $(\mathcal{S}_d, stream2)$;
16. $\mu \leftarrow \mu \times 2$;

17. **device function** LISTKEY (a, b):
18. $C_a \leftarrow \mathcal{S}_d[a], C_a \leftarrow \mathcal{S}_d[b]$;   // $C_a = \{x_1, x_2, \ldots, x_k\}, C_b = \{y_1, y_2, \ldots, y_k\}$
19.   **if** $|C_a| \neq |C_b|$ **then return** $C_a < C_b$;
20.   **if** $x_1 \neq y_1$ **then return** $x_1 < y_1$;
21.   **if** $x_2 \neq y_2$ **then return** $x_2 < y_2$;
22.   **if** $|C_a| > 2 \wedge (x_k \neq y_k)$ **then return** $x_k < y_k$;
23.   **else return** $sig(C_a) < sig(C_b)$;

---

of multiple GPU kernels concurrently, if there are enough resources. The ORDERVARI-ABLES routine produces an ordered array of authorised candidates $\mathcal{A}$ following Def. 1. The **while** loop at lines 4-16 applies VE, SUB, and BCE, for a configured number of iterations (indicated by *phases*), with increasingly large values of the threshold μ. Increasing μ exponentially allows LCVE to elect additional variables in the next elimination phase since after a phase is executed on the GPU, many elected variables are eliminated. The ERE method is computationally expensive. Therefore, it is only executed once in the final iteration, at line 10. At line 5, SYNCALL is called to synchronize all streams being executed. At line 6, the occurrence table $\mathcal{T}$ is created. The LCVE routine produces on the host side an array of elected mutually independent variables φ, in line with Def. 3.

The parallel creation of the occurrence lists in $\mathcal{T}$ results in the order of these lists being chosen non-deterministically. This results in the ELIMINATE procedure called at line 13, which performs the parallel simplifications, to produce results non-deterministically as well. To remedy this effect, the lists in $\mathcal{T}$ are sorted according to a unique key in ascending order. Besides the benefit of stability, this allows SUB to abort early when performing subsumption checks. The sorting key function is given as the device function LISTKEY at lines 17-24. It takes two references a, b and fetches the corresponding clauses C_a, C_b from $\mathcal{S}_d$ (line 18). First, clause sizes are tested at line 19. If they are equal, the first, the second, and the last literal in each clause are checked, respectively, at lines 20-22. Otherwise, clause signatures are tested at line 23. CADICAL implements a similar function, but only considers clause sizes [6]. The SORTOT routine launches a kernel to sort the lists pointed to by the variables in φ in parallel. Each thread runs an insertion sort to in-place swap clause references using LISTKEY.

The ELIMINATE procedure at line 13 calls SUB to remove any subsumed clauses or strengthen clauses if possible, after which VE is applied, followed by BCE. The SUB and BCE methods call kernels that scan the occurrence lists of all variables in φ in parallel. For more information on this, see [34]. The VE method uses a new parallel approach, which is explained in Section 6. Both the VE and SUB methods may add new unit clauses atomically to a separate array $\mathcal{U}_d$. The propagation of these units cannot be done immediately on the GPU due to possible data races, as multiple variables in a clause may occur in unit clauses. For instance, if we have unit clauses $\{a\}$ and $\{b\}$, and these would be processed by different threads, then a clause $\{\bar{a}, \bar{b}, c\}$ could be updated by both threads simultaneously. Thus, this propagation is delayed until the next iteration, and performed by the host at line 7. Note that $\mathcal{T}$ must be recreated first to consider all resolvents added by VE during the previous phase. The ERE method at line 10 is executed only once at the last phase (*phases*) before the loop is terminated. Section 7 explains in detail how ERE can be effective in simplifying both ORIGINAL and LEARNT clauses in parallel. At line 14, new units are copied from the device to the host array $\mathcal{U}_h$ asynchronously via *stream1*. The COLLECT procedure does the GC as described by Alg. 4 via *stream2*. Both streams are synchronized at line 5.

6 Three-Phase Parallel Variable Elimination

The BVIPE algorithm in our previous work [34] had a main shortcoming due to the heavy use of atomic operations to add new resolvents. Per eliminated variable, two atomic instructions were performed, one for adding new clauses and the other for adding new literals. Besides performance degradation, this also resulted in the order of added clauses being chosen non-deterministically, which impacted reproducibility (even though the produced formula would always at least be logically the same).

The approach to avoiding the excessive use of atomic instructions when adding new resolvents is to perform parallel VE in *three phases*. The first phase scans the constructed list φ to identify the elimination type (e.g., resolution or gate substitution) of each variable and to calculate the number of resolvents and their corresponding buckets.

The second phase computes an exclusive scan to determine the new references for adding resolvents, as is done in our GC mechanism (Section 4). At the last phase, we store the actual resolvents in their new locations in the simplified formula. For solution reconstruction, we use an atomic addition to count the resolved literals. The order in which they are resolved is irrelevant. The same is done for adding units. For the latter, experiments show that the number of added units is relatively small compared to the eliminated variables, hence the penalty of using atomic instructions is almost negligible. It would be overkill to use a segmented scan for adding literals or units.

At line 1 of Alg. 3, phase 1 is executed by the VARIABLESWEEP kernel (given at lines 15-27). Every thread scans the clause set of its designated literals x and $\bar{x}$ (line 17). References to these clauses are stored at $\mathcal{T}_x$ and $\mathcal{T}_{\bar{x}}$. Moreover, register variables t, β, γ are created to hold the current *type*, number of *added clauses*, and number of *added literals* of x, respectively. If x is *pure* at line 19, then there are no resolvents to add and the clause sets of x and $\bar{x}$ are directly marked as DELETED by the routine TOBLIVION. Moreover, this routine adds the marked literals atomically to resolved. At line 22, we

---

Algorithm 3: Three-Phase Parallel Variable Elimination

Input : ___global___ $\varphi, \mathcal{S}_d, \mathcal{T}, \mathcal{U}_d$, resolved, type, buckets, added, ___constant___ α

1   resolved, type, buckets, added $\leftarrow$ VARIABLESWEEP($\varphi, \mathcal{S}_d, \mathcal{T}$);
2   $last_{added} \leftarrow -1, last_{idx} \leftarrow -1, last_{cref} \leftarrow -1, last_C \leftarrow \emptyset$;
3   **for** $j : |\varphi| - 1, j - 1 \rightarrow 0$ **do**   // find index and # resolvents of last eliminated x
4 | **if** $type[j] \neq 0$ **then**
5 | | $last_{idx} \leftarrow j, last_{added} \leftarrow$ added$[j]$; **break**;
6   buckets $\leftarrow$ EXCLUSIVESCAN (buckets, SIZE(clauses), *stream0*);
7   added $\leftarrow$ EXCLUSIVESCAN (added, SIZE(references), *stream1*);
8   SYNCALL( );
9   $numCls \leftarrow last_{added} +$ added$[last_{idx}]$;
10   $last_{cref} \leftarrow$ references$[numCls - 1], last_C \leftarrow$ clauses$[last_{cref}]$;
11   $numBuckets \leftarrow last_{cref} + (\alpha +$ SIZE$(last_C) - 1)$;
12   RESIZE(clauses, *numBuckets*), RESIZE(references, *numCls*);
13   $\mathcal{S}_d, \mathcal{U}_d \leftarrow$ VARIABLERESOLVENT($\varphi, \mathcal{S}_d, \mathcal{T}$, type, buckets, added);
14

15   **kernel** VARIABLESWEEP ($\varphi, \mathcal{S}_d, \mathcal{T}$):
16 | **for all** $i \in [\![\, 0, |\varphi|\,]\!]$ **in parallel**
17 | | **register** $x \leftarrow \varphi[i], \mathcal{T}_x \leftarrow \mathcal{T}[x], \mathcal{T}_{\bar{x}} \leftarrow \mathcal{T}[x], t \leftarrow$ NONE, $\beta \leftarrow 0, \gamma \leftarrow 0$;
18 | | $type[i] \leftarrow 0$, buckets$[i] \leftarrow 0$, added$[i] \leftarrow 0$;   // initially reset
19 | | **if** $\mathcal{T}_x = \emptyset \vee \mathcal{T}_{\bar{x}} = \emptyset$ **then**   // check if x is a pure literal
20 | | | resolved $\leftarrow$ TOBLIVION($x, \mathcal{S}_d, \mathcal{T}_x, \mathcal{T}_{\bar{x}}$);
21 | | **else**
22 | | | $t, \beta, \gamma \leftarrow$ GATEREASONING ($x, \mathcal{S}_d, \mathcal{T}_x, \mathcal{T}_{\bar{x}}, \sigma$);
23 | | | **if** $t \neq$ GATE **then**
24 | | | | $t, \beta, \gamma \leftarrow$ MAYRESOLVE ($x, \mathcal{S}_d, \mathcal{T}_x, \mathcal{T}_{\bar{x}}$) ;   // t may set to RESOLUTION
25 | | | **if** $t \neq 0$ **then**   // x can be eliminated
26 | | | | $type[i] \leftarrow t$, added$[i] \leftarrow \beta$, buckets$[i] \leftarrow \alpha \times \beta + (\gamma - \beta)$;
27 | | | | resolved $\leftarrow$ TOBLIVION($x, \mathcal{S}_d, \mathcal{T}_x, \mathcal{T}_{\bar{x}}$);
28   **kernel** VARIABLERESOLVENT ($\varphi, \mathcal{S}_d, \mathcal{T}$, type, buckets, added):
29 | **for all** $i \in [\![\, 0, |\varphi|\,]\!]$ **in parallel**
30 | | **register** $x \leftarrow \varphi[i], \mathcal{T}_x \leftarrow \mathcal{T}[x], \mathcal{T}_{\bar{x}} \leftarrow \mathcal{T}[x]$;
31 | | **register** $t \leftarrow type[i], cref \leftarrow$ buckets$[i], rpos =$ added$[i]$;
32 | | **if** $t =$ RESOLUTION **then**
33 | | | $(\mathcal{S}_d, \mathcal{U}_d) \leftarrow (\mathcal{S}_d, \mathcal{U}_d) \cup$ RESOLVE($x, \mathcal{S}_d, \mathcal{T}_x, \mathcal{T}_{\bar{x}}, rpos, cref$);
34 | | **if** $t =$ GATE **then**
35 | | | $(\mathcal{S}_d, \mathcal{U}_d) \leftarrow (\mathcal{S}_d, \mathcal{U}_d) \cup$ SUBSTITUTE($x, \mathcal{S}_d, \mathcal{T}_x, \mathcal{T}_{\bar{x}}, rpos, cref$);

---

check first if x contributes to a logical gate using the routine GATEREASONING, and save the corresponding β and γ. If this is the case, the type t is set to GATE, otherwise we try resolution at line 24. The condition $\beta \leq (|\mathcal{T}_x| + |\mathcal{T}_{\bar{x}}|)$ is tested implicitly by MAYRESOLVE to limit the number of resolvents for x. If t is set to a nonzero value (line 25), the type and added arrays are updated correspondingly. The total number of buckets needed to store all added clauses is calculated by the formula $(\alpha \times \beta + (\gamma - \beta))$ and stored in buckets$[i]$ at line 26. After type and added have been completely constructed, the loop at lines 3-4 identifies the index of the last variable eliminated starting from position $|\varphi| - 1$. If the condition at line 4 holds, index j and the number of underlying resolvents are saved to $last_{idx}$ and $last_{added}$, respectively. These values will be used later to set the new size of the simplified formula $\mathcal{S}_d$ on the host side.

Phase 2 is now ready to apply EXCLUSIVESCAN on the added and buckets lists. Both clauses and references refer to the structural members of $\mathcal{S}_d$, as described in Fig. 1b. The procedure at line 6 takes the old size of clauses to offset the calculated references of the added resolvents. The SIZE routine returns the size of the input structure. Similarly, the second call at line 7 takes the old size of references and calculates the new indices for storing new references. Both scans are executed concurrently

Algorithm 4: Parallel Eager Redundancy Elimination for Inprocessing

---

Input : __global__ φ, S_d, T

```
1  kernel ERE (φ, S_d, T):
2      for all i ∈ [[ 0, |φ| ]] ^y in parallel
3          x ← φ[i];
4          for C ∈ S_d[T[x]] do
5              for C' ∈ S_d[T[x̄]] do
6                  if (C_m ←RESOLVE (x, C, C')) ≠ ∅ then
7                      if state(C) = LEARNT ∨ state(C') = LEARNT then
8                          st ← LEARNT
9                      else
10                         st ← ORIGINAL
11                     FORWARDEQUALITY (C_m, S_d, T, st);
12  device function FORWARDEQUALITY (C_m, S_d, T, st):
13      minList ← FINDMINLIST (T, C_m);
14      for all i ∈ [[ 0, |minList| ]] ^x in parallel
15          C ← S_d[minList[i]];
16          if C = C_m ∧ (state(C) = LEARNT ∨ state(C) = st) then state(C) ← DELETED ;
```

---

via *stream0* and *stream1*, and are synchronized by the SYNCALL call at line 8. After the exclusive scan, the last element in `added` gives the total number of clauses in S_d minus the resolvents added by the last eliminated variable. Therefore, adding this value to $last_{added}$ gives the total number of clauses in S_d (line 9). At line 10, the last clause $last_C$ and its reference $last_{cref}$ are fetched. At line 11, the number of buckets of $last_C$ is added to $last_{cref}$ to get the total number of buckets $numBuckets$. The $numBuckets$ and $numCls$ are used to resize `clauses` and `references`, respectively, at line 12.

Finally, in phase 3, we use the calculated indices in `added` and `buckets` to guide the new resolvents to their locations in S_d. The kernel is described at lines 28-35. Each thread either calls the procedure RESOLVE or SUBSTITUTE, based on the type stored for the designated variables. Any produced units are saved into U_d atomically. The $cref$ and $rpos$ variables indicate where resolvents should be stored in S_d per variable x.

7 Eager Redundancy Elimination

Alg. 4 describes a *two-dimensional* kernel, in which from each thread ID, an x and y coordinate is derived. This allows us to use two nested grid-stride loops. In the loops, we specify which of the two coordinates should be used to initialise i in the first iteration.

Based on the kernel's *y-dimension* ID (line 2), each thread merges where possible two clauses of its designated variable x and its complement $\bar{x}$ (lines 3-6), and writes the result in shared memory as C_m. This new clause is produced by the routine RESOLVE at line 6. At lines 7-10, we check if one of the resolved clauses is LEARNT, and if so, the state st of C_m is set to LEARNT as well, otherwise it is set to ORIGINAL. This state of C_m will guide the FORWARDEQUALITY routine called at line 11 to search for redundant clauses of the same type. This routine is a device function, as it can only be called from a kernel, and is described at lines 12-17. In this function, the x-dimension of the thread ID is used to search the clauses referenced by the minimum occurrence list *minList*, which is produced by FINDMINLIST at line 13. It has the minimum size among the lists of all literals in C_m. If a clause C is found that is equal to C_m and is either LEARNT or has a state equal to the one of C_m, it is set to DELETED (lines 16).

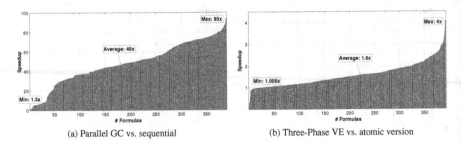

(a) Parallel GC vs. sequential   (b) Three-Phase VE vs. atomic version

Fig. 3: Speedup of the proposed VE and GC algorithms on the benchmark suite

8 Experiments

We implemented the proposed algorithms in PFROST-GPU[3] with CUDA C++ version 11.0 [31]. We evaluated all GPU experiments on an NVIDIA Titan RTX GPU. This GPU has 72 SMs (64 cores each), 24 GB global memory and 48 KB shared memory. The GPU operates at a base clock of 1.3 GHz (boost: 1.7 GHz). The GPU machine was running Linux Mint v20 with an Intel Core i5-7600 CPU of 3.5 GHz base clock speed (turbo: 4.1 GHz) and a system memory of 32 GB.

We selected 493 SAT problems from the 2013-2020 SAT competitions. All formulas larger than 5 MB in size are chosen, excluding redundancies (repeated CNFs across competitions). For very small problems, the GPU is not really needed, as only few variables and clauses can be removed. The selected problems encode around 70+ different real-world applications, with various logical properties.

In the experiments, besides the implementations of our new GPU algorithms, we involved a CPU-only version of PARAFROST (PFROST-CPU), and the CADICAL [6] SAT solver for the solving of problems, and executed these on the compute nodes of the Lisa CPU cluster[4]. Each problem was analysed in isolation on a separate computing node. Each computing node had an Intel Xeon Gold 6130 CPU running at a base clock speed of 2.1 (turbo: 3.7) GHz with 96 GB of system memory, and runs on Debian Linux operating system. With this information, we adhere to all five principles laid out in the SAT manifesto (version 1) [9], noting that we also included problems older than three years, to have a sufficient number of large problems to work with.

SAT-Simplification Speedup. Figure 3 discusses the performance evaluation of the GPU Algorithms 1 and 3 compared to their previous implementations in SIGMA [34]. For these experiments, we set μ and *phases* initially to 32 and 5, respectively. Preprocessing is only enabled to measure the speedup. Fig. 3a shows the speedup of running parallel GC against a sequential version on the host. Clearly, for almost all cases, Alg. 1 achieved a drastic acceleration when executed on the device with a maximum speed up of 93× and an average of 48×. Fig. 3b reveals how fast the 3-phase parallel VE is

---

[3] Solvers/formulas are available at https://gears.win.tue.nl/software/parafrost.

[4] This work was carried out on the Dutch national e-infrastructure with the support of SURF Cooperative.

compared to version using more atomic instructions. On average, the new algorithm is twice as fast as the old BVIPE algorithm [34]. In addition, we get reproducible results.

SAT-Solving.   These experiments provide a thorough assessment of our CPU/GPU solver, the CPU-only version, and CADICAL on SAT solving with preprocessing + inprocessing turned on. The features *walksat*, *vivification* and *probing* [6] are disabled in CADICAL as they are not yet supported in PARAFROST. As in PARAFROST, all elimination methods in CADICAL are turned on with a bound on the occurrence list size set to 30,000. The same parameters for the search heuristics are used for all experiments. However, we delay the scheduling of inprocessing in PARAFROST until 4,000 of the fixed (root) variables are removed. The occurrence limit μ is bounded by 32 in CADICAL. On the other hand, we start with 32 and double this value every new *phase* as shown in Alg. 2. These extensions increase the likelihood of doing more work on the GPU. The timeout for all experiments is set to 5,000 seconds. The timeout for the sequential solvers has a 6% tolerance (i.e., is 5,300 seconds in total) to compensate for the different CPU frequencies of the GPU machine and the cluster nodes.

Figure 4 demonstrates the runtime results for all solvers over the benchmark suite. Subplot (a) shows the total time (simplify + solving) for all formulas. Data are sorted w.r.t. the x-axis. The simplify time accounts data transfers in PFROST-GPU. Overall, PFROST-GPU dominates over PFROST-CPU and CADICAL. Subplot (b) demonstrates the solving impact of PFROST-GPU versus CADICAL on SAT/UNSAT formulas. PFROST-GPU seems more effective on UNSAT formulas than CADICAL. Collectively, PFROST-GPU performed faster on 196 instances (58% out of all solved), in which 18 formulas were unsolved by CADICAL.

Subplots (c) and (d) show simplification time and its percentage of the total processing time, respectively. Clearly, the CPU/GPU solver outperforms its sequential counterpart due to the parallel acceleration. Plot (d) tells us that PFROST-GPU keeps the workload in the region between 0 and 20% as the elimination methods are scheduled on a bulk of mutually independent variables in parallel. In CADICAL, variables and clauses are simplified sequentially, which takes more time. Plot (e) shows the effectiveness of ERE on formulas with successful clause reductions. The last plot (f) reflects the overall efficiency of parallel inprocessing on variables and clauses (learnt clauses are included). Data are sorted in descending order. Reductions can remove up to 90% and 80% of the variables and clauses, respectively.

9   Related Work

A simple GC monitor for GPU term rewriting has been proposed by van Eerd *et al.* [18]. The monitor tracks deleted terms and stores their indices in a list. New terms can be added at those indices. The authors in [1, 26] investigated the challenges for offloading garbage collectors to an Accelerated Processing Unit (APU). Matthias *et al.* [39] introduced a promising alternative for stream compaction [10] via parallel defragmentation on GPUs. Our GC, on the other hand, is tailored to SAT solving, which allows it to be simple yet efficient. Regarding inprocessing, Järvisalo *et al.* [23] introduced certain rules to determine how and when inprocessing techniques can be applied. Acceleration of the DPLL SAT solving algorithm on a GPU has been done in [15], where

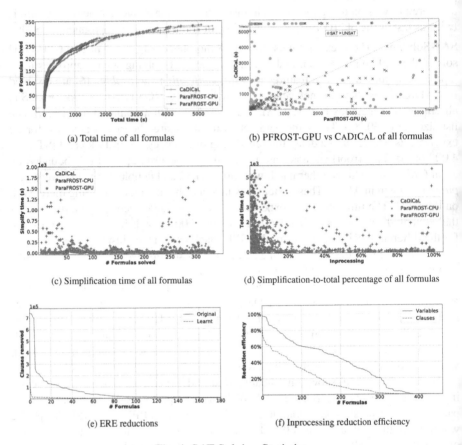

(a) Total time of all formulas

(b) PFROST-GPU vs CADICAL of all formulas

(c) Simplification time of all formulas

(d) Simplification-to-total percentage of all formulas

(e) ERE reductions

(f) Inprocessing reduction efficiency

Fig. 4: SAT Solving Statistics

some parts of the search were performed on a GPU and the remainder is handled by the CPU. Incomplete approaches are more amenable to be executed entirely on a GPU, e.g., an approach using metaheuristic algorithms [44]. We are the first to work on GPU inprocessing in modern CDCL solvers.

10 Conclusion

We have shown that GPU-accelerated inprocessing significantly reduces simplification time in SAT solving, allowing more problems to be solved. Parallel ERE and VE can be performed efficiently on many-core systems, producing impactful reductions on both original and learnt clauses in a fraction of a second, even for large problems. The proposed parallel GC achieves a substantial speedup in compacting SAT formulas on a GPU, while stimulating coalesced accessing of clauses.

Concerning future work, the results suggest to continue taking the capabilities of GPU inprocessing further by supporting more simplification techniques.

References

1. Abhinav, Nasre, R.: FastCollect: Offloading Generational Garbage Collection to integrated GPUs. In: 2016 International Conference on Compliers, Architectures, and Sythesis of Embedded Systems (CASES). pp. 1–10 (2016)
2. Audemard, G., Simon, L.: Predicting Learnt Clauses Quality in Modern SAT Solvers. In: IJCAI 2009. pp. 399–404. Morgan Kaufmann Publishers Inc., San Francisco, CA, USA (2009)
3. Bao, F.S., Gutierrez, C., Charles-Blount, J.J., Yan, Y., Zhang, Y.: Accelerating Boolean Satisfiability (SAT) solving by common subclause elimination. Artificial Intelligence Review 49(3), 439–453 (2018)
4. Biere, A.: P{re, i}coSAT@SC'09. In: SAT 2009 competitive events booklet. pp. 41–43 (2009)
5. Biere, A.: Lingeling, Plingeling, PicoSAT and PrecoSAT at SAT race 2010. FMV Report 1, Johannes Kepler University (2010)
6. Biere, A.: CaDiCaL at the SAT Race 2019. In: Proc. SAT Race 2019: Solver and Benchmark Descriptions. Department of Computer Science Report Series - University of Helsinki, vol. B-2019-1, pp. 8–9 (2019)
7. Biere, A., Cimatti, A., Clarke, E., Zhu, Y.: Symbolic model checking without BDDs. In: TACAS 1999. pp. 193–207. Springer (1999)
8. Biere, A., Järvisalo, M., Kiesl, B.: Preprocessing in SAT solving. In: Biere, A., Heule, M., van Maaren, H., Walsh, T. (eds.) Handbook of Satisfiability. Frontiers in Artificial Intelligence and Applications, IOS Press, 2nd edn. (2020), to be published
9. Biere, A., Järvisalo, M., Le Berre, D., Meel, K.S., Mengel, S.: The SAT Practitioner's Manifesto (Sep 2020). https://doi.org/10.5281/zenodo.4500928
10. Billeter, M., Olsson, O., Assarsson, U.: Efficient Stream Compaction on Wide SIMD Many-Core Architectures. In: Proceedings of the Conference on High Performance Graphics 2009. pp. 159–166. HPG '09, Association for Computing Machinery, New York, NY, USA (2009)
11. Bošnački, D., Edelkamp, S., Sulewski, D., Wijs, A.: GPU-PRISM: An Extension of PRISM for General Purpose Graphics Processing Units. In: PDMC-HiBi. pp. 17–19. IEEE Computer Society (2010)
12. Bošnački, D., Odenbrett, M., Wijs, A., Ligtenberg, W., Hilbers, P.: Efficient reconstruction of biological networks via transitive reduction on general purpose graphics processors. BMC Bioinformatics 13(281) (2012)
13. Bradley, A.R.: SAT-based model checking without unrolling. In: VMCAI 2011. pp. 70–87. Springer (2011)
14. Brown, C.E.: Reducing Higher-Order Theorem Proving to a Sequence of SAT Problems. Journal of Automated Reasoning 51(1), 57–77 (Jun 2013)
15. Dal Palù, A., Dovier, A., Formisano, A., Pontelli, E.: CUD@SAT: SAT solving on GPUs. Journal of Exper. & Theoret. Artificial Intelligence 27(3), 293–316 (2015)
16. Eén, N., Biere, A.: Effective Preprocessing in SAT Through Variable and Clause Elimination. In: SAT. LNCS, vol. 3569, pp. 61–75. Springer (2005)
17. Eén, N., Sörensson, N.: An Extensible SAT-solver. In: SAT. LNCS, vol. 2919, pp. 502–518. Springer (2004)
18. Eerd, J. van, Groote, J.F., Hijma, P., Martens, J., Wijs, A.J.: Term Rewriting on GPUs. In: FSEN. LNCS, Springer, to appear (2021)
19. Gebhardt, K., Manthey, N.: Parallel Variable Elimination on CNF Formulas. In: Timm, I.J., Thimm, M. (eds.) KI 2013: Advances in Artificial Intelligence. pp. 61–73. Springer Berlin Heidelberg, Berlin, Heidelberg (2013)
20. Han, H., Somenzi, F.: Alembic: An efficient algorithm for CNF preprocessing. In: Proc. 44th ACM/IEEE Design Automation Conference. pp. 582–587. IEEE (2007)

21. Heule, M., Järvisalo, M., Biere, A.: Clause Elimination Procedures for CNF Formulas. In: LPAR. LNCS, vol. 6397, pp. 357–371. Springer (2010)
22. Järvisalo, M., Biere, A., Heule, M.J.: Simulating circuit-level simplifications on CNF. Journal of Automated Reasoning **49**(4), 583–619 (2012)
23. Järvisalo, M., Heule, M.J., Biere, A.: Inprocessing Rules. In: IJCAR. LNCS, vol. 7364, pp. 355–370. Springer (2012)
24. Jin, H., Somenzi, F.: An incremental algorithm to check satisfiability for bounded model checking. ENTCS **119**(2), 51–65 (2005)
25. Kullmann, O.: On a generalization of extended resolution. Discrete Applied Mathematics **97**, 149–176 (1999)
26. Maas, M., Reames, P., Morlan, J., Asanović, K., Joseph, A.D., Kubiatowicz, J.: GPUs as an Opportunity for Offloading Garbage Collection. SIGPLAN Not. **47**(11), 25–36 (Jun 2012)
27. Marques-Silva, J., Glass, T.: Combinational equivalence checking using satisfiability and recursive learning. In: Design, Automation and Test in Europe Conference and Exhibition, 1999. Proceedings (Cat. No. PR00078). pp. 145–149 (March 1999)
28. Marques-Silva, J.P., Sakallah, K.A.: GRASP: A search algorithm for propositional satisfiability. IEEE Transactions on Computers **48**(5), 506–521 (1999)
29. Merrill, D.: CUB: A Parallel Primitives Library. NVLabs (2020), https://nvlabs.github.io/cub/
30. Moness, M., Mahmoud, M.O., Moustafa, A.M.: A Real-Time Heterogeneous Emulator of a High-Fidelity Utility-Scale Variable-Speed Variable-Pitch Wind Turbine. IEEE Transactions on Industrial Informatics **14**(2), 437–447 (2018)
31. NVIDIA: CUDA C Programming Guide (2020), https://docs.nvidia.com/cuda/cuda-c-programming-guide/index.html
32. Osama, M., Wijs, A.: Multiple Decision Making in Conflict-Driven Clause Learning. In: 2020 IEEE 32nd International Conference on Tools with Artificial Intelligence (ICTAI). pp. 161–169 (2020)
33. Osama, M., Gaber, L., Hussein, A.I., Mahmoud, H.: An Efficient SAT-Based Test Generation Algorithm with GPU Accelerator. Journal of Electronic Testing **34**(5), 511–527 (Oct 2018)
34. Osama, M., Wijs, A.: Parallel SAT Simplification on GPU Architectures. In: TACAS. LNCS, vol. 11427, pp. 21–40. Springer International Publishing, Cham (2019)
35. Osama, M., Wijs, A.: SIGmA: GPU Accelerated Simplification of SAT Formulas. In: iFM. LNCS, vol. 11918, pp. 514–522. Springer (2019)
36. Osama, M., Wijs, A.: ParaFROST, ParaFROST CBT, ParaFROST HRE, ParaFROST ALL at the SAT Race 2020. SAT Competition 2020 p. 42 (2020)
37. Ostrowski, R., Grégoire, E., Mazure, B., Sais, L.: Recovering and Exploiting Structural Knowledge from CNF Formulas. In: Proceedings of the 8th International Conference on Principles and Practice of Constraint Programming. pp. 185–199. CP '02, Springer-Verlag, London, UK, UK (2002)
38. Soos, M., Kulkarni, R., Meel, K.S.: Crystalball: Gazing in the black box of SAT solving. In: Janota, M., Lynce, I. (eds.) Theory and Applications of Satisfiability Testing - SAT 2019 - 22nd International Conference, SAT 2019, Lisbon, Portugal, July 9-12, 2019, Proceedings. Lecture Notes in Computer Science, vol. 11628, pp. 371–387. Springer (2019). https://doi.org/10.1007/978-3-030-24258-9_26
39. Springer, M., Masuhara, H.: Massively Parallel GPU Memory Compaction. In: ISMM. pp. 14–26. ACM (2019)
40. Stephan, P., Brayton, R.K., Sangiovanni-Vincentelli, A.L.: Combinational test generation using satisfiability. IEEE Transactions on Computer-Aided Design of Integrated Circuits and Systems **15**(9), 1167–1176 (1996)
41. Subbarayan, S., Pradhan, D.K.: NiVER: Non-increasing variable elimination resolution for preprocessing SAT instances. In: SAT. LNCS, vol. 3542, pp. 276–291. Springer (2004)

42. Wijs, A.: GPU accelerated strong and branching bisimilarity checking. In: TACAS, LNCS, vol. 9035, pp. 368–383. Springer (2015)
43. Wijs, A., Neele, T., Bošnački, D.: GPUexplore 2.0: Unleashing GPU Explicit-state Model Checking. In: FM. LNCS, vol. 9995, pp. 694–701. Springer (2016)
44. Youness, H., Ibraheim, A., Moness, M., Osama, M.: An Efficient Implementation of Ant Colony Optimization on GPU for the Satisfiability Problem. In: 2015 23rd Euromicro International Conference on Parallel, Distributed, and Network-Based Processing. pp. 230–235 (March 2015)

FOREST: An Interactive Multi-tree Synthesizer for Regular Expressions*

(✉) Margarida Ferreira[1,2], Miguel Terra-Neves[2], Miguel Ventura[2], Inês Lynce[1], and Ruben Martins[3]

[1] INESC-ID, Instituto Superior Técnico, Universidade de Lisboa, Lisbon, Portugal
{margaridaacferreira, ines.lynce}@tecnico.ulisboa.pt
[2] OutSystems, Linda-a-Velha, Portugal
{miguel.neves, miguel.ventura}@outsystems.com
[3] Carnegie Mellon University, Pittsburgh, USA
rubenm@cs.cmu.edu

Abstract Form validators based on regular expressions are often used on digital forms to prevent users from inserting data in the wrong format. However, writing these validators can pose a challenge to some users.

We present FOREST, a regular expression synthesizer for digital form validations. FOREST produces a regular expression that matches the desired pattern for the input values and a set of conditions over capturing groups that ensure the validity of integer values in the input. Our synthesis procedure is based on enumerative search and uses a Satisfiability Modulo Theories (SMT) solver to explore and prune the search space. We propose a novel representation for regular expressions synthesis, multi-tree, which induces patterns in the examples and uses them to split the problem through a divide-and-conquer approach. We also present a new SMT encoding to synthesize capture conditions for a given regular expression. To increase confidence in the synthesized regular expression, we implement user interaction based on distinguishing inputs.

We evaluated FOREST on real-world form-validation instances using regular expressions. Experimental results show that FOREST successfully returns the desired regular expression in 70% of the instances and outperforms REGEL, a state-of-the-art regular expression synthesizer.

1 Introduction

Regular expressions (also known as regexes) are powerful mechanisms for describing patterns in text with numerous applications. One notable use of regexes is to perform real-time validations on the input fields of digital forms. Regexes help filter invalid values, such as typographical mistakes ('typos') and format inconsistencies. Aside from validating the format of form input strings, regular expressions can be coupled with capturing groups. A capturing group is a sub-regex within a regex that is indicated with parenthesis and captures the text

---

* This work was supported by NSF award CCF-1762363 and through FCT under project UIDB/50021/2020, and project ANI 045917 funded by FEDER and FCT.

J. F. Groote and K. G. Larsen (Eds.): TACAS 2021, LNCS 12651, pp. 152–169, 2021.
https://doi.org/10.1007/978-3-030-72016-2_9

matched by the sub-regex inside them. Capturing groups are used to extract information from text and, in the domain of form validation, they can be used to enforce conditions over values in the input string. In this paper, we focus on the capture of integer values in input strings, and we use the notation $\$i, i \in \{0, 1, ...\}$ to refer to the integer value of the text captured by the $(i + 1)^{\text{th}}$ group.

Form validations often rely on complex regexes which require programming skills that not all users possess. To help users write regexes, prior work has proposed to synthesize regular expressions from natural language [,9, 2,2] or from positive and negative examples [,7, 0,2]. Even though these techniques assist users in writing regexes for search and replace operations, they do not specifically target digital form validation and do not take advantage of the structured format of the data.

In this paper, we propose FOREST, a new program synthesizer for regular expressions that targets digital form validations. FOREST takes as input a set of examples and returns a regex validation. FOREST accepts three types of examples: (i) **valid examples**: correct values for the input field, (ii) **invalid examples**: incorrect values for the input field due to their *format*, and (iii) **conditional invalid examples** (optional): incorrect values for the input field due to their *values*. FOREST outputs a regex validation, consisting of two components: (i) a **regular expression** that matches all valid and none of the invalid examples and (ii) **capture conditions** that express integer conditions that are satisfied by the values on all the valid but none of the conditional invalid examples.

Motivating Example. Suppose a user is writing a form where one of the fields is a date that must respect the format DD/MM/YYYY. The user wants to accept:

19/08/1996	22/09/2000	29/09/2003
26/10/1998	01/12/2001	31/08/2015

But not:

19/08/96	22.09.2000	29/9/2003
26-10-1998	1/12/2001	2015/08/31

A regular expression can be used to enforce this format. Instead of writing it, the user may simply use the two sets of values as *valid* and *invalid* input examples to FOREST, who will output the regex [0-9]{2}/[0-9]{2}/[0-9]{4}.

Additionally, if the user wants to validate not only the format, but also the values in the date, we can consider as *conditional invalid* the examples:

33/08/1996	22/13/2000	12/31/2003
26/00/1998	00/12/2001	52/03/2015

FOREST will output a regex validation complete with conditions over capturing groups that ensures only valid values are inserted as the day and month: ([0-9]{2})/([0-9]{2})/[0-9]{4}, $\$0 \leq 31 \land \$0 \geq 1 \land \$1 \leq 12 \land \$1 \geq 1$.

As we can see in the motivating example, data inserted into digital forms is usually structured and shares a common pattern among the valid examples. In this example, the data has the shape dd/dd/dddd where d represents a digit. This

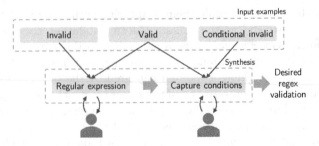

Figure 1: Regex synthesis

contrasts with general regexes for search and replace operations that are often performed over unstructured text. FOREST takes advantage of this structure by automatically detecting these patterns and using a divide-and-conquer approach to split the expression into simpler sub-expressions, solving them independently, and then merging their information to obtain the final regular expression. Additionally, FOREST computes a set of capturing groups over the regular expression, which it then uses to synthesize integer conditions that further constrain the accepted values for that form field.

Input-output examples do not require specialized knowledge and are accessible to users. However, there is one downside to using examples as a specification: they are ambiguous. There can be solutions that, despite matching the examples, do not produce the desired behavior in situations not covered in them. The ambiguity of input-output examples raises the necessity of selecting one among multiple candidate solutions. To this end, we incorporate a user interaction model based on distinguishing inputs for both the synthesis of the regular expressions and the synthesis of the capture conditions.

In summary, this paper makes the following contributions:

- We propose a multi-tree SMT representation for regular expressions that leverages the structure of the input to apply a divide-and-conquer approach.
- We propose a new method to synthesize capturing groups for a given regular expression and integer conditions over the resulting captures.
- We implemented a tool, FOREST, that interacts with the user to disambiguate the provided specification. FOREST is evaluated on real-world instances and its performance is compared with a state-of-the-art synthesizer.

2   Synthesis Algorithm Overview

The task of automatically generating a program that satisfies some desired behavior expressed as a high-level specification is known as Program Synthesis. Programming by Example (PBE) is a branch of Program Synthesis where the desired behavior is specified using input-output examples.

Our synthesis procedure is split into two stages, each relative to an output component. First, FOREST synthesizes the regular expression, which is the basis

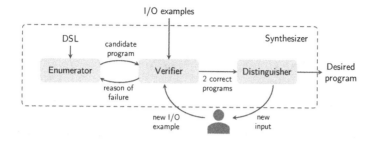

Figure 2: Interactive enumerative search

for the synthesis of capturing groups. Secondly, FOREST synthesizes the capture conditions, by first computing a set of capturing groups and then the conditions to be applied to the resulting captures. The synthesis stages are detailed in sections 3 and 4. Figure 1 shows the regex validation synthesis pipeline. Both stages of our synthesis algorithm employ enumerative search, a common approach to solve the problem of program synthesis [1,5,10,17,21]. The enumerative search cycle is depicted in Figure 2.

There are two key components for program enumeration: the *enumerator* and the *verifier*. The *enumerator* successively enumerates programs from the a predefined Domain Specific Language (DSL). Following the Occam's razor principle, programs are enumerated in increasing order of complexity. The DSL defines the set of operators that can be used to build the desired program. FOREST dynamically constructs its DSL to fit the problem at hand: it is as restricted as possible, without losing the necessary expressiveness. The regular expression DSL construction procedure is detailed in section 3.1.

For each enumerated program, the *verifier* subsequently checks whether it satisfies the provided examples. Program synthesis applications generate very large search spaces; nevertheless, the search space can be significantly reduced by pruning several infeasible expressions along with each incorrect expression found. In the first stage of the regex validation synthesis, the enumerated programs are regular expressions. The enumeration and pruning of regular expressions is described in section 3.2. In the second stage of regex validation synthesis, we deal with the enumeration of capturing groups over a pre-existing regular expression. This process is described in section 4.1.

To circumvent the ambiguity of input-output examples, FOREST implements an interaction model. A new component, the *distinguisher*, ascertains, for any two given programs, whether they are equivalent. When FOREST finds two different validations that satisfy all examples, it creates a *distinguishing input*: a new input that has a different output for each validation. To disambiguate between two programs, FOREST shows the new input to the user, who classifies it as valid or invalid, effectively choosing one program over the other. The new input-output pair is added to the examples, and the enumeration process continues until there is only one solution left. This interactive cycle is described for the synthesis of regular expressions in section 3.3 and capture conditions in section 4.3.

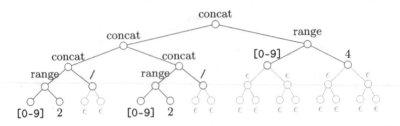

Figure 3: `[0-9]{2}/[0-9]{2}/[0-9]{4}` represented as a k-tree with $k = 2$

3   Regular Expressions Synthesis

In this section we describe the enumerative synthesis procedure that generates a regular expression that matches all valid examples and none of the invalid.

3.1   Regular Expressions DSL

Before the synthesis procedure starts, we define which operators can be used to build the desired regular expression and the values each operator can take as argument. FOREST's regular expression DSL includes the regex union and concatenation operators, as well as several regular expression quantifiers:

- *Kleene* closure: r^* matches r zero or more times,
- positive closure: r^+ matches r one or more times,
- option: r? matches r zero or one times,
- ranges: $r\{m\}$ matches r exactly m times, and $r\{m, n\}$ matches r at least m times and at most n times.

The possible values for the range operators are limited depending on the valid examples provided by the user. For the single-valued range operator, $r\{m\}$, we consider only the integer values such that $2 \leq m \leq l$, where l is the length of the longest valid example string. In the two-valued range operator, $r\{m, n\}$, the values of m and n are limited to integers such that $0 \leq m < n \leq l$. The tuple (0,1) is not considered, since it is equivalent to the option quantifier: $r\{0, 1\} = r$?.

All operators can be applied to regex literals or composed with each other to form more complex expressions. The regex literals considered in the synthesis procedure include the individual letters, digits or symbols present in the examples and all character classes that contain them. The character classes contemplated in the DSL are `[0-9]`, `[A-Z]`, `[a-z]` and all combinations of those, such as `[A-Za-z]` or `[0-9A-Za-z]`. Additionally, `[0-9A-F]` and `[0-9a-f]` are used to represent hexadecimal numbers.

3.2   Regex Enumeration

To enumerate regexes, the synthesizer requires a structure capable of representing every feasible expression. We use a tree-based representation of the search

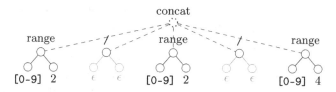

Figure 4: `[0-9]{2}/[0-9]{2}/[0-9]{4}` represented as a multi-tree with $n = 5$ and $k = 2$, resulting from the concatenation of 5 simpler regexes

space. A k-tree of depth d is a tree in which every internal node has exactly k children and every leaf node is at depth d. A program corresponds to an assignment of a DSL construct to each tree node, the node's descendants are the construct's arguments. If k is the greatest arity among all DSL constructs, then a k-tree of depth d can represent all programs of depth up to d in that DSL. The arity of constructs in FOREST's regex DSLs is at most 2, so all regexes in the search space can be represented using 2-trees. To allow constructs with arity smaller than k, some children nodes are assigned the *empty* symbol, ϵ. In Figure 3, the regex from the motivating example, `[0-9]{2}/[0-9]{2}/[0-9]{4}`, is represented as a 2-tree of depth 5.

To explore the search space in order of increasing complexity, we enumerate k-trees of lower depths first and progressively increase the depth of the trees as previous depths are exhausted. The enumerator encodes the k-tree as an SMT formula that ensures the program is well-typed. A model that satisfies the formula represents a valid regex. Due to space constraints we omit the k-tree encoding but further details can be found in the literature [2, 7].

Multi-tree representation. We considered several validators for digital forms and observed that many regexes in this domain are the concatenation of relatively simple regexes. However, the successive concatenation of simple regexes quickly becomes complex in its k-tree representation. Recall the regex for date validation presented in the motivating example: `[0-9]{2}/[0-9]{2}/[0-9]{4}`. Even though this is the concatenation of 5 simple sub-expressions, each of depth at most 2, its representation as a k-tree has depth 5, as shown in Figure 3.

The main idea behind the multi-tree constructs is to allow the number of concatenated sub-expressions to grow without it reflecting exponentially on the encoding. The multi-tree structure consists of n k-trees, whose roots are connected by an artificial root node, interpreted as an n-ary concatenation operator. This way, we are able to represent regexes using fewer nodes. Figure 4 is the multi-tree representation of the same regex as Figure 3, and shows that the multi-tree construct can represent this expression using half the nodes.

The k-tree enumerator successively explores k-trees of increasing depth. However, multi-tree has two measures of complexity: the depth of the trees, d, and the number of trees, n. FOREST employs two different methods for increasing these values: static multi-tree and dynamic multi-tree.

Static multi-tree. In the static multi-tree method, the synthesizer fixes n and progressively increases d. To find the value of n, there is a preprocessing step, in which FOREST identifies patterns in the valid examples. This is done by first identifying substrings common to all examples. A substring is considered a dividing substring if it occurs exactly the same number of times and in the same order in all examples. Then, we split each example before and after the dividing substrings. Each example becomes an array of n strings.

Example 1. Consider the valid examples from the motivating example. In these examples, '/' is a dividing substring because it occurs in every example, and exactly twice in each one. '0' is a common substring but not a dividing substring because it does not occur the same number or times in all examples. After splitting on '/', each example becomes a tuple of 5 strings:

('19', '/', '08', '/', '1996')   ('01', '/', '12', '/', '2001')
('26', '/', '10', '/', '1998')   ('29', '/', '09', '/', '2003')
('22', '/', '09', '/', '2000')   ('31', '/', '08', '/', '2015')

Then, we apply the multi-tree method with n trees. For every $i \in \{1, ..., n\}$, the ith sub-tree represents a regex that matches all strings in the ith position of the split example tuples and the concatenation of the n regexes will match the original example strings. Since each tree is only synthesizing a part of the original input strings, a reduced DSL is recomputed for each tree.

Dynamic multi-tree. The dynamic multi-tree method is employed when the examples cannot be split because there are no dividing substrings. In this scenario, the enumerator will still use a multi-tree construct to represent the regex. However, the number of trees is not fixed and all trees use the original, complete DSL. A multi-tree structure with n k-trees of depth d has $n \times (k^d - 1)$ nodes. FOREST enumerates trees with different values of (n, d) in increasing order of number of nodes, starting with $n = 1$ and $d = 2$, a simple k-tree of depth 2.

Pruning. We prune regexes which are provably equivalent to others in the search space by using algebraic rules of regular expressions like the following:

$$(r*)* \equiv r* \qquad (r?)? \equiv r? \qquad (r+)+ \equiv r+$$
$$(r+)* \equiv (r*)+ \equiv r* \qquad (r?)* \equiv (r*)? \equiv r* \qquad (r?)+ \equiv (r+)? \equiv r*$$
$$(r*)\{m\} \equiv (r\{m\})* \qquad (r+)\{m\} \equiv (r\{m\})+ \qquad (r?)\{m\} \equiv (r\{m\})?$$
$$r\{n\}\{m\} \equiv r\{m\}\{n\} \equiv r\{m \times n\}$$

To prevent the enumeration of equivalent regular expressions, we add SMT constraints that block all but one possible representation of each regex. Take, for example, the equivalence $(r?)+ \equiv r*$. We want to consider only one way to represent this regex, so we add a constraint to block the construction $(r?)+$ for any regex r. Another such equivalence results from the idempotence of union:

$r|r = r$. To prevent the enumeration of expressions of the type $r|r$, every time the union operator is assigned to a node i, we force the sub-tree underneath i's left child to be different from the sub-tree underneath i's right child by at least one node. When we enumerate a regex that is not consistent with the examples, it is eliminated from the search space. Along with the incorrect regex, we want to eliminate regexes that are equivalent to it. The union operator in the regular expressions DSL is commutative: $r|s = s|r$, for any regexes r and s. Thus, whenever an expression containing $r|s$ is discarded, we eliminate the expression that contains $s|r$ in its place as well.

3.3   Regex Disambiguation

To increase confidence in the synthesizer's solution, FOREST disambiguates the specification by interacting with the user. We employ an interaction model based on distinguishing inputs, which has been successfully used in several synthesizers [11,24,25,11]. To produce a distinguishing input, we require an SMT solver with a regex theory, such as Z3 [15,29]. Upon finding two regexes that satisfy the user-provided examples, r_1 and r_2, we use the SMT solver to solve the formula:

$$\exists s : r_1(s) \neq r_2(s), \tag{1}$$

where $r_1(s)$ (resp. $r_2(s)$) is True if and only if r_1 (resp. r_2) matches the string s. A string s that satisfies (1) is a distinguishing input. FOREST asks the user to classify this input as valid or invalid, and s is added to the respective set of examples, thus eliminating either r_1 or r_2 from the search space. After the first interaction, the synthesis procedure continues only until the end of the current depth and number of trees.

4   Capturing Groups Synthesis

In this section we describe the synthesis procedure of the second component of a regex validation: a set of integer conditions over captured values that are satisfied by all valid examples but none of the conditional invalid examples.

4.1   Capturing Groups Enumeration

To enumerate capturing groups, FOREST starts by identifying the regular expression's atomic sub-regexes: the smallest sub-regexes whose concatenation results in the original complete regex. For example, [0-9]{2} is an atomic sub-regex: there are no smaller sub-regexes whose concatenation results in it. It does not make sense to place a capturing group inside atomic sub-regexes: ([0-9]){2} does not have a clear meaning. Once identified, the atomic sub-regexes are placed in an ordered list. Enumerating capturing groups over the regular expression is done by enumerating non-empty disjoint sub-lists of this list. The elements inside each sub-list form a capturing group.

Example 2. Recall the date regex: `[0-9]{2}/[0-9]{2}/[0-9]{4}`. The respective list of atomic sub-regexes is `[[0-9]{2}, /, [0-9]{2}, /, [0-9]{4}]`. The following are examples of sub-lists of the atomic sub-regexes list and their resulting capturing groups:

$$[[[0-9]{2}], /, [0-9]{2}, /, [0-9]{4}] \rightarrow ([0-9]{2})/[0-9]{2}/[0-9]{4}$$

$$[[[0-9]{2}], /, [[0-9]{2}], /, [[0-9]{4}]] \rightarrow ([0-9]{2})/([0-9]{2})/([0-9]{4})$$

4.2 Capture Conditions Synthesis

To compute capture conditions, we need all conditional invalid examples to be matched by the regular expression. After, capturing groups are enumerated as described in section 4.1. The number of necessary capturing groups is not known beforehand, so we enumerate capturing groups in increasing number.

A capture condition is a 3-tuple: it contains the captured text, an integer comparison operator and an integer argument. FOREST considers only two integer comparison operators, $\leq$ and $\geq$. However, the algorithm can be easily expanded to include other operators. Let $\mathcal{C}$ be a set of capturing groups and $\mathcal{C}(x)$ the integer captures that result from applying $\mathcal{C}$ to example string x. Let $\mathcal{D}_{\mathcal{C}}$ be the set of all possible capture conditions over capturing groups $\mathcal{C}$. $\mathcal{D}_{\mathcal{C}}$ results from combining each capturing group with each integer operator. Finally, let $\mathcal{V}$ be the set of all valid examples, $\mathcal{I}$ the set of all conditional invalid examples, and $\mathcal{X} = \mathcal{V} \cup \mathcal{I}$ the union of these two sets.

Given capturing groups $\mathcal{C}$, FOREST uses Maximum Satisfiability Modulo Theories (MaxSMT) to select from $\mathcal{D}_{\mathcal{C}}$ the minimum set of conditions that are satisfied by all valid examples and none of the conditional invalid. To encode the problem, we define two sets of Boolean variables. First, we define $s_{cap,x}$ for every $cap \in \mathcal{C}(x)$ and $x \in \mathcal{X}$. $s_{cap,x}$ = True if capture cap in example x satisfies all used conditions that refer to it. We also define u_{cond} for all $cond \in \mathcal{D}_{\mathcal{C}}$. u_{cond} = True means condition $cond$ is used in the solution. Additionally, we define a set of integer variables b_{cond}, for all conditions $cond \in \mathcal{D}_{\mathcal{C}}$ that represent the integer argument present in each condition.

Let $\text{SMT}(cond, x)$ be the SMT representation of condition $cond$ for example x: the capture is an integer value, and the integer argument is the corresponding b_{cond} variable. Let $\mathcal{D}_{cap} \subseteq \mathcal{D}_{\mathcal{C}}$ be the set of capture conditions that refer to capture cap. Constraint (2) states that a capture cap in example x satisfies all conditions if and only if for every condition that refers to cap either it is not used in the solution or it is satisfied for the value of that capture in that example:

$$s_{cap,x} \leftrightarrow \bigwedge_{cond \in \mathcal{D}_{cap}} u_{cond} \rightarrow \text{SMT}(cond, x). \tag{2}$$

Example 3. Recall the first valid string from the motivating example: $x_0 =$ "19/08/1996". Suppose FOREST has already synthesized the desired regular expression and enumerated a capturing group that corresponds to the day: `([0-9]{2})/[0-9]{2}/[0-9]{4}`. Let $cond_0$ and $cond_1$ be the conditions that refer to the first (and only) capturing group, $0, and operators $\leq$ and $\geq$ respectively. The SMT representation for $cond_0$ and x_0 is $\mathrm{SMT}(cond_0, x_0) = 19 \leq b_{cond_0}$. Constraint (2) is:

$$s_{0,x_0} \leftrightarrow (u_{cond_0} \rightarrow 19 \leq b_{cond_0}) \wedge (u_{cond_1} \rightarrow 19 \geq b_{cond_1}).$$

Then, we ensure the used conditions are satisfied by all valid examples and none of the conditional invalid examples:

$$\bigwedge_{x \in \mathcal{V}} \bigwedge_{cap \in \mathcal{C}(x)} s_{cap,x} \wedge \bigwedge_{x \in \mathcal{I}} \bigvee_{cap \in \mathcal{C}(x)} \neg s_{cap,x}. \tag{3}$$

Since we are looking for the minimum set of capture conditions, we add soft clauses to penalize the usage of capture conditions in the solution:

$$\bigwedge_{cond \in \mathcal{D}_C} \neg u_{cond}. \tag{4}$$

We consider part of the solution only the capture conditions whose u_{cond} is True in the resulting SMT model. We also extract the values of the integer arguments in each condition from the model values of the b_{cond} variables.

4.3 Capture Conditions Disambiguation

To ensure the solution meets the user's intent, Forest disambiguates the specification using, once again, a procedure based on distinguishing inputs. Once Forest finds two different sets of capture conditions $\mathcal{S}_1$ and $\mathcal{S}_2$ that satisfy the specification, we look for a distinguishing input: a string c which satisfies all capture conditions in $\mathcal{S}_1$, but not those in $\mathcal{S}_2$, or vice-versa. First, to simplify the problem, Forest eliminates from $\mathcal{S}_1$ and $\mathcal{S}_2$ conditions which are present in both: these are not relevant to compute a distinguishing input. Let $\mathcal{S}_1^*$ (resp. $\mathcal{S}_2^*$) be the subset of $\mathcal{S}_1$ (resp. $\mathcal{S}_2$) containing only the distinguishing conditions, i.e., the conditions that differ from those in $\mathcal{S}_2$ (resp. $\mathcal{S}_1$).

We do not compute the distinguishing string c directly. Instead, we compute the integer value of the distinguishing captures in c, i.e., the captures that result from applying the regular expression and its capturing groups to the distinguishing input string. We define $|\mathcal{C}|$ integer variables, c_i, which correspond to the values of the distinguishing captures: $c_0, c_1, ..., c_{|\mathcal{C}|} = \mathcal{C}(c)$.

As before, let $\mathrm{SMT}(cond, c)$ be the SMT representation of each condition $cond$. Each capture in $\mathcal{C}(c)$ is represented by its respective c_i, the operator maintains it usual semantics and the integer argument is its value in the solution to which the condition belongs. Constraint (5) states that c satisfies the conditions in one solution but not the other.

$$\bigwedge_{cond \in \mathcal{S}_1^*} \mathrm{SMT}(cond, c) \neq \bigwedge_{cond \in \mathcal{S}_2^*} \mathrm{SMT}(cond, c). \tag{5}$$

In the end, to produce the distinguishing string c, FOREST picks an example from the valid set, applies the regular expression with the capturing groups to it, and replaces its captures with the model values for c_i.

FOREST asks the user to classify c as valid or invalid. Depending on the user's answer, c is added as a valid or conditional invalid example, effectively eliminating either S_1 or S_2 from the search space.

Example 4. Recall the examples from the motivating example. No example invalidates a date with the day 32, so FOREST will find two correct sets of capture conditions over the regular expression ([0-9]{2})/([0-9]{2})/[0-9]{4}: $S_1 = \{\$0 \leq 31, \$0 \geq 1, \$1 \leq 12, \$1 \geq 1\}$, and $S_2 = \{\$0 \leq 32, \$0 \geq 1, \$1 \leq 12, \$1 \geq 1\}$. First, we define two sets containing only the distinguishing captures: $S_1^* = \{\$0 \leq 31\}$ and $S_2^* = \{\$0 \leq 32\}$. Then, to find c_0, the value of the distinguishing capture for these solutions, we solve the constraint:

$$\exists c_0 : c_0 \leq 31 \neq c_0 \leq 32$$

and get the value $c_0 = 32$ which satisfies S_2^* (and S_2), but not S_1^* (or S_1).

If we pick the first valid example, "19/08/1996" as basis for c, the respective distinguishing input is $c =$ "32/08/1996". Once the user classifies c as invalid, c is added as a conditional invalid example and S_2 is removed from consideration.

5   Related Work

Program synthesis has been successfully used in many domains such as string processing [8,19,7,26], query synthesis [11,25,17], data wrangling [2,5], and functional synthesis [3,6]. In this section, we discuss prior work on the synthesis of regular expressions [10,1] that is most closely related to our approach.

Previous approaches that perform general string processing [7,26] restrict the form of the regular expressions that can be synthesized. In contrast, we support a wide range of regular expressions operators, including the Kleene closure, positive closure, option, and range. More recent work that targets the synthesis of regexes is done by ALPHAREGEX [10] and REGEL [1]. ALPHAREGEX performs an enumerative search and uses under- and over-approximations of regexes to prune the search space. However, ALPHAREGEX is limited to the binary alphabet and does not support the kind of regexes that we need to synthesize for form validations. REGEL [1] is a state-of-the-art synthesizer of regular expressions based on a multi-modal approach that combines input-output examples with a natural language description of user intent. They use natural language to build hierarchical sketches that capture the high-level structure of the regex to be synthesized. In addition, they prune the search space by using under- and over-approximations and symbolic regexes combined with SMT-based reasoning. REGEL's evaluation [1] has shown that their PBE engine is an order of magnitude faster than ALPHAREGEX. While REGEL targets more general regexes that are suitable for search and replace operations, we target regexes for form validation which usually have more structure. In our approach, we take advantage of this structure to split the problem into independent subproblems. This can be seen as a special case of sketching [22] where each hole is independent. Our pruning techniques are orthogonal to the ones used by REGEL and are based on removing equivalent regexes prior to the search and to remove equivalent failed regexes during search. To the best of our knowledge, no previous work focused on the synthesis of conditions over capturing groups.

Instead of using input-output examples, there are other approaches that synthesize regexes solely from natural language [9,12,27]. We see these approaches as orthogonal to ours and expect that FOREST can be improved by hints provided by a natural language component such as was done in REGEL.

6 Experimental Results

Implementation. FOREST is open-source and publicly available at https://github.com/Marghrid/FOREST. FOREST is implemented in Python 3.8 on top of TRINITY, a general-purpose synthesis framework [13]. All SMT formulas are solved using the Z3 SMT solver, version 4.8.9 [15]. To find distinguishing inputs in regular expression synthesis, FOREST uses Z3's theory of regular expressions [23]. To check the enumerated regexes against the examples, we use Python's regex library [8]. The results presented herein were obtained using an Intel(R) Xeon(R) Silver 4110 CPU @ 2.10GHz, with 64GB of RAM, running Debian GNU/Linux 10. All processes were run with a time limit of one hour.

Benchmarks. To evaluate FOREST, we used 64 benchmarks based on real-world form-validation regular expressions. These were collected from regular expression validators in validation frameworks and from `regexlib` [20], where users can upload their own regexes. Among these 64 benchmarks there are different formats: national IDs, identifiers of products, date and time, vehicle registration numbers, postal codes, email and phone numbers. For each benchmark, we generated a set of string examples. All 64 benchmarks require a regular expression to validate the examples, but only 7 require capture conditions. On average, each instance is composed of 13.2 valid examples (ranging from 4 to 33) and 9.3 invalid (ranging from 2 to 38). The 7 instances that target capture conditions have on average 6.3 conditional invalid examples (ranging from 4 to 8).

The goal of this experimental evaluation is to answer the following questions:

Q1: How does FOREST compare against REGEL? (section 6.1)
Q2: How does pruning affect multi-tree's time performance? (section 6.2)
Q3: How does static multi-tree improve on dynamic multi-tree? (section 6.2)
Q4: How does multi-tree compare against other encodings? (section 6.3)
Q5: How many examples are required to return a correct solution? (section 6.4)

FOREST, by default, uses static multi-tree (when possible) with pruning. It correctly solves 31 benchmarks (48%) in under 10 seconds. In one hour, FOREST solves 47 benchmarks (73%), with 96% accuracy: only two solutions did not correspond to the desired regex validation. FOREST disambiguates only among programs at the same depth, and so if the first solution is not at the same depth

Table 1: Comparison of time performance using different synthesis methods

Timeout (s)	10	60	3600
FOREST (with interaction)	31	39	47
FOREST's 1st regex (no interaction)	40	46	50
Multi-tree w/o pruning	20	32	38
Dynamic-only multi-tree	5	10	18
k-tree	4	9	15
Line-based (w/o pruning)	4	4	12
REGEL	29	38	47
REGEL PBE	5	7	23

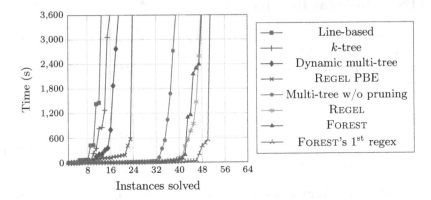

Figure 5: Instances solved using different methods

as the correct one, the correct solution is never found. After 1 hour of running time, FOREST is interrupted, but it prints its current best validation before terminating. After the timeout, FOREST returned 3 more regexes, 2 of which the correct solution for the benchmark. In all benchmarks to which FOREST returns a solution, the first matching regular expression is found in under 10 minutes. In 40 benchmarks, the first regex is found in under 10 seconds. The rest of the time is spent disambiguating the input examples. FOREST interacts with the user to disambiguate the examples in 27 benchmarks. Overall, it asks 1.8 questions and spends 38.6 seconds computing distinguishing inputs, on average.

Regarding the synthesis of capture conditions, in 5 of the benchmarks, we need only 2 capturing groups and at most 4 conditions. In these instances, the conditions' synthesis takes under 2 seconds. The remaining 2 benchmarks need 4 capturing groups and take longer: 99 seconds to synthesize 4 conditions and 1068 seconds for 6 conditions. During capture conditions synthesis, FOREST interacts 7.14 times and takes 0.1 seconds to compute distinguishing inputs, on average.

Table 1 shows the number of instances solved in under 10, 60 and 3600 seconds using FOREST, as well as using the different variations of the synthesizer which will be described in the following sections. The cactus plot in Figure 5 shows the cumulative synthesis time on the y-axis plotted against the number of benchmarks solved by each variation of FOREST (on the x-axis). The synthesis methods that correspond to lines more to the right of the plot are able to solve more benchmarks in less time. We also compare solving times with REGEL [ ]. REGEL takes as input examples and a natural description of user intent. We consider not only the complete REGEL synthesizer, but also the PBE engine of REGEL by itself, which we denote by REGEL PBE.

6.1   Comparison with REGEL

As mentioned in section 5, REGEL's synthesis procedure is split into two steps: sketch generation (using a natural language description of desired behavior) and sketch completion (using input-output examples). To compare REGEL and FOREST, we extended our 64 form validation benchmarks with a natural language description. To assess the importance of the natural language description, we also ran REGEL using only its PBE engine. Sketch generation took on average 60 seconds per instance, and successfully generated a sketch for 63 instances. The remaining instance was run without a sketch. We considered only the highest ranked sketch for each instance. In Table 1 we show how many instances can be solved with different time limits for sketch completion; note that these values do not include the sketch generation time. REGEL returned a regular expression for 47 instances within the time limit. Since REGEL does not implement a disambiguation procedure, the returned regular expression does not always exhibit the desired behavior, even though it correctly classifies all examples. Of the 47 synthesized expressions, 31 exhibit the desired intent. This is a 66% accuracy, which is the same as FOREST without disambiguation (FOREST's 1st regex) but it is much lower than FOREST with disambiguation at 96%. We also observe that REGEL's performance is severely impaired when using only its PBE engine.

51 out of the 63 generated sketches are of the form $\square\{S_1, ..., S_n\}$, where each S_i is a concrete sub-regex, i.e., has no holes. This construct indicates the desired regex must contain *at least* one of $S_1, ..., S_n$, and contains no information about the top-level operators that are used to connect them. 22 of the 47 synthesized regexes are based on sketches of that form, and they result from the direct concatenation of *all* components in the sketch. No new components are generated during sketch completion. Thus, most of REGEL's sketches could be integrated into FOREST, whose multi-tree structure holds precisely those top-level operators that were missing from REGEL's sketches.

6.2   Impact of pruning the search space and splitting examples

To evaluate the impact of pruning the search space as described in section 3.2, we ran FOREST with all pruning techniques disabled. In the scatter plot in Figure 6a, we can compare the solving time on each benchmark with and without pruning. Each mark in the plot represents an instance. The value on the y-axis shows the synthesis time of multi-tree with pruning disabled and the value on the x-axis the synthesis time with pruning enabled. The marks above the $y = x$ line

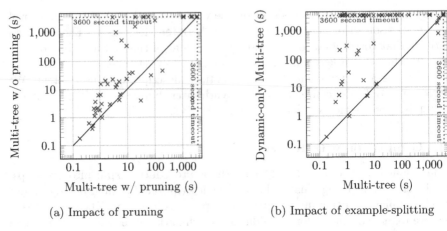

(a) Impact of pruning   (b) Impact of example-splitting

Figure 6: Comparison of synthesis time using different variations of FOREST.

(also represented in the plot) represent problems that took longer to synthesize without pruning than with pruning. On average, with pruning, FOREST can synthesize regexes in 42% of the time and enumerates about 15% of the regexes before returning. There is no significant change in the number of interactions before returning the desired solution.

FOREST is able to split the examples and use static multi-tree as described in section 3.2 in 52 benchmarks (81%). The remaining 12 are solved using dynamic multi-tree. To assess the impact of using static multi-tree we ran FOREST with a version of the multi-tree enumerator that does not split the examples, and jumps directly to dynamic multi-tree solving. In the scatter plot in Figure 6b, we compare the solving times of each benchmark. Using static multi-tree when possible, FOREST requires, on average, less than two thirds of the time (59.1%) to return the desired regex for benchmarks solved by both methods. Furthermore, with static multi-tree FOREST can synthesize more complex regexes: the maximum number of nodes in a solution returned by dynamic multi-tree is 12 (avg. 6.7), while complete multi-tree synthesizes regexes of up to 24 nodes (avg. 10.3).

6.3   Multi-tree versus k-tree and line-based encodings

To evaluate the performance of multi-tree enumeration, we ran FOREST with two other enumeration encodings: k-tree and line-based. The latter is a state of the art encoding for the synthesis of SQL queries [17]. k-tree is the default enumerator in TRINITY [13], and the line-based enumerator is available in SQUARES [10]. The k-tree encoding has a very similar structure to that of multi-tree, so our pruning techniques were easily applied to this encoding. On the other hand, line-based encoding is intrinsically different, so the pruning techniques were not implemented. We compare the line-based encoding to multi-tree without pruning. In every other aspect, the three encodings were run in the same conditions, using FOREST's regex DSL. k-tree is able to synthesize programs with up to

10 nodes, while the line-based encoding synthesizes programs of up to 9 nodes. Neither encoding outperforms multi-tree.

As seen in Table 1, line-based encoding does not outperform the tree-based encodings for the domain of regexes while it was much better for the domain of SQL queries [ ]. We conjecture this disparity arises from the different nature of DSLs. Most SQL queries, when represented as a tree, leave many branches of the tree unused, which results in a much larger tree and SMT encoding.

6.4   Impact of fewer examples

To assess the impact of providing fewer examples on the accuracy of the solution, we ran FOREST with modified versions of each benchmark. First, each benchmark was run with at most 10 valid and 10 invalid examples, chosen randomly among all examples. Conditional invalid examples are already very few per instance, so these were not altered. The accuracy of the returned regexes is slightly lower.

With only 10 valid and 10 invalid examples, FOREST returns the correct regex in 93.5% of the benchmarks, which represents a decrease of only 2.5% relative to the results with all examples. We also saw an increase in the number of interactions before returning, since fewer examples are likely to be more ambiguous. With only 10 examples, FOREST interacts on average 2.2 times per benchmark, which represents an increase of about a fifth. The increase in the number of interactions reflects on a small increase in the synthesis time (less than 1%).

After, we reduced the number of examples even further: only 5 valid and 5 invalid. The accuracy of FOREST in this setting was reduced to 71%. On average, it interacted 4.3 times per benchmark, which is over two times more than before.

7   Conclusions and Future Work

Regexes are commonly used to enforce patterns and validate the input fields of digital forms. However, writing regex validations requires specialized knowledge that not all users possess. We have presented a new algorithm for synthesis of regex validations from examples that leverages the common structure shared between valid examples. Our experimental evaluation shows that the multi-tree representation synthesizes three times more regexes than previous representations in the same amount of time and, together with the user interaction model, FOREST solves 70% of the benchmarks with the correct user intent. We verified that FOREST maintains a very high accuracy with as few as 10 examples of each kind. We also observed that our approach outperforms REGEL, a state-of-the-art synthesizer, in the domain of form validations.

As future work, we would like to explore the synthesis of more complex capture conditions, such as conditions depending on more than one capture. This would allow more restrictive validations; for example, in a date, the possible values for the day could depend on the month. Another possible extension to FOREST is to automatically separate invalid from conditional invalid examples, making this distinction imperceptible to the user.

References

1. Chen, Q., Wang, X., Ye, X., Durrett, G., Dillig, I.: Multi-modal synthesis of regular expressions. In: PLDI. ACM (2020)
2. Chen, Y., Martins, R., Feng, Y.: Maximal multi-layer specification synthesis. In: ESEC/SIGSOFT FSE. pp. 602–612. ACM (2019)
3. Fedyukovich, G., Gupta, A.: Functional synthesis with examples. In: CP. Lecture Notes in Computer Science, vol. 11802, pp. 547–564. Springer (2019)
4. Feng, Y., Martins, R., Bastani, O., Dillig, I.: Program synthesis using conflict-driven learning. In: PLDI. pp. 420–435. ACM (2018)
5. Feng, Y., Martins, R., Geffen, J.V., Dillig, I., Chaudhuri, S.: Component-based synthesis of table consolidation and transformation tasks from examples. In: PLDI. pp. 422–436. ACM (2017)
6. Golia, P., Roy, S., Meel, K.S.: Manthan: A data driven approach for boolean function synthesis. In: CAV. Springer (2020)
7. Gulwani, S.: Automating string processing in spreadsheets using input-output examples. In: POPL. pp. 317–330. ACM (2011)
8. Kini, D., Gulwani, S.: Flashnormalize: Programming by examples for text normalization. In: IJCAI. pp. 776–783. AAAI Press (2015)
9. Kushman, N., Barzilay, R.: Using semantic unification to generate regular expressions from natural language. In: HLT-NAACL. pp. 826–836. The Association for Computational Linguistics (2013)
10. Lee, M., So, S., Oh, H.: Synthesizing regular expressions from examples for introductory automata assignments. In: GPCE. pp. 70–80. ACM (2016)
11. Li, H., Chan, C., Maier, D.: Query from examples: An iterative, data-driven approach to query construction. Proc. VLDB Endow. 8(13), 2158–2169 (2015)
12. Locascio, N., Narasimhan, K., DeLeon, E., Kushman, N., Barzilay, R.: Neural generation of regular expressions from natural language with minimal domain knowledge. In: EMNLP. pp. 1918–1923. The Association for Computational Linguistics (2016)
13. Martins, R., Chen, J., Chen, Y., Feng, Y., Dillig, I.: Trinity: An Extensible Synthesis Framework for Data Science. PVLDB 12(12), 1914–1917 (2019)
14. Mayer, M., Soares, G., Grechkin, M., Le, V., Marron, M., Polozov, O., Singh, R., Zorn, B.G., Gulwani, S.: User interaction models for disambiguation in programming by example. In: UIST. pp. 291–301. ACM (2015)
15. de Moura, L.M., Bjørner, N.: Z3: an efficient SMT solver. In: TACAS. Lecture Notes in Computer Science, vol. 4963, pp. 337–340. Springer (2008)
16. Orvalho, P., Terra-Neves, M., Ventura, M., Martins, R., Manquinho, V.M.: Squares. https://squares-sql.github.io, accessed on May 27, 2020
17. Orvalho, P., Terra-Neves, M., Ventura, M., Martins, R., Manquinho, V.M.: Encodings for enumeration-based program synthesis. In: CP. Lecture Notes in Computer Science, vol. 11802, pp. 583–599. Springer (2019)
18. Python Software Foundation: Python3's regular expression module **re**. https://docs.python.org/3/library/re.html, accessed on October 11, 2020
19. Raza, M., Gulwani, S.: Automated data extraction using predictive program synthesis. In: AAAI. pp. 882–890. AAAI Press (2017)
20. Regular Expression Library: www.regexlib.com, accessed on May 27, 2020
21. Reynolds, A., Barbosa, H., Nötzli, A., Barrett, C.W., Tinelli, C.: cvc4sy: Smart and fast term enumeration for syntax-guided synthesis. In: CAV. Lecture Notes in Computer Science, vol. 11562, pp. 74–83. Springer (2019)

22. Solar-Lezama, A.: Program sketching. Int. J. Softw. Tools Technol. Transf. **15**(5-6), 475–495 (2013)
23. Stanford, C., Veanes, M., Bjørner, N.: Symbolic boolean derivatives for efficiently solving extended regular expression constraints. Tech. Rep. MSR-TR-2020-25, Microsoft (August 2020), updated November 2020.
24. Wang, C., Cheung, A., Bodík, R.: Interactive query synthesis from input-output examples. In: SIGMOD Conference. pp. 1631–1634. ACM (2017)
25. Wang, C., Cheung, A., Bodík, R.: Synthesizing highly expressive SQL queries from input-output examples. In: PLDI. pp. 452–466. ACM (2017)
26. Wang, X., Gulwani, S., Singh, R.: FIDEX: filtering spreadsheet data using examples. In: OOPSLA. pp. 195–213. ACM (2016)
27. Zhong, Z., Guo, J., Yang, W., Peng, J., Xie, T., Lou, J., Liu, T., Zhang, D.: Semregex: A semantics-based approach for generating regular expressions from natural language specifications. In: EMNLP. pp. 1608–1618. Association for Computational Linguistics (2018)

Probabilities

Finding Provably Optimal Markov Chains

Jip Spel[1]([⊠]) , Sebastian Junges[2] , and Joost-Pieter Katoen[1]

1 RWTH Aachen University, Aachen, Germany*
jip.spel@cs.rwth-aachen.de
2 University of California, Berkeley, California, USA**

Abstract. Parametric Markov chains (pMCs) are Markov chains with symbolic (aka: parametric) transition probabilities. They are a convenient operational model to treat robustness against uncertainties. A typical objective is to find the parameter values that maximize the reachability of some target states. In this paper, we consider automatically proving robustness, that is, an ε-close upper bound on the maximal reachability probability. The result of our procedure actually provides an almost-optimal parameter valuation along with this upper bound.

We propose to tackle these ETR-hard problems by a tight combination of two significantly different techniques: monotonicity checking and parameter lifting. The former builds a partial order on states to check whether a pMC is (local or global) monotonic in a certain parameter, whereas parameter lifting is an abstraction technique based on the iterative evaluation of pMCs without parameter dependencies. We explain our novel algorithmic approach and experimentally show that we significantly improve the time to determine almost-optimal synthesis.

1 Introduction

Background and problem setting. Probabilistic model checking [3, 20] is a well-established field and has various applications but assumes probabilities to be fixed constants. To deal with uncertainties, symbolic parameters are used. Parametric Markov chains (pMCs, for short) define a family of Markov chains with uncountably many family members, called instantiations, by having symbolic (aka: parametric) transition probabilities [10, 22]. We are interested in determining optimal parameter settings: which instantiation meets a given objective the best? The typical objective is to maximize the reachability probability of a set of target states. This question is inspired by practical applications such as: *what are the optimal parameter settings in randomised controllers to minimise power consumption?*, and *what is the optimal bias of coins in a randomised distributed algorithm to maximise the chance of achieving mutual exclusion?* For most applications, it suffices to achieve parameters that attain a given quality of service that is

* Supported by DFG RTG 2236 "UnRAVeL" and ERC AdG 787914 FRAPPANT.
* Supported by the NSF grants 1545126 (VeHICaL) and 1646208, by the DARPA Assured Autonomy program, by Berkeley Deep Drive, and by Toyota under the iCyPhy center.

. F. Groote and K. G. Larsen (Eds.): TACAS 2021, LNCS 12651, pp. 173–190, 2021.
https://doi.org/10.1007/978-3-030-72016-2_10

ε-close to the *unknown* optimal solution. More precisely, this paper concentrates on automatically proving ε-*robustness*, i.e., determine an upper bound which is ε-close to the maximal reachability probability. The by-product of our procedure actually provides an *almost-optimal* parameter valuation too.

Existing parameter synthesis techniques. Efficient techniques have been developed in recent years for the feasibility problem: given a parametric Markov chain, and a reachability objective, find an instantiation that reaches the target with at least a given probability. To solve this problem, it suffices to "guess" a correct family member, i.e., a correct parameter instantiation. Verifying the "guessed" instantiation against the reachability objective is readily done using off-the-shelf Markov chain model-checking algorithms. Most recent progress is based on advanced techniques that make informed guesses: This ranges from using sampling techniques [14], guided sampling such as particle swarm optimisation [7], by greedy search [24], or by solving different variants of a convex optimisation problem around a sample [8,9]. Sampling has been accelerated by reusing previous model checking results [25], or by just in time compilation of the parameter function [12]. These methods are inherently inadequate for finding *optimal* parameter settings. To the best of our knowledge, optimal parameter synthesis has received scant attention so far. A notable exception is the analysis (e.g., using SMT techniques) of rational functions, typically obtained by some form of state elimination [10,12,15], that symbolically represent reachability probabilities in terms of the parameters. These functions are exponential in the number of parameters [16] and become infeasible for more than two parameters. Parameter lifting [5,6,25] remedies this by using an abstraction technique, but due to an exponential blow-up of region splitting, is limited to a handful of parameters. *The challenge is to solve optimal parameter synthesis problems with more parameters.*

Approach. We propose to tackle the optimal synthesis problem by a deep integration of two seemingly unrelated techniques: *monotonicity checking* [27] and *parameter lifting* [25]. The former builds a partial order on the state space to check whether a pMC is (local or global) monotonic in a certain parameter, while the latter is an abstraction technique that "lifts" the parameter dependencies, obtaining interval MCs [17,21], and solves them in an iterative manner. To construct an efficient combination, we extend both methods such that they profit from each other. This is done by combining them with a tailored *divide-and-conquer* component, see Fig. 1. To prove bounds on the induced reachability probability, parameter lifting has been the undisputed state-of-the-art, despite the increased attention that parameter synthesis has received over recent years. This paper improves parameter lifting with more advanced reasoning capabilities that involve properties of the derivative, rather than the actual probabilities. These reasoning methods enable reducing the exponent of the inherently exponential-time procedure. This conceptual advantage is joined with various engineering efforts. Parameter lifting is accelerated by using side products of monotonicity analysis such as local monotonicity and shrinked parameter regions. Furthermore, bounds obtained by parameter lifting are used to obtain a cheap rule accelerating the

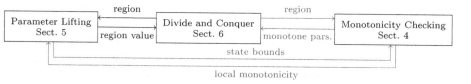

region

region

| Parameter Lifting Sect. 5 | | Divide and Conquer Sect. 6 | | Monotonicity Checking Sect. 4 |

region value

monotone pars.

state bounds

local monotonicity

Fig. 1. The symbiosis of parameter lifting and monotonicity checking. Red are new interactions, compared to earlier work. Details are given in Sect. 3.

monotonicity checker. The interplay between the two advanced techniques is tricky and requires a careful treatment.

Note that we are not the first to exploit monotonicity in the context of pMCs. Hutschenreiter *et al.* [16] showed that the complexity of model checking (a monotone fragment of) PCTL on monotonic pMC is lower than on general pMCs. Pathak *et al.* [24] provided an efficient greedy approach to repair monotonic pMCs. Recently, Gouberman *et al.* [13] used monotonicity for hitting probabilities in perturbed continuous-time MCs.

Experimental results. We realised the integrated approached on top of the Storm [11] model checker. Experiments on several benchmarks show that optimal synthesis is possible: (1) on benchmarks with up to about a few hundred parameters, (2) on benchmarks that cannot be handled without monotonicity, (3) while accelerating pure parameter lifting by up to two orders of magnitude. Our approach induces a bit of overhead on small instances for some benchmarks, and starts to pay off when increasing the number of parameters.

Main contribution. In summary, the main contribution of this paper is a tight integration of parameter lifting and monotonicity checking. Experiments indicate that this novel combination substantially improves upon the state-of-the-art in *optimal* parameter synthesis.

Organisation of the paper. Section 2 provides the necessary technical background and formalises the problem. Section 3 explains the approach—in particular the meaning of the arrows in Fig. 1. Section 4 discusses how to state bounds can be exploited in the monotonicity checker. Section 5 details how to exploit local monotonicity in parameter lifting. Section 6 then considers the tight interplay via the divide-and-conquer method. Section 7 reports on the experimental results of our prototypical implementation in Storm while Section 8 concludes the paper.

2 Problem Statement

A *probability distribution* over a finite or countably infinite set X is a function $\mu: X \to [0, 1] \subseteq \mathbb{R}$ with $\sum_{x \in X} \mu(x) = 1$. The set of all distributions on X is denoted by $Distr(X)$. Let $\vec{a} \in \mathbb{R}^n$ denote $(a_1, \dots, a_n)$. The set of multivariate polynomials over ordered variables $\vec{x} = (x_1, \ldots, x_n)$ is denoted $\mathbb{Q}[\vec{x}]$. For a polynomial f and variable x, we write $x \in f$ if the variable occurs in the polynomial f. An *instantiation* for a finite set V of real-valued variables is a function $u \colon V \to \mathbb{R}$. We often denote u as a vector $\vec{u} \in \mathbb{R}^n$ with $u_i := u(x_i)$ for $x_i \in V$. A polynomial f can be interpreted as a function $f \colon \mathbb{R}^n \to \mathbb{R}$, where $f(\vec{u})$ is obtained by substitution, i.e., $f[\vec{x} \leftarrow \vec{u}]$, where each occurrence of x_i in f is replaced by $u(x_i)$.

Definition 1 (pMC). *A* parametric Markov Chain (pMC) *is a tuple* $\mathcal{M} = (S, s_I, T, V, \mathcal{P})$ *with a finite set* S *of* states, *an* initial state $s_I \in S$, *a finite set* $T \subseteq S$ *of* target states, *a finite set* V *of* real-valued variables *(parameters) and a transition function* $\mathcal{P} \colon S \times S \to \mathbb{Q}[V]$.

A pMC $\mathcal{M}$ is a *(discrete-time) Markov chain* (MC) if the transition function yields *well-defined* probability distributions, i.e., $\mathcal{P}(s, \cdot) \in Distr(S)$ for each $s \in S$. Applying an *instantiation* $\vec{u}$ to a pMC $\mathcal{M}$ yields $\mathcal{M}[\vec{u}]$ by replacing each $f \in \mathbb{Q}[V]$ in $\mathcal{M}$ by $f(\vec{u})$. An instantiation $\vec{u}$ is *well-defined* (for $\mathcal{M}$) if $\mathcal{M}[\vec{u}]$ is an MC. A well-defined instantiation $\vec{u}$ is *graph-preserving* (for $\mathcal{M}$) if the topology is preserved, i.e., $\mathcal{P}(s, s') \neq 0$ implies $\mathcal{P}(s, s')(\vec{u}) \neq 0$ for all states s and s'. A set of instantiations is called a *region*. A region R is well-defined (graph-preserving) if $\vec{u}$ is well-defined (graph-preserving) for all $\vec{u} \in R$. In this paper, we consider only graph-preserving regions.

For a parameter-free MC $\mathcal{M}$, $\mathrm{Pr}_{\mathcal{M}}^s(\lozenge T) \in [0, 1] \subseteq \mathbb{R}$ denotes the probability that from state s the target T is eventually reached. For a formal definition, we refer to, e.g., [4, Ch. 10]. For pMC $\mathcal{M}$, $\mathrm{Pr}_{\mathcal{M}}^s(\lozenge T)$ is not a constant, but rather a function $\mathrm{Pr}_{\mathcal{M}}^{s \to T} \colon V \to [0, 1]$, with $\mathrm{Pr}_{\mathcal{M}}^{s \to T}(\vec{u}) = \mathrm{Pr}_{\mathcal{M}[\vec{u}]}^s(\lozenge T)$. The closed-form of $\mathrm{Pr}^{s \to T}$ on a graph-preserving region is a rational function over V, i.e., a fraction of two polynomials over V. On a graph-preserving region, the function $\mathrm{Pr}^{s \to T}$ is continuously differentiable [25]. We call $\mathrm{Pr}_{\mathcal{M}}^{s \to T}$ the *solution function*, and for conciseness, we often omit the subscript $\mathcal{M}$. Graph-preserving instantiations $\vec{u}, \vec{u}'$ preserve zero-one probabilities, i.e., $\mathrm{Pr}^{s \to T}(\vec{u}) = 0$ implies $\mathrm{Pr}^{s \to T}(\vec{u}') = 0$, and analogous for $=1$. We simply write $\mathrm{Pr}^{s \to T} = 0$ (or $=1$). Let $\ddot{\smile}$ ($\ddot{\frown}$) denote all states $s \in S$ with $\mathrm{Pr}^{s \to T} = 1$ ($\mathrm{Pr}^{s \to T} = 0$). By a standard preprocessing [4], we may safely assume a single $\ddot{\smile}$ and $\ddot{\frown}$ state.

Problem statement. This paper is concerned with the following questions for a given pMC $\mathcal{M}$ with target states T, and region R:

Optimal synthesis. Find the instantiation $\vec{u}^*$ such that

$$\vec{u}^* = \arg\max_{\vec{u} \in R} \mathrm{Pr}_{\mathcal{M}[\vec{u}]}(\lozenge T)$$

ϵ-*Robustness.* Given tolerance $\varepsilon \geq 0$, find an instantiation $\vec{u}^*$ such that

$$\max_{\vec{u} \in R} \mathrm{Pr}_{\mathcal{M}[\vec{u}]}(\lozenge T) - \varepsilon \leq \mathrm{Pr}_{\mathcal{M}[\vec{u}^*]}(\lozenge T) \leq \max_{\vec{u} \in R} \mathrm{Pr}_{\mathcal{M}[\vec{u}]}(\lozenge T).$$

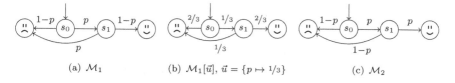

Fig. 2. Toy examples for pMCs.

The optimal synthesis problem is ETR-hard [28], i.e., as hard as finding a root of a multivariate polynomial. It is thus NP-hard and in PSPACE. The same applies to ε-robustness. The value of λ can be viewed as the optimal reachability probability of T — up to the robustness tolerance ε — over all possible parameter values while $\vec{u}^*$ is the instantiation that maximises the probability to reach T.

Like [28], we assume pMCs to be *simple*, i.e., $\mathcal{P}(s, s') \in \{x, 1-x \mid x \in V\} \cup \mathbb{Q}$ for all $s, s' \in S$ and $\sum_{s'} \mathcal{P}(s, s') = 1$. Theoretically, the above problem for simple pMCs is as hard as for general pMCs, and practically, most pMCs are simple. For simple pMCs, the graph-preserving instantiations are in $(0, 1)^{|V|}$. Regions are assumed to be *well-defined*, *rectangular* and *closed*, i.e., a region is a Cartesian product of closed intervals, $R = \times_{x \in V}[\ell_x, u_x]$. Let $R(x)$ denote the interval $[\ell_x, u_x]$ and $\mathsf{occur}(s)$ the set of variables $\{x \in V \mid \exists s' \in S. \, x \in \mathcal{P}(s, s')\}$. For simple pMCs, this set has cardinality at most one. A state s is called *parametric*, if $\mathsf{occur}(s) \neq \emptyset$; we write $\mathsf{occur}(s) = x$ if $\{x\} = \mathsf{occur}(s)$.

Example 1. Fig. 2(a) depicts a pMC. A region R is given by $p \in [1/4, 1/2]$. An instantiation $\vec{u} = \{p \mapsto 1/3\} \in R$ yields the pMC in Fig. 2(b). The solution function is $\mathrm{Pr}^{s_0 \to T}_{\mathcal{M}_1} = p \cdot (1 - p)$. Indeed $\mathrm{Pr}^{s_0 \to T}_{\mathcal{M}_1}(\vec{u}) = 2/9 = \mathrm{Pr}_{\mathcal{M}_1[\vec{u}]}(\lozenge T)$.

3 Main Ingredients in a Nutshell

To solve the problem statement, we consider an iterative method which analyzes regions, and, if necessary, splits these regions. In particular, we combine two approaches — parameter lifting and monotonicity checking — as shown in Fig. 1.

3.1 The Monotonicity Checker

We consider *local* and *global* monotonicity. We start with defining the latter.

Definition 2 (Global monotonicity). *A continuously differentiable function f on region R is monotonic increasing in variable x, denoted $f \uparrow^R_x$, if $\frac{\partial}{\partial x} f(\vec{u}) \geq 0$ for all $\vec{u} \in R^3$. The pMC $\mathcal{M} = (S, s_I, T, V, \mathcal{P})$ is monotonic increasing in parameter $x \in V$ on graph-preserving region R, written $\mathcal{M} \uparrow^R_x$, if $\mathrm{Pr}^{s_I \to T} \uparrow^R_x$.*

---

[3] To be precise, on the interior of the closed set R.

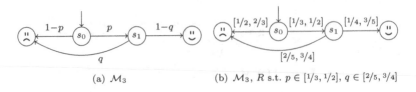

(a) $\mathcal{M}_3$ (b) $\mathcal{M}_3$, R s.t. $p \in [1/3, 1/2]$, $q \in [2/5, 3/4]$

Fig. 3. Simple pMC that indeed is an iMC.

Monotonic *decreasing*, written $\mathcal{M}{\downarrow}_x^R$, is defined analogously. Let $\mathsf{succ}(s) = \{s' \in S \mid \mathcal{P}(s, s') \neq 0\}$ be the set of direct successors of s. Given the recursive equation $\mathsf{Pr}^{s \to T} = \sum_{s' \in \mathsf{succ}(s)} \mathcal{P}(s, s') \cdot \mathsf{Pr}^{s' \to T}$ for state $s \neq \text{☺},\text{☹}$, we have

$$\mathcal{M}{\uparrow}_x^R \quad \text{iff} \quad \frac{\partial}{\partial x} \left(\sum_{s' \in \mathsf{succ}(s)} \mathcal{P}(s, s') \cdot \mathsf{Pr}^{s' \to T} \right) (\vec{u}) \geq 0 \ ,$$

for all $\vec{u} \in R$. Rather than checking global monotonicity, the monotonicity checker determines a subset of the *locally* monotone state-parameter pairs. Such pairs intuitively capture monotonicity of a parameter only locally at a state s.

Definition 3 (Local monotonicity). *Function $\mathsf{Pr}^{s \to T}$ is locally monotonic increasing in parameter x (at state s) on region R, written $\mathsf{Pr}^{s \to T}{\uparrow}_x^{\ell, R}$, if*

$$\forall \vec{u} \in R. \quad \left(\sum_{s' \in \mathsf{succ}(s)} \left(\frac{\partial}{\partial x} \mathcal{P}(s, s') \right) \cdot \mathsf{Pr}^{s' \to T} \right) (\vec{u}) \geq 0.$$

Thus, while global monotonicity considers the derivative of the entire solution function, local monotonicity (in s) only considers the derivative of the first transition (emanating from s). Local monotonicity of parameter x in every state implies global monotonicity of x, as shown in [27]. As checking global monotonicity is co-ETR hard [27], a practical approach is to check *sufficient conditions* for monotonicity. These conditions are based on constructing a pre-order on the states of the pMC; this is explained in detail in Section 4.

Example 2. For $R = \{\vec{u}(p) \in [1/10, 9/10]\}$, pMC $\mathcal{M}_1$ in Fig. 2(a) is locally monotonic increasing in p at s_0 and locally monotonic decreasing in p at s_1. From this, we cannot conclude anything about global monotonicity of p on R. Indeed, the pMC is not globally monotonic on R. $\mathcal{M}_1$ is globally monotonic on $R' = \{\vec{u}(p) \in [1/10, 1/2]\}$, but this cannot be concluded from the statement above. Contrarily, the pMC $\mathcal{M}_2$ in Fig. 2(c) is locally monotonic increasing in p at both s_0 and s_1, and is therefore globally monotonic increasing in p.

3.2   The Parameter Lifter

The key idea of parameter lifting [25] is to drop all parameter dependencies—parameters that occur at multiple states in a pMC—by introducing fresh parameters. The outcome is an *interval* Markov chain [17,21], which can be considered a special case of pMCs in which no parameter occurs at multiple states.

Definition 4 (Interval MC). *A pMC is a (simple)* interval MC (iMC)*, if* $\text{occur}(s) \cap \text{occur}(s') = \emptyset$ *for all states* $s \neq s'$.

All iMCs in this paper are simple. We typically label transitions emanating from state s in an iMC with $x = \text{occur}(s)$ by $R(x) = [\ell_x, u_x]$.

Example 3. The pMC in Fig. 3(a) is an iMC. For a fixed R, the typical notation is given in Fig. 3(b). For the pMC $\mathcal{M}_1$ in Fig. 2(a), the parameter p occurs at states s_0 and s_1, so that this pMC is not an iMC.

Definition 5 (Relaxation). *The* relaxation *of simple pMC* $\mathcal{M}=(S, s_I, T, V, \mathcal{P})$ *is the iMC* $\text{relax}(\mathcal{M}) = (S, s_I, T, V', \mathcal{P}')$ *with* $V' = \{x_s \mid s \in S, \text{occur}(s) \neq \emptyset\}$, $\mathcal{P}'(s, s') = \mathcal{P}(s, s')[\text{occur}(s) \leftarrow x_s]$.

For state s *with* $\text{occur}(s) = x$, *let* $\text{relax}(R)(x_s) = R(\text{occur}(s))$. *Likewise, an instantiation in* $\vec{u} \in R$ *is mapped to* $\text{relax}(\vec{u})$ *by* $\text{relax}(\vec{u})(x_s) = \vec{u}(\text{occur}(s))$.

Extremal reachability probabilities on iMCs are reached at the extremal values of a region. Formally [25], for each state s and region R in pMC $\mathcal{M}$:

$$\max_{\vec{u} \in R} \text{Pr}_{\mathcal{M}}^{s \to T}(\vec{u}) \leq \max_{\vec{u} \in \text{relax}(R)} \text{Pr}_{\text{relax}(\mathcal{M})}^{s \to T}(\vec{u}). \tag{1}$$

This result is a direct consequence of local monotonicity at all states implying global monotonicity. The extremal values for the reachability probabilities in the obtained iMCs are obtained by interpreting the iMCs as MDPs and applying off-the-shelf MDP model checking. We denote the right-hand side of (1) as upper bound on R, denoted $U_R(s)$. Analogously we define a lower bound $L_R(s)$.

Example 4. The pMC $\mathcal{M}_3$ in Fig. 3(a) is the relaxation of the pMC $\mathcal{M}_1$ in Fig. 2(a). Indeed, for $R = \{\vec{u}(p) \in [1/4, 3/4]\}$:

$$\max_{\vec{u} \in R} \text{Pr}_{\mathcal{M}_1}^{s_0 \to T}(\vec{u}) = 1/4 \leq 9/16 = \max_{\vec{u} \in \text{relax}(R)} \text{Pr}_{\mathcal{M}_3}^{s_0 \to T}(\vec{u}).$$

3.3   Divide and Conquer

Figure 4 shows how the extremal value for region R_ι, pMC $\mathcal{M}$, reachability property φ and precision ϵ can be computed *using only parameter lifting* [25]: This paper extends this iterative approach to include monotonicity checking. The main idea is to analyze regions and split them if the result is inconclusive. The approach uses a queue of regions that need to be checked and the current extremal value CurMax found so far. In particular, we maintain a lower bound on CurMax and know a (potentially trivial) upper bound: $(\text{CurMax}+\varepsilon) \geq \max_{\hat{R} \in Q} U_{\hat{R}}(s_I)$. We iteratively check regions and improve both bounds until a satisfactory solution is found. Initially, the queue only contains R_ι. For a selected R from the queue we compute an upper bound U_R with parameter lifting. If U_R at the initial state

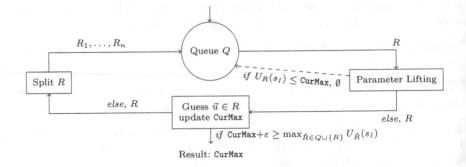

Fig. 4. Divide and conquer with pure parameter lifting

is below the current optimum, we can safely discard R. Otherwise, we want attempt to improve CurMax by guessing $u \in R$ and computing $\Pr_{\mathcal{M}}^{s \to T}(\vec{u})$ using model checking[4]. If $\Pr_{\mathcal{M}}^{s \to T}(\vec{u})$ exceeds CurMax, we update CurMax. Now, we check whether we can terminate:

In particular, let the maximum so far be bounded by $\max_{\hat{R} \in Q \cup \{R\}} U_{\hat{R}}(s_I)$. If the upper bound is below CurMax$+\varepsilon$, we are done, and return CurMax together with the u associated with CurMax. Otherwise, we continue and split R into smaller regions. By default, parameter lifting splits R along all dimensions. This algorithm converges in the limit [25].

Example 5. Reconsider Ex. 4, and assume we want to show $\max_{\vec{u} \in R} \Pr_{\mathcal{M}_1}^{s_0 \to T}(\vec{u}) \leq 1/4$, with $\varepsilon = 1/8$. We sample in (the middle of) R and obtain CurMax $= 1/4$, while the upper bound $U_R(s_I)$ from Ex. 4 is $9/16$. We split R into two regions $R_1 = \{\vec{u}(p) \in [1/4, 1/2]\}$ and $R_2 = \{\vec{u}(p) \in [1/2, 3/4]\}$. Parameter lifting reveals that for both regions the bound is $3/8$. Thus, $1/4$ is an epsilon-close instance.

The remainder of this paper integrates monotonicity checking in this loop.

> This paper addresses **three challenges**: (Sect. 4): Using state bounds in the monotonicity checker. (Sect. 5): Using local monotonicity in parameter lifting. (Sect. 6) Integrating monotonicity in the divide and conquer loop.

4   A New Rule for Sufficient Monotonicity

As discussed in Section 3.1, we aim to analyse whether for a given region R, parameter x is locally monotonic at state s. The key ingredient is a pre-order on the states of the pMC at hand that is used for checking sufficient conditions for being local monotonic. We define the pre-order and recap the "cheap" rules for efficiently determining the pre-order as adopted from [27]. We add a new, simple rule to this repertoire that lets us avoid the computationally "expensive"

---

[4] Using an *instantiation checker* that reuses model-checking results from the last guess.

rules using assumptions from [27]. The information needed to apply this new rule readily comes from parameter lifting as we will see.

Ordering states for local monotonicity. Let us consider a conceptual example showing how a pre-order on states can be used for determining local monotonicity.

Example 6. Consider the pMC $\mathcal{M}_2$ in Fig. 2(c). We reason backwards that both states are locally monotone increasing in p. First, observe that $\smile$ has a higher probability to reach the target (1) than $\frown$ (0). Now, in s_1, increasing p will move more probability mass to $\smile$, and hence, it is locally monotone. Furthermore, we know that the probability from s_1 is between $\smile$ and $\frown$. Now, for s_0 we can use that increasing p moves more probability mass to s_1, which we know has a higher probability to reach the target than $\frown$.

As in [27], we determine local monotonicity by ordering states according to their reachability probability.

Definition 6 (Reachability order). *A relation $\preceq_{R,T} \subseteq S \times S$ is a* reachability order *with respect to $T \subseteq S$ and region R if for all $s, t \in S$:*

$$s \preceq_{R,T} t \quad implies \quad \left(\forall \vec{u} \in R.\ \mathsf{Pr}^{s \to T}(\vec{u}) \le \mathsf{Pr}^{t \to T}(\vec{u}) \right).$$

The order $\preceq_{R,T}$ is called exhaustive *if the reverse implication also holds.*

The relation $\preceq_{R,T}$ is a reflexive (aka: non-strict) pre-order. The exhaustive reachability order is the union of all reachability orders, and always exists. Unless stated differently, let $\preceq$ denote the exhaustive reachability order. If the successor states of a state s are ordered, we can conclude local monotonicity in s:

Lemma 1. *Let $s, s_1, s_2 \in S$ with $\mathcal{P}(s, s_1) = x$ and $\mathcal{P}(s, s_2) = 1-x$. Then:*

$$for\ each\ region\ R: \qquad s_2 \preceq_{R,T} s_1 \quad implies \quad \mathsf{Pr}^{s \to T}\!\uparrow_x^{\ell,R}.$$

This result suggests to look for a so-called "sufficient" reachability order:

Definition 7 (Sufficient reachability order). *A reachability order $\preceq$ is* sufficient *for parameter x if for all states s with $\mathsf{occur}(s) = \{x\}$ and $s_1, s_2 \in \mathsf{succ}(s)$ it holds: $(s_1 \preceq s_2 \lor s_2 \preceq s_1)$.*

Phrased differently, the reachability order $\preceq$ is sufficient for $x \in V$ if $(\mathsf{succ}(s), \preceq)$ is a total order for all s that have transitions labelled with x. Observe that in contrast to an exhaustive order, a sufficient order does not need to exist.

Ordering states efficiently. Def. 6 provides a conceptually simple scheme to order states s_1 and s_2: compute the rational functions $\mathsf{Pr}^{s_1 \to T}$ and $\mathsf{Pr}^{s_2 \to T}$, and compare them. As the size of these multivariate rational functions can be exponential in the number of parameters [16], this is not practically viable. To avoid this, [27] has identified a set of *rules* that provide sufficient criteria to order states. Some of these rules are conceptually based on the underlying graph of a pMC and are computationally cheap; other rules reason about (a partial representation of) the full rational function $\mathsf{Pr}^{s_1 \to T}$ and are computationally expensive.

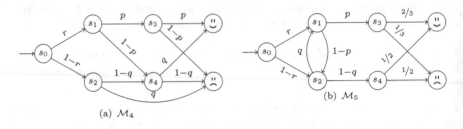

(a) $\mathcal{M}_4$ (b) $\mathcal{M}_5$

Fig. 5. Non-trivial pMCs for deducing monotonicity.

Example 7. Using bounds avoids expensive rules: See $\mathcal{M}_4$ in Fig. 5(a). Let $R = \{\vec{u}(q) \in [1/2, 3/4], \vec{u}(p) \in [1/2, 2/3]\}$. Using the solution functions $p^2 + (1-p) \cdot q$ and $q \cdot (1-q)$ for s_1 and s_2 yields $s_2 \preceq s_1$ on R. Such a rule is expensive, but the cheaper graph-based rules analogous to Ex. 6 are not applicable. However, when we use bounds from parameter lifting, we obtain $U_R(s_2) = 3/8$ and $L_R(s_1) = 1/2$, we observe $U_R(s_2) \le L_R(s_1)$ and thus $s_2 \preceq s_1$ on R. Bounds also just simplify graph-based reasoning, in particular in the presence of cycles. Consider $\mathcal{M}_5$: As $L_R(s_3) \ge U_R(s_4)$, with reasoning similar to Ex. 6, it follows that $s_2 \preceq s_1$, and we immediately get results about monotonicity.

Our aim is to avoid applying the expensive rules from [27] by imposing a new — and thanks to parameter lifting — cheap rule. To obtain this rule, we assume for state s and region R to have bounds $L_R(s)$ and $U_R(s)$ at our disposal satisfying

$$L_R(s) \le \Pr^{s \to T}(\vec{u}) \le U_R(s) \quad \text{for all } \vec{u} \in R .$$

Such bounds can be trivially assumed to be 0 and 1 respectively, but the idea is to obtain tighter bounds by exploiting the parameter lifter. This will be further detailed in Section 5. A simple observation on these bounds yields a cheap rule (provided these bounds can be easily obtained).

Lemma 2. *For $s_1, s_2 \in S$ and region R: $L_R(s_1) \ge U_R(s_2)$ implies $s_2 \preceq_{R,T} s_1$.*

In the remainder of this section, we elaborate some technical details.

Algorithmic reasoning. The pre-order $\preceq$ is stored by a representation of its Hasse diagram, referred to as RO-graph. Evaluating whether two states are ordered amounts to a graph search in the RO-graph. We start off with the initial order $\overset{..}{\frown} \preceq \overset{..}{\smile}$. Then we attempt to apply one of the cheap rules to a state s. Lemma 2 provides us with more potential to apply a cheap rule. The typical approach is to do this in a reverse topological order over the RO-graph, such that the successors of s are already ordered as much as possible. If the successor states of s are ordered, then s can be added as a vertex and directed edges can be added between s and its successors. Otherwise, state s is added between $\overset{..}{\frown}$ and $\overset{..}{\smile}$. This often allows for reasoning analogous to the example. To deal with strongly connected components, rules exist [27] that add states to the order even when not all successors are in the graph. If no cheap rule can be applied, more expensive rules using the rational functions from above or SMT-solvers are applied[5].

5   Parameter Lifting with Monotonicity Information

Recall that our aim is to compute some $\lambda \geq \max_{\vec{u} \in R} \Pr_{\mathcal{M}}^{s \to T}(\vec{u}) - \varepsilon$ for some fixed region R. In order to do so, we compute $\widehat{\lambda} := \max_{\vec{u} \in \text{relax}(R)} \Pr_{\text{relax}(\mathcal{M})}^{s \to T}(\vec{u})$ on the iMC relax($\mathcal{M}$) obtained by relaxing the pMC $\mathcal{M}$. We discuss how to speed up this computation using local monotonicity information. In the remainder, let $\mathcal{D}$ denote relax($\mathcal{M}$) and I denote relax(R). As we consider simple iMCs, let state s with $\mathcal{P}(s, s_1) = x_s$ and $\mathcal{P}(s, s_2) = 1 - x_s$ where the parameter x_s does not occur on other transitions. Assume the lower (upper) bound on x_s is l_s (u_s).

Analyzing (simple) iMCs. An iMC induces a maximal reachability bound by substituting every x_s with either l_s or u_s. Formally, let $\mathcal{V}(I)$ denote the corner points of the interval I. Then,

$$\max_{\vec{u} \in I} \Pr_{\mathcal{D}}^{s \to T}(\vec{u}) \;=\; \max_{\vec{u} \in \mathcal{V}(I)} \Pr_{\mathcal{D}}^{s \to T}(\vec{u}).$$

Thus, to maximise the probability to reach T, in every state s either the lower or the upper bound of parameter x_s has to be chosen. This induces $\mathcal{O}(2^{|S|})$ choices. They can be efficiently navigated by interpreting these choices as nondeterministic choices, interpreting the iMC as a Markov decision process (MDP) [25].

Local monotonicity helps. Assume local monotonicity establishes $s_1 \preceq s_2$, i.e., the reachability probability from s_2 is at least as high as from s_1. To maximise the reachability probability from s, the parameter x_s should be minimised. Contrary, if $s_2 \preceq s_1$, parameter x_s should be maximised. Thus, every local monotonicity result halves the amount of vertices that we are maximising over.

Example 8. Consider the iMC $\mathcal{M}_3$ in Fig. 3(a), which is the relaxation of the pMC $\mathcal{M}_1$ in Fig. 2(a). There are four combinations of lower and upper bounds that need to be investigated to compute the upper bound. Using local monotonicity, we deduce that q should be as low as possible and p as high as possible. Rather than evaluating a MDP, we thus obtain the same upper bound on the reachability probability in $\mathcal{M}_1$ by evaluating a single parameter-free Markov chain.

Accelerating value iteration. Parameter lifting [25] creates a single MDP — a comparatively expensive operation — and instantiates this MDP based on the region R to be checked. For computing the bound $\widehat{\lambda}$, specifically, it uses value iteration. Roughly, this means that for each state we start with either its lower or upper bound. The instantiated MC is then checked. Then, all bounds that can

---

[5] In an attempt to reduce the cost of these rules, the algorithm allows for deferring proof obligations in the form of assumptions. This is detailed in [27]. For this paper, however, the only relevant aspect is that these rules are computationally expensive.

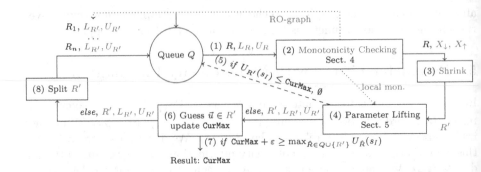

Fig. 6. The symbiosis of monotonicity checking and parameter lifting. Red are new elements compared to the vanilla approach in Fig. 4.

be improved by switching from lower to upper bound or vice versa are swapped. This procedure terminates with the optimal assignment to all bounds. We exploit the local monotonicity in this value iteration procedure by fixing the chosen bounds at locally monotonic states.

6   Lifting and Monotonocity, Together

In this section, we give a more detailed account of our approach, i.e., we will zoom in into Fig. 1 resulting in Fig. 6. In particular, we detail the divide-and-conquer block. This loop is a refinement (indicated in red in Fig. 6) of Fig. 4. We first give an overview, before discussing some aspects in greater detail.

Overall algorithm The approach considers *extended* regions, i.e., a region R is equipped with state bounds $L_R(s)$ and $U_R(s)$ such that $L_R(s) \leq \Pr_{\mathcal{M}}^{s \to T}(\vec{u}) \leq U_R(s)$ for every state s, and with monotonicity information about the monotonic increasing (and decreasing) parameters on R. Initially the input region R is extended with $L_R(s) = 0, U_R(s) = 1$ for every s, and empty monotonicity information. Additionally, we initialize a conservative approximation for the maximum probability CurMax so far as 0. Extended regions are stored in the priority queue Q where $U_R(s_I)$ are used as priority. We discuss details below. Once initialised, we start an iterative process to update the conservative approximation of L_R and U_R.

First, (1) a region R and the associated reachability order stored as RO-graph is taken from the queue Q and (2) its monotonicity is computed while using the annotated bounds L_R and U_R. Let $X_{\uparrow}^R$ denote globally monotonic increasing parameters on R, and similarly, $X_{\downarrow}^R$ denote decreasing parameters on R. For brevity, we omit the superscript R in the following.

As a next step, we (3) *shrink* a region based on global monotonicity. We define the region $\mathrm{Shrink}_{X_{\uparrow}, X_{\downarrow}}(R)$ as follows: $\mathrm{Shrink}_{X_{\uparrow}, X_{\downarrow}}(R)(x) = \ell_x$ if $x \in X_{\downarrow}$,

$\mathsf{Shrink}(R)(x) = u_x$ if $x \in X_\uparrow$, and $\mathsf{Shrink}(R)(x) = R(x)$ otherwise. In the remainder of this section, let R' denote $\mathsf{Shrink}_{X_\uparrow, X_\downarrow}(R)$. Observe that we can safely discard instantiations in $R \setminus R'$, as $\max_{\vec{u} \in R} \mathsf{Pr}_{\mathcal{M}}^{s \to T}(\vec{u}) = \max_{\vec{u} \in R'} \mathsf{Pr}_{\mathcal{M}}^{s \to T}(\vec{u})$.

Next, we (4) analyse the region R' to get bounds $L_{R'}, U_{R'}$ using parameter lifting and using the local monotonicity information from the monotonicity check. We make two observations: First, it holds that $L_R(s) \leq L_{R'}(s)$ and $U_{R'}(s) \leq U_R(s)$ for every s: Thus, there is no regret in analysing R' rather than R. Also, consider that if all parameters are globally monotone, the region R' is a singleton and straightforward to analyse.

If (5) $U_{R'}(s_I) \leq \mathtt{CurMax}$, then we discard R' altogether and go to (1). Otherwise, we (6) guess a candidate $\vec{u} \in R'$, and set $\mathtt{CurMax}$ to $\max(\mathtt{CurMax}, \mathsf{Pr}_{\mathcal{M}}^{s \to T}(\vec{u}))$. If (7) $\mathtt{CurMax} + \varepsilon \geq \max_{\hat{R} \in Q \cup \{R'\}} U_{\hat{R}}(s_I)$, then we have solved our problem statement by returning $\mathtt{CurMax}$. Otherwise, we cannot yet give a conclusive answer, and need to refine our analysis. To that end, we (8) *split* the region R' into smaller (rectangular) regions $R_1, \ldots, R_n$. Note that these sub-regions first inherit the bounds of the region R'; their bounds are refined in a subsequent iteration (if any). Termination in the limit (i.e., convergence of the lower and upper bound to the limit) follows from the termination of monotonicity checking and the termination of the loop in Fig. 4.

Incrementality A key aspect in tuning iterative approaches is the concept of incrementality; i.e., reusing previously computed information in later computation steps. Parameter lifting is already incremental [25] by reusing the MDP structure in an efficient manner. Let us address incrementality for the monotonicity checker. Notice that all monotonicity information and all bounds that are computed for region R carry over to any $\hat{R} \subseteq R$. In particular, $s \preceq_{R,T} s'$ implies $s \preceq_{\hat{R},T} s'$
. Furthermore, our monotonicity checker may give up in an iteration if no cheap rules to determine monotonicity can be applied. In that case, we annotate the current reachability order such that after refining bounds, in a subsequent iteration, we can quickly check where we gave up in a last iteration, and whether refined bounds allow progress in constructing the reachability order. Notice that in principle, we have to duplicate the order for each region. However, we do this only until the monotonicity checker does not stabilize. The checker stabilizes, e.g., if an order is sufficient. Once the checker stabilized, we do not duplicate the order anymore (as no more local or global monotonicity can be deduced).

Heuristics Our approach allows for several choices in the implementation. Whereas the correctness of the approach does not depend on how to resolve these choices, they have a significant influence on the performance. We discuss (what we believe to be) the most important choices, and how we resolved these choices in the current implementation.

Initialising $\mathtt{CurMax}$. Previously Storm was applicable only to few parameters and generously initialized $\mathtt{CurMax}$ by sampling all vertices $\mathcal{V}(R)$, which is exponential in the number of parameters. To scale to more parameters, we discard this sampling. Instead, we sample for each parameter independently to find out which parameters are definitely not monotone. Naturally, we skip parameters already known to be monotone. We select sample points as follows. We distribute the 50 points evenly along the dimension of the parameter. All other parameter values are fixed: Non-monotonic parameters are set to their middle point in their interval (as described by the region). Monotone parameters are set at the upper (lower) bound when possibly monotone increasing (decreasing).

Updating CurMax. To prove that CurMax is close to the maximum, it is essential to find a large value for CurMax fast. In our experience, sampling at too many places within regions yields significant overhead, but taking $L(s_I)$ is a too pessimistic way to update CurMax. To update CurMax, we select a single $\vec{u} \in R'$ in the middle of region R'. As we may have shrunk the region R, the middle of R' does not need to coincide with the middle of R, which yields behavior different from the vanilla refinement loop.

How and where to split? There are *two* important splitting decisions to be made. First, we need to select the dimensions (aka: parameters) in which we split. Second, we need to decide where to split along these dimensions. We had little success with trivial attempts to split at better places, so the least informative split in the middle remains our choice for splitting. However, we have changed where (in which parameter or dimensions) to split. Naturally, we do not (need to) split in monotonic parameters. Previously, parameter lifting split in every dimension at once. Let us illustrate that this quickly becomes infeasible: Assume 10 parameters. Splitting the initial region once yields 1024 regions. Splitting half of them again yields $> 500,000$ regions. Instead, we use *region estimates*, which are heuristic values for every parameter, based on the implementation of [19]. These estimates, provided by the parameter lifter, essentially consider how well the policy on the MDP (selecting upper or lower bounds in the iMC) agrees with the dependencies induced by a parameter: The more it agrees, the lower the value. The key idea is that one obtains tighter bounds if the policy adheres to the dependencies induced by the parameters[6]. We split in the dimension with the largest estimate. If the region estimate is smaller than 10^{-4}, then we split in the dimension of R with the widest interval.

Priorities in the region queue. Contrary to [25], we want to find the extremal value within the complete region, rather than partitioning the state space. Consequently, the standard technique splits based on the *size* of the region, and de-facto, a breadth-first search. When we split a region, we prioritize the subregions $\hat{R} \subseteq R'$ with $U_{R'}(s_I)$, as $U_{\hat{R}}(s_I) \leq U_{R'}(s_I)$. We use the age of a region to break ties. Here, a wild range of exploration strategies is possible. To avoid overfitting, we refrain in the experiments from weighting different aspects of the region, but the current choice is likely not the final answer.

---

[6] Technically, the value is computed as the sum of the differences between the local lower and upper bound on the reachability probability over all states with this parameter.

Table 1. Overview of the experimental results comparing vanilla parameter lifting to the integrated approach

name	instance	#states	#trans	$|V|$	ε: 0.1 integrated # i	# i$_b$	t	vanilla #i	t	ε: 0.05 integrated # i	# i$_b$	t	vanilla #i	t
NRP	(5,1)	56	75	5	469	2	<1	2575	<1	5143	2	<1	48701	3
	(10,1)	186	250	10	66219	2	11	512909	85	7168029	2	1594		TO
	(12,1)	259	348	12	425643	2	98	3304325	757			TO		TO
	(13,1)	300	403	13	1103811	2	299		TO			TO		TO
	(14,1)	344	462	14	2608869	2	718		MO			MO		MO
	(15,1)	391	525	15			TO		MO			MO		MO
EVADE	(1,2,0,1)	129	249	40	0	2	<1	2410	2	0	2	<1	4619	4
	(1,2,3,1)	513	993	160	0	2	3		MO	0	2	3		MO
	(1,2,0,2)	425	842	141	0	2	2		MO	0	2	2		MO
	(1,2,3,2)	1697	3362	561	0	2	21		MO	0	2	22		MO
Herman	(11,10)	21500	242926	1	3	3	3	3	2	9	3	14	9	3
	(11,15)	31740	369706	1	5	3	14	5	3	11	3	25	11	5
	(13,15)	126888	1713246	1	7	5	44	7	18	11	6	440	11	24
	(13,25)	208808	2889206	1	7	5	91	7	31	11	6	1415	11	41
	(13,35)	290728	4065166	1	5	4	128	5	35			TO	11	54
Maze	(25)	360	660	24	0	2	<1	1	<1	0	2	<1	40	<1
	(1000)	14985	26985	999	0	2	1	1	<1	0	2	1		MO
	(10000)	149985	269985	9999	0	2	166	1	<1	0	2	182		TO

Obtaining bounds for the monotonicity checker. While the baseline loop only computes upper-bounds, we use lower bounds to boost the monotonicity checking. We currently run these bounds until the monotonicity checker has stabilized. We observe that, mostly due to numerical computations, the time that the lower bounds take can be significant, but the overhead and the merits of getting larger lower bounds are hard to forecast.

7 Empirical Evaluation

Setup. We investigate the performance of the extended divide-and-conquer approach presented in Fig. 6. We have implemented the algorithm explained above in the probabilistic model checker Storm [11]. We compare its performance with vanilla parameter lifting, outlined in Fig. 4, as baseline. Both versions use the same underlying data structures and version of Storm. All experiments were executed on a single core Intel Xeon Platinum 8160 CPU. We did neither use any parallel processing nor randomization. We used a time out of 1800s and a memory limit of 32GB. We exclude model-building times from all experiments and emphasize that they coincide for the vanilla and new implementations.

Benchmarks and results. The common benchmarks *Crowds*, *BRP*, and *Zeroconf* have only globally monotonic parameters (and only two). Using monotonicity, they become trivial. The structure of *NAND* and *Consensus* makes them not amenable to monotonicity checking, and the performance mostly resembles the baseline. We selected additional benchmarks from [2], [23], and [18], see below. The models from the latter two sources are originally formulated as partially observable MDPs and were translated into pMC using the approach in [19].

Table 1 summarizes the results for benchmarks identified by their name and instance. We list the number of states, transitions and parameters of the pMC.

For each benchmark, we consider two values for ε: $\varepsilon=0.05$ and $\varepsilon=0.1$. For each ε, we consider the time t required and the number (**i**) of iterations that the integrated loop and the baseline require. For the integrated loop, we additionally provide the number (**i**$_b$) of extra (lower bound) parameter lifting invocations needed to assist the monotonicity checker.

Discussion of the results. We make the following observations.

- NRP: this model is globally monotonic in all its parameters. Our monotonicity checker can find this one parameter. The integrated approach is an order of magnitude faster on all instances, scaling to more parameters.
- Evade: this model is globally monotonic in some of its parameters. Our monotonicity check can find this monotonicity for a subset. The integrated approach is faster on all instances, as a better initial CurMax is guessed based on the results from the monotonicity checker.
- Herman's protocol: this is a less favourable benchmark for the integrated approach as only one parameter is not globally monotonic. The calculation of the bounds for the monotonicity checking yields significant overhead.
- Maze: this model is globally monotonic in all its parameters. This can be found directly by the monotonicity checker, so we are left to check a single valuation. This valuation is also provably the optimal valuation.

In general, for $\varepsilon=0.1$, the number of regions that need to be considered is relatively small and guessing an (almost) optimal value is not that important. This means that the results are less volatile to changes in the heuristic. For $\varepsilon=0.05$, it is significantly trickier to get this right. Monotonicity helps us in guessing a good initial point. Furthermore, it tells us in which parameters we should and should not split. Therefore, we prevent unnecessary splitting in some of the parameters.

8   Conclusion and Future Work

This paper has presented a new technique for tackling the optimal synthesis problem: what is the instance of a parametric Markov chain that satisfies a reachability objective in an optimal manner? The key concept is a deep interplay between parameter lifting, the favourable technique so far for this problem, and monotonicity checking. Experiments showed encouraging results: speed ups of up to two orders of magnitude for various benchmarks, and an increased number of parameters. Future work consists including advanced sampling techniques and applying this approach to other application areas such as optimal synthesis and monotonicity in probabilistic graphical models [26] and hyper-properties in security [1].

References

1. Ábrahám, E., Bartocci, E., Bonakdarpour, B., Dobe, O.: Parameter synthesis for probabilistic hyperproperties. In: Proc. of LPAR. EPiC Series in Computing, vol. 73, pp. 12–31. EasyChair (2020)
2. Aflaki, S., Volk, M., Bonakdarpour, B., Katoen, J.P., Storjohann, A.: Automated fine tuning of probabilistic self-stabilizing algorithms. In: SRDS. IEEE CS (2017)
3. Baier, C., de Alfaro, L., Forejt, V., Kwiatkowska, M.: Model checking probabilistic systems. In: Handbook of Model Checking. Springer (2018)
4. Baier, C., Katoen, J.P.: Principles of Model Checking. MIT Press (2008)
5. Ceska, M., Dannenberg, F., Paoletti, N., Kwiatkowska, M., Brim, L.: Precise parameter synthesis for stochastic biochemical systems. Acta Inf. **54**(6) (2017)
6. Ceska, M., Jansen, N., Junges, S., Katoen, J.: Shepherding hordes of markov chains. In: TACAS (2). Lecture Notes in Computer Science, vol. 11428, pp. 172–190. Springer (2019)
7. Chen, T., Hahn, E.M., Han, T., Kwiatkowska, M.Z., Qu, H., Zhang, L.: Model repair for Markov decision processes. In: TASE. IEEE (2013)
8. Cubuktepe, M., Jansen, N., Junges, S., Katoen, J., Papusha, I., Poonawala, H.A., Topcu, U.: Sequential convex programming for the efficient verification of parametric MDPs. In: Proc. of TACAS. LNCS, vol. 10206, pp. 133–150 (2017)
9. Cubuktepe, M., Jansen, N., Junges, S., Katoen, J.P., Topcu, U.: Synthesis in pMDPs: A tale of 1001 parameters. In: ATVA. LNCS, vol. 11138. Springer (2018)
10. Daws, C.: Symbolic and parametric model checking of discrete-time Markov chains. In: Proc. of ICTAC. LNCS, vol. 3407. Springer (2004)
11. Dehnert, C., Junges, S., Katoen, J.P., Volk, M.: A storm is coming: A modern probabilistic model checker. In: CAV (2). LNCS, vol. 10427. Springer (2017)
12. Gainer, P., Hahn, E.M., Schewe, S.: Accelerated model checking of parametric Markov chains. In: ATVA. LNCS, vol. 11138. Springer (2018)
13. Gouberman, A., Siegle, M., Tati, B.: Markov chains with perturbed rates to absorption: Theory and application to model repair. Perform. Evaluation **130**, 32–50 (2019)
14. Hahn, E.M., Han, T., Zhang, L.: Synthesis for PCTL in parametric markov decision processes. In: Proc. of NFM. LNCS, vol. 6617, pp. 146–161. Springer (2011)
15. Hahn, E.M., Hermanns, H., Zhang, L.: Probabilistic reachability for parametric Markov models. Software Tools for Technology Transfer **13**(1) (2010)
16. Hutschenreiter, L., Baier, C., Klein, J.: Parametric Markov chains: PCTL complexity and fraction-free Gaussian elimination. In: GandALF. EPTCS, vol. 256 (2017)
17. Jonsson, B., Larsen, K.G.: Specification and refinement of probabilistic processes. In: LICS. IEEE CS (1991)
18. Junges, S., Jansen, N., Seshia, S.A.: Enforcing almost-sure reachability in POMDPs. CoRR **abs/2007.00085** (2020)
19. Junges, S., Jansen, N., Wimmer, R., Quatmann, T., Winterer, L., Katoen, J.P., Becker, B.: Finite-state controllers of POMDPs using parameter synthesis. In: UAI. AUAI Press (2018)
20. Katoen, J.P.: The probabilistic model checking landscape. In: LICS. ACM (2016)
21. Kozine, I., Utkin, L.V.: Interval-valued finite Markov chains. Reliab. Comput. **8**(2), 97–113 (2002)
22. Lanotte, R., Maggiolo-Schettini, A., Troina, A.: Parametric probabilistic transition systems for system design and analysis. Formal Aspects Comput. **19**(1), 93–109 (2007)

23. Norman, G., Parker, D., Zou, X.: Verification and control of partially observable probabilistic systems. Real Time Syst. **53**(3), 354–402 (2017)
24. Pathak, S., Ábrahám, E., Jansen, N., Tacchella, A., Katoen, J.P.: A greedy approach for the efficient repair of stochastic models. In: NFM. LNCS, vol. 9058 (2015)
25. Quatmann, T., Dehnert, C., Jansen, N., Junges, S., Katoen, J.P.: Parameter synthesis for Markov models: Faster than ever. In: ATVA. LNCS, vol. 9938 (2016)
26. Rietbergen, M.T., van der Gaag, L.C.: Attaining monotonicity for Bayesian networks. In: ECSQARU. LNCS, vol. 6717, pp. 134–145. Springer (2011)
27. Spel, J., Junges, S., Katoen, J.: Are parametric Markov chains monotonic? In: Proc. of ATVA. LNCS, vol. 11781, pp. 479–496. Springer (2019)
28. Winkler, T., Junges, S., Pérez, G.A., Katoen, J.: On the complexity of reachability in parametric Markov decision processes. In: Proc. of CONCUR. LIPIcs, vol. 140, pp. 14:1–14:17. Schloss Dagstuhl - Leibniz-Zentrum für Informatik (2019)

Inductive Synthesis for Probabilistic Programs Reaches New Horizons[*]

Roman Andriushchenko[1] , Milan Češka (✉)[1] ,
Sebastian Junges[2] , and Joost-Pieter Katoen[3]

[1] Brno University of Technology, Brno, Czech Republic
ceskam@fit.vutbr.cz
[2] University of California, Berkeley, USA
[3] RWTH Aachen University, Aachen, Germany

Abstract. This paper presents a novel method for the automated synthesis of probabilistic programs. The starting point is a program sketch representing a finite family of finite-state Markov chains with related but distinct topologies, and a reachability specification. The method builds on a novel inductive oracle that greedily generates counter-examples (CEs) for violating programs and uses them to prune the family. These CEs leverage the semantics of the family in the form of bounds on its best- and worst-case behaviour provided by a deductive oracle using an MDP abstraction. The method further monitors the performance of the synthesis and adaptively switches between inductive and deductive reasoning. Our experiments demonstrate that the novel CE construction provides a significantly faster and more effective pruning strategy leading to an accelerated synthesis process on a wide range of benchmarks. For challenging problems, such as the synthesis of decentralized partially-observable controllers, we reduce the run-time from a day to minutes.

1 Introduction

Background and motivation. Controller synthesis for Markov decision processes MDPs [35]) and temporal logic constraints is a well-understood and tractable problem, with a plethora of mature tools providing efficient solving capabilities. However, the applicability of these controllers to a variety of systems is limited: Systems may be decentralized, controllers may not be able to observe the complete system state, cost constraints may apply, and so forth. Adequate operational models for these systems exist in the form of *decentralized partially-observable MDPs* (DEC-POMDPs [33]). The controller synthesis problem for these models is undecidable [30], and tool support (for verification tasks) is scarce.

This paper takes a different approach: the controller together with the environment can be modelled as probabilistic program sketches where "holes" in the probabilistic program model choices that the controller may make. Conceptually, the controllers of the DEC-POMDP are described by a user-defined finite

[*] This work has been partially supported by the Czech Science Foundation grant GJ20-02328Y and the ERC AdG Grant 787914 FRAPPANT, the NSF grants 1545126 (VeHICaL) and 1646208, by the DARPA Assured Autonomy program, by Berkeley Deep Drive, and by Toyota under the iCyPhy center.

J. F. Groote and K. G. Larsen (Eds.): TACAS 2021, LNCS 12651, pp. 191–209, 2021.
https://doi.org/10.1007/978-3-030-72016-2_11

family $\mathcal{M}$ of Markov chains. *The synthesis problem that we consider is to find a Markov chain M (i.e., a probabilistic program) in the family $\mathcal{M}$, such that $M \models \varphi$, where φ is the specification.* To allow efficient algorithms, the family must have some structure. In particular, in our setting, the family is parameterized by a set of discrete *parameters K*; an assignment $K \to V$ of these parameters with concrete values V from its associated domain yields a family member, i.e., a Markov chain (MC). Such a parameterization is naturally obtained from the probabilistic program sketch, where some constants (or program parts) can be left open. The search for a family member can thus be considered as the search for a hole-assignment. This approach fits within the realm of syntax-guided synthesis [2].

Motivating example. Herman's protocol [24] is a well-studied randomized distributed algorithm aimed to obtain fast stabilization on average. In [26], a family $\mathcal{M}$ of MCs is used to model different protocol instances. They considered each instance separately, and found which of the controllers for Herman's protocol performs best. Let us consider the protocol in a bit more detail: It considers self-stabilization of a unidirectional ring of network stations where all stations have to behave similarly—an anonymous network. Each station stores a single bit, and can read the internal bit of one (say left) neighbour. To achieve stabilization, a station for which the two legible bits coincide updates its own bit based on the outcome of a coin flip. The challenge is to select a controller that flips this coin with an optimal bias, i.e., minimizing the expected time until stabilization. In a setting where the probabilities range over $0.1, 0.2, \ldots, 0.9$, this results in analyzing nine different MCs. Does the expected time until stabilization reduce if the controllers are additionally allowed to have a single bit of memory? In every step, there are $9 \cdot 9$ combinations for selecting the coin flip and for each memory cell and coin flip outcome, the memory can now be updated, yielding $2 \cdot 2 \cdot 2$ possibilities. This one-bit extension thus results in a family of 648 models. If, in addition, one allows stations to make decisions depending on the token-bits, both the coin flips and the memory updates are multiplied by a factor 4, yielding $10,368$ models. Eventually, analyzing all individual MCs is infeasible.

Oracle-guided synthesis. To tackle the synthesis problem, we introduce an *oracle-guided inductive synthesis* approach [25,39]. A learner selects a family member and passes it to the oracle. The oracle answers whether the family member satisfies φ, and crucially, gives additional information in case this is not the case. Inspired by [9], if the family member violates the specification φ, our oracle returns a set K' of parameters such that all family members obtained by changing only the values assigned to K' violate φ. We argue that such an oracle must (1) induce little overhead in providing K', (2) be aware of the existence of parameters in the family, and (3) have (resemblance of) awareness about the semantics of the parameters and their values.

Oracles. With these requirements in mind, we construct a counterexample (CE)-based oracle from scratch. We do so by carefully exploiting existing methods. We construct critical subsystems as CEs [1]. Critical subsystems are parts of the MC that suffice to refute the specification. If a hole is absent in a CE, its value is irrelevant. To avoid the cost of finding optimal CEs—an NP-hard problem [19]—we consider greedy CEs that are similar to [9]. However, our greedy CEs are aware of the parameters, and try to limit the occurrence of parameters in the CE. Finally, to provide awareness of the semantics of parameter values, we provide lower and upper bounds on all states: Their difference indicates how much varying the value at a hole may change the overall reachability probability. These bounds are efficiently computed by another oracle. This oracle analyses a quotient MDP obtained by employing an abstraction method that is part of the abstraction-refinement loop in [10].

A hybrid variant. The two oracles are significantly different. Abstraction refinement is *deductive*: it argues about single family members by considering (an aggregation of) all family members. The critical subsystem oracle is *inductive*: by examining a single family member, it infers statements about other family members. This suggests a middle ground: a *hybrid strategy* monitors the performance of the two oracles during the synthesis and suggests their best usage. More precisely, the hybrid strategy integrates the counterexample-based oracle into the abstraction-refinement loop.

Major results. We present a novel and dedicated oracle deployed in an efficacious synthesis loop. We use model-checking results on an abstraction to tailor smaller CEs. Our greedy and family-aware CE construction is substantially faster than the use of optimal CEs. Together, these two improvements yield CEs that are on par with optimal CEs, but are found much faster. The integration of multiple abstraction-refinement steps yields a superior performance:x We compare our performance with the abstraction-refinement loop from [10] using benchmarks from [10]. Benchmarks can be classified along two dimensions: (*A*) Benchmarks with a structure good for CE-generation. (*B*) Benchmarks with a structure good for abstraction-refinement. A-benchmarks are a natural strength of our novel oracle. Our simple, efficient hybrid strategy significantly outperforms the state-of-the-art on *A*-benchmarks, while it only yields limited overhead for *B*-benchmarks. Most importantly, the novel hybrid strategy can solve benchmarks that are out of reach for pure abstraction-refinement or pure CE-based reasoning. In particular, our hybrid method is able to synthesize the optimal Herman protocol with memory—the synthesis time on a design space with 3.1 millions of candidate programs reduces from a day to minutes.

Related work The synthesis problems for parametric probabilistic systems can be divided into the following two categories.

Topology synthesis, akin to the problem considered in this paper, assumes a finite set of parameters affecting the MC topology. Finding an instantiation satisfying a reachability property is NP-complete in the number of parameters [12], and can naively be solved by analyzing all individual family members. An alternative is to model the MC family by an MDP and resort to standard MDP model-checking algorithms. Tools such as ProFeat [13] or QFLan [40] take this approach to quantitatively analyze alternative designs of software product lines [21,28]. These methods are limited to small families. This motivated (1) *abstraction-refinement* over the MDP representation [10], and (2) *counterexample-guided inductive synthesis* (CEGIS) for MCs [9], mentioned earlier. The alternative problem of sketching for probabilistic programs that fit given data is studied, e.g., in [32,38].

Parameter synthesis considers models with uncertain parameters associated to transition probabilities, and analyses how the system behaviour depends on the parameter values. The most promising techniques are based on *parameter lifting* that treats identical parameters in different transitions independently [8,36] and has been implemented in the state-of-the-art probabilistic model checkers Storm [18] and PRISM [27]. An alternative approach based on building rational functions for the satisfaction probability has been proposed in [15] and further improved in [22,17,4]. This approach has been also applied to different problems such as model repair [5,34,11].

Both synthesis problems can be also attacked by *search-based techniques* that do not ensure an exhaustive exploration of the parameter space. These include evolutionary techniques [23,31] and genetic algorithms [20]. Combinations with parameter synthesis have been used [7] to synthesize robust systems.

2   Problem Statement

We formalize the essential ingredients and the problem statement. See [3] for more material.

Sets of Markov chains. A *(discrete) distribution* over a finite set X is a function $\mu\colon S \to [0,1]$ s.t. $\sum_x \mu(x) = 1$. The set $Distr(X)$ contains all distributions over X. The *support* of $\mu \in Distr(X)$ is $\operatorname{supp}(\mu) = \{x \in X \mid \mu(x) > 0\}$.

Definition 1 (MC). *A* Markov chain (MC) *is a tuple* $D = (S, s_0, \boldsymbol{P})$, *where* S *is a finite set of* states, $s_0 \in S$ *is an* initial state, *and* $\boldsymbol{P}\colon S \to Distr(S)$ *is a* transition probability function. *We write* $\boldsymbol{P}(s,t)$ *to denote* $\boldsymbol{P}(s)(t)$. *The state* s *is* absorbing *if* $\boldsymbol{P}(s,s) = 1$.

Let K denote a finite set of discrete parameters with finite domain V_k. For brevity, we often assume that all domains are the same, and omit the subscript k. A *realization* r maps parameters to values in their domain, i.e., $r\colon K \to V$. Let $\mathcal{R}^{\mathcal{D}}$ denote the set of all realizations of a set $\mathcal{D}$ of MCs. A K-parameterized set of MCs $\mathcal{D}(K)$ contains the MCs $\mathcal{D}_r$, for every $r \in \mathcal{R}^{\mathcal{D}}$. In Sect. 3, we give an operational model for such sets. In particular, realizations will fix the targets of transitions. In our experiments, we describe these sets using the PRISM modelling language where parameters are described by undefined integer values.

Properties and specifications. For simplicity, we consider (unbounded) *reach-ability* properties[1]. For a set $T \subseteq S$ of *target states*, let $\mathbb{P}[D, s \models \Diamond T]$ denote

---

[1] Our implementation also supports expected reachability rewards.

the probability in MC D to eventually reach some state in T when starting in the state $s \in S$. A property $\varphi \equiv \mathbb{P}_{\bowtie \lambda}[\Diamond T]$ with $\lambda \in [0,1]$ and $\bowtie \in \{\leq, \geq\}$ expresses that the probability to reach T does relate to λ according to $\bowtie$. If $\bowtie = \leq$, then φ is a *safety* property; otherwise, it is a *liveness* property. Formally, state s in MC D satisfies φ if $\mathbb{P}[D, s \models \Diamond T] \geq \lambda$. The MC D satisfies φ if the above holds for its initial state. A *specification* is a set of properties $\Phi = \{\varphi_i\}_{i \in I}$, and $D \models \Phi$ if $\forall i \in I : D \models \varphi_i$.

Problem statement. The key problem statement in this paper is *feasibility*:

> Given a parameterized set of Markov chains $\mathcal{D}(K)$ over parameters K and a specification Φ, find a realization $r \colon K \to V$ such that $\mathcal{D}_r \models \Phi$.

When $\mathcal{D}$ is clear from the context, we often write $r \models \Phi$ to denote $\mathcal{D}_r \models \Phi$.

We additionally consider the optimizing variant of the synthesis problem. The *maximal synthesis* problem asks: given a maximizing property $\varphi_{\max} \equiv \mathbb{P}_{\bowtie \lambda}[\Diamond T]$, identify $r^* \in \arg\max_{r \in \mathcal{R}^{\mathcal{D}}} \{\mathbb{P}[\mathcal{D}_r \models \Diamond T] \mid \mathcal{D}_r \models \Phi\}$ provided it exists. The *minimal synthesis* problem is defined analogously.

As the state space S, the set K of parameters, and their domains are all finite, the above synthesis problems are decidable. One possible solution, called the *one-by-one approach* [14], considers each realization $r \in \mathcal{R}^{\mathcal{D}}$. The state-space and parameter-space explosion renders this approach unusable for large problems, necessitating the usage of advanced techniques that exploit the family structure.

3   Counterexample-Guided Inductive Synthesis

In this section, we recap a baseline for a counterexample-guided inductive synthesis (CEGIS) loop, as put forward in [9]. In particular, we first instantiate an oracle-guided synthesis method, discuss an operational model for families, giving structure to the parameterized set of Markov chains, and finally detail the usage of CEs to create an oracle.

Consider Fig. 1. A learner takes a set $\mathcal{R}$ of realizations, and has to find a realization $\mathcal{D}_r$ satisfying the specification Φ. The learner maintains (a symbolic representation of) a set $Q \subseteq \mathcal{R}$ of realizations that need to be checked. It iteratively asks the oracle whether a particular $r \in Q$ is a solution. If it is a solution, the oracle reports success.

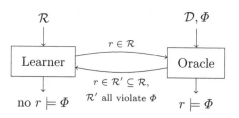

Fig. 1. Oracle-guided synthesis

Otherwise, the oracle returns a set $\mathcal{R}'$ containing r and potentially more realizations all violating Φ. The learner then prunes $\mathcal{R}'$ from Q. In Section 4, we focus on creating an efficient oracle that computes a set $\mathcal{R}'$ (with $r \in \mathcal{R}'$) of realizations that are all violating Φ. In Section 5, we provide a more advanced framework that extends this method. The remainder of this section lays the groundwork for these sections.

Families of Markov chains To avoid the need to iterate over all realizations, an efficient oracle exploits some structure of the family. In this paper, we focus on sets of Markov chains having different topologies. We explain our concepts using the operational model of families given in [10]. Our implementation supports (more expressive) PRISM programs with undefined integer constants.

Definition 2 (Family of MCs). *A family of MCs is a tuple $\mathcal{D} = (S, s_0, K, \mathcal{B})$ with S and s_0 as before, K is a finite set of parameters with domains $V_k \subseteq S$ for each $k \in K$, and $\mathcal{B} : S \to Distr(K)$ is a family of transition probability functions.*

Function $\mathcal{B}$ of a family $\mathcal{D}$ of MCs maps each state to a distribution over parameters K. In the context of the synthesis of probabilistic models, these parameters represent unknown options or features of a system under design. Realizations are now defined as follows.

Definition 3 (Realization). *A realization of a family $\mathcal{D} = (S, s_0, K, \mathcal{B})$ of MCs is a function $r : K \to S$ s.t. $r(k) \in V_k$, for all $k \in K$. We say that realization r induces MC $\mathcal{D}_r = (S, s_0, \mathcal{B}_r)$ iff $\mathcal{B}_r(s, s') = \sum_{k \in K, r(k) = s'} \mathcal{B}(s)(k)$ for any pair of states $s, s' \in S$. The set of all realizations of $\mathcal{D}$ is denoted as $\mathcal{R}^{\mathcal{D}}$.*

The set $\mathcal{R}^{\mathcal{D}} = \prod_{k \in K} V_k$ of all possible realizations is exponential in $|K|$.

Counterexample-guided oracles We first consider the feasibility synthesis for a single-property specification and later, cf. Remark 1, generalize this to multiple properties and to optimal synthesis. The notion of counterexamples is at the heart of the oracle from [9] and Sect. 4.

If an MC $D \not\models \varphi$, a *counterexample* (CE) based on a critical subsystem can serve as diagnostic information about the source of the failure. We consider the following CE, motivated by the notion of critical subsystem in [37].

Definition 4 (Counterexample). *Let $D = (S, s_0, \boldsymbol{P})$ be an MC with $s_\perp \notin S$. The sub-MC of D induced by $C \subseteq S$ is the MC $D{\downarrow}C = (S \cup \{s_\perp\}, s_0, \boldsymbol{P}')$, where the transition probability function $\boldsymbol{P}'$ is defined by:*

$$\boldsymbol{P}'(s) = \begin{cases} \boldsymbol{P}(s) & \text{if } s \in C, \\ [s_\perp \mapsto 1] & \text{otherwise.} \end{cases}$$

The set C and the sub-MC $D{\downarrow}C$ are called a counterexample *(CE) for the property $\mathbb{P}_{\leq \lambda}[\Diamond T]$ on MC D, if $D{\downarrow}C \not\models \mathbb{P}_{\leq \lambda}[\Diamond(T \cap (C \cup \{s_0\}))]$.*

Let $\mathcal{D}_r$ be an MC violating the specification φ. To compute other realizations violating φ, the oracle computes a critical subsystem $\mathcal{D}_r{\downarrow}C$, which is then used to deduce a so-called *conflict* for $\mathcal{D}_r$ and φ.

Definition 5 (Conflict). *For family of MCs $\mathcal{D} = (S, s_0, K, \mathcal{B})$ and $C \subseteq S$, the set K_C of relevant parameters (called conflict) is given by $\bigcup_{s \in C} supp(\mathcal{B}(s))$.*

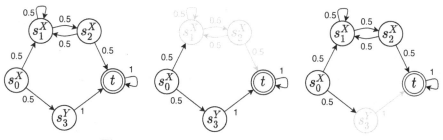

Fig. 2. Counterexamples for smaller conflicts.

It is straightforward to compute a set of violating realizations from a conflict. A *generalization* of realization r induced by the set $K_C \subseteq K$ of relevant parameters is the set $r{\uparrow}K_C = \{r' \in \mathcal{R} \mid \forall k \in K_C : r(k) = r'(k)\}$. We often use the term *conflict* to refer to its generalization. The size of a conflict, i.e., the number $|K_C|$ of relevant parameters K_C is crucial. Small conflicts potentially lead to generalizing r to larger subfamilies $r{\uparrow}K_C$. It is thus important that the CEs contain as few parameterized transitions as possible. The size of a CE in terms of the number of states is not of interest. Furthermore, the overhead of providing CEs should be bounded from below by the payoff: Finding a large generalization may take some time, but small generalizations should be returned quickly. The CE-based oracle in [9] uses an off-the-shelf CE procedure [16,41], and mostly does not provide small CEs.

4   A Smart Oracle with Counterexamples and Abstraction

This section develops an oracle based on CEs, tailored for the use in an oracle-guided inductive synthesis loop described in Sect. 3. Its main features are:

- a fast greedy approach to compute CEs that provide small conflicts: We achieve this by taking into account the position of the parameters.
- awareness about the semantics of parameters by using model-checking results from an abstraction of the family.

Before going into details, we provide some illustrative examples.

A motivating example First, we illustrate what it means to take CEs that lead to small conflicts. Consider Fig. 2, with a family member $\mathcal{D}_r$ (left), where the superscript of a state identifier s_i denotes parameters relevant to s_i. Consider the safety property $\varphi \equiv \mathbb{P}_{\leq 0.4}[\Diamond\{t\}]$. Clearly, $\mathcal{D}_r \not\models \varphi$, and we can construct two CEs: $C_1 = \{s_0, s_3, t\}$ (center) and $C_2 = \{s_0, s_1, s_2, t\}$ (right) with conflicts $K_{C_1} = \{X, Y\}$ and $K_{C_2} = \{X\}$, respectively. It illustrates that a smaller CE does not necessarily induce a smaller conflict.

We now illustrate awareness of the semantics of parameters. Consider the family $\mathcal{D} = (S, s_0, K', \mathcal{B})$, where $S = \{s_0, s_1, s_2, t, f\}$, the parameters are $K' = \{X, Y, T', F'\}$ with domains $V_X = \{s_1, s_2\}$, $V_Y = \{t, f\}$, $V_{T'} = \{t\}$, $V_{F'} = \{f\}$, and a family $\mathcal{B}$ of transition probability functions defined in Fig. 3 (left). As the

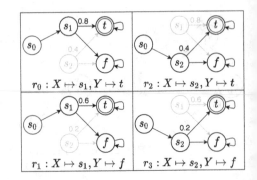

$\mathcal{B}(s_0) = [X \mapsto 1],$
$\mathcal{B}(s_1) = [T' \mapsto 0.6, Y \mapsto 0.2, F' \mapsto 0.2],$
$\mathcal{B}(s_2) = [T' \mapsto 0.2, Y \mapsto 0.2, F' \mapsto 0.6],$
$\mathcal{B}(t) = [T' \mapsto 1],$
$\mathcal{B}(f) = [F' \mapsto 1]$

Fig. 3. A family $\mathcal{D}$ of four Markov chains (unreachable states are grayed out).

parameters T' and F' each can take only one value, we consider $K = \{X, Y\}$ as the set of parameters. There are $|V_X| \times |V_Y| = 4$ family members, depicted in Fig. 3(right). For conciseness, we omit some of the transition probabilities (recall that transition probabilities sum to one). Only realization r_3 satisfies the safety property $\varphi \equiv \mathbb{P}_{\leq 0.3}[\Diamond\{t\}]$.

CEGIS [9] illustrated: Consider running CEGIS, and assume the oracle gets realization r_0 first. A model checker reveals $\mathbb{P}[\mathcal{D}_{r_0}, s_0 \models \Diamond T] = 0.8 > 0.3$. The CE for $\mathcal{D}_{r_0}$ and φ contains the (only) path to the target: $s_0 \rightarrow s_1 \rightarrow t$ having probability $0.8 > 0.3$. The corresponding CE $C = \{s_0, s_1, t\}$ induces the conflict $K_C = \{X, Y\}$. None of the parameters is generalized. The same argument applies to any subsequent realization: the constructed CEs do not allow for generalization, the oracle returns only the passed realization, and the learner keeps iterating until accidentally guessing r_3.

Can we do better? To answer this, consider CE generation as a game: The Pruner creates a critical subsystem C. The Adversary wins if it finds a MC satisfying φ containing C, thus refuting that C is a counterexample. In our setting, we change the game: The Adversary must select a family member rather than an arbitrary MC. Analogously, off-the-shelf CE generators construct a critical subsystem C that for every possible extension of C is a CE. These are *CEs without context*. In our game, the Adversary may not extend the MC arbitrarily, but must choose a family member. These are *CEs modulo a family*.

Back to the example: Observe that for a CE for $\mathcal{D}_{r_0}$, we could omit states t and s_1 from the set C of critical states: we know for sure that, once $\mathcal{D}_{r_0}$ takes transition (s_0, s_1), it will reach target state t with probability at least 0.6. This exceeds the threshold 0.3, regardless of the value of the parameter Y. Hence, for family $\mathcal{D}$, the set $C' = \{s_0\}$ is a critical subsystem. The immediate advantage is that this set induces conflict $K_{C'} = \{X\}$ (parameter Y has been generalized). This enables us to reject all realizations from the set $r_0 \uparrow K_{C'} = \{r_0, r_1\}$. *It is 'easier' to construct a CE for a (sub)family than for arbitrary MCs.* More generally, a successful oracle needs to have access to useful bounds, and effectively integrate them in the CE generation.

Counterexample construction We develop an algorithm using bounds on reachability probabilities, similar to the bounds used above. Let us assume that for some set of realizations $\mathcal{R}$ and for every state s, we have bounds $lb^{\mathcal{R}}(s)$, $ub^{\mathcal{R}}(s)$, such that for every $r \in \mathcal{R}$ we have $lb^{\mathcal{R}}(s) \leq \mathbb{P}[\mathcal{D}_r, s \models \lozenge T] \leq ub^{\mathcal{R}}(s)$. Such bounds always exist (take 0 and 1). We see later how we compute these bounds. In what follows, we fix r and denote $\mathcal{D}_r = (S, s_0, \boldsymbol{P})$. Let us assume $\mathcal{D}_r$ violates a safety property $\varphi \equiv \mathbb{P}_{\leq \lambda}[\lozenge T]$. The following definition is central:

Definition 6 (Rerouting). *Let MC $D = (S, s_0, \boldsymbol{P})$ with $s_T, s_\perp \notin S$, $C \subseteq S$ a set of* expanded *states and $\gamma \colon S \setminus C \to [0, 1]$ a* rerouting vector. *The* rerouting *of MC D w.r.t. C and γ is the MC $D{\downarrow}C[\gamma] = (S \cup \{s_\perp, s_T\}, s_0, \boldsymbol{P}^C_\gamma)$ with:*

$$\boldsymbol{P}^C_\gamma(s) = \begin{cases} \boldsymbol{P}(s) & \text{if } s \in C, \\ [s_T \mapsto \gamma(s), s_\perp \mapsto (1 - \gamma(s))] & \text{if } s \in S \setminus C, \\ [s \mapsto 1] & \text{if } s \in \{s_T, s_\perp\}. \end{cases}$$

Essentially, $D{\downarrow}C[\gamma]$ extends the MC D with additional *sink states* s_T and $s_\perp$ and replaces all outgoing transitions of any non-expanded state $s \in S \setminus C$ by a transition leading to s_T (with probability $\gamma(s)$) and a complementary one to $s_\perp$. We consider s_T to be the new target and let φ' denote the updated property. The transition $s \xrightarrow{\gamma(s)} s_T$ may be considered a 'shortcut' that by-passes successors of s and leads straight to target s_T with probability $\gamma(s)$. To ensure that $D{\downarrow}C[\gamma]$ is a CE, the value $\gamma(s)$ must be a lower bound on the reachability probability from s in D. When constructing a CE for a singular MC, we pick $\gamma = \boldsymbol{0}$, whereas when this MC is induced by a realization $r \in \mathcal{R}$, we can safely pick $\gamma = lb^{\mathcal{R}}$. The CE will be valid for every $r' \in \mathcal{R}$. It is a CE-modulo-$\mathcal{R}$.

Algorithmically, we employ a state-exploration approach and therefore start with $C^{(0)} = \emptyset$, i.e., all states are initially rerouted. If this is a CE, we are done. Otherwise, if the rerouting $D{\downarrow}C^{(0)}[\gamma]$ satisfies φ', then we 'expand' some states to obtain a CE. Naturally, we must expand reachable states to change the satisfaction of φ. By expanding some state $s \in S$, we abandon the abstraction associated with the shortcut $s \xrightarrow{\gamma(s)} s_T$ and replace it with concrete behavior that was inherent to state s in MC D. Expanding a state cannot decrease the induced reachability probability as $lb^{\mathcal{R}}$ is a valid lower bound. This gradual expansion of the reachable state space continues until for some $C \subseteq S$ the corresponding rerouting $D{\downarrow}C[\gamma]$ violates φ'. This gradual expansion process terminates as $D{\downarrow}S[\gamma] \equiv D$ and our assumption is $D \not\models \varphi$. We show this process on an example.

Example 1. Reconsider $\mathcal{D}$ in Fig. 3 with $\varphi \equiv \mathbb{P}_{\leq 0.3}[\lozenge\{t\}]$. Using the method outlined below we get: $lb^{\mathcal{R}} = [s_0 \mapsto 0.2, s_1 \mapsto 0.6, s_2 \mapsto 0.2, t \mapsto 1, f \mapsto 0]$. In absence of any bounds, the CE is $\{s_0, s_1, t\}$. Consider the gradual rerouting approach: We set $\gamma = lb^{\mathcal{R}}$, $C^{(0)} = \emptyset$ and have $D^{(0)} := \mathcal{D}_{r_0}{\downarrow}C^{(0)}[\gamma]$, see Fig. 4(a). Verifying this MC against $\varphi' = \mathbb{P}_{\leq 0.3}[\lozenge T \cup \{s_T\}]$ yields $\mathbb{P}[D^{(0)}, s_0 \models \lozenge T \cup \{s_T\}] = \gamma(s_0) = 0.2 \leq 0.3$, i.e., the set $C^{(0)}$ is not a CE. We now expand the initial state, i.e., $C^{(1)} = \{s_0\}$ and let $D^{(1)} := \mathcal{D}_{r_0}{\downarrow}C^{(1)}[\gamma]$, see Fig. 4(b). Verifying $D^{(1)}$ yields $\mathbb{P}[D^{(1)}, s_0 \models \lozenge T \cup \{s_T\}] = 1 \cdot \gamma(s_1) = 0.6 > 0.3$. Thus, the set $C^{(1)}$ is critical

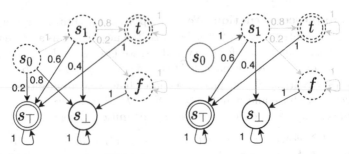

Fig. 4. Finding a CE to $\mathcal{D}_{r_0}$ and φ from Fig. 3 using the rerouting vector $\boldsymbol{\gamma} = lb^{\mathcal{R}}$.

Algorithm 1: Counterexample construction based on rerouting.

Input : An MC $\mathcal{D}_r$ a property $\varphi \equiv \mathbb{P}_{\bowtie\lambda}[\Diamond T]$ s.t. $\mathcal{D}_r \not\models \varphi$, a rerouting vector $\boldsymbol{\gamma}$.
Output : A conflict K for $\mathcal{D}_r$ and φ.

1 $i \leftarrow 0,\, K^{(i)} \leftarrow \emptyset$
2 **while** *true* **do**
3      $C^{(i)}, H^{(i)} \leftarrow$ reachableViaHoles($\mathcal{D}_r, K^{(i)}$)
4      $D^{(i)} \leftarrow \mathcal{D}_r{\downarrow}C^{(i)}[\boldsymbol{\gamma}]$
5   **if** $\mathbb{P}[D^{(i)} \models \Diamond T \cup \{s_\top\}] \not\bowtie \lambda$ **then return** $K^{(i)}$;
6      $\bar{s} \leftarrow$ chooseToExpand($H^{(i)}, K^{(i)}$)
7      $K^{(i+1)} = K^{(i)} \cup \mathrm{supp}(\mathcal{B}(\bar{s}))$
8      $i \leftarrow i + 1$
9 **end while**

---

and the corresponding conflict is $K_{C^{(1)}} = \mathrm{supp}(s_0) = \{X\}$. This is smaller than the naively computed conflict $\{X, Y\}$.

Greedy state expansion strategy Recall from Fig. 2 that for an MC $\mathcal{D}_r$ with $\mathcal{D}_r \not\models \varphi$, multiple CEs may exist inducing different conflicts. An efficient expansion strategy should yield a CE that induces a small amount of relevant parameters (to prune more family members) and this CE is preferably obtained by a small number of model-checking queries. The method presented in Alg. 1 meets these criteria. The algorithm expands multiple states between subsequent model checks, while expanding only states that are associated with parameters that are relevant. In particular, in each iteration, we keep track of the set $K^{(i)}$ of relevant parameters optimistically starting with $K^{(0)} = \emptyset$. We compute (see line 3) the set $C^{(i)}$ of states that are reachable from the initial state via states which are associated only with relevant parameters in $K^{(i)}$, i.e., via states for which $\mathrm{supp}(\mathcal{B}(s)) \subseteq K^{(i)}$. Here, $H^{(i)}$ represents a state exploration 'horizon': the set of states reachable from $C^{(i)}$ but containing some (still) irrelevant parameters. We then construct the corresponding rerouting $D{\downarrow}C^{(i)}[\boldsymbol{\gamma}]$ and check whether it is a CE. Otherwise, we greedily choose a state $\bar{s}$ from the horizon $H^{(i)}$ containing the least number of irrelevant parameters and add these parameters to our

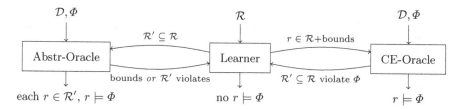

Fig. 5. Conceptual hybrid (dual-oracle) synthesis

conflict (see line 7). The resulting conflict may not be minimal, but is computed fast. Our algorithm applies to probabilistic liveness properties[2] too using $\gamma = ub^{\mathcal{R}}$.

Computing bounds We compute $lb^{\mathcal{R}}$ and $ub^{\mathcal{R}}$ using an abstraction [10]. The method considers some set $\mathcal{R}$ of realizations and computes the corresponding *quotient Markov decision process (MDP)* that over-approximates the behavior of all MCs in the family $\mathcal{R}$. Model checking this MDP yields an upper and a lower bound of the induced probabilities for all states over all realizations in $\mathcal{R}$. That is, $Bound(\mathcal{D}, \mathcal{R})$ computes $lb^{\mathcal{R}} \in \mathbb{R}^S$ and $ub^{\mathcal{R}} \in \mathbb{R}^S$ such that for each $s \in S$:

$$lb^{\mathcal{R}}(s) \ \leq \ \min_{r \in \mathcal{R}} \mathbb{P}[\mathcal{D}_r, s \models \Diamond T] \ \leq \ \max_{r \in \mathcal{R}} \mathbb{P}[\mathcal{D}_r, s \models \Diamond T] \ \leq \ ub^{\mathcal{R}}(s).$$

To allow for refinement, two properties are crucial (with point-wise inequalities):

1. $lb^{\mathcal{R}} \leq lb^{\mathcal{R}'} \wedge ub^{\mathcal{R}} \geq ub^{\mathcal{R}'}$ for $\mathcal{R}' \subseteq \mathcal{R}$ and   2. $lb^{\{r\}} = ub^{\{r\}}$ for $r \in \mathcal{R}$.

In [10], the abstraction and refinement together define an abstraction-refinement loop (AR) that addresses the feasibility problem. In the worst case, this loop analyses $2 \cdot |\mathcal{R}|$ quotient MDPs, which (as of now) may be arbitrarily larger than the number of family members they represent.

5   Hybrid Dual-Oracle Synthesis

We introduce an extended synthesis loop in which the abstraction-based reasoning is used to prune the family $\mathcal{R}$, and to accelerate the CE-based oracle from Sect. 4. The intuitive idea is outlined in Fig. 5. Note that if the CE-based oracle is not exploited, we emulate AR (explained in computing bounds above), whereas if the abstraction oracle is not used, we emulate CEGIS (with the novel oracle).

Let us motivate combining these oracles in a flexible way. The naive version outlined in the previous section assumed a single abstraction step, and invokes CEGIS with the bounds obtained from that step. Evidently, the better (tighter) the bounds γ, the better the CEs. However, the abstraction-based bounds for $\mathcal{R}$ may be very loose. These bounds can be improved by splitting the set $\mathcal{R}$ and using the bounds on the two sub-families. The idea is to run a limited number of

---

[2] Some care is required regarding loops, see [9].

Algorithm 2: Hybrid (dual-oracle) synthesis.

Input   : A family $\mathcal{D}$, a reachability property φ.
Output : Either a member r in $\mathcal{D}$ with $r \models \varphi$, or no such r exists in $\mathcal{D}$

1 $\overline{\mathcal{R}} \leftarrow \{\mathcal{R}^{\mathcal{D}}\}$;   // each analysed (sub-)family also holds bounds
2 $\delta_{CEGIS} \leftarrow 1$;   // time allocation factor for CEGIS
3 **while** *true* **do**
4   result,$\overline{\mathcal{R}}', \sigma_{AR}, t_{AR} \leftarrow$AR.run$(\overline{\mathcal{R}}, \varphi)$
5   **if** *result*.decided() **then return** *result*;
6   CEGIS.setTimeout$(t_{AR} \cdot \delta_{CEGIS})$
7   *result*, $\sigma_{CEGIS}, \overline{\mathcal{R}}'' \leftarrow$ CEGIS.run$(\overline{\mathcal{R}}', \varphi)$
8   **if** *result*.decided() **then return** *result*;
9      $\delta_{CEGIS} \leftarrow \sigma_{CEGIS}/\sigma_{AR}$
10     $\overline{\mathcal{R}} \leftarrow \overline{\mathcal{R}}''$
11 **end while**

AR steps and then invoke CEGIS. Our experiments reveal that it can be crucial to be adaptive, i.e., the integrated method must be able to detect at run time when to switch.

The proposed hybrid method switches between AR and CEGIS, where we allow for refining during the AR phase and use the obtained refined bounds during CEGIS. Additionally, we estimate the efficiency σ (e.g., the number of pruned MCs per time unit) of the two methods and allocate more time t to the method with superior performance. That is, if we detect that CEGIS prunes sub-families twice as fast as AR, we double the time in the next round for CEGIS. The resulting algorithm is summarized in Alg. 2. Recall that AR (at line 5) takes one family from $\overline{\mathcal{R}}$, either solves it or splits it and returns the set of undecided families $\overline{\mathcal{R}}'$. In contrast, CEGIS processes multiple families from $\overline{\mathcal{R}}'$ until the timeout and then returns the set of undecided families $\overline{\mathcal{R}}''$. This workflow is motivated by the fact that one iteration of AR (i.e., the involved MDP model-checking) is typically significantly slower that one CEGIS iteration.

Remark 1. Although the developed framework for integrated synthesis has been discussed in the context of feasibility with respect to a single property φ, it can be easily generalized to handle *multiple*-property specifications as well as to treat *optimal* synthesis. Regarding multiple properties, the idea remains the same: Analyzing the quotient MDP with respect to multiple properties yields multiple probability bounds. After initiating a CEGIS-loop and obtaining an unsatisfiable realization, we can construct a separate conflict for each unsatisfied property, while using the corresponding probability bound to enhance the CE generation process. Optimal synthesis is handled similarly to feasibility, but, after obtaining a satisfiable solution, we update the optimizing property to exclude this solution: e.g., for maximal synthesis this translates to increasing the threshold of the maximizing property. Having exhausted the search space of family members, the last obtained solution is declared to be the optimal one.

model	$\lvert K\rvert$	$\lvert\mathcal{R}^{\mathcal{D}}\rvert$	MDP size	avg. MC size	model	$\lvert K\rvert$	$\lvert\mathcal{R}^{\mathcal{D}}\rvert$	MDP size	avg. MC size
Grid	8	65k	11.5k	1.2k	*Pole*	17	1.3M	6.6k	5.6k
Maze	20	1M	9k	5.4k	*Herman*	8	0.5k	48k	5.2k
DPM	16	43M	9.5k	2.2k	*Herman**	7	3.1M	6k	1k

Table 1. Summary of the benchmarks and their statistics

6   Experimental evaluation

Implementation. We implemented the hybrid oracle on top of the probabilistic model checker Storm [18]. While the high-performance parts were implemented in C++, we used a python API to flexibly construct the overall synthesis loop. For SMT solving, we used Z3 [29]. The tool chain takes a PRISM [27] or JANI [6] sketch and a set of temporal properties, and returns a satisfying realization, if such exists, or outputs that such realization does not exist. The implementation in the form of an artefact is available at https://zenodo.org/record/4422543.

Set-up. We compare the adaptive oracle-guided synthesis with two state-of-the-art synthesis methods: program-level CEGIS [9] using a MaxSat CE generation [16,41] and AR [10]. These use the same architecture and data structures from Storm. All experiments are run on an Ubuntu 19.04 machine with Intel i5-8300H (4 cores at 2.3 GHz) and using up to 8 GB RAM, with all the algorithms being executed on a single thread. The benchmarks consists of five different models, see Table 1, from various domains that were used in [9,10]. As opposed to the benchmark considered in [9,10], we use larger variants of *Grid* and *Herman* to better demonstrate differences in the performance of individual methods.

To investigate the scalability of the methods, we consider a new variant of the *Herman* model, that allows us to scale the number of randomization strategies and thus the family size. In particular, we will compare performance on two instances of different sizes: *small Herman** (5k members) and *large Herman** (3.1M members, other statistics are reported in Table 1).

To reason about the pruning efficiency of different synthesis methods, we want to avoid feasible synthesis problems, where the order of family exploration can lead to inconsistent performance. Instead, we will primarily focus on non-feasible problems, where all realizations need to be explored in order to prove unsatisfiability. The experimental evaluation is presented in three parts. (1) We evaluate the novel CE construction method and compare it with the MaxSat-based oracle from [9]. (2) We compare the hybrid synthesis loop with the two baselines AR and CEGIS. (3) We consider novel hard synthesis instances (multi-property synthesis, finding optimal programs) on instances of the model *Herman**.

Comparing CE construction methods We consider *the quality of the CEs* and *their generation time*. In particular, we want to investigate (1) whether using CEs-modulo-families yields better CEes, (2) how the quality of CEs from the smart oracle compares to the MaxSat-based oracle, and how their time consumption compares. As a measure of quality of a CE, the average number of its relevant parameters w.r.t. the total number of its parameters is taken. That is, smaller

| model | MaxSat [16] | CE quality | | performance | | | | | |
| | | state expansion (new) | | CEGIS [9] | | AR [10] | | Hybrid (new) | |
		trivial	non-trivial	iters	time	iters	time	iters	time
Grid	0.59 (0.025)	0.50 (0.001)	0.50	613	30	5325	486	(285, 11)	6
*	0.74 (0.026)	0.65 (0.001)	0.65	1801	93	6139	540	(2100, 127)	33
Maze	0.21 (0.247)	0.55 (0.009)	0.38	290	5449	49	17	(105, 13)	7
*	0.24 (2.595)	0.63 (0.012)	0.46	301	6069	63	26	(146, 17)	9
DPM	0.32 (0.447)	0.61 (0.007)	0.53	2906	2488	299	25	(631, 143)	23
*	0.33 (0.525)	0.49 (0.006)	0.42	3172	2782	1215	81	(2374, 545)	76
Pole	-	0.87 (0.062)	0.16	-	-	309	12	(3, 5)	1
*	-	0.54 (0.041)	0.29	-	-	615	23	(80, 61)	6
Herman	-	0.91 (0.011)	0.50	-	-	171	86	(24, 1)	9
*	-	0.88 (0.016)	0.87	-	-	643	269	(485, 13)	29

Table 2. CE quality for different methods and performance of three synthesis methods. For each model/property, we report results for two different thresholds where the symbol '*' marks the one closer to the feasibility threshold, representing the more difficult synthesis problem. Symbol '-' marks a two-hour timeout. **CE quality**: The presented numbers give the CE quality (i.e., the smaller, the better). The numbers in parentheses represent the average run-time of constructing one CE in seconds (run-times for constructing CE using non-trivial bounds are similar as for trivial ones and are thus not reported). **Performance**: for each method, we report the number of iterations (for the hybrid method, the reported values are iterations of the CEGIS and AR oracle, respectively) and the run-time in seconds.

ratios imply better CEs. To measure the influence of using CEs-modulo-families, two types of bounds are used: (i) trivial bounds (i.e., $\gamma = 0$ for safety and $\gamma = 1$ for liveness properties), and (ii) non-trivial bounds corresponding to the entire family $\mathcal{R}^{\mathcal{D}}$ representing the most conservative estimate. The results are reported in (the left part of) Table 2. In the next subsection, we investigate this same benchmark from the point of view of the performance of the synthesis methods, which also shows the immediate effect of the new CE generation strategy.

The first observation is that using non-trivial bounds (as opposed to trivial ones) for the state expansion approach can drastically decrease the conflict size. It turns out that the CEs obtained using the greedy approach are mostly larger than those obtained with the MaxSat method. However (see *Grid*), even for trivial bounds, we may obtain smaller CEs than for MaxSat: computing a minimal-command CE does not necessarily induce an optimal conflict. On the other hand, comparing the run-times in the parentheses, one can see that computing CEs via the greedy state expansion is orders of magnitude faster than computing command-optimal ones using MaxSat. It is good to realize that the greedy method makes at most $|K|$ model-checking queries to compute CEs, while the MaxSat method may make exponentially many such queries. Overall, the greedy method using the non-trivial bounds is able to obtain CEs of comparable quality as the MaxSat method, while being orders of magnitude faster.

Performance comparison with AR/CEGIS We compare the hybrid synthesis loop from Sect. 5 with two state-of-the-art baselines: CEGIS and AR. The results are displayed in (the right half of) Table 2. *In all 10 cases, the hybrid method outperforms the baselines. It is up to an order of magnitude faster.*

Let us discuss the performance of the hybrid method. We classify benchmarks along two dimensions: (1) the performance of CEGIS and (2) the performance of AR. Based on the empirical performance, we classify (*Grid*) as good-for-CEGIS (and not for AR), *Maze*, *Pole* and *DPM* as good-for-AR (and not for CEGIS), and *Herman* as hard (for both). Roughly, AR works well when the quotient MDP does not blow up and its analysis is precise due to consistent schedulers, i.e., when the parameter dependencies are not crucial for a precise analysis. CEGIS performs well when the CEs are small and fast to compute. On the other hand, synthesis problems for which neither pure CEGIS nor pure AR are able to effectively reason about non-trivial subfamilies, inherently profit from a hybrid method. The main point we want to discuss is *how the hybrid method reinforces the strengths of both methods, rather than their weaknesses.*

In the hybrid method, there are two factors that determine the efficiency: (i) *how fast do we get bounds on the reachability probability that are tight enough to enable construction of good counterexamples?* and (ii) *how good are the constructed counterexamples?* The former factor is attributed to the proposed adaptive scheme (see Alg. 2), where the method will prefer AR-like analysis and continue refinement until the computed bounds allow construction of small counterexamples. The latter is reflected above. Let us now discuss how these two aspects are reflected in the benchmarks.

In good-for-CEGIS benchmarks like *Grid*, after analyzing a quotient MDP for the whole family, the hybrid method mostly profits from better CEs yielding better bounds, thus outperforming CEGIS. Indeed, the CEs are found so fast that the bottleneck is no longer their generation. This also explains why the speedup is not immediately translated to the speedup on the overall synthesis loop. In the good-for-AR benchmark *DPM*, the hybrid method provides only a minor improvement as it has to perform a large number of AR-iterations before the novel CE-based pruning can be effectively used. This can be considered as the worst-case scenario for the hybrid method. On other good-for-AR benchmarks like *Maze* and *Pole*, the good performance on AR allows to quickly obtain tight bounds which can then be exploited by CEGIS. Finally, in hard models like *Herman*, abstraction-refinement is very expensive, but even the bounds from the first round yield bounds that, as opposed to the trivial bounds, now enable good CEs: CEGIS can keep using these bounds to quickly prune the state space.

More complicated synthesis problems Our new approach can push the limits of synthesis benchmarks significantly. We illustrate this by considering a new variant of the *Herman* model, *Herman**, and a property imposing an upper bound on the expected number of rounds until stabilization. We put this bound just below the optimal (i.e., the minimal) value, yielding a hard non-feasible problem. The synthesis results are summarized in Table 3. As CEGIS performs poorly on *Herman*, it is excluded here.

synthesis	AR		Hybrid		synthesis	AR		Hybrid	
problem	iters	time	iters	time	problem	iters	time	iters	time
feasibility	81	30s	(274, 1)	**7s**	feasibility	69k	47h	(14280, 2)	**13.4m**
two properties	97	38s	(274, 1)	**8s**	optimality	83k	55h	(16197, 3)	**16.8m**
optimality	531	150s	(571, 7)	**12s**	5%-optimality	60k	42h	(6421, 7)	**5.1m**

Table 3. The impact of scaling the family size (of the *Herman** model) and handling more complex synthesis problems. The left part shows the results for the smaller variant (5k members), the right part for the larger one (3.1M members).

First, we investigate on *small Herman** how the methods can handle the synthesis for multi-property specifications. We add one feasible property to the (still non-feasible) specification (row 'two properties'). While including more properties typically slows down the AR computation, the performance of the hybrid method is not affected as the corresponding overhead is mitigated by additional pruning opportunities. Second, we consider optimal synthesis for the property as used in the feasibility synthesis. The hybrid method requires only a minor overhead to find an optimal solution compared to checking feasibility. This overhead is significantly larger for AR.

Next, we consider *larger Herman** model having significantly more randomization strategies (3.1M members) that include solutions leading to a considerably faster stabilization. This model is out of reach for existing synthesis approaches: one-by-one enumeration takes more than 27 hours and the AR performs even worse—solving the feasibility and optimality problems requires 47 and 55 hours, respectively. On the other hand, the proposed hybrid method is able to solve these problems within minutes. Finally, we consider a relaxed variant of optimal synthesis (5%-optimality) guaranteeing that the found solution is up to 5% worse than the optimal. Relaxing the optimally criterion speeds up the hybrid synthesis method by about a factor three.

These experiments clearly demonstrate that scaling up the synthesis problem several orders of magnitude renders existing synthesis methods infeasible: they need tens of hours to solve the synthesis problems. Meanwhile, the hybrid method tackles these difficult synthesis problems without significant penalty and is capable of producing a solution within minutes.

7   Conclusion

We present a novel method for the automated synthesis of probabilistic programs. Pairing the counterexample-guided inductive synthesis with the deductive oracle using an MDP abstraction, we develop a synthesis technique enabling faster construction of smaller counterexamples. Evaluating the method on case studies from different domains, we demonstrate that the novel CE construction and the adaptive strategy lead to a significant acceleration of the synthesis process. The proposed method is able to reduce the run-time for challenging problems from days to minutes. In our future work, we plan to investigate counterexamples on the quotient MDPs and improve the abstraction refinement strategy.

References

1. Ábrahám, E., Becker, B., Dehnert, C., Jansen, N., Katoen, J.P., Wimmer, R.: Counterexample generation for discrete-time Markov models: An introductory survey. In: SFM. LNCS, vol. 8483, pp. 65–121. Springer (2014)
2. Alur, R., Bodík, R., Dallal, E., Fisman, D., Garg, P., Juniwal, G., Kress-Gazit, H., Madhusudan, P., Martin, M.M.K., Raghothaman, M., Saha, S., Seshia, S.A., Singh, R., Solar-Lezama, A., Torlak, E., Udupa, A.: Syntax-guided synthesis. In: Dependable Software Systems Engineering, NATO Science for Peace and Security Series, vol. 40, pp. 1–25. IOS Press (2015)
3. Baier, C., de Alfaro, L., Forejt, V., Kwiatkowska, M.: Model checking probabilistic systems. In: Handbook of Model Checking, pp. 963–999. Springer (2018)
4. Baier, C., Hensel, C., Hutschenreiter, L., Junges, S., Katoen, J., Klein, J.: Parametric markov chains: PCTL complexity and fraction-free gaussian elimination. Inf. Comput. **272**, 104504 (2020)
5. Bartocci, E., Grosu, R., Katsaros, P., Ramakrishnan, C.R., Smolka, S.A.: Model repair for probabilistic systems. In: TACAS'11. LNCS, vol. 6605, pp. 326–340 (2011)
6. Bornholt, J., Torlak, E., Grossman, D., Ceze, L.: Optimizing synthesis with metasketches. In: POPL'16. p. 775–788. Association for Computing Machinery (2016)
7. Calinescu, R., Češka, M., Gerasimou, S., Kwiatkowska, M., Paoletti, N.: Efficient synthesis of robust models for stochastic systems. J. of Systems and Softw. **143**, 140–158 (2018)
8. Češka, M., Dannenberg, F., Paoletti, N., Kwiatkowska, M., Brim, L.: Precise parameter synthesis for stochastic biochemical systems. Acta Inf. **54**(6), 589–623 (2017)
9. Češka, M., Hensel, C., Junges, S., Katoen, J.P.: Counterexample-driven synthesis for probabilistic program sketches. In: FM. LNCS, vol. 11800, pp. 101–120. Springer (2019)
10. Češka, M., Jansen, N., Junges, S., Katoen, J.P.: Shepherding hordes of Markov chains. In: TACAS (2). LNCS, vol. 11428, pp. 172–190. Springer (2019)
11. Chatzieleftheriou, G., Katsaros, P.: Abstract model repair for probabilistic systems. Inf. Comput. **259**(1), 142–160 (2018)
12. Chonev, V.: Reachability in augmented interval Markov chains. In: RP'2019. LNCS, vol. 11674, pp. 79–92. Springer (2019)
13. Chrszon, P., Dubslaff, C., Klüppelholz, S., Baier, C.: ProFeat: feature-oriented engineering for family-based probabilistic model checking. Formal Asp. Comput. **30**(1), 45–75 (2018)
14. Classen, A., Cordy, M., Heymans, P., Legay, A., Schobbens, P.Y.: Model checking software product lines with SNIP. Int. J. on Softw. Tools for Technol. Transf. **14**, 589–612 (2012)
15. Daws, C.: Symbolic and parametric model checking of discrete-time Markov chains. In: ICTAC. LNCS, vol. 3407, pp. 280–294. Springer (2004)
16. Dehnert, C., Jansen, N., Wimmer, R., Ábrahám, E., Katoen, J.P.: Fast debugging of PRISM models. In: ATVA. LNCS, vol. 8837, pp. 146–162. Springer (2014)
17. Dehnert, C., Junges, S., Jansen, N., Corzilius, F., Volk, M., Bruintjes, H., Katoen, J.P., Ábrahám, E.: PROPhESY: A PRObabilistic ParamEter SYNthesis Tool. In: CAV'15. LNCS, vol. 9206, pp. 214–231. Springer (2015)
18. Dehnert, C., Junges, S., Katoen, J.P., Volk, M.: A Storm is coming: A modern probabilistic model checker. In: CAV. LNCS, vol. 10427, pp. 592–600. Springer (2017)

19. Funke, F., Jantsch, S., Baier, C.: Farkas certificates and minimal witnesses for probabilistic reachability constraints. In: TACAS (1). LNCS, vol. 12078, pp. 324–345. Springer (2020)

20. Gerasimou, S., Calinescu, R., Tamburrelli, G.: Synthesis of probabilistic models for quality-of-service software engineering. Autom. Softw. Eng. 25(4), 785–831 (2018)

21. Ghezzi, C., Sharifloo, A.M.: Model-based verification of quantitative non-functional properties for software product lines. Inf. & Softw. Technol. 55(3), 508–524 (2013)

22. Hahn, E.M., Hermanns, H., Zhang, L.: Probabilistic reachability for parametric Markov models. Int. J. on Softw. Tools for Technol. Transf. 13(1), 3–19 (2011)

23. Harman, M., Mansouri, S.A., Zhang, Y.: Search-based software engineering: Trends, techniques and applications. ACM Comp. Surveys 45(1), 11:1–11:61 (2012)

24. Herman, T.: Probabilistic self-stabilization. Inf. Process. Lett. 35(2), 63–67 (1990)

25. Jha, S., Gulwani, S., Seshia, S.A., Tiwari, A.: Oracle-guided component-based program synthesis. In: ICSE. p. 215–224. ACM (2010)

26. Kwiatkowska, M., Norman, G., Parker, D.: Probabilistic verification of Herman's self-stabilisation algorithm. Formal Aspects of Computing 24(4), 661–670 (2012)

27. Kwiatkowska, M., Norman, G., Parker, D.: PRISM 4.0: Verification of probabilistic real-time systems. In: CAV. LNCS, vol. 6806, pp. 585–591. Springer (2011)

28. Lanna, A., Castro, T., Alves, V., Rodrigues, G., Schobbens, P.Y., Apel, S.: Feature-family-based reliability analysis of software product lines. Inf. and Softw. Technol. 94, 59–81 (2018)

29. Lindemann, C.: Performance modelling with deterministic and stochastic Petri nets. SIGMETRICS Perform. Eval. Rev. 26(2), 3 (1998)

30. Madani, O., Hanks, S., Condon, A.: On the undecidability of probabilistic planning and infinite-horizon partially observable Markov decision problems. In: AAAI/IAAI. pp. 541–548. AAAI Press / The MIT Press (1999)

31. Martens, A., Koziolek, H., Becker, S., Reussner, R.: Automatically improve software architecture models for performance, reliability, and cost using evolutionary algorithms. In: WOSP/SIPEW. pp. 105–116. ACM (2010)

32. Nori, A.V., Ozair, S., Rajamani, S.K., Vijaykeerthy, D.: Efficient synthesis of probabilistic programs. In: PLDI'14. pp. 208–217. ACM (2015)

33. Oliehoek, F.A., Amato, C.: A Concise Introduction to Decentralized POMDPs. Springer Briefs in Intelligent Systems, Springer (2016)

34. Pathak, S., Ábrahám, E., Jansen, N., Tacchella, A., Katoen, J.P.: A greedy approach for the efficient repair of stochastic models. In: NFM'15. LNCS, vol. 9058, pp. 295–309. Springer (2015)

35. Puterman, M.L.: Markov Decision Processes: Discrete Stochastic Dynamic Programming. Wiley Series in Probability and Statistics, Wiley (1994)

36. Quatmann, T., Dehnert, C., Jansen, N., Junges, S., Katoen, J.P.: Parameter synthesis for Markov models: Faster than ever. In: ATVA'16. LNCS, vol. 9938, pp. 50–67 (2016)

37. Quatmann, T., Jansen, N., Dehnert, C., Wimmer, R., Ábrahám, E., Katoen, J.P., Becker, B.: Counterexamples for expected rewards. In: FM. pp. 435–452. Springer (2015)

38. Saad, F.A., Cusumano-Towner, M.F., Schaechtle, U., Rinard, M.C., Mansinghka, V.K.: Bayesian synthesis of probabilistic programs for automatic data modeling. Proceedings of the ACM on Programming Languages 3(POPL), 1–32 (2019)

39. Solar-Lezama, A., Rabbah, R., Bodík, R., Ebcioğlu, K.: Programming by sketching for bit-streaming programs. In: PLDI'05. pp. 281–294. ACM (2005)

40. Vandin, A., ter Beek, M.H., Legay, A., Lluch-Lafuente, A.: Qflan: A tool for the quantitative analysis of highly reconfigurable systems. In: FM. LNCS, vol. 10951, pp. 329–337. Springer (2018)
41. Wimmer, R., Jansen, N., Vorpahl, A., Ábrahám, E., Katoen, J.P., Becker, B.: High-level counterexamples for probabilistic automata. Logical Methods in Computer Science **11**(1) (2015)

Analysis of Markov Jump Processes under Terminal Constraints

Michael Backenköhler[1,✉], Luca Bortolussi[2,3], Gerrit Großmann[1], Verena Wolf[1,3]

[1]Saarbrücken Graduate School of Computer Science, Saarland University, Saarland Informatics Campus E1 3, Saarbrücken, Germany
✉ michael.backenkoehler@uni-saarland.de
[2]Univeristy of Trieste, Trieste, Italy
[3] Saarland University, Saarland Informatics Campus E1 3, Saarbrücken, Germany

Abstract. Many probabilistic inference problems such as stochastic filtering or the computation of rare event probabilities require model analysis under initial and terminal constraints. We propose a solution to this *bridging problem* for the widely used class of population-structured Markov jump processes. The method is based on a state-space lumping scheme that aggregates states in a grid structure. The resulting approximate bridging distribution is used to iteratively refine relevant and truncate irrelevant parts of the state-space. This way, the algorithm learns a well-justified finite-state projection yielding guaranteed lower bounds for the system behavior under endpoint constraints. We demonstrate the method's applicability to a wide range of problems such as Bayesian inference and the analysis of rare events.

Keywords: Bayesian Inference · Bridging problem · Smoothing · Lumping · Rare Events.

1 Introduction

Discrete-valued continuous-time Markov Jump Processes (MJP) are widely used to model the time evolution of complex discrete phenomena in continuous time. Such problems naturally occur in a wide range of areas such as chemistry [16], systems biology [49,46], epidemiology [36] as well as queuing systems [10] and finance [39]. In many applications, an MJP describes the stochastic interaction of populations of agents. The state variables are counts of individual entities of different populations.

Many tasks, such as the analysis of rare events or the inference of agent counts under partial observations naturally introduce terminal constraints on the system. In these cases, the system's initial state is known, as well as the system's (partial) state at a later time-point. The probabilities corresponding to this so-called *bridging problem* are often referred to as *bridging probabilities* [17,19]. For instance, if the exact, full state of the process X_t has been observed at time 0 and T, the bridging distribution is given by

$$\Pr(X_t = x \mid X_0 = x_0, X_T = x_g)$$

© The Author(s) 2021
J. F. Groote and K. G. Larsen (Eds.): TACAS 2021, LNCS 12651, pp. 210–229, 2021.
https://doi.org/10.1007/978-3-030-72016-2_12

for all states x and times $t \in [0, T]$. Often, the condition is more complex, such that in addition to an initial distribution, a terminal distribution is present. Such problems typically arise in a Bayesian setting, where the a priori behavior of a system is filtered such that the posterior behavior is compatible with noisy, partial observations [11,25]. For example, time-series data of protein levels is available while the mRNA concentration is not [1,25]. In such a scenario our method can be used to identify a good truncation to analyze the probabilities of mRNA levels.

Bridging probabilities also appear in the context of rare events. Here, the rare event is the terminal constraint because we are only interested in paths containing the event. Typically researchers have to resort to Monte-carlo simulations in combination with variance reduction techniques in such cases [14,26].

Efficient numerical approaches that are not based on sampling or ad-hoc approximations have rarely been developed.

Here, we combine state-of-the-art truncation strategies based on a forward analysis [28,4] with a refinement approach that starts from an abstract MJP with lumped states. We base this lumping on a grid-like partitioning of the state-space. Throughout a lumped state, we assume a uniform distribution that gives an efficient and convenient abstraction of the original MJP. Note that the lumping does not follow the classical paradigm of Markov chain lumpability [12] or its variants [15]. Instead of an approximate block structure of the transition-matrix used in that context, we base our partitioning on a segmentation of the molecule counts. Moreover, during the iterative refinement of our abstraction, we identify those regions of the state-space that contribute most to the bridging distribution. In particular, we refine those lumped states that have a bridging probability above a certain threshold δ and truncate all other macro-states. This way, the algorithm learns a truncation capturing most of the bridging probabilities. This truncation provides guaranteed lower bounds because it is at the granularity of the original model.

In the rest of the paper, after presenting related work (Section 2) and background (Section 3), we discuss the method (Section 4) and several applications, including the computation of rare event probabilities as well as Bayesian smoothing and filtering (Section 5).

2   Related Work

The problem of endpoint constrained analysis occurs in the context of Bayesian estimation [41]. For population-structured MJPs, this problem has been addressed by Huang et al. [25] using moment closure approximations and by Wildner and Köppl [48] further employing variational inference. Golightly and Sherlock modified stochastic simulation algorithms to approximatively augment generated trajectories [17]. Since a statistically exact augmentation is only possible for few simple cases, diffusion approximations [18] and moment approximations [35] have been employed. Such approximations, however, do not give any guarantees on the approximation error and may suffer from numerical instabilities [43].

The bridging problem also arises during the estimation of first passage times and rare event analysis. Approaches for first-passage times are often of heuristic nature [42,22,8]. Rigorous approaches yielding guaranteed bounds are currently limited by the performance of state-of-the-art optimization software [6]. In biological applications, rare events of interest are typically related to the reachability of certain thresholds on molecule counts or mode switching [45]. Most methods for the estimation of rare event probabilities rely on importance sampling [26,14]. For other queries, alternative variance reduction techniques such as control variates are available [5]. Apart from sampling-based approaches, dynamic finite-state projections have been employed by Mikeev et al. [34], but are lacking automated truncation schemes.

The analysis of countably infinite state-spaces is often handled by a predefined truncation [27]. Sophisticated state-space truncations for the (unconditioned) forward analysis have been developed to give lower bounds and rely on a trade-off between computational load and tightness of the bound [37,28,4,24,31].

Reachability analysis, which is relevant in the context of probabilistic verification [8,38], is a bridging problem where the endpoint constraint is the visit of a set of goal states. Backward probabilities are commonly used to compute reachability likelihoods [2,50]. Approximate techniques for reachability, based on moment closure and stochastic approximation, have also been developed in [8,9], but lack error guarantees. There is also a conceptual similarity between computing bridging probabilities and the forward-backward algorithm for computing state-wise posterior marginals in hidden Markov models (HMMs) [40]. Like MJPs, HMMs are a generative model that can be conditioned on observations. We only consider two observations (initial and terminal state) that are not necessarily noisy but the forward and backward probabilities admit the same meaning.

3   Preliminaries

3.1   Markov Jump Processes with Population Structure

A population-structured Markov jump process (MJP) describes the stochastic interactions among agents of distinct types in a well-stirred reactor. The assumption of all agents being equally distributed in space, allows to only keep track of the overall copy number of agents for each type. Therefore the state-space is $\mathcal{S} \subseteq \mathbb{N}^{n_S}$ where n_S denotes the number of agent types or populations. Interactions between agents are expressed as *reactions*. These reactions have associated gains and losses of agents, given by non-negative integer vectors v_j^- and v_j^+ for reaction j, respectively. The overall effect is given by $v_j = v_j^+ - v_j^-$. A reaction between agents of types $S_1, \ldots, S_{n_S}$ is specified in the following form:

$$\sum_{\ell=1}^{n_S} v_{j\ell}^- S_\ell \xrightarrow{\alpha_j(x)} \sum_{\ell=1}^{n_S} v_{j\ell}^+ S_\ell. \tag{1}$$

The propensity function α_j gives the rate of the exponentially distributed firing time of the reaction as a function of the current system state $x \in S$. In population models, *mass-action* propensities are most common. In this case the firing rate is given by the product of the number of reactant combinations in x and a *rate constant* c_j, i.e.

$$\alpha_j(x) := c_j \prod_{\ell=1}^{n_S} \binom{x_\ell}{v_{j\ell}^-}. \tag{2}$$

In this case, we give the rate constant in (1) instead of the function α_j. For a given set of n_R reactions, we define a stochastic process $\{X_t\}_{t \geq 0}$ describing the evolution of the population sizes over time t. Due to the assumption of exponentially distributed firing times, X is a continuous-time Markov chain (CTMC) on S with infinitesimal generator matrix Q, where the entries of Q are

$$Q_{x,y} = \begin{cases} \sum_{j:x+v_j=y} \alpha_j(x), & \text{if } x \neq y, \\ -\sum_{j=1}^{n_R} \alpha_j(x), & \text{otherwise.} \end{cases} \tag{3}$$

The probability distribution over time can be analyzed as an initial value problem. Given an initial state x_0, the distribution[1]

$$\pi(x_i, t) = \Pr(X_t = x_i \mid X_0 = x_0), \quad t \geq 0 \tag{4}$$

evolves according to the Kolmogorov forward equation

$$\frac{d}{dt}\pi(t) = \pi(t)Q, \tag{5}$$

where $\pi(t)$ is an arbitrary vectorization $(\pi(x_1, t), \pi(x_2, t), \ldots, \pi(x_{|S|}, t))$ of the states.

Let $x_g \in S$ be a fixed goal state. Given the terminal constraint $\Pr(X_T = x_g)$ for some $T \geq 0$, we are interested in the so-called backward probabilities

$$\beta(x_i, t) = \Pr(X_T = x_g \mid X_t = x_i), \quad t \leq T. \tag{6}$$

Note that $\beta(\cdot, t)$ is a function of the conditional event and thus is no probability distribution over the state-space. Instead $\beta(\cdot, t)$ gives the reaching probabilities for all states over the time span of $[t, T]$. To compute these probabilities, we can employ the Kolmogorov backward equation

$$\frac{d}{dt}\beta(t) = Q\beta(t)^\top, \tag{7}$$

where we use the same vectorization to construct $\beta(t)$ as we used for $\pi(t)$. The above equation is integrated backwards in time and yields the reachability probability for each state x_i and time $t < T$ of ending up in x_g at time T.

---

[1] In the sequel, x_i denotes a state with index i instead of its i-th component.

The state-space of many MJPs with population structure, even simple ones, is countably infinite. In this case, we have to truncate the state-space to a *reasonable* finite subset. The choice of this truncation heavily depends on the goal of the analysis. If one is interested in the most "common" behavior, for example, a dynamic mass-based truncation scheme is most appropriate [32]. Such a scheme truncates states with small probability during the numerical integration. However, common mass-based truncation schemes are not as useful for the bridging problem. This is because trajectories that meet the specific terminal constraints can be far off the main bulk of the probability mass. We solve this problem by a state-space lumping in connection with an iterative refinement scheme.

Consider as an example a birth-death process. This model can be used to model a wide variety of phenomena and often constitutes a sub-module of larger models. For example, it can be interpreted as an M/M/1 queue with service rates being linearly dependent on the queue length. Note, that even for this simple model, the state-space is countably infinite.

Model 1 (Birth-Death Process). *The model consists of exponentially distributed arrivals and service times proportional to queue length. It can be expressed using two mass-action reactions:*

$$\varnothing \xrightarrow{10} X \qquad and \qquad X \xrightarrow{.1} \varnothing .$$

The initial condition $X_0 = 0$ holds with probability one.

3.2   Bridging Distribution

The process' probability distribution given both initial and terminal constraints is formally described by the conditional probabilities

$$\gamma(x_i, t) = \Pr(X_t = x_i \mid X_0 = x_0, X_T = x_g), \quad 0 \le t \le T \qquad (8)$$

for fixed initial state x_0 and terminal state x_g. We call these probabilities the *bridging probabilities*. It is straight-forward to see that γ admits the factorization

$$\gamma(x_i, t) = \pi(x_i, t)\beta(x_i, t)/\pi(x_g, T) \qquad (9)$$

due to the Markov property. The normalization factor, given by the reachability probability $\pi(x_g, T) = \beta(x_0, 0)$, ensures that $\gamma(\cdot, t)$ is a distribution for all time points $t \in [0, T]$. We call each $\gamma(\cdot, t)$ a *bridging distribution*. From the Kolmogorov equations (5) and (7) we can obtain both the forward probabilities $\pi(\cdot, t)$ and the backward probabilities $\beta(\cdot, t)$ for $t < T$.

We can easily extend this procedure to deal with hitting times constrained by a finite time-horizon by making the goal state x_g absorbing.

In Figure 1 we plot the forward, backward, and bridging probabilities for Model 1. The probabilities are computed on a $[0, 100]$ state-space truncation. The approximate forward solution $\hat{\pi}$ shows how the probability mass drifts upwards towards the stationary distribution Poisson(100). The backward probabilities

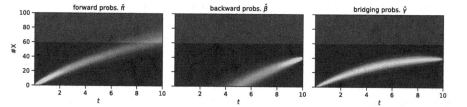

Fig. 1. Forward, backward, and bridging probabilities for Model 1 with initial constraint $X_0 = 0$ and terminal constraint $X_{10} = 40$ on a truncated state-space. Probabilities over 0.1 in $\hat{\pi}$ and $\hat{\beta}$ are given full intensity for visual clarity. The lightly shaded area (≥ 60) indicates a region being more relevant for the forward than for the bridging probabilities.

are highest for states below the goal state $x_g = 40$. This is expected because upwards drift makes reaching x_g more probable for "lower" states. Finally, the approximate bridging distribution $\hat{\gamma}$ can be recognized to be proportional to the product of forward $\hat{\pi}$ and backward probabilities $\hat{\beta}$.

4   Bridge Truncation via Lumping Approximations

We first discuss the truncation of countably infinite state-spaces to analyze backward and forward probabilities (Section 4.1). To identify effective truncations we employ a lumping scheme. In Section 4.2, we explain the construction of macrostates and assumptions made, as well as the efficient calculation of transition rates between them. Finally, in Section 4.3 we present an iterative refinement algorithm yielding a suitable truncation for the bridging problem.

4.1   Finite State Projection

Even in simple models such as a birth-death Process (Model 1), the reachable state-space is countably infinite. Direct analyzes of backward (6) and forward equations (4) are often infeasible. Instead, the integration of these differential equations requires working with a finite subset of the infinite state-space [37]. If states are truncated, their incoming transitions from states that are not truncated can be re-directed to a *sink state*. The accumulated probability in this sink state is then used as an error estimate for the forward integration scheme. Consequently, many truncation schemes, such as dynamic truncations [4], aim to minimize the amount of "lost mass" of the forward probability. We use the same truncation method but base the truncation on bridging probabilities rather than the forward probabilities.

4.2   State-Space Lumping

When dealing with bridging problems, the most likely trajectories from the initial to the terminal state are typically not known a priori. Especially if the event in question is rare, obtaining a state-space truncation adapted to its constraints is difficult. We devise a lumping scheme that groups nearby states, i.e. molecule counts, into larger *macro-states*. A macro-state is a collection of states treated as one state in a lumped model, which can be seen as an abstraction of the original model. These macro-states form a partitioning of the state-space. In this lumped model, we assume a uniform distribution over the constituent micro-states inside each macro-state. Thus, given that the system is in a particular macro-state, all of its micro-states are equally likely. This partitioning allows us to analyze significant regions of the state-space efficiently albeit under a rough approximation of the dynamics. Iterative refinement of the state-space after each analysis moves the dynamics closer to the original model. In the final step of the iteration, the considered system states are at the granularity of the original model such that no approximation error is introduced by assumptions of the lumping scheme. Computational efficiency is retained by truncating in each iteration step those states that contribute little probability mass to the (approximated) bridging distributions.

We choose a lumping scheme based on a grid of hypercube macro-states whose endpoints belong to a predefined grid. This topology makes the computation of transition rates between macro-states particularly convenient. Mass-action reaction rates, for example, can be given in a closed-form due to the Faulhaber formulae. More complicated rate functions such as Hill functions can often be handled as well by taking appropriate integrals.

Our choice is a scheme that uses n_S-dimensional hypercubes. A macro-state $\bar{x}_i(\ell^{(i)}, u^{(i)})$ (denoted by $\bar{x}_i$ for notational ease) can therefore be described by two vectors $\ell^{(i)}$ and $u^{(i)}$. The vector $\ell^{(i)}$ gives the corner closest to the origin, while $u^{(i)}$ gives the corner farthest from the origin. Formally,

$$\bar{x}_i = \bar{x}_i(\ell^{(i)}, u^{(i)}) = \{x \in \mathbb{N}^{n_S} \mid \ell^{(i)} \leq x \leq u^{(i)}\}, \tag{10}$$

where '$\leq$' stands for the element-wise comparison. This choice of topology makes the computation of transition rates between macro-states particularly convenient: Suppose we are interested in the set of micro-states in macro-state $\bar{x}_i$ that can transition to macro-state $\bar{x}_k$ via reaction j. It is easy to see that this set is itself an interval-defined macro-state $\bar{x}_{i \xrightarrow{j} k}$. To compute this macro-state we can simply shift $\bar{x}_i$ by v_j, take the intersection with $\bar{x}_k$ and project this set back. Formally,

$$\bar{x}_{i \xrightarrow{j} k} = ((\bar{x}_i + v_j) \cap \bar{x}_k) - v_j, \tag{11}$$

where the additions are applied element-wise to all states making up the macro-states. For the correct handling of the truncation it is useful to define a general exit state

$$\bar{x}_{i \xrightarrow{j}} = ((\bar{x}_i + v_j) \setminus \bar{x}_i) - v_j. \tag{12}$$

This state captures all micro-states inside $\bar{x}_i$ that can leave the state via reaction j. Note that all operations preserve the structure of a macro-state as defined in (10). Since a macro-state is based on intervals the computation of the transition rate is often straight-forward. Under the assumption of polynomial rates, as

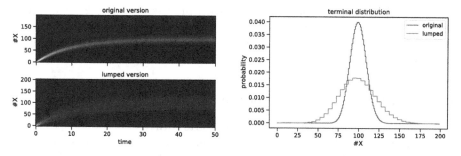

Fig. 2. A lumping approximation of Model 1 on the state-space truncation to $[0, 200]$ on $t \in [0, 50]$. On the left-hand side solutions of a regular truncation approximation and a lumped truncation (macro-state size is 5) are given. On the right-hand side the respective terminal distributions $\Pr(X_{50} = x_i)$ are contrasted.

it is the case for mass-action systems, we can compute the sum of rates over this transition set efficiently using Faulhaber's formula. We define the lumped transition function

$$\bar{\alpha}_j(\bar{x}) = \sum_{x \in \bar{x}} \alpha_j(x) \tag{13}$$

for macro-state $\bar{x}$ and reaction j. As an example consider the following mass-action reaction $2X \xrightarrow{c} \varnothing$. For macro-state $\bar{x} = \{0, \dots, n\}$ we can compute the corresponding lumped transition rate

$$\bar{\alpha}(\bar{x}) = \frac{c}{2} \sum_{i=1}^{n} i(i-1) = \frac{c}{2} \sum_{i=1}^{n} (i^2 - i) = \frac{c}{2} \left(\frac{2n^3 + 3n^2 + n}{6} - \frac{n^2 + n}{2} \right)$$

eliminating the explicit summation in the lumped propensity function.

For polynomial propensity functions α such formulae are easily obtained automatically. For non-polynomial propensity functions, we can use the continuous integral as an approximation. This is demonstrated on a case study in Section 5.2.

Using the transition set computation (11) and the lumped propensity function (13) we can populate the Q-matrix of the finite lumping approximation:

$$\bar{Q}_{\bar{x}_i, \bar{x}_k} = \begin{cases} \sum_{j=1}^{n_R} \bar{\alpha}_j \left(\bar{x}_{i \xrightarrow{j} k} \right) / \mathrm{vol}\,(\bar{x}_i), & \text{if } \bar{x}_i \neq \bar{x}_k \\ -\sum_{j=1}^{n_R} \bar{\alpha}_j \left(\bar{x}_{i \xrightarrow{j}} \right) / \mathrm{vol}\,(\bar{x}_i), & \text{otherwise} \end{cases} \tag{14}$$

In addition to the lumped rate function over the transition state $\bar{x}_{i \xrightarrow{j} k}$, we need to divide by the total volume of the lumped state $\bar{x}_i$. This is due to the assumption of a uniform distribution inside the macro-states. Using this Q-matrix, we can compute the forward and backward solution using the respective Kolmogorov equations (5) and (7).

Interestingly, the lumped distribution tends to be less concentrated. This is due to the assumption of a uniform distribution inside macro-states. This effect is illustrated by the example of a birth-death process in Figure 2. Due to this effect, an iterative refinement typically keeps an over-approximation in terms of state-space area. This is a desirable feature since relevant regions are less likely to be pruned due to lumping approximations.

4.3   Iterative Refinement Algorithm

The iterative refinement algorithm (Alg. 1) starts with a set of large macro-states that are iteratively refined, based on approximate solutions to the bridging problem. We start by constructing square macro-states of size 2^m in each dimension for some $m \in \mathbb{N}$ such that they form a large-scale grid $\mathcal{S}^{(0)}$. Hence, each initial macro-state has a volume of $(2^m)^{n_S}$. This choice of grid size is convenient because we can halve states in each dimension. Moreover, this choice ensures that all states have equal volume and we end up with states of volume $2^0 = 1$ which is equivalent to a truncation of the original non-lumped state-space.

An iteration of the state-space refinement starts by computing both the forward and backward probabilities (lines 2 and 3) via integration of (5) and (7), respectively, using the lumped $\hat{Q}$-matrix. Based on the resulting approximate forward and backward probabilities, we compute an approximation of the bridging distributions (line 4). This is done for each time-point in an equispaced grid on $[0, T]$. The time grid granularity is a hyper-parameter of the algorithm. If the grid is too fine, the memory overhead of storing backward $\hat{\beta}^{(i)}$ and forward solutions $\hat{\pi}^{(i)}$ increases.[2] If, on the other hand, the granularity is too low, too much of the state-space might be truncated. Based on a threshold parameter $\delta > 0$ states are either removed or split (line 7), depending on the mass assigned to them by the approximate bridging probabilities $\hat{\gamma}_t^{(i)}$. A state can be split by the split-function which halves the state in each dimension. Otherwise, it is removed. Thus, each macro-state is either split into 2^{n_S} new states or removed entirely. The result forms the next lumped state-space $\mathcal{S}^{(i+1)}$. The Q-matrix is adjusted (line 10) such that transition rates for $\mathcal{S}^{(i+1)}$ are calculated according to (14). Entries of truncated states are removed from the transition matrix. Transitions leading to them are re-directed to a sink state (see Section 4.1). After m iterations (we started with states of side lengths 2^m) we have a standard finite state projection scheme on the original model tailored to computing an approximation of the bridging distribution.

In Figure 3 we give a demonstration of how Algorithm 1 works to refine the state-space iteratively. Starting with an initial lumped state-space $\mathcal{S}^{(0)}$ covering a large area of the state-space, repeated evaluations of the bridging distributions are performed. After five iterations the remaining truncation includes all states that significantly contribute to the bridging probabilities over the times $[0, T]$.

It is important to realize that determining the most relevant states is *the* main challenge. The above algorithm solves this problem by considering only

---

[2] We denote the approximations with a hat (e.g. $\hat{\pi}$) rather than a bar (e.g. $\bar{\pi}$) to indicate that not only the lumping approximation but also a truncation is applied and similarly for the Q-matrix.

Algorithm 1: Iterative refinement for the bridging problem

---

    input : Initial partitioning $\mathcal{S}^{(0)}$, truncation threshold δ
    output: approximate bridging distribution $\hat{\gamma}$

1 **for** $i = 1, \ldots, m$ **do**
2      $\hat{\pi}_t^{(i)} \leftarrow$ solve approximate forward equation on $\mathcal{S}^{(i)}$;
3      $\hat{\beta}_t^{(i)} \leftarrow$ solve approximate backward equation on $\mathcal{S}^{(i)}$;
4      $\hat{\gamma}_t^{(i)} \leftarrow \hat{\beta}^{(i)} \hat{\pi}^{(i)} / \hat{\pi}(x_g, T)$;   /* approximate bridging distribution */
5      $\mathcal{S}^{(i+1)} \leftarrow \emptyset$;
6   **foreach** $\bar{x} \in \mathcal{S}^{(i)}$ **do**
7   **if** $\exists t. \hat{\gamma}_t^{(i)}(\bar{x}) \geq \delta$;   /* refine based on bridging probabilities */
8   **then**
9             $\mathcal{S}^{(i+1)} \leftarrow \mathcal{S}^{(i+1)} \cup \mathtt{split}(\bar{x})$;
10   update $\hat{Q}$-matrix;
11 **return** $\hat{\gamma}^{(i)}$;

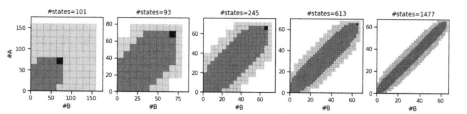

Fig. 3. The state-space refinement algorithm on two parallel unit-rate arrival processes. The bridging problem from $(0, 0)$ to $(64, 64)$ and $T = 10$ and truncation threshold $\delta = 5e\text{-}3$. States with a bridging probability below δ are light grey. The macro-state containing the goal state is marked in black. The initial macro-states are of size 16×16.

those parts of the state-space that contribute most to the bridging probabilities. The truncation is tailored to this condition and might ignore regions that are likely in the unconditioned case. For instance, in Fig. 1 the bridging probabilities mostly remain below a population threshold of $\#X = 60$ (as indicated by the lighter/darker coloring), while the forward probabilities mostly exceed this bound. Hence, in this example a significant portion of the forward probabilities $\hat{\pi}_t^{(i)}$ is captured by the sink state. However, the condition in line 7 in Algorithm 1 ensures that states contributing significantly to $\hat{\gamma}_t^{(i)}$ will be kept and refined in the next iteration.

5   Results

We present four examples in this section to evaluate our proposed method. A prototype was implemented in Python 3.8. For numerical integration we

threshold δ	1e-2	1e-3	1e-4	1e-5
truncation size	1154	2354	3170	3898
overall states	2074	3546	4586	5450
estimate	8.8851e-30	1.8557e-29	1.8625e-29	1.8625e-29
rel. error	5.2297e-01	3.6667e-03	3.7423e-05	9.5259e-08

Table 1. Estimated reachability probabilities based on varying truncation thresholds δ: The true probability is 1.8625e-29. We also report the size of the final truncation and the accumulated size of all truncations during refinement iterations (overall states).

used the Scipy implementation [47] of the implicit method based on backward-differentiation formulas [13]. The analysis as a Jupyter notebook is made available online[3].

5.1   Bounding Rare Event Probabilities

We consider a simple model of two parallel Poisson processes describing the production of two types of agents. The corresponding probability distribution has Poisson product form at all time points $t \geq 0$ and hence we can compare the accuracy of our numerical results with the exact analytic solution. We use the proposed approach to compute lower bounds for rare event probabilities. [4]

Model 2 (Parallel Poisson Processes). *The model consists of two parallel independent Poisson processes with unit rates.*

$$\varnothing \xrightarrow{1} A \qquad and \qquad \varnothing \xrightarrow{1} B .$$

The initial condition $X_0 = (0,0)$ holds with probability one. After t time units each species abundance is Poisson distributed with rate $\lambda = t$.

We consider the final constraint of reaching a state where both processes exceed a threshold of 64 at time 20. Without prior knowledge, a reasonable truncation would have been 160×160. But our analysis shows that just 20% of the states are necessary to capture over 99.6% of the probability mass reaching the target event (cf. Table 1). Decreasing the threshold δ leads to a larger set of states retained after truncation as more of the bridging distribution is included (cf. Figure 4). We observe an increase in truncation size that is approximately logarithmic in δ, which, in this example, indicates robustness of the method with respect to the choice of δ.

---

[3] https://www.github.com/mbackenkoehler/mjp_bridging

[4] These bounds are rigorous up to the approximation error of the numerical integration scheme. However, the forward solution could be replaced by an adaptive uniformization approach [3] for a more rigorous integration error control.

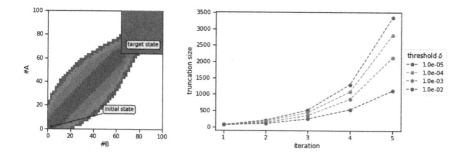

Fig. 4. State-space truncation for varying values of the threshold parameter δ: Two parallel Poisson processes under terminal constraints $X_{20}^{(A)} \geq 64$ and $X_{20}^{(B)} \geq 64$. The initial macro-states are 16×16 such that the final states are regular micro states.

Comparison to other methods The truncation approach that we apply is similar to the one used by Mikeev et al. [34] for rare event estimation. However, they used a given linearly biased MJP model to obtain a truncation. A general strategy to compute an appropriate biasing was not proposed. It is possible to adapt our truncation approach to the dynamic scheme in Ref. [34] where states are removed in an on-the-fly fashion during numerical integration.

A finite state-space truncation covering the same area as the initial lumping approximation would contain 25,600 states.[5] The standard approach would be to build up the entire state-space for such a model [27]. Even using a conservative truncation threshold $\delta = $ 1e-5, our method yields an accurate estimate using only about a fifth (5450) of this accumulated over all intermediate lumped approximations.

5.2   Mode Switching

Mode switching occurs in models exhibiting *multi-modal* behavior [44] when a trajectory traverses a potential barrier from one mode to another. Often, mode switching is a rare event and occurs in the context of gene regulatory networks where a mode is characterized by the set of genes being currently active [30]. Similar dynamics also commonly occur in queuing models where a system may for example switch its operating behavior stochastically if traffic increases above or decreases below certain thresholds. Using the presented method, we can get both a qualitative and quantitative understanding of switching behavior without resorting to Monte-Carlo methods such as importance sampling.

Exclusive Switch The exclusive switch [7] has three different modes of operation, depending on the DNA state, i.e. on whether a protein of type one or two is bound to the DNA.

---

[5] Here, the goal is not treated as a single state. Otherwise, it consists of 24,130 states.

Model 3 (Exclusive Switch). *The exclusive switch model consists of a promoter region that can express both proteins P_1 and P_2. Both can bind to the region, suppressing the expression of the other protein. For certain parameterizations, this leads to a bi-modal or even tri-modal behavior.*

$$D \xrightarrow{\rho} D + P_1 \qquad D \xrightarrow{\rho} D + P_2 \qquad P_1 \xrightarrow{\lambda} \varnothing \qquad P_2 \xrightarrow{\lambda} \varnothing$$

$$D + P_1 \xrightarrow{\beta} D.P_1 \qquad D.P1 \xrightarrow{\gamma} D + P_1 \qquad D.P_1 \xrightarrow{\alpha} D.P_1 + P_1$$

$$D + P_2 \xrightarrow{\beta} D.P_2 \qquad D.P2 \xrightarrow{\gamma} D + P_2 \qquad D.P_2 \xrightarrow{\alpha} D.P_2 + P_2$$

The parameter values are $\rho = 1e\text{-}1$, $\lambda = 1e\text{-}3$, $\beta = 1e\text{-}2$, $\gamma = 8e\text{-}3$, and $\alpha = 1e\text{-}1$.

Since we know a priori of the three distinct operating modes, we adjust the method slightly: The state-space for the DNA states is not lumped. Instead we "stack" lumped approximations of the P_1-P_2 phase space upon each other. Special treatment of DNA states is common for such models [28].

To analyze the switching, we choose the transition from (variable order: P_1, P_2, D, $D.P_1$, $D.P_2$) $x_1 = (32, 0, 0, 0, 1)$ to $x_2 = (0, 32, 0, 1, 0)$ over the time interval $t \in [0, 10]$. The initial lumping scheme covers up to 80 molecules of P_1 and P_2 for each mode. Macro-states have size 8×8 and the truncation threshold is $\delta = 1e\text{-}4$.

In the analysis of biological switches, not only the switching probability but also the switching dynamics is a central part of understanding the underlying biological mechanisms. In Figure 5 (left), we therefore plot the time-varying probabilities of the gene state conditioned on the mode. We observe a rapid unbinding of P_2, followed by a slow increase of the binding probability for P_1. These dynamics are already qualitatively captured by the first lumped approximation (dashed lines).

Toggle Switch Next, we apply our method to a toggle switch model exhibiting non-polynomial rate functions. This well-known model considers two proteins A and B inhibiting the production of the respective other protein [29].

Model 4. *Toggle Switch (Hill functions) We have population types A and B with the following reactions and reaction rates.*

$$\varnothing \xrightarrow{\alpha_1(\cdot)} A, \quad \text{where} \quad \alpha_1(x) = \frac{\rho}{1 + x_B}, \qquad A \xrightarrow{\lambda} \varnothing$$

$$\varnothing \xrightarrow{\alpha_1(\cdot)} B, \quad \text{where} \quad \alpha_1(x) = \frac{\rho}{1 + x_A}, \qquad B \xrightarrow{\lambda} \varnothing$$

The parameterization is $\rho = 10$, $\lambda = 0.1$.

Due to the non-polynomial rate functions α_1 and α_2, the transition rates between macro-states are approximated by using the continuous integral

$$\bar{\alpha}_1(\bar{x}) \approx \int_{a-0.5}^{b+0.5} \frac{\rho}{1+x}\, dx = \rho\left(\log\left(b + 1.5\right) - \log\left(a + 0.5\right)\right)$$

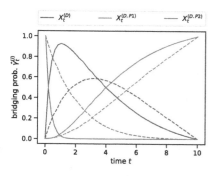
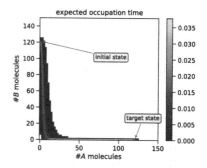

Fig. 5. (left) Mode probabilities of the exclusive switch bridging problem over time for the first lumped approximation (dashed lines) and the final approximation (solid lines) with constraints $X_0 = (32, 0, 0, 1, 0)$ and $X_{10} = (0, 32, 0, 0, 1)$. (right) The expected occupation time (excluding initial and terminal states) for the switching problem of the toggle switch using Hill-type functions. The bridging problem is from initial $(0, 120)$ to a first passage of $(120, 0)$ in $t \in [0, 10]$.

for a macro-state $\bar{x} = \{a, \ldots, b\}$.

We analyze the switching scenario from $(0, 120)$ to the first visit of state $(120, 0)$ up to time $T = 10$. The initial lumping scheme covers up to 352 molecules of A and B and macro-states have size 32×32. The truncation threshold is $\delta = 1\text{e-}4$. The resulting truncation is shown in Figure 5 (right). It also illustrates the kind of insights that can be obtained from the bridging distributions. For an overview of the switching dynamics, we look at the expected occupation time under the terminal constraint of having entered state $(120, 0)$. Letting the corresponding hitting time be $\tau = \inf\{t \geq 0 \mid X_t = (120, 0)\}$, the expected occupation time for some state x is $E\left(\int_0^T 1_{=x}(X_t)\, dt \mid \tau \leq 10\right)$. We observe that in this example the switching behavior seems to be asymmetrical. The main mass seems to pass through an area where initially a small number of A molecules is produced followed by a total decay of B molecules.

5.3   Recursive Bayesian Estimation

We now turn to the method's application in recursive Bayesian estimation. This is the problem of estimating the system's past, present, and future behavior under given observations. Thus, the MJP becomes a hidden Markov model (HMM). The observations in such models are usually noisy, meaning that we cannot infer the system state with certainty.

This estimation problem entails more general distributional constraints on terminal $\beta(\cdot, T)$ and initial $\pi(\cdot, 0)$ distributions than the point mass distributions considered up until now. We can easily extend the forward and backward probabilities to more general initial distributions and terminal distributions $\beta(T)$. For the forward probabilities we get

$$\pi(x_i, t) = \sum_j \Pr(X_t = x_i \mid X_0 = x_j)\pi(x_j, 0), \tag{15}$$

and similarly the backward probabilities are given by

$$\beta(x_i, t) = \sum_j \Pr(X_T = x_j \mid X_t = x_i)\beta_T(x_j). \tag{16}$$

We apply our method to an SEIR (susceptible-exposed-infected-removed) model. This is widely used to describe the spreading of an epidemic such as the current COVID-19 outbreak [23,20]. Temporal snapshots of the epidemic spread are mostly only available for a subset of the population and suffer from inaccuracies of diagnostic tests. Bayesian estimation can then be used to infer the spreading dynamics given uncertain temporal snapshots.

Model 5 (Epidemics Model). *A population of susceptible individuals can contract a disease from infected agents. In this case, they are exposed, meaning they will become infected but cannot yet infect others. After being infected, individuals change to the removed state. The mass-action reactions are as follows.*

$$S + I \xrightarrow{\lambda} E + I \qquad E \xrightarrow{\mu} I \qquad I \xrightarrow{\rho} R$$

The parameter values are $\lambda = 0.5$, $\mu = 3$, $\rho = 3$. *Due to the stoichiometric invariant* $X_t^{(S)} + X_t^{(E)} + X_t^{(I)} + X_t^{(R)} = $ const., *we can eliminate R from the system.*

We consider the following scenario: We know that initially ($t = 0$) one individual is infected and the rest is susceptible. At time $t = 0.3$ all individuals are tested for the disease. The test, however, only identifies infected individuals with probability 0.99. Moreover, the probability of a false positive is 0.05. We like to identify the distribution given both the initial state and the measurement at time $t = 0.3$. In particular, we want to infer the distribution over the latent counts of S and E by *recursive Bayesian estimation*.

The posterior for n_I infected individuals at time t, given measurement $Y_t = \hat{n}_I$ can be computed using Bayes' rule

$$\Pr(X_t^{(I)} = n_I \mid Y_t = \hat{n}_I) \propto \Pr(Y_t = \hat{n}_I \mid X_t^{(I)} = n_I)\Pr(X_t^{(I)} = n_I). \tag{17}$$

This problem is an extension of the bridging problem discussed up until now. The difference is that the terminal posterior is estimated it using the result of the lumped forward equation and the measurement distribution using (17). Based on this estimated terminal posterior, we compute the bridging probabilities and refine the truncation tailored to the location of the posterior distribution. In Figure 6 (left), we illustrate the bridging distribution between the terminal posterior and initial distribution. In the context of filtering problems this is commonly referred to as smoothing. Using the learned truncation, we can obtain the posterior distribution for the number of infected individuals at $t = 0.3$ (Figure 6 (middle)). Moreover, can we infer a distribution over the unknown number of susceptible and exposed individuals (Figure 6 (right)).

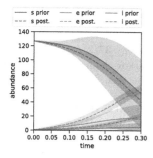
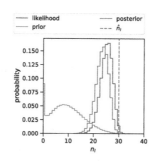
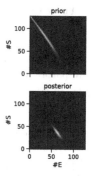

Fig. 6. (left) A comparison of the prior dynamics and the posterior smoothing (bridging) dynamics. (middle) The prior, likelihood, and posterior of the number of infected individuals n_I at time $t = 0.3$ given the measurement $\hat{n}_I = 30$. (right) The prior and posterior distribution over the latent types E and S.

6   Conclusion

The analysis of Markov Jump processes with constraints on the initial and terminal behavior is an important part of many probabilistic inference tasks such as parameter estimation using Bayesian or maximum likelihood estimation, inference of latent system behavior, the estimation of rare event probabilities, and reachability analysis for the verification of temporal properties. If endpoint constraints correspond to atypical system behaviors, standard analysis methods fail as they have no strategy to identify those parts of the state-space relevant for meeting the terminal constraint.

Here, we proposed a method that is not based on stochastic sampling and statistical estimation but provides a direct numerical approach. It starts with an abstract lumped model, which is iteratively refined such that only those parts of the model are considered that contribute to the probabilities of interest. In the final step of the iteration, we operate at the granularity of the original model and compute lower bounds for these bridging probabilities that are rigorous up to the error of the numerical integration scheme.

Our method exploits the population structure of the model, which is present in many important application fields of MJPs. Based on experience with other work based on truncation, the approach can be expected to scale up to at least a few million states [33]. Compared to previous work, our method neither relies on approximations of unknown accuracy nor additional information such as a suitable change of measure in the case of importance sampling. It only requires a truncation threshold and an initial choice for the macro-state sizes.

In future work, we plan to extend our method to hybrid approaches, in which a moment representation is employed for large populations while discrete counts are maintained for small populations. Moreover, we will apply our method to model checking where constraints are described by some temporal logic [21].

Acknowledgements This project was supported by the DFG project MULTI-MODE and Italian PRIN project SEDUCE.

References

1. Adan, A., Alizada, G., Kiraz, Y., Baran, Y., Nalbant, A.: Flow cytometry: basic principles and applications. Critical reviews in biotechnology **37**(2), 163–176 (2017)
2. Amparore, E.G., Donatelli, S.: Backward solution of Markov chains and Markov regenerative processes: Formalization and applications. Electron. Notes Theor. Comput. Sci. **296**, 7–26 (2013)
3. Andreychenko, A., Crouzen, P., Mikeev, L., Wolf, V.: On-the-fly uniformization of time-inhomogeneous infinite Markov population models. arXiv preprint arXiv:1006.4425 (2010)
4. Andreychenko, A., Mikeev, L., Spieler, D., Wolf, V.: Parameter identification for Markov models of biochemical reactions. In: International Conference on Computer Aided Verification. pp. 83–98. Springer (2011)
5. Backenköhler, M., Bortolussi, L., Wolf, V.: Control variates for stochastic simulation of chemical reaction networks. In: Bortolussi, L., Sanguinetti, G. (eds.) Computational Methods in Systems Biology. pp. 42–59. Springer, Cham (2019)
6. Backenköhler, M., Bortolussi, L., Wolf, V.: Bounding mean first passage times in population continuous-time Markov chains. To appear in Proc. of QEST'20 (2020)
7. Barzel, B., Biham, O.: Calculation of switching times in the genetic toggle switch and other bistable systems. Physical Review E **78**(4), 041919 (2008)
8. Bortolussi, L., Lanciani, R.: Stochastic approximation of global reachability probabilities of Markov population models. In: Computer Performance Engineering - 11th European Workshop, EPEW 2014, Florence, Italy, September 11-12, 2014. Proceedings. pp. 224–239 (2014)
9. Bortolussi, L., Lanciani, R., Nenzi, L.: Model checking markov population models by stochastic approximations. Inf. Comput. **262**, 189–220 (2018)
10. Breuer, L.: From Markov jump processes to spatial queues. Springer Science & Business Media (2003)
11. Broemeling, L.D.: Bayesian Inference for Stochastic Processes. CRC Press (2017)
12. Buchholz, P.: Exact and ordinary lumpability in finite Markov chains. Journal of applied probability pp. 59–75 (1994)
13. Byrne, G.D., Hindmarsh, A.C.: A polyalgorithm for the numerical solution of ordinary differential equations. ACM Transactions on Mathematical Software (TOMS) **1**(1), 71–96 (1975)
14. Daigle Jr, B.J., Roh, M.K., Gillespie, D.T., Petzold, L.R.: Automated estimation of rare event probabilities in biochemical systems. The Journal of Chemical Physics **134**(4), 01B628 (2011)
15. Dayar, T., Stewart, W.J.: Quasi lumpability, lower-bounding coupling matrices, and nearly completely decomposable Markov chains. SIAM Journal on Matrix Analysis and Applications **18**(2), 482–498 (1997)
16. Gillespie, D.T.: Exact stochastic simulation of coupled chemical reactions. The journal of physical chemistry **81**(25), 2340–2361 (1977)
17. Golightly, A., Sherlock, C.: Efficient sampling of conditioned Markov jump processes. Statistics and Computing **29**(5), 1149–1163 (2019)
18. Golightly, A., Wilkinson, D.J.: Bayesian inference for stochastic kinetic models using a diffusion approximation. Biometrics **61**(3), 781–788 (2005)
19. Golightly, A., Wilkinson, D.J.: Bayesian parameter inference for stochastic biochemical network models using particle Markov chain monte carlo. Interface focus **1**(6), 807–820 (2011)

20. Grossmann, G., Backenköhler, M., Wolf, V.: Importance of interaction structure and stochasticity for epidemic spreading: A COVID-19 case study. In: Seventeenth international conference on the quantitative evaluation of systems (QEST 2020). IEEE (2020)
21. Hajnal, M., Nouvian, M., Šafránek, D., Petrov, T.: Data-informed parameter synthesis for population markov chains. In: International Workshop on Hybrid Systems Biology. pp. 147–164. Springer (2019)
22. Hayden, R.A., Stefanek, A., Bradley, J.T.: Fluid computation of passage-time distributions in large Markov models. Theoretical Computer Science **413**(1), 106–141 (2012)
23. He, S., Peng, Y., Sun, K.: SEIR modeling of the COVID-19 and its dynamics. Nonlinear Dynamics pp. 1–14 (2020)
24. Henzinger, T.A., Mateescu, M., Wolf, V.: Sliding window abstraction for infinite Markov chains. In: International Conference on Computer Aided Verification. pp. 337–352. Springer (2009)
25. Huang, L., Pauleve, L., Zechner, C., Unger, M., Hansen, A.S., Koeppl, H.: Reconstructing dynamic molecular states from single-cell time series. Journal of The Royal Society Interface **13**(122), 20160533 (2016)
26. Kuwahara, H., Mura, I.: An efficient and exact stochastic simulation method to analyze rare events in biochemical systems. The Journal of chemical physics **129**(16), 10B619 (2008)
27. Kwiatkowska, M., Norman, G., Parker, D.: Prism 4.0: Verification of probabilistic real-time systems. In: International conference on computer aided verification. pp. 585–591. Springer (2011)
28. Lapin, M., Mikeev, L., Wolf, V.: SHAVE: stochastic hybrid analysis of Markov population models. In: Proceedings of the 14th international conference on Hybrid systems: computation and control. pp. 311–312 (2011)
29. Lipshtat, A., Loinger, A., Balaban, N.Q., Biham, O.: Genetic toggle switch without cooperative binding. Physical review letters **96**(18), 188101 (2006)
30. Loinger, A., Lipshtat, A., Balaban, N.Q., Biham, O.: Stochastic simulations of genetic switch systems. Physical Review E **75**(2), 021904 (2007)
31. Mikeev, L., Neuhäußer, M.R., Spieler, D., Wolf, V.: On-the-fly verification and optimization of DTA-properties for large Markov chains. Formal Methods in System Design **43**(2), 313–337 (2013)
32. Mikeev, L., Sandmann, W.: Approximate numerical integration of the chemical master equation for stochastic reaction networks. arXiv preprint arXiv:1907.10245 (2019)
33. Mikeev, L., Sandmann, W., Wolf, V.: Efficient calculation of rare event probabilities in Markovian queueing networks. In: Proceedings of the 5th International ICST Conference on Performance Evaluation Methodologies and Tools. pp. 186–196 (2011)
34. Mikeev, L., Sandmann, W., Wolf, V.: Numerical approximation of rare event probabilities in biochemically reacting systems. In: International Conference on Computational Methods in Systems Biology. pp. 5–18. Springer (2013)
35. Milner, P., Gillespie, C.S., Wilkinson, D.J.: Moment closure based parameter inference of stochastic kinetic models. Statistics and Computing **23**(2), 287–295 (2013)
36. Mode, C.J., Sleeman, C.K.: Stochastic processes in epidemiology: HIV/AIDS, other infectious diseases, and computers. World Scientific (2000)
37. Munsky, B., Khammash, M.: The finite state projection algorithm for the solution of the chemical master equation. The Journal of chemical physics **124**(4), 044104 (2006)

38. Neupane, T., Myers, C.J., Madsen, C., Zheng, H., Zhang, Z.: Stamina: Stochastic approximate model-checker for infinite-state analysis. In: International Conference on Computer Aided Verification. pp. 540–549. Springer (2019)
39. Pardoux, E.: Markov processes and applications: algorithms, networks, genome and finance, vol. 796. John Wiley & Sons (2008)
40. Rabiner, L., Juang, B.: An introduction to hidden Markov models. IEEE ASSP Magazine **3**(1), 4–16 (1986)
41. Särkkä, S.: Bayesian filtering and smoothing, vol. 3. Cambridge University Press (2013)
42. Schnoerr, D., Cseke, B., Grima, R., Sanguinetti, G.: Efficient low-order approximation of first-passage time distributions. Phys. Rev. Lett. **119**, 210601 (Nov 2017). https://doi.org/10.1103/PhysRevLett.119.210601
43. Schnoerr, D., Sanguinetti, G., Grima, R.: Validity conditions for moment closure approximations in stochastic chemical kinetics. The Journal of chemical physics **141**(8), 08B616_1 (2014)
44. Siegal-Gaskins, D., Mejia-Guerra, M.K., Smith, G.D., Grotewold, E.: Emergence of switch-like behavior in a large family of simple biochemical networks. PLoS Comput Biol **7**(5), e1002039 (2011)
45. Strasser, M., Theis, F.J., Marr, C.: Stability and multiattractor dynamics of a toggle switch based on a two-stage model of stochastic gene expression. Biophysical journal **102**(1), 19–29 (2012)
46. Ullah, M., Wolkenhauer, O.: Stochastic approaches for systems biology. Springer Science & Business Media (2011)
47. Virtanen, P., Gommers, R., Oliphant, T.E., Haberland, M., Reddy, T., Cournapeau, D., Burovski, E., Peterson, P., Weckesser, W., Bright, J., van der Walt, S.J., Brett, M., Wilson, J., Jarrod Millman, K., Mayorov, N., Nelson, A.R.J., Jones, E., Kern, R., Larson, E., Carey, C., Polat, İ., Feng, Y., Moore, E.W., Vand erPlas, J., Laxalde, D., Perktold, J., Cimrman, R., Henriksen, I., Quintero, E.A., Harris, C.R., Archibald, A.M., Ribeiro, A.H., Pedregosa, F., van Mulbregt, P., Contributors, S...: SciPy 1.0: Fundamental Algorithms for Scientific Computing in Python. Nature Methods **17**, 261–272 (2020). https://doi.org/https://doi.org/10.1038/s41592-019-0686-2
48. Wildner, C., Koeppl, H.: Moment-based variational inference for Markov jump processes. arXiv preprint arXiv:1905.05451 (2019)
49. Wilkinson, D.J.: Stochastic modelling for systems biology. CRC press (2018)
50. Zapreev, I., Katoen, J.P.: Safe on-the-fly steady-state detection for time-bounded reachability. In: Third International Conference on the Quantitative Evaluation of Systems-(QEST'06). pp. 301–310. IEEE (2006)

Multi-objective Optimization of Long-run Average and Total Rewards

Tim Quatmann[1][✉] and Joost-Pieter Katoen[1]

RWTH Aachen University, Aachen, Germany
tim.quatmann@cs.rwth-aachen.de

Abstract This paper presents an efficient procedure for multi-objective model checking of long-run average reward (aka: mean pay-off) and total reward objectives as well as their combination. We consider this for Markov automata, a compositional model that captures both traditional Markov decision processes (MDPs) as well as a continuous-time variant thereof. The crux of our procedure is a generalization of Forejt *et al.*'s approach for total rewards on MDPs to arbitrary combinations of long-run and total reward objectives on Markov automata. Experiments with a prototypical implementation on top of the STORM model checker show encouraging results for both model types and indicate a substantial improved performance over existing multi-objective long-run MDP model checking based on linear programming.

1 Introduction

MDP model checking In various applications, multiple decision criteria and uncertainty frequently co-occur. Stochastic decision processes for which the objective is to achieve multiple—possibly partly conflicting—objectives occur in various fields. These include operations research, economics, planning in AI, and game theory, to mention a few. This has stimulated model checking of Markov decision processes (MDPs) [46], a prominent model in decision making under uncertainty, against multiple objectives. This development enlarges the rich plethora of automated MDP verification algorithms against single objectives [7].

Multi-objective MDP Various types of objectives known from conventional—single-objective—model checking have been lifted to the multi-objective case. These objectives range over ω-regular specifications including LTL [26,27], expected (discounted and non-discounted) total rewards [21,27,28,52,22], step-bounded and reward-bounded reachability probabilities [28,35], and—most relevant for this work—*expected long-run average (LRA) rewards* [18,11,20], also known as mean pay-offs. For the latter, all current approaches build upon linear programming (LP) which yields a theoretical time-complexity polynomial in the model size. However, in practice, LP-based methods are often outperformed by approaches based on value- or strategy iteration [28,1,42]. The LP-based approach of [27] and the iterative approach of [28] are both implemented in PRISM [45] and STORM [40]. The LP formulation of [11,20] is implemented in MULTIGAIN [12], an extension of PRISM for multi-objective LRA rewards.

© The Author(s) 2021
J. F. Groote and K. G. Larsen (Eds.): TACAS 2021, LNCS 12651, pp. 230–249, 2021.
https://doi.org/10.1007/978-3-030-72016-2_13

Contributions of this paper We present a computationally efficient procedure for multi-objective model checking of LRA reward and total reward objectives as well as their mixture. The crux of our procedure is *a generalization* of Forejt *et al.*'s iterative approach [28] for total rewards on MDPs *to expected LRA reward objectives*. In fact, our approach supports the arbitrary *mixtures* of expected LRA and total reward objectives. To our knowledge, such mixtures have not been considered so far. Experiments on various benchmarks using a prototypical implementation in STORM indicate that this generalized iterative algorithm outperforms the LP approach implemented in MULTIGAIN.

In addition, we extend this approach towards *Markov automata* (MA) [25,23], a continuous-time variant of MDP that is amenable to compositional modeling. This model is well-suited, among others, to provide a formal semantics for dynamic fault trees and generalized stochastic Petri nets [24]. Our multi-objective LRA approach for MA builds upon the value-iteration approach for single-objective expected LRA rewards on MA [17] which—on practical models—outperforms the LP-based approach of [30]. To the best of our knowledge, this is the *first multi-objective expected LRA reward approach for MA*. Experimental results on MA benchmarks show that the treatment of a continuous-time variant of LRA comes at almost no time penalty compared to the MDP setting.

Other related work Mixtures of various other objectives have been considered for MDPs. This includes conditional expectations or ratios of reward functions [5,4]. [31] considers LTL formulae with probability thresholds while maximizing an expected LRA reward. [35,41] address multi-objective quantiles on reachability properties while [50,20] consider multi-objective combinations of percentile queries on MDP and LRA objectives. [6] treats resilient systems ensuring constraints on the repair mechanism while maximizing the expected LRA reward when being operational. The trade-off between expected LRA rewards and their variance is analyzed in [13]. [33] studies multiple objectives on interval MDP, where transition probabilities can be specified as intervals in cases where the concrete probabilities are unknown. Multiple LRA reward objectives for *stochastic games* have been treated using LP [19] and value iteration over convex sets [8,9]; the latter is included in PRISM-GAMES [44,43]. These approaches can also be applied to MDPs when viewed as one-player stochastic games. Algorithms for single-objective model checking of MA deal with objectives such as expected total rewards, time-bounded reachability probabilities, and expected long-run average rewards [38,29,30,15]. The only multi-objective approach for MA so far [47] shows that any method for multi-objective MDP can be applied on (a discretized version of) an MA for queries involving unbounded or time-bounded reachability probabilities and expected total rewards, but no long-run average rewards.

2   Preliminaries

The set of *probability distributions* over a finite set Ω is given by $Dist(\Omega) = \{\mu\colon \Omega \mapsto [0,1] \mid \sum_{\omega\in\Omega} \mu(\omega) = 1\}$. For a distribution $\mu \in Dist(\Omega)$ we let $supp(\mu) = \{\omega \in \Omega \mid \mu(\omega) > 0\}$ denote its support. μ is *Dirac* if $|supp(\mu)| = 1$.

Let $\mathbb{R}_{\geq 0} = \{x \in \mathbb{R} \mid x \geq 0\}$, $\mathbb{R}_{>0} = \{x \in \mathbb{R} \mid x > 0\}$, and $\bar{\mathbb{R}} = \mathbb{R} \cup \{-\infty, \infty\}$ denote the non-negative, positive, and extended real numbers, respectively. For a point $\mathbf{p} = \langle p_1, \ldots, p_\ell \rangle \in \mathbb{R}^\ell$, $\ell \in \mathbb{N}$ and $i \in \{1, \ldots, \ell\}$ we write $\mathbf{p}[\![i]\!]$ for its ith entry p_i. For $\mathbf{p}, \mathbf{q} \in \mathbb{R}^\ell$ let $\mathbf{p} \cdot \mathbf{q}$ denote the dot product. We further write $\mathbf{p} \leq \mathbf{q}$ iff $\forall i \colon \mathbf{p}[\![i]\!] \leq \mathbf{q}[\![i]\!]$ and $\mathbf{p} \lneq \mathbf{q}$ iff $\mathbf{p} \leq \mathbf{q} \wedge \mathbf{p} \neq \mathbf{q}$. The *closure* of a set $P \subseteq \mathbb{R}^\ell$ is the union of P and its boundary, denoted by $cl(P)$. The *convex hull* of P is given by $conv(P) = \left\{ \sum_{i=1}^\ell \mu(i) \cdot \mathbf{p}_i \mid \mu \in Dist(\{1, \ldots, \ell\}), \mathbf{p}_1, \ldots, \mathbf{p}_\ell \in P \right\}$. The *downward convex hull* of P is given by $dwconv(P) = \left\{ \mathbf{q} \in \mathbb{R}^\ell \mid \exists \mathbf{p} \in conv(P) \colon \mathbf{q} \leq \mathbf{p} \right\}$.

2.1 Markov Automata

Markov automata (MA) [25,23] provide an expressive formalism that allows one to model exponentially distributed delays, nondeterminism, probabilistic branching, and instantaneous (undelayed) transitions.

Definition 1. *A Markov Automaton is a tuple $\mathcal{M} = \langle S, Act, \Delta, \mathbf{P} \rangle$ where S is a finite set of states, Act is a finite set of actions, $\Delta \colon S \to \mathbb{R}_{>0} \cup 2^{Act}$ is a transition function assigning exit rates to Markovian states $MS^{\mathcal{M}} = \{s \in S \mid \Delta(s) \in \mathbb{R}_{>0}\}$ and sets of enabled actions to probabilistic states $PS^{\mathcal{M}} = \{s \in S \mid \Delta(s) \subseteq Act\}$, and $\mathbf{P} \colon MS^{\mathcal{M}} \cup SA^{\mathcal{M}} \to Dist(S)$ with $SA^{\mathcal{M}} = \{\langle s, \alpha \rangle \in PS \times Act \mid \alpha \in \Delta(s)\}$ is a probability function that assigns a distribution over possible successor states for each Markovian state and enabled state-action pair.*

Let $\mathcal{M} = \langle S, Act, \Delta, \mathbf{P} \rangle$ be an MA. If $\mathcal{M}$ is clear from the context, we may omit the superscript from $MS^{\mathcal{M}}$, $PS^{\mathcal{M}}$, $SA^{\mathcal{M}}$, and further notations introduced below. Intuitively, the time $\mathcal{M}$ stays in a Markovian state $s \in MS$ is governed by an *exponential distribution* with rate $\Delta(s) \in \mathbb{R}_{>0}$, i.e., the probability to take a transition from s within $t \in \mathbb{R}_{\geq 0}$ time units is $1 - e^{-\Delta(s) \cdot t}$. Upon taking a transition, a successor state $s' \in S$ is drawn from the distribution $\mathbf{P}(s)$, i.e., $\mathbf{P}(s)(s')$ is the probability that the transition leads to $s' \in S$. For probabilistic states $\hat{s} \in PS$, an enabled action $\alpha \in \Delta(\hat{s})$ has to be picked and a successor state is drawn from $\mathbf{P}(\langle \hat{s}, \alpha \rangle)$ (without any delay). Nondeterminism is thus only possible at probabilistic states. We assume deadlock free MA, i.e., $\forall s \in PS^{\mathcal{M}} \colon \Delta(s) \neq \emptyset$.

Remark 1. To enable more flexible modeling such as parallel compositions, the literature (e.g., [25,30]) often considers a more liberal variant of MA where (i) different successor distributions can be assigned to the same state-action pair and (ii) states can be both, Markovian *and* probabilistic. MAs as in Definition 1— also known as closed MA—are equally expressive: they can be constructed via action renaming and by applying the so-called *maximal progress assumption* [25].

An *infinite path* in $\mathcal{M}$ is a sequence $\pi = s_0 \kappa_1 s_1 \kappa_2 \ldots$ where for each $i \geq 0$ either $s_i \in MS$, $\kappa_{i+1} \in \mathbb{R}_{\geq 0}$, and $\mathbf{P}(s_i)(s_{i+1}) > 0$ or $s_i \in PS$, $\kappa_{i+1} \in \Delta(s_i)$, and $\mathbf{P}(\langle s_i, \kappa_{i+1} \rangle)(s_{i+1}) > 0$. Intuitively, if s_i is Markovian, $\kappa_{i+1} \in \mathbb{R}_{\geq 0}$ reflects the time we have stayed in s_i until transitioning to s_{i+1}. If s_i is probabilistic, $\kappa_{i+1} \in Act$ is the performed action via which we transition to s_{i+1}. A finite path

$\hat{\pi} = s_0\kappa_1 s_1 \kappa_2 \ldots \kappa_n s_n$ is a finite prefix of an infinite path π. We set $last(\hat{\pi}) = s_n$ and $|\hat{\pi}| = n$ for finite $\hat{\pi}$ and $|\pi| = \infty$ for infinite π. For (finite or infinite) path $\bar{\pi} = s_0\kappa_1 s_1 \kappa_2 \ldots$ let $dur(\bar{\pi}) = \sum_{i=1}^{|\bar{\pi}|} dur(\kappa_i)$ be the total duration of $\bar{\pi}$ where $dur(\kappa) = \kappa$ if $\kappa \in \mathbb{R}_{\geq 0}$ and 0 otherwise. If $\bar{\pi}$ is infinite and $dur(\bar{\pi}) < \infty$, the path is called *Zeno*. For $k \in \mathbb{N}$ with $k \leq |\bar{\pi}|$ we let $prefix_{steps}(\bar{\pi}, k)$ denote the unique prefix π' of $\bar{\pi}$ with $|\pi'| = k$ and for $t \in \mathbb{R}_{\geq 0}$ we let $prefix_{time}(\bar{\pi}, t)$ denote the largest prefix of $\bar{\pi}$ with total duration at most t. The sets of infinite and finite paths of $\mathcal{M}$ are given by $Paths_{inf}^{\mathcal{M}}$ and $Paths_{fin}^{\mathcal{M}}$, respectively.

A *component* of $\mathcal{M}$ is a set $C \subseteq MS \cup SA$. We set $states(C) = (C \cap MS) \cup \{s \in PS \mid \exists \alpha \colon \langle s, \alpha \rangle \in C\}$. C is *closed* if $\forall c \in C \colon supp(\mathbf{P}(c)) \subseteq states(C)$ and *connected* if for all $s, s' \in states(C)$ there is $s_0\kappa_1 \ldots \kappa_n s_n \in Paths_{fin}$ with $s = s_0$, $s' = s_n$, and for each $i \geq 0$ either $s_i \in C \cap MS$ or $\langle s_i, \kappa_{i+1} \rangle \in C \cap SA$. An *end component (EC)* is a closed and connected component. An EC is *maximal* if it is not a proper subset of another EC. $MECS(\mathcal{M})$ denotes the maximal ECs of $\mathcal{M}$. For an EC C let $exits(C) = \{\langle s, \alpha \rangle \in SA^{\mathcal{M}} \mid s \in states(C) \text{ and } \langle s, \alpha \rangle \notin C\}$.

Definition 2. *The* sub-MA *of* $\mathcal{M}$ *induced by a closed component* C *is given by* $\mathcal{M}[\![C]\!] = \langle states(C), Act, \Delta_C, \mathbf{P}_C \rangle$ *where* $\Delta_C(s) = \Delta(s)$ *if* $s \in C \cap MS^{\mathcal{M}}$ *and otherwise* $\Delta_C(s) = \{\alpha \in \Delta(s) \mid \langle s, \alpha \rangle \in C\}$, *and* $\mathbf{P}_C$ *is the restriction of* $\mathbf{P}$ *to* C.

A *strategy* for $\mathcal{M}$ resolves the nondeterminism at probabilistic states by providing probability distributions over enabled actions based on the execution history.

Definition 3. *A (general)* strategy *for MA* $\mathcal{M} = \langle S, Act, \Delta, \mathbf{P} \rangle$ *is a function* $\sigma \colon Paths_{fin} \to Dist(Act) \cup \{\tau\}$ *such that for* $\hat{\pi} \in Paths_{fin}$ *we have* $\sigma(\hat{\pi}) \in Dist(\Delta(last(\hat{\pi})))$ *if* $last(\hat{\pi}) \in PS$ *and* $\sigma(\hat{\pi}) = \tau$ *otherwise*.

A strategy σ is called *memoryless* if the choice only depends on the current state, i.e., $\forall \hat{\pi}, \hat{\pi}' \in Paths_{fin} \colon last(\hat{\pi}) = last(\hat{\pi}')$ implies $\sigma(\hat{\pi}) = \sigma(\hat{\pi}')$. If all assigned distributions are Dirac, σ is called *deterministic*. Let $\Sigma^{\mathcal{M}}$ and $\Sigma_{md}^{\mathcal{M}}$ denote the set of general and memoryless deterministic strategies of $\mathcal{M}$, respectively. For simplicity, we often interpret $\sigma \in \Sigma_{md}^{\mathcal{M}}$ as a function $\sigma \colon S \to Act \cup \{\tau\}$. The *induced sub-MA* for $\sigma \in \Sigma_{md}^{\mathcal{M}}$ is given by $\mathcal{M}[\![MS \cup \{\langle s, \sigma(s) \rangle \mid s \in PS\}]\!]$. Strategy $\sigma \in \Sigma^{\mathcal{M}}$ and initial state $s_I \in S$ define a *probability measure* $\mathrm{Pr}_\sigma^{\mathcal{M}, s_I}$ that assigns probabilities to sets of infinite paths [38]. The expected value of $f \colon Paths_{inf} \to \bar{\mathbb{R}}$ is given by the Lebesque integral $\mathrm{Ex}_\sigma^{\mathcal{M}, s_I}(f) = \int_{\pi \in Paths_{inf}} f(\pi) \, d\mathrm{Pr}_\sigma^{\mathcal{M}, s_I}(\pi)$.

2.2 Reward-based Objectives

MA can be equipped with *rewards* to model various quantities like, e.g., energy consumption or the number of produced units. We distinguish between *transition rewards* $\mathcal{R}_{trans} \colon MS \cup SA \times S \to \mathbb{R}$ that are collected when transitioning from one state to another and *state rewards* $\mathcal{R}_{state} \colon S \to \mathbb{R}$ that are collected over time, i.e., staying in state s for t time units yields a reward of $\mathcal{R}_{state}(s) \cdot t$. Since no time passes in probabilistic states, state rewards $\mathcal{R}_{state}(s)$ for $s \in PS$ are not relevant. A reward assignment combines the two notions.

Definition 4. *A reward assignment for MA $\mathcal{M}$ and $\mathcal{R}_{state}, \mathcal{R}_{trans}$ as above is a function $\mathcal{R}: (MS \times \mathbb{R}_{\geq 0}) \cup SA \times S \to \mathbb{R}$ with*

$$\mathcal{R}(\langle s, \kappa \rangle, s') = \begin{cases} \mathcal{R}_{state}(s) \cdot \kappa + \mathcal{R}_{trans}(s, s') & \text{if } s \in MS, \kappa \in \mathbb{R}_{\geq 0} \\ \mathcal{R}_{trans}(\langle s, \kappa \rangle, s') & \text{if } s \in PS, \kappa \in \Delta(s). \end{cases}$$

We fix a reward assignment $\mathcal{R}$ for $\mathcal{M}$. $\mathcal{R}$ can also be applied to any sub-MA $\mathcal{M}[\![C]\!]$ of $\mathcal{M}$ in a straightforward way. For a component $C \subseteq MS \cup SA$ we write $\mathcal{R}(C) \geq 0$ if all rewards assigned within C are non-negative, formally $\forall \langle s, \kappa \rangle \in (C \cap SA) \cup ((C \cap MS) \times \mathbb{R}_{\geq 0}): \forall s' \in states(C): \mathcal{R}(\langle C, \kappa \rangle, s') \geq 0$. The shortcuts $\mathcal{R}(C) \leq 0$ and $\mathcal{R}(C) = 0$ are similar. The reward of a finite path $\hat{\pi} = s_0 \kappa_1 s_1 \kappa_2 \ldots \kappa_n s_n$ is denoted by $\mathcal{R}(\hat{\pi}) = \sum_{i=1}^{|\hat{\pi}|} \mathcal{R}(\langle s_{i-1}, \kappa_i \rangle, s_i)$.

Definition 5. *The total reward objective for reward assignment $\mathcal{R}$ is given by $tot(\mathcal{R}): Paths_{inf} \to \bar{\mathbb{R}}$ with $tot(\mathcal{R})(\pi) = \limsup_{k \to \infty} \mathcal{R}(prefix_{steps}(\pi, k))$.*

Definition 6. *The long-run average (LRA) reward objective for $\mathcal{R}$ is given by $lra(\mathcal{R}): Paths_{inf} \to \bar{\mathbb{R}}$ with $lra(\mathcal{R})(\pi) = \limsup_{t \to \infty} \frac{1}{t} \cdot \mathcal{R}(prefix_{time}(\pi, t))$.*

Sect. 4 considers assumptions under which the limit in both definitions can be attained, i.e., $\limsup$ can be replaced by $\lim$. The incorporation of other objectives such as *reachability probabilities* are discussed in Remark 3.

2.3   Markov Decision Processes

A *Markov Decision Process (MDP)* $\mathcal{M}$ is an MA with only probabilistic states, i.e., $MS^{\mathcal{M}} = \emptyset$. All notions above also apply to MDP. However, since all paths of an MDP have duration 0, there is no timing information available. For MDP, we therefore usually consider *steps* instead of time. In particular, for reward assignment $\mathcal{R}$ we consider $lra_{steps}(\mathcal{R})$ instead of $lra(\mathcal{R})$, where $lra_{steps}(\mathcal{R})(\pi) = \limsup_{k \to \infty} \frac{1}{k} \cdot \mathcal{R}(prefix_{steps}(\pi, k))$. Below, we focus on MA. Applying our results to step-based LRA rewards on MDPs is straightforward. Time-based LRA reward objectives for MA can not straightforwardly be reduced to step-based measures for MDP due to the interplay of delayed- and undelayed transitions.

3   Efficient Multi-objective Model Checking

We formalize common tasks in multi-objective model checking and sketch our solution method based on [28]. We fix an MA $\mathcal{M} = \langle S, Act, \Delta, \mathbf{P} \rangle$ with initial state $s_I \in S$ and $\ell > 0$ objectives $f_1, \ldots, f_\ell: Paths_{inf} \to \mathbb{R}$ with $\mathcal{F} = \langle f_1, \ldots, f_\ell \rangle$. The notation for expected values is lifted to tuples: $\mathrm{Ex}_\sigma(\mathcal{F}) = \langle \mathrm{Ex}_\sigma(f_1), \ldots, \mathrm{Ex}_\sigma(f_\ell) \rangle$.

3.1   Multi-objective Model Checking Queries

Our aim is to maximize the expected value for each (potentially conflicting) objective f_j. We impose the following assumption which can be asserted using single-objective model checking. We further discuss the assumption in Remark 2.

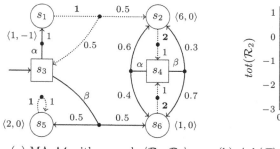
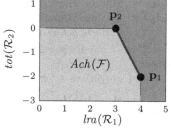

(a) MA $\mathcal{M}$ with rewards $\langle \mathcal{R}_1, \mathcal{R}_2 \rangle$ (b) $Ach(\mathcal{F})$ (green) and $Pareto(\mathcal{F})$ (blue)

Figure 1: MA with achievable points and Pareto front for $\mathcal{F} = \langle lra(\mathcal{R}_1), tot(\mathcal{R}_2) \rangle$

Assumption 1 (Objective Finiteness) $\forall j\colon \sup\{\mathrm{Ex}_\sigma(f_j) \mid \sigma \in \Sigma\} < \infty.$

Definition 7. *For $\mathcal{F}$ as above, $Ach(\mathcal{F}) = \{\mathbf{p} \in \mathbb{R}^\ell \mid \exists \sigma \in \Sigma\colon \mathbf{p} \le \mathrm{Ex}_\sigma(\mathcal{F})\}$ is the set of* achievable points. *The* Pareto front *is given by $Pareto(\mathcal{F}) = \{\mathbf{p} \in cl(Ach(\mathcal{F})) \mid \forall \mathbf{p}' \gneqq \mathbf{p}\colon \mathbf{p}' \notin cl(Ach(\mathcal{F}))\}.$*

A point $\mathbf{p} \in Ach(\mathcal{F})$ is called *achievable* and there is a single strategy σ that for each objective f_j *achieves* an expected value of at least $\mathbf{p}[\![j]\!]$. Due to Assumption 1, the Pareto front is the *frontier* of the set of achievable points, meaning that it is the smallest set $P \subseteq \mathbb{R}^\ell$ with $dwconv(P) = cl(Ach(\mathcal{F}))$. We can thus interpret $Pareto(\mathcal{F})$ as a representation for $cl(Ach(\mathcal{F}))$ and vice versa. The set of achievable points is closed iff all points on the Pareto front are achievable.

Example 1. Fig. 1a shows an MA with initial state s_3. Transitions are annotated with actions, rates (boldfaced), and successor probabilities. We also depict two reward assignments $\mathcal{R}_1$ and $\mathcal{R}_2$ by labeling states and transitions with tuples $\langle r_1, r_2 \rangle$ where, e.g., $\mathcal{R}_2(s_3, \alpha, s_1) = -1$ and for $t \in \mathbb{R}_{\ge 0}\colon \mathcal{R}_1(s_2, t, s_4) = 6 \cdot t$.

For $\sigma_1 \in \Sigma_{\mathrm{md}}$ with $\sigma_1\colon s_3, s_4 \mapsto \alpha$, the EC $\{s_2, \langle s_4, \alpha \rangle, \langle s_4, \beta \rangle, s_6\}$ is reached almost surely (with probability 1), yielding $\mathrm{Ex}_{\sigma_1}(lra(\mathcal{R}_1)) = 0.6 \cdot 6 + 0.4 \cdot 1 = 4$ and $\mathrm{Ex}_{\sigma_1}(tot(\mathcal{R}_2)) = \sum_{i=0}^{\infty} -1 \cdot (0.5)^i = -2$. It follows that the point $\mathbf{p}_1 = \langle 4, -2 \rangle$ as indicated in Fig. 1b is achievable. Similarly, $\sigma_2 \in \Sigma_{\mathrm{md}}$ with $\sigma_2\colon s_3 \mapsto \beta, s_4 \mapsto \alpha$ achieves the point $\mathbf{p}_2 = \langle 3, 0 \rangle$. With strategies that randomly pick an action at s_3, we can also achieve any point on the blue line in Fig. 1b that connects $\mathbf{p}_1$ and $\mathbf{p}_2$. This line coincides with the Pareto front $Pareto(\mathcal{F})$ for $\mathcal{F} = \langle lra(\mathcal{R}_1), tot(\mathcal{R}_2) \rangle$. The set of achievable points $Ach(\mathcal{F})$ (indicated in green) coincides with the downward convex hull of the Pareto front.

For multi-objective model checking we are concerned with the following queries:

MULTI-OBJECTIVE MODEL CHECKING QUERIES

Qualitative Achievability: Given point $\mathbf{p} \in \mathbb{R}^\ell$, decide if $\mathbf{p} \in Ach(\mathcal{F})$.

Quantitative Achievability: Given $p_2, p_3, \ldots, p_\ell \in \mathbb{R}$, compute or approximate $\sup\{p \in \mathbb{R} \mid \langle p, p_2, p_3, \ldots, p_\ell \rangle \in Ach(\mathcal{F})\}$.

Pareto: Compute or approximate $Pareto(\mathcal{F})$.

Input : MA $\mathcal{M}$ with initial state s_I, objectives $\mathcal{F} = \langle f_1, \ldots, f_\ell \rangle$
Output : An approximation of $Ach(\mathcal{F})$
1 $P \leftarrow \emptyset$ // *Collects achievable points found so far.*
2 $Q \leftarrow \mathbb{R}^\ell$ // *Excludes points that are known to be unachievable.*
3 **repeat**
4   Select weights $\mathbf{w} \in \{\mathbf{w}' \in (\mathbb{R}_{\geq 0})^\ell \mid \sum_{j=1}^\ell \mathbf{w}'[\![j]\!] = 1\}$ and $\varepsilon > 0$
5   Find $v_{\mathbf{w}} \geq \sup\{\mathbf{w} \cdot \mathrm{Ex}_\sigma(\mathcal{F}) \mid \sigma \in \Sigma\}$, $\sigma_{\mathbf{w}} \in \Sigma$ s.t. $|v_{\mathbf{w}} - \mathbf{w} \cdot \mathrm{Ex}_{\sigma_{\mathbf{w}}}(\mathcal{F})| \leq \varepsilon$
6   Compute $\mathbf{p}_{\mathbf{w}} \in \mathbb{R}^\ell$ with $\forall j \colon \mathbf{p}_{\mathbf{w}}[\![j]\!] = \mathrm{Ex}_{\sigma_{\mathbf{w}}}(f_j)$
7     $P \leftarrow P \cup \{\mathbf{p}_{\mathbf{w}}\}$; $Q \leftarrow Q \cap \{\mathbf{p} \in \mathbb{R}^\ell \mid \mathbf{w} \cdot \mathbf{p} \leq v_{\mathbf{w}}\}$
8 **until** Approximation $dwconv(P) \subseteq Ach(\mathcal{F}) \subseteq Q$ answers multi-obj. query

Algorithm 1: Approximating the set of achievable points

3.2 Approximation of Achievable Points

A practically efficient approach that tackles the above queries for expected total rewards in MDP was given in [28]. It is based on so-called *sandwich algorithms* known from convex multi-objective optimization [53,51]. We extend the algorithm to arbitrary combinations of objectives f_j on MA, including—and this is the main algorithmic novelty—mixtures of total- and LRA reward objectives.

The idea is to iteratively refine an approximation of the set of achievable points $Ach(\mathcal{F})$. The refinement loop is outlined in Algorithm 1. At the start of each iteration, the algorithm chooses a weight vector $\mathbf{w}$ and a precision parameter ε after some heuristic (details below). Then, Line 5, considers the weighted sum of the expected values of the objectives f_j. More precisely, an upper bound $v_{\mathbf{w}}$ for $\sup\{\mathbf{w} \cdot \mathrm{Ex}_\sigma(\mathcal{F}) \mid \sigma \in \Sigma\}$ as well as a "near optimal" strategy $\sigma_{\mathbf{w}}$ need to be found such that the difference between the bound $v_{\mathbf{w}}$ and the weighted sum induced by $\sigma_{\mathbf{w}}$ is at most ε. In Sect. 4, we outline the computation of $v_{\mathbf{w}}$ and $\sigma_{\mathbf{w}}$ for the case where $\mathcal{F}$ consists of total-and LRA reward objectives. Next, in Line 6 the algorithm computes a point $\mathbf{p}_{\mathbf{w}}$ that contains the expected values for each individual objective f_j under strategy $\sigma_{\mathbf{w}}$. These values can be computed using off-the-shelf single-objective model checking algorithms on the model induced by $\sigma_{\mathbf{w}}$. By definition, $\mathbf{p}_{\mathbf{w}}$ is achievable. Finally, Line 7 inserts the found point into the initially empty set P and excludes points from the set Q (which initially contains all points) that are known to be unachievable. The following theorem establishes the correctness of the approach. We prove it using Lemmas 1 and 2.

Theorem 1. *Algorithm 1 maintains the invariant* $dwconv(P) \subseteq Ach(\mathcal{F}) \subseteq Q$.

Lemma 1. $\forall \mathbf{p} \in Ach(\mathcal{F}), \mathbf{w} \in (\mathbb{R}_{\geq 0})^\ell \colon \mathbf{w} \cdot \mathbf{p} \leq \sup\{\mathbf{w} \cdot \mathrm{Ex}_\sigma(\mathcal{F}) \mid \sigma \in \Sigma\}$.

Proof. Let $\mathbf{p} \in Ach(\mathcal{F})$ be achieved by strategy $\sigma_{\mathbf{p}} \in \Sigma$. The claim follows from

$$\mathbf{w} \cdot \mathbf{p} = \sum_{j=1}^\ell \mathbf{w}[\![j]\!] \cdot \mathbf{p}[\![j]\!] \leq \sum_{j=1}^\ell \mathbf{w}[\![j]\!] \cdot \mathrm{Ex}_{\sigma_{\mathbf{p}}}(f_j) \leq \sup\left\{ \sum_{j=1}^\ell \mathbf{w}[\![j]\!] \cdot \mathrm{Ex}_\sigma(f_j) \,\Big|\, \sigma \in \Sigma \right\}.$$

Lemma 2. $Ach(\mathcal{F})$ *is convex, i.e.,* $Ach(\mathcal{F}) = conv(Ach(\mathcal{F}))$.

Proof. We need to show that for two points $\mathbf{p}_1, \mathbf{p}_2 \in Ach(\mathcal{F})$ with achieving strategies $\sigma_1, \sigma_2 \in \Sigma$, any point $\mathbf{p}$ on the line connecting $\mathbf{p}_1$ and $\mathbf{p}_2$ is also achievable. Formally, for $w \in [0,1]$ show that $\mathbf{p}_w = w \cdot \mathbf{p}_1 + (1-w) \cdot \mathbf{p}_2 \in Aeh(\mathcal{F})$. Consider the strategy σ_w that initially makes a coin flip[1]: With probability w it mimics σ_1 and otherwise it mimics σ_2. We can show for all objectives f_j:

$$\mathbf{p_w}[\![j]\!] = w \cdot \mathbf{p}_1[\![j]\!] + (1-w) \cdot \mathbf{p}_2[\![j]\!] \leq w \cdot \mathrm{Ex}_{\sigma_1}(f_j) + (1-w) \cdot \mathrm{Ex}_{\sigma_2}(f_j) = \mathrm{Ex}_{\sigma_w}(f_j).$$

We now show Theorem 1. A similar proof was given in [28].

Proof (of Theorem 1). All $\mathbf{p_w} \in P$ are achievable, i.e., $P \subseteq Ach(\mathcal{F})$. By Definition 7 and Lemma 2 we get $dwconv(P) \subseteq dwconv(Ach(\mathcal{F})) = conv(Ach(\mathcal{F})) = Ach(\mathcal{F})$. Now let $\mathbf{p} \in Ach(\mathcal{F})$ and let $\mathbf{w}$ be an arbitrary weight vector considered in some iteration of Algorithm 1 with corresponding value $v_\mathbf{w}$ computed in Line 5. Lemma 1 yields $\mathbf{w} \cdot \mathbf{p} \leq \sup\{\mathbf{w} \cdot \mathrm{Ex}_\sigma(\mathcal{F}) \mid \sigma \in \Sigma\} \leq v_\mathbf{w}$ and thus $\mathbf{p} \in Q$.

Algorithm 1 can be stopped at any time and the current approximation of $Ach(\mathcal{F})$ can be used to (i) decide qualitative achievability, (ii) provide a lower and an upper bound for quantitative achievability, and (iii) obtain an approximative representation of the Pareto front.

The *precision parameter* ε can be decreased dynamically to obtain a gradually finer approximation. If $Ach(\mathcal{F})$ is closed, the supremum $\sup\{\mathbf{w} \cdot \mathrm{Ex}_\sigma(\mathcal{F}) \mid \sigma \in \Sigma\}$ can be attained by some strategy $\sigma_\mathbf{w}$, allowing us to set $\varepsilon = 0$.

We briefly sketch the *selection of weight vectors* as proposed in [28]. In the first ℓ iterations of Algorithm 1, we optimize each objective f_j individually, i.e., we consider for all j the weight vector $\mathbf{w}$ with $\mathbf{w}[\![i]\!] = 0$ for $i \neq j$ and $\mathbf{w}[\![j]\!] = 1$. After that, we consider weight vectors that are orthogonal to a facet of the downward convex hull of the current set of points P. To approximate the Pareto front, facets with a large distance to $\mathbb{R}^\ell \setminus Q$ are considered first. To answer a qualitative or quantitative achievability query, the selection can be guided further based on the input point $\mathbf{p} \in \mathbb{R}^\ell$ or the input values $p_2, p_3, \ldots, p_\ell \in \mathbb{R}$. More details and further discussions on these heuristics can be found in [28].

Remark 2. Assumption 1 does not exclude $\mathrm{Ex}_\sigma(f_j) = -\infty$ which occurs, e.g., when objectives reflect resource consumption and some (bad) strategies require infinite resources. Moreover, if Assumption 1 is violated for an objective f_j we observe that for this objective, any (arbitrarily high) value $p \in \mathbb{R}$ can be achieved with some strategy $\sigma \in \Sigma$ such that $p \leq \mathrm{Ex}_\sigma(f_j)$. Similar to the proof of Lemma 2, a strategy can be constructed that—with a small probability—mimics a strategy inducing a very high expected value for f_j and—with the remaining (high) probability—optimizes for the other objectives. Let $\mathcal{F}_{-j}$ be the tuple $\mathcal{F}$ without f_j and similarly for $\mathbf{p} \in \mathbb{R}^\ell$ let $\mathbf{p}_{-j} \in \mathbb{R}^{\ell-1}$ be the point $\mathbf{p}$ without the jth entry. Assuming $\inf\{\mathrm{Ex}_\sigma(f_j) \mid \sigma \in \Sigma\} > -\infty$, we can show that $cl(Ach(\mathcal{F})) = \{\mathbf{p} \in \mathbb{R}^\ell \mid \mathbf{p}_{-j} \in cl(Ach(\mathcal{F}_{-j}))\}$. Put differently, $cl(Ach(\mathcal{F}))$ can be constructed from the achievable points obtained without the objective f_j.

---

[1] Strategies as in Definition 3 can not "store" the outcome of the initial coin flip. Thus, given $\hat{\pi} \in Paths_{\mathrm{fin}}$, strategy σ_w actually has to consider the *conditional* probability for the outcome of the coin flip, given that $\hat{\pi}$ has been observed. Alternatively, we could have also introduced strategies with memory.

4 Optimizing Weighted Combinations of Objectives

We now analyze weighted sums of expected values as in Line 5 of Algorithm 1.

WEIGHTED SUM OPTIMIZATION PROBLEM

Input: MA $\mathcal{M}$ with initial state s_I, objectives $\mathcal{F} = \langle f_1, \ldots, f_\ell \rangle$,

weight vector $\mathbf{w} \in \{\mathbf{w}' \in (\mathbb{R}_{\geq 0})^\ell \mid \sum_{j=1}^\ell \mathbf{w}'[\![j]\!] = 1\}$, precision $\varepsilon > 0$

Output: Value $v_\mathbf{w} \in \mathbb{R}$, with $v_\mathbf{w} \geq \sup\{\mathbf{w} \cdot \mathrm{Ex}_\sigma(\mathcal{F}) \mid \sigma \in \Sigma\}$ and

strategy $\sigma_\mathbf{w} \in \Sigma$ such that $|v_\mathbf{w} - \mathbf{w} \cdot \mathrm{Ex}_{\sigma_\mathbf{w}}(\mathcal{F})| \leq \varepsilon$.

We only consider total- and LRA reward objectives. Remark 3 discusses other objectives. We show that instead of a weighted sum of the expected values we can consider weighted sums of the rewards. This allows us to combine all objectives into a single reward assignment and then apply single-objective model checking.

4.1 Pure Long-run Average Queries

Initially, we restrict ourselves to LRA objectives and show a reduction of the weighted sum optimization problem to a single-objective long-run average reward computation. As usual for MA [38,29,17] we forbid so-called Zeno behavior.

Assumption 2 (Non-Zenoness) $\forall \sigma \in \Sigma^\mathcal{M} : \mathrm{Pr}_\sigma^\mathcal{M}(\{\pi \mid dur(\pi) < \infty\}) = 0$.

The assumption is equivalent to assuming that every EC of $\mathcal{M}$ contains at least one Markovian state. If the assumption holds, the limit in Definition 6 can be attained almost surely (with probability 1) and corresponds to a value $v \in \mathbb{R}$. Thus, Assumption 1 for LRA objectives is already implied by Assumption 2. Let $\mathcal{F}_{lra} = \langle lra(\mathcal{R}_1), \ldots, lra(\mathcal{R}_\ell) \rangle$ with reward assignments $\mathcal{R}_j$. Moreover, for weight vector $\mathbf{w}$ let $\mathcal{R}_\mathbf{w}$ be the reward assignment with $\mathcal{R}_\mathbf{w}(\langle s, \kappa \rangle, s') = \sum_{j=1}^\ell \mathbf{w}[\![j]\!] \cdot \mathcal{R}_j(\langle s, \kappa \rangle, s')$.

Theorem 2. $\forall \sigma \in \Sigma : \mathbf{w} \cdot \mathrm{Ex}_\sigma(\mathcal{F}_{lra}) = \mathrm{Ex}_\sigma(lra(\mathcal{R}_\mathbf{w}))$.

Proof. Due to Assumption 2 we have for almost all paths $\pi \in Paths_{\mathrm{inf}}$ that for all $j \in \{1, \ldots, \ell\}$ the limit $\lim_{t\to\infty} \frac{1}{t} \cdot \mathcal{R}_j(prefix_{time}(\pi, t))$ exists and

$$\sum_{j=1}^\ell \mathbf{w}[\![j]\!] \cdot lra(\mathcal{R}_j)(\pi) = \lim_{t\to\infty} \frac{1}{t} \cdot \sum_{j=1}^\ell \mathbf{w}[\![j]\!] \cdot \mathcal{R}_j(prefix_{time}(\pi, t)) = lra(\mathcal{R}_\mathbf{w})(\pi).$$

The theorem follows with

$$\sum_{j=1}^\ell \mathbf{w}[\![j]\!] \cdot \mathrm{Ex}_\sigma(lra(\mathcal{R}_j)) = \int_\pi \sum_{j=1}^\ell \mathbf{w}[\![j]\!] \cdot lra(\mathcal{R}_j) \, d\mathrm{Pr}_\sigma(\pi) = \mathrm{Ex}_\sigma(lra(\mathcal{R}_\mathbf{w})).$$

Due to Theorem 2, it suffices to consider the expected LRA reward for the *single* reward assignment $\mathcal{R}_\mathbf{w}$. The supremum $\sup\{\mathrm{Ex}_\sigma(lra(\mathcal{R}_\mathbf{w})) \mid \sigma \in \Sigma\}$ is attained by some memoryless deterministic strategy $\sigma_\mathbf{w} \in \Sigma_{md}$ [30]. Such a strategy and the induced value $v_\mathbf{w} = \mathrm{Ex}_{\sigma_\mathbf{w}}(lra(\mathcal{R}_\mathbf{w}))$ can be computed (or approximated) with *linear programming* [30], *strategy iteration* [42] or *value iteration* [17,1].

4.2   A Two-phase Approach for Single-objective LRA

The computation of single-objective expected LRA rewards for reward assignment $\mathcal{R}_\mathbf{w}$ can be divided in two phases [29,17,1]. First, each maximal end component $C \in MECS(\mathcal{M})$ is analyzed individually by computing for sub-MA $\mathcal{M}[\![C]\!]$ and some[2] $s \in states(C)$ the value $v_C = \max\{Ex_\sigma^{\mathcal{M}[\![C]\!],s}(lra(\mathcal{R}_\mathbf{w})) \mid \sigma \in \Sigma_{md}^{\mathcal{M}[\![C]\!]}\}$.

Secondly, we consider a quotient model $\mathcal{M}' = \mathcal{M}_{\backslash MECS(\mathcal{M})}$ of $\mathcal{M}$ that replaces the states of each $C \in MECS(\mathcal{M})$ by a single state.

Definition 8. *For $\mathcal{M} = \langle S, Act, \Delta, \mathbf{P} \rangle$ and a set of ECs $\mathcal{C}$, the quotient is the MA $\mathcal{M}_{\backslash \mathcal{C}} = \langle S_{\backslash \mathcal{C}}, Act_{\backslash \mathcal{C}}, \Delta_{\backslash \mathcal{C}}, \mathbf{P}_{\backslash \mathcal{C}} \rangle$ where*
- *$S_{\backslash \mathcal{C}} = (S \setminus \bigcup_{C \in \mathcal{C}} states(C)) \uplus \mathcal{C} \uplus \{s_\perp\}$, $Act_{\backslash \mathcal{C}} = Act \uplus (\bigcup_{C \in \mathcal{C}} exits(C)) \uplus \{\perp\}$,*
- *$\Delta_{\backslash \mathcal{C}}(\hat{s}) = \begin{cases} \Delta(\hat{s}) & \text{if } \hat{s} \in S \\ exits(\hat{s}) \cup \{\perp\} & \text{if } \hat{s} \in \mathcal{C} \\ 1 & \text{if } \hat{s} = s_\perp, \text{ and} \end{cases}$*
- *$\mathbf{P}_{\backslash \mathcal{C}}(c) = \begin{cases} \mathbf{P}(c) & \text{if } c \in MS^{\mathcal{M}} \cup SA^{\mathcal{M}} \\ \mathbf{P}(\langle s, \alpha \rangle) & \text{if } c = \langle C, \langle s, \alpha \rangle \rangle \text{ for } C \in \mathcal{C} \text{ and } \langle s, \alpha \rangle \in exits(C) \\ \{s_\perp \mapsto 1\} & \text{if } c \in \mathcal{C} \times \{\perp\} \cup \{s_\perp\} \end{cases}$*

Intuitively, selecting action $\perp$ at a state $C \in MECS(\mathcal{M})$ in $\mathcal{M}'$ reflects any strategy of $\mathcal{M}$ that upon visiting the EC C will stay in this EC forever. We can thus mimic any strategy of the sub-MA $\mathcal{M}[\![C]\!]$, in particular a memoryless deterministic strategy that maximizes the expected value of $lra(\mathcal{R}_\mathbf{w})$ in $\mathcal{M}[\![C]\!]$. Contrarily, selecting an action $\langle s, \alpha \rangle$ at a state C of $\mathcal{M}'$ reflects a strategy of $\mathcal{M}$ that upon visiting the EC C enforces that the states of C will be left via the exiting state-action pair $\langle s, \alpha \rangle$. Let $\mathcal{R}^*$ be the reward assignment for $\mathcal{M}'$ that yields $\mathcal{R}^*(\langle C, \perp \rangle, s_\perp) = v_C$ and 0 in all other cases. It can be shown that $\max\{Ex_\sigma^{\mathcal{M}, s_I}(lra(\mathcal{R}_\mathbf{w})) \mid \sigma \in \Sigma^{\mathcal{M}}\} = \max\{Ex_\sigma^{\mathcal{M}', s_I'}(tot(\mathcal{R}^*)) \mid \sigma \in \Sigma^{\mathcal{M}'}\}$, where $s_I' = C_I$ if s_I is contained in some $C_I \in MECS(\mathcal{M})$ and $s_I' = s_I$ otherwise.

The maximal total reward in $\mathcal{M}'$ can be computed using standard techniques such as *value iteration* and *policy iteration* [46] as well as the more recent *sound value iteration* and *optimistic value iteration* [48,36]. The latter two provide sound precision guarantees for the output value v, i.e., $|v - \max\{Ex_\sigma^{\mathcal{M}', s_I'}(tot(\mathcal{R}^*)) \mid \sigma \in \Sigma^{\mathcal{M}'}\}| \leq \varepsilon$ for a given $\varepsilon > 0$.

4.3   Combining Long-run Average and Total Rewards

We now consider arbitrary combinations of total- and long-run average reward objectives $\mathcal{F} = \langle tot(\mathcal{R}_1), \dots, tot(\mathcal{R}_k), lra(\mathcal{R}_{k+1}), \dots, lra(\mathcal{R}_\ell) \rangle$ with $0 < k < \ell$.

The above-mentioned procedure for LRA reduces the analysis to an expected total reward computation on the quotient model $\mathcal{M}_{\backslash MECS(\mathcal{M})}$. This approach suggests to also incorporate other total-reward objectives for $\mathcal{M}$ in the quotient

---

[2] The value v_C does not depend on the selected state s. Intuitively, this is because any other state $s' \in states(C)$ can be reached from s almost surely.

model. However, special care has to be taken concerning total rewards collected within ECs of $\mathcal{M}$ that would no longer be present in the quotient $\mathcal{M}_{\setminus MECS(\mathcal{M})}$. We discuss how to deal with this issue by considering the quotient only for ECs in which no (total) reward is collected. We start with restricting the (total) rewards that might be assigned to transitions within EC.

Assumption 3 (Sign-Consistency) *For all total reward objectives* $tot(\mathcal{R}_j)$ *either* $\forall C \in MECS(\mathcal{M}): \mathcal{R}_j(C) \geq 0$ *or* $\forall C \in MECS(\mathcal{M}): \mathcal{R}_j(C) \leq 0$.

The assumption implies that paths on which infinitely many positive *and* infinitely many negative reward is collected have probability 0. One consequence is that the limit in Definition 5 exists for almost all paths [3]. A discussion on objectives $tot(\mathcal{R}_j)$ that violate Assumption 3 for single-objective MDP is given in [3]. Their multi-objective treatment is left for future work.

When Assumptions 1 and 3 hold, we get $\mathcal{R}_j(C) \leq 0$ for all objectives $tot(\mathcal{R}_i)$ and EC C. Put differently, all non-zero total rewards collected in an EC have to be negative. Strategies that induce a total reward of $-\infty$ for some objective $tot(\mathcal{R}_i)$ will not be taken into account for the set of achievable points. Therefore, transitions within ECs that yield negative reward should only be taken finitely often. These transitions can be disregarded when computing the expected LRA rewards, i.e., only the 0-ECs [3] are relevant for the LRA computation.

Definition 9. *A 0-EC of $\mathcal{M}$ and $\mathcal{R}_1, \ldots, \mathcal{R}_k$ is an EC C of $\mathcal{M}$ with $\mathcal{R}_i(C) = 0$ for all $\mathcal{R}_i$. The set of maximal 0-ECs is given by $MECS_0(\mathcal{M}, \langle \mathcal{R}_1, \ldots, \mathcal{R}_i \rangle)$.*

$MECS_0(\mathcal{M}, \langle \mathcal{R}_1, \ldots, \mathcal{R}_k \rangle)$ can be computed by constructing the maximal ECs of the sub-MA of $\mathcal{M}$ where transitions with a non-zero reward are erased.

We are ready to describe our approach that combines LRA rewards of 0-ECs and the remaining total rewards into a single total-reward objective. Let $\mathcal{R}_{\mathbf{w}}^{tot}$ and $\mathcal{R}_{\mathbf{w}}^{lra}$ be reward assignments with $\mathcal{R}_{\mathbf{w}}^{tot}(\langle s, \kappa \rangle, s') = \sum_{i=1}^{k} \mathbf{w}[\![i]\!] \cdot \mathcal{R}_i(\langle s, \kappa \rangle, s')$ and $\mathcal{R}_{\mathbf{w}}^{lra}(\langle s, \kappa \rangle, s') = \sum_{j=k}^{\ell} \mathbf{w}[\![j]\!] \cdot \mathcal{R}_j(\langle s, \kappa \rangle, s')$. Moreover, for $\pi \in Paths_{\inf}$ we set $(tot(\mathcal{R}_{\mathbf{w}}^{tot}) + lra(\mathcal{R}_{\mathbf{w}}^{lra}))(\pi) = tot(\mathcal{R}_{\mathbf{w}}^{tot})(\pi) + lra(\mathcal{R}_{\mathbf{w}}^{lra})(\pi)$.

Theorem 3. $\forall \sigma \in \Sigma: \mathbf{w} \cdot Ex_{\sigma}(\mathcal{F}) = Ex_{\sigma}(tot(\mathcal{R}_{\mathbf{w}}^{tot}) + lra(\mathcal{R}_{\mathbf{w}}^{lra}))$.

Proof. Using a similar reasoning as in the proof of Theorem 2, we get:

$$\mathbf{w} \cdot Ex_{\sigma}(\mathcal{F}) = \left(\sum_{i=1}^{k} \mathbf{w}[\![i]\!] \cdot Ex_{\sigma}(tot(\mathcal{R}_i)) \right) + \left(\sum_{j=k+1}^{\ell} \mathbf{w}[\![j]\!] \cdot Ex_{\sigma}(lra(\mathcal{R}_j)) \right)$$

$$= Ex_{\sigma}(tot(\mathcal{R}_{\mathbf{w}}^{tot})) + Ex_{\sigma}(lra(\mathcal{R}_{\mathbf{w}}^{lra})) = Ex_{\sigma}(tot(\mathcal{R}_{\mathbf{w}}^{tot}) + lra(\mathcal{R}_{\mathbf{w}}^{lra})).$$

Algorithm 2 outlines the procedure for solving the weighted sum optimization problem. It first computes optimal LRA rewards and inducing strategies for each maximal 0-EC (Lines 1 to 3). Then, a quotient model $\mathcal{M}^*$ and a reward assignment $\mathcal{R}^*$ incorporating all total- and LRA rewards is build and analyzed (Lines 4 to 6). $\mathcal{M}^*$ might still contain ECs other than $\{s_\perp\}$. Those ECs shall be left eventually to avoid collecting infinite negative reward for a total reward objective $tot(\mathcal{R}_i)$. Note that the weight $\mathbf{w}[\![i]\!]$ for such an objective might be zero,

Input : MA $\mathcal{M}$ with initial state s_I, objectives
$\mathcal{F} = \langle tot(\mathcal{R}_1), \ldots, tot(\mathcal{R}_k), lra(\mathcal{R}_{k+1}), \ldots, lra(\mathcal{R}_\ell)\rangle$, weight vector $\mathbf{w}$
Output : Value $v_{\mathbf{w}}$, strategy $\sigma_{\mathbf{w}}$ as in the weighted sum optimization problem

1 $\mathcal{C} \leftarrow MECS_0(\mathcal{M}, \langle \mathcal{R}_1, \ldots, \mathcal{R}_i \rangle)$ // Compute maximal 0-ECs and their LRA.
2 **foreach** $C \in \mathcal{C}$ **do**
3 $\quad$ Compute $v_C = \max \left\{ \mathrm{Ex}_\sigma^{\mathcal{M}[\![C]\!]}(lra(\mathcal{R}_{\mathbf{w}}^{lra})) \mid \sigma \in \Sigma_{\mathrm{md}}^{\mathcal{M}[\![C]\!]} \right\}$
$\quad$ and inducing strategy $\sigma_C \in \Sigma_{\mathrm{md}}^{\mathcal{M}[\![C]\!]}$

4 $\mathcal{M}^* \leftarrow \mathcal{M}_{\backslash \mathcal{C}}$ // Build and analyze quotient model.
5 Build reward assignment $\mathcal{R}^*$ with

$$\mathcal{R}^*(\langle s, \kappa \rangle, s') = \begin{cases} v_C & \text{if } s = C, \kappa = \bot, \text{ and } s' = s_\bot \\ \mathcal{R}_{\mathbf{w}}^{tot}(\langle \hat{s}, \alpha \rangle, s') & \text{if } s = C, \kappa = \langle \hat{s}, \alpha \rangle \in exits(C) \\ \mathcal{R}_{\mathbf{w}}^{tot}(\langle s, \alpha \rangle, s') & \text{otherwise} \end{cases}$$

6 Compute $v_{\mathbf{w}} = \max \left\{ \mathrm{Ex}_\sigma^{\mathcal{M}^*}(tot(\mathcal{R}^*)) \,\middle|\, \sigma \in \Sigma_{\mathrm{md}}^{\mathcal{M}^*}, \Pr_\sigma^{\mathcal{M}^*}(\Diamond \{s_\bot\}) = 1 \right\}$
$\quad$ and inducing strategy $\sigma^* \in \Sigma_{\mathrm{md}}^{\mathcal{M}^*}$
7 Build strategy $\sigma_{\mathbf{w}} \in \Sigma_{\mathrm{md}}^{\mathcal{M}}$ with

$$\sigma_{\mathbf{w}}(s) = \begin{cases} \sigma_C(s) & \text{if } \exists C \in \mathcal{C}: s \in states(C) \text{ and } \sigma^*(C \in \mathcal{C}) = \bot \\ \alpha & \text{if } \exists C \in \mathcal{C}: s \in states(C) \text{ and } \sigma^*(C) = \langle s, \alpha \rangle \\ \sigma_{C \Diamond \{s'\}}(s) & \text{if } \exists C \in \mathcal{C}: s \in states(C) \text{ and } \sigma^*(C) = \langle s', \alpha \rangle \text{ for } s' \neq s \\ \sigma^*(s) & \text{otherwise} \end{cases}$$

Algorithm 2: Optimizing the weighted sum for total and LRA objectives

i.e., the rewards of $\mathcal{R}_i$ are not present in $\mathcal{R}^*$. It is therefore necessary to explicitly restrict the analysis to strategies that almost surely (i.e., with probability 1) reach $s_\bot$. To compute the maximal expected total reward in Line 6 with, e.g., standard value iteration, we can consider another quotient model for $\mathcal{M}^*$ and the 0-ECs of $\mathcal{M}^*$ and $\mathcal{R}^*$. In contrast to Definition 8, this quotient should not introduce the $\bot$ action since it shall not be possible to remain in an EC forever. In Line 7, the strategies for the 0-ECs and for the quotient $\mathcal{M}^*$ are combined into one strategy $\sigma_{\mathbf{w}}$ for $\mathcal{M}$. Here, $\sigma_{C \Diamond s'}$ refers to a strategy of $\mathcal{M}[\![C]\!]$ for which every state $s \in states(C)$ eventually reaches $s' \in states(C)$ almost surely.

Since Algorithm 2 produces a memoryless deterministic strategy $\sigma_{\mathbf{w}}$, the point $\mathbf{p}_{\mathbf{w}} \in \mathbb{R}^\ell$ in Line 6 of Algorithm 1 can be computed on the induced sub-MA for $\sigma_{\mathbf{w}}$. Assuming exact single-objective solution methods, the resulting value $v_{\mathbf{w}}$ and strategy $\sigma_{\mathbf{w}} \in \Sigma_{\mathrm{md}}^{\mathcal{M}}$ of Algorithm 2 satisfy $v_{\mathbf{w}} = \mathbf{w} \cdot \mathrm{Ex}_{\sigma_{\mathbf{w}}}(\mathcal{F})$, yielding an exact solution to the weighted sum optimization problem. As the number of memoryless deterministic strategies is bounded, we conclude the following, extending results for pure LRA queries [11] to mixtures with total rewards.

Corollary 1. *For total- and LRA reward objectives* $\mathcal{F}$, *$Ach(\mathcal{F})$ is closed and is the downward convex hull of at most* $|\Sigma_{\mathrm{md}}^{\mathcal{M}}| = \prod_{s \in PS} |\Delta(s)|$ *points.*

Remark 3. Our framework can be extended to support objectives beyond total- and LRA rewards. *Minimizing objectives* where one is interested in a strategy σ

that induces a *small* expected value can be considered by multiplying all rewards with -1. Since we already allow negative values in reward assignments, no further adaptions are necessary. We emphasize that our framework lifts a restriction imposed in [28] that disabled a simultaneous analysis of maximizing *and* minimizing total reward objectives. *Reachability probabilities* can be transformed to expected total rewards on a modified model in which the information whether a goal state has already been visited is stored in the state-space. *Goal-bounded* total rewards as in [30], where no further rewards are collected as soon as one of the goal states is reached can be transformed similarly. For MDP, *step- and reward-bounded* reachability probabilities can be converted to total reward objectives by unfolding the current amount of steps (or rewards) into the state-space of the model. Approaches that avoid such an expensive unfolding have been presented in [28] for objectives with step-bounds and in [34,35] for objectives with one or multiple reward-bounds. *Time-bounded* reachability probabilities for MA have been considered in [47]. Finally, ω-regular specifications such as *linear temporal logic (LTL)* formulae have been transformed to total reward objectives in [27]. However, the optimization of LRA rewards within the ECs of the model might interfere with the satisfaction of one or more ω-regular specifications [31].

5   Experimental Evaluation

Implementation details Our approach has been implemented in the model checker STORM [40]. Given an MA or MDP (specified using the PRISM language or JANI [14]), the tool answers qualitative- and quantitative achievability as well as Pareto queries. Beside of mixtures of total- and LRA reward objectives, STORM also supports most of the extensions in Remark 3—with the notable exception of LTL. We use LRA value iteration [17,1] and sound value iteration [48] for calls to single-objective model checking. Both provide sound precision guarantees, i.e., the relative error of these computations is at most ε, where we set $\varepsilon = 10^{-6}$.

Workstation cluster To showcase the capabilities of our implementation, we present a workstation cluster—originally considered in [39] as a CTMC—now modeled as an MA. The cluster considers two sub-clusters each consisting of one *switch* and N *workstations*. Within each sub-cluster the workstations are connected to the switch in a star topology and the two switches are connected with a *backbone*. Each of the components may fail with a certain rate. A controller can (i) acquire additional repair units (up to M) and (ii) control the movements of the repair units. In Fig. 2a we depict the resulting sets of achievable points—as computed by our implementation—for $N = 16$ and $M = 4$. As objectives, we considered the long-run average number of operating workstations $lra(\mathcal{R}_{\#op})$, the long-run average probability that at least N workstations are operational $lra(\mathcal{R}_{\#op \geq N})$, and the total number of acquired repair units $tot(\mathcal{R}_{\#rep})$.

Related tools MULTIGAIN [12] is an extension of PRISM [45] that implements the LP-based approach of [11] for multiple LRA objectives on MDP to answer

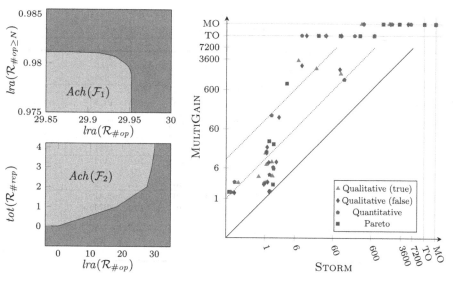

(a) Results for workstation cluster   (b) Comparison of STORM and MULTIGAIN

Figure 2: Exemplary results and runtime comparison with MULTIGAIN

qualitative and quantitative achievability as well as Pareto queries. For the latter, it is briefly mentioned in [12] that ideas of [28] were used similar to our approach but no further details are provided. MULTIGAIN does not support MA, *mixtures* with total reward objectives, and Pareto queries with $\ell > 2$ objectives. However, it does support more general quantitative achievability queries.

PRISM-GAMES [44,43] implements value iteration over convex sets [8,9] to analyze multiple LRA reward objectives on stochastic games (SGs). By converting MDPs to 1-player SGs, PRISM-GAMES could also be applied in our setting. However, some experiments on 1-player SGs indicated that this approach is not competitive compared to the dedicated MDP implementations in MULTIGAIN and STORM. We therefore do not consider PRISM-GAMES in our evaluation.

Benchmarks We consider 10 different case studies including the workstation cluster (clu) as well as benchmarks from QVBS [37] (dpm, rqs, res), from MULTI-GAIN [12] (mut, phi, vir), from [42] (csn, sen), and from [47] (pol). For each case study we consider 3 concrete instances resulting in 12 MAs and 18 MDPs. The analyzed objectives range over LRA rewards, (goal-bounded) total rewards, and time-, step- and unbounded reachability probabilities.

Set-up We evaluated the performance of STORM and MULTIGAIN Version 1.0.2[3]. All experiments were run on 4 cores[4] of an Intel Xeon Platinum 8160 CPU with

---

[3] Obtained from http://qav.cs.ox.ac.uk/multigain and invoked with GUROBI [32].

[4] STORM uses one core, MULTIGAIN uses multiple cores due to JAVA's garbage collection and GUROBI's parallel solving techniques.

Table 1: Results for pure LRA Pareto queries

Model	Par.	#lra	$\lvert S\rvert$	$\lvert MS\rvert$	$\lvert\Delta\rvert$	$\lvert\mathcal{C}\rvert$	$\lvert S_{\mathcal{C}}\rvert$	#iter	Storm	MultiGain
csn	3	3	177		427	38	158	9	1.23	
csn	4	4	945		2753	176	880	30	109	
csn	5	5	4833		$2\cdot10^4$	782	4622		TO	
mut	3	2	$3\cdot10^4$		$5\cdot10^4$	1	$3\cdot10^4$	15	3.7	859
mut	4	2	$7\cdot10^5$		$1\cdot10^6$	1	$7\cdot10^5$	14	91.4	TO
mut	5	2	$1\cdot10^7$		$3\cdot10^7$	1	$1\cdot10^7$	12	3197	MO
phi	4	2	9440		$4\cdot10^4$	1	9440	6	1.7	24.7
phi	5	2	$9\cdot10^4$		$4\cdot10^5$	1	$9\cdot10^4$	18	24.5	TO
phi	6	2	$2\cdot10^6$		$1\cdot10^7$	1	$2\cdot10^6$	12	1221	MO
res	5-5	2	2618		8577	1	2618	16	1.64	2.31
res	15-15	2	$2\cdot10^5$		$7\cdot10^5$	1	$2\cdot10^5$	3	712	TO
res	20-20	2	$8\cdot10^5$		$2\cdot10^6$	1	$8\cdot10^5$	7	299	TO
sen	2	3	7855		$2\cdot10^4$	3996	6105	13	3.41	
sen	3	3	$8\cdot10^4$		$3\cdot10^5$	$5\cdot10^4$	$7\cdot10^4$	14	274	
sen	4	3	$6\cdot10^5$		$3\cdot10^6$	$4\cdot10^5$	$5\cdot10^5$		TO	
vir	2	2	80		393	2	66	4	<1	1.47
vir	3	2	$2\cdot10^4$		$2\cdot10^5$	2	$2\cdot10^4$	2	1.3	29.3
vir	4	2	$4\cdot10^7$		$7\cdot10^8$	?	?		MO	MO
clu	8-3	2	$2\cdot10^5$	$1\cdot10^5$	$4\cdot10^5$	4	$2\cdot10^5$	11	287	
clu	16-4	2	$2\cdot10^6$	$9\cdot10^5$	$4\cdot10^6$	5	$2\cdot10^6$	10	4199	
clu	32-3	2	$2\cdot10^6$	$1\cdot10^6$	$5\cdot10^6$	4	$2\cdot10^6$		TO	
dpm	3-3	2	2640	1008	3240	1	2640	32	19.5	
dpm	4-4	2	$3\cdot10^4$	$1\cdot10^4$	$4\cdot10^4$	1	$3\cdot10^4$	33	1179	
dpm	5-5	2	$6\cdot10^5$	$2\cdot10^5$	$7\cdot10^5$	1	$6\cdot10^5$		TO	
pol	3-3	2	9522	4801	$2\cdot10^4$	1	9522	17	3.44	
pol	4-3	2	$5\cdot10^4$	$3\cdot10^4$	$1\cdot10^5$	1	$5\cdot10^4$	19	19.2	
pol	4-4	2	$8\cdot10^5$	$5\cdot10^5$	$2\cdot10^6$	1	$8\cdot10^5$	29	3350	
rqs	2-2	2	1619	628	2296	1	1618	63	4.52	
rqs	3-3	2	$9\cdot10^4$	$4\cdot10^4$	$1\cdot10^5$	1	$9\cdot10^4$	106	162	
rqs	5-3	2	$2\cdot10^6$	$1\cdot10^6$	$4\cdot10^6$	1	$2\cdot10^6$	97	4345	

a time limit of 2 hours and 32 GB RAM. For each experiment we measured the total runtime (including model building) to solve one query. For qualitative and quantitative achievability we consider thresholds close to the Pareto front. For Pareto queries, the approximation precision 10^{-4} was set to both tools.

Results Fig. 2b visualizes the runtime comparison with MultiGain. A point $\langle x,y\rangle$ in the plot corresponds to a query that has been solved by Storm in x seconds and by MultiGain in y seconds. Points on the solid diagonal mean that both tools were equally fast. The two dotted lines indicate experiments where Storm only required $\frac{1}{10}$ resp. $\frac{1}{100}$ of the time of MultiGain. TO and MO indicate a time- or memory out. Tables 1 and 2 provide further data for Pareto queries. The columns indicate model name and parameters, the number of LRA reward, total reward, and bounded reachability objectives, the number of states ($\lvert S\rvert$), Markovian states ($\lvert MS\rvert$), successor distributions ($\lvert\Delta\rvert$), 0-ECs ($\lvert\mathcal{C}\rvert$), and states within 0-ECs ($\lvert S_{\mathcal{C}}\rvert$) of the MA or MDP, the number of iterations (#iters) of Algorithm 1 performed by Storm, and the total runtime of Storm and MultiGain in seconds. Runtimes are omitted if the tool does not support the query. MDP (MA) benchmarks are at the top (bottom) of each table. Table 1 considers pure LRA queries, whereas Table 2 considers mixtures.

Table 2: Results for Pareto queries with other objective types

Model	Par.	#lra/tot/bnd	$|S|$	$|MS|$	$|\Delta|$	$|C|$	$|S_C|$	#iter	STORM
res	5-5	2-0-1	2618		8577	1	2618	17	4.27
res	5-5	2-1-0	2618		8577	1	1705	6	1.43
res	15-15	2-0-1	$2\cdot10^5$		$7\cdot10^5$	1	$2\cdot10^5$	4	792
res	15-15	2-1-0	$2\cdot10^5$		$7\cdot10^5$	1	$1\cdot10^5$	8	1061
res	20-20	2-0-1	$8\cdot10^5$		$2\cdot10^6$	1	$8\cdot10^5$	8	641
res	20-20	2-1-0	$8\cdot10^5$		$2\cdot10^6$	1	$4\cdot10^5$	4	101
clu	8-3	1-1-0	$2\cdot10^5$	$1\cdot10^5$	$4\cdot10^5$	4	$2\cdot10^5$	7	163
clu	16-4	1-1-0	$2\cdot10^6$	$9\cdot10^5$	$4\cdot10^6$	5	$2\cdot10^6$	9	3432
clu	32-3	1-1-0	$2\cdot10^6$	$1\cdot10^6$	$5\cdot10^6$	4	$2\cdot10^6$	7	3328
dpm	3-3	1-0-1	5232	1980	6408	46	3045	2	11.2
dpm	3-3	1-1-0	4584	1656	5562	25	2856	4	<1
dpm	4-4	1-0-1	$7\cdot10^4$	$2\cdot10^4$	$8\cdot10^4$	497	$4\cdot10^4$	2	214
dpm	4-4	1-1-0	$6\cdot10^4$	$2\cdot10^4$	$7\cdot10^4$	301	$4\cdot10^4$	4	3.32
dpm	5-5	1-0-1	$1\cdot10^6$	$3\cdot10^5$	$1\cdot10^6$	6476	$6\cdot10^5$		TO
dpm	5-5	1-1-0	$1\cdot10^6$	$3\cdot10^5$	$1\cdot10^6$	4321	$6\cdot10^5$	4	329
pol	3-3	1-1-0	$1\cdot10^4$	5309	$2\cdot10^4$	1	9522	3	1.37
pol	4-3	1-1-0	$6\cdot10^4$	$3\cdot10^4$	$1\cdot10^5$	1	$5\cdot10^4$	3	2.52
pol	4-4	1-1-0	$9\cdot10^5$	$5\cdot10^5$	$2\cdot10^6$	1	$8\cdot10^5$	3	237
rqs	2-2	1-1-0	2805	1039	4159	1	1618	3	<1
rqs	3-3	1-1-0	$1\cdot10^5$	$6\cdot10^4$	$3\cdot10^5$	1	$9\cdot10^4$	3	4.51
rqs	5-3	1-1-0	$3\cdot10^6$	$2\cdot10^6$	$7\cdot10^6$	1	$2\cdot10^6$	3	182

Discussion As indicated in Fig. 2b, our implementation outperforms MULTIGAIN on almost all benchmarks and for all types of queries and is often orders of magnitude faster. According to MULTIGAIN's log files, the majority of its runtime is spend for solving LPs, suggesting that the better performance of STORM is likely due to the iterative approach presented in this work.

Table 1 shows that *pure LRA queries on models with millions of states can be handled*. There were no significant runtime gaps between MA and MDP models. For csn, the increased number of objectives drastically increases the overall runtime. This is partly due to our naive implementation of the geometric set representations used in Algorithm 1. Table 2 indicates that the performance and scalability for mixtures of LRA and other types of objectives is similar. One exception are queries involving time-bounded reachability on MA (e.g., dpm). Here, our implementation is based on the single-objective approach of [29] that is known to be slower than more recent methods [16,15].

Data availability The implementation, models, and log files are available at [49].

6   Conclusion

The analysis of multi-objective model checking queries involving multiple long-run average rewards can be incorporated into the framework of [28] enabling (i) the use of off-the-shelf single-objective algorithms for LRA and (ii) the combination with other kinds of objectives such as total rewards. Our experiments indicate that this approach clearly outperforms existing algorithms based on linear programming. Future work includes lifting the approach to *partially observable MDP* and *stochastic games*, potentially using ideas of [10] and [2], respectively.

References

1. Ashok, P., Chatterjee, K., Daca, P., Kretínský, J., Meggendorfer, T.: Value iteration for long-run average reward in Markov decision processes. In: CAV (1). LNCS, vol. 10426, pp. 201–221. Springer (2017). https://doi.org/10.1007/978-3-319-63387-9_10
2. Ashok, P., Chatterjee, K., Kretínský, J., Weininger, M., Winkler, T.: Approximating values of generalized-reachability stochastic games. In: LICS. pp. 102–115. ACM (2020). https://doi.org/10.1145/3373718.3394761
3. Baier, C., Bertrand, N., Dubslaff, C., Gburek, D., Sankur, O.: Stochastic shortest paths and weight-bounded properties in Markov decision processes. In: LICS. pp. 86–94. ACM (2018). https://doi.org/10.1145/3209108.3209184
4. Baier, C., Dubslaff, C., Klüppelholz, S.: Trade-off analysis meets probabilistic model checking. In: CSL-LICS. pp. 1:1–1:10. ACM (2014). https://doi.org/10.1145/2603088.2603089
5. Baier, C., Dubslaff, C., Klüppelholz, S., Daum, M., Klein, J., Märcker, S., Wunderlich, S.: Probabilistic model checking and non-standard multi-objective reasoning. In: Gnesi, S., Rensink, A. (eds.) FASE. LNCS, vol. 8411, pp. 1–16. Springer (2014). https://doi.org/10.1007/978-3-642-54804-8_1
6. Baier, C., Dubslaff, C., Korenciak, L., Kucera, A., Rehák, V.: Synthesis of optimal resilient control strategies. In: ATVA. LNCS, vol. 10482, pp. 417–434. Springer (2017). https://doi.org/10.1007/978-3-319-68167-2_27
7. Baier, C., Hermanns, H., Katoen, J.: The 10, 000 facets of MDP model checking. In: Computing and Software Science, LNCS, vol. 10000, pp. 420–451. Springer (2019). https://doi.org/10.1007/978-3-319-91908-9_21
8. Basset, N., Kwiatkowska, M.Z., Topcu, U., Wiltsche, C.: Strategy synthesis for stochastic games with multiple long-run objectives. In: TACAS. LNCS, vol. 9035, pp. 256–271. Springer (2015). https://doi.org/10.1007/978-3-662-46681-0_22
9. Basset, N., Kwiatkowska, M.Z., Wiltsche, C.: Compositional strategy synthesis for stochastic games with multiple objectives. Inf. Comput. **261**(Part), 536–587 (2018). https://doi.org/10.1016/j.ic.2017.09.010
10. Bork, A., Junges, S., Katoen, J., Quatmann, T.: Verification of indefinite-horizon POMDPs. In: ATVA. LNCS, vol. 12302, pp. 288–304. Springer (2020). https://doi.org/10.1007/978-3-030-59152-6_16
11. Brázdil, T., Brozek, V., Chatterjee, K., Forejt, V., Kucera, A.: Two views on multiple mean-payoff objectives in Markov decision processes. LMCS **10**(1) (2014). https://doi.org/10.2168/LMCS-10(1:13)2014
12. Brázdil, T., Chatterjee, K., Forejt, V., Kucera, A.: MultiGain: A controller synthesis tool for MDPs with multiple mean-payoff objectives. In: TACAS. LNCS, vol. 9035, pp. 181–187. Springer (2015). https://doi.org/10.1007/978-3-662-46681-0_12
13. Brázdil, T., Chatterjee, K., Forejt, V., Kucera, A.: Trading performance for stability in Markov decision processes. J. Comput. Syst. Sci. **84**, 144–170 (2017). https://doi.org/10.1016/j.jcss.2016.09.009
14. Budde, C.E., Dehnert, C., Hahn, E.M., Hartmanns, A., Junges, S., Turrini, A.: JANI: quantitative model and tool interaction. In: TACAS (2). LNCS, vol. 10206, pp. 151–168 (2017). https://doi.org/10.1007/978-3-662-54580-5_9
15. Butkova, Y., Fox, G.: Optimal time-bounded reachability analysis for concurrent systems. In: TACAS (2). LNCS, vol. 11428, pp. 191–208. Springer (2019), https://doi.org/10.1007/978-3-030-17465-1_11

16. Butkova, Y., Hatefi, H., Hermanns, H., Krcál, J.: Optimal continuous time Markov decisions. In: ATVA. LNCS, vol. 9364, pp. 166–182. Springer (2015). https://doi.org/10.1007/978-3-319-24953-7_12

17. Butkova, Y., Wimmer, R., Hermanns, H.: Long-run rewards for Markov automata. In: TACAS (2). LNCS, vol. 10206, pp. 188–203 (2017). https://doi.org/10.1007/978-3-662-54580-5_11

18. Chatterjee, K.: Markov decision processes with multiple long-run average objectives. In: FSTTCS. LNCS, vol. 4855, pp. 473–484. Springer (2007). https://doi.org/10.1007/978-3-540-77050-3_39

19. Chatterjee, K., Doyen, L.: Perfect-information stochastic games with generalized mean-payoff objectives. In: LICS. pp. 247–256. ACM (2016). https://doi.org/10.1145/2933575.2934513

20. Chatterjee, K., Kretínská, Z., Kretínský, J.: Unifying two views on multiple mean-payoff objectives in Markov decision processes. LMCS 13(2) (2017). https://doi.org/10.23638/LMCS-13(2:15)2017

21. Chatterjee, K., Majumdar, R., Henzinger, T.A.: Markov decision processes with multiple objectives. In: STACS. LNCS, vol. 3884, pp. 325–336. Springer (2006), https://doi.org/10.1007/11672142_26

22. Delgrange, F., Katoen, J., Quatmann, T., Randour, M.: Simple strategies in multi-objective MDPs. In: TACAS (1). LNCS, vol. 12078, pp. 346–364. Springer (2020). https://doi.org/10.1007/978-3-030-45190-5_19

23. Deng, Y., Hennessy, M.: On the semantics of Markov automata. Inf. Comput. 222, 139–168 (2013). https://doi.org/10.1016/j.ic.2012.10.010

24. Eisentraut, C., Hermanns, H., Katoen, J., Zhang, L.: A semantics for every GSPN. In: Petri Nets. LNCS, vol. 7927, pp. 90–109. Springer (2013)

25. Eisentraut, C., Hermanns, H., Zhang, L.: On probabilistic automata in continuous time. In: LICS. pp. 342–351. IEEE Computer Society (2010). https://doi.org/10.1109/LICS.2010.41

26. Etessami, K., Kwiatkowska, M.Z., Vardi, M.Y., Yannakakis, M.: Multi-objective model checking of Markov decision processes. LMCS 4(4) (2008). https://doi.org/10.2168/LMCS-4(4:8)2008

27. Forejt, V., Kwiatkowska, M.Z., Norman, G., Parker, D., Qu, H.: Quantitative multi-objective verification for probabilistic systems. In: TACAS. LNCS, vol. 6605, pp. 112–127. Springer (2011), https://doi.org/10.1007/978-3-642-19835-9_11

28. Forejt, V., Kwiatkowska, M.Z., Parker, D.: Pareto curves for probabilistic model checking. In: ATVA. LNCS, vol. 7561, pp. 317–332. Springer (2012). https://doi.org/10.1007/978-3-642-33386-6_25

29. Guck, D., Hatefi, H., Hermanns, H., Katoen, J., Timmer, M.: Analysis of timed and long-run objectives for Markov automata. LMCS 10(3) (2014). https://doi.org/10.2168/LMCS-10(3:17)2014

30. Guck, D., Timmer, M., Hatefi, H., Ruijters, E., Stoelinga, M.: Modelling and analysis of Markov reward automata. In: ATVA. LNCS, vol. 8837, pp. 168–184. Springer (2014). https://doi.org/10.1007/978-3-319-11936-6_13

31. Guo, M., Zavlanos, M.M.: Probabilistic motion planning under temporal tasks and soft constraints. IEEE Trans. Autom. Control. 63(12), 4051–4066 (2018). https://doi.org/10.1109/TAC.2018.2799561

32. Gurobi Optimization, L.: Gurobi optimizer reference manual (2020), http://www.gurobi.com

33. Hahn, E.M., Hashemi, V., Hermanns, H., Lahijanian, M., Turrini, A.: Interval Markov decision processes with multiple objectives: From robust strategies to

pareto curves. ACM Trans. Model. Comput. Simul. **29**(4), 27:1–27:31 (2019). https://doi.org/10.1145/3309683

34. Hartmanns, A., Junges, S., Katoen, J., Quatmann, T.: Multi-cost bounded reachability in MDP. In: TACAS (2). LNCS, vol. 10806, pp. 320–339. Springer (2018). https://doi.org/10.1007/978-3-319-89963-3_19

35. Hartmanns, A., Junges, S., Katoen, J., Quatmann, T.: Multi-cost bounded tradeoff analysis in MDP. J. Autom. Reason. **64**(7), 1483–1522 (2020). https://doi.org/10.1007/s10817-020-09574-9

36. Hartmanns, A., Kaminski, B.L.: Optimistic value iteration. In: CAV (2). LNCS, vol. 12225, pp. 488–511. Springer (2020). https://doi.org/10.1007/978-3-030-53291-8_26

37. Hartmanns, A., Klauck, M., Parker, D., Quatmann, T., Ruijters, E.: The Quantitative Verification Benchmark Set. In: TACAS (1). LNCS, vol. 11427, pp. 344–350. Springer (2019). https://doi.org/10.1007/978-3-030-17462-0_20

38. Hatefi, H., Hermanns, H.: Model checking algorithms for Markov automata. Electron. Commun. Eur. Assoc. Softw. Sci. Technol. **53** (2012). https://doi.org/10.14279/tuj.eceasst.53.783

39. Haverkort, B.R., Hermanns, H., Katoen, J.: On the use of model checking techniques for dependability evaluation. In: SRDS. pp. 228–237. IEEE Computer Society (2000). https://doi.org/10.1109/RELDI.2000.885410

40. Hensel, C., Junges, S., Katoen, J., Quatmann, T., Volk, M.: The probabilistic model checker Storm. CoRR **abs/2002.07080** (2020)

41. Klein, J., Baier, C., Chrszon, P., Daum, M., Dubslaff, C., Klüppelholz, S., Märcker, S., Müller, D.: Advances in probabilistic model checking with PRISM: variable reordering, quantiles and weak deterministic büchi automata. Int. J. Softw. Tools Technol. Transf. **20**(2), 179–194 (2018). https://doi.org/10.1007/s10009-017-0456-3

42. Kretínský, J., Meggendorfer, T.: Efficient strategy iteration for mean payoff in Markov decision processes. In: ATVA. LNCS, vol. 10482, pp. 380–399. Springer (2017). https://doi.org/10.1007/978-3-319-68167-2_25

43. Kwiatkowska, M., Norman, G., Parker, D., Santos, G.: Prism-games 3.0: Stochastic game verification with concurrency, equilibria and time. In: CAV (2). LNCS, vol. 12225, pp. 475–487. Springer (2020). https://doi.org/10.1007/978-3-030-53291-8_25

44. Kwiatkowska, M., Parker, D., Wiltsche, C.: PRISM-games: verification and strategy synthesis for stochastic multi-player games with multiple objectives. STTT **20**(2), 195–210 (2018). https://doi.org/10.1007/s10009-017-0476-z

45. Kwiatkowska, M.Z., Norman, G., Parker, D.: PRISM 4.0: Verification of probabilistic real-time systems. In: CAV. LNCS, vol. 6806, pp. 585–591. Springer (2011). https://doi.org/10.1007/978-3-642-22110-1_47

46. Puterman, M.L.: Markov Decision Processes. John Wiley and Sons (1994)

47. Quatmann, T., Junges, S., Katoen, J.: Markov automata with multiple objectives. In: CAV (1). LNCS, vol. 10426, pp. 140–159. Springer (2017). https://doi.org/10.1007/978-3-319-63387-9_7

48. Quatmann, T., Katoen, J.: Sound value iteration. In: CAV (1). LNCS, vol. 10981, pp. 643–661. Springer (2018). https://doi.org/10.1007/978-3-319-96145-3_37

49. Quatmann, T., Katoen, J.: Multi-objective optimization of long-run average and total rewards: Supplemental material. Zenodo (2020). https://doi.org/10.5281/zenodo.4094999

50. Randour, M., Raskin, J., Sankur, O.: Percentile queries in multi-dimensional Markov decision processes. FMSD **50**(2-3), 207–248 (2017). https://doi.org/10.1007/s10703-016-0262-7
51. Rennen, G., van Dam, E.R., den Hertog, D.: Enhancement of sandwich algorithms for approximating higher-dimensional convex Pareto sets. INFORMS J. Comput. **23**(4), 493–517 (2011). https://doi.org/10.1287/ijoc.1100.0419
52. Roijers, D.M., Scharpff, J., Spaan, M.T.J., Oliehoek, F.A., de Weerdt, M., Whiteson, S.: Bounded approximations for linear multi-objective planning under uncertainty. In: ICAPS. AAAI (2014), http://www.aaai.org/ocs/index.php/ICAPS/ICAPS14/paper/view/7929
53. Solanki, R.S., Appino, P.A., Cohon, J.L.: Approximating the noninferior set in multiobjective linear programming problems. European Journal of Operational Research **68**(3), 356 – 373 (1993). https://doi.org/10.1016/0377-2217(93)90192-P

Inferring Expected Runtimes of Probabilistic Integer Programs Using Expected Sizes*

Fabian Meyer[ID], Marcel Hark[(✉)][ID], and Jürgen Giesl[(✉)][ID]

LuFG Informatik 2, RWTH Aachen University, Aachen, Germany
fabian.niklas.meyer@rwth-aachen.de, {marcel.hark,giesl}@cs.rwth-aachen.de

Abstract. We present a novel modular approach to infer upper bounds on the expected runtimes of probabilistic integer programs automatically. To this end, it computes bounds on the runtimes of program parts and on the sizes of their variables in an alternating way. To evaluate its power, we implemented our approach in a new version of our open-source tool KoAT.

1 Introduction

There exist several approaches and tools for automatic complexity analysis of non-probabilistic programs, e.g., [2–6, 8, 9, 18, 20, 21, 27, 28, 30, 34–36, 51, 57, 58]. While most of them rely on basic techniques like *ranking functions* (see, e.g., [6, 12–14, 17, 53]), they usually combine these basic techniques in sophisticated ways. For example, in [18] we developed a modular approach for automated complexity analysis of integer programs, based on an alternation between finding symbolic runtime bounds for program parts and using them to infer bounds on the sizes of variables in such parts. So each analysis step is restricted to a small part of the program. The implementation of this approach in KoAT [18] (which is integrated in AProVE [30]) is one of the leading tools for complexity analysis [31].

While there exist several adaptions of basic techniques like ranking functions to *probabilistic programs* (e.g., [1, 11, 15, 16, 22–26, 29, 32, 37, 38, 48, 62]), most of the sophisticated full approaches for complexity analysis have not been adapted to probabilistic programs yet, and there are only few powerful tools available which analyze the runtimes of probabilistic programs automatically [10, 50, 61, 62].

We study probabilistic integer programs (Sect. 2) and define suitable notions of non-probabilistic and expected runtime and size bounds (Sect. 3). Then, we adapt our modular approach for runtime and size analysis of [18] to probabilistic programs (Sect. 4 and 5). So such an adaption is not only possible for *basic techniques* like ranking functions, but also for *full approaches* for complexity analysis.

For this adaption, several problems had to be solved. When computing expected runtime or size bounds for new program parts, the main difficulty is to determine when it is sound to use *expected* bounds on previous program parts and when one has to use *non-probabilistic* bounds instead. Moreover, the semantics of probabilistic programs is significantly different from classical integer programs. Thus, the proofs of our techniques differ substantially from the ones in [18], e.g.,

---

* funded by the Deutsche Forschungsgemeinschaft (DFG, German Research Foundation) - 235950644 (Project GI 274/6-2) & DFG Research Training Group 2236 UnRAVeL

J. F. Groote and K. G. Larsen (Eds.): TACAS 2021, LNCS 12651, pp. 250–269, 2021.
https://doi.org/10.1007/978-3-030-72016-2_14

we have to use concepts from measure theory like ranking supermartingales.

In Sect. 6, we evaluate the implementation of our new approach in the tool KoAT [18,43] and compare with related work. We refer to [47] for an appendix of our paper containing all proofs, preliminaries from probability and measure theory, and an overview on the benchmark collection used in our evaluation.

2 Probabilistic Integer Programs

For any set $M \subseteq \overline{\mathbb{R}}$ (with $\overline{\mathbb{R}} = \mathbb{R} \cup \{\infty\}$) and $w \in M$, let $M_{\geq w} = \{v \in M \mid v \geq w \vee v = \infty\}$. For a set $\mathcal{PV}$ of *program variables*, we first introduce the kind of *bounds* that our approach computes. Similar to [18], our bounds represent *weakly monotonically increasing* functions from $\mathcal{PV} \to \overline{\mathbb{R}}_{\geq 0}$. Such bounds have the advantage that they can easily be "composed", i.e., if f and g are both weakly monotonically increasing upper bounds, then so is $f \circ g$.

Definition 1 (Bounds). *The set of bounds* $\mathcal{B}$ *is the smallest set with* $\mathcal{PV} \cup \overline{\mathbb{R}}_{\geq 0}$ $\subseteq \mathcal{B}$, *and where* $b_1, b_2 \in \mathcal{B}$ *and* $v \in \mathbb{R}_{\geq 1}$ *imply* $b_1 + b_2$, $b_1 \cdot b_2 \in \mathcal{B}$ *and* $v^{b_1} \in \mathcal{B}$.

Our notion of probabilistic programs combines classical integer programs (as in, e.g., [18]) and probabilistic control flow graphs (see, e.g., [1]). A *state* s is a variable assignment $s: \mathcal{V} \to \mathbb{Z}$ for the (finite) set $\mathcal{V}$ of all variables in the program, where $\mathcal{PV} \subseteq \mathcal{V}$, $\mathcal{V} \setminus \mathcal{PV}$ is the set of *temporary variables*, and Σ is the set of all states. For any $s \in \Sigma$, the state $|s|$ is defined by $|s|(x) = |s(x)|$ for all $x \in \mathcal{V}$. The set $\mathcal{C}$ of *constraints* is the smallest set containing $e_1 \leq e_2$ for all polynomials $e_1, e_2 \in \mathbb{Z}[\mathcal{V}]$ and $c_1 \wedge c_2$ for all $c_1, c_2 \in \mathcal{C}$. In addition to "$\leq$", in examples we also use relations like "$>$", which can be simulated by constraints (e.g., $e_1 > e_2$ is equivalent to $e_2 + 1 \leq e_1$ when regarding integers). We also allow the application of states to arithmetic expressions e and constraints c. Then the number $s(e)$ resp. $s(c) \in \{\mathbf{t}, \mathbf{f}\}$ results from evaluating the expression resp. the constraint when substituting every variable x by $s(x)$. So for bounds $b \in \mathcal{B}$, we have $|s|(b) \in \mathbb{R}_{\geq 0}$.

In the transitions of a program, a program variable $x \in \mathcal{PV}$ can also be updated by adding a value according to a *bounded distribution function* $d : \Sigma \to \text{Dist}(\mathbb{Z})$. Here, for any state s, $d(s)$ is the probability distribution of the values that are added to x. As usual, a *probability distribution* on $\mathbb{Z}$ is a mapping $pr : \mathbb{Z} \to \mathbb{R}$ with $pr(v) \in [0, 1]$ for all $v \in \mathbb{Z}$ and $\sum_{v \in \mathbb{Z}} pr(v) = 1$. Let $\text{Dist}(\mathbb{Z})$ be the set of distributions pr whose expected value $\mathbb{E}(pr) = \sum_{v \in \mathbb{Z}} v \cdot pr(v)$ is well defined and finite, i.e., $\mathbb{E}_{\text{abs}}(pr) = \sum_{v \in \mathbb{Z}} |v| \cdot pr(v) < \infty$. A distribution function $d : \Sigma \to \text{Dist}(\mathbb{Z})$ is *bounded* if there is a finite bound $\mathfrak{E}(d) \in \mathcal{B}$ with $\mathbb{E}_{\text{abs}}(d(s)) \leq |s|(\mathfrak{E}(d))$ for all $s \in \Sigma$. Let $\mathcal{D}$ denote the set of all bounded distribution functions (our implementation supports Bernoulli, uniform, geometric, hypergeometric, and binomial distributions, see [43] for details).

Definition 2 (PIP). $(\mathcal{PV}, \mathcal{L}, \mathcal{GT}, \ell_0)$ *is a* probabilistic integer program *with*

1. *a finite set of* program variables $\mathcal{PV} \subseteq \mathcal{V}$
2. *a finite non-empty set of* program locations $\mathcal{L}$
3. *a finite non-empty set of* general transitions $\mathcal{GT}$. *A* general transition g *is a finite non-empty set of transitions* $t = (\ell, p, \tau, \eta, \ell')$, *consisting of*

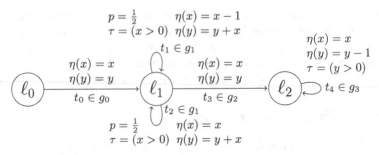

Fig. 1: PIP with non-deterministic and probabilistic branching

(a) the start and target locations $\ell, \ell' \in \mathcal{L}$ of transition t,
(b) the probability $p \geq 0$ that transition t is chosen when g is executed,
(c) the guard $\tau \in C$ of t, and
(d) the update function $\eta \colon \mathcal{PV} \to \mathbb{Z}[\mathcal{V}] \cup \mathcal{D}$ of t, mapping every program variable to an update polynomial or a bounded distribution function.
All $t \in g$ must have the same start location ℓ and the same guard τ. Thus, we call them the start location and guard of g, and denote them by ℓ_g and τ_g. Moreover, the probabilities p of the transitions in g must add up to 1.
4. an initial location $\ell_0 \in \mathcal{L}$, where no transition has target location ℓ_0

PIPs allow for both probabilistic and non-deterministic branching and sampling. Probabilistic branching is modeled by selecting a transition out of a non-singleton general transition. Non-deterministic branching is represented by several general transitions with the same start location and non-exclusive guards. Probabilistic sampling is realized by update functions that map a program variable to a bounded distribution function. Non-deterministic sampling is modeled by updating a program variable with an expression containing temporary variables from $\mathcal{V} \setminus \mathcal{PV}$, whose values are non-deterministic (but can be restricted in the guard). The set of *initial* general transitions $\mathcal{GT}_0 \subseteq \mathcal{GT}$ consists of all general transitions with start location ℓ_0.

Example 3 (PIP). Consider the PIP in Fig. 1 with initial location ℓ_0 and the program variables $\mathcal{PV} = \{x, y\}$. Here, let $p = 1$ and $\tau = \mathbf{t}$ if not stated explicitly. There are four general transitions: $g_0 = \{t_0\}$, $g_1 = \{t_1, t_2\}$, $g_2 = \{t_3\}$, and $g_3 = \{t_4\}$, where g_1 and g_2 represent a non-deterministic branching. When choosing the general transition g_1, the transitions t_1 and t_2 encode a probabilistic branching. If we modified the update η and the guard τ of t_0 to $\eta(x) = u \in \mathcal{V} \setminus \mathcal{PV}$ and $\tau = (u > 0)$, then x would be updated to a non-deterministically chosen positive value. In contrast, if $\eta(x) = \mathrm{GEO}(\frac{1}{2})$, then t_0 would update x by adding a value sampled from the geometric distribution with parameter $\frac{1}{2}$.

In the following, we regard a fixed PIP $\mathcal{P}$ as in Def. 2. A *configuration* is a tuple (ℓ, t, s), with the current location $\ell \in \mathcal{L}$, the current state $s \in \Sigma$, and the transition t that was evaluated last and led to the current configuration. Let $\mathcal{T} = \bigcup_{g \in \mathcal{GT}} g$. Then $\mathrm{Conf} = (\mathcal{L} \uplus \{\ell_\perp\}) \times (\mathcal{T} \uplus \{t_{\mathrm{in}}, t_\perp\}) \times \Sigma$ is the set of all configurations, with a special location $\ell_\perp$ indicating the termination of a run, and special transitions t_{in} (used in the first configuration of a run) and $t_\perp$ (for the configurations of the run after termination). The (virtual) general transition $g_\perp = \{t_\perp\}$ only contains $t_\perp$.

A *run* of a PIP is an infinite sequence $\vartheta = c_0\, c_1 \cdots \in \mathsf{Conf}^\omega$. Let $\mathsf{Runs} = \mathsf{Conf}^\omega$ and let $\mathsf{FPath} = \mathsf{Conf}^*$ be the set of all *finite paths* of configurations.

In our setting, deterministic Markovian schedulers suffice to resolve all non-determinism (see, e.g., [54, Prop. 6.2.1]). For $c = (\ell, t, s) \in \mathsf{Conf}$, such a *scheduler* $\mathfrak{S}$ yields a pair $\mathfrak{S}(c) = (g, s')$ where g is the next general transition to be taken (with $\ell = \ell_g$) and s' chooses values for the temporary variables where $s'(\tau_g) = \mathbf{t}$ and $s(x) = s'(x)$ for all $x \in \mathcal{PV}$. If $\mathcal{GT}$ contains no such g, we get $\mathfrak{S}(c) = (g_\perp, s)$.

For each scheduler $\mathfrak{S}$ and initial state s_0, we first define a probability mass function $pr_{\mathfrak{S},s_0}$. For all $c \in \mathsf{Conf}$, $pr_{\mathfrak{S},s_0}(c)$ is the probability that a run starts in c. Thus, $pr_{\mathfrak{S},s_0}(c) = 1$ if $c = (\ell_0, t_{\mathrm{in}}, s_0)$ and $pr_{\mathfrak{S},s_0}(c) = 0$, otherwise. Moreover, for all $c', c \in \mathsf{Conf}$, $pr_{\mathfrak{S},s_0}(c' \to c)$ is the probability that the configuration c' is followed by the configuration c (see [47] for the formal definition of $pr_{\mathfrak{S},s_0}$).

For any $f = c_0 \cdots c_n \in \mathsf{FPath}$, let $pr_{\mathfrak{S},s_0}(f) = pr_{\mathfrak{S},s_0}(c_0) \cdot pr_{\mathfrak{S},s_0}(c_0 \to c_1) \cdot \\ \cdots pr_{\mathfrak{S},s_0}(c_{n-1} \to c_n)$. We say that f is *admissible* for $\mathfrak{S}$ and s_0 if $pr_{\mathfrak{S},s_0}(f) > 0$. A run ϑ is admissible if all its finite prefixes are admissible. A configuration $c \in \mathsf{Conf}$ is admissible if there is some admissible finite path ending in c.

The semantics of PIPs can now be defined by giving a corresponding probability space, which is obtained by a standard cylinder construction (see, e.g., [7,60]). Let $\mathbb{P}_{\mathfrak{S},s_0}$ denote the corresponding probability measure which lifts $pr_{\mathfrak{S},s_0}$ to cylinder sets: For any $f \in \mathsf{FPath}$, we have $pr_{\mathfrak{S},s_0}(f) = \mathbb{P}_{\mathfrak{S},s_0}(\mathrm{Pre}_f)$ for the set Pre_f of all runs with prefix f. So $\mathbb{P}_{\mathfrak{S},s_0}(\Theta)$ is the probability that a run from $\Theta \subseteq \mathsf{Runs}$ is obtained when using the scheduler $\mathfrak{S}$ and starting in s_0.

We denote the associated expected value operator by $\mathbb{E}_{\mathfrak{S},s_0}$. So for any random variable $X : \mathsf{Runs} \to \overline{\mathbb{N}} = \mathbb{N} \cup \{\infty\}$, we have $\mathbb{E}_{\mathfrak{S},s_0}(X) = \sum_{n \in \overline{\mathbb{N}}} n \cdot \mathbb{P}_{\mathfrak{S},s_0}(X = n)$. For details on the preliminaries from probability theory we refer to [47].

3 Complexity Bounds

In Sect. 3.1, we first recapitulate the concepts of (non-probabilistic) runtime and size bounds from [18]. Then we introduce *expected* runtime and size bounds in Sect. 3.2 and connect them to their non-probabilistic counterparts.

3.1 Runtime and Size Bounds

Again, let $\mathcal{P}$ denote the PIP which we want to analyze. Def. 4 recapitulates the notions of runtime and size bounds from [18] in our setting. Recall that bounds from $\mathcal{B}$ do not contain temporary variables, i.e., we always try to infer bounds in terms of the initial values of the *program variables*. Let $\sup \varnothing = 0$, as all occurring sets are subsets of $\overline{\mathbb{R}}_{\geq 0}$, whose minimal element is 0.

Definition 4 (Runtime and Size Bounds [18]). $\mathcal{RB} \colon \mathcal{T} \to \mathcal{B}$ *is a* runtime *bound and* $\mathcal{SB} \colon \mathcal{T} \times \mathcal{V} \to \mathcal{B}$ *is a* size bound *if for all transitions* $t \in \mathcal{T}$, *all variables* $x \in \mathcal{V}$, *all schedulers* $\mathfrak{S}$, *and all states* $s_0 \in \Sigma$, *we have*

$$|s_0|\,(\mathcal{RB}(t)) \geq \sup \{\, |\{i \mid t_i = t\}| \mid f = (\_, t_0, \_) \cdots (\_, t_n, \_) \wedge pr_{\mathfrak{S},s_0}(f) > 0 \,\},$$
$$|s_0|\,(\mathcal{SB}(t,x)) \geq \sup \{\, |s(x)| \mid f = \cdots (\_, t, s) \wedge pr_{\mathfrak{S},s_0}(f) > 0 \,\}.$$

So $\mathcal{RB}(t)$ is a bound on the number of executions of t and $\mathcal{SB}(t, x)$ over-approximates the greatest absolute value that $x \in \mathcal{V}$ takes after the application of the transition t in any admissible finite path. Note that Def. 4 does not apply to t_{in} and $t_\perp$, since they are not contained in $\mathcal{T}$.

We call a tuple $(\mathcal{RB}, \mathcal{SB})$ a (non-probabilistic) *bound pair*. We will use such non-probabilistic bound pairs for an initialization of expected bounds (Thm. 10) and to compute improved expected runtime and size bounds in Sect. 4 and 5.

Example 5 (Bound Pair). The technique of [18] computes the following bound pair for the PIP of Fig. 1 (by ignoring the probabilities of the transitions).

$$\mathcal{RB}(t) = \begin{cases} 1, & \text{if } t = t_0 \text{ or } t = t_3 \\ x, & \text{if } t = t_1 \\ \infty, & \text{if } t = t_2 \text{ or } t = t_4 \end{cases} \qquad \mathcal{SB}(t, x) = \begin{cases} x, & \text{if } t \in \{t_0, t_1, t_2\} \\ 3 \cdot x, & \text{if } t \in \{t_3, t_4\} \end{cases}$$

$$\mathcal{SB}(t, y) = \begin{cases} y, & \text{if } t = t_0 \\ \infty, & \text{if } t \in \{t_1, t_2, t_3, t_4\} \end{cases}$$

Clearly, t_0 and t_3 can only be evaluated once. Since t_1 decrements x and no transition increments it, t_1's runtime is bounded by $|s_0|(x)$. However, t_2 can be executed arbitrarily often if $s_0(x) > 0$. Thus, the runtimes of t_2 and t_4 are unbounded (i.e., $\mathcal{P}$ is not terminating when regarding it as a non-probabilistic program). $\mathcal{SB}(t, x)$ is finite for all transitions t, since x is never increased. In contrast, the value of y can be arbitrarily large after all transitions but t_0.

3.2 Expected Runtime and Size Bounds

We now define the *expected* runtime and size complexity of a PIP $\mathcal{P}$.

Definition 6 (Expected Runtime Complexity, PAST [15]). *For $g \in \mathcal{GT}$, its runtime is the random variable $\mathcal{R}(g)$ where $\mathcal{R}: \mathcal{GT} \to \mathsf{Runs} \to \overline{\mathbb{N}}$ with*

$$\mathcal{R}(g)((\_, t_0, \_)(\_, t_1, \_) \cdots) = |\{i \mid t_i \in g\}|.$$

For a scheduler $\mathfrak{S}$ and $s_0 \in \Sigma$, the expected runtime complexity of $g \in \mathcal{GT}$ is $\mathbb{E}_{\mathfrak{S}, s_0}(\mathcal{R}(g))$ and the expected runtime complexity of $\mathcal{P}$ is $\sum_{g \in \mathcal{GT}} \mathbb{E}_{\mathfrak{S}, s_0}(\mathcal{R}(g))$.

If $\mathcal{P}$'s expected runtime complexity is finite for every scheduler $\mathfrak{S}$ and every initial state s_0, then $\mathcal{P}$ is called positively almost surely terminating (PAST).

So $\mathcal{R}(g)(\vartheta)$ is the number of executions of a transition from g in the run ϑ.

While non-probabilistic size bounds refer to pairs (t, x) of transitions $t \in \mathcal{T}$ and variables $x \in \mathcal{V}$ (so-called *result variables* in [18]), we now introduce expected size bounds for *general result variables* (g, ℓ, x), which consist of a general transition g, one of its target locations ℓ, and a program variable $x \in \mathcal{PV}$. So x must not be a temporary variable (which represents *non-probabilistic* non-determinism), since general result variables are used for *expected* size bounds.

Definition 7 (Expected Size Complexity). *The set of general result variables is $\mathcal{GRV} = \{(g, \ell, x) \mid g \in \mathcal{GT}, x \in \mathcal{PV}, (\_, \_, \_, \_, \ell) \in g\}$. The size of $\alpha = (g, \ell, x) \in \mathcal{GRV}$ is the random variable $\mathcal{S}(\alpha)$ where $\mathcal{S}: \mathcal{GRV} \to \mathsf{Runs} \to \overline{\mathbb{N}}$ with*

$$\mathcal{S}(g, \ell, x)((\ell_0, t_0, s_0)(\ell_1, t_1, s_1) \cdots) = \sup\{|s_i(x)| \mid \ell_i = \ell \wedge t_i \in g\}.$$

For a scheduler $\mathfrak{S}$ *and* s_0, *the expected size complexity of* $\alpha \in \mathcal{GRV}$ *is* $\mathbb{E}_{\mathfrak{S},s_0}(\mathcal{S}(\alpha))$.

So for any run ϑ, $\mathcal{S}(g, \ell, x)(\vartheta)$ is the greatest absolute value of x in location ℓ, whenever ℓ was entered with a transition from g. We now define bounds for the expected runtime and size complexity which hold *independent* of the scheduler.

Definition 8 (Expected Runtime and Size Bounds).

- $\mathcal{RB}_{\mathbb{E}} : \mathcal{GT} \to \mathcal{B}$ *is an* expected runtime bound *if for all* $g \in \mathcal{GT}$, *all schedulers* $\mathfrak{S}$, *and all* $s_0 \in \Sigma$, *we have* $|s_0| (\mathcal{RB}_{\mathbb{E}}(g)) \geq \mathbb{E}_{\mathfrak{S},s_0}(\mathcal{R}(g))$.
- $\mathcal{SB}_{\mathbb{E}} : \mathcal{GRV} \to \mathcal{B}$ *is an* expected size bound *if for all* $\alpha \in \mathcal{GRV}$, *all schedulers* $\mathfrak{S}$, *and all* $s_0 \in \Sigma$, *we have* $|s_0| (\mathcal{SB}_{\mathbb{E}}(\alpha)) \geq \mathbb{E}_{\mathfrak{S},s_0}(\mathcal{S}(\alpha))$.
- *A pair* $(\mathcal{RB}_{\mathbb{E}}, \mathcal{SB}_{\mathbb{E}})$ *is called an* expected bound pair.

Example 9 (Expected Runtime and Size Bounds).   Our new techniques from Sect. 4 and 5 will derive the following expected bounds for the PIP from Fig. 1.

$$\mathcal{RB}_{\mathbb{E}}(g) = \begin{cases} 1, & \text{if } g \in \{g_0, g_2\} \\ 2 \cdot x, & \text{if } g = g_1 \\ 6 \cdot x^2 + 2 \cdot y, & \text{if } g = g_3 \end{cases} \qquad \mathcal{SB}_{\mathbb{E}}(g, \_, x) = \begin{cases} x, & \text{if } g = g_0 \\ 2 \cdot x, & \text{if } g = g_1 \\ 3 \cdot x, & \text{if } g \in \{g_2, g_3\} \end{cases}$$

$$\mathcal{SB}_{\mathbb{E}}(g_0, \ell_1, y) = y \qquad\qquad \mathcal{SB}_{\mathbb{E}}(g_2, \ell_2, y) = 6 \cdot x^2 + 2 \cdot y$$
$$\mathcal{SB}_{\mathbb{E}}(g_1, \ell_1, y) = 6 \cdot x^2 + y \qquad\qquad \mathcal{SB}_{\mathbb{E}}(g_3, \ell_2, y) = 12 \cdot x^2 + 4 \cdot y$$

While the runtimes of t_2 and t_4 were unbounded in the non-probabilistic case (Ex. 5), we obtain finite bounds on the expected runtimes of $g_1 = \{t_1, t_2\}$ and $g_3 = \{t_4\}$. For example, we can expect x to be non-positive after at most $|s_0| (2 \cdot x)$ iterations of g_1. Based on the above expected runtime bounds, the expected runtime complexity of the PIP is at most $|s_0| (\mathcal{RB}_{\mathbb{E}}(g_0) + \ldots + \mathcal{RB}_{\mathbb{E}}(g_3)) = |s_0| (2 + 2 \cdot x + 2 \cdot y + 6 \cdot x^2)$, i.e., it is in $\mathcal{O}(n^2)$ where n is the maximal absolute value of the program variables at the start of the program.

The following theorem shows that non-probabilistic bounds can be lifted to expected bounds, since they do not only bound the expected value of $\mathcal{R}(g)$ resp. $\mathcal{S}(\alpha)$, but the whole distribution. As mentioned, all proofs can be found in [47].

Theorem 10 (Lifting Bounds).   *For a bound pair* $(\mathcal{RB}, \mathcal{SB})$, $(\mathcal{RB}_{\mathbb{E}}, \mathcal{SB}_{\mathbb{E}})$ *with* $\mathcal{RB}_{\mathbb{E}}(g) = \sum_{t \in g} \mathcal{RB}(t)$ *and* $\mathcal{SB}_{\mathbb{E}}(g, \ell, x) = \sum_{t = (\_,\_,\_,\_,\ell) \in g} \mathcal{SB}(t, x)$ *is an expected bound pair.*

Here, we over-approximate the maximum of $\mathcal{SB}(t, x)$ for $t = (\_, \_, \_, \_, \ell) \in g$ by their sum. For asymptotic bounds, this does not affect precision, since $\max(f, g)$ and $f + g$ have the same asymptotic growth for any non-negative functions f, g.

Example 11 (Lifting of Bounds).   When lifting the bound pair of Ex. 5 to expected bounds according to Thm. 10, one would obtain $\mathcal{RB}_{\mathbb{E}}(g_0) = \mathcal{RB}_{\mathbb{E}}(g_2) = 1$ *and* $\mathcal{RB}_{\mathbb{E}}(g_1) = \mathcal{RB}_{\mathbb{E}}(g_3) = \infty$. *Moreover,* $\mathcal{SB}_{\mathbb{E}}(g_0, \ell_1, x) = x$, $\mathcal{SB}_{\mathbb{E}}(g_1, \ell_1, x) = 2 \cdot x$, $\mathcal{SB}_{\mathbb{E}}(g_2, \ell_2, x) = \mathcal{SB}_{\mathbb{E}}(g_3, \ell_2, x) = 3 \cdot x$, $\mathcal{SB}_{\mathbb{E}}(g_0, \ell_1, y) = y$, *and* $\mathcal{SB}_{\mathbb{E}}(g, \_, y) = \infty$ *whenever* $g \neq g_0$. *Thus, with these lifted bounds one cannot show that* $\mathcal{P}$'s *expected runtime complexity is finite, i.e., they are substantially less precise than the finite expected bounds from Ex. 9. Our approach will compute such finite expected bounds by repeatedly improving the lifted bounds of Thm. 10.*

4 Computing Expected Runtime Bounds

We first present a new variant of probabilistic linear ranking functions in Sect. 4.1. Based on this, in Sect. 4.2 we introduce our modular technique to infer expected runtime bounds by using expected size bounds.

4.1 Probabilistic Linear Ranking Functions

For probabilistic programs, several techniques based on ranking supermartingales have been developed. In this section, we define a class of probabilistic ranking functions that will be suitable for our modular analysis.

We restrict ourselves to ranking functions $\mathfrak{r} : \mathcal{L} \to \mathbb{R}[\mathcal{PV}]_{\text{lin}}$ that map every location to a *linear polynomial* (i.e., of at most degree 1) without temporary variables. The linearity restriction is common to ease the automated inference of ranking functions. Moreover, this restriction will be needed for the soundness of our technique. Nevertheless, our approach of course also infers non-linear expected runtimes (by combining the linear bounds obtained for different program parts).

Let $\exp_{\mathfrak{r},g,s}$ denote the expected value of $\mathfrak{r}$ after an execution of $g \in \mathcal{GT}$ in state $s \in \Sigma$. Here, $s_\eta(x)$ is the expected value of $x \in \mathcal{PV}$ after performing the update η in state s. So if $\eta(x) \in \mathcal{D}$, then x's expected value after the update results from adding the expected value of the probability distribution $\eta(x)(s)$:

$$\exp_{\mathfrak{r},g,s} = \sum_{(\ell,p,\tau,\eta,\ell') \in g} p \cdot s_\eta(\mathfrak{r}(\ell')) \quad \text{with } s_\eta(x) = \begin{cases} s(\eta(x)), & \text{if } \eta(x) \in \mathbb{Z}[\mathcal{V}] \\ s(x) + \mathbb{E}(\eta(x)(s)), & \text{if } \eta(x) \in \mathcal{D} \end{cases}$$

Definition 12 (PLRF). *Let* $\mathcal{GT}_> \subseteq \mathcal{GT}_{\text{ni}} \subseteq \mathcal{GT}$. *Then* $\mathfrak{r} : \mathcal{L} \to \mathbb{R}[\mathcal{PV}]_{\text{lin}}$ *is a probabilistic linear ranking function (PLRF) for* $\mathcal{GT}_>$ *and* $\mathcal{GT}_{\text{ni}}$ *if for all* $g \in \mathcal{GT}_{\text{ni}} \setminus \mathcal{GT}_>$ *and* $c' \in \mathsf{Conf}$ *there is a* $\bowtie_{g,c'} \in \{<, \geq\}$ *such that for all finite paths* $\cdots c' c$ *that are admissible for some* $\mathfrak{S}$ *and* $s_0 \in \Sigma$, *and where* $c = (\ell, t, s)$ *(i.e., where* t *is the transition that is used in the step from* c' *to* c*), we have:*

Boundedness (a): *If* $t \in g$ *for a* $g \in \mathcal{GT}_{\text{ni}} \setminus \mathcal{GT}_>$, *then* $s(\mathfrak{r}(\ell)) \bowtie_{g,c'} 0$.
Boundedness (b): *If* $t \in g$ *for a* $g \in \mathcal{GT}_>$, *then* $s(\mathfrak{r}(\ell)) \geq 0$.
Non-Increase: *If* $\ell = \ell_g$ *for a* $g \in \mathcal{GT}_{\text{ni}}$ *and* $s(\tau_g) = \mathbf{t}$, *then* $s(\mathfrak{r}(\ell)) \geq \exp_{\mathfrak{r},g,s}$.
Decrease: *If* $\ell = \ell_g$ *for a* $g \in \mathcal{GT}_>$ *and* $s(\tau_g) = \mathbf{t}$, *then* $s(\mathfrak{r}(\ell)) - 1 \geq \exp_{\mathfrak{r},g,s}$.

So if one is restricted to the sub-program with the non-increasing transitions $\mathcal{GT}_{\text{ni}}$, then $\mathfrak{r}(\ell)$ is an upper bound on the expected number of applications of transitions from $\mathcal{GT}_>$ when starting in ℓ. Hence, a PLRF for $\mathcal{GT}_> = \mathcal{GT}_{\text{ni}} = \mathcal{GT}$ would imply that the program is PAST (see, e.g., [1,16,24,25]). However, our PLRFs differ from the standard notion of probabilistic ranking functions by considering arbitrary subsets $\mathcal{GT}_{\text{ni}} \subseteq \mathcal{GT}$. This is needed for the modularity of our approach which allows us to analyze program parts separately (e.g., $\mathcal{GT} \setminus \mathcal{GT}_{\text{ni}}$ is ignored when inferring a PLRF). Thus, our "Boundedness" conditions differ slightly from the corresponding conditions in other definitions. Condition (b) requires that $g \in \mathcal{GT}_>$ never leads to a configuration where $\mathfrak{r}$ is negative. Condition (a) states that in an admissible path where $g = \{t_1, t_2, \ldots\} \in \mathcal{GT}_{\text{ni}} \setminus \mathcal{GT}_>$ is used for continuing in configuration c', if executing t_1 in c' makes $\mathfrak{r}$ negative, then executing t_2 must make $\mathfrak{r}$ negative as well. Thus, such a g can never come before a general transition from $\mathcal{GT}_>$ in an admissible path and hence, g can be ignored when inferring upper bounds on the runtime. This increases the power of our approach and it allows us to consider only *non-negative* random variables in our correctness proofs.

We use SMT solvers to generate PLRFs automatically. Then for "Boundedness", we regard all $s' \in \Sigma$ with $s'(\tau_g) = \mathfrak{t}$ and require "Boundedness" for any state s that is reachable from s'.

Example 13 (PLRFs). Consider again the PIP in Fig. 1 and the sets $\mathcal{GT}_> = \mathcal{GT}_{ni} = \{g_1\}$ and $\mathcal{GT}'_> = \mathcal{GT}'_{ni} = \{g_3\}$, which correspond to its two loops.

The function $\mathfrak{r}$ with $\mathfrak{r}(\ell_1) = 2 \cdot x$ and $\mathfrak{r}(\ell_0) = \mathfrak{r}(\ell_2) = 0$ is a PLRF for $\mathcal{GT}_> = \mathcal{GT}_{ni}$: For every admissible configuration (ℓ, t, s) with $t \in g_1$ we have $\ell = \ell_1$ and $s(\mathfrak{r}(\ell_1)) = 2 \cdot s(x) \geq 0$, since x was positive before (due to g_1's guard) and it was either decreased by 1 or not changed by the update of t_1 resp. t_2. Hence $\mathfrak{r}$ is bounded. Moreover, for $s_1(x) = s(x-1) = s(x) - 1$ and $s_2(x) = s(x)$ we have:

$$\exp_{\mathfrak{r},g,s} = \tfrac{1}{2} \cdot s_1(\mathfrak{r}(\ell_1)) + \tfrac{1}{2} \cdot s_2(\mathfrak{r}(\ell_1)) = 2 \cdot s(x) - 1 = s(\mathfrak{r}(\ell_1)) - 1$$

So $\mathfrak{r}$ is decreasing on g_1 and as $\mathcal{GT}_> = \mathcal{GT}_{ni}$, also the non-increase property holds. Similarly, $\mathfrak{r}'$ with $\mathfrak{r}'(\ell_2) = y$ and $\mathfrak{r}'(\ell_0) = \mathfrak{r}'(\ell_1) = 0$ is a PLRF for $\mathcal{GT}'_> = \mathcal{GT}'_{ni}$.

In our implementation, $\mathcal{GT}_>$ is always a singleton and we let $\mathcal{GT}_{ni} \subseteq \mathcal{GT}$ be a cycle in the call graph where we find a PLRF for $\mathcal{GT}_> \subseteq \mathcal{GT}_{ni}$. The next subsection shows how we can then obtain an expected runtime bound for the overall program by searching for suitable ranking functions repeatedly.

4.2   Inferring Expected Runtime Bounds

Our approach to infer expected runtime bounds is based on an underlying (non-probabilistic) bound pair $(\mathcal{RB}, \mathcal{SB})$ which is computed by existing techniques (in our implementation, we use [18]). To do so, we abstract the PIP to a standard integer transition system by ignoring the probabilities of transitions and replacing probabilistic with non-deterministic sampling (e.g., the update $\eta(x) = \text{GEO}(\tfrac{1}{2})$ would be replaced by $\eta(x) = x + u$ with $u \in \mathcal{V} \setminus \mathcal{PV}$, where $u > 0$ is added to the guard). Of course, we usually have $\mathcal{RB}(t) = \infty$ for some transitions t.

We start with the expected bound pair $(\mathcal{RB}_\mathbb{E}, \mathcal{SB}_\mathbb{E})$ that is obtained by lifting $(\mathcal{RB}, \mathcal{SB})$ as in Thm. 10. Afterwards, the expected runtime bound $\mathcal{RB}_\mathbb{E}$ is improved repeatedly by applying the following Thm. 16 (and similarly, $\mathcal{SB}_\mathbb{E}$ is improved repeatedly by applying Thm. 23 and 25 from Sect. 5). Our approach alternates the improvement of $\mathcal{RB}_\mathbb{E}$ and $\mathcal{SB}_\mathbb{E}$, and it uses expected size bounds on "previous" transitions to improve expected runtime bounds, and vice versa.

To improve $\mathcal{RB}_\mathbb{E}$, we generate a PLRF $\mathfrak{r}$ for a part of the program. To obtain a bound for the *full* program from $\mathfrak{r}$, one has to determine which transitions can enter the program part and from which locations it can be entered.

Definition 14 (Entry Locations and Transitions). *For $\mathcal{GT}_{ni} \subseteq \mathcal{GT}$ and $\ell \in \mathcal{L}$, the entry transitions are $\mathcal{ET}_{\mathcal{GT}_{ni}}(\ell) = \{g \in \mathcal{GT} \setminus \mathcal{GT}_{ni} \mid \exists t \in g. t = (\_,\_,\_,\_,\ell)\}$. Then the entry locations are all start locations of $\mathcal{GT}_{ni}$ whose entry transitions* *are not empty, i.e., $\mathcal{EL}_{\mathcal{GT}_{ni}} = \{\ell \mid \mathcal{ET}_{\mathcal{GT}_{ni}}(\ell) \neq \varnothing \land (\ell, \_, \_, \_, \_) \in \bigcup \mathcal{GT}_{ni}\}$.*[1]

Example 15 (Entry Locations and Transitions). For the PIP from Fig. 1 and $\mathcal{GT}_{ni} = \{g_1\}$, we have $\mathcal{EL}_{\mathcal{GT}_{ni}} = \{\ell_1\}$ and $\mathcal{ET}_{\mathcal{GT}_{ni}}(\ell_1) = \{g_0\}$. So the loop formed by g_1 is entered at location ℓ_1 and the general transition g_0 has to be executed before. Similarly, for $\mathcal{GT}'_{ni} = \{g_3\}$ we have $\mathcal{EL}_{\mathcal{GT}'_{ni}} = \{\ell_2\}$ and $\mathcal{ET}_{\mathcal{GT}'_{ni}}(\ell_2) = \{g_2\}$.

Recall that if $\mathfrak{r}$ is a PLRF for $\mathcal{GT}_> \subseteq \mathcal{GT}_{ni}$, then in a program that is restricted to $\mathcal{GT}_{ni}$, $\mathfrak{r}(\ell)$ is an upper bound on the expected number of executions of transitions from $\mathcal{GT}_>$ when starting in ℓ. Since $\mathfrak{r}(\ell)$ may contain negative coefficients, it is not weakly monotonically increasing in general. To turn expressions $e \in \mathbb{R}[\mathcal{PV}]$ into bounds from $\mathcal{B}$, let the over-approximation $\lceil \cdot \rceil$ replace all coefficients by their absolute value. So for example, $\lceil x - y \rceil = \lceil x + (-1) \cdot y \rceil = x + y$. Clearly, we have $|s|(\lceil e \rceil) \geq |s|(e)$ for all $s \in \Sigma$. Moreover, if $e \in \mathbb{R}[\mathcal{PV}]$ then $\lceil e \rceil \in \mathcal{B}$.

To turn $\lceil \mathfrak{r}(\ell) \rceil$ into a bound for the full program, one has to take into account how often the sub-program with the transitions $\mathcal{GT}_{ni}$ is reached via an entry transition $h \in \mathcal{ET}_{\mathcal{GT}_{ni}}(\ell)$ for some $\ell \in \mathcal{EL}_{\mathcal{GT}_{ni}}$. This can be over-approximated by $\sum_{t=(\_,\_,\_,\_,\ell)\in h} \mathcal{RB}(t)$, which is an upper bound on the number of times that transitions in h to the entry location ℓ of $\mathcal{GT}_{ni}$ are applied in a full program run.

The bound $\lceil \mathfrak{r}(\ell) \rceil$ is expressed in terms of the program variables at the entry location ℓ of $\mathcal{GT}_{ni}$. To obtain a bound in terms of the variables at the start of the program, one has to take into account which value a program variable x may have when the sub-program $\mathcal{GT}_{ni}$ is reached. For every entry transition $h \in \mathcal{ET}_{\mathcal{GT}_{ni}}(\ell)$, this value can be over-approximated by $\mathcal{SB}_{\mathbb{E}}(h, \ell, x)$. Thus, we have to instantiate each variable x in $\lceil \mathfrak{r}(\ell) \rceil$ by $\mathcal{SB}_{\mathbb{E}}(h, \ell, x)$. Let $\mathcal{SB}_{\mathbb{E}}(h, \ell, \cdot) : \mathcal{PV} \to \mathcal{B}$ be the mapping with $\mathcal{SB}_{\mathbb{E}}(h, \ell, \cdot)(x) = \mathcal{SB}_{\mathbb{E}}(h, \ell, x)$. Hence, $\mathcal{SB}_{\mathbb{E}}(h, \ell, \cdot)(\lceil \mathfrak{r}(\ell) \rceil)$ over-approximates the expected number of applications of $\mathcal{GT}_>$ if $\mathcal{GT}_{ni}$ is entered in location ℓ, where this bound is expressed in terms of the input variables of the program. Here, weak monotonic increase of $\lceil \mathfrak{r}(\ell) \rceil$ ensures that instantiating its variables by an over-approximation of their size yields an over-approximation of the runtime.

Theorem 16 (Expected Runtime Bounds). *Let $(\mathcal{RB}_{\mathbb{E}}, \mathcal{SB}_{\mathbb{E}})$ be an expected bound pair, $\mathcal{RB}$ a (non-probabilistic) runtime bound, and $\mathfrak{r}$ a PLRF for $\mathcal{GT}_> \subseteq \mathcal{GT}_{ni} \subseteq \mathcal{GT}$. Then $\mathcal{RB}'_{\mathbb{E}} : \mathcal{GT} \to \mathcal{B}$ is an expected runtime bound where*

$$\mathcal{RB}'_{\mathbb{E}}(g) = \begin{cases} \displaystyle\sum_{\substack{\ell \in \mathcal{EL}_{\mathcal{GT}_{ni}} \\ h \in \mathcal{ET}_{\mathcal{GT}_{ni}}(\ell)}} \Big(\sum_{t=(\_,\_,\_,\_,\ell)\in h} \mathcal{RB}(t) \Big) \cdot (\mathcal{SB}_{\mathbb{E}}(h, \ell, \cdot)(\lceil \mathfrak{r}(\ell) \rceil)), & \text{if } g \in \mathcal{GT}_> \\[4pt] \mathcal{RB}_{\mathbb{E}}(g), & \text{if } g \notin \mathcal{GT}_> \end{cases}$$

Example 17 (Expected Runtime Bounds). For the PIP from Fig. 1, our approach starts with $(\mathcal{RB}_{\mathbb{E}}, \mathcal{SB}_{\mathbb{E}})$ from Ex. 11 which results from lifting the bound pair from Ex. 5. To improve the bound $\mathcal{RB}_{\mathbb{E}}(g_1) = \infty$, we use the PLRF $\mathfrak{r}$ for $\mathcal{GT}_> = \mathcal{GT}_{ni} = \{g_1\}$ from Ex. 13. By Ex. 15, we have $\mathcal{EL}_{\mathcal{GT}_{ni}} = \{\ell_1\}$ and $\mathcal{ET}_{\mathcal{GT}_{ni}}(\ell_1) = \{g_0\}$ with $g_0 = \{t_0\}$, whose runtime bound is $\mathcal{RB}(t_0) = 1$, see Ex. 5. Using the expected size bound $\mathcal{SB}_{\mathbb{E}}(g_0, \ell_1, x) = x$ from Ex. 9, Thm. 16 yields

$$\mathcal{RB}'_{\mathbb{E}}(g_1) = \mathcal{RB}(t_0) \cdot \mathcal{SB}_{\mathbb{E}}(g_0, \ell_1, \cdot)(\lceil \mathfrak{r}(\ell_1) \rceil) = 1 \cdot 2 \cdot x = 2 \cdot x.$$

---

[1] For a set of sets like $\mathcal{GT}_{ni}$, $\bigcup \mathcal{GT}_{ni}$ denotes their union, i.e., $\bigcup \mathcal{GT}_{ni} = \bigcup_{g \in \mathcal{GT}_{ni}} g$.

To improve $\mathcal{RB}_{\mathbb{E}}(g_3)$, *we use the PLRF* $\mathfrak{r}'$ *for* $\mathcal{GT}'_{\geq} = \mathcal{GT}'_{\text{ni}} = \{g_3\}$ *from Ex. 13. As* $\mathcal{EL}_{\mathcal{GT}'_{\text{ni}}} = \{\ell_2\}$ *and* $\mathcal{ET}_{\mathcal{GT}'_{\text{ni}}}(\ell_2) = \{g_2\}$ *by Ex. 15, where* $g_2 = \{t_3\}$ *and* $\mathcal{RB}(t_3) = 1$ *(Ex. 5), with the bound* $\mathcal{SB}_{\mathbb{E}}(g_2, \ell_2, y) = 6 \cdot x^2 + 2 \cdot y$ *from Ex. 9, Thm. 16 yields*

$$\mathcal{RB}'_{\mathbb{E}}(g_3) = \mathcal{RB}(t_3) \cdot \mathcal{SB}_{\mathbb{E}}(g_2, \ell_2, \cdot)\left(\lceil \mathfrak{r}'(\ell_2) \rceil\right) = 1 \cdot \mathcal{SB}_{\mathbb{E}}(g_2, \ell_2, y) = 6 \cdot x^2 + 2 \cdot y.$$

So based on the expected size bounds of Ex. 9, we have shown how to compute the expected runtime bounds of Ex. 9 automatically.

Similar to [18], our approach relies on combining bounds that one has computed earlier in order to derive new bounds. Here, bounds may be combined *linearly*, bounds may be *multiplied*, and bounds may even be *substituted* into other bounds. But in contrast to [18], sometimes one may combine *expected* bounds that were computed earlier and sometimes it is only sound to combine *non-probabilistic* bounds: If a new bound is computed by *linear combinations* of earlier bounds, then it is sound to use the "expected versions" of these earlier bounds. However, if two bounds are *multiplied*, then it is in general not sound to use their "expected versions". Thus, it would be *unsound* to use the *expected* runtime bounds $\mathcal{RB}_{\mathbb{E}}(h)$ instead of the *non-probabilistic* bounds $\sum_{t=(\_,\_,\_,\_,\ell)\in h} \mathcal{RB}(t)$ on the entry transitions in Thm. 16 (a counterexample is given in [47]).[2]

In general, if bounds $b_1, \ldots, b_n$ are *substituted* into another bound b, then it is sound to use "expected versions" of the bounds $b_1, \ldots, b_n$ if b is *concave*, see, e.g., [10, 11, 40]. Since bounds from $\mathcal{B}$ do not contain negative coefficients, we obtain that a finite[3] bound $b \in \mathcal{B}$ is concave iff it is a linear polynomial (see [47]).

Thus, in Thm. 16 we may substitute *expected* size bounds $\mathcal{SB}_{\mathbb{E}}(h, \ell, x)$ into $\lceil \mathfrak{r}(\ell) \rceil$, since we restricted ourselves to *linear* ranking functions $\mathfrak{r}$ and hence, $\lceil \mathfrak{r}(\ell) \rceil$ is also linear. Note that in contrast to [11], where a notion of concavity was used to analyze probabilistic term rewriting, a multilinear expression like $x \cdot y$ is not concave when regarding both arguments simultaneously. Hence, it is unsound to use such ranking functions in Thm. 16. See [47] for a counterexample to show why substituting expected bounds into a non-linear bound is incorrect in general.

5   Computing Expected Size Bounds

We first compute *local* bounds for one application of a transition (Sect. 5.1). To turn them into *global* bounds, we encode the data flow of a PIP in a graph. Sect. 5.2 then presents our technique to compute expected size bounds.

5.1   Local Change Bounds and General Result Variable Graph

We first compute a bound on the expected change of a variable during an update. More precisely, for every general result variable (g, ℓ, x) we define a bound $\mathcal{CB}_{\mathbb{E}}(g, \ell, x)$ on the change of the variable x that we can expect in one

---

[2]   An exception is the special case where $\mathfrak{r}(\ell)$ is *constant*. Then, our implementation indeed uses the expected bound $\mathcal{RB}_{\mathbb{E}}(h)$ instead of $\sum_{t=(\_,\_,\_,\_,\ell)\in h} \mathcal{RB}(t)$ [47].

[3]   A bound is *finite* if it does not contain ∞. We always simplify expressions and thus, a bound like $0 \cdot \infty$ is also finite, because it simplifies to 0, as usual in measure theory.

execution of the general transition g when reaching location ℓ. So we consider all $t = (\_, p, \_, \eta, \ell) \in g$ and the expected difference between the current value of x and its update $\eta(x)$. However, for $\eta(x) \in \mathbb{Z}[\mathcal{V}]$, $\eta(x) - x$ is not necessarily from $\mathcal{B}$ because it may contain negative coefficients. Thus, we use the over-approximation $\lceil \eta(x) - x \rceil$ (where we always simplify expressions before applying $\lceil \cdot \rceil$, e.g., $\lceil x - x \rceil = \lceil 0 \rceil = 0$). Moreover, $\lceil \eta(x) - x \rceil$ may contain temporary variables. Let $\mathrm{tv}_t : \mathcal{V} \to \mathcal{B}$ instantiate all temporary variables by the largest possible value they can have after evaluating the transition t. Hence, we then use $\mathrm{tv}_t(\lceil \eta(x) - x \rceil)$ instead. For tv_t, we have to use the underlying *non-probabilistic* size bound $\mathcal{SB}$ for the program (since the scheduler determines the values of temporary variables by non-deterministic *(non-probabilistic)* choice). If x is updated according to a bounded distribution function $d \in \mathcal{D}$, then as in Sect. 2, let $\mathfrak{E}(d) \in \mathcal{B}$ denote a finite bound on d, i.e., $\mathbb{E}_{\mathrm{abs}}(d(s)) \leq |s| \, (\mathfrak{E}(d))$ for all $s \in \Sigma$.

Definition 18 (Expected Local Change Bound). *Let $\mathcal{SB}$ be a size bound. Then $\mathcal{CB}_{\mathbb{E}} : \mathcal{GRV} \to \mathcal{B}$ with $\mathcal{CB}_{\mathbb{E}}(g, \ell, x) = \displaystyle\sum_{t=(\_,p,\_,\eta,\ell)\in g} p \cdot \mathrm{ch}_t(\eta(x), x)$, where*

$$\mathrm{ch}_t(\eta(x), x) = \begin{cases} \mathfrak{E}(d), & \text{if } \eta(x) = d \in \mathcal{D} \\ \mathrm{tv}_t(\lceil \eta(x) - x \rceil), & \text{otherwise} \end{cases} \quad \text{and} \quad \mathrm{tv}_t(y) = \begin{cases} \mathcal{SB}(t, y), & \text{if } y \notin \mathcal{PV} \\ y, & \text{if } y \in \mathcal{PV} \end{cases}$$

Example 19 ($\mathcal{CB}_{\mathbb{E}}$). For the PIP of Fig. 1, we have $\mathcal{CB}_{\mathbb{E}}(g_0, \_, \_) = \mathcal{CB}_{\mathbb{E}}(g_2, \_, \_) = \mathcal{CB}_{\mathbb{E}}(g_3, \ell_2, x) = 0$, since the respective updates are identities. Moreover,

$$\mathcal{CB}_{\mathbb{E}}(g_1, \ell_1, x) = \tfrac{1}{2} \cdot \lceil (x-1) - x \rceil + \tfrac{1}{2} \cdot \lceil x - x \rceil = \tfrac{1}{2} \cdot 1 + \tfrac{1}{2} \cdot 0 = \tfrac{1}{2}.$$

In a similar way, we obtain $\mathcal{CB}_{\mathbb{E}}(g_1, \ell_1, y) = x$ and $\mathcal{CB}_{\mathbb{E}}(g_3, \ell_2, y) = 1$.

The following theorem shows that for any admissible configuration in a state s', $\mathcal{CB}_{\mathbb{E}}(g, \ell, x)$ is an upper bound on the expected value of $|s(x) - s'(x)|$ if s is the next state obtained when applying g in state s' to reach location ℓ.

Theorem 20 (Soundness of $\mathcal{CB}_{\mathbb{E}}$). *For any $(g, \ell, x) \in \mathcal{GRV}$, scheduler $\mathfrak{S}$, $s_0 \in \Sigma$, and admissible configuration $c' = (\_, \_, s')$, we have*

$$|s'| \, (\mathcal{CB}_{\mathbb{E}}(g, \ell, x)) \geq \sum_{c=(\ell,t,s)\in\mathrm{Conf},\ t\in g} pr_{\mathfrak{S},s_0}(c' \to c) \cdot |s(x) - s'(x)|.$$

To obtain *global* bounds from the local bounds $\mathcal{CB}_{\mathbb{E}}(g, \ell, x)$, we construct a *general result variable graph* which encodes the data flow between variables. Let $\mathrm{pre}(g) = \mathcal{ET}_\varnothing(\ell_g)$ be the the set of *pre-transitions* of g which lead into g's start location ℓ_g. Moreover, for $\alpha = (g, \ell, x) \in \mathcal{GRV}$ let its *active variables* $\mathrm{actV}(\alpha)$ consist of all variables occurring in the bound $x + \mathcal{CB}_{\mathbb{E}}(\alpha)$ for α's expected size.

Definition 21 (General Result Variable Graph). *The general result variable graph has the set of nodes $\mathcal{GRV}$ and the set of edges $\mathcal{GRVE}$, where*

$$\mathcal{GRVE} = \{ ((g', \ell', x'), (g, \ell, x)) \mid g' \in \mathrm{pre}(g) \wedge \ell' = \ell_g \wedge x' \in \mathrm{actV}(g, \ell, x) \}.$$

Example 22 (General Result Variable Graph). The general result variable graph for the PIP of Fig. 1 is shown below. For $\mathcal{CB}_{\mathbb{E}}$ from Ex. 19, we have $\mathrm{actV}(g_1, \ell_1, x) = \{x\}$, as $x + \mathcal{CB}_{\mathbb{E}}(\alpha) = x + \tfrac{1}{2}$ contains no variable except x.

Similarly, $\text{actV}(g_1, \ell_1, y) = \{x, y\}$, as x and y are contained in $y + C\mathcal{B}_\mathbb{E}(g_1, \ell_1, y) = y + x$. For all other $\alpha \in \mathcal{GRV}$, we have $\text{actV}(\_, \_, x) = \{x\}$ and $\text{actV}(\_, \_, y) = \{y\}$. As $\text{pre}(g_1) = \{g_0, g_1\}$, the graph captures the dependence of (g_1, ℓ_1, x) on (g_0, ℓ_1, x) and (g_1, ℓ_1, x), and of (g_1, ℓ_1, y) on (g_0, ℓ_1, x), (g_0, ℓ_1, y), (g_1, ℓ_1, x), and (g_1, ℓ_1, y). The other edges are obtained in a similar way.

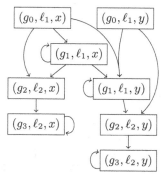

5.2   Inferring Expected Size Bounds

We now compute global expected size bounds for the general result variables by considering the SCCs of the general result variable graph separately. As usual, an SCC is a maximal subgraph with a path from each node to every other node. An SCC is *trivial* if it consists of a single node without an edge to itself. We first handle trivial SCCs in Sect. 5.2.1 and consider non-trivial SCCs in Sect. 5.2.2.

5.2.1   Inferring Expected Size Bounds for Trivial SCCs
By Thm. 20, $x + C\mathcal{B}_\mathbb{E}(g, \ell, x)$ is a *local* bound on the expected value of x after applying g once in order to enter ℓ. However, this bound is formulated in terms of the values of the variables immediately before applying g. We now want to compute *global* bounds in terms of the *initial* values of the variables at the start of the program.

If g is *initial* (i.e., $g \in \mathcal{GT}_0$ since g starts in the initial location ℓ_0), then $x + C\mathcal{B}_\mathbb{E}(g, \ell, x)$ is already a global bound, as the values of the variables before the application of g are the initial values of the variables at the program start.

Otherwise, the variables y occurring in the local bound $x + C\mathcal{B}_\mathbb{E}(g, \ell, x)$ have to be replaced by the values that they can take in a full program run before applying the transition g. Thus, we have to consider all transitions $h \in \text{pre}(g)$ and instantiate every variable y by the maximum of the values that y can have after applying h. Here, we again over-approximate the maximum by the sum.

If $C\mathcal{B}_\mathbb{E}(g, \ell, x)$ is *concave* (i.e., a *linear* polynomial), then we can instantiate its variables by *expected* size bounds $S\mathcal{B}_\mathbb{E}(h, \ell_g, y)$. However, this is unsound if $C\mathcal{B}_\mathbb{E}(g, \ell, x)$ is not linear, i.e., not concave (see [47] for a counterexample). So in this case, we have to use *non-probabilistic* bounds $S\mathcal{B}(t, y)$ instead.

As in Sect. 4.2, we use an underlying non-probabilistic bound pair $(\mathcal{RB}, S\mathcal{B})$ and start with the expected pair $(\mathcal{RB}_\mathbb{E}, S\mathcal{B}_\mathbb{E})$ obtained by lifting $(\mathcal{RB}, S\mathcal{B})$ according to Thm. 10. While Thm. 16 improves $\mathcal{RB}_\mathbb{E}$, we now improve $S\mathcal{B}_\mathbb{E}$. Here, the SCCs of the general result variable graph should be treated in topological order, since then one may first improve $S\mathcal{B}_\mathbb{E}$ for result variables corresponding to $\text{pre}(g)$, and use that when improving $S\mathcal{B}_\mathbb{E}$ for result variables of the form $(g, \_, \_)$.

Theorem 23 (Expected Size Bounds for Trivial SCCs). *Let $S\mathcal{B}_\mathbb{E}$ be an expected size bound, $S\mathcal{B}$ a (non-probabilistic) size bound, and let $\alpha = (g, \ell, x)$ form a trivial SCC of the general result variable graph. Let $\text{size}_\mathbb{E}^\alpha$ and size^α be mappings from $\mathcal{PV} \to \mathcal{B}$ with $\text{size}_\mathbb{E}^\alpha(y) = \sum_{h \in \text{pre}(g)} S\mathcal{B}_\mathbb{E}(h, \ell_g, y)$ and $\text{size}^\alpha(y) = \sum_{h \in \text{pre}(g),\, t = (\_,\_,\_,\_,\ell_g) \in h} S\mathcal{B}(t, y)$. Then $S\mathcal{B}_\mathbb{E}' : \mathcal{GRV} \to \mathcal{B}$ is an expected size bound,* *where* $SB'_{\mathbb{E}}(\beta) = SB_{\mathbb{E}}(\beta)$ *for* $\beta \neq \alpha$ *and*

$$SB'_{\mathbb{E}}(\alpha) = \begin{cases} x + CB_{\mathbb{E}}(\alpha), & \text{if } g \in \mathcal{GT}_0 \\ \text{size}^{\alpha}_{\mathbb{E}}(x + CB_{\mathbb{E}}(\alpha)), & \text{if } g \notin \mathcal{GT}_0, CB_{\mathbb{E}}(\alpha) \text{ is linear} \\ \text{size}^{\alpha}_{\mathbb{E}}(x) + \text{size}^{\alpha}(CB_{\mathbb{E}}(\alpha)), & \text{if } g \notin \mathcal{GT}_0, CB_{\mathbb{E}}(\alpha) \text{ is not linear} \end{cases}$$

Example 24 (SB$_{\mathbb{E}}$ for Trivial SCCs). The general result variable graph in Ex. 22 contains 4 trivial SCCs formed by $\alpha_x = (g_0, \ell_1, x)$, $\alpha_y = (g_0, \ell_1, y)$, $\beta_x = (g_2, \ell_2, x)$, and $\beta_y = (g_2, \ell_2, y)$. For all these general result variables, the expected local change bound $CB_{\mathbb{E}}$ is 0 (see Ex. 19). Thus, it is linear. Since $g_0 \in \mathcal{GT}_0$, Thm. 23 yields $SB'_{\mathbb{E}}(\alpha_x) = x + CB_{\mathbb{E}}(\alpha_x) = x$ and $SB'_{\mathbb{E}}(\alpha_y) = y + CB_{\mathbb{E}}(\alpha_y) = y$.

By treating SCCs in topological order, when handling β_x, β_y, we can assume that we already have $SB_{\mathbb{E}}(\alpha_x) = x$, $SB_{\mathbb{E}}(\alpha_y) = y$ and $SB_{\mathbb{E}}(g_1, \ell_1, x) = 2 \cdot x$, $SB_{\mathbb{E}}(g_1, \ell_1, y) = 6 \cdot x^2 + y$ (see Ex. 9) for the result variables corresponding to $\text{pre}(g_2) = \{g_0, g_1\}$. We will explain in Sect. 5.2.2 how to compute such expected size bounds for non-trivial SCCs. Hence, by Thm. 23 we obtain $SB'_{\mathbb{E}}(\beta_x) = \text{size}^{\beta_x}_{\mathbb{E}}(x + CB_{\mathbb{E}}(\beta_x)) = SB_{\mathbb{E}}(\alpha_x) + SB_{\mathbb{E}}(g_1, \ell_1, x) = 3 \cdot x$ and $SB'_{\mathbb{E}}(\beta_y) = \text{size}^{\beta_y}_{\mathbb{E}}(y + CB_{\mathbb{E}}(\beta_y)) = SB_{\mathbb{E}}(\alpha_y) + SB_{\mathbb{E}}(g_1, \ell_1, y) = 6 \cdot x^2 + 2 \cdot y$.

5.2.2 Inferring Expected Size Bounds for Non-Trivial SCCs

Now we handle non-trivial SCCs C of the general result variable graph. An upper bound for the expected size of a variable x when entering C is obtained from $SB_{\mathbb{E}}(\beta)$ for all general result variables $\beta = (\_, \_, x)$ which have an edge to C.

To turn $CB_{\mathbb{E}}(g, \ell, x)$ into a global bound, as in Thm. 23 its variables y have to be instantiated by the values $\text{size}^{(g, \ell, x)}(y)$ that they can take in a full program run before applying a transition from g. Thus, $\text{size}^{(g, \ell, x)}(CB_{\mathbb{E}}(g, \ell, x))$ is a global bound on the expected change resulting from *one* application of g. To obtain an upper bound for the whole SCC C, we add up these global bounds for all $(g, \_, x) \in C$ and take into account how often the general transitions in the SCC are expected to be executed, i.e., we multiply with their expected runtime bound $RB_{\mathbb{E}}(g)$. So while in Thm. 16 we improve $RB_{\mathbb{E}}$ using expected size bounds for previous transitions, we now improve $SB_{\mathbb{E}}(C)$ using expected runtime bounds for the transitions in C and expected size bounds for previous transitions.

Theorem 25 (Expected Size Bounds for Non-Trivial SCCs). *Let* $(RB_{\mathbb{E}}, SB_{\mathbb{E}})$ *be an expected bound pair,* (RB, SB) *a (non-probabilistic) bound pair, and let* $C \subseteq \mathcal{GRV}$ *form a non-trivial SCC of the general result variable graph where* $\mathcal{GT}_C = \{g \in \mathcal{GT} \mid (g, \_, \_) \in C\}$. *Then* $SB'_{\mathbb{E}}$ *is an expected size bound:*

$$SB'_{\mathbb{E}}(\alpha) = \begin{cases} \sum_{(\beta,\alpha)\in\mathcal{GRVE}, \, \beta\notin C, \, \alpha\in C, \, \beta=(\_,\_,x)} SB_{\mathbb{E}}(\beta) \; + \\ \quad \sum_{g\in\mathcal{GT}_C} RB_{\mathbb{E}}(g) \cdot \left(\sum_{\alpha'=(g,\_,x)\in C} \text{size}^{\alpha'}(CB_{\mathbb{E}}(\alpha')) \right), & \text{if } \alpha = (\_,\_,x) \in C \\ SB_{\mathbb{E}}(\alpha), & \text{otherwise} \end{cases}$$

Here we really have to use the *non-probabilistic* size bound $\text{size}^{\alpha'}$ instead of $\text{size}^{\alpha'}_{\mathbb{E}}$, even if $CB_{\mathbb{E}}(\alpha')$ is linear, i.e., concave. Otherwise we would multiply the expected values of two random variables which are not independent.

Example 26 (SB$_{\mathbb{E}}$ for Non-Trivial SCCs). The general result variable graph in

Ex. 22 contains 4 non-trivial SCCs formed by $\alpha'_x = (g_1, \ell_1, x)$, $\alpha'_y = (g_1, \ell_1, y)$, $\beta'_x = (g_3, \ell_2, x)$, *and* $\beta'_y = (g_3, \ell_2, y)$. *By the results on* $\mathcal{SB}_{\mathbb{E}}$, $\mathcal{RB}_{\mathbb{E}}$, $\mathcal{CB}_{\mathbb{E}}$, *and* $\mathcal{SB}$ *from Ex. 24, 17, 19, and 5, Thm. 25 yields the expected size bound in Ex. 9:*

$$\mathcal{SB}'_{\mathbb{E}}(\alpha'_x) = \mathcal{SB}_{\mathbb{E}}(\alpha_x) + \mathcal{RB}_{\mathbb{E}}(g_1) \cdot \text{size}^{\alpha'_x}(\mathcal{CB}_{\mathbb{E}}(\alpha'_x)) = x + 2 \cdot x \cdot \tfrac{1}{2} = 2 \cdot x$$

$$\mathcal{SB}'_{\mathbb{E}}(\alpha'_y) = \mathcal{SB}_{\mathbb{E}}(\alpha_y) + \mathcal{RB}_{\mathbb{E}}(g_1) \cdot \text{size}^{\alpha'_y}(\mathcal{CB}_{\mathbb{E}}(\alpha'_y)) = y + 2 \cdot x \cdot \text{size}^{\alpha'_y}(x)$$

$$= y + 2 \cdot x \cdot \sum\nolimits_{i \in \{0,1,2\}} \mathcal{SB}(t_i, x) \qquad = 6 \cdot x^2 + y$$

$$\mathcal{SB}'_{\mathbb{E}}(\beta'_x) = \mathcal{SB}_{\mathbb{E}}(\beta_x) + \mathcal{RB}_{\mathbb{E}}(g_3) \cdot \text{size}^{\beta'_x}(\mathcal{CB}_{\mathbb{E}}(\beta'_x)) = 3 \cdot x + (6x^2 + 2y) \cdot 0 = 3 \cdot x$$

$$\mathcal{SB}'_{\mathbb{E}}(\beta'_y) = \mathcal{SB}_{\mathbb{E}}(\beta_y) + \mathcal{RB}_{\mathbb{E}}(g_3) \cdot \text{size}^{\beta'_y}(\mathcal{CB}_{\mathbb{E}}(\beta'_y)) = 6 \cdot x^2 + 2 \cdot y + (6x^2 + 2y) \cdot 1$$

$$= 12 \cdot x^2 + 4 \cdot y$$

6   Related Work, Implementation, and Conclusion

Related Work Our approach adapts techniques from [18] to probabilistic programs. As explained in Sect. 1, this adaption is not at all trivial (see our proofs in [47]).

There has been a lot of work on proving PAST and inferring bounds on expected runtimes using supermartingales, e.g., [1, 11, 15, 16, 22–25, 29, 32, 48, 62]. While these techniques infer one (lexicographic) ranking supermartingale to analyze the complete program, our approach deals with information flow between different program parts and analyzes them separately.

There is also work on modular analysis of almost sure termination (AST) [1, 25, 26, 37, 38, 48], i.e., termination with probability 1. This differs from our results, since AST is compositional, in contrast to PAST (see, e.g., [41, 42]).

A fundamentally different approach to ranking supermartingales (i.e., to *forward-reasoning*) is *backward-reasoning* by so-called expectation transformers, see, e.g., [10, 41, 42, 44–46, 50, 52, 61]. In this orthogonal reasoning, [10, 41, 42, 52] consider the connection of the expected runtime and size. While expectation transformers apply backward- instead of forward-reasoning, their correctness can also be justified using supermartingales. More precisely, Park induction for upper bounds on the expected runtime via expectation transformers essentially ensures that a certain stochastic process is a supermartingale (see [33] for details).

To the best of our knowledge, the only available tools for the inference of upper bounds on the expected runtimes of probabilistic programs are [10, 50, 61, 62]. The tool of [61] deals with data types and higher order functions in probabilistic ML programs and does not support programs whose complexity depends on (possibly negative) integers (see [55]). Furthermore, the tool of [48] focuses on proving or refuting (P)AST of probabilistic programs for so-called *Prob-solvable* loops, which do not allow for nested or sequential loops or non-determinism. So both [61] and [48] are orthogonal to our work. We discuss [10, 50, 62] below.

Implementation We implemented our analysis in a new version of our tool **KoAT** [18]. KoAT is an open-source tool written in **OCaml**, which can also be downloaded as a Docker image and accessed via a web interface [43].

Given a PIP, the analysis proceeds as in Alg. 1. The preprocessing in Line 1 adds invariants to guards (using **APRON** [39] to generate (non-probabilistic) invariants), unfolds transitions [19], and removes unreachable locations, transitions with probability 0, and transitions with unsatisfiable guards (using **Z3** [49]).

Input: PIP $(\mathcal{PV}, \mathcal{L}, \mathcal{GT}, \ell_0)$
1 preprocess the PIP
2 $(\mathcal{RB}, \mathcal{SB}) \leftarrow$ perform non-probabilistic analysis using [18]
3 $(\mathcal{RB}_\mathbb{E}, \mathcal{SB}_\mathbb{E}) \leftarrow$ lift $(\mathcal{RB}, \mathcal{SB})$ to an expected bound pair with Thm. 10
4 **repeat**
5   **for all** SCCs C of the general result variable graph in topological order **do**
6   **if** $C = \{\alpha\}$ is trivial **then** $\mathcal{SB}'_\mathbb{E} \leftarrow$ improve $\mathcal{SB}_\mathbb{E}$ for C by Thm. 23
7   **else** $\mathcal{SB}'_\mathbb{E} \leftarrow$ improve $\mathcal{SB}_\mathbb{E}$ for C by Thm. 25
8   **for all** $\alpha \in C$ **do** $\mathcal{SB}_\mathbb{E}(\alpha) \leftarrow \min\{\mathcal{SB}_\mathbb{E}(\alpha), \mathcal{SB}'_\mathbb{E}(\alpha)\}$
9   **for all** general transitions $g \in \mathcal{GT}$ **do**
10         $\mathcal{RB}'_\mathbb{E} \leftarrow$ improve $\mathcal{RB}_\mathbb{E}$ for $\mathcal{GT}_> = \{g\}$ by Thm. 16
11         $\mathcal{RB}_\mathbb{E}(g) \leftarrow \min\{\mathcal{RB}_\mathbb{E}(g), \mathcal{RB}'_\mathbb{E}(g)\}$
12 **until** no bound is improved anymore
Output: $\sum_{g \in \mathcal{GT}} \mathcal{RB}_\mathbb{E}(g)$

Algorithm 1: Overall approach to infer bounds on expected runtimes

We start by a non-probabilistic analysis and lift the resulting bounds to an initial expected bound pair (Lines 2 and 3). Afterwards, we first try to improve the expected size bounds using Thm. 23 and 25, and then we attempt to improve the expected runtime bounds using Thm. 16 (if we find a PLRF using Z3). To determine the "minimum" of the previous and the new bound, we use a heuristic which compares polynomial bounds by their degree. While we over-approximated the maximum of expressions by their sum to ease readability in this paper, KoAT also uses bounds containing "min" and "max" to increase precision.

This alternating modular computation of expected size and runtime bounds is repeated so that one can benefit from improved expected runtime bounds when computing expected size bounds and vice versa. We abort this improvement of expected bounds in Alg. 1 if they are all finite (or when reaching a timeout).

To assess the power of our approach, we performed an experimental evaluation of our implementation in KoAT. We did not compare with the tool of [62], since [62] expects the program to be annotated with already computed invariants. But for many of the examples in our experiments, the invariant generation tool [56] used by [62] did not find invariants strong enough to enable a meaningful analysis (and we could not apply APRON [39] due to the different semantics of invariants).

Instead, we compare KoAT with the tools Absynth [50] and eco-imp [10] which are both based on a conceptionally different *backward-reasoning* approach. We ran the tools on all 39 examples from Absynth's evaluation in [50] (except recursive, which contains non-tail-recursion and thus cannot be encoded as a PIP), and on the 8 additional examples from the artifact of [50]. Moreover, our collection has 29 additional benchmarks: 14 examples that illustrate different aspects of PIPs, 5 PIPs based on examples from [50] where we removed assumptions, and 10 PIPs based on benchmarks from the *TPDB* [59] where some transitions were enriched with probabilistic behavior. The *TPDB* is a collection of typical programs used in the annual *Termination and Complexity Competition* [31]. We ran the experiments on an iMac with an Intel i5-2500S CPU and 12 GB of RAM under macOS Sierra for Absynth and NixOS 20.03 for KoAT and eco-imp. A timeout of 5 minutes per

Bound	KoAT	Absynth	eco-imp
$\mathcal{O}(1)$	6	6	6
$\mathcal{O}(n)$	32	32	29
$\mathcal{O}(n^2)$	3	8	9
$\mathcal{O}(n^{>2})$	0	0	0
EXP	0	0	0
∞	5	0	2
TO	0	0	0

Fig. 2: Results on benchmarks from [50]

Bound	KoAT	Absynth	eco-imp
$\mathcal{O}(1)$	2	1	2
$\mathcal{O}(n)$	10	3	6
$\mathcal{O}(n^2)$	12	1	6
$\mathcal{O}(n^{>2})$	2	0	0
EXP	1	0	0
∞	2	15	12
TO	0	9	3

Fig. 3: Results on our new benchmarks

example was applied for all tools. The average runtime of successful runs was 4.26 s for KoAT, 3.53 s for Absynth, and just 0.93 s for eco-imp.

Fig. 2 and 3 show the generated asymptotic bounds, where n is the maximal absolute value of the program variables at the program start. Here, "∞" indicates that no finite time bound could be computed and "TO" means "timeout". The detailed asymptotic results of all tools on all examples can be found in [43, 47].

Absynth and eco-imp slightly outperform KoAT on the examples from Absynth's collection, while KoAT is considerably stronger than both tools on the additional benchmarks. In particular, Absynth and eco-imp outperform our approach on examples with nested probabilistic loops. While our modular approach can analyze inner loops separately when searching for probabilistic ranking functions, Thm. 16 then requires *non-probabilistic* time bounds for all transitions entering the inner loop. But these bounds may be infinite if the outer loop has probabilistic behavior itself. Moreover, in contrast to our work and [10], the approach of [50] does not require weakly monotonic bounds.

On the other hand, KoAT is superior to Absynth and eco-imp on large examples with many loops, where only a few transitions have probabilistic behavior (this might correspond to the typical application of randomization in practical programming). Here, we benefit from the modularity of our approach which treats loops independently and combines their bounds afterwards. Absynth and eco-imp also fail for our leading example of Fig. 1, while KoAT infers a quadratic bound. Hence, the tools have particular strengths on orthogonal kinds of examples.

KoAT's source code is available at https://github.com/aprove-developers/ KoAT2-Releases/tree/probabilistic. To obtain a KoAT artifact, see https:// aprove-developers.github.io/ExpectedUpperBounds/ for a static binary and Docker image. This web site also provides all examples from our evaluation, detailed outputs of our experiments, and a *web interface* to run KoAT directly online.

Conclusion We presented a new modular approach to infer upper bounds on the expected runtimes of probabilistic integer programs. To this end, non-probabilistic and expected runtime and size bounds on parts of the program are computed in an alternating fashion and then combined to an overall expected runtime bound. In the evaluation, our tool KoAT succeeded on 91% of all examples, while the main other related tools (Absynth and eco-imp) only inferred finite bounds for 68% resp. 77% of the examples. In future work, it would be interesting to consider a modular combination of these tools (resp. of their underlying approaches).

Acknowledgements We thank Carsten Fuhs for discussions on initial ideas.

References

1. Agrawal, S., Chatterjee, K., Novotný, P.: Lexicographic ranking supermartingales: An efficient approach to termination of probabilistic programs. Proc. ACM Program. Lang. **2**(POPL) (2017), https://doi.org/10.1145/3158122
2. Albert, E., Arenas, P., Genaim, S., Puebla, G.: Closed-form upper bounds in static cost analysis. J. Autom. Reasoning **46**(2), 161–203 (2011), https://doi.org/10.1007/s10817-010-9174-1
3. Albert, E., Arenas, P., Genaim, S., Puebla, G., Zanardini, D.: Cost analysis of object-oriented bytecode programs. Theor. Comput. Sci. **413**(1), 142–159 (2012), https://doi.org/10.1016/j.tcs.2011.07.009
4. Albert, E., Genaim, S., Masud, A.N.: On the inference of resource usage upper and lower bounds. ACM Trans. Comput. Log. **14**(3) (2013), https://doi.org/10.1145/2499937.2499943
5. Albert, E., Bofill, M., Borralleras, C., Martin-Martin, E., Rubio, A.: Resource analysis driven by (conditional) termination proofs. Theory Pract. Log. Program. **19**(5-6), 722–739 (2019), https://doi.org/10.1017/S1471068419000152
6. Alias, C., Darte, A., Feautrier, P., Gonnord, L.: Multi-dimensional rankings, program termination, and complexity bounds of flowchart programs. In: Proc. SAS '10. LNCS, vol. 6337, pp. 117–133 (2010), https://doi.org/10.1007/978-3-642-15769-1_8
7. Ash, R.B., Doléans-Dade, C.A.: Probability and Measure Theory. Harcourt Academic Press, 2nd edn. (2000)
8. Avanzini, M., Moser, G.: A combination framework for complexity. In: Proc. RTA 13. LIPIcs, vol. 21, pp. 55–70 (2013), https://doi.org/10.4230/LIPIcs.RTA.2013.55
9. Avanzini, M., Moser, G., Schaper, M.: TcT: Tyrolean Complexity Tool. In: Proc. TACAS '16. LNCS, vol. 9636, pp. 407–423 (2016), https://doi.org/10.1007/978-3-662-49674-9_24
10. Avanzini, M., Moser, G., Schaper, M.: A modular cost analysis for probabilistic programs. Proc. ACM Program. Lang. **4**(OOPSLA) (2020), https://doi.org/10.1145/3428240
11. Avanzini, M., Dal Lago, U., Yamada, A.: On probabilistic term rewriting. Sci. Comput. Program. **185** (2020), https://doi.org/10.1016/j.scico.2019.102338
12. Ben-Amram, A.M., Genaim, S.: Ranking functions for linear-constraint loops. J. ACM **61**(4) (2014), https://doi.org/10.1145/2629488
13. Ben-Amram, A.M., Genaim, S.: On multiphase-linear ranking functions. In: Proc. CAV '17. LNCS, vol. 10427, pp. 601–620 (2017), https://doi.org/10.1007/978-3-319-63390-9_32
14. Ben-Amram, A.M., Doménech, J.J., Genaim, S.: Multiphase-linear ranking functions and their relation to recurrent sets. In: Proc. SAS '19. LNCS, vol. 11822, pp. 459–480 (2019), https://doi.org/10.1007/978-3-030-32304-2_22
15. Bournez, O., Garnier, F.: Proving positive almost-sure termination. In: Proc. RTA '05. LNCS, vol. 3467, pp. 323–337 (2005), https://doi.org/10.1007/978-3-540-32033-3_24
16. Bournez, O., Garnier, F.: Proving positive almost sure termination under strategies. In: Proc. RTA '06. LNCS, vol. 4098, pp. 357–371 (2006), https://doi.org/10.1007/11805618_27
17. Bradley, A.R., Manna, Z., Sipma, H.B.: Linear ranking with reachability. In: Proc. CAV '05. LNCS, vol. 3576, pp. 491–504 (2005), https://doi.org/10.1007/11513988_48
18. Brockschmidt, M., Emmes, F., Falke, S., Fuhs, C., Giesl, J.: Analyzing runtime and size complexity of integer programs. ACM Trans. Program. Lang. Syst. **38**(4) (2016), https://doi.org/10.1145/2866575

19. Burstall, R.M., Darlington, J.: A transformation system for developing recursive programs. J. ACM **24**(1), 44–67 (1977), https://doi.org/10.1145/321992.321996
20. Carbonneaux, Q., Hoffmann, J., Shao, Z.: Compositional certified resource bounds. In: Proc. PLDI '15. pp. 467–478 (2015), https://doi.org/10.1145/2737924.2737955
21. Carbonneaux, Q., Hoffmann, J., Reps, T.W., Shao, Z.: Automated resource analysis with Coq proof objects. In: CAV '17. LNCS, vol. 10427, pp. 64–85 (2017), https://doi.org/10.1007/978-3-319-63390-9_4
22. Chakarov, A., Sankaranarayanan, S.: Probabilistic program analysis with martingales. In: Proc. CAV '13. LNCS, vol. 8044, pp. 511–526 (2013), https://doi.org/10.1007/978-3-642-39799-8_34
23. Chatterjee, K., Novotný, P., Zikelic, D.: Stochastic invariants for probabilistic termination. In: Proc. POPL '17. pp. 145–160 (2017), https://doi.org/10.1145/3093333.3009873
24. Chatterjee, K., Fu, H., Novotný, P., Hasheminezhad, R.: Algorithmic analysis of qualitative and quantitative termination problems for affine probabilistic programs. ACM Trans. Program. Lang. Syst. **40**(2) (2018), https://doi.org/10.1145/3174800
25. Chatterjee, K., Fu, H., Novotný, P.: Termination analysis of probabilistic programs with martingales. In: Barthe, G., Katoen, J., Silva, A. (eds.) Foundations of Probabilistic Programming, pp. 221—258. Cambridge University Press (2020), https://doi.org/10.1017/9781108770750.008
26. Ferrer Fioriti, L.M., Hermanns, H.: Probabilistic termination: Soundness, completeness, and compositionality. In: Proc. POPL '15. pp. 489–501 (2015), https://doi.org/10.1145/2676726.2677001
27. Flores-Montoya, A., Hähnle, R.: Resource analysis of complex programs with cost equations. In: Proc. APLAS '14. LNCS, vol. 8858, pp. 275–295 (2014), https://doi.org/10.1007/978-3-319-12736-1_15
28. Flores-Montoya, A.: Upper and lower amortized cost bounds of programs expressed as cost relations. In: Proc. FM '16. LNCS, vol. 9995, pp. 254–273 (2016), https://doi.org/10.1007/978-3-319-48989-6_16
29. Fu, H., Chatterjee, K.: Termination of nondeterministic probabilistic programs. In: Proc. VMCAI '19. LNCS, vol. 11388, pp. 468–490 (2019), https://doi.org/10.1007/978-3-030-11245-5_22
30. Giesl, J., Aschermann, C., Brockschmidt, M., Emmes, F., Frohn, F., Fuhs, C., Hensel, J., Otto, C., Plücker, M., Schneider-Kamp, P., Ströder, T., Swiderski, S., Thiemann, R.: Analyzing program termination and complexity automatically with AProVE. J. Autom. Reasoning **58**(1), 3–31 (2017), https://doi.org/10.1007/s10817-016-9388-y
31. Giesl, J., Rubio, A., Sternagel, C., Waldmann, J., Yamada, A.: The termination and complexity competition. In: Proc. TACAS '19. LNCS, vol. 11429, pp. 156–166 (2019), https://doi.org/10.1007/978-3-030-17502-3_10
32. Giesl, J., Giesl, P., Hark, M.: Computing expected runtimes for constant probability programs. In: Proc. CADE '19. LNAI, vol. 11716, pp. 269–286 (2019), https://doi.org/10.1007/978-3-030-29436-6_16
33. Hark, M., Kaminski, B.L., Giesl, J., Katoen, J.: Aiming low is harder: Induction for lower bounds in probabilistic program verification. Proc. ACM Program. Lang. **4**(POPL) (2020), https://doi.org/10.1145/3371105
34. Hoffmann, J., Aehlig, K., Hofmann, M.: Multivariate amortized resource analysis. ACM Trans. Program. Lang. Syst. **34**(3) (2012), https://doi.org/10.1145/2362389.2362393
35. Hoffmann, J., Shao, Z.: Type-based amortized resource analysis with integers and arrays. J. Funct. Program. **25** (2015), https://doi.org/10.1017/S0956796815000192

36. Hoffmann, J., Das, A., Weng, S.C.: Towards automatic resource bound analysis for OCaml. In: Proc. POPL '17. pp. 359–373 (2017), https://doi.org/10.1145/3009837.3009842

37. Huang, M., Fu, H., Chatterjee, K.: New approaches for almost-sure termination of probabilistic programs. In: Proc. APLAS '18. LNCS, vol. 11275, pp. 181–201 (2018), https://doi.org/10.1007/978-3-030-02768-1_11

38. Huang, M., Fu, H., Chatterjee, K., Goharshady, A.K.: Modular verification for almost-sure termination of probabilistic programs. Proc. ACM Program. Lang. 3(OOPSLA) (2019), https://doi.org/10.1145/3360555

39. Jeannet, B., Miné, A.: Apron: A library of numerical abstract domains for static analysis. In: Proc. CAV '09. pp. 661–667 (2009), https://doi.org/10.1007/978-3-642-02658-4_52

40. Kallenberg, O.: Foundations of Modern Probability. Springer, New York (2002), https://doi.org/10.1007/978-1-4757-4015-8

41. Kaminski, B.L., Katoen, J., Matheja, C., Olmedo, F.: Weakest precondition reasoning for expected runtimes of randomized algorithms. J. ACM **65** (2018), https://doi.org/10.1145/3208102

42. Kaminski, B.L., Katoen, J., Matheja, C.: Expected runtime analyis by program verification. In: Barthe, G., Katoen, J., Silva, A. (eds.) Foundations of Probabilistic Programming, pp. 185—220. Cambridge University Press (2020), https://doi.org/10.1017/9781108770750.007

43. KoAT: Web interface, binary, Docker image, and examples available at the web site https://aprove-developers.github.io/ExpectedUpperBounds/. The source code is available at https://github.com/aprove-developers/KoAT2-Releases/tree/probabilistic.

44. Kozen, D.: Semantics of probabilistic programs. J. Comput. Syst. Sci. **22**(3), 328–350 (1981), https://doi.org/10.1016/0022-0000(81)90036-2

45. McIver, A., Morgan, C.: Abstraction, Refinement and Proof for Probabilistic Systems. Springer (2005), https://doi.org/10.1007/b138392

46. McIver, A., Morgan, C., Kaminski, B.L., Katoen, J.: A new proof rule for almost-sure termination. Proc. ACM Program. Lang. **2**(POPL) (2018), https://doi.org/10.1145/3158121

47. Meyer, F., Hark, M., Giesl, J.: Inferring expected runtimes of probabilistic integer programs using expected sizes. CoRR **abs/2010.06367** (2020), https://arxiv.org/abs/2010.06367

48. Moosbrugger, M., Bartocci, E., Katoen, J., Kovács, L.: Automated termination analysis of polynomial probabilistic programs. In: Proc. ESOP '21. LNCS (2021), to appear.

49. de Moura, L., Bjørner, N.: Z3: An efficient SMT solver. In: Proc. TACAS '08. LNCS, vol. 4963, pp. 337–340 (2008), https://doi.org/10.1007/978-3-540-78800-3_24

50. Ngo, V.C., Carbonneaux, Q., Hoffmann, J.: Bounded expectations: Resource analysis for probabilistic programs. In: Proc. PLDI '18. pp. 496–512 (2018), https://doi.org/10.1145/3192366.3192394, tool artifact and benchmarks available from https://channgo2203.github.io/zips/tool_benchmark.zip

51. Noschinski, L., Emmes, F., Giesl, J.: Analyzing innermost runtime complexity of term rewriting by dependency pairs. J. Autom. Reasoning **51**(1), 27–56 (2013), https://doi.org/10.1007/s10817-013-9277-6

52. Olmedo, F., Kaminski, B.L., Katoen, J., Matheja, C.: Reasoning about recursive probabilistic programs. In: Proc. LICS '16. pp. 672–681 (2016), https://doi.org/10.1145/2933575.2935317

53. Podelski, A., Rybalchenko, A.: A complete method for the synthesis of linear ranking functions. In: Proc. VMCAI '04. LNCS, vol. 2937, pp. 239–251 (2004), https://doi.org/10.1007/978-3-540-24622-0_20
54. Puterman, M.L.: Markov Decision Processes: Discrete Stochastic Dynamic Programming. John Wiley & Sons (2005)
55. RaML (Resource Aware ML), https://www.raml.co/interface/
56. Sankaranarayanan, S., Sipma, H.B., Manna, Z.: Constraint-based linear-relations analysis. In: Proc. SAS '04. LNCS, vol. 3148, pp. 53–68 (2004), https://doi.org/10.1007/978-3-540-27864-1_7
57. Sinn, M., Zuleger, F., Veith, H.: Complexity and resource bound analysis of imperative programs using difference constraints. J. Autom. Reasoning **59**(1), 3–45 (2017), https://doi.org/10.1007/s10817-016-9402-4
58. Srikanth, A., Sahin, B., Harris, W.R.: Complexity verification using guided theorem enumeration. In: Proc. POPL '17. pp. 639–652 (2017), https://doi.org/10.1145/3009837.3009864
59. TPDB (Termination Problems Data Base), http://termination-portal.org/wiki/TPDB
60. Vardi, M.Y.: Automatic verification of probabilistic concurrent finite-state programs. In: Proc. FOCS '85. pp. 327–338 (1985), https://doi.org/10.1109/SFCS.1985.12
61. Wang, D., Kahn, D.M., Hoffmann, J.: Raising expectations: automating expected cost analysis with types. Proc. ACM Program. Lang. **4**(ICFP) (2020), https://doi.org/10.1145/3408992
62. Wang, P., Fu, H., Goharshady, A.K., Chatterjee, K., Qin, X., Shi, W.: Cost analysis of nondeterministic probabilistic programs. In: Proc. PLDI '19. pp. 204–220 (2019), https://doi.org/10.1145/3314221.3314581

Probabilistic and Systematic Coverage of Consecutive Test-Method Pairs for Detecting Order-Dependent Flaky Tests

Anjiang Wei[1], Pu Yi[1], Tao Xie[1] (✉), Darko Marinov[2], and Wing Lam[2]

[1] Peking University, Beijing, China**
{weianjiang,lukeyi,taoxie}@pku.edu.cn
[2] University of Illinois at Urbana-Champaign, Urbana, IL, USA
{marinov,winglam2}@illinois.edu

Abstract. Software developers frequently check their code changes by running a *set* of tests against their code. Tests that can nondeterministically pass or fail when run on the same code version are called *flaky tests*. These tests are a major problem because they can mislead developers to debug their recent code changes when the failures are unrelated to these changes. One prominent category of flaky tests is order-dependent (OD) tests, which can deterministically pass or fail depending on the *order* in which the set of tests are run. By detecting OD tests in advance, developers can fix these tests before they change their code. Due to the high cost required to explore all possible orders ($n!$ permutations for n tests), prior work has developed tools that randomize orders to detect OD tests. Experiments have shown that randomization can detect many OD tests, and that most OD tests depend on just one other test to fail. However, there was no analysis of the probability that randomized orders detect OD tests. In this paper, we present the first such analysis and also present a simple change for sampling random test orders to increase the probability. We finally present a novel algorithm to systematically explore all consecutive pairs of tests, guaranteeing to detect all OD tests that depend on one other test, while running substantially fewer orders and tests than simply running all test pairs.

Keywords: Flaky tests · Order dependent · Test-pair coverage

1 Introduction

The most common way that developers check their software is through frequent regression testing performed while they develop software. Developers run regression tests to check that recent code changes do not break existing functionality. A major problem for regression testing is *flaky tests* [27], which can nondeterministically pass or fail when run on the same code version. The failures from

---

** Tao Xie is with the Key Laboratory of High Confidence Software Technologies (Peking University), Ministry of Education, China, and is the corresponding author.

© The Author(s) 2021
J. F. Groote and K. G. Larsen (Eds.): TACAS 2021, LNCS 12651, pp. 270–287, 2021.
https://doi.org/10.1007/978-3-030-72016-2_15

these tests can mislead developers to debug their recent changes while the failures can be due to a variety of reasons unrelated to the changes. Many software organizations have reported flaky tests as one of their biggest problems in software development, including Apple [18], Facebook [5,10], Google [8,30,31,43,48], Huawei [16], Microsoft [11,12,20,21], and Mozilla [40].

These flaky tests are among the tests, called *test suite*, that developers run during regression testing; a test suite is most often specified as a *set*, not a sequence, of tests. Having a test suite as a set provides benefits for regression testing techniques such as selection, prioritization, and parallelization [23,45]. The test execution platform can choose to run these tests in various *test orders*. For example, for projects using Java, the most popular testing framework is JUnit [17], and the most popular build system is Maven [28]. Tests in JUnit are organized in a set of *test classes*, each of which has a set of *test methods*. By default, Maven runs tests using the Surefire plugin [29], which does not guarantee any order of test classes or test methods. However, the use of Surefire and JUnit does *not* interleave the test methods from different test classes in a test order. The same structure is common for many other testing frameworks such as TestNG [41], Cucumber [4], and Spock [38].

One prominent category of flaky tests is deterministic *order-dependent (OD) tests* [22,24,32,47], which can deterministically pass or fail in various test orders, with at least one order in which these tests pass and at least one other order in which they fail. Other flaky tests are non-deterministic (ND) tests, which are flaky due to reasons other than solely the test order [24]; for at least one test order, these tests can nondeterministically pass or fail even in that same test order. Our iDFlakies work [22] has released the iDFlakies dataset [15] of flaky tests in open-source Java projects. We obtained this dataset by running test suites many times in randomized test orders, collecting test failures, and classifying failed tests as OD or ND flaky tests. In total, 50.5% of the dataset are OD tests, while the remaining 49.5% are ND tests.

Prior research has proposed multiple tools [2,6,9,14,22,47] to detect OD tests. Some of the tools [9,14] search for *potential* OD tests and may therefore report false alarms, i.e., tests that cannot fail in the current test suite (but may fail in some extended test suite). The other tools [2,6,22,47] detect OD tests that actually fail by running multiple randomized orders of the test suite. Running tests in random orders is also available in many testing platforms, e.g., Surefire for Java has a mode to randomize the order of test classes, pytest [35] for Python has the --random-order option, and rspec [36] for Ruby has the --order random option. While these tools can detect many OD tests, the tools run random orders and hence can miss running test orders in which OD tests would fail. The listed prior work has *not* studied the *flake rates*, i.e., the probability that an OD test would fail when run in (uniformly) sampled test orders.

Our iFixFlakies work [37] has studied the *causes* of failures for OD tests. We find that the vast majority of OD tests are related to *pairs* of tests, i.e., each OD test would pass or fail due to the sharing of some global state with just one other test. Our iFixFlakies work has also defined multiple kinds of tests related to OD tests. Each OD test belongs to one of two kinds: (1) *brittle*, which is a test that fails when run by itself but passes in a test order where the test is preceded by a *state-setter*; and (2) *victim*, which is a test that passes when run by itself but fails in a test order where the test is preceded by a (state-)*polluter* unless a (state-)*cleaner* runs in between the polluter and the victim. Most of the work in this paper focuses on victim tests because most OD tests are victims rather than brittles (e.g., 91% of the truly OD tests in the iDFlakies dataset are victims [15]), and the analysis for brittles often follows as a simple special case of the analysis for victims.

This paper makes the following two main contributions.

Probability Analysis. We develop a methodology to analytically obtain the flake rates of OD tests and propose a simple change to the random sampling of test orders to increase the probability of detecting OD tests. A flake rate is defined as the ratio of the number of test orders in which an OD test fails divided by the total number of orders. Flake rates can help researchers analytically compare various algorithms (e.g., comparing reversing a passing order to sampling a random order as shown in Section 4.4) and help practitioners prioritize the fixing of flaky tests. Specifically, we study the following problem: determine the flake rate for a given victim test with its set of polluters and a set of cleaners for each polluter. We first derive simple formulas with two main assumptions: (A1) all polluters have the same set of cleaners and (A2) all of the victim, polluters, and cleaners are in the same test class. We then derive formulas that keep A1 but relax A2. Our results on 249 real flaky tests show that our formulas are applicable to 236 tests (i.e., only 13 tests violate A1). To relax both assumptions, we propose an approach to estimate the flake rate without running test orders. Our analysis finds that some OD tests have a rather low flake rate, as low as 1.2%.

Systematic Test-Pair Exploration. Because random sampling of test orders may miss test orders in which OD tests fail, we propose a systematic approach to cover all consecutive test pairs to detect OD tests. We present an algorithm that systematically explores all consecutive test pairs, guaranteeing the detection of all OD tests that depend on one other test, while running substantially fewer tests than a naive exploration that runs every pair by itself. Our algorithm builds on the concept of Tuscan squares [7], studied in the field of combinatorics. Given a test suite, the algorithm generates a set of test orders, each consisting of at least two distinct tests and at most all of the tests from the test suite, that cover all of the consecutive test pairs, while trying to minimize the cost of running those test orders. The algorithm can cover pairs of tests from the same and different classes, while considering only the test orders that do not interleave tests from different test classes, being a common constraint of testing frameworks such as JUnit [17]. Our analysis shows that the algorithm runs substantially fewer tests than naive exploration. To experiment with the new algorithm based on Tuscan squares, we run some of the test orders generated by the algorithm for some of the test suites in the iDFlakies dataset. Our experiments detect 44 new OD tests, not detected in prior work [22,24,25], and we have added the newly detected tests to the Illinois Dataset of Flaky Tests [19].

```
1   public void testMRAppMasterSuccessLock() { // testV for short
2     ... // setup MapReduce job, e.g., set conf and userName
3     MRAppMaster appMaster =
4       new MRAppMasterTest("appattempt_...", "container_...", "host", -1,
5           -1, System.currentTimeMillis(), false, false);
6     try {
7       MRAppMaster.initAndStartAppMaster(appMaster, conf, userName);
8     } catch (IOException e) { ... }
9     ... // assert the state and some properties of appMaster
10    appMaster.stop();
11  }
```

Fig. 1. Victim OD test from Hadoop's TestMRAppMaster class.

```
1   public void testSigTermedFunctionality() { // testP for short
2     JHEventHandlerForSigtermTest jheh =
3       new JHEventHandlerForSigtermTest(Mockito.mock(AppContext.class), 0);
4     jheh.addToFileMap(Mockito.mock(JobId.class));
5     ... // have jheh handle a few events
6     jheh.stop();
7     ... // assert whether the events were handled properly
8   }
```

Fig. 2. Polluter test from Hadoop's TestJobHistoryEventHandler class.

2   Background and Example

We use an example to introduce some key concepts for OD tests and to illustrate challenges in debugging these tests. We represent a test order as a sequence of tests $\langle t_1, t_2, \ldots, t_l \rangle$. In Java, each test order is executed by a Java Virtual Machine (JVM) that starts from the initial state (e.g., all shared pointer variables initialized to null) and then runs each test, which potentially modifies the shared state. Each test is run *at most once* in one JVM run. (Thus, covering test orders and test pairs has to be done with a *set* of test orders and cannot be done with just one very long order, e.g., using superpermutations [13].) A test v is a *victim* if it passes in the order $\langle v \rangle$ but fails in another order; the other order usually contains a single *polluter* test p (besides many other tests) such that v fails even in the order $\langle p, v \rangle$. Moreover, the test suite may contain a *cleaner* test c such that v passes in the order $\langle p, c, v \rangle$. Note that test orders *may contain more tests* besides polluters and cleaners for a victim v, but these other tests do not modify the relevant state and do not affect whether v passes or not in any order. Precise definitions for these tests are in our previous work [37].

Figure 1 shows a snippet of a victim test, testMRAppMasterSuccessLock (in short testV), from the widely used Hadoop project [1]. The test suite for this test has 392 tests. This test is from the MapReduce (MR) framework and aims to check an MR application. This test is a victim because it passes when run by itself but has two polluter tests. If the victim is run after either one of its polluter tests (and no cleaner runs in between the polluter and the victim), then the victim fails with a NullPointerException. Figure 2 shows a snippet of one of these two polluter tests, testSigTermedFunctionality (in short testP).

These tests form a polluter-victim pair because they share a global state, namely all "active" jobs stored in a *static* map in the JobHistoryEventHandler class. (In JUnit 4, only the heap state reachable from the class fields declared as static is shared across tests; JUnit does *not* automatically reset that state, but developers can add `setup` and `teardown` methods to reset the state.) To check an MR application, `testV` first sets up some state (Line 2), then creates an MR application (Line 3), and starts the application (Line 7). The `NullPointerException` arises when the test tries to stop the MR application (Line 10). Specifically, the `appMaster` accesses the shared map data structure that tracks all jobs run by any application. When `testV` is run after `testP`, then `appMaster` will attempt to stop a job created by the polluter, although the job has already been stopped.

This static map is empty when the JVM starts running a test order, and it is also explicitly cleared by some tests. In fact, we find 11 cleaner tests that clear the map, and the victim passes when any one of these 11 tests is run between `testP` and `testV`. Interestingly, for the other polluter test, `testTimelineEventHandling` (in short `testP'`), the victim fails for the same reason, but `testP'` has 31 cleaners—the same 11 as `testP` and 20 other cleaners. Our manual inspection finds that the `testP'` polluter has other cleaners because the job created by `testP'` is named `job_200_0001`, while the job created by the `testP` polluter is a mock object. The 20 other cleaners also create and stop jobs named `job_200_0001` and therefore act as cleaners for the `testP'` polluter but not the `testP` polluter. This example illustrates not only how victims and polluters work but also the complexity in how these tests interact with cleaners.

In Section 4.2, we explore how to compute the *flake rate* for a victim test, i.e., the probability that the test fails in a randomly sampled test order of all tests in the test suite. For this example, the 392 tests could, in theory, be run in 392! ($\sim 10^{848}$) test orders (permutations), but in practice, JUnit never interleaves test methods from different test classes. These tests are split into 48 classes that actually have $\sim 10^{234}$ test orders that JUnit could run. The relevant 34 tests (1 victim, 2 polluters, and 31 cleaners) belong to 8 test classes: 2 polluters belong to one class (`TestJobHistoryEventHandler`), 11 cleaners belong to the same class as the polluters, 1 cleaner belongs to the same class as the victim (`TestMRAppMaster`), and the remaining 19 cleaners belong to six other classes. For this victim, randomly sampling the orders that JUnit could run gives a flake rate of 4.5%. In Section 4.4, we propose a simple change to increase the probability of detecting OD tests by running a reverse of each passing test order. For this victim, the conditional probability that the reverse order fails is 4.9%.

A commonly asked question is whether all detected OD tests should be fixed. While ideally all flaky tests should be fixed, some are not fixed [21,23]. For the majority of OD tests, fixing them is good to prevent flaky-test failures that can mislead the developers into debugging the wrong parts of the code; also, fixing OD tests enables tests to be run in any order, which then enables the use of beneficial regression-testing techniques [23]. Some OD tests are intentionally run in specific orders (e.g., using the `@FixMethodOrder` annotation in JUnit) to speed up testing by reusing states. We have submitted fixes for a large number of flaky tests in our prior work [19].

3   Preliminaries

We next formalize the concepts that we have introduced informally and define some new concepts. Let $T = \{t_1, t_2, \ldots, t_n\}$ be a set of n tests partitioned in k classes $\mathbb{C} = \{C_1, C_2, \ldots, C_k\}$. We use class$(t)$ to denote the class of test t. Each class C_i has $n_i = |\{t \in T \mid \text{class}(t) = C_i\}|$ tests.

We use $\omega(T')$ to denote a test order, i.e., a permutation of tests in $T' \subseteq T$, and drop T' when clear from the context. We use ω_i to denote the i-th test in the test order ω, and $|\omega|$ to denote the length of a test order as measured by the number of tests. We use $t \prec_\omega t'$ to denote that test t is before t' in the test order ω. We will analyze some cases that allow all $n!$ permutations, potentially interleaving tests from different classes. We use $\Omega_A(T)$ to denote the set of all test orders for T. Some testing tools [47] explore all these test orders, potentially generating false alarms because most testing frameworks [4,17,38,41] do not allow all these test orders.

We are primarily concerned with *class-compatible* test orders where all tests from each class are consecutive, i.e., if class$(\omega_i) = $ class$(\omega_{i'})$, then for all j with $i < j < i'$, class$(\omega_i) = $ class(ω_j). We use $\Omega_C(T)$ to denote the set of all class-compatible test orders for T. The number of such class-compatible test orders is $k! \prod_{i=1}^{k} n_i!$. Section 4.2 presents how to compute the flake rate, i.e., the percentage of test orders in which a given victim test (with its polluters and cleaners) fails.

Section 5 presents how to systematically generate test orders to ensure that all test pairs are covered. A *test pair* $\langle t, t' \rangle$ consists of two distinct tests $t \neq t'$. We say that a test order ω *covers* a test pair $\langle t, t' \rangle$, in notation cover$(\omega, \langle t, t' \rangle)$, iff the two tests are consecutive in ω, i.e., $\omega = \langle \ldots, t, t', \ldots \rangle$. Considering consecutive tests is important because a victim may not fail if not run right after a polluter, i.e., when a cleaner is run between the polluter and the victim. A set of test orders Ω covers the union of test pairs covered by each test order $\omega \in \Omega$. In general, test orders in a set can be of different lengths. Each test order ω covers $|\omega| - 1$ test pairs.

We distinguish *intra-class* test pairs, where class$(t) = $ class(t'), and *inter-class* test pairs, where class$(t) \neq $ class(t'). Of the total $n(n-1)$ test pairs, each class C_i has $n_i(n_i - 1)$ intra-class test pairs, and the number of inter-class test pairs is $2 \sum_{1 \leq i < j \leq k} n_i n_j$. Each class-compatible test order of all T tests covers $n_i - 1$ intra-class test pairs for each class C_i and $k - 1$ inter-class test pairs.

We aim to generate a set of test orders Ω that cover all test pairs[3]. If we consider $\Omega_A(T)$ that allows all test orders, we need at least n test orders to cover all $n(n-1)$ test pairs. When we have only one class or all classes have only one test, then all test orders are class-compatible. However, consider the more common case when we have more than one class and some class has more than one test. If we consider $\Omega_C(T)$ that allows only class-compatible test orders, we need at least $\max_{i=1}^{k} n_i$ test orders to cover all intra-class test pairs and at

---

[3] This problem should not be confused with *pairwise testing* [33], which typically aims to cover pairs of values from different test parameters.

least $M = 2\sum_{1\leq i<j\leq k} n_i n_j/(k-1)$ test orders to cover all inter-class test pairs; because $M > \max_{i=1}^k n_i$, we need at least M class-compatible test orders to cover all test pairs.

More precisely, we aim to generate a set of test orders Ω that has the lowest cost for test execution. The cost for each test order ω can be modeled well as a sum of a fixed cost Cost_0 (e.g., corresponding to the time required to start a JVM and load required classes) and a cost for each test (e.g., the time to execute the test method): $\text{Cost}(\omega) = \text{Cost}_0 + \sum_{t\in\omega} \text{Cost}(t)$. The cost for a set of test orders is then simply the sum of individual costs $\text{Cost}(\Omega) = \sum_{\omega\in\Omega} \text{Cost}(\omega)$. For example, a trivial way to cover all test pairs is with a set of test orders where each test order is just a test pair: $\Omega_p = \{\langle t, t'\rangle \mid t, t' \in T \wedge t \neq t'\}$; however, the cost is unnecessarily high: $\text{Cost}(\Omega_p) = n(n-1)\text{Cost}_0 + 2(n-1)\text{Cost}(T)$, where $\text{Cost}(T) = \sum_{t\in T} \text{Cost}(t)$.

To simplify, we can assume that each test in T has the same cost, say, Cost_1, and then $\text{Cost}(\Omega_p) = n(n-1)\text{Cost}_0 + 2n(n-1)\text{Cost}_1$. In the optimal case, each test order would be a permutation of n tests covering $n-1$ test pairs, and the number of test orders would be just $n(n-1)/(n-1) = n$. Therefore, the lowest cost is $\text{Cost}(\Omega_{opt}) = n\text{Cost}_0 + n^2\text{Cost}_1$, demonstrating that the factor for Cost_0 can be substantially reduced, while the factor for Cost_1 is nearly halved ($\frac{n}{2(n-1)}$). However, in most realistic cases, due to the constraints of class-compatible test orders and the big differences in the number of tests across different classes, we cannot reach the optimal case.

3.1   Dataset for Evaluation

Besides deriving some analytical results, we also run some empirical experiments on flaky tests from Java projects. Our recent work [25] ran the iDFlakies tool on most test suites in the projects from the iDFlakies dataset [15] using the configurations recommended by our iDFlakies work [22]. Specifically, we ran 100 randomly sampled test orders from $\Omega_C(T)$ and 1 test order that is the reverse order of what Maven Surefire [29] runs by default. Note that unlike our work in Section 4.4, where we propose running a reverse test order of *every* test order where all tests passed, the one reverse order that we ran in our recent work [25] may or may not have been from a passing test order, and the reverse order is run only once and not for every passing test order.

Each project in the iDFlakies dataset is a Maven-based, Java project organized into one or more *modules*, which are (sub)directories that organize code under test and test code. Each module contains its own test suite. For the remainder of the paper, we use the 121 modules in which our recent work [25] found at least one flaky test (but not necessarily OD test). To illustrate diversity among these 121 modules, the number of classes ranges from 1 to 2215, with an average of 61, and the total number of tests ranges from 1 to 4781, with an average of 287. The number of tests per class ranges from 1 to 200, with an average of 4.8.

When we run some of the test orders generated by our systematic test-pair exploration as described in Section 5.2, we detect a total of 249 OD tests in 44 of the 121 modules. Of the 249 OD tests, 57 are brittles and 192 are victims. Compared to the OD tests detected in our prior work [22,24,25] that used the iDFlakies dataset, we find 44 new OD tests that have not been detected before. Of the 44 OD tests, 1 is brittle and 43 are victims. One of the newly detected victim tests (testMRAppMasterSuccessLock) is shown in Section 2.

4   Analysis of Flake Rate and Simple Algorithm Change

We next discuss how to compute the flake rate for each OD test. Let T be a test suite with an OD test. Prior work [22,24,25,47] would run many test orders of T and compute the flake rate for each test as a ratio of the number of test failures and the number of test runs. However, failures of flaky tests are probabilistic, and running even many test orders may not suffice to obtain the true flake rate for each test. Running more test orders is rather costly in machine time; in the limit, we may need to run all $|T|!$ permutations to obtain the true flake rate for OD tests. To reduce machine time needed for computing the flake rate for OD tests, we first propose a new procedure, and then derive formulas based on this procedure. We finally show a simple change for sampling random test orders to increase the probability of detecting OD tests.

4.1   Determining Test Outcome without Running a Test Order

We use a two-step procedure to determine the test outcome for a given OD test. We assume that some prior runs already detected the OD test, and the goal is to determine the test outcome for some new test orders that were not run.

In Step 1, we classify how each test from T relates to each OD test in a simple setting that runs only *up to three* tests. Specifically, we first determine whether an OD test t is a victim or a brittle by running the test in isolation, i.e., just $\langle t \rangle$, by itself 10 times: if t always passes, it is considered a victim (although it may be an ND test); if t always fails, it is considered a brittle (although it may be an ND test); and if t sometimes passes and sometimes fails, it is definitely an ND, not OD, test. This approach was proposed for iFixFlakies [37], and using 10 runs is a common industry practice to check whether a test is flaky [31,40].

We then find (1) for each victim, *all* its single polluters in T and also *all* single cleaners for each polluter, and (2) for each brittle, *all* its single state-setters in T. To find polluters (resp. state-setters) of a victim (resp. brittle) test, iFixFlakies [37] takes as input a test order (of entire T) where the test failed (resp. passed) and then searches the prefix of the test in that test order using delta debugging [46] (an extended version of binary search). While iFixFlakies can find all polluters (resp. state-setters) in the prefix, it does not necessarily find all polluters in T, and it takes substantial time to find these polluters using delta debugging. The experiments show that in 98% of cases, binary search finds one test to be a polluter, although some rare cases need a *polluter group* that consists of two tests.

We propose a simpler and faster approach to find polluters (resp. state-setters) for the most common case: for each victim v (resp. brittle b) and each test $t \in T \setminus \{v\}$ (resp. $t \in T \setminus \{b\}$), we run a pair of the test and the victim (resp. brittle), i.e., $\langle t, v \rangle$ (resp. $\langle t, b \rangle$). If the victim fails (resp. brittle passes), then the test t is a polluter (resp. state-setter). Further, for each victim v, its polluter p, and a test $t \in T \setminus \{v, p\}$, we run a triple of $\langle p, t, v \rangle$, and if v passes, then t is a cleaner for the pair of v and p. Note that for the same victim v, different polluters may have different cleaners such as the example presented in Section 2.

In Step 2, we determine whether each OD test passes or fails in a given test order using only the abstraction from Step 1, without actually running the test order. We focus on victims because they are more complex than brittles; brittles can be viewed as special cases with slight changes (requiring a state-setter to *run* before a brittle to pass, rather than requiring a polluter *not* to run before a victim to pass). Without loss of generality, we consider one victim at a time. Intuitively, the victim fails in a test order if a polluter is run before the victim without a cleaner between the polluter and the victim. Formally, we define the test outcome as follows.

Definition 1 (Test Outcome from Abstraction). *Let T be a test suite with one victim $v \in T$, polluters $P \subset T$, and a family of cleaners $C_p \subset T$ indexed by each polluter $p \in P$. The outcome of v in a test order ω is defined as follows:*

$$\text{fail}(\omega) \equiv \exists p \in P.\, p \prec_\omega v \wedge \nexists c \in C_p.\, p \prec_\omega c \wedge c \prec_\omega v; \quad \text{pass}(\omega) \equiv \neg\text{fail}(\omega).$$

This definition is an estimate of what one would obtain for all (repeated) runs of $|T|!$ permutations, for three main reasons: (1) tests may behave differently in test orders than in isolation [24] (and an OD test may even be an ND test in some orders [24]); (2) polluters, cleaners, and state-setters may not be single tests but groups (iFixFlakies [37] reports that groups are rather rare); and (3) a test that fails in some prefix may behave differently for the tests that come after it in a test order than when the test passes (again, iFixFlakies [37] reports this issue to be rare, finding just one such case). Despite these potential sources of error, our evaluation shows that our use of abstraction obtains flake rates similar to iDFlakies for orders that iDFlakies ran. Most importantly, our use of abstraction allows us to evaluate many more orders without actually running them, thus taking much less machine time.

4.2 Computing Flake Rate

We next define flake rate, derive formulas for computing flake rate for two cases, and show why we need to sample test orders for other cases.

Definition 2 (Flake Rate). *For a test suite T with exactly one victim, given a set of test orders $\Omega(T)$, the flake rate is defined as the ratio:*

$$f(T) = |\{\omega \in \Omega(T) \,|\, \text{fail}(\omega)\}| \,/\, |\Omega(T)|;$$

we use the subscript f_A and f_C when we need to refer specifically to the flake rate for $\Omega_A(T)$ and $\Omega_C(T)$ (defined in Section 3), respectively.

We derive the formula for flake rate based on the number of polluters P and cleaners C for two special cases. In general, computing the flake rate can ignore tests that are not *relevant*, i.e., not in $\{v\} \cup P \cup \bigcup_{p \in P} C_p$. It is easy to prove that $f(T) = f(T')$ if T and T' have the same victim, polluters, and cleaners—the reason is that the tests from $T \setminus T'$ are irrelevant in any order and do not affect the outcome of v; we omit the proof due to space limit. The further analysis thus focuses only on the relevant tests.

Special Case 1: Assume that (A1) all polluters have the same set C of cleaners: $C = C_p, \forall p \in P$; and (A2) all of the victim, polluters, and cleaners are in the same class: $\forall t, t' \in \{v\} \cup P \cup C.\text{class}(t) = \text{class}(t')$; it means that $\Omega_A(T) = \Omega_C(T)$ and $f_A = f_C$. Let $\pi = |P|$ and $\gamma = |C|$. The total number of permutations of the relevant tests is $(\pi + \gamma + 1)!$. While we can obtain $|\{\omega \in \Omega(T) \mid \text{fail}(\omega)\}|$ purely by definition, counting test orders where the victim fails, we prefer to take a probabilistic approach that will simplify further proofs. A victim fails if (1) it is not in the first position, with probability $(\pi + \gamma)/(\pi + \gamma + 1)$, and (2) its immediate predecessor is a polluter, with probability $\pi/(\pi + \gamma)$, giving the overall flake rate $f(T) = \pi/(\pi + \gamma + 1)$. This formula is simple, but real test suites often violate A1 or A2. Of the 249 tests used in our experiments, 13 violate both A1 and A2, 207 violate only A2, and only 29 do not violate either.

Special Case 2: Keeping A1 but relaxing A2, assume that the victim is in class C_1 with π_1 polluters and γ_1 cleaners, and the other $k-1$ classes have π_i polluters and γ_i cleaners, $2 \le i \le k$, where in general, either π_i or γ_i, but not both, can be zero for any class except for the victim's own class where both π_1 and γ_1 can be zero. Per Special Case 1, we have $f_A(T) = (\sum_{i=1}^{k} \pi_i)/(\sum_{i=1}^{k} \pi_i + \sum_{i=1}^{k} \gamma_i + 1)$. Next, consider class-compatible test orders, which do not interleave tests from different classes. The victim fails if (1) it fails in its own class, with probability $\pi_1/(\pi_1 + \gamma_1 + 1)$, or (2) the following three conditions hold: (2.1) the victim is the first in its own class, with probability $1/(\pi_1 + \gamma_1 + 1)$, (2.2) the class is *not* the first among classes, with probability $(k-1)/k$, and (2.3) the immediately preceding class ends with a polluter, with probability $\pi_i/(\pi_i + \gamma_i)$ for each class i and thus the probability $\sum_{i=2}^{k}(\pi_i/(\pi_i + \gamma_i))/(k-1)$ across all classes. Overall,

$$f_C(T) = \frac{\pi_1 + \frac{1}{k}\sum_{i=2}^{k} \frac{\pi_i}{\pi_i + \gamma_i}}{\pi_1 + \gamma_1 + 1}.$$

The formula is already more complex. It is important to note that we can have either $f_A(T) \ge f_C(T)$ or $f_C(T) \ge f_A(T)$, based on the ratio of polluters and cleaners in the victim's own class vs. the ratio of polluters and victims in other classes, i.e., neither set of test orders ensures a higher flake rate. We show in Section 4.3 that both cases arise in practice.

General Case: In the most general case, relaxing A1 to allow different polluters to have a different set of cleaners, while also having all these relevant tests in different classes, it appears challenging to derive a closed-form expression for $f_A(T)$, let alone for $f_C(T)$. We thus resort to estimating flake rates by sampling orders from $\Omega_A(T)$ or $\Omega_C(T)$, and counting what ratio of them fail based on Definition 1 in Section 4.3.

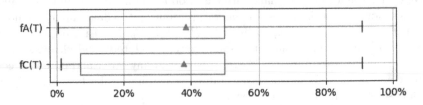

Fig. 3. Distribution of flake rate for two sets of test orders.

4.3   Comparing Flake Rate for Different Sets of Test Orders

While tools such as iDFlakies [22] incorporate the requirement of not interleaving tests from different classes in a test order, some other tools [47] do not incorporate this requirement, so they allow all test orders. Recall that $\Omega_A(T)$ denotes the set of all test orders and $\Omega_C(T)$ denotes the set of test orders that satisfy the requirement. The reason to run $\Omega_A(T)$ is to try to maximize the detection of all potential OD tests at the risk that some detected failures would be false positives. In particular, a test failure observed in some non-class-compatible order may not be reproducible in any class-compatible prefix of that order, e.g., due to the various ways to customize JUnit [17] (with annotations such as @Before, @BeforeClass, @Rule) or similar testing frameworks. The reason to run only $\Omega_C(T)$ is to detect OD-test failures that developers can observe from running the tests and are therefore motivated to fix.

While both sets of test orders can detect all true positive OD tests, it is not clear which set of test orders are *more likely* to detect *true positive* OD tests. Intuitively, running $\Omega_A(T)$ test orders can more likely detect failures if cleaners and victims are in the same class, while polluters are in different classes; in such cases, polluters are less likely to come in between cleaners and the victim. For example, for the victim presented in Section 2, the $\Omega_A(T)$ flake rate is 10.5%, while the $\Omega_C(T)$ flake rate is 4.5%. On the other hand, running $\Omega_C(T)$ test orders can more likely detect failures if polluters and victims are in the same class, while cleaners are in different classes. Similar reasoning applies to brittles: if state-setters are more often in the same test class as the brittle, then the brittle is less likely to fail than if state-setters are more often in other classes.

To compare these sets of test orders on real OD tests, we use the dataset of 192 victim and 57 brittle tests described in Section 3.1. We collect all single test polluters for each victim and all single test cleaners for each polluter-victim pair. We also collect all single test state-setters for the brittles. We then use either the formulas presented in Section 4.2 or a large number of uniformly sampled test orders to obtain the flake rates, $f_A(T)$ and $f_C(T)$, for each test. Specifically, our formulas apply for 236 of the 249 tests. For the remaining 13 tests (all victims), we sample 100,000 test orders from each of $\Omega_A(T)$ and $\Omega_C(T)$ to estimate their flake rates.

Figure 3 summarizes the results. For each set of test orders, the figure shows a boxplot that visualizes the distribution of flake rates for 249 OD tests. The

$f_A(T)$ flake rates have a slightly higher mean (38.4%) than the $f_C(T)$ flake rates (38.0%). Statistical tests for paired samples of the flake rates—specifically, dependent Student's t-test obtains a p-value of 0.47 and Wilcoxon signed-rank test obtains a p-value of 0.01—show that the differences could be statistically significant (at $\alpha = 0.05$ level). However, if we omit the 13 tests that required samplings, the means are 38.3% for $f_A(T)$ and 38.6% for $f_C(T)$, and the difference is not statistically significant (dependent Student's t-test obtains a p-value of 0.55, and Wilcoxon signed-rank test obtains a p-value of 0.19).

Prior work [6,22,24,47] has not performed any explicit comparison between the two sets of test orders. Our results demonstrate that running $\Omega_A(T)$ might be more likely to detect true positive OD tests. However, using such test orders may contain false positives. Future work on detecting OD tests should explore how to address false positives if $\Omega_A(T)$ test orders are run.

4.4   Simple Change to Increase Probability of Detecting OD Tests

Inspired by our probability analysis, we propose a simple change to increase the probability of detecting OD tests. The standard algorithm for sampling S random test orders simply repeats S times the following steps: (1) $\omega \leftarrow$ sample a random test order from possible test orders ($\Omega_A(T)$ or $\Omega_C(T)$); (2) obtain result $r \leftarrow \text{run}(\omega)$; (3) if r is FAIL, then print ω. (A variant [22] may store previously sampled test orders to avoid repetition, but the number of possible test orders is usually so large that sampling the same one is highly unlikely, so one can save space and time by not tracking previously sampled test orders.)

Our key change is to select the next test order as a *reverse* of the prior test order that passed: (4) if r is PASS, then $\omega_R \leftarrow \text{reverse}(\omega)$. The intuition for this change is that a passing order may have the polluter *after* the victim. Therefore, reversing the passing order would have the polluter *before* the victim, and thus the reverse of the passing order should have a higher probability to fail than a random order that may have the polluter before or after the victim. Note that the reverse of a class-compatible test order is also a class-compatible test order, so this change applies to $\Omega_C(T)$. The other changes are to run ω_R, print if it fails, and properly count the test orders to select exactly S samples of test orders.

We next compute the probability that the reverse of a passing order fails. **Special Case 1:** Consider the Special Case 1 scenario from Section 4.2 with π polluters and γ cleaners. For the standard algorithm, $f(T) = f_A(T) = f_C(T) = \pi/(\pi + \gamma + 1)$. For our change, the conditional probability that the second test order fails given that the first test order passes is $P(\text{fail}(\omega_R)|\text{pass}(\omega)) = P(\text{fail}(\omega_R) \wedge \text{pass}(\omega))/P(\text{pass}(\omega))$. We already have $P(\text{pass}(\omega)) = 1 - f(T) = (\gamma + 1)/(\pi + \gamma + 1)$.

To compute $P(\text{fail}(\omega_R) \wedge \text{pass}(\omega))$, we consider two cases based on the position of the victim in the passing test order ω. (1) If the victim is first, with the probability of $1/(\pi + \gamma + 1)$, then the second test should be a polluter, with the probability of $\pi/(\pi + \gamma)$, so we get $\pi/((\pi + \gamma)(\pi + \gamma + 1))$ for this case. (2) If the victim is not first, it cannot be the last in ω because otherwise, ω_R would not fail, so the victim is in the middle, with the probability of $(\pi + \gamma - 1)/(\pi + \gamma + 1)$.

We also need a cleaner right before the victim, with probability $\gamma/(\pi+\gamma)$, and a polluter right after the victim, with probability $\pi/(\pi+\gamma-1)$. Overall, we get the probability $\pi\gamma/((\pi+\gamma)(\pi+\gamma+1))$ for this case. We can sum up the two cases to get $P(\text{fail}(\omega_R) \wedge \text{pass}(\omega)) = \pi(\gamma+1)/((\pi+\gamma)(\pi+\gamma+1))$.

Finally, the conditional probability that the reverse test order fails given the first test order passes is $P(\text{fail}(\omega_R)|\text{pass}(\omega)) = (\frac{\pi(\gamma+1)}{(\pi+\gamma)(\pi+\gamma+1)})/(\frac{\gamma+1}{\pi+\gamma+1}) = \pi/(\pi+\gamma)$. This probability is strictly larger than $f(T) = \pi/(\pi+\gamma+1)$, because $\pi > 0$ must be true for the victim to be a victim.

Special Case 2: For the Special Case 2 scenario from Section 4.2, the common case is $\pi_1 + \gamma_1 > 0$ (i.e., the victim's class C_1 has at least one other relevant test). Based on the relative position of the victim in class C_1, we consider three cases: the victim runs first, in the middle, or last in class C_1. After calculating the probability for the three cases separately and summing them up, we get the probability that the reverse test order fails and the first test order passes as $P(\text{fail}(\omega_R) \wedge \text{pass}(\omega)) = \frac{\pi_1+k\pi_1\gamma_1+\pi_1 S_\gamma+\gamma_1(\pi_1+\gamma_1+1)S_\pi}{k(\pi_1+\gamma_1)(\pi_1+\gamma_1+1)}$ where $S_\pi = \sum_{i=2}^{k}\frac{\pi_i}{\pi_i+\gamma_i}$ and $S_\gamma = \sum_{i=2}^{k}\frac{\gamma_i}{\pi_i+\gamma_i}$. In Section 4.2, we have computed $P(\text{pass}(\omega))$, so dividing $P(\text{fail}(\omega_R) \wedge \text{pass}(\omega))$ by $P(\text{pass}(\omega))$ gives the conditional probability that the reverse test order fails given the first test order passes. Due to the complexity of the formulas, it is difficult to show a detailed proof that $P(\text{fail}(\omega_R)|\text{pass}(\omega)) > f(T)$, so we sample test orders instead.

When we sample both $\Omega_A(T)$ and $\Omega_C(T)$ for 100,000 random test orders on all 249 OD tests without reverse (i.e., the standard algorithm) and with reverse when a test order passes (i.e., our change), we find that our change does statistically significantly increase the chance to detect OD tests. Specifically, for $\Omega_A(T)$, test orders without reverse obtain a mean of 38.6%, while test orders with reverse of passing test orders obtain a mean of 45.3%. Statistical tests for paired samples on the flake rates without and with reverse for $\Omega_A(T)$ show a p-value of $\sim 10^{-38}$ for dependent Student's t-test and a p-value of $\sim 10^{-43}$ for Wilcoxon signed-rank test. Similarly, for $\Omega_C(T)$, test orders without reverse obtain a mean of 38.0%, while test orders with reverse of passing test orders obtain a mean of 45.3%. Statistical tests for paired samples on the flake rates without and with reverse for $\Omega_C(T)$ show a p-value of $\sim 10^{-42}$ for dependent Student's t-test and a p-value of $\sim 10^{-42}$ for Wilcoxon signed-rank test.

Based on these positive results, we have changed the iDFlakies tool [22] so that, by default, it runs the reverse of the previous order, instead of running a random order, if the previous order found no new flaky test.

5   Generating Test Orders to Cover Test Pairs

We next discuss our algorithm to generate test orders that systematically cover all test pairs for a given set T with n tests. The motivation is that even with our change to increase the probability to detect OD tests, the randomization-based sampling remains inherently probabilistic and can fail to detect an OD test.

5.1 Special Case: All Orders are Class-Compatible

We first focus on the special case where we have only one class, or many classes that each have only one test, so all $n!$ permutations are class-compatible. For example, for $n = 2$ we can cover both pairs with $\Omega_2 = \{\langle t_1, t_2 \rangle, \langle t_2, t_1 \rangle\}$, and for $n = 4$ we can cover all 12 pairs with 4 test orders $\Omega_4 = \{\langle t_1, t_4, t_2, t_3 \rangle, \langle t_2, t_1, t_3, t_4 \rangle, \langle t_3, t_2, t_4, t_1 \rangle, \langle t_4, t_3, t_1, t_2 \rangle\}$. Recall that n is the minimum number of test orders needed to cover all test pairs, so the cases for $n = 2$ and $n = 4$ are optimal. The reader is invited to consider for $n = 3$ whether we can cover all 6 test pairs with just 3 test orders. The answer is upcoming in this section.

To address this problem, we consider *Tuscan squares* [7], objects studied in the field of combinatorics. Given a natural number n, a Tuscan square consists of n rows, each of which is a permutation of the numbers $\{1, 2, \ldots, n\}$, and every pair $\langle i, j \rangle$ of distinct numbers occurs consecutively in some row. Tuscan squares are sometimes called "row-complete Latin squares" [34], but note that Tuscan squares need *not* have each column be a permutation of all numbers.

A Tuscan square of size n is equivalent to a decomposition of the complete graph on n vertices, K_n, into n Hamiltonian paths [42]. The decomposition for even n has been known since the 19th century and is often attributed to Walecki [26]. The decomposition for odd $n \geq 7$ was published in 1980 by Tillson [42]. Tillson presented a beautiful construction for $n = 4m + 3$ and a rather involved construction for $n = 4m + 1$ with a recursive step and manually constructed base case for $n = 9$. In brief, Tuscan squares can be constructed for all values of n except $n = 3$ or $n = 5$. We did not find a public implementation for generating Tuscan squares, and considering the complexity of the case $n = 4m+1$ in Tillson's construction, we have made our implementation public [44].

We can directly translate permutations from Tuscan squares into n test orders that cover all test pairs in this special case (where all test pairs are either only intra-class test pairs of one class or only inter-class test pairs of n classes). These sets of test orders have the minimal possible cost: $\text{Cost}(\Omega_n) = n(\text{Cost}_0 + \text{Cost}(T))$, substantially lower than $\text{Cost}(\Omega_p)$ for running all test pairs in isolation. For $n = 3$ and $n = 5$, we have to use 4 and 6 test orders, respectively, to cover all test orders. For example, for $n = 3$ we can cover all 6 pairs with 4 orders $\{\langle t_1, t_2, t_3 \rangle, \langle t_2, t_1, t_3 \rangle, \langle t_3, t_1 \rangle, \langle t_3, t_2 \rangle\}$.

5.2 General Case

Algorithm 1 shows the pseudo-code algorithm to generate test orders that cover all test pairs in the general case where we have more than one class and at least one class has more than one test. The main function calls two functions to generate test orders that cover intra-class and inter-class test pairs.

The function `cover_intra_class_pairs` generates test orders that cover all intra-class test pairs. For each class, the function `compute_tuscan_square` is used to generate test orders of tests within the class to cover all intra-class test pairs. These test orders for each class are then appended to form a test order for the entire test suite T. The function `pick`, invoked on multiple lines,

---

Algorithm 1: Generate test orders that cover all intra-test-class and inter-test-class test-method pairs

```
 1  Input: T          # test suite, a set of test methods partitioned into test classes
 2  Output: Ω                                      # output is a set of test orders
 3  Function cover_all_pairs():
 4  |    Ω = {}                                                       # empty set
 5  |    cover_intra_class_pairs()
 6  |    cover_inter_class_pairs()

 7  Function cover_intra_class_pairs():
 8  |    map = {}                    # map each class to all its intra-class orders
 9  |    for C ∈ classes(T) do
10  |    |    map = map ∪ {⟨C, ωC⟩ | ωC ∈ compute_tuscan_square(C)}
11  |    while map ≠ {} do
12  |    |    ω = ⟨⟩                                             # empty order
13  |    |    Cs = {C | ∃ωC. ⟨C, ωC⟩ ∈ map}
14  |    |    for C ∈ Cs do
15  |    |    |    ωC = pick({ωC | ⟨C, ωC⟩ ∈ map})
16  |    |    |    map = map \ {⟨C, ωC⟩}
17  |    |    |    ω = ω ⊕ ωC                                   # append order
18  |    |    Ω = Ω ∪ {ω}

19  Function cover_inter_class_pairs():
20  |    pairs = {⟨t, t′⟩ | t, t′ ∈ T ∧ class(t) ≠ class(t′)}\   # from all inter-class pairs..
21  |          {⟨t, t′⟩ | ∃ω ∈ Ω. cover(ω, ⟨t, t′⟩)}   # ..remove covered by intra-class orders
22  |    while pairs ≠ {} do
23  |    |    ω = pick(pairs)        # start with a randomly chosen not-covered pair
24  |    |    pairs = pairs \ {ω}
25  |    |    while true do
26  |    |    |    tp = ω|ω|−1                            # previously last test
27  |    |    |    ts = {t | ⟨tp, t⟩ ∈ pairs ∧ class(t) ∉ classes(ω)}
28  |    |    |    if ts = {} then
29  |    |    |    |    break
30  |    |    |    tn = pick(ts)                          # next test to extend order
31  |    |    |    pairs = pairs\{⟨tp, tn⟩}
32  |    |    |    ω = ω ⊕ tn
33  |    |    Ω = Ω ∪ {ω}
```

---

chooses a random element from a set. The outer loop iterates as many times as the maximum number of intra-class test orders for any class. When the loop finishes, Ω contains a set of test orders that cover *all intra-class* and *some inter-class* test pairs. Each test order that concatenates tests from l classes covers $l - 1$ inter-class test pairs. (Using just these test orders, we already detected 44 new OD tests in the test suites from the iDFlakies dataset.) Each intra-class test pair is covered by exactly one test order. Modulo the special cases for $n = 3$ and $n = 5$, each *covered* inter-class pair appears in *exactly one* test order in Ω, because Tuscan squares satisfy the invariant that each element appears only once as the first and once as the last in the permutations in a Tuscan square.

The function `cover_inter_class_pairs` generates more test orders to cover the remaining inter-class test pairs. It uses a greedy algorithm to first initialize a test order with a randomly selected not-covered test pair and then extend the test order with a randomly selected not-covered test pair as long as an appropriate test pair exists. Extending the test order as long as possible reduces both the number of test orders and the number of times each test needs to be run.

We evaluate our randomized algorithm on 121 modules from the iDFlakies dataset as described in Section 3.1. We use the total cost, which considers the number of test orders and the number of tests in all of those test orders. The number of test orders is related to $Cost_0$, while the number of tests is related to $Cost_1$ as defined in Section 3. We run our algorithm 10 times for various random seeds. The coefficient of variation [3] for each module shows that the algorithm is fairly stable, with the average for all modules being only 1.1% and 0.25% for the number of test orders and the number of tests, respectively.

Compared with Ω_p that has all test orders of just test pairs, our randomized algorithm's average number of test orders and the average number of tests are only 3.68% and 51.8%, respectively, that of all the Ω_p test orders. The overall cost of the test orders generated by our randomized algorithm is close to the optimal, because the number of test orders is reduced by almost two orders of magnitude, and 51.8% of the number of tests is close to the theoretical minimum of 50% that of Ω_p test orders for $Cost_1$.

6   Conclusion

Order-dependent (OD) tests are one prominent category of flaky tests. Prior work [22,24,47] has used randomized test orders to detect OD tests. In this paper, we have presented the first analysis of the probability that randomized test orders detect OD tests. We have also proposed a simple change for sampling random test orders to increase the probability of detecting OD tests. We have finally proposed a novel algorithm that systematically explores all consecutive pairs of tests, guaranteeing to find all OD tests that depend on one other test. Our experimental results show that our algorithm runs substantially fewer tests than a naive exploration that runs all pairs of tests. Our runs of some test orders generated by the algorithm detect 44 new OD tests, not detected in prior work [22,24,25] on the same evaluation dataset.

Acknowledgments

We are grateful to Peter Taylor for a StackExchange post [39] that led us to the concept of Tuscan squares. We thank Dragan Stevanović, Wenyu Wang, and Zhengkai Wu for discussions about Tuscan squares and Reed Oei for comments on the paper draft. This work was partially supported by NSF grants CNS-1564274, CNS-1646305, CCF-1763788, and CCF-1816615. We also acknowledge support for research on flaky tests from Facebook and Google.

References

1. Apache Hadoop (2020), https://github.com/apache/hadoop
2. Bell, J., Kaiser, G., Melski, E., Dattatreya, M.: Efficient dependency detection for safe Java test acceleration. In: ESEC/FSE (2015)
3. Coefficient of variation (2020), https://en.wikipedia.org/wiki/Coefficient_of_variation
4. Cucumber (2020), https://cucumber.io/docs/cucumber
5. Facebook testing and verification request for proposals (2019), https://research.fb.com/programs/research-awards/proposals/facebook-testing-and-verification-request-for-proposals-2019
6. Gambi, A., Bell, J., Zeller, A.: Practical test dependency detection. In: ICST (2018)
7. Golomb, S.W., Taylor, H.: Tuscan squares – A new family of combinatorial designs. Ars Combinatoria (1985)
8. Google: Avoiding flakey tests (2008), http://googletesting.blogspot.com/2008/04/tott-avoiding-flakey-tests.html
9. Gyori, A., Shi, A., Hariri, F., Marinov, D.: Reliable testing: Detecting state-polluting tests to prevent test dependency. In: ISSTA (2015)
10. Harman, M., O'Hearn, P.: From start-ups to scale-ups: Opportunities and open problems for static and dynamic program analysis. In: SCAM (2018)
11. Herzig, K., Greiler, M., Czerwonka, J., Murphy, B.: The art of testing less without sacrificing quality. In: ICSE (2015)
12. Herzig, K., Nagappan, N.: Empirically detecting false test alarms using association rules. In: ICSE (2015)
13. Houston, R.: Tackling the minimal superpermutation problem (2014), arXiv
14. Huo, C., Clause, J.: Improving oracle quality by detecting brittle assertions and unused inputs in tests. In: FSE (2014)
15. iDFlakies: Flaky test dataset (2020), https://sites.google.com/view/flakytestdataset
16. Jiang, H., Li, X., Yang, Z., Xuan, J.: What causes my test alarm? Automatic cause analysis for test alarms in system and integration testing. In: ICSE (2017)
17. JUnit (2020), https://junit.org
18. Kowalczyk, E., Nair, K., Gao, Z., Silberstein, L., Long, T., Memon, A.: Modeling and ranking flaky tests at Apple. In: ICSE SEIP (2020)
19. Lam, W.: Illinois Dataset of Flaky Tests (IDoFT) (2020), http://mir.cs.illinois.edu/flakytests
20. Lam, W., Godefroid, P., Nath, S., Santhiar, A., Thummalapenta, S.: Root causing flaky tests in a large-scale industrial setting. In: ISSTA (2019)
21. Lam, W., Muşlu, K., Sajnani, H., Thummalapenta, S.: A study on the lifecycle of flaky tests. In: ICSE (2020)
22. Lam, W., Oei, R., Shi, A., Marinov, D., Xie, T.: iDFlakies: A framework for detecting and partially classifying flaky tests. In: ICST (2019)
23. Lam, W., Shi, A., Oei, R., Zhang, S., Ernst, M.D., Xie, T.: Dependent-test-aware regression testing techniques. In: ISSTA (2020)
24. Lam, W., Winter, S., Astorga, A., Stodden, V., Marinov, D.: Understanding reproducibility and characteristics of flaky tests through test reruns in Java projects. In: ISSRE (2020)
25. Lam, W., Winter, S., Wei, A., Xie, T., Marinov, D., Bell, J.: A large-scale longitudinal study of flaky tests. In: OOPSLA (2020)
26. Lucas, E.: Récréations mathématiques (1894)

27. Luo, Q., Hariri, F., Eloussi, L., Marinov, D.: An empirical analysis of flaky tests. In: FSE (2014)
28. Maven (2020), https://maven.apache.org
29. Maven Surefire plugin (2020), https://maven.apache.org/surefire/maven-surefire-plugin
30. Memon, A., Gao, Z., Nguyen, B., Dhanda, S., Nickell, E., Siemborski, R., Micco, J.: Taming Google-scale continuous testing. In: ICSE SEIP (2017)
31. Micco, J.: The state of continuous integration testing at Google. In: ICST (2017)
32. Muşlu, K., Soran, B., Wuttke, J.: Finding bugs by isolating unit tests. In: ESEC/FSE (2011)
33. Nie, C., Leung, H.: A survey of combinatorial testing. ACM Comput. Surv. (2011)
34. Ollis, M.: Sequenceable groups and related topics. Electronic Journal of Combinatorics (2013)
35. pytest (2020), https://docs.pytest.org
36. RSpec (2020), https://rspec.info
37. Shi, A., Lam, W., Oei, R., Xie, T., Marinov, D.: iFixFlakies: A framework for automatically fixing order-dependent flaky tests. In: ESEC/FSE (2019)
38. Spock (2019), http://docs.spockframework.org
39. StackExchange – Covering pairs with permutations (2020), https://math.stackexchange.com/questions/1769877/covering-pairs-with-permutations
40. Test Verification (2019), https://developer.mozilla.org/en-US/docs/Mozilla/QA/Test_Verification
41. TestNG (2019), https://testng.org/doc/documentation-main.html
42. Tillson, T.W.: A Hamiltonian decomposition of K_{2m}^*, $2m \geq 8$. Journal of Combinatorial Theory, Series B (1980)
43. TotT: Avoiding flakey tests (2019), http://goo.gl/vHE47r
44. TuscanSquare (2020), https://github.com/Anjiang-Wei/TuscanSquare
45. Yoo, S., Harman, M.: Regression testing minimization, selection and prioritization: A survey. Software Testing, Verification & Reliability (2012)
46. Zeller, A., Hildebrandt, R.: Simplifying and isolating failure-inducing input. TSE (2002)
47. Zhang, S., Jalali, D., Wuttke, J., Muşlu, K., Lam, W., Ernst, M.D., Notkin, D.: Empirically revisiting the test independence assumption. In: ISSTA (2014)
48. Ziftci, C., Reardon, J.: Who broke the build?: Automatically identifying changes that induce test failures in continuous integration at Google scale. In: ICSE (2017)

Timed Systems

Timed Automata Relaxation for Reachability

Jaroslav Bendík ✉[1], Ahmet Sencan[2], Ebru Aydin Gol[2], and Ivana Černá[1]

[1] Faculty of Informatics, Masaryk University, Brno, Czech Republic
{xbendik,cerna}@fi.muni.cz
[2] Department of Computer Engineering, Middle East Technical University, Ankara, Turkey {sencan.ahmet,ebrugol}@metu.edu.tr

Abstract. Timed automata (TA) have shown to be a suitable formalism for modeling real-time systems. Moreover, modern model-checking tools allow a designer to check whether a TA complies with the system specification. However, the exact timing constraints of the system are often uncertain during the design phase. Consequently, the designer is able to build a TA with a correct structure, however, the timing constraints need to be tuned to make the TA comply with the specification.

In this work, we assume that we are given a TA together with an existential property, such as reachability, that is not satisfied by the TA. We propose a novel concept of a minimal sufficient reduction (MSR) that allows us to identify the minimal set S of timing constraints of the TA that needs to be tuned to meet the specification. Moreover, we employ mixed-integer linear programming to actually find a tuning of S that leads to meeting the specification.

Keywords: Timed Automata · Relaxation · Design · Reachability.

1   Introduction

A timed automaton (TA) [4] is a finite automaton extended with a set of real-time variables, called clocks, which capture the time. The clocks enrich the semantics and the constraints on the clocks restrict the behavior of the automaton, which are particularly important in modeling time-critical systems. The examples of TA models of critical systems include scheduling of real-time systems [30,29,33], medical devices [43,38], and rail-road crossing systems [52].

Model-checking methods allow for verifying whether a given TA meets a given system specification. Contemporary model-checking tools, such as UPPAAL [17] or Imitator [9], have proved to be practically applicable on various industrial case studies [17,10,34]. Unfortunately, during the system design phase, the system information is often incomplete. A designer is often able to build a TA with correct structure, i.e., exactly capturing locations and transitions of the modeled system, however the exact clock (timing) constraints that enable/trigger the transitions are uncertain. Thus, the produced TA often does not meet the specification (i.e., it does not pass the model-checking) and it needs to be fixed. If the specification declares universal properties, e.g., safety or unavoidability, that need to hold on

ⓒ The Author(s) 2021
J. F. Groote and K. G. Larsen (Eds.): TACAS 2021, LNCS 12651, pp. 291–310, 2021.
https://doi.org/10.1007/978-3-030-72016-2_16

each trace of the TA, a model-checker either returns "yes", or it returns "no" and generates a trace along which the property is violated. This trace can be used to repair the model in an automated way [42]. However, in the case of existential properties, such as reachability, the property has to hold on a trace of the TA. The model-checker either returns "yes" and generates a witness trace satisfying the property, or returns just "no" and does not provide any additional information that would help the designer to correct the TA.

Contribution. In this paper, we study the following problem: given a timed automaton $\mathcal{A}$ and a reachability property that is not satisfied by $\mathcal{A}$, relax clock constraints of $\mathcal{A}$ such that the resultant automaton $\mathcal{A}'$ satisfies the reachability property. Moreover, the goal is to minimize the number of the relaxed clock constraints and, secondary, also to minimize the overall change of the timing constants used in the clock constraints. We propose a two step solution for this problem. In the first step, we identify a *minimal sufficient reduction (MSR)* of $\mathcal{A}$, i.e., an automaton $\mathcal{A}''$ that satisfies the reachability property and originates from $\mathcal{A}$ by removing only a minimal necessary set of clock constraints. In the second step, instead of completely removing the clock constraints, we employ mixed integer linear programming (MILP) to find a minimal relaxation of the constraints that leads to a satisfaction of the reachability property along a witness path.

The underlying assumption is that during the design the most suitable timing constants reflecting the system properties are defined. Thus, our goal is to generate a TA satisfying the reachability property by changing a minimum number of timing constants. Some of the constraints of the initial TA can be strict (no relaxation is possible), which can easily be integrated to the proposed solution. Thus, the proposed method can be viewed as a way to handle design uncertainties: develop a TA $\mathcal{A}$ in a best-effort basis and apply our algorithm to find a $\mathcal{A}'$ that is *as close as* possible to $\mathcal{A}$ and satisfies the given reachability property.

Related Work. Another way to handle uncertainties about timing constants is to build a *parametric* timed automaton (PTA), i.e., a TA where clock constants can be represented with parameters. Subsequently, a parameter synthesis tool, such as [46,9,26], can be used to find suitable values of the parameters for which the resultant TA satisfies the specification. However, most of the parameter synthesis problems are undecidable [6]. While symbolic algorithms without termination guarantees exist for some subclasses [25,39,12], these algorithms are computationally very expensive compared to model checking (see [5]). Moreover, minimizing the number of modified clock constraints is not straightforward.

A related TA repair problem has been studied in a recent work [7], where the authors also assumed that some of the constraints are incorrect. To repair the TA, they parametrized the initial TA and generated parameters by analyzing traces of the TA. However, the authors [7] do not focus on repairing the TA w.r.t. reachability properties as we do. Instead, their goal is to make the TA compliant with an oracle that decides if a trace of the TA belongs to a system or not. Thus, their approach cannot handle reachability properties. Furthermore in [7], the total change of the timing constraints is minimized, while we primarily minimize the number of changed constraints, then the total change.

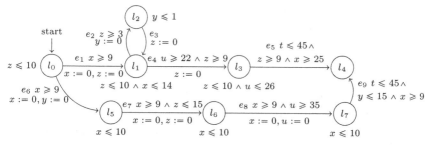

Fig. 1. An example of a timed automaton.

2 Preliminaries and Problem Formulation

2.1 Timed Automata

A *timed automaton* (TA) [3,4,44] is a finite-state machine extended with a finite set C of real-valued clocks. A *clock* $x \in C$ measures the time spent after its last reset. In a TA, clock constraints are defined for locations (states) and transitions. A *simple clock constraint* is defined as $x - y \sim c$ where $x, y \in C \cup \{0\}$, $\sim \in \{<, \leqslant\}$ and $c \in \mathbb{Z} \cup \{\infty\}$.[3] Simple clock constraints and constraints obtained by combining these with conjunction operator ($\wedge$) are called *clock constraints*. The sets of simple and all clock constraints are denoted by $\varPhi_S(C)$ and $\varPhi(C)$, respectively. For a clock constraint $\phi \in \varPhi(C)$, $\mathcal{S}(\phi)$ denotes the simple constraints from ϕ, e.g., $\mathcal{S}(x - y < 10 \wedge y \leqslant 20) = \{x - y < 10, y \leqslant 20\}$. A *clock valuation* $v : C \to \mathbb{R}_+$ assigns non-negative real values to each clock. The notation $v \models \phi$ denotes that the clock constraint ϕ evaluates to true when each clock x is replaced with $v(x)$. For a clock valuation v and $d \in \mathbb{R}_+$, $v + d$ is the clock valuation obtained by *delaying* each clock by d, i.e., $(v + d)(x) = v(x) + d$ for each $x \in C$. For $\lambda \subseteq C$, $v[\lambda := 0]$ is the clock valuation obtained after *resetting* each clock from λ, i.e., $v[\lambda := 0](x) = 0$ for each $x \in \lambda$ and $v[\lambda := 0](x) = v(x)$ for each $x \in C \backslash \lambda$.

Definition 1 (Timed Automata). *A timed automaton* $\mathcal{A} = (L, l_0, C, \Delta, Inv)$ *is a tuple, where L is a finite set of locations, $l_0 \in L$ is the initial location, C is a finite set of clocks, $\Delta \subseteq L \times 2^C \times \varPhi(C) \times L$ is a finite transition relation, and $Inv : L \to \varPhi(C)$ is an invariant function.*

For a transition $e = (l_s, \lambda, \phi, l_t) \in \Delta$, l_s is the source location, l_t is the target location, λ is the set of clocks reset on e and ϕ is the guard (i.e., a clock constraint) tested for enabling e. The semantics of a TA is given by a labelled transition system (LTS). An LTS is a tuple $\mathcal{T} = (S, s_0, \Sigma, \to)$, where S is a set of states, $s_0 \in S$ is an initial state, Σ is a set of symbols, and $\to \subseteq S \times \Sigma \times S$ is a transition relation. A transition $(s, a, s') \in \to$ is also shown as $s \xrightarrow{a} s'$.

Definition 2 (LTS semantics for TA). *Given a TA $\mathcal{A} = (L, l_0, C, \Delta, Inv)$, the labelled transition system $T(\mathcal{A}) = (S, s_0, \Sigma, \to)$ is defined as follows:*

---

[3] Simple constraints are only defined as upper bounds to ease the presentation. This definition is not restrictive since $x - y \geqslant c$ and $x \geqslant c$ are equivalent to $y - x \leqslant -c$ and $0 - x \leqslant -c$, respectively. A similar argument holds for strict inequality ($>$).

- $S = \{(l, v) \mid l \in L, v \in \mathbb{R}_+^{|C|}, v \models Inv(l)\}$,
- $s_0 = (l_0, \mathbf{0})$, where $\mathbf{0}(x) = 0$ for each $x \in C$,
- $\Sigma = \{act\} \cup \mathbb{R}_+$, and
- the transition relation $\rightarrow$ is defined by the following rules:
  - delay transition: $(l, v) \xrightarrow{d} (l, v + d)$ if $v + d \models Inv(l)$
  - discrete transition: $(l, v) \xrightarrow{act} (l', v')$ if there exists $(l, \lambda, \phi, l') \in \Delta$ such that $v \models \phi$, $v' = v[\lambda := 0]$, and $v' \models Inv(l')$.

The notation $s \rightarrow_d s'$ is used to denote a delay transition of duration d followed by a discrete transition from s to s', i.e., $s \xrightarrow{d} s \xrightarrow{act} s'$. A run ρ of $\mathcal{A}$ is either a finite or an infinite alternating sequence of delay and discrete transitions, i.e., $\rho = s_0 \rightarrow_{d_0} s_1 \rightarrow_{d_1} s_2 \rightarrow_{d_2} \cdots$. The set of all runs of $\mathcal{A}$ is denoted by $[[\mathcal{A}]]$.

A path π of $\mathcal{A}$ is an interleaving sequence of locations and transitions, $\pi = l_0, e_1, l_1, e_2, \ldots$, where $e_{i+1} = (l_i, \lambda_{i+1}, \phi_{i+1}, l_{i+1}) \in \Delta$ for each $i \geq 0$. A path $\pi = l_0, e_1, l_1, e_2, \ldots$ is said to be realizable if there exists a delay sequence $d_0, d_1, \ldots$ such that $(l_0, \mathbf{0}) \rightarrow_{d_0} (l_1, v_1) \rightarrow_{d_1} (l_1, v_2) \rightarrow_{d_2} \cdots$ is a run of $\mathcal{A}$ and for every $i \geq 1$, the ith discrete transition is taken according to e_i, i.e., $e_i = (l_{i-1}, \lambda_i, \phi_i, l_i)$, $v_{i-1} + d_{i-1} \models \phi_i$, $v_i = (v_{i-1} + d_{i-1})[\lambda_i := 0]$ and $v_i \models Inv'(l_i)$.

Given a TA $\mathcal{A}$, a subset $L_T \subset L$ of its locations is reachable on $\mathcal{A}$ if there exists $\rho = (l_0, \mathbf{0}) \rightarrow_{d_0} (l_1, v_1) \rightarrow_{d_1} \cdots \rightarrow_{d_{n-1}} (l_n, v_n) \in [[\mathcal{A}]]$ such that $l_n \in L_T$; otherwise, L_T is unreachable. The reachability problem is decidable and implemented in various verification tools, e.g., [17,9]. The verifier either returns "No" when the location is unreachable, or it generates a run (witness) reaching the set L_T.

Example 1. Figure 1 illustrates a TA with 8 locations: $\{l_0, \ldots, l_7\}$, 9 transitions: $\{e_1, \ldots, e_9\}$, an initial location l_0, and an unreachable set of locations $L_T = \{l_4\}$.

2.2 Timed Automata Relaxations and Reductions

For a timed automaton $\mathcal{A} = (L, l_0, C, \Delta, Inv)$, the set of pairs of transition and associated simple constraints is defined in (1) and the set of pairs of location and associated simple constraints is defined in (2).

$$\Psi(\Delta) = \{(e, \varphi) \mid e = (l_s, \lambda, \phi, l_t) \in \Delta, \varphi \in \mathcal{S}(\phi)\} \tag{1}$$

$$\Psi(Inv) = \{(l, \varphi) \mid l \in L, \varphi \in \mathcal{S}(Inv(l))\} \tag{2}$$

Definition 3 (constraint-relaxation). *Let $\phi \in \Phi(C)$ be a constraint over C, $\Theta \subseteq \mathcal{S}(\phi)$ be a subset of its simple constraints and $\mathbf{r} : \Theta \rightarrow \mathbb{N} \cup \{\infty\}$ be a positive valued relaxation valuation. The relaxed constraint is defined as:*

$$R(\phi, \Theta, \mathbf{r}) = \left(\bigwedge_{\varphi \in \mathcal{S}(\phi) \setminus \Theta} \varphi \right) \wedge \left(\bigwedge_{\varphi = x - y \sim c \in \Theta} x - y \sim c + \mathbf{r}(\varphi) \right) \tag{3}$$

Intuitively, $R(\phi, \Theta, \mathbf{r})$ relaxes only the thresholds of simple constraints from Θ with respect to $\mathbf{r}$, e.g., $R(x - y \leq 10 \wedge y < 20, \{y < 20\}, \mathbf{r}) = x - y \leq 10 \wedge y < 23$, where $\mathbf{r}(y < 20) = 3$. Setting a threshold to ∞ implies removing the corresponding simple constraint, e.g., $R(x - y \leq 10 \wedge y < 20, \{y < 20\}, \mathbf{r}) = x - y \leq 10$, where $\mathbf{r}(y < 20) = \infty$. Note that $R(\phi, \Theta, \mathbf{r}) = \phi$ when Θ is empty.

Definition 4 ($(D, I, \mathbf{r})$-relaxation). *Let $\mathcal{A} = (L, l_0, C, \Delta, Inv)$ be a TA, $D \subseteq \Psi(\Delta)$ and $I \subseteq \Psi(Inv)$ be transition and location constraint sets, and $\mathbf{r} : D \cup I \to \mathbb{N} \cup \{\infty\}$ be a positive valued relaxation valuation. The $(D, I, \mathbf{r})$-relaxation of $\mathcal{A}$, denoted $\mathcal{A}_{<D,I,\mathbf{r}>}$, is a TA $\mathcal{A}' = (L', l_0', C', \Delta', Inv')$ such that:*

- *$L = L'$, $l_0 = l_0'$, $C = C'$, and*
- *Δ' originates from Δ by relaxing D via $\mathbf{r}$. For $e = (l_s, \lambda, \phi, l_t) \in \Delta$, let $D|_e = \{\varphi \mid (e, \varphi) \in D\}$, and let $\mathbf{r}|_e(\varphi) = \mathbf{r}(e, \varphi)$, then $\Delta' = \{(l_s, \lambda, R(\phi, D|_e, \mathbf{r}|_e), l_t) \mid e = (l_s, \lambda, \phi, l_t) \in \Delta\}$*
- *Inv' originates from Inv by relaxing I via $\mathbf{r}$. For $l \in L$, let $I|_l = \{\varphi \mid (l, \varphi) \in I\}$, and $\mathbf{r}|_l(\varphi) = \mathbf{r}(l, \varphi)$, then $Inv'(l) = R(Inv(l), I|_l, \mathbf{r}|_l)$.*

Intuitively, the TA $\mathcal{A}_{<D,I,\mathbf{r}>}$ emerges from $\mathcal{A}$ by relaxing the guards of the transitions from the set D and relaxing invariants of the locations from I with respect to $\mathbf{r}$. In the special case of setting the threshold of each constraint from D and I to ∞, i.e., when $\mathbf{r}(a) = \infty$ for each $a \in D \cup I$, the corresponding simple constraints are effectively removed, which is called a (D,I)-reduction and denoted by $\mathcal{A}_{<D,I>}$. Note that $\mathcal{A} = \mathcal{A}_{<\varnothing,\varnothing>}$.

Proposition 1. *Let $\mathcal{A} = (L, l_0, C, \Delta, Inv)$ be a timed automaton, $D \subseteq \Psi(\Delta)$ and $I \subseteq \Psi(Inv)$ be sets of simple guard and invariant constraints, and $\mathbf{r} : D \cup I \to \mathbb{N} \cup \{\infty\}$ be a relaxation valuation. Then $[[\mathcal{A}]] \subseteq [[\mathcal{A}_{<D,I,\mathbf{r}>}]]$.*

Proof. Observe that for a clock constraint $\phi \in \Phi(C)$, a subset of its simple constraints $\Theta \subseteq \mathcal{S}(\phi)$, a relaxation valuation $\mathbf{r}'$ for Θ, and the relaxed constraint $R(\phi, \Theta, \mathbf{r}')$ as in Definition 3, it holds that for any clock valuation $v : v \models \phi \implies v \models R(\phi, \Theta, \mathbf{r}')$. Now, consider a run $\rho = (l_0, \mathbf{0}) \to_{d_0} (l_1, v_1) \to_{d_1} (l_2, v_2) \to_{d_2} \cdots \in [[\mathcal{A}]]$. Let $\pi = l_0, e_1, l_1, e_2, \ldots$ with $e_i = (l_{i-1}, \lambda_i, \phi_i, l_i) \in \Delta$ for each $i \geq 1$ be the path realized as ρ via delay sequence $d_0, d_1, \ldots$. By Definition 4 for each $(l, \lambda, \phi, l') \in \Delta$, there is $(l, \lambda, R(\phi, D|_e, \mathbf{r}|_e), l') \in \Delta'$. We define a path induced by π on $\mathcal{A}_{<D,I,\mathbf{r}>}$ as:

$$M(\pi) = l_0, (l_0, \lambda_1, R(\phi_1, D|_{e_1}, \mathbf{r}|_{e_1}), l_1), l_1, (l_1, \lambda_2, R(\phi_2, D|_{e_2}, \mathbf{r}|_{e_2}), l_2), \ldots \quad (4)$$

For each $i = 0, \ldots, n - 1$ it holds that $v_i \models R(Inv(l_i), D|_{l_i}, \mathbf{r}|_{l_i})$, $v_i + d_i \models R(Inv(l_i), D|_{l_i}, \mathbf{r}|_{l_i})$ and $v_i + d_i \models R(\phi_{i+1}, D|_{e_{i+1}}, \mathbf{r}|_{e_{i+1}})$. Thus $M(\pi)$ is realizable on $\mathcal{A}_{<D,I,\mathbf{r}>}$ via the same delay sequence and $\rho \in [[\mathcal{A}_{<D,I,\mathbf{r}>}]]$. As $\rho \in [[\mathcal{A}]]$ is arbitrary, we conclude that $[[\mathcal{A}]] \subseteq [[\mathcal{A}_{<D,I,\mathbf{r}>}]]$.

2.3 Problem Statement

Problem 1. Given a TA $\mathcal{A} = (L, l_0, C, \Delta, Inv)$ and a set of target locations $L_T \subset L$ that is unreachable on $\mathcal{A}$, find a $(D, I, \mathbf{r})$-relaxation $\mathcal{A}_{<D,I,\mathbf{r}>}$ of $\mathcal{A}$ such that L_T is reachable on $\mathcal{A}_{<D,I,\mathbf{r}>}$. Moreover, the goal is to identify a $(D, I, \mathbf{r})$-relaxation that minimizes the number $|D \cup I|$ of relaxed constraints, and, secondary, we tend to minimize the overall change of the clock constraints $\sum_{c \in D \cup I} \mathbf{r}(c)$.

We propose a two step solution to this problem. In the first step, we identify a subset $D \cup I$ of the simple constraints $\Psi(\Delta) \cup \Psi(Inv)$ such that L_T is reachable on the (D, I)-reduction $\mathcal{A}_{<D,I>}$ and $|D \cup I|$ is minimized. Consequently, we can obtain a witness path of the reachability on $\mathcal{A}_{<D,I>}$ from the verifier. The path would be realizable on $\mathcal{A}$ if we remove the constraints $D \cup I$. In the second step, instead of completely removing the constraints $D \cup I$, we find a relaxation valuation $\mathbf{r} : D \cup I \to \mathbb{N} \cup \{\infty\}$ such that the path found in the first step is realizable on $\mathcal{A}_{<D,I,\mathbf{r}>}$. To find $\mathbf{r}$, we introduce relaxation parameters for constraints in $D \cup I$. Subsequently, we solve an MILP problem to find a valuation of the parameters, i.e., $\mathbf{r}$, that makes the path realizable on $\mathcal{A}_{<D,I,\mathbf{r}>}$ and minimizes $\sum_{c \in D \cup I} \mathbf{r}(c)$. Note that it might be the case that the reduction $\mathcal{A}_{<D,I>}$ contains multiple realizable paths that lead to L_T, and another path might result in a smaller overall change. Also, there might exist another candidate subset $D' \cup I'$ with $|D' \cup I'| = |D \cup I|$ that would lead to a smaller overall change. While our approach can be applied to a number of paths and a number of candidate subsets $D \cup I$, processing all of them can be practically intractable.

3   Minimal Sufficient (D,I)-Reductions

Throughout this section, we simply write a *reduction* when talking about a (D,I)-reduction of $\mathcal{A}$. To name a reduction, we either simply use capital letters, e.g., M, N, K, or we use the notation $\mathcal{A}_{<D,I>}$ to also specify the sets D, I of simple clock constraints. Given a reduction $N = \mathcal{A}_{<D,I>}$, $|N|$ denotes the cardinality $|D \cup I|$. Furthermore, $\mathcal{R}_{\mathcal{A}}$ denotes the set of all reductions. We define a partial order relation $\sqsubseteq$ on $\mathcal{R}_{\mathcal{A}}$ as $\mathcal{A}_{<D,I>} \sqsubseteq \mathcal{A}_{<D',I'>}$ iff $D \cup I \subseteq D' \cup I'$. Similarly, we write $\mathcal{A}_{<D,I>} \sqsubsetneq \mathcal{A}_{<D',I'>}$ iff $D \cup I \subsetneq D' \cup I'$. We say that a reduction $\mathcal{A}_{<D,I>}$ is a *sufficient reduction* (w.r.t. $\mathcal{A}$ and L_T) iff L_T is reachable on $\mathcal{A}_{<D,I>}$; otherwise, $\mathcal{A}_{<D,I>}$ is an *insufficient reduction*. Crucial observation for our work is that the property of being a sufficient reduction is monotone w.r.t. the partial order:

Proposition 2. *Let $\mathcal{A}_{<D,I>}$ and $\mathcal{A}_{<D',I'>}$ be reductions such that $\mathcal{A}_{<D,I>} \sqsubseteq \mathcal{A}_{<D',I'>}$. If $\mathcal{A}_{<D,I>}$ is sufficient then $\mathcal{A}_{<D',I'>}$ is also sufficient.*

Proof. Note that $\mathcal{A}_{<D',I'>}$ is a $(D'\backslash D, I'\backslash I)$-reduction of $\mathcal{A}_{<D,I>}$. By Proposition 1, $[[\mathcal{A}_{<D,I>}]] \subseteq [[\mathcal{A}_{<D',I'>}]]$, i.e., the run of $\mathcal{A}_{<D,I>}$ that witnesses the reachability of L_T is also a run of $\mathcal{A}_{<D',I'>}$.

Definition 5 (MSR). *A sufficient reduction $\mathcal{A}_{<D,I>}$ is a minimal sufficient reduction (MSR) iff there is no $c \in D \cup I$ such that the reduction $\mathcal{A}_{<D\backslash\{c\},I\backslash\{c\}>}$ is sufficient. Equivalently, due to Proposition 2, $\mathcal{A}_{<D,I>}$ is an MSR iff there is no sufficient reduction $\mathcal{A}_{<D',I'>}$ such that $\mathcal{A}_{<D',I'>} \sqsubsetneq \mathcal{A}_{<D,I>}$.*

Recall that a reduction $\mathcal{A}_{<D,I>}$ is determined by $D \subseteq \Psi(\Delta)$ and $I \subseteq \Psi(Inv)$. Consequently, $|\mathcal{R}_{\mathcal{A}}| = 2^{|\Psi(\Delta) \cup \Psi(Inv)|}$. Moreover, there can be up to $\binom{k}{k/2}$ MSRs where $k = |\Psi(\Delta) \cup \Psi(Inv)|$ (see Sperner's theorem [51]). Also note, that the *minimality* of a reduction does not mean a *minimum* number of simple clock

---

Algorithm 1: Minimum MSR Extraction Scheme

---

1 $N \leftarrow \mathcal{A}_{<\Psi(\Delta),\Psi(Inv)>}; \mathcal{M} \leftarrow \varnothing; \mathcal{I} \leftarrow \varnothing$
2 **while** $N \neq$ `null` **do**
3     $M, \mathcal{I} \leftarrow$ `shrink`$(N, \mathcal{I})$ // Algorithm 2
4     $\mathcal{M} \leftarrow \mathcal{M} \cup \{M\}$
5     $N, \mathcal{I} \leftarrow$ `findSeed`$(M, \mathcal{M}, \mathcal{I})$ // Algorithm 3
6 **return** M

---

constraints that are reduced by the reduction; there can exist two MSRs, M and N, such that $|M| < |N|$. Since our overall goal is to relax $\mathcal{A}$ as little as possible, we identify a *minimum* MSR, i.e., an MSR M such that there is no MSR M' with $|M'| < |M|$, and then use the minimum MSR for the MILP part (Section 4) of our overall approach. There can be also up to $\binom{k}{k/2}$ minimum MSRs.

Example 2. Assume the TA $\mathcal{A}$ and $L_T = \{l_4\}$ from Example 1 (Fig. 1). There are 24 MSRs and 4 of them are minimum. For example, $\mathcal{A}_{<D,I>}$ with $D = \{(e_5, x \geqslant 25)\}$ and $I = \{(l_3, u \leqslant 26)\}$ is a minimum MSR, and $\mathcal{A}_{<D',I'>}$ with $D' = \{(e_9, y \leqslant 15), (e_7, z \leqslant 15)\}$ and $I' = \{(l_6, x \leqslant 10)\}$ is a non-minimum MSR.

3.1 Base Scheme For Computing a Minimum MSR

Algorithm 1 shows a high-level scheme of our approach for computing a minimum MSR. The algorithm iteratively identifies an ordered set of MSRs, $|M_1| > |M_2| > \cdots > |M_k|$, such that the last MSR M_k is a minimum MSR. Each of the MSRs, say M_i, is identified in two steps. First, the algorithm finds a *seed*, i.e., a reduction N_i such that N_i is sufficient and $|N_i| < |M_{i-1}|$. Second, the algorithm *shrinks* N_i into an MSR M_i such that $M_i \sqsubseteq N_i$ (and thus $|M_i| \leqslant |N_i|$). The initial seed N_1 is $\mathcal{A}_{<\Psi(\Delta),\Psi(Inv)>}$, i.e., the reduction that removes all simple clock constraints (which makes all locations of $\mathcal{A}$ trivially reachable). Once there is no sufficient reduction N_i with $|N_i| < |M_{i-1}|$, we know that $M_{i-1} = M_k$ is a minimum MSR.

Note that the algorithm also maintains two auxiliary sets, $\mathcal{M}$ and $\mathcal{I}$, to store all identified MSRs and insufficient reductions, respectively. The two sets are used during the process of finding and shrinking a seed which we describe below.

3.2 Shrinking a Seed

Our approach for shrinking a seed N into an MSR M is based on two concepts: a *critical simple clock constraint* and a *reduction core*.

Definition 6 (critical constraint). *Given a sufficient reduction $\mathcal{A}_{<D,I>}$, a simple clock constraint c is critical for $\mathcal{A}_{<D,I>}$ iff $\mathcal{A}_{<D\setminus\{c\},I\setminus\{c\}>}$ is insufficient.*

Proposition 3. *If $c \in D \cup I$ is critical for a sufficient reduction $\mathcal{A}_{<D,I>}$ then c is critical for every sufficient reduction $\mathcal{A}_{<D',I'>}$, $\mathcal{A}_{<D',I'>} \sqsubseteq \mathcal{A}_{<D,I>}$. Moreover, by Definitions 5 and 6, $\mathcal{A}_{<D,I>}$ is an MSR iff every $c \in D \cup I$ is critical for $\mathcal{A}_{<D,I>}$.*

Algorithm 2: shrink($\mathcal{A}_{<D,I>}, \mathcal{I}$)

---

1 $X \leftarrow \emptyset$
2 **while** $(D \cup I) \neq X$ **do**
3 $\quad$ $c \leftarrow$ pick a simple clock constraint from $(D \cup I) \backslash X$
4 $\quad$ **if** $\mathcal{A}_{<D\backslash\{c\},I\backslash\{c\}>} \notin \mathcal{I}$ **and** $\mathcal{A}_{<D\backslash\{c\},I\backslash\{c\}>}$ *is sufficient* **then**
5 $\quad\quad$ $\rho \leftarrow$ a witness run of the sufficiency of $\mathcal{A}_{<D\backslash\{c\},I\backslash\{c\}>}$
6 $\quad\quad$ $\mathcal{A}_{<D,I>} \leftarrow$ the reduction core of $\mathcal{A}_{<D\backslash\{c\},I\backslash\{c\}>}$ w.r.t. ρ
7 $\quad$ **else**
8 $\quad\quad$ $X \leftarrow X \cup \{c\}$
9 $\quad\quad$ $\mathcal{I} \leftarrow \mathcal{I} \cup \{N \in \mathcal{R}_{\mathcal{A}} \mid N \sqsubseteq \mathcal{A}_{<D\backslash\{c\},I\backslash\{c\}>}\}$

10 **return** $\mathcal{A}_{<D,I>}, \mathcal{I}$

Proof. By contradiction, assume that c is critical for $\mathcal{A}_{<D,I>}$ but not for $\mathcal{A}_{<D',I'>}$, i.e., $\mathcal{A}_{<D\backslash\{c\},I\backslash\{c\}>}$ is insufficient and $\mathcal{A}_{<D'\backslash\{c\},I'\backslash\{c\}>}$ is sufficient. As $\mathcal{A}_{<D',I'>} \sqsubseteq \mathcal{A}_{<D,I>}$, we have $\mathcal{A}_{<D'\backslash\{c\},I'\backslash\{c\}>} \sqsubseteq \mathcal{A}_{<D\backslash\{c\},I\backslash\{c\}>}$. By Proposition 2, if the reduction $\mathcal{A}_{<D'\backslash\{c\},I'\backslash\{c\}>}$ is sufficient then $\mathcal{A}_{<D\backslash\{c\},I\backslash\{c\}>}$ is also sufficient.

Definition 7 (reduction core). *Let $\mathcal{A}_{<D,I>}$ be a sufficient reduction, ρ a witness run of the sufficiency (i.e., reachability of L_T on $\mathcal{A}_{<D,I>}$), and π the path corresponding to ρ. Futhermore, let $M(\pi) = l_0, e_1, \ldots, e_n, l_n$ be the path corresponding to π on the original TA $\mathcal{A}$ defined as in (4). The reduction core of $\mathcal{A}_{<D,I>}$ w.r.t. ρ is the reduction $A_{<D',I'>}$ where $D' = \{(e, \varphi) \mid (e, \varphi) \in D \wedge e = e_i$ for some $1 \leq i \leq n\}$ and $I' = \{(l, \varphi) \mid (l, \varphi) \in I \wedge l = l_i$ for some $0 \leq l \leq n\}$.*

Intuitively, the reduction core of $\mathcal{A}_{<D,I>}$ w.r.t. ρ reduces from $\mathcal{A}$ only the simple clock constraints that appear on the witness path in $\mathcal{A}$.

Proposition 4. *Let $\mathcal{A}_{<D,I>}$ be a sufficient reduction, ρ the witness of reachability of L_T on $\mathcal{A}_{<D,I>}$, and $\mathcal{A}_{<D',I'>}$ the reduction core of $\mathcal{A}_{<D,I>}$ w.r.t. ρ. Then $\mathcal{A}_{<D',I'>}$ is a sufficient reduction and $\mathcal{A}_{<D',I'>} \sqsubseteq \mathcal{A}_{<D,I>}$.*

Proof. By Definition 7, $D' \subseteq D$ and $I' \subseteq I$, thus $\mathcal{A}_{<D',I'>} \sqsubseteq \mathcal{A}_{<D,I>}$. As for the sufficiency of $\mathcal{A}_{<D',I'>}$, we only sketch the proof. Intuitively, both $\mathcal{A}_{<D,I>}$ and $\mathcal{A}_{<D',I'>}$ originate from $\mathcal{A}$ by only removing some simple clock constraints ($D \cup I$, and $D' \cup I'$, respectively), i.e., the graph structure of $\mathcal{A}_{<D,I>}$ and $\mathcal{A}_{<D',I'>}$ is the same, however, some corresponding paths of $\mathcal{A}_{<D,I>}$ and $\mathcal{A}_{<D',I'>}$ differ in the constraints that appear on the paths. By Definition 7, the path π that corresponds to the witness run ρ of $\mathcal{A}_{<D,I>}$ is also a path of $\mathcal{A}_{<D',I'>}$. Since realizability of a path depends only on the constraints along the path, if π is realizable on $\mathcal{A}_{<D,I>}$ then π is also realizable on $\mathcal{A}_{<D',I'>}$.

Our approach for shrinking a sufficient reduction N is shown in Algorithm 2. The algorithm iteratively maintains a sufficient reduction $\mathcal{A}_{<D,I>}$ and a set X of known critical constraints for $\mathcal{A}_{<D,I>}$. Initially, $\mathcal{A}_{<D,I>} = N$ and $X = \emptyset$. In each iteration, the algorithm picks a simple clock constraint $c \in (D \cup$

$I)\backslash X$ and checks the reduction $\mathcal{A}_{<D\backslash\{c\},I\backslash\{c\}>}$ for sufficiency. If $\mathcal{A}_{<D\backslash\{c\},I\backslash\{c\}>}$ is insufficient, the algorithm adds c to X. Otherwise, if $\mathcal{A}_{<D\backslash\{c\},I\backslash\{c\}>}$ is sufficient, the algorithm obtains a witness run ρ of the sufficiency from the verifier and reduces $\mathcal{A}_{<D,I>}$ to the corresponding reduction core. The algorithm terminates when $(D \cup I) = X$. An invariant of the algorithm is that every $c \in X$ is critical for $\mathcal{A}_{<D,I>}$. Thus, when $(D \cup I) = X$, $\mathcal{A}_{<D,I>}$ is an MSR (Proposition 3).

Note that the algorithm also uses the set $\mathcal{I}$ of known insufficient reductions. In particular, before calling a verifier to check a reduction for sufficiency (line 4), the algorithm first checks (in a lazy manner) whether the reduction is already known to be insufficient. Also, whenever the algorithm determines a reduction $\mathcal{A}_{<D\backslash\{c\},I\backslash\{c\}>}$ to be insufficient, it adds $\mathcal{A}_{<D\backslash\{c\},I\backslash\{c\}>}$ and every N, $N \sqsubseteq \mathcal{A}_{<D\backslash\{c\},I\backslash\{c\}>}$ to $\mathcal{I}$ (by Proposition 2, every such N is also insufficient).

3.3   Finding a Seed

We now describe the procedure findSeed. The input is the latest identified MSR M, the set $\mathcal{M}$ of known MSRs, and the set $\mathcal{I}$ of known insufficient reductions. The output is a seed, i.e., a sufficient reduction N such that $|N| < |M|$, or null if there is no seed. Let us denote by CAND the set of all *candidates* on a seed, i.e., CAND $= \{N \in \mathcal{R}_{\mathcal{A}} \,|\, |N| < |M|\}$. A brute-force approach would be to check individual reductions in CAND for sufficiency until a sufficient one is found, however, this can be practically intractable since $|\text{CAND}| = \sum_{i=1}^{|M|} \binom{|\Psi(\Delta) \cup \Psi(Inv)|}{i-1}$.

We provide three observations to prune the set CAND of candidates that need to be tested for being a seed. The first observation exploits the set $\mathcal{I}$ of already known insufficient reductions: no $N \in \mathcal{I}$ can be a seed. The second observation exploits the set $\mathcal{M}$ of already known MSRs. By the definition of an MSR, for every $M' \in \mathcal{M}$ and every N such that $N \subsetneq M'$, the reduction N is necessarily insufficient and hence cannot be a seed. The third observation is stated below:

Observation 1. *For every sufficient reduction $N \in$ CAND there exists a sufficient reduction $N' \in$ CAND such that $N \sqsubseteq N'$ and $|N'| = |M| - 1$.*

Proof. If $|N| = |M| - 1$, then $N = N'$. For the other case, when $|N| < |M| - 1$, let $N = \mathcal{A}_{<D^N,I^N>}$ and $M = \mathcal{A}_{<D^M,I^M>}$. We construct $N' = \mathcal{A}_{<D^{N'},I^{N'}>}$ by adding arbitrary $(|M| - |N|) - 1$ simple clock constraint from $(D^M \cup I^M) \backslash (D^N \cup I^N)$ to $(D^N \cup I^N)$, i.e., $D^N \cup I^N \subseteq D^{N'} \cup I^{N'} \subseteq (D^M \cup I^M \cup D^N \cup I^N)$ and $|D^{N'} \cup I^{N'}| = |M| - 1$. By definition of CAND, $N' \in$ CAND. Moreover, since $N \subsetneq N'$ and N is sufficient, then N' is also sufficient (Proposition 2).

Based on the above observations, we build a set $\mathcal{C}$ of indispensable candidates on seeds that need to be tested for sufficiency:

$$\mathcal{C} = \{N \in \mathcal{R}_{\mathcal{A}} \,|\, N \notin \mathcal{I} \wedge \forall M' \in \mathcal{M}.\, N \not\sqsubseteq M' \wedge |N| = |M| - 1\} \qquad (5)$$

The procedure findSeed, shown in Algorithm 3, in each iteration picks a reduction $N \in \mathcal{C}$ and checks it for sufficiency (via the verifier). If N is sufficient, findSeed returns N as the seed. Otherwise, when N is insufficient, the algorithm first attempts to *enlarge* N into an insufficient reduction E such that $N \sqsubseteq E$. By Proposition 2, every reduction N' such that $N' \sqsubseteq E$ is also insufficient, thus all these reductions are subsequently added to $\mathcal{I}$ and hence removed from $\mathcal{C}$ (note that this includes also N). If $\mathcal{C}$ becomes empty, then there is no seed.

The purpose of *enlarging* N into E is to quickly prune the candidate set $\mathcal{C}$. We could just add all the insufficient reductions $\{N' \mid N' \sqsubseteq N\}$ to $\mathcal{I}$, but note that $|\{N' \mid N' \sqsubseteq E\}|$ is exponentially larger than $|\{N' \mid N' \sqsubseteq N\}|$ w.r.t. $|E| - |N|$. The enlargement, shown in Algorithm 4, works almost dually to shrinking. Let $N = \mathcal{A}_{<D,I>}$. The algorithm attempts to one by one add the constraints from $\Psi(\Delta) \backslash D$ and $\Psi(Inv) \backslash I$ to D and I, respectively, checking each emerged reduction for sufficiency, and keeping only the changes that preserve $\mathcal{A}_{<D,I>}$ to be insufficient.

3.4   Representation of $\mathcal{I}$ and $\mathcal{C}$

The final piece of the puzzle is how to efficiently manipulate with the sets $\mathcal{I}$ and $\mathcal{C}$. In particular, we are adding reductions to $\mathcal{I}$ and $\mathcal{C}$, removing reductions from $\mathcal{C}$, checking if a reduction belongs to $\mathcal{I}$, checking if $\mathcal{C}$ is empty, and picking a reduction from $\mathcal{C}$. The problem is that the size these sets can be exponential w.r.t. $|\Psi(\Delta) \cup \Psi(Inv)|$ (there are exponentially many reductions), and thus, it is practically intractable to maintain the sets explicitly. Instead, we use a symbolic representation. Given a TA $\mathcal{A}$ with simple clock constraints $\Psi(\Delta) = \{(e_1, \varphi_1), \ldots, (e_p, \varphi_p)\}$ and $\Psi(Inv) = \{(l_1, \varphi_1), \ldots, (l_q, \varphi_q)\}$, we introduce two sets $X = \{x_1, \ldots, x_p\}$ and $Y = \{y_1, \ldots, y_q\}$ of Boolean variables. Note that every valuation of the variables $X \cup Y$ one-to-one maps to the reduction $\mathcal{A}_{<D,I>}$ such that $(e_i, \varphi_i) \in D$ iff x_i is assigned *True* and $(l_j, \varphi_j) \in I$ iff y_j is assigned *True*.

The set $\mathcal{I}$ is gradually built during the whole computation of Algorithm 1. To represent $\mathcal{I}$, we build a Boolean formula $\mathbb{I}$ such that a reduction N **does not** belong to $\mathcal{I}$ iff N **does** correspond to a model of $\mathbb{I}$. Initially, $\mathcal{I} = \varnothing$, thus $\mathbb{I} = True$. To add an insufficient reduction $\mathcal{A}_{<D,I>}$ and all reductions N, $N \sqsubseteq \mathcal{A}_{<D,I>}$, to $\mathcal{I}$, we add to $\mathbb{I}$ the clause $(\bigvee_{(e_i,\varphi_i) \in \Psi(\Delta) \backslash D} x_i) \vee (\bigvee_{(l_j,\varphi_j) \in \Psi(Inv) \backslash I} y_j)$.

The set $\mathcal{C}$ is repeatedly built during each call of the procedure findSeed based on Eq. 5 and it is encoded via a Boolean formula $\mathbb{C}$ such that every model of $\mathbb{C}$ **does** correspond to a reduction $N \in \mathcal{C}$:

$$\mathbb{C} = \mathbb{I} \wedge \bigwedge_{\mathcal{A}_{<D,I>} \in \mathcal{M}} ((\bigvee_{(e_i,\varphi_i) \in \Psi(\Delta) \backslash D} x_i) \vee (\bigvee_{(l_j,\varphi_j) \in \Psi(Inv) \backslash I} y_j)) \wedge \mathbf{trues}(|\mathsf{M}| - 1) \quad (6)$$

where $\mathbf{trues}(|\mathsf{M}| - 1)$ is a cardinality encoding forcing that exactly $|\mathsf{M}| - 1$ variables from $X \cup Y$ are set to *True*. To check if $\mathcal{C} = \varnothing$ or to pick a reduction $N \in \mathcal{C}$, we ask a SAT solver for a model of $\mathbb{C}$. To remove an insufficient reduction from $\mathcal{C}$, we update the formula $\mathbb{I}$ (and thus also $\mathbb{C}$) as described above.

3.5   Related Work

Although the concept of minimal sufficient reductions (MSRs) is novel in the context of timed automata, similar concepts appear in other areas of computer

---

Algorithm 3: findSeed($M, \mathcal{M}, \mathcal{I}$)

1 **while** $\{N \in \mathcal{R}_A \mid N \notin \mathcal{I} \wedge \forall M' \in \mathcal{M}. N \nsubseteq M' \wedge |N| = |M| - 1\} \neq \varnothing$ **do**

2 $\quad$ $N \leftarrow$ pick from $\{N \in \mathcal{R}_A \mid N \notin \mathcal{I} \wedge \forall M' \in \mathcal{M}. N \nsubseteq M' \wedge |N| = |M| - 1\}$

3 $\quad$ **if** N *is sufficient* **then return** $N, \mathcal{I}$

4 $\quad$ **else** $\mathcal{I} \leftarrow \mathcal{I} \cup \{N' \in \mathcal{R}_A \mid N' \sqsubseteq \text{enlarge}(N)\}$

5 **return** null, $\mathcal{I}$

Algorithm 4: enlarge($\mathcal{A}_{<D,I>}$)

1 **foreach** $c \in (\Psi(\Delta) \cup \Psi(Inv)) \backslash (D \cup I)$ **do**

2 $\quad$ **if** $c \in \Psi(\Delta)$ *and* $\mathcal{A}_{<D \cup \{c\}, I>}$ *is sufficient* **then** $D \leftarrow D \cup \{c\}$

3 $\quad$ **if** $c \in \Psi(Inv)$ *and* $\mathcal{A}_{<D, I \cup \{c\}>}$ *is sufficient* **then** $I \leftarrow I \cup \{c\}$

4 **return** $\mathcal{A}_{<D,I>}$

---

science. For example, see minimal unsatisfiable subsets [15], minimal correction subsets [47], minimal inconsistent subsets [16,18], or minimal inductive validity cores [32]. All these concepts can be generalized as *minimal sets over monotone predicates (MSMPs)* [48,49]. The input is a reference set R and a monotone predicate $\mathbf{P} : \mathcal{P}(R) \rightarrow \{1, 0\}$, and the goal is to find minimal subsets of R that satisfy the predicate. In the case of MSRs, the reference set is the set of all simple constraints $\Psi(\Delta) \cup \Psi(Inv)$ and, for every $D \cup I \subseteq \Psi(\Delta) \cup \Psi(Inv)$, the predicate is defined as $\mathbf{P}(D \cup I) = 1$ iff $\mathcal{A}_{<D,I>}$ is sufficient. Many algorithms were proposed (e.g., [45,14,19,22,20,47,21,37,32,23]) for finding MSMPs for particular instances of the MSMP problem. However, the algorithms are dedicated to the particular instances and extensively exploit specific properties of the instances (such as we exploit reduction cores in case of MSRs). Consequently, the algorithms either cannot be used for finding MSRs, or they would be rather inefficient.

4 Synthesis of Relaxation Parameters

The main objective of this study is to make the target locations L_T of a given TA $\mathcal{A} = (L, l_0, C, \Delta, Inv)$ reachable by only modifying the constants of simple constraints of $\mathcal{A}$. In the previous section, we presented an efficient algorithm to find a set of simple clock constraints $D \subseteq \Psi(\Delta)$ (1) (over transitions) and $I \subseteq \Psi(Inv)$ (2) (over locations) such that the target set is reachable when constraints D and I are removed from $\mathcal{A}$. In other words, L_T is reachable on $\mathcal{A}_{<D,I>}$. Consequently, a verifier generates a finite run $\rho'_{L_T} = (l_0, \mathbf{0}) \rightarrow_{d_0} (l_1, v_1) \rightarrow_{d_1} \ldots \rightarrow_{d_{n-1}} (l_n, v_n)$ of $\mathcal{A}_{<D,I>}$ such that $l_n \in L_T$. Let $\pi'_{L_T} = l_0, e'_1, l_1, \ldots, e'_{n-1}, l_n$ be the corresponding path on $\mathcal{A}_{<D,I>}$, i.e., π'_{L_T} is realizable on $\mathcal{A}_{<D,I>}$ due to the delay sequence $d_0, d_1, \ldots, d_{n-1}$ and the resulting run is ρ'_{L_T}. The corresponding path on the original TA $\mathcal{A}$ defined as in (4) is:

$$\pi'_{L_T} = M(\pi_{L_T}), \text{ and } \pi_{L_T} = l_0, e_1, l_1, \ldots, e_{n-1}, l_n, \tag{7}$$

While π'_{L_T} is realizable on $\mathcal{A}_{<D,I>}$, π_{L_T} is not realizable on $\mathcal{A}$ since L_T is not reachable on $\mathcal{A}$. We present an MILP based method to find a relaxation valuation $\mathbf{r} : D \cup I \to \mathbb{N} \cup \{\infty\}$ such that the path induced by π_{L_T} is realizable on $\mathcal{A}_{<D,I,\mathbf{r}>}$.

Given an automaton path $\pi = l_0, e_1, l_1, \ldots, e_{n-1}, l_n$ with $e_i = (l_{i-1}, \lambda_i, \phi_i, l_i)$ for each $i = 1, \ldots, n-1$, we introduce real valued delay variables $\delta_0, \ldots, \delta_{n-1}$ that represent the time spent in each location along the path. Since clocks measure the time passed since their last resets, for a fixed path, a clock on a given constraint (invariant or guard) can be mapped to a sum of delay variables:

$$\Gamma(x, \pi, i) = \delta_k + \delta_{k+1} + \ldots + \delta_{i-1} \text{ where } k = \max(\{m \mid x \in \lambda_m, m < i\} \cup \{0\}) \quad (8)$$

The value of clock x equals to $\Gamma(x, \pi, i)$ on the i-th transition e_i along π. In (8), k is the index of the transition where x is last reset before e_i along π, and it is 0 if it is not reset. $\Gamma(0, \pi, i)$ is defined as 0 for notational convenience.

Guards. For transition e_i, each simple constraint $\varphi = x - y \sim c \in \mathcal{S}(\phi_i)$ on the guard ϕ_i is mapped to the new delay variables as:

$$\Gamma(x, \pi, i) - \Gamma(y, \pi, i) \sim c + p_{e_i, \varphi} \quad (9)$$

where $p_{e_i, \varphi}$ is a new integer valued relaxation variable if $(e_i, \varphi) \in D$, otherwise it is set to 0.

Invariants. Each clock constraint $\varphi = x - y \sim c \in \mathcal{S}(Inv(l_i))$ of the invariant of location l_i is mapped to arriving (10) and leaving (11) constraints over the delay variables, since the invariant should be satisfied when arriving and leaving the location (and hence, due to the invariant convexity, also in the location).

$$\Gamma(x, \pi, i) \cdot \mathbf{I}(x \notin \lambda_i) - \Gamma(y, \pi, i) \cdot \mathbf{I}(y \notin \lambda_i) \sim c + p_{l_i, \varphi_i} \quad \text{if } i > 0 \text{(arriving)} \quad (10)$$

$$\Gamma(x, \pi, i+1) - \Gamma(y, \pi, i+1) \sim c + p_{l_i, \varphi_i} \quad \text{(leaving)} \quad (11)$$

where $\mathbf{I}$ is a binary function mapping *true* to 1 and *false* to 0, p_{l_i, φ_i} is a new integer valued variable if $(l_i, \varphi_i) \in I$, otherwise it is set to 0.

Finally, we define an MILP (12) for the path π. The constraint relaxation variables $\{p_{l,\varphi} \mid (l, \varphi) \in I\}$ and $\{p_{e,\varphi} \mid (e, \varphi) \in D\}$ (integer valued), and the delay variables $\delta_0, \ldots, \delta_{n-1}$ (real valued) are the decision variables of the MILP.

$$\text{minimize} \sum_{(l,\varphi)\in I} p_{l,\varphi} + \sum_{(e,\varphi)\in D} p_{e,\varphi} \quad (12)$$

subject to (9) for each $i = 1, \ldots, n - 1$, and $x - y \sim c \in \mathcal{S}(\phi_i)$

(10) for each $i = 1, \ldots, n$, and $x - y \sim c \in \mathcal{S}(Inv(l_i))$

(11) for each $i = 0, \ldots, n - 1$, and $x - y \sim c \in \mathcal{S}(Inv(l_i))$

$p_{l,\varphi} \in \mathbb{Z}_+$ for each $(l, \varphi) \in I$, and $p_{e,\varphi} \in \mathbb{Z}_+$ for each $(e, \varphi) \in D$

Let $\{p^\star_{l,\varphi} \mid (l, \varphi) \in I\}$, $\{p^\star_{e,\varphi} \mid (e, \varphi) \in D\}$, and $\delta^\star_0, \ldots, \delta^\star_{n-1}$ denote the solution of MILP (12). Define a relaxation valuation $\mathbf{r}$ with respect to the solution as

$$\mathbf{r}(l, \varphi) = p^\star_{l,\varphi} \text{ for each } (l, \varphi) \in I, \quad \mathbf{r}(e, \varphi) = p^\star_{e,\varphi} \text{ for each } (e, \varphi) \in D. \quad (13)$$

Theorem 1. *Let $\mathcal{A} = (L, l_0, C, \Delta, Inv)$ be a timed automaton, $\pi = l_0, e_1, l_1, \ldots,$ e_n, l_n be a finite path of $\mathcal{A}$, and $D \subset \Psi(\Delta)$, $I \subset \Psi(I)$ be guard and invariant constraint sets. If the MILP constructed from $\mathcal{A}$, π, D and I as defined in (12) is feasible, then l_n is reachable on $\mathcal{A}_{<D, I, \mathbf{r}>}$ with $\mathbf{r}$ as defined in (13).*

Proof sketch Let $\{p^\star_{l,\varphi} \mid (l, \varphi) \in I\}$, $\{p^\star_{e,\varphi} \mid (e, \varphi) \in D\}$, and $\delta^\star_0, \ldots, \delta^\star_{n-1}$ be the optimal solution of MILP (12). Define clock value sequence $v_0, v_1, \ldots, v_n$ with respect to the path π with $e_i = (l_{i-1}, \lambda_i, \phi_i, l_i)$ and the delay sequence $\delta^\star_0, \ldots, \delta^\star_{n-1}$ iteratively as $v_i = \mathbf{0}$ and $v_i = (v_{i-1} + \delta^\star_{i-1})[\lambda_i := 0]$ for each $i = 1, \ldots, n$. Along the path π, v_i is consistent with $\Gamma(\cdot, \pi, i)$ (8) such that

$$a)\ v_i(x) = \Gamma(x, \pi, i).I(x \notin \lambda_i) \qquad and \quad b)\ v_i(x) + \delta^\star_i = \Gamma(x, \pi, i+1) \quad (14)$$

MILP (12) constraints and (14) imply that the path $M(\pi)$ that end in l_n is realizable on $\mathcal{A}_{<D, I, \mathbf{r}>}$ via the delay sequence $\delta^\star_0, \ldots, \delta^\star_{n-1}$.

A linear programming (LP) based approach was used in [27] to generate the optimal delay sequence for a given path of a weighted timed automata. In our case, the optimization problem is in MILP form since we find an integer valued relaxation valuation ($\mathbf{r}$) in addition to the delay variables.

Recall that we construct relaxation sets D and I via Algorithm 1, and define π_{L_T} (7) that reach L_T such that the corresponding path π'_{L_T} is realizable on $\mathcal{A}_{<D, I>}$. Then, we define MILP (12) with respect to π_{L_T}, D and I, and define $\mathbf{r}$ (13) according to the optimal solution. Note that this MILP is always feasible since π'_{L_T} is realizable on $\mathcal{A}_{<D, I>}$. Finally, by Theorem 1, we conclude that L_T is reachable on $\mathcal{A}_{<D, I, \mathbf{r}>}$.

Example 3. For the TA shown in Fig. 1, Algorithm 1 generates $\mathcal{A}_{<D, I>}$ with $D = \{(e_5, x \geqslant 25)\}$ and $I = \{(l_3, u \leqslant 26)\}$ such that $\pi = l_0, e_1, l_1, e_2, l_2, e_3, l_1, e_4, l_3, e_5,$ l_4 is realizable on $\mathcal{A}_{<D, I>}$. The MILP is constructed for π, D and I with decision variables $p_{e_5, x \geqslant 25}$, $p_{l_3, u \leqslant 26}$, $\delta_0, \delta_1, \delta_2, \delta_3, \delta_4$ and δ_5 as in (12). The solution is $p_{e_5, x \geqslant 25} = 3$, $p_{l_3, u \leqslant 26} = 5$, and the delay sequence is $9, 4, 0, 9, 9, 0$. Consequently, l_4 is reachable on $\mathcal{A}_{<D, I, \mathbf{r}>}$ with $\mathbf{r}(e_5, x \geqslant 25) = 3$ and $\mathbf{r}(l_3, u \leqslant 26) = 5$.

5   Case Study

We implemented the proposed reduction and relaxation methods in a tool called Tamus. We use UPPAAL for sufficiency checks and witness computation, and CBC solver from Or-tools library [50] for the MILP part. All experiments were run on a laptop with Intel i5 quad core processor at 2.5 GHz and 8 GB ram. The tool and used benchmarks are available at https://github.com/jar-ben/tamus.

As discussed in Section 1, an alternative approach to solve our problem (Problem 1) is to parameterize each simple clock constraint of the TA. Then, we can run a parameter synthesis tool on the parameterized TA to identify the set of all possible valuations of the parameters for which the TA satisfies the reachability property. Subsequently, we can choose the valuations that assign non-zero values (i.e., relax) to the minimum number of parameters, and out of these, we

Table 1. Results for the scheduler TA, where $|\Psi| = |\Psi(\Delta) \cup \Psi(I)|$ is the total number of constraints, $d = |D \cup U|$ is the minimum MSR size, v is the number of reachability checks, t is the computation time in seconds (including the reachability checks), and c_m is the optimal cost of (12).

Model	$|\Psi|$	d	v	t	c_m	Model	$|\Psi|$	d	v	t	c_m	Model	$|\Psi|$	d	v	t	c_m
$\mathcal{A}_{(3,1,12)}$	11	2	33	0.18	6	$\mathcal{A}_{(5,1,12)}$	16	3	120	0.63	10	$\mathcal{A}_{(7,1,12)}$	19	3	120	0.63	11
$\mathcal{A}_{(3,2,12)}$	17	1	13	0.13	13	$\mathcal{A}_{(5,2,12)}$	24	1	42	0.35	13	$\mathcal{A}_{(7,2,12)}$	28	1	95	0.72	13
$\mathcal{A}_{(3,1,18)}$	16	3	61	0.37	9	$\mathcal{A}_{(5,1,18)}$	23	4	149	0.90	16	$\mathcal{A}_{(7,1,18)}$	28	5	313	1.87	25
$\mathcal{A}_{(3,2,18)}$	24	1	40	0.40	6	$\mathcal{A}_{(5,2,18)}$	35	1	57	0.58	6	$\mathcal{A}_{(7,2,18)}$	42	1	70	0.74	6
$\mathcal{A}_{(3,1,24)}$	21	4	97	0.65	12	$\mathcal{A}_{(5,1,24)}$	31	6	327	2.16	24	$\mathcal{A}_{(7,1,24)}$	38	7	709	4.76	35
$\mathcal{A}_{(3,2,24)}$	32	1	80	0.85	16	$\mathcal{A}_{(5,2,24)}$	47	2	169	1.80	31	$\mathcal{A}_{(7,2,24)}$	57	2	201	2.21	21
$\mathcal{A}_{(3,1,30)}$	26	5	141	1.05	15	$\mathcal{A}_{(5,1,30)}$	39	7	541	4.17	31	$\mathcal{A}_{(7,1,30)}$	48	10	1680	14.12	47
$\mathcal{A}_{(3,2,30)}$	40	1	65	0.84	9	$\mathcal{A}_{(5,2,30)}$	59	2	330	3.95	14	$\mathcal{A}_{(7,2,30)}$	72	2	403	5.01	14

can choose the one with a minimum cumulative change of timing constants. In our experimental evaluation, we evaluate a state-of-the-art parameter synthesis tool called Imitator [9] to run such analysis. Although Imitator is not tailored for our problem, it allows us to measure the relative scalability of our approach compared to a well-established synthesis technique.

We used two collections of benchmarks: one is obtained from literature, and the other are crafted timed automata modeling a machine scheduling problem. All experiments were run using a time limit of 20 minutes per benchmark.

Machine Scheduling A scheduler automaton is composed of a set of paths from location l_0 to location l_1. Each path $\pi = l_0 e_k l_k e_{k+1} \ldots l_{k+M-1} e_{k+M} l_1$ represents a particular scheduling scenario where an intermediate location, e.g. l_i for $i = k, \ldots, k + M - 1$, belongs to a unique path (only one incoming and one outgoing transition). Thus, a TA that has p paths with M intermediate locations in each path has $M \cdot p + 2$ locations and $(M + 1) \cdot p$ transitions. Each intermediate location represents a machine operation, and periodic simple clock constraints are introduced to mimic the limitations on the corresponding durations. For example, assume that the total time to use machines represented by locations l_{k+i} and l_{k+i+1} is upper (or lower) bounded by c for $i = 0, 2, \ldots, M - 2$. To capture such a constraint with a period of $t = 2$, a new clock x is introduced and it is reset and checked on every t^{th} transition along the path, i.e., for every $m \in \{i \cdot t + k \mid i \cdot t \leq M - 1\}$, let $e_m = (l_m, \lambda_m, \phi_m, l_{m+1})$, add x to λ_m, set $\phi_m := \phi_m \land x \leq c$ ($x \geq c$ for lower bound). A periodic constraint is denoted by $(t, c, \sim)$, where t is its period, c is the timing constant, and $\sim \in \{<, \leq, >, \geq\}$. A set of such constraints are defined for each path to capture possible restrictions. In addition, a bound T on the total execution time is captured with the constraint $x \leq T$ on transition e_{k+M} over a clock x that is not reset on any transition. A realizable path to l_1 represents a feasible scheduling scenario, thus the target set is $L_T = \{l_1\}$. We have generated 24 test cases. A test case $\mathcal{A}_{(c,p,M)}$ represents a timed automaton with $c \in \{3, 5, 7\}$ clocks, and $p \in \{1, 2\}$ paths with $M \in \{12, 18, 24, 30\}$ intermediate locations in each path. $R_{c,i}$ is the set of

Table 2. Experimental results for the benchmarks, where $|\Psi|$, d, v t and c_m are as defined in Table 1, $|\Psi^u|$ is the number of constraints considered in the analysis and m is the number of mutated constraints. t^I, t^{IT}, t^{Ic} and t^{ITc} are the Imitator computation times, where c indicates that the early termination flag ("counterexample") is used, otherwise the largest set of parameters is searched, and T indicates that only the constraints from the MSR identified by Tamus are parametrized, otherwise all constraints from Ψ^u are parametrized. to shows that the timeout limit is reached (20 min.). We ran the Imitator with the flag "incl". Note that when run with the flag "merge", the performance of Imitator increases on 2 benchmarks, however, it decreases on other 2 benchmarks.

Model	Source	Spec.	$|\Psi|$	$|\Psi^u|$	d	m	v	t	c_m	t^I	t^{IT}	t^{Ic}	t^{ITc}
accel1000	[11][35]	reach.	7690	13	2	3	22	1.83	-	182.5	2.08	1.77	1.03
CAS	[2]	reach.	18	18	2	9	46	0.31	16	0.75	0.11	0.09	0.01
coffee	[12]	reach.	10	10	2	3	18	0.07	14	0.008	0.002	0.007	0.003
Jobshop4	[1]	reach.	64	48	5	5	272	1.99	-	to	949.5	to	942.3
Pipeline3-3	[41]	reach.	41	41	1	12	42	0.37	-	to	0.08	to	0.05
RCP	[28]	reach.	42	42	1	11	181	2.51	-	to	0.02	24.23	0.02
SIMOP3	[8]	reach.	80	80	6	40	903	10.65	-	to	7.26	to	0.49
Fischer	[36]	safety	24	16	1	0	14	0.08	-	to	to	0.21	0.01
JLR13-3tasks	[40][13]	safety	42	36	1	0	40	0.41	-	to	2.60	0.05	0.08
WFAS	[24][31]	safety	32	24	1	0	10	0.08	-	16.20	0.01	0.03	0.006

periodic restrictions defined for the ith path of an automaton with c clocks:

$$R_{3,1} = \{(2,11,\geqslant),(3,15,\leqslant)\} \qquad R_{3,2} = \{(4,17,\geqslant),(5,20,\leqslant)\}$$
$$R_{5,1} = R_{3,1} \cup \{(4,21,\geqslant),(5,25,\leqslant)\} \qquad R_{5,2} = R_{3,2} \cup \{(8,33,\geqslant),(9,36,\leqslant)\}$$
$$R_{7,1} = R_{5,1} \cup \{(6,31,\geqslant),(7,35,\leqslant)\} \qquad R_{7,2} = R_{5,2} \cup \{(12,49,\geqslant),(12,52,\leqslant)\}$$

Note that $\mathcal{A}_{(c,2,M)}$ emerges from $\mathcal{A}_{(c,1,M)}$ by adding a path with restrictions $R_{c,2}$.

Table 1 shows results achieved by Tamus on these models. Tamus solved all models and the hardest one $\mathcal{A}_{(7,1,30)}$ took only 14.12 seconds. As expected, the computation time t increases with the number $|\Psi|$ of simple clock constraints in the model. Moreover, the computation time highly correlates with the size d of the minimum MSR. Especially, if we compare two generic models $\mathcal{A}_{(c,1,M)}$ and $\mathcal{A}_{(c,2,M)}$, although $\mathcal{A}_{(c,2,M)}$ has one more path and more constraints, Tamus is faster on $\mathcal{A}_{(c,2,M)}$ since it quickly converges to the path with smaller MSRs.

Imitator solved $\mathcal{A}_{(3,1,12)}$, $\mathcal{A}_{(3,2,12)}$, $\mathcal{A}_{(3,1,18)}$, and $\mathcal{A}_{(5,1,12)}$ within 0.08, 0.5, 61, and 67 seconds, and timeouted for the other models. In addition, we run Imitator with a flag "counterexample" that terminates the computation when a satisfying valuation is found. The use of this flag reduced the computation time for the aforementioned cases, and it allowed to solve two more models: $\mathcal{A}_{(3,2,18)}$ and $\mathcal{A}_{(5,2,12)}$. However, using this flag, Imitator often did not provide a solution that minimizes the number of relaxed simple clock constraints.

Benchmarks from Literature We collected 10 example models from literature that include models with a safety specification that requires avoiding a set of locations L_A, and models with a reachability specification with a set of target locations L_T as considered in this paper. In both cases, the original models satisfy the given specification. For the first case, we define L_A as the target set and apply our method. Here, we find the minimal number of timing constants that should be changed to reach L_A, i.e., to violate the original safety specification. For the second case, inspired from mutation testing [2], we change a number of constraints on the original model so that L_T becomes unreachable. Eight of the examples are networks of TAs, and while a network of TAs can be represented as a single product TA and hence our approach can handle it, Tamus currently supports only MSR computation for networks of TA, but not MILP relaxation.

The results are shown in Table 2. Tamus computed a minimum MSR for all the models and also provided the MILP relaxation for the non-network models. Note that the bottle-neck of our approach is the MSR computation and especially the verifier calls; the MILP part always took only few milliseconds (including models from Table 1), thus we believe that it would be also the case for the networks of TAs. The base variant of Imitator that computes the set of all satisfying parameter valuations solved only 4 of the 10 models. When run with the early termination flag, Imitator solved 3 more models, however, as discussed above, the provided solutions might not be optimal. We have also evaluated a combination of Tamus and Imitator. In particular, we first run Tamus to compute a minimum MSR $\mathcal{A}_{<D,I>}$, then parameterized the constraints $D \cup I$ in the original TA $\mathcal{A}$, and run Imitator on the parameterized TA. In this case, Imitator solved 9 out of 10 models. Moreover, we have the guarantee that we found the optimal solution: the MSR ensures that we relax the minimum number of simple clock constraints, and Imitator finds all satisfying parameterizations of the constraints hence also the one with minimum cumulative change of timing constants.

Conclusion In this work, we proposed the novel concept of a minimum MSR for a TA, that is a minimum set of simple constraints that need to be relaxed to satisfy a reachability specification. We developed efficient methods to find a minimum MSR, and presented an MILP based solution to tune these constraints. Our analysis on benchmarks showed that our tool Tamus can generate a minimum MSR within seconds even for large systems. In addition, we compared our results with Imitator and observed that Tamus scales much better. However, Tamus minimizes the cumulative change of the constraints from a minimum MSR by considering a single witness path. If the goal is to find a minimal relaxation globally, i.e., w.r.t. all witness paths for the MSR, we recommend to use the combined version of Tamus and Imitator, i.e., first run Tamus to find a minimum MSR, parametrize each constraint from the MSR and run Imitator to find all satisfying parameter valuations, including the global optimum.

Acknowledgements This research was supported in part by ERDF "Cyber-Security, CyberCrime and Critical Information Infrastructures Center of Excellence" (No. CZ.02.1.01/0.0/0.0/16_019/0000822) and in part by the European Union's Horizon 2020 research and innovation programme under the Marie Sklodowska-Curie grant agreement No. 798482.

References

1. Abdeddaïm, Y., Maler, O.: Job-shop scheduling using timed automata. In: Berry, G., Comon, H., Finkel, A. (eds.) Computer Aided Verification. pp. 478–492. Springer Berlin Heidelberg, Berlin, Heidelberg (2001). https://doi.org/10.1007/3-540-44585-4_46
2. Aichernig, B.K., Lorber, F., Ničković, D.: Time for mutants — model-based mutation testing with timed automata. In: Veanes, M., Viganò, L. (eds.) Tests and Proofs. pp. 20–38. Springer Berlin Heidelberg, Berlin, Heidelberg (2013). https://doi.org/10.1007/978-3-642-38916-0_2
3. Alur, R.: Timed automata. In: International Conference on Computer Aided Verification. pp. 8–22. Springer (1999). https://doi.org/10.1007/3-540-48683-6_3
4. Alur, R., Dill, D.L.: A theory of timed automata. Theoretical computer science 126(2), 183–235 (1994). https://doi.org/10.1016/0304-3975(94)90010-8
5. André, É.: A benchmark library for parametric timed model checking. In: Artho, C., Ölveczky, P.C. (eds.) Formal Techniques for Safety-Critical Systems. pp. 75–83. Springer International Publishing, Cham (2019). https://doi.org/10.1007/978-3-030-12988-0_5
6. André, E.: What's decidable about parametric timed automata? Int. J. Softw. Tools Technol. Transf. 21(2), 203–219 (Apr 2019). https://doi.org/10.1007/s10009-017-0467-0
7. André, É., Arcaini, P., Gargantini, A., Radavelli, M.: Repairing timed automata clock guards through abstraction and testing. In: Beyer, D., Keller, C. (eds.) Tests and Proofs. pp. 129–146. Springer International Publishing, Cham (2019). https://doi.org/10.1007/978-3-030-31157-5_9
8. André, É., Chatain, T., De Smet, O., Fribourg, L., Ruel, S.: Synthèse de contraintes temporisées pour une architecture d'automatisation en réseau. Journal Européen des Systèmes Automatisés 43 (November 2009). https://doi.org/10.3166/jesa.43.1049-1064
9. André, É., Fribourg, L., Kühne, U., Soulat, R.: Imitator 2.5: A tool for analyzing robustness in scheduling problems. In: Giannakopoulou, D., Méry, D. (eds.) FM 2012: Formal Methods. pp. 33–36. Springer Berlin Heidelberg, Berlin, Heidelberg (2012). https://doi.org/10.1007/978-3-642-32759-9_6
10. André, É., Fribourg, L., Mota, J.M., Soulat, R.: Verification of an industrial asynchronous leader election algorithm using abstractions and parametric model checking. In: Enea, C., Piskac, R. (eds.) Verification, Model Checking, and Abstract Interpretation. pp. 409–424. Springer International Publishing, Cham (2019). https://doi.org/10.1007/978-3-030-11245-5_19
11. André, É., Hasuo, I., Waga, M.: Offline timed pattern matching under uncertainty. In: ICECCS. pp. 10–20. IEEE Computer Society (2018). https://doi.org/10.1109/ICECCS2018.2018.00010
12. André, É., Knapik, M., Lime, D., Penczek, W., Petrucci, L.: Parametric verification: An introduction. Trans. Petri Nets Other Model. Concurr. 14, 64–100 (2019). https://doi.org/10.1007/978-3-662-60651-3_3
13. André, É., Lipari, G., Nguyen, H.G., Sun, Y.: Reachability preservation based parameter synthesis for timed automata. In: Havelund, K., Holzmann, G., Joshi, R. (eds.) NASA Formal Methods. pp. 50–65. Springer International Publishing, Cham (2015). https://doi.org/10.1007/978-3-319-17524-9_5
14. Bacchus, F., Katsirelos, G.: Finding a collection of muses incrementally. In: CPAIOR. Lecture Notes in Computer Science, vol. 9676, pp. 35–44. Springer (2016). https://doi.org/10.1007/978-3-319-33954-2_3

15. de la Banda, M.G., Stuckey, P.J., Wazny, J.: Finding all minimal unsatisfiable subsets. In: PPDP. pp. 32–43. ACM (2003). https://doi.org/10.1145/888251.888256
16. Barnat, J., Bauch, P., Beneš, N., Brim, L., Beran, J., Kratochvíla, T.: Analysing sanity of requirements for avionics systems. FAoC pp. 1–19 (2016). https://doi.org/10.1007/s00165-015-0348-9
17. Behrmann, G., David, A., Larsen, K.G., Hakansson, J., Petterson, P., Yi, W., Hendriks, M.: Uppaal 4.0. In: Proceedings of the 3rd International Conference on the Quantitative Evaluation of Systems. pp. 125–126. QEST '06, IEEE Computer Society, Washington, DC, USA (2006). https://doi.org/10.1109/QEST.2006.59
18. Bendík, J.: Consistency checking in requirements analysis. In: ISSTA. pp. 408–411. ACM (2017). https://doi.org/10.1145/3092703.3098239
19. Bendík, J., Beneš, N., Černá, I., Jiří: Tunable online MUS/MSS enumeration. In: FSTTCS. LIPIcs, vol. 65, pp. 50:1–50:13. Schloss Dagstuhl - Leibniz-Zentrum für Informatik (2016). https://doi.org/10.4230/LIPIcs.FSTTCS.2016.50
20. Bendík, J., Černá, I.: Replication-guided enumeration of minimal unsatisfiable subsets. In: CP. LNCS, vol. 12333, pp. 37–54. Springer (2020). https://doi.org/10.1007/978-3-030-58475-7_3
21. Bendík, J., Černá, I.: Rotation based MSS/MCS enumeration. In: LPAR. EPiC Series in Computing, vol. 73, pp. 120–137. EasyChair (2020). https://doi.org/10.29007/8btb
22. Bendík, J., Černá, I., Beneš, N.: Recursive online enumeration of all minimal unsatisfiable subsets. In: ATVA. Lecture Notes in Computer Science, vol. 11138, pp. 143–159. Springer (2018). https://doi.org/10.1007/978-3-030-01090-4_9
23. Bendík, J., Ghassabani, E., Whalen, M.W., Černá, I.: Online enumeration of all minimal inductive validity cores. In: SEFM. Lecture Notes in Computer Science, vol. 10886, pp. 189–204. Springer (2018). https://doi.org/10.1007/978-3-319-92970-5_12
24. Beneš, N., Bezděk, P., Larsen, K.G., Srba, J.: Language emptiness of continuous-time parametric timed automata. In: ICALP (2). Lecture Notes in Computer Science, vol. 9135, pp. 69–81. Springer (2015). https://doi.org/10.1007/978-3-662-47666-6_6
25. Bezděk, P., Beneš, N., Barnat, J., Černá, I.: LTL parameter synthesis of parametric timed automata. In: De Nicola, R., Kühn, E. (eds.) Software Engineering and Formal Methods. pp. 172–187. Springer International Publishing, Cham (2016). https://doi.org/10.1007/978-3-319-41591-8_12
26. Bezděk, P., Beneš, N., Černá, I., Barnat, J.: On clock-aware LTL parameter synthesis of timed automata. J. Log. Algebraic Methods Program. **99**, 114–142 (2018). https://doi.org/10.1016/j.jlamp.2018.05.004
27. Bouyer, P., Brihaye, T., Bruyère, V., Raskin, J.F.: On the optimal reachability problem of weighted timed automata. Formal Methods in System Design **31**, 135–175 (2007). https://doi.org/10.1007/s10703-007-0035-4
28. Collomb-Annichini, A., Sighireanu, M.: Parameterized reachability analysis of the IEEE 1394 root contention protocol using trex (08 2001)
29. David, A., Illum, J., Larsen, K.G., Skou, A.: Model-based framework for schedulability analysis using UPPAAL 4.1. In: Model-based design for embedded systems, pp. 117–144 (2009)
30. Fehnker, A.: Scheduling a steel plant with timed automata. In: Proceedings Sixth International Conference on Real-Time Computing Systems and Applications. RTCSA'99 (Cat. No.PR00306). pp. 280–286 (1999). https://doi.org/10.1109/RTCSA.1999.811256

31. Feo-Arenis, S., Westphal, B., Dietsch, D., Muñiz, M., Andisha, A.S.: The wireless fire alarm system: Ensuring conformance to industrial standards through formal verification. In: Jones, C., Pihlajasaari, P., Sun, J. (eds.) FM 2014: Formal Methods. pp. 658–672. Springer International Publishing, Cham (2014). https://doi.org/10.1007/978-3-319-06410-9_44
32. Ghassabani, E., Whalen, M.W., Gacek, A.: Efficient generation of all minimal inductive validity cores. In: FMCAD. pp. 31–38. IEEE (2017). https://doi.org/10.23919/FMCAD.2017.8102238
33. Guan, N., Gu, Z., Deng, Q., Gao, S., Yu, G.: Exact schedulability analysis for static-priority global multiprocessor scheduling using model-checking. In: Proc. of SEUS. pp. 263–272 (2007). https://doi.org/10.1007/978-3-540-75664-4_26
34. Henzinger, T.A., Preussig, J., Wong-Toi, H.: Some lessons from the hytech experience. In: Proceedings of the 40th IEEE Conference on Decision and Control (Cat. No.01CH37228). vol. 3, pp. 2887–2892 vol.3 (2001)
35. Hoxha, B., Abbas, H., Fainekos, G.: Benchmarks for temporal logic requirements for automotive systems. In: Frehse, G., Althoff, M. (eds.) ARCH14-15. 1st and 2nd International Workshop on Applied veRification for Continuous and Hybrid Systems. EPiC Series in Computing, vol. 34, pp. 25–30. EasyChair (2015). https://doi.org/10.29007/xwrs, https://easychair.org/publications/paper/4bfq
36. Hune, T., Romijn, J., Stoelinga, M., Vaandrager, F.: Linear parametric model checking of timed automata. In: Margaria, T., Yi, W. (eds.) Tools and Algorithms for the Construction and Analysis of Systems. pp. 189–203. Springer Berlin Heidelberg, Berlin, Heidelberg (2001). https://doi.org/10.1007/3-540-45319-9_14
37. Ivrii, A., Malik, S., Meel, K.S., Vardi, M.Y.: On computing minimal independent support and its applications to sampling and counting. Constraints An Int. J. 21(1), 41–58 (2016). https://doi.org/10.1007/s10601-015-9204-z
38. Jiang, Z., Pajic, M., Alur, R., Mangharam, R.: Closed-loop verification of medical devices with model abstraction and refinement. Int. J. Softw. Tools Technol. Transf. 16(2), 191–213 (Apr 2014). https://doi.org/10.1007/s10009-013-0289-7, https://doi.org/10.1007/s10009-013-0289-7
39. Jovanovic, A., Lime, D., Roux, O.H.: Integer parameter synthesis for real-time systems. IEEE Transactions on Software Engineering 41(5), 445–461 (2015). https://doi.org/10.1109/TSE.2014.2357445
40. Jovanović, A., Lime, D., Roux, O.H.: Integer parameter synthesis for timed automata. In: Piterman, N., Smolka, S.A. (eds.) Tools and Algorithms for the Construction and Analysis of Systems. pp. 401–415. Springer Berlin Heidelberg, Berlin, Heidelberg (2013). https://doi.org/10.1007/978-3-642-36742-7_28
41. Knapik, M., Penczek, W.: Bounded model checking for parametric timed automata. Trans. Petri Nets Other Model. Concurr. 5, 141–159 (2010)
42. Kölbl, M., Leue, S., Wies, T.: Clock bound repair for timed systems. In: Dillig, I., Tasiran, S. (eds.) Computer Aided Verification. pp. 79–96. Springer International Publishing, Cham (2019). https://doi.org/10.1007/978-3-030-25540-4_5
43. Kwiatkowska, M., Mereacre, A., Paoletti, N., Patanè, A.: Synthesising robust and optimal parameters for cardiac pacemakers using symbolic and evolutionary computation techniques. In: Abate, A., Šafránek, D. (eds.) Hybrid Systems Biology. pp. 119–140. Springer International Publishing, Cham (2015). https://doi.org/10.1007/978-3-319-26916-0_7
44. Larsen, K.G., Yi, W.: Time abstracted bisimulation: Implicit specifications and decidability. In: International Conference on Mathematical Foundations of Programming Semantics. pp. 160–176. Springer (1993). https://doi.org/10.1006/inco.1997.2623

45. Liffiton, M.H., Previti, A., Malik, A., Marques-Silva, J.: Fast, flexible MUS enumeration. Constraints **21**(2), 223–250 (2016). https://doi.org/10.1007/s10601-015-9183-0
46. Lime, D., Roux, O.H., Seidner, C., Traonouez, L.: Romeo: A parametric model-checker for petri nets with stopwatches. In: TACAS. Lecture Notes in Computer Science, vol. 5505, pp. 54–57. Springer (2009). https://doi.org/10.1007/978-3-642-00768-2_6
47. Marques-Silva, J., Heras, F., Janota, M., Previti, A., Belov, A.: On computing minimal correction subsets. In: IJCAI. pp. 615–622. IJCAI/AAAI (2013)
48. Marques-Silva, J., Janota, M., Belov, A.: Minimal sets over monotone predicates in boolean formulae. In: CAV. Lecture Notes in Computer Science, vol. 8044, pp. 592–607. Springer (2013). https://doi.org/10.1007/978-3-642-39799-8_39
49. Marques-Silva, J., Janota, M., Mencía, C.: Minimal sets on propositional formulae. problems and reductions. Artif. Intell. **252**, 22–50 (2017). https://doi.org/10.1016/j.artint.2017.07.005
50. Perron, L., Furnon, V.: Or-tools, https://developers.google.com/optimization/
51. Sperner, E.: Ein satz über untermengen einer endlichen menge. Mathematische Zeitschrift **27**(1), 544–548 (1928)
52. Wang, F.: Formal verification of timed systems: a survey and perspective. Proceedings of the IEEE **92**(8), 1283–1305 (Aug 2004). https://doi.org/10.1109/JPROC.2004.831210

Iterative Bounded Synthesis for Efficient Cycle Detection in Parametric Timed Automata*

Étienne André[1], Jaime Arias[2], Laure Petrucci[2], and Jaco van de Pol[3]

[1] Université de Lorraine, CNRS, Inria, LORIA, Nancy, France
[2] LIPN, CNRS UMR 7030, Université Sorbonne Paris Nord, Villetaneuse, France
[3] Aarhus University, Aarhus, Denmark, jaco@cs.au.dk

Abstract. We study semi-algorithms to synthesise the constraints under which a Parametric Timed Automaton satisfies some liveness requirement. The algorithms traverse a possibly infinite parametric zone graph, searching for accepting cycles. We provide new search and pruning algorithms, leading to successful termination for many examples. We demonstrate the success and efficiency of these algorithms on a benchmark. We also illustrate parameter synthesis for the classical Bounded Retransmission Protocol. Finally, we introduce a new notion of completeness in the limit, to investigate if an algorithm enumerates all solutions.

Keywords: Parameter Synthesis, Liveness Properties, IMITATOR

1 Introduction

Many critical devices and processes in our society are controlled by software, in which real-time aspects often play a crucial role. Timed Automata (TA [1]) are an important formalism to design and study real-time systems; they extend finite automata with real-valued *clocks*. Their success is based on the decidability of the basic analysis problems of checking *reachability* and *liveness* properties.

Precise timing information is often unknown during the design phase. Therefore, Parametric Timed Automata (PTA [2]) extend TA with *parameters*, representing unknown waiting times, deadlines, network speed, etc. A single PTA represents an infinite class of TA. To facilitate design exploration, *parameter constraint synthesis* aims at a description of all parameter values for which the system meets some requirement. Unfortunately, it is already undecidable to check if a PTA admits a parameter valuation for which a bad state can be reached [2,3].

In this paper, we study the parameter constraint synthesis problem for liveness properties of the full class of PTA. In particular, the goal is to compute the parameter valuations for which a Parametric Timed Büchi Automaton has a non-empty language. Note that this allows handling requirements in LTL and MITL [24]. We represent the solution concisely as a disjunction of conjunctions

---

*This work is partially supported by projects CNRS-INS2I TrAVAIL, IFD SE-CReTS and ANR-NRF ProMiS (ANR-19-CE25-0015).

J. F. Groote and K. G. Larsen (Eds.): TACAS 2021, LNCS 12651, pp. 311–329, 2021.
https://doi.org/10.1007/978-3-030-72016-2_17

of linear inequalities between the parameters (a set of convex polyhedra).

We will consider semi-algorithms that operate on the so-called parametric zone graph (PZG), where a parametric zone is a conjunction of linear inequalities over clock and parameter values. These semi-algorithms may not terminate since the PZG can be infinite. However, even in that case, we are interested in the soundness and completeness of the set of all enumerated solutions.

Our contributions to the parameter constraint synthesis for liveness of PTA are: 1) A definition of soundness and completeness for non-terminating algorithms. 2) A new synthesis algorithm, using bounded search with iterative deepening; this is the first algorithm that enumerates all accepting cycles in the possibly infinite PZG, in contrast to previous NDFS-based algorithms [25]. 3) An experimental benchmark, comparing the successful termination and runtime efficiency of all algorithms. 4) A case study on the Bounded Retransmission Protocol.

Related Work. Decidability for (subclasses of) PTA has been extensively studied [2,19,3]. We study the emptiness and related synthesis problem for *Parametric Timed Büchi Automata* with unrestricted use of rational parameters and real-valued clocks. In this general case, the model checking problem is undecidable [2] and therefore exact synthesis is out of reach (in contrast to the setting with bounded integers [20,11]). Decidability of *liveness* properties for a subclass of PTA, where the occurrence of parameters is restricted, is discussed in [8].

Our approach inherits basic techniques from Timed Automata, in particular the zone graph. For TA, the zone graph is finite after LU-abstraction [27,23,17]. Another technique prunes states that are subsumed by larger states. Subsumption must be applied with care, in order to preserve liveness properties [22,18].

Previous semi-algorithms were based on Nested Depth-First Search (NDFS). They search the (possibly infinite) parametric zone graph (PZG) for accepting cycles. Their zones are projected onto the parameters and accumulated into the global constraint. The basic *cumulative* algorithm [11] prunes states whose projected zone is already included in the accumulated constraint. The cumulative algorithm was extended with *subsumption* and *layering* for PTA [25]. The problem with all NDFS-based algorithms is that the computation can diverge in one branch, missing solutions for accepting cycles in other branches forever.

Our main improvement is a *bounded* approach, which can be combined with breadth- and depth-first search. We check for accepting cycles up to a certain bound, and keep increasing the bound to achieve completeness in the limit. Eventually, this will enumerate all parametric constraints corresponding to all accepting cycles in the PZG. Sometimes, the combination of bounded search and subsumption can even identify infinite paths that do not form a cycle, but this is not guaranteed. A previous proposal for Bounded Model Checking for PTA [21] considers the region graph and has not been implemented. We will provide several small illustrative examples inspired by the invited talk [26].

To evaluate our algorithms, we implemented them in the IMITATOR toolset [6], extending its functionality from reachability to liveness properties. This way, we can reuse its PTA benchmark [4]. We also reimplemented the algorithms of [11,25] in a single NDFS framework. We illustrate our method on the Bounded

Retransmission Protocol (BRP). We synthesize parameter constraints for liveness properties of BRP for the first time. Our constraints are more liberal than the constraints reported in previous work [14,19].

2   PTA, Parametric Zone Graphs and Accepted Runs

Let X be a set of real-valued clocks (e.g. x, y) and let P be a set of rational parameters (e.g. p, q). A linear term over parameters (plt) is an expression of the form $\sum_i \alpha_i p_i + \beta$, where $p_i \in P$, and coefficients $\alpha_i, \beta \in \mathbb{Q}$. A (diagonal) inequality is of the form $x_1 - x_2 \bowtie plt$, with $x_i \in X \cup \{0\}$ and $\bowtie \in \{<, \leq, =, \geq, >\}$. Examples are $x - y \leq 2p + q$, $x > q - 1$ and $2 \leq p$. A (convex) constraint (or zone Z) is a conjunction of inequalities. We write $\mathcal{C}$ for the set of zones.

We define a PTA $\mathcal{A} = (L, \ell_0, F, I, E)$, where L is a finite set of locations, $\ell_0 \in L$ is the initial location and $F \subseteq L$ is the set of accepting locations. $I : L \rightarrow \mathcal{C}$ denotes an invariant for each location and E is a set of transitions of the form (ℓ, g, R, ℓ'), with source $\ell \in L$, target $\ell' \in L$, guard $g \in \mathcal{C}$ and clock reset $R \subseteq X$.

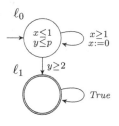

Fig. 1. PTA $\mathcal{A}_1$

The concrete semantics of a PTA is defined in terms of valuations. A parameter valuation is a function $v : P \rightarrow \mathbb{Q}_{\geq 0}$ and a clock valuation is a function $w : X \rightarrow \mathbb{R}_{\geq 0}$. Let $d \in \mathbb{R}_{\geq 0}$ be a delay, then we define the clock valuation $w + d$ such that $(w + d)(x) := w(x) + d$. Let $R \subseteq X$ be a clock reset, then we define the clock valuation $w[R](x) := 0$ if $x \in R$ and $w(x)$ otherwise. We write $\mathbf{0}$ for the clock valuation s.t. $\forall x \in X : \mathbf{0}(x) = 0$. We extend parameter valuations to linear terms. We write $v, w \models (x_i - x_j \bowtie plt)$ iff $w(x_i) - w(x_j) \bowtie v(plt)$, and $v, w \models Z$ iff $v, w \models e$ for all inequalities e in Z.

Given a parameter valuation v, we write $v(\mathcal{A})$ for the timed automaton obtained by replacing all parameters p in invariants and guards by $v(p)$. The concrete semantics of a PTA $\mathcal{A}$ is derived from the TA $v(\mathcal{A})$, and defined as a timed transition system with states (ℓ, w), initial state $(\ell_0, \mathbf{0})$ (we assume that $\mathbf{0} \models I(\ell_0)$), and transitions $\rightarrow = \xrightarrow{d} \cdot \xrightarrow{e}$, where continuous time delay $(\xrightarrow{d})$ and discrete transitions $(\xrightarrow{e})$ are defined as

- If $d \in \mathbb{R}_{\geq 0}$ and $w + d \models I(\ell)$, then $(\ell, w) \xrightarrow{d} (\ell, w + d)$.
- If $e = (\ell, g, R, \ell') \in E$ and $w \models g$ and $w[R] \models I(\ell')$ then $(\ell, w) \xrightarrow{e} (\ell', w[R])$.

An infinite run $(\ell_0, w_0) \rightarrow (\ell_1, w_1) \rightarrow \cdots$ is *accepted* if it passes through an accepting location infinitely often, i.e. the set $\{i \mid \ell_i \in F\}$ is infinite. We ignore the problem of Zeno runs, which can be avoided by a syntactic transformation [9].

Example 1. The PTA $\mathcal{A}_1$ in Fig. 1 has locations $\{\ell_0, \ell_1\}$, clocks $\{x, y\}$ and parameter p. Only ℓ_1 is accepting. The initial location ℓ_0 has an invariant consisting of two inequalities. Its self-loop is enabled if $x \geq 1$ and it resets clock x. Note that clock y is never reset. For $p = 2.5$, we have the following example run:
$$(\ell_0, (0, 0)) \xrightarrow{1} ((\ell_0, (1, 1)) \rightarrow ((\ell_0, (0, 1)) \xrightarrow{1} ((\ell_0, (1, 2)) \rightarrow ((\ell_1, (1, 2)).$$
Note that the accepting location ℓ_1 would not be reachable for $p < 2$. On the other hand, for all $p \geq 2$, there exists an infinite accepted run through ℓ_1.

We will now recall from [5,20] the parametric zone graph (PZG), providing an abstract semantics to a PTA. A single PZG treats all parameter valuations symbolically. Also, the PZG avoids the uncountably infinite timed transition system. The PZG can still be (countably) infinite.

We first define some operations on zones, in terms of their valuations. It is well known that convex polyhedra are closed under these operations, and our implementation in IMITATOR uses the Parma Polyhedra Library [10].

- Time elapse: $Z^\nearrow$ corresponds to $\{(v, w + d) \mid d \in \mathbb{R}_{\geq 0} \land v, w \models Z\}$.
- Clock reset: $Z[R]$ corresponds to $\{(v, w[R]) \mid v, w \models Z\}$.

The PZG is a transition system where each abstract state consists of a location and a non-empty zone. The PZG of $\mathcal{A} = (L, \ell_0, F, I, E)$ is $(S, s_0, \Rightarrow, A)$, with $S \subseteq L \times \mathcal{C}$, initial state $s_0 = (\ell_0, (\bigwedge_{x \in X} x = 0)^\nearrow \cap I(\ell_0))$, and accepting states $A = \{(\ell, Z) \mid \ell \in F\}$. A transition step $(\ell, Z) \Rightarrow (\ell', Z')$ exists if for some $(\ell, g, R, \ell') \in E$ we have $Z' = ((Z \cap g)[R] \cap I(\ell'))^\nearrow \cap I(\ell') \neq \emptyset$. We write $\Rightarrow^+$ ($\Rightarrow^*$) for the transitive (reflexive) closure of $\Rightarrow$.

Example 2. The PZG of $\mathcal{A}_1$ from Ex. 1 is shown in Fig. 2; it extends infinitely to the right. We use that $(x = 0 \land y = 0)^\nearrow = (y - x = 0)$. The loop on ℓ_0 can only be executed when $x = 1$, and it resets $x := 0$, while y is never reset. So after n executions of the loop, $y - x = n$. These n steps are only possible if $p \geq n$.

The PZG obeys two important properties (Prop. 1 and 2). First, the parametric constraint can only decrease along the transitions in the PZG. Second, a state simulates the behaviour of any state that it subsumes. We first define these notions. We write $Z \subseteq Z'$ iff $v, w \models Z$ implies $v, w \models Z'$.

- Parametric constraint: $(\ell, Z){\downarrow}_P$ corresponds to $\{v \mid \exists w.v, w \models Z\}$.
- Subsumption: $(\ell, Z) \sqsubseteq (\ell', Z')$ iff $\ell = \ell'$ and $Z \subseteq Z'$.

Proposition 1 ([25]). *If $s_1 \Rightarrow s_2$ then $s_2{\downarrow}_P \subseteq s_1{\downarrow}_P$.*

Proposition 2 ([25]). *If $s_1 \Rightarrow s_2$ and $s_1 \sqsubseteq s_1'$ then for some s_2', $s_1' \Rightarrow s_2'$ and $s_2 \sqsubseteq s_2'$.*

Example 3. The first ℓ_1 state in Fig. 2 shows that there is an infinite loop when $p \geq 2$. By Prop. 1, the parametric zone of all states following the dashed red edge are contained in $p \geq 2$. So we can prune the PZG at the dashed red arrow, since no new parameter valuations will be found.

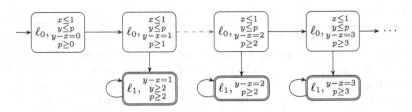

Fig. 2. PZG of the PTA $\mathcal{A}_1$ from Fig. 1

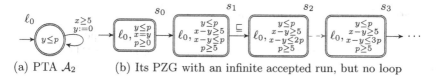

(a) PTA $\mathcal{A}_2$ (b) Its PZG with an infinite accepted run, but no loop

Fig. 3. PTA $\mathcal{A}_2$ with the corresponding PZG

Example 4. Fig. 3 shows PTA $\mathcal{A}_2$ and its infinite PZG. The transition can only become enabled when $p \geq 5$. Each transition must happen within the following p time units, so after $n > 0$ iterations, $5 \leq x - y \leq n \times p$. Note that $s_1 \Rightarrow s_2$ and $s_1 \sqsubseteq s_2$. By Prop. 2, for some s', $s_2 \Rightarrow s'$ and $s_2 \sqsubseteq s'$. Repeating the argument, we can construct an infinite trace. So, although the PZG has no cycle, the presence of an infinite path can be deduced even if we prune the PZG at the dashed edge.

3   Sound and Complete Liveness Parameter Synthesis

Given a PTA $\mathcal{A}$, we aim at synthesising the parameter valuations v for which the TA $v(\mathcal{A})$ contains an infinite accepted run. Our algorithms operate by searching the PZG $(S, s_0, \Rightarrow, A)$ for accepting "lassos" or, as in Ex. 4, 6 and 7, even for accepting "spirals". We write $\Rightarrow^+$ ($\Rightarrow^*$) for the transitive (reflexive) closure of $\Rightarrow$. An accepting lasso on s_1 consists of two finite paths $s_0 \Rightarrow^* s_1 \Rightarrow^+ s_1$, such that $s_1 \in A$. More generally, an accepting spiral on s_1 consists of two finite paths $s_0 \Rightarrow^* s_1 \Rightarrow^+ s_2$, with $s_1 \in A$ and $s_1 \sqsubseteq s_2$.

Proposition 3. *If the PZG of PTA $\mathcal{A}$ contains an accepting spiral on s_1, then for all $v \in s_1\!\downarrow_P$, $v(\mathcal{A})$ contains an (infinite) accepted run.*

Proof. Assume $s_0 \Rightarrow^* s_1 \Rightarrow^+ s_2$ with $s_1 \in A$ and $s_1 \sqsubseteq s_2$. Note that $s_2 \in A$, since $\sqsubseteq$ only holds between states with the same location. Then by monotonicity, $s_1\!\downarrow_P \sqsubseteq s_2\!\downarrow_P$ and by Prop. 1, $s_2\!\downarrow_P \sqsubseteq s_1\!\downarrow_P$, so $s_1\!\downarrow_P = s_2\!\downarrow_P$. By Prop. 2, there exists some s_3 such that $s_2 \Rightarrow s_3$ and $s_2 \sqsubseteq s_3$. We can repeat this to construct an infinite accepted run from s_1, with the constant parametric constraint $s_1\!\downarrow_P$. The states from $s_0 \Rightarrow^* s_1$ have an even larger constraint (Prop. 1). By the correspondence between runs in the PTA and runs in the PZG, we obtain an infinite accepted run in $v(\mathcal{A})$ for every $v \vDash s_1\!\downarrow_P$.   □

The reverse of Prop. 3 is not true. An infinite PZG could contain an infinite path that does not form a lasso (or even a spiral). Such an infinite path in the PZG may or may not correspond to a concrete TA run.

Example 5. The situation of $\mathcal{A}_3$ in Fig. 4 is quite different from Ex. 4. The PZG of $\mathcal{A}_3$ has an infinite path (ℓ_0, Z_i), where Z_i contains the invariant $x \leq 1 \wedge y \leq p$ and the additional constraints $y - x = i \wedge p \geq i$. Note that at most p transitions can happen in $\mathcal{A}_3$, since we cannot wait longer when $y \geq p$. So $v(\mathcal{A}_3)$ has only finite runs for any v. We call this infinite path infeasible, since $\cap_i(Z_i\!\downarrow_P) = \emptyset$.

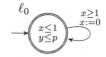

Fig. 4. PTA $\mathcal{A}_3$.

3.1   Soundness and Completeness

In contrast to TA, where both reachability and liveness properties are decidable [1], it is well-known that even reachability-emptiness for PTA is undecidable [2,3]. So in particular, we cannot expect a terminating, sound and complete algorithm for liveness synthesis. Instead, our algorithms are *semi-algorithms*, which enumerate a number of aggregate solutions, but may not terminate. Each aggregate solution will be presented as a convex polyhedral constraint on the parameters ("parametric zone").

Such semi-algorithms can either enumerate a finite number of aggregate solutions (after which they could terminate or diverge), or enumerate an infinite number of aggregates (and hence never terminate). Fig. 5 shows an example where the set of solutions, $p \in \{1, 2, 3, \ldots\}$, is not equivalent to a finite disjunction of convex polyhedra, so no terminating algorithm can enumerate all aggregate solutions.[1]

Fig. 5. PTA $\mathcal{A}_4$

In the rest of this section, we introduce and discuss various soundness and completeness requirements for semi-algorithms. Assume that the algorithm is run on an input PTA $\mathcal{A}$ and let *Sol* be the set of all solutions, *i.e.* $Sol = \{v \mid v(\mathcal{A}) \text{ has an accepted run}\}$. Assume that the algorithm enumerates a finite or infinite collection of aggregate solutions, in the form of parametric zones Z_i.

Partial correctness: This traditional correctness criterion requires that if the algorithm terminates, then $\bigcup_i Z_i = Sol$, *i.e.* the finite output characterizes exactly all correct parameter valuations.

Soundness: This criterion also provides some guarantee when the algorithm diverges. It requires that all enumerated solutions are correct, *i.e.* $\bigcup_i Z_i \subseteq Sol$.

Completeness: We call a semi-algorithm *complete* if it enumerates all solutions, *i.e.* $Sol \subseteq \bigcup_i Z_i$. Enumerating $p = 1$, $p = 2$, ... is complete for $\mathcal{A}_4$.

Note that for reachability, a simple Breadth-First Search (BFS) over the PZG would yield a sound and complete (but not always terminating) semi-algorithm. For liveness, this is insufficient: the algorithm would miss infinite paths that do not form a cycle. Still, the following trivial semi-algorithm, EnumQ, would be sound and complete: "Enumerate all rational parameter valuations v, decide if $v(\mathcal{A})$ has an accepting loop [1] and, if so, emit $\{v\}$." Although it is sound and complete, this algorithm is quite unsatisfactory, since it will never terminate, and it will never aggregate solutions in larger polyhedra. To distinguish PZG-based algorithms, we need a weaker form of completeness.

Completeness for symbolic lassos: A semi-algorithm is *complete for symbolic lassos* if it enumerates all parameter valuations leading to accepting lassos in the PZG, *i.e.* $\bigcup_i Z_i$ contains $s \!\downarrow_P$, when the PZG contains an accepting lasso on s.

Completeness for symbolic lassos is weaker than completeness, since it may miss parameter valuations v for which $v(\mathcal{A})$ has an accepted run, but this only happens when the PZG has an infinite path that does not end in a cycle.

---

[1]It is not even obvious that $\cap_i(Z_i \!\downarrow_P)$ can be represented by a finite conjunction.

4 Semi-Algorithms for Liveness Parameter Synthesis

In this section, we discuss three semi-algorithms for liveness parameter synthesis. In Sec. 4.1, we discuss the previous approach [11,25], based on Nested Depth-First Search (NDFS). All NDFS-based variants turn out to be incomplete for symbolic lassos. In Sec. 4.2, we introduce a simple algorithm based on Breadth-First Search (BFS), which analyses the Strongly Connected Components (SCC) at each new level. We show that the BFS-based algorithm is complete for symbolic lassos. Finally, Sec. 4.3 introduces our new Bounded Synthesis with Iterative Deepening (BSID) algorithm. BSID is also complete for symbolic lassos, and it is compatible with all NDFS enhancements.

4.1 Nested Depth-First Search with Enhancements

The NDFS algorithm (Alg. 1) is run on the PZG, with initial state s_0, accepting states A, and NEXT-STATE(s) enumerating the $\Rightarrow$-successors. We first explain basic NDFS [13], cf. the uncoloured parts of Alg. 1. The goal of the outer *blue search* (ll.4–13) is to visit all states in DFS order, and just before backtracking, call the red search on all accepting states (l.12). Note that states on the DFS stack are cyan (l.6), and states that are handled completely are blue (l.13). The goal of the inner *red search* (ll.14–21) is to detect if there is an accepting cycle. It colours visited states red (l.16), to ensure that states are visited at most once. It reports an accepting cycle (l.20) when a cyan state is encountered.

Cumulative pruning (pink) [11,25]. For synthesis, we collect the *Constraints* that lead to accepting cycles (l.20). We prune the search when the parametric constraint of some state is included in *Constraints* (l.5,15). This is justified by Prop. 1, since all successors of the pruned state will have an even smaller parametric constraint. Prop. 1 also implies that all states on a cycle have the same parametric constraint. So we also prune the red search, by restricting the search for a cycle to the current parametric constraint (l.18).

Subsumption (grey) [22,25]. This pruning strategy takes advantage of the subsumption relation between states. The accepting lassos reachable from red states s are already included in *Constraints*. By Prop. 3, any lasso on state $t \sqsubseteq t'$ can be simulated by t'. Hence, we immediately prune the search when we encounter a state $t \sqsubseteq Red$, i.e. $\exists t'. t \sqsubseteq t' \in Red$ (l.11,21). We exploit the subsumption structure once more: if $t \sqsupseteq Cyan$, i.e. $\exists t'. t \sqsupseteq t' \in Cyan$ (l.19), we have found an accepting spiral, which implies there is an accepted run, Prop. 3.

Lookahead (yellow) . The *lookahead* strategy is new (in this context) and allows for early detection of accepting cycles in *dfsBlue*. It looks for a transition to a *cyan* state (l.7), which is on the DFS stack. If the source or target of this transition is accepting, then the cycle is accepting as well and reported at l.8.

Accepting First (blue). This is a new strategy, aimed at increasing the chance of finding an accepting cycle early in the search, to promote more pruning. It simply works by picking accepting successors before their siblings at l.10,17.

Alg. 1 Collecting NDFS with strategies:
cumulative pruning ▓subsumption▓ lookahead ▓accepting first▓

1: **procedure** NDFS
2:    $Cyan := Blue := Red := \emptyset$; $Constraints := \emptyset$
3:    $dfsBlue(s_0)$

4: **procedure** $dfsBlue(s)$
5:    **if** $s{\downarrow}_P \subseteq Constraints$ **then** $Blue := Blue \cup \{s\}$; **return**
6:    $Cyan := Cyan \cup \{s\}$
7:    **if** $\exists s' \in$ NEXT-STATE$(s) \cap Cyan : (s \in A \vee s' \in A)$ **then**
8:       $Constraints := Constraints \cup \{s'{\downarrow}_P\}$ ▷ Report cycle at state s'
9:    **else**
10:       **for all** $t \in$ REORDERED-NEXT-STATE(s) **do**
11:          **if** $t \notin Blue \cup Cyan$ ▓$\wedge t \not\sqsubseteq Red$▓ **then** $dfsBlue(t)$
12:       **if** $s \in A$ **then** $dfsRed(s)$
13:       $Blue := Blue \cup \{s\}$; $Cyan := Cyan \setminus \{s\}$

14: **procedure** $dfsRed(s)$
15:    **if** $s{\downarrow}_P \not\subseteq Constraints$ **then**
16:       $Red := Red \cup \{s\}$
17:       **for all** $t \in$ REORDERED-NEXT-STATE(s) **do**
18:          **if** $t{\downarrow}_P = s{\downarrow}_P$ **then**
19:             **if** ▓$Cyan \sqsubseteq t$▓ **then**
20:                $Constraints := Constraints \cup t{\downarrow}_P$ ▷ Report cycle at state t
21:             **else if** ▓$t \not\sqsubseteq Red$▓ **then** $dfsRed(t)$

Layering (not shown here) [25]. The layering strategy gives priority to states with large parametric constraints, since these potentially prune many other states. To this end, successors in the next parametric layer are delayed, which is sound, since every cycle must lie entirely in the same parametric layer (Prop. 1).

Proposition 4. *All mentioned NDFS variants are sound and partially correct.*

Proof. Partial correctness is shown in [25]. Soundness follows from Prop. 3, since all collected constraints correspond to accepting spirals.   □

Example 6. None of the mentioned NDFS is complete for symbolic lassos. Consider $\mathcal{A}_5$ in Fig. 6. Its PZG extends Fig. 3(b) with a transition from all states to one additional accepting state with self-loop, $s = (\ell_1, p + x \geq y \geq 6 + x)$, where $s{\downarrow}_P = (p \geq 6)$. All NDFS variants (including all combinations of cumulative pruning, subsumption, lookahead, accept-first, and layering) allow the execution that diverges on the infinite $p \geq 5$ path, so they will never detect the accepting cycle on $p \geq 6$.

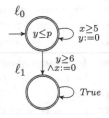

Fig. 6. PTA $\mathcal{A}_5$

4.2 Breadth-First Search

We now describe a BFS-based synthesis algorithm for accepting cycle detection. As in Alg. 1, our BFS algorithm maintains a parameter constraint *Constraints*, initially empty. The algorithm basically explores the newly computed symbolic states in a breadth-first search manner, *i.e.* by iteratively computing all siblings at a given depth level, before computing their own children states. Then, whenever one of these new states is *identical* to a state already present in the state space, a cycle may exist. In this case, we run an SCC-detection algorithm (inspired by Tarjan) and, if there is indeed a cycle, we add the cycle parameter constraint to the result *Constraints*. Remember that, from Prop. 1, all states in such a cycle have the same parametric constraint.

Note that, in contrast to the algorithms in Sec. 4.1 and 4.3, we have to use state *equality*, since using unrestricted subsumption could introduce spurious cycles (cf. examples in [22]). However, we do use *cumulative pruning*, as in Sec. 4.1: whenever the parametric constraint of a new state s is included in the current result *Constraints* (*i.e.* $s\downarrow_P \subseteq Constraints$), we discard it, as no potential loop starting from this state, or from its successors, can improve *Constraints* anyhow.

In contrast to the NDFS-based algorithms in Sec. 4.1, our BFS algorithm is complete for symbolic lassos, since every lasso will appear at some level, and the SCC algorithm will eventually detect it.

Proposition 5. *The BFS+SCC algorithm is sound, partially correct, and complete for symbolic lassos.*

4.3 Bounded Synthesis with Iterative Deepening

One way to enforce termination is to explore the PZG up to a given depth (Bounded Synthesis). However, this could make the result incomplete. Therefore, as long as there are unexplored states, the bound should be increased (Iterative Deepening), to synthesize parameter valuations for deeper accepting cycles.

Alg. 2 presents this procedure, called BSID. Although all strategies in Sec. 4.1 are compatible with this approach, only cumulative pruning and subsumption are shown in the algorithm. It repeatedly explores the PZG from an initial depth *depthinit*, incrementing the depth by *depthstep* at each iteration (1.8). The termination criterion is that the current exploration did terminate without reaching its current depth (1.7). In this case, the result is complete. Both *dfsBlue* and *dfsRed* do not go beyond the current exploration depth (at 1.10,20).

To avoid some duplicate work at different iterations, the set of blue states is split using two colours: *Green states* have a descendent not completely processed due to the depth limit, and should thus be considered in further iterations; *Blue states* are those whose children have already been completely explored and thus should not be considered anymore. Hence, at the beginning of an iteration, all colours but blue are reset (1.5). States are coloured green when they are at the depth limit (1.10) or if they have a green successor (1.16). Note that *dfsBlue* is not called for blue states at 1.14, but it may be called for states that have been coloured green at the previous iteration but have been uncoloured.

Proposition 6. *The BSID algorithm is sound, partially correct, and complete for symbolic lassos.*

Proof. Soundness follows from Prop. 3, since every collected constraint corresponds to an accepting spiral. Completeness for symbolic lassos follows, since every accepting cycle in the PZG is entirely present at some depth. When NDFS is run beyond that depth, it will report the constraint leading to that cycle. Partial correctness follows, since the algorithm only terminates if the last run did not reach the depth-bound, in which case the PZG is searched exhaustively. □

Example 7. On both $\mathcal{A}_2$ (Fig. 3, Ex. 4) and $\mathcal{A}_5$ (Fig. 6, Ex. 6), BSID will correctly report $p \geq 5$ and then terminate; for $\mathcal{A}_5$ it may first report $p \geq 6$, depending on the search order. It is actually the combination of *bounded* synthesis and *subsumption* that makes the algorithm complete for this example. The bound ensures that NDFS is run after the first iteration, and subsumption ensures that an accepting spiral is found as explained in Ex. 4. At this point, the constraint $p \geq 5$ is discovered, which prunes the rest of the PZG, ensuring termination.

Alg. 2 Iterative deepening NDFS with cumulative constraint pruning and subsumption

```
 1: procedure ITERATIVECOLLECTNDFSSUB(depthinit,depthstep)
 2:     Cyan := Blue := Red := Green := ∅ ; Constraints := ∅
 3:     depth := depthinit; again := true
 4:     while again do
 5:         Cyan := Red := Green := ∅ ; depthreached := false
 6:         dfsBlue(s₀,0)
 7:         if ¬depthreached then again := false
 8:         if again then depth := depth + depthstep

 9: procedure dfsBlue(s,dₛ)
10:     if dₛ ≥ depth then depthreached := true ; Green := Green ∪ {s} ; return
11:     if s↓P ⊆ Constraints then Blue := Blue ∪ {s} ; return
12:     Cyan := Cyan ∪ {s}
13:     for all t ∈ NEXT-STATE(s) do
14:         if t ∉ Blue ∪ Green ∪ Cyan ∧ t ⋢ Red then dfsBlue(t,dₛ+1)
15:     if s ∈ A then dfsRed(s,dₛ)
16:     if ∃s' ∈ Green ∩ NEXT-STATE(s) then Green := Green ∪ {s}
17:     else Blue := Blue ∪ {s}
18:     Cyan := Cyan \ {s}

19: procedure dfsRed(s,dₛ)
20:     if dₛ < depth ∧ s↓P ⋢ Constraints then
21:         Red := Red ∪ {s}
22:         for all t ∈ NEXT-STATE(s) do
23:             if t↓P= s↓P then
24:                 if Cyan ⊑ t then
25:                     Constraints := Constraints ∪ t↓P        ▷ Report cycle at state t
26:                 else if t ⋢ Red then dfsRed(t,dₛ+1)
```

5   Experimental Evaluation

We conducted some experiments, to compare all algorithms on the number of cases they can solve and on their efficiency. In order to compare cases in which an algorithm does not terminate, we also counted the number of reported cycles.

To this end, we implemented our new algorithms BFS and BSID in IMI-TATOR 3,[2] and we also reimplemented all NDFS-based algorithms [11,25] in a unified DFS framework. We ran all algorithms on a benchmark, distributed with IMITATOR [4] and also used in [25]. The size of the benchmarks is shown in Tab. 1 (columns L,X,P). We used a timeout of 120 s.[3]

In Tab. 1, we compare some combinations of NDFS enhancements (Sec. 4.1), extending the baseline (*cumulative pruning*). The results show that *subsumption* alone performs worst, while *lookahead* solves more cases, *e.g.* ll.3–6 of Tab. 1. Interestingly, adding our new *accepting first* strategy succeeds to find cycles (l.12) that are missed by all other strategies. Finally, adding the *layering* approach leads to success in most cases and provides the fastest results on average, but it finds no accepting cycles at all for five cases where others found some.

Tab. 2 compares the new algorithms BFS (Sec. 4.2) and BSID (Sec. 4.3), including all enhancements (except layering) under various depth settings. BSID is generally faster than BFS, in particular with an iterative depth-step of 5. The performance of BFS is closest to BSID with depth-step 1. The first two columns evaluate the effectiveness of using the green colour (ng = -no-green). Without green, no information from previous iterations is reused. Avoiding recomputation is faster, leading to a deeper exploration within the time limit (*e.g.* on l.2).

Comparing both tables, we notice that for ll.15–17 NDFS synthesised some parameter values that are missed by BSID and BFS. BSID is generally faster than its NDFS counterpart A+L+Sub, but NDFS with layering is even faster.

6   Case Study: the Bounded Retransmission Protocol

The *Bounded Retransmission Protocol* (BRP) has been analysed in [16,14,19], but we now *synthesise* the most liberal parameter constraints to obtain some reachability and liveness guarantees. For reachability, these constraints are more liberal than proposed in previous work. Synthesising parameter constraints for liveness properties is new, and our new algorithms were required to achieve this.

Our starting point is the PTA model from [14]. Each session starts with a transmission request S_in and is terminated by an indication S_ok, S_nok or S_dk ("don't know"). The BRP is regulated by clocks, with some timing parameters: TD is the delay in the communication channel, TS and TR indicate the time that the sender (receiver) should wait. Finally, SYNC models the waiting time in case sender and receiver get out of sync. The maximum number of retransmissions is a discrete parameter, which we fixed in most experiments to MAX = 2.

---

[2]Algorithms are integrated in IMITATOR v.3. The artifact is at doi.org/10.5281/zenodo.4115919 and can be run at: imitator.lipn.univ-paris13.fr/artifact.

[3]The experiment ran on a DELL PowerEdge FC640, 2 processors (Intel Xeon Silver 4114 @ 2.20 GHz), Debian GNU/Linux 10, 187.50 GiB memory.

Table 1. Comparing various NDFS enhancements. For each model, L denotes the number of locations, X the number of clocks, and P the number of parameters. For each algorithm, column d indicates the actual depth reached, m the minimum depth at which a cycle was found, c the total number of cycles found, s the number of states explored, and t the time spent in the algorithm (discarding parsing the model) in seconds. # terminations indicates the number of benchmarks for which the algorithm terminates, and # fastest how many times it performed best. Finally, we computed for each algorithm the Average Normalised Time over all benchmarks, where we normalised the time w.r.t. the largest time used by any algorithm in Tab. 1 and 2. Timeout values get a normalised time of 1.

#	Model	L	X	P	Subsumption					Lookahead					Accept.+Look					A+L+Sub					A+L+Sub+Lvars				
					d	m	c	s	t	d	m	c	s	t	d	m	c	s	t	d	m	c	s	t	d	m	c	s	t
1	BRP	22	7	2	32	18	17	8370	TO	32	15	17	8336	TO	32	14	17	8340	TO	32	14	17	8350	TO	31	16	10	4666	TO
2	coffee	4	2	3	3580	0		3581	TO	3590	0		3591	TO	3591	0		3592	TO	3581	0		3582	TO	3545	4	1	3550	TO
3	critical-region	20	2	2	10980			10981	TO	10	7	2	7	0.013	4	3	2	6	0.015	4	3	2	6	0.013	3	3	1	4	0.012
4	critical-region4	38	4	2	11564			11565	TO	10	7	2	17	0.042	10	7	2	16	0.044	10	7	2	16	0.043	3	3	1	8	0.026
5	F3	18	3	0	7607			7608	TO	0	0	1	1	0.009	0	0	1	1	0.007	0	0	1	1	0.009	0	0	0	1	0.007
6	F4	23	4	2	6260			6261	TO	0	0	1	1	0.011	0	0	1	1	0.009	0	0	1	1	0.009	0	0	1	1	0.012
7	FDDI4	34	13	2	90	36	2	742	1.960	90	32	2	690	1.695	90	32	2	690	1.692	90	32	2	690	1.696	110	101	1	660	1.718
8	FischerAHV93	13	2	4	15	4	2	24	0.022	4	3	1	11	0.013	4	3	1	11	0.013	4	3	1	11	0.012	4	3	1	11	0.013
9	flipflop	49	5	2	7	5	6	20	0.024	7	5	6	18	0.022	7	5	6	18	0.022	7	5	6	18	0.023	7	7	1	8	0.014
10	fmtv1A1-v2	15	3	3	30	13	75	4229	TO	30	13	75	4235	TO	30	13	66	4538	TO	30	13	66	4539	TO	29	13	55	5929	67.651
11	fmtv1A3-v2	15	3	3	40	26	116	4949	TO	40	26	116	4975	TO	40	26	108	5065	TO	40	26	108	5041	TO	45			10898	TO
12	JLR-TACAS13	2	2	1	6443		1	6444	0.008	6506		1	6507	0.009	1309	1	1	2619	0.011	1308	1	1	2616	0.009	6362			6363	TO
13	lynch	18	2	1	10	9	1	24	0.005	7	7	1	19	0.025	3	3	1	19	0.009	3	3	1	19	0.011	3	3	1	4	0.012
14	lynch5	45	5	1	45		1	24	0.033	7	7	1	19	0.027	7	7	1	19	0.027	7	7	1	19	0.028	7	7	1	19	0.025
15	Pipeline-KP12-2-3	14	4	6	544	81	29	3256	TO	560	36	59	2227	TO	73	29	80	1643	TO	73	29	80	1645	TO	49	32	46	2146	TO
16	Pipeline-KP12-2-5	18	4	6	997	756	10	2989	TO	110	50	64	2401	TO	101	39	69	1711	TO	101	39	69	1713	TO	69	44	33	2201	TO
17	Pipeline-KP12-3-3	19	5	6	689	448	6	1263	TO	132	57	23	869	TO	122	50	21	706	TO	122	50	21	707	TO	112	59	1	1239	TO
18	RCP	48	6	5	74	8	12	237	0.886	74	8	12	237	0.877	74	8	12	237	0.871	74	8	12	237	0.866	50	50	1	105	0.152
19	Sched2.100.0	17	6	2	132	3	19	872	5.890	132	3	19	872	5.870	132	2	19	869	5.842	132	2	19	869	5.844	174	20	4	592	2.465
20	Sched2.100.2	17	6	2	990	3	21	2430	TO	990	3	21	2453	TO	990	2	21	2453	TO	990	2	21	2461	TO	3433	21	5	3838	TO
21	Sched2.50.0	17	6	2	132	7	19	756	4.434	132	7	19	756	4.398	132	6	19	752	4.348	132	6	19	752	4.368	242	31	5	636	2.853
22	Sched2.50.2	17	6	2	1559	7	22	3037	TO	1561	7	22	3039	TO	1563	6	22	3037	TO	1567	6	22	3041	TO	2737	22	0	4584	TO
23	simop	46	8	2	2533			2534	TO	2520			2521	TO	2520			2521	TO	2521		142	2522	TO	2520		142	2521	TO
24	spsmall	52	11	2	34	30	142	4036	17.637	34	26	142	3445	13.812	34	25	142	2634	10.952	34	25	142	2634	10.987	34	25	142	2663	7.436
25	tgcTogether2	12	3	6	32	13	7	137	0.410	18	13	4	79	0.410	18	13	4	79	0.193	18	13	4	79	0.193	14	13	2	47	0.060
26	WFAS-BBLS15-det	10	4	2	6682	3	12	6737	TO	6749	3	12	6804	TO	6643	3	14	6698	TO	6576	3	14	6631	TO	7048	3	14	7049	TO

	# terminations	# fastest	Avg. Norm. Time
Subsumption	10	1	0.853
Lookahead	13	0	0.754
Accept.+Look	13	3	0.743
A+L+Sub	14	3	0.720
A+L+Sub+Lvars	15	11	0.651

	Model	Depth 5, step 5				Depth 5, step 5 (ng)				Depth 10, step 5				Depth 10, step 10				Depth 0, step 1				BFS			
		d	m	c	t	d	m	c	t	d	m	c	t	d	m	c	t	d	m	c	t	d	m	c	t
1	BRP	20	12	19	TO	20	12	19	TO	20	12	19	TO	20	12	26	TO	20	12	15	TO	21	13	41	TO
2	coffee	2280	4	2	0.012	2055	4	1	0.013	2273	4	3	0.015	2674	4	6	0.014	1345	4	1	0.015	3664	5	4	TO
3	critical-region	4	3	2	TO	5	5	2	TO	10	7	2	0.042	10	7	2	0.044	4	4	1	0.009	5	3	2	0.023
4	critical-region4	5	5	1	0.141	5	5	2	0.141	7	7	1	0.044	7	7	1	TO	4	4	1	0.432	7	5	29	3.321
5	F3	0	0	1	0.007	0	0	1	0.007	0	0	1	0.008	0	0	1	0.007	0	0	1	0.011	3	1	4	0.010
6	F4	0	0	1	0.009	0	0	1	0.011	0	0	1	0.010	0	0	1	0.009	0	0	1	TO	3	1	5	0.014
7	FDDI4	70	32	2	2.279	70	32	2	2.658	70	32	2	2.308	70	32	2	2.010	70	32	2	3.366	72	33	10	2.907
8	FischerAHV93	4	3	1	0.010	4	3	1	0.013	4	3	1	0.014	4	3	1	0.014	4	3	1	0.017	6	1	14	0.010
9	flipflop	7	5	6	0.022	7	5	6	0.023	7	5	6	0.022	7	5	6	0.021	7	5	6	0.026	9	6	8	0.024
10	fmtv1A1-v2	30	13	51	119.408	30	13	51	TO	30	13	51	TO	30	13	60	TO	29	13	45	102.716	32	14	321	113.084
11	fmtv1A3-v2	20	13	21	TO	20	13	21	TO	20	13	21	TO	20	13	22	TO	20	13	10	TO	21	14	101	TO
12	JLR-TACAS13	2065	1	2065	TO	1490	1	1490	TO	2065	1	2065	TO	2690	1	2690	TO	1030	1	1030	TO	1299	2	1298	TO
13	lynch	3	3	1	0.008	3	3	1	0.011	3	3	1	0.013	3	3	1	0.010	3	3	1	0.012	6	4	1	0.013
14	lynch5	5	5	1	0.100	5	5	1	0.094	7	7	1	0.025	7	7	1	0.028	3	3	1	0.120	6	4	1	0.437
15	Pipeline-KP12-2-3	15	15	0	TO	15	15	0	TO	15	15	0	TO	20	20	0	TO	13	8	0	TO	15	9	0	TO
16	Pipeline-KP12-2-5	15	15	0	TO	15	15	0	TO	15	15	0	TO	20	20	0	TO	15	8	0	TO	17		0	TO
17	Pipeline-KP12-3-3	15	15	0	TO	15	15	0	TO	15	15	0	TO	20	20	0	TO	13	8	0	TO	16		0	TO
18	RCP	10	8	6	0.507	10	8	6	0.511	10	8	6	0.352	10	8	6	0.351	10	8	7	0.834	12	9	104	1.855
19	Sched2.100.0	104	2	10	5.709	107	2	10	7.044	104	2	10	5.715	104	2	10	4.322	104	2	9	19.068	54	3	56	2.861
20	Sched2.100.2	130	2	14	TO	130	2	14	TO	130	2	14	TO	140	2	14	TO	120	2	13	TO	92	3	348	TO
21	Sched2.50.0	104	6	9	4.054	107	6	9	5.044	104	6	9	4.048	104	6	9	3.043	104	6	8	13.177	36	7	52	1.900
22	Sched2.50.2	135	6	12	TO	135	6	12	TO	135	6	12	TO	140	6	12	TO	131	6	11	TO	106	7	278	TO
23	simop	25	15	53	TO	25	15	53	TO	25	15	53	TO	30	20	59	TO	21	13	44	TO	22	14	304	TO
24	spsmall	34	25	142	9.632	34	25	142	9.633	34	25	142	9.581	34	25	142	11.246	34	25	142	11.318	36	26	368	12.480
25	tgcTogether2	15	13	3	0.149	15	13	3	0.155	15	13	3	0.154	18	13	4	0.197	14	13	3	0.197	16	14	5	0.159
26	WFAS-BBLS15-det	2090	3	9	TO	1465	3	9	TO	2090	3	9	TO	2800	3	12	TO	991	3	9	TO	6748	4	17	TO
	# terminations	15				14				15				14				15				15			
	# fastest	6				1				3				5				1				3			
	Avg. Norm. Time	0.701				0.735				0.725				0.704				0.835				0.863			

Table 2. Comparing exploration of BSID (Alg. 2) with different depth settings, using all strategies except layering (A+L+Sub), and BFS (Sec. 4.2). For each algorithm, column d indicates the actual depth reached, m the minimum depth at which a cycle was found, c the total number of cycles found, and t the time spent in the algorithm (discarding parsing the model) in seconds. # terminations indicates the number of benchmarks for which the algorithm terminates, and # fastest how many times it performed best. Finally, we computed for each algorithm the Average Normalised Time over all benchmarks, where we normalised the time w.r.t. the largest time used by any algorithm in Tab. 1 and 2. Timeout values get a normalised time of 1.

6.1   Synthesis for Reachability Properties: deriving sharper bounds

To illustrate synthesis for reachability properties, we first enhance the parametric verification experiments from [14,19] in IMITATOR. The reachability properties are: **(C)** the channels will never be used simultaneously; and **(R)** the receiver gets a correct initial frame in each session. Property **(C)** is formalised as:

```
property := #synth AGnot(loc[channelK] = in_transitK & loc[channelL] = in_transitL)
```

We synthesise the safe parameter constraints for "unreachability" by:[4]

```
imitator -mergeq -comparison inclusion brp_Channels.imi brp_Channels.imiprop
```

IMITATOR derives within 2 s the exact constraint $TS > 2*TD$: The sender should wait (TS) for the round-trip time of a message + acknowledgement (2*TD).

Property **(R)** is formalised by adding an error location `FailureR` to the receiver, which should be unreachable. Since we learned the constraint $TS > 2*TD$ in the previous run, we now include this constraint in the initial condition. Within 1 s, IMITATOR synthesizes the exact constraint for this safety property:

```
imitator -mergeq -comparison inclusion brp_RC.imi brp_RC.imiprop
SYNC + TS >= TR + TD & TS > 2*TD & TR > 4*TS + 3*TD
```

The fact that this can be computed is not surprising, but it *is* surprising that this constraint is more liberal than the one derived in [14,19], which was:

```
SYNC >= TR & TS > 2*TD & TR > 2*MAX*TS + 3*TD
```

One can easily check that, for $MAX = 2$, their constraint is strictly stronger than ours. *So we found more parameter values for which BRP is correct.* By construction, we found the most liberal constraint for $MAX = 2$, and we confirmed a similar result for up to $MAX = 20$. We cannot handle a parametric MAX.

6.2   Liveness: approximations by bounded synthesis

Next, we want to measure the overhead of liveness checking. To this end, we make the failureR location an accepting cycle, and use a liveness property. Note that in this case, the synthesised constraint will indicate the error condition.

```
accepting loc FailureR: invariant True when True goto FailureR;
init := ... & TS > 2 * TD
property := #synth CycleThrough(accepting)
```

Since we search for an accepting loop, inclusion and merging are unsound, but still complete. However, we can safely apply subsumption in NDFS. Without inclusion, the zone graph is infinite, so we are forced to resort to bounded synthesis, which only provides an under-approximation. Hence, we also use iterative deepening (BSID, Sec. 4.3). The depth limit is reached in 6 s.

---

[4]Inclusion and merging are sound and complete for reachability [7]. Inclusion applies maximal subsumption, while merging combines zones with exact convex hull.

```
imitator brp_RC.imi accepting.imiprop -depth-step=5 -depth-limit=25 -recompute-green
    4*TS + 3*TD >= TR & TS > 2*TD
OR TR + TD > SYNC + TS & TS > 2*TD
```

We could have searched even deeper for more liberal constraints, but it can be easily checked that this error constraint is equivalent to the complement of the safety constraint (within the initial condition), see Sec. 6.1, property **(R)**. Hence, we can conclude that we have already synthesised the exact constraint.

6.3 Proper Liveness Properties

GF(S_in). Next, we will synthesise constraints for an actual liveness property, stating that the number of new sessions is infinite. We use Spot [15] to generate a Büchi automaton for the *negation* of this formula, and add the result as a monitor to the IMITATOR model, synchronising with the sender process. We add the constraints on correctness that we learned before to the initial constraints:

```
init := ... & SYNC >= TR & TS > 2*TD & TR > 4*TS + 3*TD
```

The following command tries to synthesize all parameters (within the initial constraint) for which an accepting loop is reachable, *i.e.* **GF** S_in is violated. We replaced subsumption by full inclusion, since otherwise IMITATOR gets lost in the infinite parametric zone graph. Recall that inclusion is complete but unsound for NDFS, so this provides an over-approximation of the constraints.

```
imitator -no-subsumption -comparison inclusion brp_GF_S_in_RC.imi accepting.imiprop
```

IMITATOR replies *False* in 1 second, so there is no reachable accepting cycle. Since this was an over-approximation, the result is conclusive: **GF** S_in holds under all parameter values inside this initial constraint. Note that, in principle, the property could be violated outside this initial condition. We can rerun the same experiment with the more general initial condition TS > 2*TD. IMITATOR confirms that the property still holds, but checking this larger space takes 19 s.

G(S_in ⇒ F(S_ok ∨ S_nok ∨ S_dk)). Using the same method, IMITATOR confirms in 16 s, that also this response property holds: every sessions start is followed by some indication.

```
imitator -no-subsumption -comparison inclusion brp_GSinFSdk.imi accepting.imiprop
```

G(S_in ⇒ F(S_ok ∨ S_nok)). Let us pretend that we forgot the indication S_dk (don't know). This time, we search for a symbolic counter-example (using the option -witness), under the initial condition TS > 2*TD.

```
property := #witness CycleThrough(accepting)
imitator brp_GSinFSnok.imi accepting_one.imiprop
```

As expected, IMITATOR finds a counter-example quickly (within 0.04s).

7   Conclusion

We presented and evaluated new semi-algorithms solving the liveness parameter synthesis problem for Parametric Timed Automata. We also introduced new soundness and completeness notions for such semi-algorithms. The new algorithms, based on BFS and Bounded Synthesis (BSID), at least enumerate all parameters leading to accepting lassos in the parametric zone graph. We showed that this property does not hold for all previous algorithms, which were based on NDFS. Our new algorithms are less sensitive to the particular search order than the previous NDFS algorithms, that could get stuck in some branch of the PZG.

Tab. 3 (left) shows the soundness and completeness status of all considered algorithms. Full inclusion and BS-n can only provide an over-approximation (resp. under-approximation). The enumQ algorithm is complete, but never terminates (indicated by $\times\times$), so its partial soundness and completeness results are vacuous (indicated by $(\checkmark)$). Although the problem is undecidable, one might still hope for an algorithm that enumerates all possible solutions (like enumQ, generating and testing all rational solutions) *and* produces a finite set of aggregate solutions (if it exists). The algorithm should terminate for practical cases.

Tab. 3 (right) shows the results of our algorithms for examples $\mathcal{A}_1$–$\mathcal{A}_6$. They either terminate with an exact $(\checkmark)$ or partial $((\checkmark))$ result, or diverge $(\times)$. In one case the addition of the layers strategy is needed to obtain a partial result $((L))$.

Our last example shows another challenge to obtain a complete approach. The PZG of PTA $\mathcal{A}_6$ has a non-cyclic infinite path. It seems non-trivial to compute its limit constraint automatically. After n steps, the parametric constraint is $p \geq n \times q$. So the limit constraint is $q = 0 \wedge p \geq q$.

In order to handle cases where the set of solutions is not even a finite union of convex sets (Fig. 5), an entirely different representation of the solutions would be required.

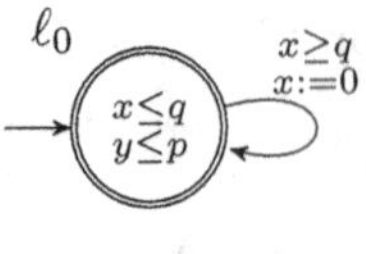

Fig. 7. PTA $\mathcal{A}_6$.

Finally, exploiting the component-based structure of networks of PTA using a compositional approach, such as the one developed recently for fair paths in infinite systems [12], would be an exciting extension.

Table 3. Soundness and completeness properties of various algorithms.

Algorithm	terminates	partially sound	partially complete	sound in the limit	complete in limit	complete for lassos	$\mathcal{A}_1$	$\mathcal{A}_2$	$\mathcal{A}_3$	$\mathcal{A}_4$	$\mathcal{A}_5$	$\mathcal{A}_6$
NDFS (enhanced)	×	✓	✓	✓	×	×	✓	×	×	$(\checkmark)$	(L)	×
NDFS + inclusion	×	×	✓	×	×	×	✓	×	×	$(\checkmark)$	(L)	×
BFS + SCC	×	✓	✓	✓	×	✓	✓	×	×	$(\checkmark)$	$(\checkmark)$	×
BSID	×	✓	✓	✓	×	✓	✓	✓	×	$(\checkmark)$	✓	×
BS-n (fixed bound)	✓	✓	×	✓	×	×						
Naïve enumQ	××	$(\checkmark)$	$(\checkmark)$	✓	✓	✓						

References

1. Alur, R., Dill, D.L.: A theory of timed automata. Theoretical Computer Science **126**(2), 183–235 (1994). https://doi.org/10.1016/0304-3975(94)90010-8
2. Alur, R., Henzinger, T.A., Vardi, M.Y.: Parametric real-time reasoning. In: Kosaraju, S.R., Johnson, D.S., Aggarwal, A. (eds.) STOC. pp. 592–601. ACM, New York, NY, USA (1993). https://doi.org/10.1145/167088.167242
3. André, É.: What's decidable about parametric timed automata? International Journal on Software Tools for Technology Transfer (2019). https://doi.org/10.1007/s10009-017-0467-0
4. André, É.: A benchmark library for parametric timed model checking. In: Artho, C., Ölveczky, P.C. (eds.) FTSCS. Communications in Computer and Information Science, vol. 1008, pp. 75–83. Springer (2019). https://doi.org/10.1007/978-3-030-12988-0_5
5. André, É., Chatain, Th., Encrenaz, E., Fribourg, L.: An inverse method for parametric timed automata. International Journal of Foundations of Computer Science **20**(5), 819–836 (2009). https://doi.org/10.1142/S0129054109006905
6. André, É., Fribourg, L., Kühne, U., Soulat, R.: IMITATOR 2.5: A tool for analyzing robustness in scheduling problems. In: Giannakopoulou, D., Méry, D. (eds.) FM. Lecture Notes in Computer Science, vol. 7436, pp. 33–36. Springer (2012). https://doi.org/10.1007/978-3-642-32759-9_6
7. André, É., Fribourg, L., Soulat, R.: Merge and conquer: State merging in parametric timed automata. In: Hung, D.V., Ogawa, M. (eds.) ATVA. Lecture Notes in Computer Science, vol. 8172, pp. 381–396. Springer (Oct 2013). https://doi.org/10.1007/978-3-319-02444-8_27
8. André, É., Lime, D.: Liveness in L/U-parametric timed automata. In: Legay, A., Schneider, K. (eds.) ACSD. pp. 9–18. IEEE (2017). https://doi.org/10.1109/ACSD.2017.19
9. André, É., Nguyen, H.G., Petrucci, L., Sun, J.: Parametric model checking timed automata under non-Zenoness assumption. In: Barrett, C., Kahsai, T. (eds.) NFM. Lecture Notes in Computer Science, vol. 10227, pp. 35–51. Springer (2017). https://doi.org/10.1007/978-3-319-57288-8_3
10. Bagnara, R., M., H.P., Zaffanella, E.: The Parma Polyhedra Library: Toward a complete set of numerical abstractions for the analysis and verification of hardware and software systems. Science of Computer Programming **72**(1–2), 3–21 (2008). https://doi.org/10.1016/j.scico.2007.08.001
11. Bezděk, P., Beneš, N., Barnat, J., Černá, I.: LTL parameter synthesis of parametric timed automata. In: Nicola, R.D., eva Kühn (eds.) SEFM. Lecture Notes in Computer Science, vol. 9763, pp. 172–187. Springer (2016). https://doi.org/10.1007/978-3-319-41591-8_12
12. Cimatti, A., Griggio, A., Magnago, E.: Proving the existence of fair paths in infinite-state systems. In: Henglein, F., Shoham, S., Vizel, Y. (eds.) VMCAI. Lecture Notes in Computer Science, vol. 12597, pp. 104–126. Springer (2021). https://doi.org/10.1007/978-3-030-67067-2_6
13. Courcoubetis, C., Vardi, M., Wolper, P., Yannakakis, M.: Memory-efficient algorithms for the verification of temporal properties. Formal Methods in System Design **1**(2/3), 275–288 (1992). https://doi.org/10.1007/BF00121128
14. D'Argenio, P.R., Katoen, J.P., Ruys, T.C., Tretmans, J.: The bounded retransmission protocol must be on time! In: Brinksma, E. (ed.) TACAS. Lecture Notes in Computer Science, vol. 1217, pp. 416–431. Springer (1997). https://doi.org/10.1007/BFb0035403

15. Duret-Lutz, A., Lewkowicz, A., Fauchille, A., Michaud, T., Renault, É., Xu, L.: Spot 2.0 — A framework for LTL and ω-automata manipulation. In: ATVA. Lecture Notes in Computer Science, vol. 9938, pp. 122–129. Springer (2016). https://doi.org/10.1007/978-3-319-46520-3_8

16. Groote, J.F., van de Pol, J.: A bounded retransmission protocol for large data packets. In: Wirsing, M., Nivat, M. (eds.) AMAST. Lecture Notes in Computer Science, vol. 1101, pp. 536–550. Springer (1996). https://doi.org/10.1007/BFb0014338

17. Herbreteau, F., Srivathsan, B.: Efficient on-the-fly emptiness check for timed Büchi automata. In: Bouajjani, A., Chin, W.N. (eds.) ATVA. Lecture Notes in Computer Science, vol. 6252, pp. 218–232. Springer (2010). https://doi.org/10.1007/978-3-642-15643-4_17

18. Herbreteau, F., Srivathsan, B., Tran, T.T., Walukiewicz, I.: Why liveness for timed automata is hard, and what we can do about it. ACM Transactions on Computational Logic **21**(3), 17:1–17:28 (2020). https://doi.org/10.1145/3372310

19. Hune, T., Romijn, J., Stoelinga, M., Vaandrager, F.W.: Linear parametric model checking of timed automata. Journal of Logic and Algebraic Programming **52-53**, 183–220 (2002). https://doi.org/10.1016/S1567-8326(02)00037-1

20. Jovanović, A., Lime, D., Roux, O.H.: Integer parameter synthesis for real-time systems. IEEE Transactions on Software Engineering **41**(5), 445–461 (2015). https://doi.org/10.1109/TSE.2014.2357445

21. Knapik, M., Penczek, W.: Bounded model checking for parametric timed automata. Transactions on Petri Nets and Other Models of Concurrency **5**, 141–159 (2012). https://doi.org/10.1007/978-3-642-29072-5_6

22. Laarman, A., Olesen, M.C., Dalsgaard, A.E., Larsen, K.G., van de Pol, J.: Multicore emptiness checking of timed Büchi automata using inclusion abstraction. In: Sharygina, N., Veith, H. (eds.) CAV. Lecture Notes in Computer Science, vol. 8044, pp. 968–983. Springer, Heidelberg, Germany (2013). https://doi.org/10.1007/978-3-642-39799-8_69

23. Li, G.: Checking timed Büchi automata emptiness using LU-abstractions. In: Ouaknine, J., Vaandrager, F.W. (eds.) FORMATS, Lecture Notes in Computer Science, vol. 5813, pp. 228–242. Springer (2009). https://doi.org/10.1007/978-3-642-04368-0_18

24. Maler, O., Nickovic, D., Pnueli, A.: From MITL to timed automata. In: Asarin, E., Bouyer, P. (eds.) FORMATS. Lecture Notes in Computer Science, vol. 4202, pp. 274–289. Springer (2006). https://doi.org/10.1007/11867340_20

25. Nguyen, H.G., Petrucci, L., van de Pol, J.: Layered and collecting NDFS with subsumption for parametric timed automata. In: Lin, A.W., Sun, J. (eds.) ICECCS. pp. 1–9. IEEE Computer Society (2018). https://doi.org/10.1109/ICECCS2018.2018.00009

26. van de Pol, J., Petrucci, L.: On completeness of liveness synthesis for parametric timed automata (extended abstract, invited talk). In: Roggenbach, M. (ed.) WADT 2020 (2021), to appear

27. Tripakis, S., Yovine, S., Bouajjani, A.: Checking timed Büchi automata emptiness efficiently. Formal Methods in System Design **26**(3), 267–292 (2005). https://doi.org/10.1007/s10703-005-1632-8

Algebraic Quantitative Semantics for Efficient Online Temporal Monitoring

Konstantinos Mamouras$^{(\boxtimes)}$, Agnishom Chattopadhyay, and Zhifu Wang

Rice University, Houston TX 77005, USA
{mamouras, agnishom, zfwang}@rice.edu

Abstract. We investigate efficient algorithms for the online monitoring of properties written in metric temporal logic (MTL). We employ an abstract algebraic semantics based on semirings. It encompasses the Boolean semantics and a quantitative semantics capturing the robustness of satisfaction, which is based on the max-min semiring over the extended real numbers. We provide a precise equational characterization of the class of semirings for which our semantics can be viewed as an approximation to an alternative semantics that quantifies the distance of a system trace from the set of all traces that satisfy the desired property.

Keywords: Online Monitoring · Verification · Quantitative Semantics.

1 Introduction

Online monitoring is a lightweight verification technique for checking during runtime that a system behaves as desired. It has proved to be effective for evaluating the correctness of the behavior of complex systems, which includes cyber-physical systems (CPSs) that consist of both computational and physical processes. An *online monitor* is a program that observes the execution trace of the system and emits values that indicate events of interest or other actionable information.

It is common to specify monitors using special-purpose formalisms such as variants of temporal logic and domain-specific programming languages. In the context of cyber-physical systems, logics that are interpreted over signals are frequently used. This includes Metric Temporal Logic (MTL) [30] and Signal Temporal Logic (STL) [33]. We focus here on properties specified with MTL and interpreted over discrete-time signals. We do not restrict the outputs of the monitor to Boolean (qualitative) verdicts, but allow for a quantitative interpretation of property satisfaction that admits various degrees of truth or falsity. Such quantitative interpretations of temporal logic have been considered before, including several variants of the so-called robust semantics of MTL [22,20,5].

Our starting point is the widely-used spatial robust semantics of MTL [22]. This uses the set $\mathbb{R}^{\pm\infty} = \mathbb{R} \cup \{-\infty, \infty\}$ of the extended real numbers as truth values, where a positive number indicates truth, a negative number indicates falsity, and zero is ambiguous. Disjunction is interpreted as max, and conjunction is interpreted as min. Two quantitative semantic notions are considered in [22]:

© The Author(s) 2021
J. F. Groote and K. G. Larsen (Eds.): TACAS 2021, LNCS 12651, pp. 330–348, 2021.
https://doi.org/10.1007/978-3-030-72016-2_18

(1) the *robustness degree* degree(φ, u) of a trace u w.r.t. a formula φ, which is defined in a global way using distances between signals, and (2) the *robust semantics* $\rho(\varphi, u)$ of a formula φ w.r.t. a trace u, which is defined by induction on the structure of φ. The former notion is the primary definition that captures the intuitive idea of the degree of satisfaction, whereas the latter is used as an approximate estimate. The usefulness of this estimate is justified by establishing a precise relationship between the two values [22]. The robust semantics of [22] has been used in prior work on online monitoring [16,15].

We embark on an investigation of how to generalize the robustness framework of [22] to other notions of quantitative truth values. Instead of focusing exclusively on the concrete structure $(\mathbb{R}^{\pm\infty}, \sup, \inf, -\infty, \infty)$, we take an *abstract algebraic* approach and look at classes of structures that are defined axiomatically. We start by considering the class of semirings, algebraic structures of the form $(V, +, \cdot, 0, 1)$ with an addition operation $+$ (which models disjunction) and a multiplication operation $\cdot$ (which models conjunction) satisfying a set of equational laws. The class of semirings contains $\mathbb{B} = \{\bot, \top\}$ (the Boolean values), $(\mathbb{R}^{\pm\infty}, \max, \min, -\infty, \infty)$, the max-plus (tropical) semiring $(\mathbb{R} \cup \{-\infty\}, \max, +, -\infty, 0)$, and $(\mathbb{R}, +, \cdot, 0, 1)$. The semiring of intervals with (semiring) addition given by $[a, b] \oplus [c, d] = [\max(a, c), \max(b, d)]$ and (semiring) multiplication given by $[a, b] \otimes [c, d] = [\min(a, c), \min(b, d)]$ is an especially interesting example, as it can be used to model uncertainty in the truth value: an element $[a, b]$ indicates that the truth value lies somewhere within this interval.

We use an algebraic generalization of the inductively-defined robust semantics of [22], as our goal is to obtain online monitors that are time- and space-efficient. Our main results are the following:

- The theorem of [22] that relates degree(φ, u) and $\rho(\varphi, u)$ is generalized from $\mathbb{R}^{\pm\infty}$ to a class of semirings. The class of semirings for which the theorem holds admits a precise axiomatic characterization (Theorem 7). To obtain this, we develop a notion of symbolic quantitative languages that forms a semantic bridge between quantitative specifications and sets of traces.
- We propose a new algorithm for efficient online monitoring (Theorem 11) that goes beyond existing algorithms. Prior monitors [16,15] compute max or min over sliding-windows and therefore apply only to semirings that are linear orders (e.g., $\mathbb{B}$ and $\mathbb{R}^{\pm\infty}$). Our monitoring algorithm applies to values V that are partial orders or more general semirings. In order to obtain this algorithm, we reduce the monitoring of formulas of the form $\varphi \, \mathsf{S}_{[a,b]} \, \psi$ and $\varphi \, \mathsf{U}_{[a,b]} \, \psi$ to a sliding-window aggregation (which is neither max nor min).

We provide an implementation of our algebraic monitoring framework in Rust. Our experiments show that our monitors scale reasonably well and they compare favorably against the state-of-the-art monitoring tool Reelay [40].

2   Algebraic Semantics using Semirings

A *semiring* is an algebraic structure $(V, +, \cdot, 0, 1)$, where $+$ is called addition and $\cdot$ is called multiplication, that satisfies the following properties: (1) $(V, +, 0)$ is a commutative monoid, (2) $(V, \cdot, 1)$ is a monoid, (3) multiplication distributes over addition, and (4) 0 is an annihilator for multiplication. The last two properties say that $x(y+z) = xy + xz$, $(x+y)z = xz + yz$, and $0x = x0 = 0$ for all $x, y, z \in V$. We sometimes write xy to mean $x \cdot y$. A semiring V is called *idempotent* if addition is idempotent, that is, $x + x = x$ for every $x \in V$. For an idempotent semiring, we define the partial order induced by $+$ as follows: $x \leq y$ iff $x + y = y$. A *homomorphism* from a semiring U to a semiring V is a function $h : U \to V$ that commutes with the semiring operations. An *epimorphism* is a surjective homomorphism. Let U and V be idempotent semirings and $h : U \to V$ be a semiring homomorphism. Then, h is *monotone* (i.e., *order-preserving*).

Example 1. The set $\mathbb{B} = \{\bot, \top\}$ of Boolean values with disjunction and conjunction is a semiring. The set $\mathbb{T} = \{\bot, ?, \top\}$ can be endowed with semiring structure as follows: $x + \bot = x$, $x + \top = \top$, $? + ? = ?$, $x \cdot \bot = \bot$, $x \cdot \top = x$, and $? \cdot ? = ?$, where $\cdot$ is commutative. The structure $\mathbb{T}$ is used to give a *three-valued* interpretation of formulas (? is inconclusive). The structure $(\mathbb{R}^{\pm\infty}, \max, \min, -\infty, \infty)$ is the *max-min semiring* over the extended reals. The structure $(\mathbb{R}, +, \cdot, 0, 1)$ is a semiring and $\mathbb{Z}$ (integers) and $\mathbb{N}$ (natural numbers) are subsemirings of it.

We interpret the max-min semiring $\mathbb{R}^{\pm\infty}$ as degrees of truth, where positive means true and negative means false. The value 0 is ambiguous. For this reason we also consider a variant of $\mathbb{R}^{\pm\infty}$, where the value 0 is refined into a positive $+0$ (true) and a negative -0 (false). We thus obtain the max-min semiring $\mathbb{R}^{\pm\infty}_{\pm 0}$, which is isomorphic to $\mathbb{B} \times \mathbb{R}_{\geq 0}$, where $\mathbb{R}_{\geq 0} = \{x \in \mathbb{R} \mid x \geq 0\}$.

For integers $i, j \in \mathbb{Z}$ we define the intervals $[i, j] = \{n \in \mathbb{Z} \mid i \leq n \leq j\}$ and $[i, \infty) = \{n \in \mathbb{Z} \mid i \leq n\}$. For a set I of integers and $n \in \mathbb{Z}$, define $n + I = \{n + i \mid i \in I\}$ and $n - I = \{n - i \mid i \in I\}$.

For a semiring V, an interval $I = [i, j]$ (where i, j are natural numbers) and an I-indexed tuple $\bar{x} = (x_i)_{i \in I}$ whose components are in V, we define $\sum \bar{x} = \sum_{k \in I} x_k = \sum_{k=i}^{j} x_k = x_i + \cdots + x_j$ and $\prod \bar{x} = \prod_{k \in I} x_k = \prod_{k=i}^{j} x_k = x_i \cdots x_j$. If the tuple $\bar{x}$ is empty (i.e., $I = \emptyset$) then we define $\sum \bar{x} = 0$ and $\prod \bar{x} = 1$.

We will consider formulas of Metric Temporal Logic (MTL) interpreted over *traces* that are finite or infinite sequences of *data items* from a set D. We write D^* (resp., D^+) for the set of all finite (resp., non-empty finite) sequences over D, and $D^\omega = \omega \to D$ for the set of all infinite sequences over D, where ω is the first infinite ordinal (i.e., the set of natural numbers). We also define $D^\infty = D^* \cup D^\omega$. We write ε for the empty sequence and $|u|$ for the length of a trace, where $|u| = \omega$ if u is infinite. A finite sequence $u \in D^*$ can be viewed as a function from $\{0, \ldots, |u| - 1\}$ to D, that is, $u = u(0)u(1)\ldots u(|u| - 1)$. We also consider a semiring V whose elements represent quantitative truth values, and *unary quantitative predicates* $p : D \to V$. We write $\mathbb{1}, \mathbb{0} : D \to V$ for the predicates given by $\mathbb{1}(d) = 1$ and $\mathbb{0}(d) = 0$ for every $d \in D$.

The set $\mathsf{MTL}(D, V)$ of ***temporal formulas*** is built from the atomic predicates $p : D \to V$ using the Boolean connectives $\vee$ and $\wedge$, the unary temporal connectives $\mathsf{P}_I, \mathsf{H}_I, \mathsf{F}_I, \mathsf{G}_I$, and the binary temporal connectives $\mathsf{S}_I, \bar{\mathsf{S}}_I, \mathsf{U}_I, \bar{\mathsf{U}}_I$, where I is an interval of the form $[i, j]$ or $[i, \infty)$ with $i, j < \omega$. For every temporal

$$\rho(p, u, i) = p(u(i))$$

$$\rho(\varphi \vee \psi, u, i) = \rho(\varphi, u, i) + \rho(\psi, u, i) \qquad \rho(\varphi \wedge \psi, u, i) = \rho(\varphi, u, i) \cdot \rho(\psi, u, i)$$

$$\rho(\mathsf{P}_I \varphi, u, i) = \sum_{j \in i-I,\, j \geq 0} \rho(\varphi, u, j) \qquad \rho(\mathsf{H}_I \varphi, u, i) = \prod_{j \in i-I,\, j \geq 0} \rho(\varphi, u, j)$$

$$\rho(\mathsf{F}_I \varphi, u, i) = \sum_{j \in i+I,\, j < |u|} \rho(\varphi, u, j) \qquad \rho(\mathsf{G}_I \varphi, u, i) = \prod_{j \in i+I,\, j < |u|} \rho(\varphi, u, j)$$

$$\rho(\varphi \, \mathsf{S}_I \, \psi, u, i) = \sum_{j \in i-I,\, j \geq 0} \left(\rho(\psi, u, j) \cdot \prod_{k=j+1}^{i} \rho(\varphi, u, k) \right)$$

$$\rho(\varphi \, \bar{\mathsf{S}}_I \, \psi, u, i) = \prod_{j \in i-I,\, j \geq 0} \left(\rho(\psi, u, j) + \sum_{k=j+1}^{i} \rho(\varphi, u, k) \right)$$

$$\rho(\varphi \, \mathsf{U}_I \, \psi, u, i) = \sum_{j \in i+I,\, j < |u|} \left(\prod_{k=i}^{j-1} \rho(\varphi, u, k) \right) \cdot \rho(\psi, u, j)$$

$$\rho(\varphi \, \bar{\mathsf{U}}_I \, \psi, u, i) = \prod_{j \in i+I,\, j < |u|} \left(\sum_{k=i}^{j-1} \rho(\varphi, u, k) + \rho(\psi, u, j) \right)$$

Fig. 1: Semiring-based quantitative semantics for MTL.

connective $X \in \{\mathsf{P}, \mathsf{H}, \mathsf{S}, \bar{\mathsf{S}}, \mathsf{F}, \mathsf{G}, \mathsf{U}, \bar{\mathsf{U}}\}$, we write X_i as an abbreviation for $X_{[i,i]}$ and X as an abbreviation for $X_{[0,\infty)}$.

Since we focus in this paper on online monitoring, we restrict attention to the **future-bounded** fragment of MTL, where the future-time temporal connectives are bounded. That is, every U_I connective is of the form $\mathsf{U}_{[a,b]}$ for $a \leq b < \omega$ (and similarly for F_I, G_I, $\bar{\mathsf{U}}_I$). We always assume this restriction on formulas.

We interpret the formulas in $\mathsf{MTL}(D, V)$ over traces from D^∞ and at specific time points. The *interpretation function* $\rho : \mathsf{MTL}(D, V) \times D^\infty \times \omega \to V$, where $\rho(\varphi, u, i)$ is defined when $i < |u|$, is shown in Fig. 1. We say that the formulas φ and ψ are *equivalent*, and we write $\varphi \equiv \psi$, if $\rho(\varphi, u, i) = \rho(\psi, u, i)$ for every $u \in D^\infty$ and $i < |u|$. For every formula φ and every interval I, it holds that $\mathsf{P}_I \varphi \equiv \mathbb{1} \, \mathsf{S}_I \, \varphi$, $\mathsf{H}_I \varphi \equiv \mathbb{0} \, \bar{\mathsf{S}}_I \, \varphi$, $\mathsf{F}_I \varphi \equiv \mathbb{1} \, \mathsf{U}_I \, \varphi$, and $\mathsf{G}_I \varphi \equiv \mathbb{0} \, \bar{\mathsf{U}}_I \, \varphi$.

We say that a semiring V *refines* $\mathbb{B}$ if there is a semiring homomorphism $h : V \to \mathbb{B}$. Notice that h is necessarily an epimorphism because $h(0) = \bot$ and $h(1) = \top$. Informally, we think of $h^{-1}(\bot)$ as the subset of "false" values and $h^{-1}(\top)$ as the subset of "true" values. In particular, this means that V can be partitioned into true and false values. There are semirings that cannot refine $\mathbb{B}$. For example, the semiring $(\mathbb{Z}, +, \cdot, 0, 1)$ of the integers cannot refine $\mathbb{B}$.

Let $h : V \to \mathbb{B}$. For a predicate $p : D \to V$, we say that $d \in D$ *h-satisfies* p, and we write $d \models_h p$, if $h(p(d)) = \top$. For $u \in D^\infty$ and $i < |u|$ we define the *satisfaction relation* $\models_h$ as usual (for atomic formulas: $u, i \models_h p$ iff $u(i) \models_h p$).

Lemma 2. Let D be a set of data items, V be a semiring, and $h : V \to \mathbb{B}$. The following are equivalent:

(1) The function h is a semiring homomorphism.
(2) $u, i \models_h \varphi$ iff $h(\rho(\varphi, u, i)) = \top$ for every $\varphi : \mathsf{MTL}(D, V)$, $u \in D^\infty$ and $i < |u|$.

Lemma 2 says that the qualitative semantics $\models_h$ agrees with the quantitative semantics ρ exactly when $h : V \to \mathbb{B}$ is a semiring homomorphism. In this case, ρ is more fine-grained and loses no information regarding Boolean satisfaction.

Lemma 3. Let D be a set of data items and V be a semiring. The identities of Fig. 2 hold for all formulas $\varphi, \psi \in \mathsf{MTL}(D, V)$.

$$P\varphi \equiv P_1(P\varphi) \vee \varphi \quad \text{and} \quad H\varphi \equiv H_1(H\varphi) \wedge \varphi$$
$$\varphi \, S \, \psi \equiv (P_1(\varphi \, S \, \psi) \wedge \varphi) \vee \psi$$
$$P_{[a,\infty)}\varphi \equiv P_a P\varphi \quad \text{and} \quad H_{[a,\infty)}\varphi \equiv H_a H\varphi$$
$$\varphi \, S_{[a,\infty)} \, \psi \equiv P_a(\varphi \, S \, \psi) \wedge H_{[0,a-1]}\varphi, \quad \text{for } a \geq 1$$
$$P_{[a,b]}\varphi \equiv P_a P_{[0,b-a]}\varphi \quad \text{and} \quad H_{[a,b]}\varphi \equiv H_a H_{[0,b-a]}\varphi$$
$$\varphi \, S_{[a,b]} \, \psi \equiv P_a(\varphi \, S_{[0,b-a]} \, \psi) \wedge H_{[0,a-1]}\varphi, \quad \text{for } a \geq 1$$
$$F_{[0,b]}\varphi \equiv F_b P_{[0,b]}\varphi \quad \text{and} \quad G_{[0,b]}\varphi = G_b H_{[0,b]}\varphi$$
$$F_{[a,b]}\varphi \equiv F_b P_{[0,b-a]}\varphi \quad \text{and} \quad G_{[a,b]}\varphi \equiv G_b H_{[0,b-a]}\varphi$$
$$\varphi \, U_{[a,b]} \, \psi \equiv G_{[0,a-1]}\varphi \wedge F_a(\varphi \, U_{[0,b-a]} \, \psi), \quad \text{for } a \geq 1$$

Fig. 2: Equivalences between temporal formulas.

The identities of Fig. 2 are all shown using the semiring axioms. The identity below can be used to reduce the monitoring of $S_{[0,a]}$ to $P_{[0,a]}$.

$$\varphi \, S_{[0,a]} \, \psi \equiv (\varphi \, S \, \psi) \wedge P_{[0,a]}\psi \tag{1}$$

An early occurrence of this idea is in [19], where they consider the more general (future-time) form $\varphi \, U_{[a,b]} \, \psi \equiv (\varphi \, U_{[a,\infty)} \, \psi) \wedge F_{[a,b]}\psi$. Prior work on efficient monitoring [15] uses an algorithm based on it. Specifically, [15] uses a sliding-max algorithm [32], which can be applied to the max-min semiring $\mathbb{R}^{\pm\infty}$ and other similar linear orders, but is not applicable to partial orders or other semirings.

Proposition 4. For a set D with at least two elements and a semiring V, the following are equivalent:
(1) The semiring V is a bounded distributive lattice.
(2) Equivalence (1) holds for all formulas $\varphi, \psi \in \mathsf{MTL}(D, V)$.

Proposition 4 gives a precise characterization of when the identity (1) applies. This characterization is axiomatic and identifies the class of bounded distributive lattices as the most general class for which the identity is valid. One important implication is that monitors that are based on this identity cannot be used for other semirings such as $(\mathbb{R}, +, \cdot, 0, 1)$ and $(\mathbb{N}, +, \cdot, 0, 1)$.

Example 5 (Uncertainty). We want to identify a notion of quantitative truth values in situations where we interpret formulas over a signal $x[n]$ that is not known with perfect accuracy, but we can put an upper and lower bound on each sample, i.e., $a \leq x[n] \leq b$. For example, suppose that we know that $99.9 \leq x[0] \leq 100.1$ and we want to evaluate the atomic predicate $p = $ "$x \geq 99$" at time 0. The truth value can be taken to be the interval $[0.9, 1.1]$ in this case, since there is uncertainty in the distance of signal value from the threshold.

More concretely, this situation of uncertain input signal can arise in the monitoring of systems where the raw signal is captured at one site, then compressed and transmitted to another site for monitoring. In many resource-constrained settings (e.g., certain IoT systems), the signal has to be compressed with a lossy compression scheme in order to meet network bandwidth constraints. So, at the monitoring site, the exact signal values are not known but can possibly be placed within intervals (depending on the used compression scheme).

In order to model this kind of uncertainty, we consider the set $\mathcal{I}(\mathbb{R}^{\pm\infty})$ of intervals of the form $[a, b]$ with $a \leq b$ and $a, b \in \mathbb{R}^{\pm\infty}$. An interval $[a, b] \subseteq \mathbb{R}^{\pm\infty}$ can be thought of as an uncertain truth value (it can be any one of those contained in $[a, b]$). For intervals $[a, b]$ and $[c, d]$ we define $[a, b] \oplus [c, d] = [\max(a, c), \max(b, d)]$ and $[a, b] \otimes [c, d] = [\min(a, c), \min(b, d)]$. An interval of the form $[a, a]$ is equal to the singleton set $\{a\}$. The structure $(\mathcal{I}(\mathbb{R}^{\pm\infty}), \oplus, \otimes, \{-\infty\}, \{\infty\})$ is a semiring.

The semiring $\mathcal{I}(\mathbb{R}^{\pm\infty})$ is a partial order (more specifically, it is a bounded distributive lattice) and therefore does not fit existing monitoring frameworks that consider only linear orders (e.g., the max-min semiring $\mathbb{R}^{\pm\infty}$ of the extended reals and the associated sliding-max/min algorithms).

3   Symbolic Quantitative Traces and Languages

In this section we start with our investigation of how to generalize the "robustness degree" of [22] to our abstract algebraic setting. The result of [22] that relates the robustness degree with the robust semantics is an inequality. For this reason, we focus on idempotent semirings, for which there is a natural partial order $\leq$ that is induced by semiring addition ($x \leq y$ iff $x + y = y$). Since our approach is abstract algebraic (i.e., axiomatic), we have no notion of real-valued distance between elements of D. Moreover, V does not need to be a semiring of real numbers. Instead, we rely on the intuition that for an atomic predicate $p : D \to V$ and a data item $d \in D$, the value $p(d)$ gives a degree of truth or falsity. We propose using *symbolic traces* $\mathbf{x} = p_0 p_1 \ldots p_{n-1}$, which are sequences of atomic predicates, in order to compactly represent sets of *concrete traces*, which are sequences of data items. If each p_i represents a subset $S_i \subseteq D$, then $\mathbf{x}$ represents the set $L = S_0 \times S_1 \times \cdots \times S_{n-1} = \{v_0 v_1 \ldots v_{n-1} \mid v_i \in S_i \text{ for each } i\}$ of concrete traces. Moreover, given a concrete trace $u = u_0 u_1 \ldots u_{n-1} \in D^n$, we can use the value $p_0(u_0) \cdot p_1(u_1) \cdots p_{n-1}(u_{n-1}) \in V$ as a quantitative measure of how close the trace u is to the set of traces L. We propose the interpretation of a formula φ as a *language of symbolic traces*. This will allow us to define the "closeness" of a trace $u \in D^n$ to the specification φ as a (semiring) sum of all the closeness values w.r.t. each symbolic trace in the symbolic language of φ. We will also see that this interpretation of a formula φ as a symbolic language is compatible with the standard interpretation of φ as a set of concrete traces. Using these definitions we obtain a generalization of the theorem of [22] that relates the robustness degree with the robust semantics. Additionally, we characterize precisely the class of semirings for which this generalization is possible.

Let V be an idempotent semiring. For predicates $p, q : D \to V$ we define $p \leq q$ if $p(d) \leq q(d)$ for every $d \in D$. The intuition for $p \leq q$ is that p is a stronger predicate than q. We write $\mathsf{F}(D, V)$ to denote the set of atomic quantitative predicates, which always includes the predicates $\mathbb{1}$ and $\mathbb{0}$. For symbolic traces $\mathbf{x}, \mathbf{y} \in \mathsf{F}(D, V)^\infty$ with $\lambda = |\mathbf{x}| = |\mathbf{y}|$ we define $\mathbf{x} \leq \mathbf{y}$ if $\mathbf{x}(i) \leq \mathbf{y}(i)$ for every $i < \lambda$. These relations $\leq$ on predicates and traces are partial orders. We define the *symbolic satisfaction relation* $\models$, where $\mathbf{x}, i \models \varphi$ says that the formula φ : $\mathsf{MTL}(D, V)$ is satisfied by the symbolic trace $\mathbf{x} \in \mathsf{F}(D, V)^\infty$ at position $i < |\mathbf{x}|$. For atomic formulas, we put $\mathbf{x}, i \models p$ iff $\mathbf{x}(i) \leq p$. The definition is given by induction on φ in the usual way. For a formula φ : $\mathsf{MTL}(D, V)$, length $\lambda \in \omega \cup \{\omega\}$ and a position $i < \lambda$, we define the *symbolic language* $\mathsf{SL}(\varphi, \lambda, i) = \{\mathbf{x} \in \mathsf{F}(D, V)^\lambda \mid \mathbf{x}, i \models \varphi\}$. For nonempty finite traces $\mathbf{x} \in \mathsf{F}(D, V)^n$ and $u \in D^n$ of the same length, we define $\mathbf{x}[u] = \prod_{i=1}^n \mathbf{x}(i)(u(i))$, where $n = |\mathbf{x}| = |u|$. Since the semiring multiplication is monotone w.r.t. $\leq$, we see that $\mathbf{x} \leq \mathbf{y}$ implies $\mathbf{x}[u] \leq \mathbf{y}[u]$ for every $u \in D^n$. Informally, the value $\mathbf{x}[u]$ quantifies how close the concrete trace u is to the symbolic trace $\mathbf{x}$.

Example 6. Let $D = \mathbb{R}$ and $V = \mathbb{R}^{\pm\infty}$. For $c \in \mathbb{R}$, the predicate $p = \text{"}x \geq c\text{"}$ is defined by $p(d) = d - c$ for every $d \in D$. The predicate $q = \text{"}x \leq c\text{"}$ is given by $q(d) = c - d$ for every $d \in D$. For the symbolic trace $\mathbf{x} = \text{"}x \geq 1\text{"} \text{ "}x \leq 5\text{"} \text{ "}x \geq 2\text{"}$ and the concrete trace $u = 3\,6\,8$ we get that $\mathbf{x}[u] = \min(2, -1, 6) = -1$.

Let $c, d \in \mathbb{R}$. For the predicates $p = \text{"}x \geq c\text{"}$ and $q = \text{"}x \geq d\text{"}$ we have that $p \leq q$ iff $d \leq c$. Similarly, for the predicates $p = \text{"}x \leq c\text{"}$ and $q = \text{"}x \leq d\text{"}$ it holds that $p \leq q$ iff $c \leq d$. Finally, notice that the predicates $\text{"}x \geq c\text{"}$ and $\text{"}x \leq d\text{"}$ are incomparable. Consider $\mathbf{y} = \text{"}x \geq 0\text{"} \text{ "}x \leq 7\text{"} \text{ "}x \geq 1\text{"}$ and observe that $\mathbf{x} \leq \mathbf{y}$.

For the formula $\varphi = p \wedge \mathsf{F}_1 q$, where p and q are atomic predicates, we have that $\mathsf{SL}(\varphi, 2, 0) = \{p'q' \in \mathsf{F}(D, V)^2 \mid p' \leq p \text{ and } q' \leq q\}$.

The definition of the robustness degree in [22] involves the value $-\mathsf{dist}(u, L) = -\inf_{v \in L} \mathsf{dist}(u, v) = \sup_{v \in L} -\mathsf{dist}(u, v)$, where u is a trace, L is a set of traces, and dist is a metric. Notice that this is a supremum over a potentially infinite set. The semirings that we have considered so far have an addition operation that can model a *finitary* supremum. In order to model an *infinitary* supremum, we need to consider semirings that have an infinitary addition operation. A *complete semiring* is an algebraic structure $(V, +, \sum, \cdot, 0, 1)$, where $\sum_{i \in I} x_i$ is the sum of the I-indexed tuple of elements $(x_i)_{i \in I}$, that satisfies: (1) $\sum_{i \in \emptyset} x_i = 0$, $\sum_{i \in \{j\}} x_i = x_j$, $\sum_{i \in \{j,k\}} x_i = x_j + x_k$ for $j \neq k$, and $\sum_{k \in K} \sum_{i \in I_k} x_i = \sum_{i \in I} x_i$ where $I = \bigcup_{k \in K} I_k$ and the index sets $(I_k)_{k \in K}$ are pairwise disjoint, (2) $(V, \cdot, 1)$ is a monoid, (3) the infinite distributivity properties $(\sum_{i \in I} x_i) \cdot y = \sum_{i \in I} (x_i y)$ and $x \cdot (\sum_{i \in I} y_i) = \sum_{i \in I} (x y_i)$ hold for every index set I and all $x_i, y \in V$, and (4) 0 is an annihilator for multiplication. A complete semiring V is *idempotent* if $\sum_{i \in I} x_i = x$ for every non-empty index set I with $x_i = x$ for every $i \in I$. For example, $(\mathbb{R}^{\pm\infty}, \max, \sup, \min, -\infty, +\infty)$ is an idempotent complete semiring. For a formula φ : $\mathsf{MTL}(D, V)$, a trace $u \in D^+$ and $i < n = |u|$, we define

$$\mathsf{val}(\varphi, u, i) = \sum_{\mathbf{x} \in \mathsf{SL}(\varphi, n, i)} \mathbf{x}[u]. \tag{2}$$

Informally, $\mathsf{val}(\varphi, u, i)$ is a measure of how close the trace u is to satisfying φ at position i. It is an abstract algebraic variant of the robustness degree [22].

Theorem 7 (Approximation). Let D be a set of data items and V be an idempotent complete semiring. Then, the following are equivalent:
(1) The multiplication of V is idempotent and 1 is the top element of V.

(2) For every $\varphi : \mathsf{MTL}(D,V)$, $u \in D^+$ and $i < |u|$, $\mathsf{val}(\varphi, u, i) \leq \rho(\varphi, u, i)$.

Proof. Assume that (1) holds. Let $n \geq 1$ be an integer. For a symbolic language $\mathcal{L} \subseteq \mathsf{F}(D,V)^n$ and for $u \in D^n$, we define $\mathsf{val}(\mathcal{L}, u) = \sum_{\mathbf{x} \in \mathcal{L}} \mathbf{x}(u)$. Let $\{\mathcal{L}_i\}_{i \in I}$ be a collection of languages with $\mathcal{L}_i \subseteq \mathsf{F}(D,V)^n$. Then,

$$\mathsf{val}(\textstyle\bigcup_{i \in I} \mathcal{L}_i, u) = \sum_{\mathbf{x} \in \bigcup_{i \in I} \mathcal{L}_i} \mathbf{x}[u] \leq \sum_{i \in I} \sum_{\mathbf{x} \in \mathcal{L}_i} \mathbf{x}[u] = \sum_{i \in I} \mathsf{val}(\mathcal{L}_i, u). \qquad (3)$$

For symbolic languages $\mathcal{L}_1, \mathcal{L}_2 \subseteq \mathsf{F}(D,V)^n$, define $\mathcal{L} = \mathcal{L}_1 \cap \mathcal{L}_2$, $\mathcal{L}'_1 = \mathcal{L}_1 \setminus \mathcal{L}_2$ and $\mathcal{L}'_2 = \mathcal{L}_2 \setminus \mathcal{L}_1$. Then, $\mathcal{L}_1 = \mathcal{L}'_1 \cup \mathcal{L}$ and $\mathcal{L}_2 = \mathcal{L}'_2 \cup \mathcal{L}$. The languages $\mathcal{L}'_1, \mathcal{L}'_2, \mathcal{L}$ are pairwise disjoint. So, we have that $\mathsf{val}(\mathcal{L}_1, u) = x + z$ and $\mathsf{val}(\mathcal{L}_2, u) = y + z$, where $x = \mathsf{val}(\mathcal{L}'_1, u)$, $y = \mathsf{val}(\mathcal{L}'_2, u)$ and $z = \mathsf{val}(\mathcal{L}, u)$. It follows that

$$\mathsf{val}(\mathcal{L}_1 \cap \mathcal{L}_2, u) = z = zz \leq (x + z)(y + z) = \mathsf{val}(\mathcal{L}_1, u) \cdot \mathsf{val}(\mathcal{L}_2, u) \qquad (4)$$

by the idempotence of multiplication. This property extends to $\mathsf{val}(\mathcal{L}_1 \cap \cdots \cap \mathcal{L}_k, u) \leq \mathsf{val}(\mathcal{L}_1, u) \cdots \mathsf{val}(\mathcal{L}_k, u)$. Now, we will prove (2) by induction on φ.

- For the base case we have $\mathsf{SL}(p, n, i) = \{\mathbf{x} \in \mathsf{F}(D,V)^n \mid \mathbf{x}(i) \leq p\}$. Define $\mathbf{y} \in \mathsf{F}(D,V)^n$ by $\mathbf{y}(i) = p$ and $\mathbf{y}(j) = \mathbb{1}$ for every $j \neq i$. That is, $\mathbf{y} = \mathbb{1}^i \, p \, \mathbb{1}^{n-i-1}$. For every $\mathbf{x} \in \mathsf{SL}(p, n, i)$ we have $\mathbf{x}(i) \leq p$ and therefore $\mathbf{x} \leq \mathbf{y}$ (since $\mathbb{1}$ is the top element of V). It follows that $\mathbf{x}[u] \leq \mathbf{y}[u] = p(u(i))$. So, $\mathsf{val}(p, u, i) = \sum_{\mathbf{x} \in \mathsf{SL}(p,n,i)} \mathbf{x}[u] \leq p(u(i)) = \rho(p, u, i)$.
- For the case of disjunction, we have $\mathsf{SL}(\varphi \vee \psi, n, i) = \mathsf{SL}(\varphi, n, i) \cup \mathsf{SL}(\psi, n, i)$. It follows that $\mathsf{val}(\varphi \vee \psi, u, i) \leq \mathsf{val}(\varphi, u, i) + \mathsf{val}(\psi, u, i) \leq \rho(\varphi, u, i) + \rho(\psi, u, i) = \rho(\varphi \vee \psi, u, i)$ by the induction hypothesis and (3).
- For the case of conjunction we observe that $\mathsf{val}(\varphi \wedge \psi, u, i) = \mathsf{val}(\mathsf{SL}(\varphi, n, i) \cap \mathsf{SL}(\psi, n, i), u) \leq \mathsf{val}(\varphi, u, i) \cdot \mathsf{val}(\psi, u, i) \leq \rho(\varphi, u, i) \cdot \rho(\psi, u, i) = \rho(\varphi \wedge \psi, u, i)$ by the induction hypothesis and (4).

The rest of the cases S, $\bar{\mathsf{S}}$, U, $\bar{\mathsf{U}}$ can be dealt with similarly using (3) and (4). The proof that (2) implies (1) is not too difficult, and we therefore omit it. □

Theorem 7 could be considered an abstract algebraic counterpart of the result of [22] (page 4268, Theorem 13) for discrete finite traces. We will discuss later how it can be used to obtain the original result (for the max-min semiring $\mathbb{R}^{\pm\infty}$) as a corollary. Additionally, Theorem 7 gives a precise equational characterization of the class of semirings for which the relationship between the two semantics holds.

Let D be a set of data items, V be a semiring and $h : V \to \mathbb{B}$. For a formula $\varphi : \mathsf{MTL}(D,V)$, length $\lambda \in \omega \cup \{\omega\}$ and $i < \lambda$, we define the *concrete trace language* $\mathsf{CL}_h(\varphi, \lambda, i) = \{u \in D^\lambda \mid u, i \models_h \varphi\}$. For a symbolic trace $\mathbf{x} \in \mathsf{F}(D,V)^\lambda$, we define its (concrete) *trace language* by $\mathsf{CL}_h(\mathbf{x}) = \{u \in D^\lambda \mid u \models_h \mathbf{x}\}$, where $u \models_h \mathbf{x}$ means that $u(i) \models_h \mathbf{x}(i)$ for every $i < n$. Lemma 8 below establishes a correspondence between the symbolic and concrete language of a formula φ, which we need to connect Theorem 7 to the concrete setting of [22].

Lemma 8 (Concrete and Symbolic Languages). Let D be a set of data items, V be an idempotent semiring with top element 1, and $h : V \to \mathbb{B}$ be a semiring homomorphism. For every formula $\varphi : \mathsf{MTL}(D,V)$, length $\lambda \in \omega \cup \{\omega\}$, and position $i < \lambda$, it holds that $\mathsf{CL}_h(\varphi, \lambda, i) = \bigcup_{\mathbf{x} \in \mathsf{SL}(\varphi, \lambda, i)} \mathsf{CL}_h(\mathbf{x})$.

4   Relationship with robust semantics

In this section, we consider the concrete quantitative setting where V is the max-min semiring $\mathbb{R}^{\pm\infty}$. We will obtain the result of [22] that relates the robustness degree with the robust semantics as a consequence of Theorem 7.

A *metric space* is a set M together with a function $\mathsf{dist} : M \times M \to \mathbb{R}_{\geq 0}$, called *metric*, satisfying: (1) $\mathsf{dist}(x, y) = 0$ iff $x = y$ for all $x, y \in M$, (2) $\mathsf{dist}(x, y) = \mathsf{dist}(y, x)$ for all $x, y \in M$, and (3) $\mathsf{dist}(x, z) \leq \mathsf{dist}(x, y) + \mathsf{dist}(y, z)$ for all $x, y, z \in M$. Given a metric dist on M we define the *distance function* Dist as follows:

$$\mathsf{dist} : M \times \mathcal{P}(M) \to \mathbb{R}_{\geq 0}^{\infty} \qquad\qquad \mathsf{Dist} : M \times \mathcal{P}(M) \to \mathbb{R}^{\pm\infty}$$

$$\mathsf{dist}(x, S) = \inf_{y \in S} \mathsf{dist}(x, y) \qquad \mathsf{Dist}(d, S) = \begin{cases} -\mathsf{dist}(d, S), & \text{if } d \notin S \\ \mathsf{dist}(d, {\sim}S), & \text{if } d \in S \end{cases}$$
$$\mathsf{dist}(x, \emptyset) = \infty$$

where ${\sim}S = M \setminus S$ is the complement of S. Notice that $\mathsf{Dist}(x, \emptyset) = -\infty$.

Let D be a metric space of points (data items). Let $\mathbf{p}$ be a propositional letter (symbol), and $\mathcal{O}(\mathbf{p}) \subseteq D$ be its interpretation, that is, the set of points for which $\mathbf{p}$ is true. The corresponding quantitative predicate is $p : D \to \mathbb{R}^{\pm\infty}$ given by $p(d) = \mathsf{Dist}(d, \mathcal{O}(\mathbf{p}))$ for every $d \in D$. Given the metric dist on D, we obtain a metric $\mathsf{dist} : D^\lambda \times D^\lambda \to \mathbb{R}_{\geq 0}^{\infty}$ (on the set of traces of length λ, where $\lambda \in \omega \cup \{\omega\}$) as follows: $\mathsf{dist}(u, v) = \sup_{i < \lambda} \mathsf{dist}(u(i), v(i))$. Let $\mathsf{CL}_{\mathcal{O}}(\varphi, n, i) = \{u \in D^n \mid u, i \models_{\mathcal{O}} \varphi\}$ be the set of traces (of length n) that satisfy φ at i (defined using the interpretation function $\mathcal{O}$). Corollary 9 below was proved in [22]. We will give a proof that relies on the algebraic variant that we presented earlier.

Corollary 9. Let D be a set of data items, and $V = \mathbb{R}^{\pm\infty}$. Let $\varphi : \mathsf{MTL}(D, V)$, $u \in D^n$ and $i < n$ (where $n \geq 1$). Then, $-\mathsf{dist}(u, \mathsf{CL}_{\mathcal{O}}(\varphi, n, i)) \leq \rho(\varphi, u, i)$.

Proof. We will use the semiring $\mathbb{R}_{\pm 0}^{\pm\infty} \cong \mathbb{B} \times \mathbb{R}_{\geq 0}^{\infty}$ instead of $\mathbb{R}^{\pm\infty}$, so that the value 0 is not ambiguous (it can be either true or false when we use $\mathbb{R}^{\pm\infty}$). That is, we will have a positive zero $+0$ (true) and a negative zero -0 (false). The semiring homomorphism $h : \mathbb{R}_{\pm 0}^{\pm\infty} \to \mathbb{B}$ sends the positive (resp., negative) elements to $\top$ (resp., $\bot$). We will interpret a predicate symbol $\mathbf{p}$ as the quantitative predicate $p : D \to \mathbb{R}_{\pm 0}^{\pm\infty}$ given by $p(d) = -\mathsf{dist}(d, \mathcal{O}(\mathbf{p}))$ if $d \notin \mathcal{O}(\mathbf{p})$ and $p(d) = +\mathsf{dist}(d, {\sim}\mathcal{O}(\mathbf{p}))$ if $d \in \mathcal{O}(\mathbf{p})$. Using these definitions, the satisfaction relations $\models_{\mathcal{O}}$ and $\models_h$ are the same, hence $\mathsf{CL}_{\mathcal{O}}$ and CL_h are the same. Now,

$$\begin{aligned} \mathsf{dist}(u, \mathsf{CL}_h(\varphi, n, i)) &= \mathsf{dist}(u, \textstyle\bigcup_{\mathbf{x} \in \mathsf{SL}(\varphi, n, i)} \mathsf{CL}_h(\mathbf{x})) && [\text{Lemma 8}] \\ &= \inf_{\mathbf{x} \in \mathsf{SL}(\varphi, n, i)} \inf_{v \in \mathsf{CL}_h(\mathbf{x})} \sup_{i < n} \mathsf{dist}(u(i), v(i)) && [\text{def. of dist}] \\ &\geq \inf_{\mathbf{x} \in \mathsf{SL}(\varphi, n, i)} \sup_{i < n} \inf_{v \in \mathsf{CL}_h(\mathbf{x})} \mathsf{dist}(u(i), v(i)) && [\sup \inf \leq \inf \sup] \\ &= \inf_{\mathbf{x} \in \mathsf{SL}(\varphi, n, i)} \sup_{i < n} \inf_{v(i) \in \mathcal{O}(\mathbf{x}(i))} \mathsf{dist}(u(i), v(i)) && [\text{def. of CL}] \\ &= \inf_{\mathbf{x} \in \mathsf{SL}(\varphi, n, i)} \sup_{i < n} \mathsf{dist}(u(i), \mathcal{O}(\mathbf{x}(i))). && [\text{def. of dist}] \end{aligned}$$

By negating the above inequality we get that

$$-\mathrm{dist}(u, \mathsf{CL}_h(\varphi, n, i)) \leq \sup_{\mathbf{x} \in \mathsf{SL}(\varphi, n, i)} \inf_{i < n} -\mathrm{dist}(u(i), \mathcal{O}(\mathbf{x}(i))),$$

which is $\leq \sum_{\mathbf{x} \in \mathsf{SL}(\varphi, n, i)} \mathbf{x}[u] = \mathsf{val}(\varphi, u, i)$. From Theorem 7 we get $\mathsf{val}(\varphi, u, i) \leq \rho(\varphi, u, i)$ and therefore $-\mathrm{dist}(u, \mathsf{CL}_{\mathcal{O}}(\varphi, n, i)) \leq \rho(\varphi, u, i)$. $\qquad\Box$

From Corollary 9 we can also obtain $\rho(\varphi, u, i) \leq \mathrm{dist}(u, \sim\mathsf{CL}_{\mathcal{O}}(\varphi, n, i))$. This inequality is equivalent to $-\mathrm{dist}(u, \sim\mathsf{CL}_{\mathcal{O}}(\varphi, n, i)) \leq -\rho(\varphi, u, i)$, which in turn is equivalent to $-\mathrm{dist}(u, \mathsf{CL}_{\mathcal{O}}(\sim\varphi, n, i)) \leq \rho(\sim\varphi, u, i)$. The operation $\sim$ on formulas is a pseudo-negation, that is, $\sim\varphi$ is the formula that results by "dualizing" all connectives and negating the atomic predicates. This operation is meaningful for the semiring $\mathbb{R}^{\pm\infty}$. The final inequality is an instance of Corollary 9 for $\sim\varphi$.

Theorem 7 and Corollary 9 are not used later for the monitoring algorithm. The significance of our theorem is that it can be instantiated to give the existing result from [22]. This serves as a sanity check for our algebraic framework and it supports the semiring-based semantics of Sect. 2.

5   Online Monitoring

For an infinite input trace $u \in D^\omega$, the output of the monitor for the time instant t should be $\rho(\varphi, u, t)$, but the monitor has to compute it by observing only a finite prefix of u. In order for the output value of the monitor to agree with the standard temporal semantics over infinite traces we may need to delay an output item until some part of the future input is seen. For example, in the case of $\mathsf{F}_1 p$ we need to wait for one time unit: the output at time t is given after the input item at time $t + 1$ is seen. In other words, the monitor for $\mathsf{F}_1 p$ has a *delay* (the output is falling behind the input) of one time unit. Symmetrically, we can allow monitors to emit output early when the correct value is known. For example, the output value for $\mathsf{P}_1 p$ is 0 in the beginning and the value at time t is already known from time $t - 1$. So, we also allow monitors to have negative delay (the output is running ahead of the input). The function $\mathsf{dl} : \mathsf{MTL} \to \mathbb{Z}$ gives the amount of delay required to monitor a formula. It is defined by $\mathsf{dl}(p) = 0$ and

$$\mathsf{dl}(\varphi \wedge \psi) = \max(\mathsf{dl}(\varphi), \mathsf{dl}(\psi)) \qquad \mathsf{dl}(\varphi \, \mathsf{S}_{[a,b]} \, \psi) = \max(\mathsf{dl}(\varphi), \mathsf{dl}(\psi)) - a$$
$$\mathsf{dl}(\varphi \, \mathsf{S}_{[a,\infty)} \, \psi) = \max(\mathsf{dl}(\varphi), \mathsf{dl}(\psi)) - a \quad \mathsf{dl}(\varphi \, \mathsf{U}_{[a,b]} \, \psi) = \max(\mathsf{dl}(\varphi), \mathsf{dl}(\psi)) + b.$$

The monitor $\mathsf{TL}(\varphi)$ for a formula φ is a variant of a Mealy machine. If $\mathsf{dl}(\varphi) = 0$, the $\mathsf{TL}(\varphi)$ is precisely a Mealy machine (one output item per input item) with inputs D and outputs V. If $\ell = \mathsf{dl}(\varphi) > 0$, then $\mathsf{TL}(\varphi)$ emits no output for the first ℓ steps and then behaves like a Mealy machine. If $\ell = \mathsf{dl}(\varphi) < 0$, then $\mathsf{TL}(\varphi)$ emits ℓ items upon initialization and continues to behave like a Mealy machine.

Let A and B be sets. A *monitor* of type $\mathsf{M}(A, B)$ is a state machine $G = (\mathsf{St}, \mathsf{init}, \mathsf{o}, \mathsf{next}, \mathsf{out})$, where St is a set of *states*, $\mathsf{init} \in \mathsf{St}$ is the *initial state*, $\mathsf{o} \in B^*$ is the *initial output*, $\mathsf{next} : \mathsf{St} \times A \to \mathsf{St}$ is the *transition function*, and $\mathsf{out} : \mathsf{St} \times A \to \mathsf{Opt}(B)$ is the *output function*, where $\mathsf{Opt}(B) = B \cup \{\mathsf{nil}\}$.

$$\begin{array}{ccc}
\mathrm{map}(op) : \mathrm{M}(A, B) & \mathrm{aggr}(b, op) : \mathrm{M}(A, B) & \mathrm{emit}(n, v) : \mathrm{M}(A, A) \\
\mathrm{St} = \mathrm{Unit} & \mathrm{St} = B & \mathrm{St} = \mathrm{Unit} \\
\mathrm{init} = u & \mathrm{init} = b & \mathrm{init} = u \\
\mathrm{o} = \varepsilon & \mathrm{o} = \varepsilon & \mathrm{o} = v^n \\
\mathrm{next}(s, a) = s & \mathrm{next}(s, a) = op(s, a) & \mathrm{next}(s, a) = s \\
\mathrm{out}(s, a) = op(a) & \mathrm{out}(s, a) = op(s, a) & \mathrm{out}(s, a) = a
\end{array}$$

$$\begin{array}{ccc}
\mathrm{ignore}(n) : \mathrm{M}(A, A) & \mathrm{wnd}(n, v, op) : \mathrm{M}(A, A) & \mathrm{wndV}(n, op) : \mathrm{M}(A, A) \\
\mathrm{St} = [0, n] & \mathrm{St} = \mathrm{Buf}(A) & \mathrm{St} = \mathrm{Buf}(A) \\
\mathrm{init} = 0 & \mathrm{init} = \mathrm{Buf}(n, v) & \mathrm{init} = \mathrm{Buf}() \\
\mathrm{o} = \varepsilon & \mathrm{o} = \varepsilon & \mathrm{o} = \varepsilon \\
\mathrm{next}(s, a) = s + 1, \text{ if } s < n & \mathrm{next}(s, a) = s.\mathrm{ins}(a) & \mathrm{next}(s, a) = s.\mathrm{ins}(a) \\
\mathrm{next}(s, a) = s, \text{ if } s = n & \mathrm{out}(s, a) = s.\mathrm{ins}(a).\mathrm{agg}(op) & \mathrm{out}(s, a) = \varepsilon, \text{ if } \mathrm{size}(s) < n - 1 \\
\mathrm{out}(s, a) = \mathrm{nil}, \text{ if } s < n & & \mathrm{out}(s, a) = s.\mathrm{ins}(a).\mathrm{agg}(op), \text{ o/w} \\
\mathrm{out}(s, a) = a, \text{ if } s = n & &
\end{array}$$

Fig. 3: Basic building blocks for constructing temporal quantitative monitors.

In Fig. 3 we give several examples of simple monitors that can be used as building blocks. The monitor $\mathrm{map}(op)$ applies the function $op : A \to B$ elementwise. The monitor $\mathrm{aggr}(b, op)$ applies a running aggregation to the input trace that is specified by the initial aggregate $b : B$ and the aggregation function $op : B \times A \to B$ (similar to the fold combinator used in functional programming). The monitor $\mathrm{emit}(n, v)$ emits n copies of the value $v \in A$ upon initialization and then echoes the input trace. The monitor $\mathrm{ignore}(n)$ discards the first n items of the trace and proceeds to echo the rest of the trace. The monitor $\mathrm{wnd}(n, v, op)$ performs an aggregation, given by the associative function $op : A \times A \to A$, over a sliding window of size n. It initializes the window using the value $v : A$ and emits output at the arrival of every item. The monitor $\mathrm{wndV}(n, op)$ is different in that it starts with an empty window and it only starts emitting output when the window fills up with n items. We will combine monitors using the operations *serial composition* $\gg$ and *parallel composition* **par**. In the serial composition $G \gg H$ the output trace of G is propagated as input trace to H. In the parallel composition $\mathrm{par}(G, H)$ the input trace to copied to two concurrently executing monitors G and H and their output traces are combined. Both combinators $\gg$ and **par** are given by variants of the product construction on state machines. In the case of **par** the output traces of G and H may not be synchronized (one may be ahead of the other), which requires some bounded buffering in order to properly align them. The construction for **par** is described in [37]. Some variants of the combinators of Figure 3 are part of the StreamQL language [29], which has been proposed for the processing of streaming time series.

The identities of Fig. 2 suggest that MTL monitoring can be reduced to a small set of computational primitives. In fact, the primitives described earlier are sufficient to specify the monitors, as shown in Fig. 4. We write $\pi_1 : A \times B \to A$ for the left projection and $\pi_2 : A \times B \to B$ for the right projection.

Let $u \in D^+$ and $n = |u|$. If $n > a$ then $\rho(\varphi \, \mathsf{S}_{[0,a]} \, \psi, u, n - 1) = \rho(\varphi \, \mathsf{S} \, \psi, v, a)$, where v is the suffix of u with $a + 1$ items. If $n \le a$ then $\rho(\varphi \, \mathsf{S}_{[0,a]} \, \psi, u, n - 1) =$

$$\text{TL}(p) = \text{map}(p)$$
$$\text{TL}(\varphi \vee \psi) = \text{par}(\text{TL}(\varphi), \text{TL}(\psi)) \gg \text{map}(+)$$
$$\text{TL}(\mathsf{P}\varphi) = \text{TL}(\varphi) \gg \text{aggr}(0, +)$$
$$\text{TL}(\mathsf{P}_a\varphi) = \text{TL}(\varphi) \gg \text{emit}(a, 0)$$
$$\text{TL}(\mathsf{P}_{[a,\infty)}\varphi) = \text{TL}(\mathsf{P}_a\mathsf{P}\varphi)$$
$$\text{TL}(\varphi \mathsf{S}\, \psi) = \text{par}(\text{TL}(\varphi), \text{TL}(\psi)) \gg \text{aggr}(0, opS)$$
$$opS : V \times (V \times V) \to V, \text{ where}$$
$$opS(s, \langle x, y \rangle) = (s \cdot x) + y$$
$$\text{TL}(\varphi \mathsf{S}_{[a,\infty)}\, \psi) = \text{TL}(\mathsf{P}_a(\varphi \mathsf{S}\, \psi) \wedge \mathsf{H}_{[0,a-1]}\varphi)$$
$$\text{TL}(\varphi \mathsf{S}_{[0,b]}\, \psi) = \text{par}(\text{TL}(\varphi), \text{TL}(\psi)) \gg$$
$$\text{wnd}(b + 1, 0, \otimes_{\mathsf{S}}) \gg \text{map}(\pi_2)$$
$$\text{TL}(\varphi \mathsf{S}_{[a,b]}\, \psi) = \text{TL}(\mathsf{P}_a(\varphi \mathsf{S}_{[0,b-a]}\, \psi) \wedge \mathsf{H}_{[0,a-1]}\varphi)$$
$$\text{TL}(\mathsf{F}_a\varphi) = \text{TL}(\varphi) \gg \text{ignore}(a)$$
$$\text{TL}(\mathsf{F}_{[a,b]}\varphi) = \text{TL}(\mathsf{F}_b\mathsf{P}_{[0,b-a]}\varphi)$$
$$\text{TL}(\varphi \mathsf{U}_{[0,b]}\, \psi) = \text{par}(\text{TL}(\varphi), \text{TL}(\psi)) \gg$$
$$\text{wndV}(b + 1, \otimes_{\mathsf{U}}) \gg \text{map}(\pi_2)$$
$$\text{TL}(\varphi \mathsf{U}_{[a,b]}\, \psi) = \text{TL}(\mathsf{G}_{[0,a-1]}\varphi \wedge \mathsf{F}_a(\varphi \mathsf{U}_{[0,b-a]}\, \psi))$$

```
// fill buffer with v (initial values)
T[n] buf ← [n; v]
// calculate partial aggregates
for i ← n − 2 to 0 do
|  buf[i] ← buf[i] ⊗ buf[i + 1]
// initial total aggregate
T agg ← buf[0]
Nat m ← 0  // size of new block
T z ← nil  // aggregate of new block
Function Add(T d):
    if m = n then // full new block
        // convert new block to old
        for i ← n − 2 to 1 do
        |  buf[i] ← buf[i] ⊗ buf[i + 1]
        m ← 0  // empty new block
        z ← nil
    // evict oldest item, replace with d
    buf[m] ← d
    m ← m + 1  // new block enlarged
    z ← z ⊗ d  // where nil ⊗ d = d
    if m < n then
    |  agg ← buf[m] ⊗ z
    else // m = n
    |  agg ← z
```

Fig. 4: Online monitors for bounded-future MTL formulas & sliding aggregation.

$\rho(\varphi \mathsf{S}\, \psi, 0^{a+1-n}u, a)$. So, we can implement a monitor for the connective $\mathsf{S}_{[0,a]}$ by computing S over a window of exactly $a + 1$ data items.

Proposition 10 (Aggregation for S, U). Let V be a semiring. For every trace $u = u_0u_1 \ldots u_{n-1} \in (V \times V)^+$ of length $n = |u|$, the values $\rho(\pi_1 \mathsf{S}\, \pi_2, u, n-1)$ and $\rho(\pi_1 \mathsf{U}\, \pi_2, u, 0)$ can be written as aggregates of the form $\pi_2(u_0 \otimes u_1 \otimes \cdots \otimes u_{n-1})$.

Proposition 10 justifies the translation of $\mathsf{S}_{[0,b]}/\mathsf{U}_{[0,b]}$ into monitors (Fig. 4). Now, we will describe the data structure that performs the sliding aggregation. It is used in Fig. 3 in the monitors wnd and wndV. The implementation is shown in Fig. 4. Suppose that the current window (of size n) is $[x_0, x_1, \ldots, x_{n-1}]$. We maintain a buffer of the form $[x_{n-m}, \ldots, x_{n-1}, y_0, \ldots, y_{n-1-m}]$, where the part $[x_{n-m}, \ldots, x_{n-1}]$ is the block of newer elements ("new block") and the part $[y_0, \ldots, y_{n-1-m}]$ contains aggregates of the older elements ("old block"). They satisfy the invariant $y_i = x_i \otimes \cdots \otimes x_{n-1-m}$ for every $i = 0, \ldots, n-1-m$. We also maintain the aggregate $z = x_{n-m} \otimes \cdots \otimes x_{n-1}$ of the new block. So, the overall aggregate of the window is $agg = y_0 \otimes z$. When a new item d arrives, we evict the aggregate y_0 corresponding to the oldest item x_0 and replace it by d. Thus, the new block is expanded with the additional item d and therefore we also update the aggregates z and agg. When the new block becomes full (i.e., $m = n$) then we convert it to an old block by performing all partial aggregations from right to left. This conversion requires $n - 1$ applications of $\otimes$, but it is performed once every n items. So, the algorithm needs $O(1)$ amortized time-per-item.

Theorem 11. Let D be a set of data items, V be a semiring, and $\varphi : \text{MTL}(D, V)$ be a bounded-future formula. The monitor $\text{TL}(\varphi) : \mathsf{M}(D, V)$ is a streaming algorithm that needs $O(2^{|\varphi|})$ space and $O(|\varphi|)$ amortized time-per-item.

Proof. The algorithm needs space that is exponential in the size of φ because of the connectives of the form $X_{[a,\infty)}$ and $X_{[a,b]}$. The monitor uses buffers of size a or $b - a$. Since the constants a, b are written in binary notation, we need space that is exponential in the size. The $O(|\varphi|)$ amortized time per element hinges on the algorithm of Fig. 4, which is used for $\mathsf{S}_{[0,b]}$ and $\mathsf{U}_{[0,b]}$. As discussed earlier, this algorithm needs $O(1)$ amortized time-per-item.

6   Experimental Evaluation

We have implemented our semiring-based monitoring framework in Rust. We compare our implementation with the verified lattice-based monitors of [13] and the monitoring tool Reelay [40]. We perform our experiments using the $(\mathbb{R}^{\pm\infty}, \max, \min)$ semiring for truth values, which are approximately represented using 64-bit floating-point numbers.

We have observed that all three tools process items at a roughly constant rate. We summarize the performance of a monitor with the average time it takes to process one data item (i.e., amortized time-per-item). In Fig. 5, we consider formulas $X_{[0,n]}$, X_n, $X_{[n,2n]}$, $X_{[n,\infty)}$ where $X \in \{\mathsf{S}, \mathsf{P}\}$. We show the time-per-item for the monitors for $n = 1, 10, 10^2, 10^3, 10^4, 10^5, 10^6$. We have also evaluated how the monitors for future temporal connectives scale with respect to the constants in the intervals. In Fig. 6, we benchmark all tools using formulas from the Timescales benchmark [39]. Our monitors are generally more than 100 (resp., 10) times faster than Reelay (resp., the lattice-based tool of [13]).

The profiling tools Valgrind [38] and Heaptrack [41] are used to analyze the memory consumption of the monitors. Our Rust implementation, given a formula, begins by allocating a fixed amount of memory and does not allocate any more memory during the rest of the computation. Reelay allocates and de-allocates memory throughout its execution. The lattice-based monitor is implemented in OCaml (which is a garbage-collected language) and consumes a larger amount of memory. In Fig. 5, we plot the peak memory usage of the monitors. We note that our tool does not seem to be allocating an increasing amount of memory for P_n and similar formulas. This is because the corresponding monitor for P_n emits output as early as possible and therefore does not need to use a buffer. In the case of the lattice-based monitor and our tool, we observe that the memory consumption does not depend on the input trace (it only depends on the formula). In the case of Reelay, it appears that the memory consumption depends on the input trace. We have plotted the behavior for two different input traces: one that consists of an increasing sequence of values ("reelay-ascending"), and another one that is decreasing ("reelay-descending"). We have only measured the memory usage of Reelay for up to $n = 2^{13}$, as the execution becomes very slow beyond this value.

We use *case studies* from the automotive domain, which have been suggested as benchmarks for hybrid system verification [25]. The **A**utomatic Transmission System has two input signals (a throttle and a break) and three output signals: the gear sequence (g_i for each gear i), the engine rotation speed (in

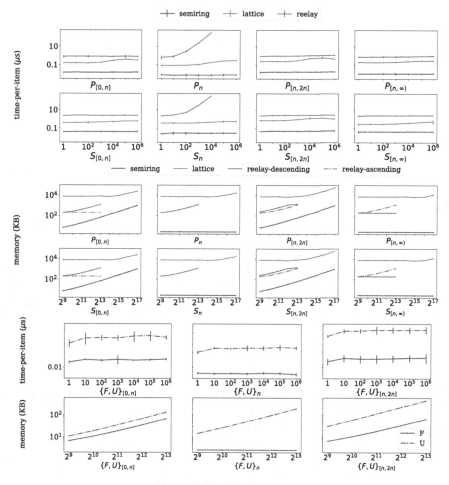

Fig. 5: Microbenchmark

rpm, denoted ω) and the vehicle speed (denoted v). Based on the suggestions in [25], we consider five properties: $A_1 = \omega < \overline{\omega}$, $A_2 = (\omega < \overline{\omega}) \wedge (v < \overline{v})$, $A_3 = g_1 \wedge \mathsf{Y}(g_2) \to \mathsf{Y}\mathsf{H}_{[0,2.5]}g_2$ (where Y is notation for P_1), $A_4 = \mathsf{H}_{[0,5]}(\omega < \overline{\omega}) \to \mathsf{H}_{[0,2.5]}(v < \overline{v})$ and $A_5 = (v > \overline{v}) \, \overline{\mathsf{S}}_{[0,1]} ((\omega > \overline{\omega}) \, \overline{\mathsf{S}}_{[0,2]} ((\neg g_4) \, \overline{\mathsf{S}}_{[0,10]} ((\neg g_3) \, \overline{\mathsf{S}} ((\neg g_2) \, \overline{\mathsf{S}} (\neg g_1)))))$. All constants in the temporal connectives are in seconds, and we choose the constants $\overline{v} = 120$ and $\overline{\omega} = 4500$. Formula A_3 says that before changing from the second to the first gear, at least 2.5 seconds must first pass. Formula A_4 says that keeping the engine speed low enough should ensure that the vehicle does not exceed a certain speed. Formula A_5 says that changing the gear from the first to the fourth within 10 seconds, and then having the engine speed exceed $\overline{\omega}$ will cause the vehicle speed to exceed $\overline{v}$. The other case study is a **Fault-Tolerant Fuel Control System**. We monitor two properties. The first is

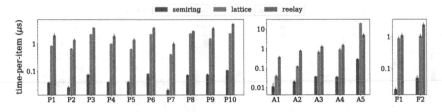

Fig. 6: Macrobenchmarks

that the fuel flow rate should frequently become and remain non-zero for a sufficient amount of time. We encode this as $F_1 = H_{[0,10]}P_{[0,1]}(FuelFlowRate > 0)$.
The other property is to ensure that whenever the air-to-fuel ratio goes out of
bounds, then within 1 second it should settle back and stay there for a second.
This is written as $F_2 = (H_{[0,1]}airFuelRatio < 1)\, \bar{S}_{[0,2]}\, airFuelRatio < 1$. The
experimental results are shown in Fig. 6.

All of our experiments were executed on a laptop with an Intel Core i7
10610U CPU clocked at 2.30GHz and 16GB of memory. Each value reported is
the mean of 20 executions of the experiment. The whiskers in the plots indicate
the standard deviation across all executions.

7   Related Work

Fainekos and Pappas [22] define the robustness degree of satisfaction in terms
of the distance of the signal from the set of desirable ones (or its complement).
They also suggest an under-approximation of the robustness degree which can
be effectively monitored. This is called the *robust semantics* and is defined by
induction on STL formulas, by interpreting conjunction (resp., disjunction) as
min (resp., max) of $\mathbb{R}^{\pm\infty}$. Our paper explores this robust semantics (and the
related approximation guarantee) in the general algebraic setting of semirings.

In [27], the authors study a generalization of the robustness degree by considering idempotent semirings of real numbers. They also propose an online monitoring algorithm that uses symbolic weighted automata. While this approach
computes the precise robustness degree in the sense of [22], the construction
of the relevant automata incurs a doubly exponential blowup if one considers
STL specifications. In [13], it is observed that an extension of the robust semantics to bounded distributive lattices can be effectively monitored. In this paper,
we generalize this semantics by considering semirings (bounded distributive lattices are semirings). Semirings are also used in [9], where the authors consider
a spatio-temporal logic. They consider the class of constraint semirings, which
require the semiring order to induce a complete lattice. Efforts have been made
to define notions of robustness that take temporal discrepancies into account.
In [20], we see a definition of temporal robustness by considering the effect of
shifting the signal in time. The "edit distance" between discretized signals is proposed as a measure of robustness in [26]. Abbas et al. [3] define a notion of (τ, ε)

closeness between signals, which considers temporal and value-based guarantees separately. In [2], a metric based on conformance is put forward for applications in cardiac electrophysiology. Averaging temporal operators are used in [5], which assign a higher value to temporal obligations that are satisfied earlier.

A key ingredient for the efficient monitoring of STL is a streaming algorithm for sliding-window maximum [19,15]. The tool Breach [17,18], which is used for the falsification of temporal specifications over hybrid systems, uses the sliding-maximum algorithm of [32]. In contrast, we use a more general sliding aggregation which applies to any associative operation (not only max/min) and does not require the truth values to be totally ordered.

Different approaches for interpreting future temporal connectives in the context of online monitoring have been studied. While [16] assumes the availability of a predictor to interpret future connectives, [21] considers robustness intervals: the tightest intervals which cover the robustness for all possible extensions of the available trace prefix. Reelay [40] exclusively uses past-time connectives. The transducer-based framework of [37] can be used to monitor rich temporal properties which depend on bounded future input by allowing some bounded delay in the output.

There is a large amount of work on formalisms, domain-specific languages and associated tools for quantitative online monitoring and, more generally, for data stream processing. The synchronous language LOLA [14] has served as the basis for the StreamLAB tool [23], which is used for monitoring cyber-physical systems. Quantitative Regular Expressions [36] and associated automata-theoretic models with registers [7,8,6] have been used to express complex online detection algorithms for medical monitoring [1,4]. There are many synchronous languages and models of computation based on Kahn's dataflow model [28] that have been used for signal processing [31] and embedded controller design [12,11,10]. The construction of online monitors described in Sect. 5 relies on a set of combinators that constitute a simple domain-specific language for stream processing. Our focus here, however, is on providing efficient monitors for MTL formulas with a quantitative semantics, rather than designing a general-purpose language for monitor specification. The compositional construction of automata-based monitors from temporal specifications has also been considered in [34,35,24].

8   Conclusion

We have presented a new efficient algorithm for the online monitoring of MTL properties over discrete traces. We have used an abstract algebraic semantics based on semirings, which can be instantiated to the widely-used Boolean (qualitative) and robustness (quantitative) semantics, as well as to other partially ordered semirings. We also provide a theorem that relates our quantitative semantics with an algebraic generalization of the robustness degree of [22]. We have provided an implementation of our algebraic monitoring framework, and we have shown experimentally that our monitors scale reasonably well and are competitive against the state-of-the-art tool Reelay [40].

References

1. Abbas, H., Alur, R., Mamouras, K., Mangharam, R., Rodionova, A.: Real-time decision policies with predictable performance. Proceedings of the IEEE, Special Issue on Design Automation for Cyber-Physical Systems **106**(9), 1593–1615 (2018). https://doi.org/10.1109/JPROC.2018.2853608
2. Abbas, H., Mangharam, R.: Generalized robust MTL semantics for problems in cardiac electrophysiology. In: ACC 2018. pp. 1592–1597. IEEE (2018). https://doi.org/10.23919/ACC.2018.8431460
3. Abbas, H., Mittelmann, H.D., Fainekos, G.E.: Formal property verification in a conformance testing framework. In: MEMOCODE 2014. pp. 155–164. IEEE (2014). https://doi.org/10.1109/MEMCOD.2014.6961854
4. Abbas, H., Rodionova, A., Mamouras, K., Bartocci, E., Smolka, S.A., Grosu, R.: Quantitative regular expressions for arrhythmia detection. IEEE/ACM Transactions on Computational Biology and Bioinformatics **16**(5), 1586–1597 (2019). https://doi.org/10.1109/TCBB.2018.2885274
5. Akazaki, T., Hasuo, I.: Time robustness in MTL and expressivity in hybrid system falsification. In: Kroening, D., Păsăreanu, C.S. (eds.) CAV 2015. LNCS, vol. 9207, pp. 356–374. Springer, Cham (2015). https://doi.org/10.1007/978-3-319-21668-3_21
6. Alur, R., Fisman, D., Mamouras, K., Raghothaman, M., Stanford, C.: Streamable regular transductions. Theoretical Computer Science **807**, 15–41 (2020). https://doi.org/10.1016/j.tcs.2019.11.018
7. Alur, R., Mamouras, K., Stanford, C.: Automata-based stream processing. In: ICALP 2017. Leibniz International Proceedings in Informatics (LIPIcs), vol. 80, pp. 112:1–112:15. Schloss Dagstuhl–Leibniz-Zentrum fuer Informatik, Dagstuhl, Germany (2017). https://doi.org/10.4230/LIPIcs.ICALP.2017.112
8. Alur, R., Mamouras, K., Stanford, C.: Modular quantitative monitoring. Proceedings of the ACM on Programming Languages **3**(POPL), 50:1–50:31 (2019). https://doi.org/10.1145/3290363
9. Bartocci, E., Bortolussi, L., Loreti, M., Nenzi, L.: Monitoring mobile and spatially distributed cyber-physical systems. In: MEMOCODE 2017. pp. 146–155. ACM (2017). https://doi.org/10.1145/3127041.3127050
10. Benveniste, A., Le Guernic, P., Jacquemot, C.: Synchronous programming with events and relations: The SIGNAL language and its semantics. Science of Computer Programming **16**(2), 103–149 (1991). https://doi.org/10.1016/0167-6423(91)90001-E
11. Berry, G., Gonthier, G.: The Esterel synchronous programming language: Design, semantics, implementation. Science of Computer Programming **19**(2), 87–152 (1992). https://doi.org/10.1016/0167-6423(92)90005-V
12. Caspi, P., Pilaud, D., Halbwachs, N., Plaice, J.A.: LUSTRE: A declarative language for real-time programming. In: Proceedings of the 14th ACM SIGACT-SIGPLAN Symposium on Principles of Programming Languages. pp. 178–188. POPL '87, ACM, New York, NY, USA (1987). https://doi.org/10.1145/41625.41641
13. Chattopadhyay, A., Mamouras, K.: A verified online monitor for metric temporal logic with quantitative semantics. In: Deshmukh, J., Ničković, D. (eds.) RV 2020. LNCS, vol. 12399, pp. 383–403. Springer, Cham (2020). https://doi.org/10.1007/978-3-030-60508-7_21
14. D'Angelo, B., Sankaranarayanan, S., Sanchez, C., Robinson, W., Finkbeiner, B., Sipma, H.B., Mehrotra, S., Manna, Z.: LOLA: Runtime monitor-

ing of synchronous systems. In: TIME 2005. pp. 166–174. IEEE (2005). https://doi.org/10.1109/TIME.2005.26

15. Deshmukh, J.V., Donzé, A., Ghosh, S., Jin, X., Juniwal, G., Seshia, S.A.: Robust online monitoring of signal temporal logic. Formal Methods in System Design **51**(1), 5–30 (2017). https://doi.org/10.1007/s10703-017-0286-7

16. Dokhanchi, A., Hoxha, B., Fainekos, G.: On-line monitoring for temporal logic robustness. In: Bonakdarpour, B., Smolka, S.A. (eds.) RV 2014. LNCS, vol. 8734, pp. 231–246. Springer, Cham (2014). https://doi.org/10.1007/978-3-319-11164-3_19

17. Donzé, A.: Breach, a toolbox for verification and parameter synthesis of hybrid systems. In: Touili, T., Cook, B., Jackson, P. (eds.) CAV 2010. LNCS, vol. 6174, pp. 167–170. Springer, Heidelberg (2010). https://doi.org/10.1007/978-3-642-14295-6_17

18. Donzé, A.: Breach: A MATLAB toolbox for simulation-based design of dynamical/CPS/hybrid systems. https://github.com/decyphir/breach (2021), [Online; accessed January 22, 2021]

19. Donzé, A., Ferrère, T., Maler, O.: Efficient robust monitoring for STL. In: Sharygina, N., Veith, H. (eds.) CAV 2013. LNCS, vol. 8044, pp. 264–279. Springer, Heidelberg (2013). https://doi.org/10.1007/978-3-642-39799-8_19

20. Donzé, A., Maler, O.: Robust satisfaction of temporal logic over real-valued signals. In: Chatterjee, K., Henzinger, T.A. (eds.) FORMATS 2010. LNCS, vol. 6246, pp. 92–106. Springer, Heidelberg (2010). https://doi.org/10.1007/978-3-642-15297-9_9

21. Dreossi, T., Dang, T., Donzé, A., Kapinski, J., Jin, X., Deshmukh, J.V.: Efficient guiding strategies for testing of temporal properties of hybrid systems. In: Havelund, K., Holzmann, G., Joshi, R. (eds.) NFM 2015. LNCS, vol. 9058, pp. 127–142. Springer, Cham (2015). https://doi.org/10.1007/978-3-319-17524-9_10

22. Fainekos, G.E., Pappas, G.J.: Robustness of temporal logic specifications for continuous-time signals. Theoretical Computer Science **410**(42), 4262–4291 (2009). https://doi.org/10.1016/j.tcs.2009.06.021

23. Faymonville, P., Finkbeiner, B., Schledjewski, M., Schwenger, M., Stenger, M., Tentrup, L., Torfah, H.: StreamLAB: Stream-based monitoring of cyber-physical systems. In: Dillig, I., Tasiran, S. (eds.) CAV 2019. LNCS, vol. 11561, pp. 421–431. Springer, Cham (2019). https://doi.org/10.1007/978-3-030-25540-4_24

24. Ferrère, T., Maler, O., Ničković, D., Pnueli, A.: From real-time logic to timed automata. Journal of the ACM **66**(3), 19:1–19:31 (2019). https://doi.org/10.1145/3286976

25. Hoxha, B., Abbas, H., Fainekos, G.E.: Benchmarks for temporal logic requirements for automotive systems. In: ARCH@CPSWeek 2014, 2015. EPiC Series in Computing, vol. 34, pp. 25–30. EasyChair (2014). https://doi.org/10.29007/xwrs

26. Jakšić, S., Bartocci, E., Grosu, R., Nguyen, T., Ničković, D.: Quantitative monitoring of STL with edit distance. Formal Methods in System Design **53**(1), 83–112 (2018). https://doi.org/10.1007/s10703-018-0319-x

27. Jakšić, S., Bartocci, E., Grosu, R., Ničković, D.: An algebraic framework for runtime verification. IEEE Transactions on Computer-Aided Design of Integrated Circuits and Systems **37**(11), 2233–2243 (2018). https://doi.org/10.1109/TCAD.2018.2858460

28. Kahn, G.: The semantics of a simple language for parallel programming. Information Processing **74**, 471–475 (1974)

29. Kong, L., Mamouras, K.: StreamQL: A query language for processing streaming time series. Proceedings of the ACM on Programming Languages **4**(OOPSLA) (2020). https://doi.org/10.1145/3428251

30. Koymans, R.: Specifying real-time properties with metric temporal logic. Real-Time Systems **2**(4), 255–299 (1990). https://doi.org/10.1007/BF01995674

31. Lee, E.A., Messerschmitt, D.G.: Static scheduling of synchronous data flow programs for digital signal processing. IEEE Transactions on Computers **C-36**(1), 24–35 (1987). https://doi.org/10.1109/TC.1987.5009446

32. Lemire, D.: Streaming maximum-minimum filter using no more than three comparisons per element. Nordic Journal of Computing **13**(4), 328–339 (2006)

33. Maler, O., Nickovic, D.: Monitoring temporal properties of continuous signals. In: Lakhnech, Y., Yovine, S. (eds.) FTRTFT 2004, FORMATS 2004. LNCS, vol. 3253, pp. 152–166. Springer, Heidelberg (2004). https://doi.org/10.1007/978-3-540-30206-3_12

34. Maler, O., Nickovic, D., Pnueli, A.: Real time temporal logic: Past, present, future. In: Pettersson, P., Yi, W. (eds.) FORMATS 2005. LNCS, vol. 3829, pp. 2–16. Springer, Heidelberg (2005). https://doi.org/10.1007/11603009_2

35. Maler, O., Nickovic, D., Pnueli, A.: From MITL to timed automata. In: Asarin, E., Bouyer, P. (eds.) FORMATS 2006. LNCS, vol. 4202, pp. 274–289. Springer, Heidelberg (2006). https://doi.org/10.1007/11867340_20

36. Mamouras, K., Raghothaman, M., Alur, R., Ives, Z.G., Khanna, S.: StreamQRE: Modular specification and efficient evaluation of quantitative queries over streaming data. In: PLDI 2017. pp. 693–708. ACM (2017). https://doi.org/10.1145/3062341.3062369

37. Mamouras, K., Wang, Z.: Online signal monitoring with bounded lag. IEEE Transactions on Computer-Aided Design of Integrated Circuits and Systems (2020). https://doi.org/10.1109/TCAD.2020.3013053

38. The Valgrind Developers: Valgrind: An instrumentation framework for building dynamic analysis tools. `https://valgrind.org/` (2021), [Online; accessed January 22, 2021]

39. Ulus, D.: Timescales: A benchmark generator for MTL monitoring tools. In: Finkbeiner, B., Mariani, L. (eds.) RV 2019. LNCS, vol. 11757, pp. 402–412. Springer, Cham (2019). https://doi.org/10.1007/978-3-030-32079-9_25

40. Ulus, D.: The Reelay monitoring tool. `https://doganulus.github.io/reelay/` (2020), [Online; accessed August 20, 2020]

41. Wolff, M.: Heaptrack: A heap memory profiler for Linux. `https://github.com/KDE/heaptrack` (2021), [Online; accessed January 22, 2021]

Neural Networks

Synthesizing Context-free Grammars from Recurrent Neural Networks

Daniel M. Yellin[1] ✉ and Gail Weiss[2]

[1] IBM, Givatayim, Israel
dannyyellin@gmail.com
[2] Technion, Haifa, Israel
sgailw@cs.technion.ac.il

Abstract. We present an algorithm for extracting a subclass of the context free grammars (CFGs) from a trained recurrent neural network (RNN). We develop a new framework, *pattern rule sets* (PRSs), which describe sequences of deterministic finite automata (DFAs) that approximate a non-regular language. We present an algorithm for recovering the PRS behind a sequence of such automata, and apply it to the sequences of automata extracted from trained RNNs using the L^* algorithm. We then show how the PRS may converted into a CFG, enabling a familiar and useful presentation of the learned language.

Extracting the learned language of an RNN is important to facilitate understanding of the RNN and to verify its correctness. Furthermore, the extracted CFG can augment the RNN in classifying correct sentences, as the RNN's predictive accuracy decreases when the recursion depth and distance between matching delimiters of its input sequences increases.

Keywords: Model Extraction · Learning Context Free Grammars · Finite State Machines · Recurrent Neural Networks

1 Introduction

Recurrent Neural Networks (RNNs) are a class of neural networks adapted to sequential input, enjoying wide use in a variety of sequence processing tasks. Their internal process is opaque, prompting several works into extracting interpretable rules from them. Existing works focus on the extraction of deterministic or weighted finite automata (DFAs and WFAs) from trained RNNs [18,6,26,3].

However, DFAs are insufficient to fully capture the behavior of RNNs, which are known to be theoretically Turing-complete [20], and for which there exist architecture variants such as LSTMs [14] and features such as stacks [9,23] or attention [4] increasing their practical power. Several recent investigations explore the ability of different RNN architectures to learn Dyck, counter, and other non-regular languages [19,5,28,21], with mixed results.

While the data indicates that RNNs can generalize and achieve high accuracy, they do not learn hierarchical rules, and generalization deteriorates as the length and 'depth' of the input grows [19,5,28]. Sennhauser and Berwick conjecture that

© The Author(s) 2021
J. F. Groote and K. G. Larsen (Eds.): TACAS 2021, LNCS 12651, pp. 351–369, 2021.
https://doi.org/10.1007/978-3-030-72016-2_19

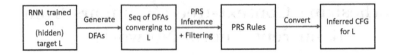

Fig. 1. Overview of steps in algorithm to synthesize the hidden language L

"what the LSTM has in fact acquired is sequential statistical approximation to this solution" instead of "the 'perfect' rule-based solution" [19]. Similarly, Yu et. al. conclude that "the RNNs can not truly model CFGs, even when powered by the attention mechanism" [28]. This is line with Hewitt et. al., who note that a fixed precision RNN can only learn a language of fixed depth strings [13].

Goal of this paper We wish to extract a CFG from a trained RNN. In particular, we wish to find the CFG that not only explains the finite language learnt by the RNN, but generalizes it to strings of unbounded depth and distance.

Our approach Our method builds on the DFA extraction work of Weiss et al. [26], which uses the L^* algorithm [2] to learn the DFA of a given RNN. As part of the learning process, L^* creates a sequence of *hypothesis DFAs* approximating the target language. Our main insight is in treating these hypothesis DFAs as coming from a set of underlying rules, that recursively improve each DFA's approximation of the target CFG by increasing the distance and embedded depth of the sequences it can recognize. In this light, synthesizing the target CFG becomes the problem of recovering these rules.

We propose the framework of *pattern rule sets* (PRSs) for describing such rule applications, and present an algorithm for recovering a PRS from a sequence of DFAs. We also provide a method for converting a PRS to a CFG, and test our method on RNNs trained on several PRS languages. Pattern rule sets are expressive enough to cover several variants of the Dyck languages, which are prototypical context-free languages (CFLs): the Chomsky–Schützenberger representation theorem shows that any CFL can be expressed as a homomorphic image of a Dyck language intersected with a regular language[16].

A significant issue we address is that the extracted DFAs are often inexact, either through inaccuracies in the RNN, or as an artifact of the L^* algorithm.

To the best of our knowledge, this is the first work on synthesizing a CFG from a general RNN (though some works extract push-down automata [23,9] from RNNs with an external stack, they do not apply to plain RNNs). The overall steps in our technique are given in Figure 1.

Contributions The main contributions of this paper are:

- *Pattern Rule Sets* (PRSs), a framework for describing a sequence of DFAs approximating a CFL.
- An algorithm for recovering the PRS generating a sequence of DFAs, that may also be applied to noisy DFAs elicited from an RNN using L^* .
- An algorithm converting a PRS to a CFG.

– An implementation of our technique[1], and an evaluation of its success on recovering various CFLs from trained RNNs.

2 Definitions and Notations

2.1 Deterministic Finite Automata

Definition 1 (Deterministic Finite Automata). *A deterministic finite automaton (DFA) over an alphabet Σ is a 5-tuple $\langle \Sigma, q_0, Q, F, \delta \rangle$ such that Q is a finite set of states, $q_0 \in Q$ is the initial state, $F \subseteq Q$ is a set of final (accepting) states and $\delta : Q \times \Sigma \rightarrow Q$ is a (possibly partial) transition function.*

Unless stated otherwise, we assume each DFA's states are unique to itself, i.e., for any two DFAs A, B – including two instances of the same DFA – $Q_A \cap Q_B = \emptyset$. A DFA A is said to be *complete* if δ is complete, i.e., the value $\delta(q, \sigma)$ is defined for every $q, \sigma \in Q \times \Sigma$. Otherwise, it is *incomplete*.

We define the extended transition function $\hat{\delta} : Q \times \Sigma^* \rightarrow Q$ and the language $L(A)$ accepted by A in the typical fashion. We also associate a language with intermediate states of A: $L(A, q_1, q_2) \triangleq \{w \in \Sigma^* \mid \hat{\delta}(q_1, w) = q_2\}$. The states from which no sequence $w \in \Sigma^*$ is accepted are known as the *sink reject states*.

Definition 2. *The* sink reject states *of a DFA $A = \langle \Sigma, q_0, Q, F, \delta \rangle$ are the maximal set $Q_R \subseteq Q$ satisfying: $Q_R \cap F = \emptyset$, and for every $q \in Q_R$ and $\sigma \in \Sigma$, either $\delta(q, \sigma) \in Q_R$ or $\delta(q, \sigma)$ is not defined.*

Definition 3 (Defined Tokens). *Let $A = \langle \Sigma, q_0, Q, F, \delta \rangle$ be a complete DFA with sink reject states Q_R. For every $q \in Q$, its defined tokens are $\text{def}(A, q) \triangleq \{\sigma \in \Sigma \mid \delta(q, \sigma) \notin Q_R\}$. When the DFA A is clear from context, we write $\text{def}(q)$.*

All definitions for complete DFAs are extended to incomplete DFAs A by considering their *completion* - an extension of A in which all missing transitions are connected to a (possibly new) sink reject state.

Definition 4 (Set Representation of δ). *A (possibly partial) transition function $\delta : Q \times \Sigma \rightarrow Q$ may be equivalently defined as the set $S_\delta = \{(q, \sigma, q') \mid \delta(q, \sigma) = q'\}$. We use δ and S_δ interchangeably.*

Definition 5 (Replacing a State). *For a transition function $\delta : Q \times \Sigma \rightarrow Q$, state $q \in Q$, and new state $q_n \notin Q$, we denote by $\delta_{[q \leftarrow q_n]} : Q' \times \Sigma \rightarrow Q'$ the transition function over $Q' = (Q \setminus \{q\}) \cup \{q_n\}$ and Σ that is identical to δ except that it redirects all transitions into or out of q to be into or out of q_n.*

---

[1] The implementation for this paper, and a link to all trained RNNs, is available at https://github.com/tech-srl/RNN_to_PRS_CFG.

2.2   Dyck Languages

A Dyck language *of order* N is expressed by the grammar D ::= ε | L_1 D R_1 | ... | L_N D R_N | D D with unique symbols $L_1, \ldots, L_N, D_1, \ldots, D_N$. A common measure of complexity for a Dyck word is its maximum *distance* (number of characters) between matching delimiters and *embedded depth* (number of unclosed delimiters) [19]. We generalize and refer to *Regular Expression Dyck (RE-Dyck)* languages as languages expressed by the same CFG, except that each L_i and each R_i derive some regular expression.

We present regular expressions as is standard, for example: $L(\{a|b\}\cdot c) \triangleq \{ac, bc\}$.

3   Patterns

Patterns are DFAs with a single *exit* state q_X in place of a set of final states, and with no cycles on their initial or exit states unless $q_0 = q_X$.

Definition 6 (Patterns). *A pattern* $p = \langle \Sigma, q_0, Q, q_X, \delta \rangle$ *is a DFA* $A^p = \langle \Sigma, q_0, Q, \{q_X\}, \delta \rangle$, *satisfying: 1.* $L(A^p) \neq \emptyset$, *and 2. either* $q_0 = q_X$, *or* $\mathrm{def}(q_X) = \emptyset$ *and* $L(A, q_0, q_0) = \{\varepsilon\}$. *If* $q_0 = q_X$ *then* p *is called* circular, *otherwise, it is* non-circular. *Patterns are always given in minimal incomplete presentation.*

We refer to a pattern's initial and exit states as its *edge states*. All the definitions for DFAs apply to patterns through A^p. We denote each pattern p's language $L_p \triangleq L(p)$, and if it is marked by some superscript i, we refer to all of its components with superscript i: $p^i = \langle \Sigma, q_0^i, Q^i, q_X^i, \delta^i \rangle$.

3.1   Pattern Composition

We can compose two non-circular patterns p^1, p^2 by merging the exit state of p^1 with the initial state of p^2, creating a new pattern p^3 satisfying $L_{p^3} = L_{p^1} \cdot L_{p^2}$.

Definition 7 (Serial Composition). *Let* p^1, p^2 *be two non-circular patterns. Their* serial composite *is the pattern* $p^1 \circ p^2 = \langle \Sigma, q_0^1, Q, q_X^2, \delta \rangle$ *in which* $Q = Q^1 \cup Q^2 \setminus \{q_X^1\}$ *and* $\delta = \delta^1_{[q_X^1 \leftarrow q_0^2]} \cup \delta^2$. *We call* q_0^2 *the* join state *of this operation.*

If we additionally merge the exit state of p_2 with the initial state of p_1, we obtain a circular pattern p which we call the *circular composition* of p_1 and p_2. This composition satisfies $L_p = \{L_{p_1} \cdot L_{p_2}\}^*$.

Definition 8 (Circular Composition). *Let* p^1, p^2 *be two non-circular patterns. Their* circular composite *is the circular pattern* $p_1 \circ_c p_2 = \langle \Sigma, q_0^1, Q, q_0^1, \delta \rangle$ *in which* $Q = Q^1 \cup Q^2 \setminus \{q_X^1, q_X^2\}$ *and* $\delta = \delta^1_{[q_X^1 \leftarrow q_0^2]} \cup \delta^2_{[q_X^2 \leftarrow q_0^1]}$. *We call* q_0^2 *the* join state *of this operation.*

Figure 2 shows 3 examples of serial and circular compositions of patterns.

Patterns do not carry information about whether or not they have been composed from other patterns. We maintain such information using *pattern pairs*.

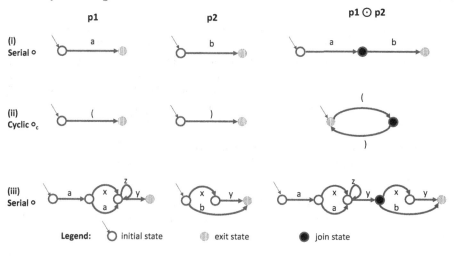

Fig. 2. Examples of the composition operator

Definition 9 (Pattern Pair). *A pattern pair is a pair $\langle P, P_c \rangle$ of pattern sets, such that $P_c \subset P$ and for every $p \in P_c$ there exists exactly one pair $p_1, p_2 \in P$ satisfying $p = p_1 \odot p_2$ for some $\odot \in \{\circ, \circ_c\}$. We refer to the patterns $p \in P_c$ as the composite patterns of $\langle P, P_c \rangle$, and to the rest as its base patterns.*

We will often discuss patterns that have been composed into larger DFAs.

Definition 10 (Pattern Instances). *Let $A = \langle \Sigma, q_0^A, Q^A, F, \delta^A \rangle$ be a DFA, $p = \langle \Sigma, q_0, Q, q_X, \delta \rangle$ be a pattern, and $\hat{p} = \langle \Sigma, q_0', Q', q_X', \delta' \rangle$ be a pattern 'inside' A, i.e., $Q' \subseteq Q^A$ and $\delta' \subseteq \delta^A$. We say that $\hat{p}$ is an* instance *of p in A if $\hat{p}$ is isomorphic to p.*

A pattern instance in a DFA A is uniquely determined by its structure and initial state: (p, q). If p is a composite pattern with respect to some pattern pair $\langle P, P_c \rangle$, the join state of its composition within A is also uniquely defined.

Definition 11. *For every pattern pair $\langle P, P_c \rangle$, for each composite pattern $p \in P_c$, DFA A, and initial state q of an instance $\hat{p}$ of p in A, $\mathrm{join}(p, q, A)$ returns the join state of $\hat{p}$ with respect to its composition in $\langle P, P_c \rangle$.*

4   Pattern Rule Sets

For any infinite sequence $S = A_1, A_2, \ldots$ of DFAs satisfying $L(A_i) \subset L(A_{i+1})$, for all i, we define the language of S as the union of the languages of all these DFAs: $L(S) = \cup_i L(A_i)$. Such sequences may be used to express CFLs.

In this work we take a finite sequence $A_1, A_2, \ldots, A_n$ of DFAs, and assume it is a (possibly noisy) finite prefix of an infinite sequence of approximations for a language, as above. We attempt to reconstruct the language by guessing how the sequence may continue. To allow such generalization, we must make assumptions about how the sequence is generated. For this we introduce *pattern rule sets*.

Pattern rule sets (PRSs) create sequences of DFAs with a single accepting state. Each PRS is built around a pattern pair $\langle P, P_c \rangle$, and each rule application connects a new pattern instance to the current DFA A_i, at the join state of a composite-pattern inserted into A_i at some earlier point. To define where a pattern can be connected to A_i, we introduce an *enabled instance* set $\mathcal{I}$.

Definition 12. *An* enabled DFA *over a pattern pair* $\langle P, P_c \rangle$ *is a tuple* $\langle A, \mathcal{I} \rangle$ *such that* $A = \langle \Sigma, q_0, Q, F, \delta \rangle$ *is a DFA and* $\mathcal{I} \subseteq P_c \times Q$ *marks enabled instances of composite patterns in* A.

Intuitively, for every enabled DFA $\langle A, \mathcal{I} \rangle$ and $(p, q) \in \mathcal{I}$, we know: (i) there is an instance of pattern p in A starting at state q, and (ii) this instance is *enabled*; i.e., we may connect new pattern instances to its join state $\mathrm{join}(p, q, A)$.

Definition 13. *A PRS* **P** *is a tuple* $\langle \Sigma, P, P_c, R \rangle$ *where* $\langle P, P_c \rangle$ *is a pattern pair over the alphabet* Σ *and* R *is a set of* rules. *Each rule has one of the following forms, for some* $p, p^1, p^2, p^3, p^I \in P$, *with* p^1 *and* p^2 *non-circular:*

(1) $\perp \twoheadrightarrow p^I$
(2) $p \twoheadrightarrow_c (p^1 \odot p^2) \propto p^3$, *where* $p = p^1 \odot p^2$ *for* $\odot \in \{\circ, \circ_c\}$, *and* p^3 *is circular*
(3) $p \twoheadrightarrow_s (p^1 \circ p^2) \propto p^3$, *where* $p = p^1 \circ p^2$ *and* p^3 *is non-circular*

A PRS derives sequences of enabled DFAs as follows: first, a rule of type (1) creates $\langle A_1, \mathcal{I}_1 \rangle$ according to p^I. Then, for every $\langle A_i, \mathcal{I}_i \rangle$, each rule may connect a new pattern instance to A_i, specifically at a state determined by $\mathcal{I}_i$.

Definition 14 (Initial Composition). $\mathcal{D}_1 = \langle A_1, \mathcal{I}_1 \rangle$ *is generated from a rule* $\perp \twoheadrightarrow p^I$ *as follows:* $A_1 = A^{p^I}$, *and* $\mathcal{I}_i = \{(p^I, q_0^I)\}$ *if* $p^I \in P_c$ *and otherwise* $\mathcal{I}_1 = \emptyset$.

Let $\mathcal{D}_i = \langle A_i, \mathcal{I}_i \rangle$ be the enabled DFA at step i and denote $A_i = \langle \Sigma, q_0, Q, F, \delta \rangle$. Note that for A_1, $|F| = 1$, and for all A_{i+1}, F is unchanged (by future definitions).

Rules of type (1) extend A_i by grafting a circular pattern to q_0, and then enabling that pattern if it is composite.

Definition 15 (Rules of type (1)). *A rule* $\perp \twoheadrightarrow p^I$ *with circular* p^I *may extend* $\langle A_i, \mathcal{I}_i \rangle$ *at the initial state* q_0 *of* A_i *iff* $\mathrm{def}(q_0) \cap \mathrm{def}(q_0^I) = \emptyset$. *This creates the DFA* $A_{i+1} = \langle \Sigma, q_0, Q \cup Q^I \setminus \{q_0^I\}, F, \delta \cup \delta^I_{[q_0^I \leftarrow q_0]} \rangle$. *If* $p^I \in P_c$ *then* $\mathcal{I}_{i+1} = \mathcal{I}_i \cup \{(p^I, q_0)\}$, *else* $\mathcal{I}_{i+1} = \mathcal{I}_i$.

Rules of type (2) graft a circular pattern $p^3 = \langle \Sigma, q_0^3, q_x^3, F, \delta^3 \rangle$ onto the join state q_j of an enabled pattern instance $\hat{p}$ in A_i, by merging q_0^3 with q_j. In doing so, they also enable the patterns composing $\hat{p}$, if they are composite.

Definition 16 (Rules of type (2)). *A rule* $p \twoheadrightarrow_c (p^1 \odot p^2) \propto p^3$ *may extend* $\langle A_i, \mathcal{I}_i \rangle$ *at the join state* $q_j = \mathrm{join}(p, q, A_i)$ *of any instance* $(p, q) \in \mathcal{I}_i$, *provided* $\mathrm{def}(q_j) \cap \mathrm{def}(q_0^3) = \emptyset$. *This creates* $\langle A_{i+1}, \mathcal{I}_{i+1} \rangle$ *as follows:* $A_{i+1} = \langle \Sigma, q_0, Q \cup Q^3 \setminus q_0^3, F, \delta \cup \delta^3_{[q_0^3 \leftarrow q_j]} \rangle$, *and* $\mathcal{I}_{i+1} = \mathcal{I}_i \cup \{(p^k, q^k) \mid p^k \in P_c, k \in \{1, 2, 3\}\}$, *where* $q^1 = q$ *and* $q^2 = q^3 = q_j$.

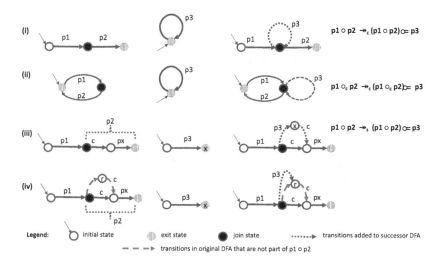

Fig. 3. Structure of DFA after applying rule of type 2 or type 3

Example applications of rule (2) are shown in Figures 3(i) and 3(ii).

We also wish to graft a non-circular pattern p^3 between p^1 and p^2, but this time we must avoid connecting the exit state q_X^3 to q_j lest we loop over p^3 multiple times. We therefore replicate the outgoing transitions of q_j in $p^1 \circ p^2$ to the inserted state q_X^3 so that they may act as the connections back into the DFA.

Definition 17 (Rules of type (3)). *A rule* $p \rightarrow_s (p^1 \circ p^2) \propto p^3$ *may extend* $\langle A_i, \mathcal{I}_i \rangle$ *at the join state* $q_j = \mathrm{join}(p, q, Ai)$ *of any instance* $(p, q) \in \mathcal{I}_i$, *provided* $\mathrm{def}(q_j) \cap \mathrm{def}(q_0^3) = \emptyset$. *This creates* $\langle A_{i+1}, \mathcal{I}_{i+1} \rangle$ *as follows:* $A_{i+1} = \langle \Sigma, q_0, Q \cup Q^3 \setminus q_0^3, F, \delta \cup \delta^3_{[q_0^3 \leftarrow q_j]} \cup C \rangle$ *where* $C = \{ (q_X^3, \sigma, \delta(q_j, \sigma)) | \ \sigma \in \mathrm{def}(p^2, q_0^3) \}$, *and* $\mathcal{I}_{i+1} = \mathcal{I}_i \cup \{ (p^k, q^k) | \ p^k \in P_c, k \in \{1, 2, 3\} \}$ *where* $q^1 = q$ *and* $q^2 = q^3 = q_j$.

We call C the *connecting transitions*. We depict this rule application in example in Fig. 3 (iii), in which a member of C is labeled 'c'.

Multiple applications of rules of type (3) to the same instance $\hat{p}$ will create several equivalent states in the resulting DFAs, as all of their exit states will have the same connecting transitions. These states are merged in a minimized representation, as depicted in Diagram (iv) of Figure 3.

We write $A \in G(\mathbf{P})$ if there exists a sequence of enabled DFAs derived from $\mathbf{P}$ s.t. $A = A_i$ for some A_i in this sequence.

Definition 18 (Language of a PRS). *The language of a PRS* $\mathbf{P}$ *is the union of the languages of the DFAs it can generate:* $L(\mathbf{P}) = \cup_{A \in G(\mathbf{P})} L(A)$.

4.1 Examples

Example 1: Let p^1 and p^2 be the patterns accepting 'a' and 'b' respectively. Consider the PRS R_{ab} with rules, $\perp \rightarrow p^1 \circ p^2$ and $p^1 \circ p^2 \rightarrow_s (p^1 \circ p^2) \propto (p^1 \circ p^2)$.

This PRS creates only one sequence of DFAs. Once the first rule creates the initial DFA, by continuously applying the second rule we obtain the infinite sequence of DFAs each satisfying $L(A_i) = \{a^j b^j : 1 \leq j \leq i\}$, and so $L(R_{ab}) = \{a^i b^i : i > 0\}$. Figure 2(i) presents A_1, while A_2 and A_3 appear in Figure 4(i). We can substitute any non-circular patterns for p^1 and p^2, creating the language $\{x^i y^i : i > 0\}$ for any non-circular pattern regular expressions x and y.

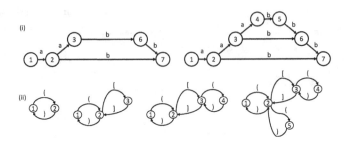

Fig. 4. DFA sequences for R_{ab} and R_{Dyck2}

Example 2: Let p^1, p^2, p^4, and p^5 be the non-circular patterns accepting '(', ')', '[', and ']' respectively. Let $p^3 = p^1 \circ_c p^2$ and $p^6 = p^4 \circ_c p^5$. Let R_{Dyck2} be the PRS containing rules $\perp \twoheadrightarrow p^3$, $\perp \twoheadrightarrow p^6$, $p^3 \twoheadrightarrow_c (p^1 \circ_c p^2) \propto p^3$, $p^3 \twoheadrightarrow_c (p^1 \circ_c p^2) \propto p^6$, $p^6 \twoheadrightarrow_c (p^4 \circ_c p^5) \propto p^3$, and $p^6 \twoheadrightarrow_c (p^4 \circ_c p^5) \propto p^6$. R_{Dyck2} defines the Dyck language of order 2. Figure 4 (ii) shows one of its possible DFA-sequences.

5   PRS Inference Algorithm

A PRS can generate a sequence of DFAs defining, in the limit, a context-free language. We are now interested in inverting this process: given a sequence of DFAs generated by a PRS **P**, can we reconstruct **P**? Coupled with an L^* extraction of DFAs from a trained RNN, solving this problem will enable us to extract a PRS from an RNN – provided the extraction follows a PRS (as we often find it does).

We present an algorithm for this problem, and show its correctness. In practice the DFAs we are given are not "perfect"; they contain noise that deviates from the PRS. We therefore augment this algorithm, allowing it to operate smoothly even on imperfect DFA sequences created from RNN extraction.

In the following, for each pattern instance $\hat{p}$ in A_i, we denote by p the pattern that it is an instance of. We use similar notation $\hat{p}^1, \hat{p}^2$, and $\hat{p}^I$ to refer to specific instances of patterns p^1, p^2 and p^I. Additionally, for each consecutive DFA pair A_i and A_{i+1}, we refer by $\hat{p}^3$ to the new pattern instance in A_{i+1}.

Main steps of inference algorithm. Given a sequence of DFAs $S = A_1 \cdots A_n$, the algorithm infers $\mathbf{P} = \langle \Sigma, P, P_c, R \rangle$ in the following stages:

1. Discover the initial pattern instance $\hat{p}^I$ in A_1. Insert p^I into P and mark $\hat{p}^I$ as enabled. Insert the rule $\perp \to p^I$ into R.

2. For $i, 1 \leq i \leq n - 1$:
   (a) Discover the new pattern instance $\hat{p}^3$ in A_{i+1} that extends A_i.
   (b) If $\hat{p}^3$ starts at the state q_0 of A_{i+1}, then it is an application of a rule of type (1). Insert p^3 into P, mark $\hat{p}^3$ as enabled, and add $\perp \twoheadrightarrow p^3$ to R.
   (c) Otherwise ($\hat{p}^3$ does not start at q_0), find the unique enabled pattern $\hat{p} = \hat{p}^1 \odot \hat{p}^2$ in A_i s.t. $\hat{p}^3$'s initial state q is the join state of $\hat{p}$. Add p^1, p^2, and p^3 to P, p to P_c, and mark $\hat{p}^1, \hat{p}^2$, and $\hat{p}^3$ as enabled. If $\hat{p}^3$ is non-circular, add $p \twoheadrightarrow_s (p^1 \circ p^2) \propto p^3$ to R; otherwise add $p \twoheadrightarrow_c (p^1 \odot p^2) \propto p^3$.

3. Define Σ to be the set of symbols used by the patterns P.

We now elaborate on how we determine the patterns $\hat{p}^I$, $\hat{p}^3$, and $\hat{p}$.

Discovering new patterns $\hat{p}^I$ and $\hat{p}^3$ A_1 provides an initial pattern p^I. For subsequent DFAs, we need to identify which states in $A_{i+1} = \langle \Sigma, q_0', Q', F', \delta' \rangle$ are 'new' relative to $A_i = \langle \Sigma, q_0, Q, F, \delta \rangle$. From the PRS definitions, we know that there is a subset of states and transitions in A_{i+1} that is isomorphic to A_i:

Definition 19. *(Existing states and transitions)* For every $q' \in Q'$, we say that q' exists in A_i with parallel state $q \in Q$ iff there exists a sequence $w \in \Sigma^*$ such that $q = \hat{\delta}(q_0, w)$, $q' = \hat{\delta}'(q_0, w)$, and neither is a sink reject state. Additionally, for every $q_1', q_2' \in Q'$ with parallel states $q_1, q_2 \in Q$, we say that $(q_1', \sigma, q_2') \in \delta'$ exists in A_i iff $(q_1, \sigma, q_2) \in \delta$. We denote A_{i+1}'s existing states and transitions by $Q_E \subseteq Q'$ and $\delta_E \subseteq \delta'$, and the new ones as $Q_N = Q' \setminus Q_E$ and $\delta_N = \delta' \setminus \delta_E$.

By construction of PRSs, each state in A_{i+1} has at most one parallel state in A_i, which can be found in one simultaneous traversal of the two DFAs.

The new states and transitions form a new pattern instance $\hat{p}$ in A_{i+1}, excluding its initial and possibly its exit state. The initial state of $\hat{p}$ is the existing state $q_s' \in Q_E$ that has outgoing new transitions. The exit state q_X' of $\hat{p}$ is identified by the *Exit State Discovery* algorithm:

1. If there exists a $(q, \sigma, q_s') \in \delta_N$, then $\hat{p}$ is circular: $q_X' = q_s'$. (Fig. 3(i), (ii)).
2. Otherwise, $\hat{p}$ is non-circular. If it is the first (with respect to S) non-circular pattern grafted onto q_s', then q_X' is the unique new state whose transitions into A_{i+1} are the *connecting* transitions from Definition 17 (Fig. 3 (iii)).
3. If there is no such state, then $\hat{p}$ is not the first non-circular pattern grafted onto q_s', and q_X' is the unique existing state $q_X' \neq q_s'$ with new incoming transitions. (Fig. 3(iv)).

Finally, the new pattern instance is $p = \langle \Sigma, q_s', Q_p, q_X', \delta_p \rangle$, where $Q_p = Q_N \cup \{q_s', q_X'\}$ and δ_p is the restriction of δ_N to the states of Q_p.

Discovering the pattern $\hat{p}$ (step 2c) In [27] we show that no two enabled pattern instances in a DFA can share a join state, that if they share any non-edge states, then one is contained in the other, and finally that a pattern's join states is never one of its edge states. This makes finding $\hat{p}$ straightforward: denoting q_j

as the parallel of $\hat{p}^3$'s initial state in A_i, we seek the enabled composite pattern instance $(p, q) \in \mathcal{I}_i$ for which $\mathrm{join}(p, q, A_i) = q_j$. If none is present, we seek the only enabled instance $(p, q) \in \mathcal{I}_i$ that contains q_j as a non-edge state, but is not yet marked as a composite. (Note that if two enabled instances share a non-edge state, then the containing one is already marked as a composite: otherwise we would not have found and enabled the other).

In [27] we define the concept of a *minimal generator* and prove the following:

Theorem 1. *Let $A_1, A_2, ...A_n$ be a finite sequence of DFAs that has a minimal generator* **P**. *Then the PRS Inference Algorithm will discover* **P**.

5.1 Deviations from the PRS framework

Given a sequence of DFAs generated by the rules of PRS **P**, the inference algorithm given above will faithfully infer **P**. In practice however, we want to apply the algorithm to a sequence of DFAs extracted from a trained RNN using the L^* algorithm (as in [26]). Such a sequence may contain noise: artifacts from an imperfectly trained RNN, or from the behavior of L^*. The major deviations are incorrect pattern creation, simultaneous rule applications, and slow initiation.

Incorrect pattern creation Whether due to inaccuracies in the RNN classification, or as artifacts of the L^* process, incorrect patterns are often inserted into the DFA sequence. Fortunately, these patterns rarely repeat, and so we can discern between them and 'legitimate' patterns using a *voting* and *threshold* scheme.

The *vote* for each discovered pattern $p \in P$ is the number of times it has been inserted as the new pattern between a pair of DFAs A_i, A_{i+1} in S. We set a *threshold* for the minimum vote a pattern needs to be considered valid, and only build rules around the connection of valid patterns onto the join states of other valid patterns. To do this, we modify the flow of the algorithm: before discovering rules, we first filter invalid patterns by splitting step 2 into two phases. *Phase 1:* Mark all the inserted patterns between each pair of DFAs, and compute their votes. Add to P those whose vote is above the threshold. *Phase 2:* Consider each DFA pair A_i, A_{i+1} in order. If the new pattern in A_{i+1} is valid, and its initial state's parallel state in A_i also lies in a valid pattern, then synthesize the rule according to the original algorithm. If a pattern is discovered to be composite, add its composing patterns to P.

As almost every DFA sequence produced by our method has some noise, the voting scheme greatly extended the reach of our algorithm.

Simultaneous rule applications In the theoretical framework, A_{i+1} differs from A_i by applying a *single* PRS rule, and therefore q'_s and q'_X are uniquely defined. L^* however does not guarantee such minimal increments between DFAs. In particular, it may apply multiple PRS rules between two subsequent DFAs, extending A_i with several patterns. To handle this, we expand the initial and exit state discovery methods given above.

1. Mark the new states and transitions Q_N and δ_N as before.

2. Identify the *set* of new pattern instance initial states (*pattern heads*): the set $H \subseteq Q' \setminus Q_N$ of states in A_{i+1} with outgoing new transitions.
3. For each pattern head $q' \in H$, compute the *relevant* sets $\delta_{N|q'} \subseteq \delta_N$ and $Q_{N|q'} \subseteq Q_N$ of new transitions and states: the members of δ_N and Q_N that are reachable from q' *without passing through any existing transitions*.
4. For each $q' \in H$, restrict to $Q_{N|q'}$ and $\delta_{N|q'}$ and compute q'_X and p as before.

If A_{i+1}'s new patterns have no overlap and do not create an ambiguity around join states, then they may be handled independently and in arbitrary order. They are used to discover rules and then enabled, as in the original algorithm.

Simultaneous but dependent rule applications – such as inserting a pattern and then grafting another onto its join state – are more difficult to handle, as it is not always possible to determine which pattern was grafted onto which. However, there is a special case which appeared in several of our experiments (examples L13 ad L14 of Section 7) for which we developed a technique as follows.

Suppose we discover a rule $r_1 : p_0 \rightarrow_s (p_l \circ p_r) \propto p$ and p contains a cycle c around some internal state q_j. If later another rule inserts a pattern p_n at the state q_j, we understand that p is in fact a composite pattern, with $p = p_1 \circ p_2$ and join state q_j. However, as patterns do not contain cycles at their edge states, c cannot be a part of either p_1 or p_2. We conclude that the addition of p was in fact a simultaneous application of two rules: $r'_1 : p_0 \rightarrow_s (p_l \circ p_r) \propto p'$ and $r_2 : p' \rightarrow_c (p_1 \circ p_2) \propto c$, where p' is p without the cycle c, and update our PRS and our DFAs' enabled pattern instances accordingly. The case when p is circular and r_1 is of rule type (2) is handled similarly.

Slow initiation Ideally, A_1 directly supplies an initial rule $\bot \twoheadrightarrow p^I$ to our PRS. In practice, the first few DFAs generated by L^* have almost random structure. We solve this by leaving discovery of the initial rules to the *end* of the algorithm, at which point we have a set of 'valid' patterns that we are sure are part of the PRS. From there we examine the *last* DFA A_n generated in the sequence, note all the enabled instances (p^I, q_0) at its initial state, and generate a rule $\bot \twoheadrightarrow p^I$ for each of them. This technique has the weakness that it will not recognise patterns p^I that do not also appear as extending patterns p_3 elsewhere in the sequence, unless the threshold for patterns is minimal.

6   Converting a PRS to a CFG

We present an algorithm to convert a given PRS to a context free grammar (CFG), making the rules extracted by our algorithm more accessible.

A restriction: Let $\mathbf{P} = \langle \Sigma, P, P_c, R \rangle$ be a PRS. For simplicity, we restrict the PRS so that every pattern p can only appear on the LHS of rules of type (2) or only appear on the LHS of rules of type (3) but cannot only appear on the LHS of both types of rules. Similarly, we assume that for each rule $\bot \twoheadrightarrow p_I$, the RHS patterns p_I are all circular or non-circular. This restriction is natural: all of the examples in Sections 4.1 and 7.3 conform to it. Still, in [27] we show how to remove this restriction.

We create a CFG $G = \langle \Sigma, N, S, Prod \rangle$. Σ is the same alphabet of $\mathbf{P}$ and we take S as a special start symbol. For every pattern $p \in P$, let $G_p = \langle \Sigma_p, N_p, Z_p, Prod_p \rangle$ be a CFG describing $L(p)$. Let $P_Y \subseteq P_C$ be those composite patterns that appear on the LHS of a rule of type (2). Create the non-terminal C_S and for each $p \in P_Y$, create an additional non-terminal C_p. We set $N = \{S, C_S\} \bigcup_{p \in P} \{N_p\} \bigcup_{p \in P_Y} \{C_p\}$.

Let $\bot \twoheadrightarrow p_I$ be a rule in $\mathbf{P}$. If p_I is non-circular, create a production $S ::= Z_{p_I}$. If p_I is circular, create the productions $S ::= S_C$, $S_C ::= S_C S_C$ and $S_C ::= Z_{p_I}$. For each rule $p \twoheadrightarrow_s (p_1 \circ p_2) \propto p_3$ create a production $Z_p ::= Z_{p_1} Z_{p_3} Z_{p_2}$. For each rule $p \twoheadrightarrow_c (p_1 \circ p_2) \propto p_3$ create productions $Z_p ::= Z_{p_1} C_p Z_{p_2}$, $C_p ::= C_p C_p$, and $C_p ::= Z_{p_3}$. Let $Prod'$ be the all the productions defined by the above process. We set $Prod = \{\bigcup_{p \in P} Prod_p\} \cup Prod'$.

Theorem 2. *Let G and $\mathbf{P}$ be as above. Then $L(\mathbf{P}) = L(G)$.*

The proof is given in the extended version of this paper [27].

Expressibility Every RE-Dyck language (Section 2.2) can be expressed by a PRS, but the converse is not true; RE-Dyck languages nest delimiters arbitrarily, while PRS grammars may not. For instance, language L12 of Section 7.3 is not a Dyck language. Meanwhile, not every CFL can be expressed by a PRS [27].

Succinctness The construction above does not necessarily yield a minimal CFG G. For a PRS defining the Dyck language of order 2 – which can be expressed by a CFG with 4 productions and 1 non-terminal – our construction yields a CFG with 10 non-terminals and 12 productions. In this case, and often in others, we can recognise and remove the spurious productions from the generated grammar.

7   Experimental results

7.1   Methodology

We test the algorithm on several PRS-expressible context free languages, attempting to extract them from trained RNNs using the process outlined in Figure 1. For each language, we create a probabilistic CFG generating it, train an RNN on samples from this grammar, extract a sequence of DFAs from the RNN, and apply our PRS inference algorithm. Finally, we convert the extracted PRS back to a CFG, and compare it to our target CFG.

In all of our experiments, we use a vote-threshold s.t. patterns with less than 2 votes are not used to form any PRS rules (Section 5.1). Using no threshold significantly degraded the results by including too much noise, while higher thresholds often caused us to overlook correct patterns and rules.

7.2   Generating a sequence of DFAs

We obtain a sequence of DFAs for a given CFG using only positive samples[11,1] by training a *language-model RNN* (LM-RNN) on these samples and then extracting DFAs from it with the aid of the L^* algorithm [2], as described in [26]. To apply L^* we must treat the LM-RNN as a binary classifier. We set an 'acceptance threshold' t and define the RNN's language as the set of sequences s satisfying: 1. the RNN's probability for an end-of-sequence token after s is greater than t, and 2. at no point during s does the RNN pass through a token with probability $< t$. This is identical to the concept of *locally t-truncated support* defined in [13].

To create the samples for the RNNs, we write a weighted version of the CFG, in which each non-terminal is given a probability over its rules. We then take N samples from the weighted CFG according to its distribution, split them into train and validation sets, and train an RNN on the train set until the validation loss stops improving. In our experiments, we used $N = 10,000$. For our languages, we used very small 2-layer LSTMs: hidden dimension 10 and input dimension 4.

In some cases, especially when all of the patterns in the rules are several tokens long, the extraction of [26] terminates too soon: neither L^* nor the RNN abstraction consider long sequences, and equivalence is reached between the L^* hypothesis and the RNN abstraction despite neither being equivalent to the 'true' language of the RNN. In these cases we push the extraction a little further using two methods: first, if the RNN abstraction contains only a single state, we make an arbitrary initial refinement by splitting 10 hidden dimensions, and restart the extraction. If this is also not enough, we sample the RNN according to its distribution, in the hope of finding a counterexample to return to L^*. The latter approach is not ideal: sampling the RNN may return very long sequences, effectively increasing the next DFA by many rule applications. We place a time limit of $1,000$ seconds (~ 17 minutes) on the extraction.

7.3   Languages

We experiment on 15 PRS-expressible languages $L_1 - L_{15}$, grouped into 3 classes:

1. Languages of the form X^nY^n, for various regular expressions X and Y. In particular, the languages L_1 through L_6 are $X_i^n Y_i^n$ for: (X_1,Y_1)=(a,b), (X_2,Y_2)=(a|b,c|d), (X_3,Y_3)=(ab|cd,ef|gh), (X_4,Y_4)=(ab,cd), (X_5,Y_5)=(abc,def), and (X_6,Y_6)=(ab|c,de|f).
2. Dyck and RE-Dyck languages. In particular, languages L_7 through L_9 are the Dyck languages of order 2 through 4, and L_{10} and L_{11} are RE-Dyck languages of order 1 with the delimiters (L_{10},R_{10})=(abcde,vwxyz) and (L_{11},R_{11})=(ab|c,de|f).
3. Variations of the Dyck languages. L_{12} is the language of alternating single-nested delimiters, generating only sequences of the sort ([([])]) or [([])]. L_{13} and L_{14} are Dyck-1 and Dyck-2 with additional neutral tokens a,b,c that may appear multiple times anywhere in the sequence. L_{15} is like L_{13} except that the neutral additions are the token d and the sequence abc, eg: (abc()())d is in L_{15}, but a(bc()())d is not.

LG	DFAs	Init Pats	Final Pats	Min/Max Votes	CFG Correct	LG	DFAs	Init Pats	Final Pats	Min/Max Votes	CFG Correct
L_1	18	1	1	16/16	Correct	L_9	30	6	4	5/8	Correct
L_2	16	1	1	14/14	Correct	L_{10}	6	2	1	3/3	Correct
L_3	14	6	4	2/4	Incorrect	L_{11}	24	6	3	5/12	Incorrect
L_4	8	2	1	5/5	Correct	L_{12}	28	2	2	13/13	Correct
L_5	10	2	1	7/7	Correct	L_{13}	9	6	1	2/2	Correct
L_6	22	9	4	3/16	Incorrect	L_{14}	17	5	2	5/7	Correct
L_7	24	2	2	11/11	Correct	L_{15}	13	6	4	3/6	Incorrect
L_8	22	5	4	2/9	Partial						

Table 1. Results of experiments on DFAs extracted from RNNs

7.4   Results

Table 1 shows the results. The 2nd column shows the number of DFAs extracted from the RNN. The 3rd and 4th columns present the number of patterns found by the algorithm before and after applying vote-thresholding to remove noise. The 5th column gives the minimum and maximum votes received by the final patterns (we count only patterns introduced as a new pattern p^3 in some A_{i+1}). The 6th column notes whether the algorithm found a correct CFG, according to our manual inspection. For languages where our algorithm only missed or included 1 or 2 valid/invalid productions, we label it as partially correct.

Alternating Patterns Our algorithm struggled on the languages L_3, L_6, and L_{11}, which contained patterns whose regular expressions had alternations (such as ab|cd in L_3, and ab|c in L_6 and L_{11}). Investigating their DFA sequences uncovered the that the L^* extraction had 'split' the alternating expressions, adding their parts to the DFAs over multiple iterations. For example, in the sequence generated for L_3, ef appeared in A_7 without gh alongside it. The next DFA corrected this mistake but the inference algorithm could not piece together these two separate steps into a single rule. It will be valuable to expand the algorithm to these cases.

Simultaneous Applications Originally our algorithm failed to accurately generate L_{13} and L_{14} due to simultaneous rule applications. However, using the technique described in Section 5.1 we were able to correctly infer these grammars. However, more work is needed to handle simultaneous rule applications in general.

Additionally, sometimes a very large counterexample was returned to L^* , creating a large increase in the DFAs: the 9th iteration of the extraction on L_3 introduced almost 30 new states. The algorithm does not manage to infer anything meaningful from these nested, simultaneous applications.

Missing Rules For the Dyck languages $L_7 - L_9$, the inference algorithm was mostly successful. However, due to the large number of possible delimiter combinations, some patterns and nesting relations did not appear often enough in the DFA sequences. As a result, for L_8, some productions were missing in the generated grammar. L_8 also created one incorrect production due to noise in the sequence (one erroneous pattern was generated two times,passing the threshold).

RNN Noise In L_{15}, the extracted DFAs for some reason always forced that a single character d be included between every pair of delimiters. Our inference algorithm of course maintained this peculiarity. It correctly allowed the allowed optional embedding of "abc" strings. But due to noisy (incorrect) generated DFAs, the patterns generated did not maintain balanced parenthesis.

8 Related work

Training RNNs to recognize Dyck Grammars. Recently there has been a surge of interest in whether RNNs can learn Dyck languages [5,19,21,28]. While these works report very good results on learning the language for sentences of similar distance and depth as the training set, with the exception of [21], they report significantly lower accuracy for out-of-sample sentences.

Among these, Sennhauser and Berwick [19] use LSTMs, and show that in order to keep the error rate within a 5 percent tolerance, the number of hidden units must grow exponentially with the distance or depth of the sequences (though Hewitt et. al. [13] find much lower theoretical bounds). They conclude that LSTMs do not learn rules, but rather statistical approximations. Bernardy [5] experimented with various RNN architectures, finding in particular that the LSTM has more difficulty in predicting closing delimiters in the middle of a sentence than at the end. Based on this, he conjectures that the RNN is using a counting mechanism, but has not truly learnt the Dyck language (its CFG). For the simplified task of predicting only the final closing delimiter of a legal sequence, Skachkova, Trost and Klakow [21] find that LSTMs have nearly perfect accuracy across words with large distances and embedded depth.

Yu, Vu and Kuhn [28] compare the three works above, and note that the task of predicting only the closing bracket of a balanced Dyck word is not sufficient for checking if an RNN has learnt the language, as it can be computed by only a counter. In their experiments, they present a prefix of a Dyck word and train the RNN to predict the next valid closing bracket. They experiment with an LSTM using 4 different models, and show that the generator-attention model [17] performs the best, and is able to generalize quite well at the tagging task . However, they find that it degrades rapidly with out-of-domain tests. They also conclude that RNNs do not really learn the Dyck language. These experimental results are reinforced by the theoretical work in [13], who remark that no finite precision RNN can learn a Dyck language of unbounded depth, and give precise bounds on the memory required to learn a Dyck language of bounded depth.

Despite these findings, our algorithm nevertheless extracts a CFG from a trained RNN, discovering rules based on DFAs synthesized from the RNN using the algorithm in [26]. Because we can use a short sequence of DFAs to extract the rules, and because the first DFAs in the sequence describe Dyck words with increasing but limited distance and depth, we are often able to extract the CFG perfectly even when the RNN does not generalize well. Moreover, we show that our approach works with more complex types of delimiters, and on Dyck languages with expressions between delimiters.

Extracting DFAs from RNNs. There have been many approaches to extract higher level representations from a neural network (NN), both to facilitate comprehension and to verify correctness. One of the oldest approaches is to extract rules from a NN [24,12]. In particular, several works attempt to extract FSAs from RNNs [18,15,25]. We base our work on [26]. Its ability to generate sequences of DFAs providing increasingly better approximations of the CFL is critical to our method.

There has been less research on extracting a CFG from an RNN. One exception is [23], where they develop a Neural Network Pushdown Automata (NNPDA) framework, a hybrid system augmenting an RNN with external stack memory. They show how to extract a push-down automaton from an NNPDA, however, their technique relies on the PDA-like structure of the inspected architecture. In contrast, we extract CFGs from RNNs without stack augmentation.

Learning CFGs from samples. There is a wide body of work on learning CFGs from samples. An overview is given in [10] and a survey of work for grammatical inference applied to software engineering tasks can be found in [22].

Clark et. al. studies algorithms for learning CFLs given only positive examples [11]. In [7], Clark and Eyraud show how one can learn a subclass of CFLs called *CF substitutable* languages. There are many languages that can be expressed by a PRS but are not substitutable, such as $x^n b^n$. However, there are also substitutable languages that cannot be expressed by a PRS (wxw^R - see [27]). In [8], Clark, Eyraud and Habrard present Contextual Binary Feature Grammars. However, it does not include Dyck languages of arbitrary order. None of these techniques deal with noise in the data, essential to learning a language from an RNN.

9   Future Directions

Currently, for each experiment, we train the RNN on that language and then apply the PRS inference algorithm on a single DFA sequence generated from that RNN. Perhaps the most substantial improvement we can make is to extend our technique to learn from multiple DFA sequences. We can train multiple RNNs and generate DFA sequences for each one. We can then run the PRS inference algorithm on each of these sequences, and generate a CFG based upon rules that are found in a significant number of the runs. This would require care to guarantee that the final rules form a cohesive CFG. It would also address the issue that not all rules are expressed in a single DFA sequence, and that some grammars may have rules that are executed only once per word of the language.

Our work generates CFGs for generalized Dyck languages, but it is possible to generalize PRSs to express a greater range of languages. Work will then be needed to extend the PRS inference algorithm.

References

1. Angluin, D.: Inductive inference of formal languages from positive data. Inf. Control. **45**(2), 117–135 (1980), https://doi.org/10.1016/S0019-9958(80)90285-5
2. Angluin, D.: Learning regular sets from queries and counterexamples. Inf. Comput. **75**(2), 87–106 (1987). https://doi.org/10.1016/0890-5401(87)90052-6
3. Ayache, S., Eyraud, R., Goudian, N.: Explaining black boxes on sequential data using weighted automata. In: Unold, O., Dyrka, W., Wieczorek, W. (eds.) Proceedings of the 14th International Conference on Grammatical Inference, ICGI 2018. Proceedings of Machine Learning Research, vol. 93, pp. 81–103. PMLR (2018), http://proceedings.mlr.press/v93/ayache19a.html
4. Bahdanau, D., Cho, K., Bengio, Y.: Neural machine translation by jointly learning to align and translate. In: Bengio, Y., LeCun, Y. (eds.) 3rd International Conference on Learning Representations, ICLR 2015 (2015), http://arxiv.org/abs/1409.0473
5. Bernardy, J.P.: Can recurrent neural networks learn nested recursion? In: Linguistic Issues in Language Technology, Volume 16, 2018. CSLI Publications (2018), https://www.aclweb.org/anthology/2018.lilt-16.1
6. Cechin, A.L., Simon, D.R.P., Stertz, K.: State automata extraction from recurrent neural nets using k-means and fuzzy clustering. In: 23rd International Conference of the Chilean Computer Science Society (SCCC 2003). pp. 73–78. IEEE Computer Society (2003). https://doi.org/10.1109/SCCC.2003.1245447
7. Clark, A., Eyraud, R.: Polynomial identification in the limit of substitutable context-free languages. J. Mach. Learn. Res. **8**, 1725–1745 (2007), http://dl.acm.org/citation.cfm?id=1314556
8. Clark, A., Eyraud, R., Habrard, A.: A polynomial algorithm for the inference of context free languages. In: Clark, A., Coste, F., Miclet, L. (eds.) Grammatical Inference: Algorithms and Applications, 9th International Colloquium, ICGI 2008, Proceedings. Lecture Notes in Computer Science, vol. 5278, pp. 29–42. Springer (2008). https://doi.org/10.1007/978-3-540-88009-7_3
9. Das, S., Giles, C.L., Sun, G.: Learning context-free grammars: Capabilities and limitations of a recurrent neural network with an external stack memory. In: Conference of the Cognitive Science Society. pp. 791–795. Morgan Kaufmann Publishers (1992)
10. D'Ulizia, A., Ferri, F., Grifoni, P.: A survey of grammatical inference methods for natural language learning. Artif. Intell. Rev. **36**(1), 1–27 (2011). https://doi.org/10.1007/s10462-010-9199-1
11. Gold, E.M.: Language identification in the limit. Information and Control **10**(5), 447–474 (May 1967), https://doi.org/10.1016/S0019-9958(67)91165-5
12. Hailesilassie, T.: Rule extraction algorithm for deep neural networks: A review. International Journal of Computer Science and Information Security (IJCSIS) **14**(7) (July 2016)
13. Hewitt, J., Hahn, M., Ganguli, S., Liang, P., Manning, C.D.: RNNs can generate bounded hierarchical languages with optimal memory. In: Proceedings of the 2020 Conference on Empirical Methods in Natural Language Processing (EMNLP). pp. 1978–2010. Association for Computational Linguistics (2020), https://www.aclweb.org/anthology/2020.emnlp-main.156
14. Hochreiter, S., Schmidhuber, J.: Long short-term memory. Neural Computation **9**(8), 1735–1780 (1997). https://doi.org/10.1162/neco.1997.9.8.1735
15. Jacobsson, H.: Rule extraction from recurrent neural networks: A taxonomy and review. Neural Computation **17**(6), 1223–1263 (2005). https://doi.org/10.1162/0899766053630350

16. Kozen, D.C.: The Chomsky—Schützenberger theorem. In: Automata and Computability. pp. 198–200. Springer Berlin Heidelberg, Berlin, Heidelberg (1977)

17. Luong, T., Pham, H., Manning, C.D.: Effective approaches to attention-based neural machine translation. In: Màrquez, L., Callison-Burch, C., Su, J., Pighin, D., Marton, Y. (eds.) Proceedings of the 2015 Conference on Empirical Methods in Natural Language Processing, EMNLP 2015. pp. 1412–1421. The Association for Computational Linguistics (2015). https://doi.org/10.18653/v1/d15-1166

18. Omlin, C.W., Giles, C.L.: Extraction of rules from discrete-time recurrent neural networks. Neural Networks 9(1), 41–52 (1996). https://doi.org/10.1016/0893-6080(95)00086-0

19. Sennhauser, L., Berwick, R.: Evaluating the ability of LSTMs to learn context-free grammars. In: Proceedings of the 2018 EMNLP Workshop BlackboxNLP: Analyzing and Interpreting Neural Networks for NLP. pp. 115–124. Association for Computational Linguistics (Nov 2018). https://doi.org/10.18653/v1/W18-5414

20. Siegelmann, H.T., Sontag, E.D.: On the Computational Power of Neural Nets. J. Comput. Syst. Sci. 50(1), 132–150 (1995). https://doi.org/10.1006/jcss.1995.1013

21. Skachkova, N., Trost, T., Klakow, D.: Closing brackets with recurrent neural networks. In: Proceedings of the 2018 EMNLP Workshop BlackboxNLP: Analyzing and Interpreting Neural Networks for NLP. pp. 232–239. Association for Computational Linguistics (Nov 2018). https://doi.org/10.18653/v1/W18-5425

22. Stevenson, A., Cordy, J.R.: A survey of grammatical inference in software engineering. Sci. Comput. Program. 96(P4), 444–459 (Dec 2014). https://doi.org/10.1016/j.scico.2014.05.008

23. Sun, G., Giles, C.L., Chen, H.: The neural network pushdown automaton: Architecture, dynamics and training. In: Giles, C.L., Gori, M. (eds.) Adaptive Processing of Sequences and Data Structures, International Summer School on Neural Networks. Lecture Notes in Computer Science, vol. 1387, pp. 296–345. Springer (1997). https://doi.org/10.1007/BFb0054003

24. Thrun, S.: Extracting rules from artifical neural networks with distributed representations. In: Tesauro, G., Touretzky, D.S., Leen, T.K. (eds.) Advances in Neural Information Processing Systems 7, NIPS Conference, 1994. pp. 505–512. MIT Press (1994), http://papers.nips.cc/paper/924-extracting-rules-from-artificial-neural-networks-with-distributed-representations

25. Wang, Q., Zhang, K., Liu, X., Giles, C.L.: Connecting first and second order recurrent networks with deterministic finite automata. CoRR abs/1911.04644 (2019), http://arxiv.org/abs/1911.04644

26. Weiss, G., Goldberg, Y., Yahav, E.: Extracting automata from recurrent neural networks using queries and counterexamples. In: Dy, J.G., Krause, A. (eds.) Proceedings of the 35th International Conference on Machine Learning, ICML 2018. Proceedings of Machine Learning Research, vol. 80, pp. 5244–5253. PMLR (2018), http://proceedings.mlr.press/v80/weiss18a.html

27. Yellin, D.M., Weiss, G.: Synthesizing context-free grammars from recurrent neural networks (extended version) (2021), http://arxiv.org/abs/2101.08200

28. Yu, X., Vu, N.T., Kuhn, J.: Learning the Dyck language with attention-based Seq2Seq models. In: Proceedings of the 2019 ACL Workshop BlackboxNLP: Analyzing and Interpreting Neural Networks for NLP. pp. 138–146. Association for Computational Linguistics (2019), https://www.aclweb.org/anthology/W19-4815

Automated and Formal Synthesis of Neural Barrier Certificates for Dynamical Models

Andrea Peruffo[1]([✉])[iD], Daniele Ahmed[2][iD], Alessandro Abate[1][iD]

[1] Department of Computer Science, University of Oxford,
Oxford, UK
{name.surname}@cs.ox.ac.uk
[2] Amazon Inc, London, UK

Abstract. We introduce an automated, formal, counterexample-based approach to synthesise Barrier Certificates (BC) for the safety verification of continuous and hybrid dynamical models. The approach is underpinned by an inductive framework: this is structured as a sequential loop between a learner, which manipulates a candidate BC structured as a neural network, and a sound verifier, which either certifies the candidate's validity or generates counter-examples to further guide the learner. We compare the approach against state-of-the-art techniques, over polynomial and non-polynomial dynamical models: the outcomes show that we can synthesise sound BCs up to two orders of magnitude faster, with in particular a stark speedup on the verification engine (up to three orders less), whilst needing a far smaller data set (up to three orders less) for the learning part. Beyond improvements over the state of the art, we further challenge the new approach on a hybrid dynamical model and on larger-dimensional models, and showcase the numerical robustness of our algorithms and codebase.

1 Introduction

Barrier Certificates (BC) are an effective and powerful technique to prove safety properties on models of continuous dynamical systems, as well as hybrid models (featuring both continuous and discrete states) [21,22]. Whenever found, a BC partitions the state space of the model into two parts, ensuring that all trajectories starting from a given initial set, located within one side of the BC, cannot reach a given set of states (deemed to be unsafe), located on the other side. Thus a successful synthesis of a BC (which is in general not a unique object) represents a formal proof of safety for the dynamical model. BC find various applications spanning robotics, multi-agent systems, and biology [7,32].

This work addresses the safety of dynamical systems modelled in general by non-linear ordinary differential equations (ODE), and presents a novel method for the automated and formal synthesis of BC. The approach leverages Satisfiability Modulo Theory (SMT) and inductive reasoning (CEGIS, Figure 1, introduced later), to guarantee the correctness of the automated synthesis procedure: this rules out both algorithmic and numerical errors related to BC synthesis [10].

© The Author(s) 2021
J. F. Groote and K. G. Larsen (Eds.): TACAS 2021, LNCS 12651, pp. 370–388, 2021.
https://doi.org/10.1007/978-3-030-72016-2_20

Background and Related Work A few techniques have been developed to synthesise BC. For polynomial models, sum-of-squares (SOS) and semi-definite programming relaxations [14,16,29] convert the BC synthesis problem into constraints expressed as linear or bilinear matrix inequalities: these are numerically solved as a convex optimisation problem, however unsoundly. To increase scalability and to enhance expressiveness, numerous barrier formats have been considered: BC based on exponential conditions are presented in [14]; BC based on Darboux polynomials are outlined in [33]; [30] newly introduces a multi-dimensional generalisation of BC, thus broadening their scope and applicability. BC can also be used to verify safety of uncertain (e.g. parametric) models [20]. Let us remark that SOS approaches are typically *unsound*, namely they rely on iterative and numerical methods to synthesise the BC. [10] a-posteriori verifies SOS candidates via computer-aided design (CAD) techniques [15].

Model *invariants* (namely, regions that provably contain model trajectories, such as *basins of attractions* [28]) can be employed as BC, though their synthesis is less general, as it does not comprise an unsafe set and tacitly presupposes the initial set to be "well placed" within the state space (that is, within the aforementioned basin): [19] introduces a fixpoint algorithm to find algebraic-differential invariants for hybrid models; invariants can be characterised analytically [4] or synthesised computationally [8]. Invariants can be alternatively studied by *Lyapunov theory* [5], which provides *stability* guarantees for dynamical models, and thus can characterise invariants (and barriers) as side products: however this again requires that initial conditions are positioned around stable equilibria, and does not explicitly encompass unsafe sets in the synthesis. Whilst Lyapunov theory is classically approached either analytically (explicit synthesis) or numerically (with unsound techniques), an approach that is relevant for the results of this work looks at automated and sound Lyapunov function synthesis: in [27] Lyapunov functions are soundly found within parametric templates, by constructing a system of linear inequality constraints over unknown coefficients. [23,24,25] employ a counterexample-based approach to synthesise control Lyapunov functions, which inspires this work, using a combination of SMT solvers and convex optimisation engines: however unlike this work, SMT solvers are never used for verification, which is instead handled by solving optimisation problems that are numerically unsound. As argued above, let us emphasise again that the BC synthesis problem, as studied in this work, cannot in general be reduced to a problem of Lyapunov stability analysis, and is indeed more general.

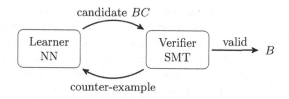

Fig. 1. Schematic representation of the CEGIS loop.

Core approach We introduce a method that efficiently exploits machine learning, whilst guaranteeing formal proofs of correctness via SMT. We leverage a CounterExample-Guided Inductive Synthesis (CEGIS) procedure [31], which is structured as an inductive loop between a *Learner* and a *Verifier* (cf. Fig. 1). A learner numerically (and unsoundly) trains a neural network (NN) to fit over a finite set of samples the requirements for a BC, which are expressed through a loss function; then a verifier either formally proves the validity of the BC or provides (a) counter-example(s) through an SMT solver: the counter-examples indicate where the barrier conditions are violated, and are passed back to the learner for further training. This synthesis method for neural BC is formally sound and fully automated, and thanks to its specific new features, is shown to be much faster and to clearly require less data than state-of-the-art results.

Contributions beyond the State of the Art Cognate work [34] presents a method to compute BC using neural networks and to verify their correctness a-posteriori: as such, it does not generate counter-examples within an inductive loop, as in this work. [34] considers large sample sets that are randomly divided into batches and fed to a feed-forward NN; the verification at the end of the (rather long) training either validates the candidate, or invalidates it and the training starts anew on the same dataset. In Section 4 the method in [34] is shown to be slower (both in the training and in the verification), and to require more data than the CEGIS-based approach of this work, which furthermore introduces numerous bespoke optimisations, as outlined in Section 3: our CEGIS-based technique exploits fast learning, verification simplified by the candidates passed by the Learner, and an enhanced communication between Learner and Verifier. Our approach further showcases numerical robustness and scalability features.

Related to the work on BC is the synthesis of Lyapunov functions, mentioned above. The construction of *Lyapunov Neural Networks* (LNNs) has been studied with approaches based on simulations and numerical optimisation, which are in general unsound [26]. Formal methods for Lyapunov synthesis are introduced in [5], together with a counterexample-based approach using polynomial candidates. The work is later extended in [2], which employs NN as candidates over polynomial dynamical models. The generation of control Lyapunov functions using counterexample-based NN is similarly considered in [9], however this is done by means of differing architectural details and does not extend to BC synthesis. Beyond the work in [5], this contribution is not limited to a specific polynomial template, since it supports more general mixtures of polynomial functions obtained through the NN structure, as well as the canonical tanh, sigmoid, ReLU activations (we provide one example of BC using tanh activations). Compared to [5], where we use LP programming to synthesise Lyapunov functions, in this work: *a)* we use a template-free procedure, thanks to the integration of NNs - these are needed since template-based SOS-programming approaches are not sufficient to provide BCs for several of the presented benchmarks (see Section 4 and [34]); *b)* we provide an enhanced loss function (naturally absent from [5]), enriched counter-example generation, prioritised check of the verification constraints, and *c)* we newly synthesise verified barrier certificates for hybrid models, which are generated using counterexample-based, neural architectures. Finally, beyond [5] the new approach is endowed with numerical robustness features.

SOS programming solutions [14,16,29] are not quite comparable to this work. Foremostly, they are not sound, i.e. do not offer a formal guarantee of numerical and algorithmic correctness. The exception is [10], which verifies SOS candidates a-posteriori by means of CAD [15] techniques that are known not to scale well. Furthermore, they can be hardly embedded within a CEGIS loop - we experimentally show that SOS candidates are handled with difficulty by SMT solvers. Finally, they hardly cope with the experiments we have considered, as already observed in [34]. We instead use SMT solvers (Z3 [11] and dReal [13]) within CEGIS to provide sound outcomes based on NN candidates, proffering a new approach that synthesises and formally verifies candidate BCs altogether, with minimum effort from the user.

Organisation The remainder of the paper is organised as follows: Section 2 presents preliminary notions on BCs and outlines the problem. Section 3 describes the approach: training of the NN in Sec. 3.1 and verification in Sec. 3.2. Section 4 presents case studies, Section 5 delineates future work.

2 Safety Analysis with Barrier Certificates

We address the safety verification of continuous-time dynamical models by designing barrier certificates (BC) over the continuous state space X of the model. We consider n-dimensional dynamical models described by

$$\dot{x}(t) = \frac{dx}{dt} = f(x), \quad x(0) = x_0 \in X_0 \subset X, \tag{1}$$

where $f : X \to \mathbb{R}^n$ is a continuous vector field, $X \subseteq \mathbb{R}^n$ is an open set defining the state space of the system, and X_0 represents the set of initial states. Given model (1) and an unsafe set $X_u \subset X$, the safety verification problem concerns checking whether or not all trajectories of the model originating from X_0 reach the unsafe region X_u. BC offer a sufficient condition asserting the safety of the model, namely when no trajectory enters the unsafe region.

Definition 1. *The Lie derivative of a continuously differentiable scalar function $B : X \to \mathbb{R}$, with respect to a vector field f, is defined as follows*

$$\dot{B}(x) = \nabla B(x) \cdot f(x) = \sum_{i=1}^{n} \frac{\partial B}{\partial x_i} \frac{dx_i}{dt} = \sum_{i=1}^{n} \frac{\partial B}{\partial x_i} f_i(x). \tag{2}$$

Intuitively, this derivative denotes the rate of change of function B along the model trajectories.

Proposition 1 (Barrier Certificate for Safety Verification, [21]). *Let the model in (1) and the sets X, X_0 and X_u be given. Suppose there exists a function*

$B : X \to \mathbb{R}$ *that is differentiable with respect to its argument and satisfies the following conditions:*

$$B(x) \leq 0 \ \forall x \in X_0, \quad B(x) > 0 \ \forall x \in X_u, \quad \dot{B}(x) < 0 \ \forall x \in X \ s.t. \ B(x) = 0, \tag{3}$$

then the safety of the model is guaranteed. That is, there is no trajectory of the model contained in X, starting from the initial set X_0, that ever enters set X_u.

Consider a trajectory $x(t)$ starting in $x_0 \in X_0$ and the evolution of $B(x(t))$ along this trajectory. Whilst the first of the three conditions guarantees that $B(x_0) \leq 0$, the last condition asserts that the value of $B(x(t))$ along a trajectory $x(t)$ must decrease. Hence such a trajectory $x(t)$ cannot enter the set X_u, where $B(x) > 0$ (second condition), thus ensuring the safety of the model.

3 Synthesis of Neural Barrier Certificates via Learning and Verification

We introduce an automated and formal approach for the construction of barrier certificates (BC) that are expressed as feed-forward neural networks (NN). The procedure leverages CEGIS (see Fig. 1) [31], an automated and sound procedure for solving second-order logic synthesis problems, which comprises two interacting parts. The first component is a *Learner*, which provides candidate BC functions by training a NN over a finite set of sample inputs. The network is then translated into a logical formula in an appropriate theory, by evaluating it with symbolic inputs, instead of canonical floating point numbers. The details of this conversion are outlined in [2]. This encoded candidate is passed to the second component, a *Verifier*, which acts as an oracle: either it proves that the solution is valid, or it finds one (or more) instance (called a counter-example) where the candidate BC does not comply with required conditions. The verifier consists of an SMT solver [15], namely an algorithmic decision procedure that extends Boolean SAT problems to richer, more expressive theories, such as non-linear arithmetics.

More precisely, the learner trains a NN composed of n input neurons (this matches the dimension of the model f), k hidden layers, and one output neuron (recall that $B(x)$ is a scalar function): this NN candidate B is required to closely match the conditions in Eq. (3) over a discrete set of samples S, which is initialised randomly. The verifier checks whether the candidate B violates any of the conditions in Eq. (3) over the entire set X and, if so, produces one (or more, as in this work) counter-examples c. We add c to the samples set S as the loop restarts, hence forcing the NN to be trained *also* over the generated counter-examples c. Note that the NN retains its old weights, and restarts the training from the weights obtained at the end of the previous session. This loop repeats until the SMT verifier proves that no counter-examples exist or until a timeout is reached. CEGIS offers a scalable and flexible alternative for BC synthesis: on the one hand, the learner does not require soundness, and ensures a rapid synthesis exploiting the training of NN architectures; on the other, the algorithm is *sound*, i.e. a valid output from the SMT-based verifier is provably correct; of course we cannot claim any *completeness*, since CEGIS might in general not terminate with a solution because it operates over a continuous model.

The performance of the CEGIS algorithm in practice hinges on the effective exchange of information between the learner and the verifier [3]. A core contribution of this work is to tailor the CEGIS architecture to the problem of BC synthesis: we devise several improvements to NN training, such as a bespoke loss function and a multi-layer NN architecture that ensures robustness and outputs a function that is tailored to the verification engine. Over consecutive loops, the verifier may return similar counter-examples: we thus propose a more informative counter-examples generation by the SMT verifier that is adapted to the candidate BC and the underlying dynamical model. These tailored architectural details generate in practice a rapid, efficient, and robust CEGIS loop, which is shown in this work to clearly outperform state-of-the-art methods.

3.1 Training of the Barrier Neural Network

The learner instantiates the candidate BC using the hyper-parameters k and h (depth and width of the NN), trains it over the N samples in the set S, and later refines its training whenever the verifier adds counter-examples to the set S. The class of candidate BC comprises multi-layered, feed-forward NN with *polynomial* and non-polynomial activation functions. Unlike most learning applications, the choice of polynomial activations comes from the need for interpretable outputs from the NN, whose analytical expression must be readily processed by the verifier. The order γ of the polynomial activations is a hyper-parameter fed at the start of the procedure: we split the i-th hidden layer into γ portions and apply polynomial activations of order j to the neurons of the j-th portion.

Example 1 (Polynomial Activations). Assume a NN composed of an input x, 3 hidden neurons and 1 activation-free output, with γ-th order polynomial activation, $\gamma = 3$. We split the hidden layer in γ sub-vectors, each containing one neuron. The hidden layer after the activation results in

$$z = \left[W_1^{(1)}x + b_1 \qquad (W_2^{(1)}x + b_2)^2 \qquad (W_3^{(1)}x + b_3)^3 \right]^T,$$

where the $W_i^{(1)}$ are the i-th row of the first-layer weight matrix, and the b_i form the bias vector.   □

The learning process updates the NN parameters to improve the satisfaction of the BC conditions in (3): $B(x) \leq 0$ for $x \in X_0$, $B(x) > 0$ for $x \in X_u$, and a negative Lie derivative $\dot{B}$ (Eq. (2)) over the set implicitly defined by $B(x) = 0$. The training minimises a loss comprising three terms, namely

$$L = L_0 + L_u + L_d = \frac{1}{N} \sum_{i=1}^{N} \left(\max_{s_i \in X_0} \{\tau_0, B(s_i)\} + \max_{s_i \in X_u} \{\tau_u, -B(s_i)\} \right.$$

$$\left. + \max_{s_i : B(s_i) = 0} \{\tau_d, \dot{B}(s_i)\} \right), \quad (4)$$

where s_i, $i = 1, \ldots, N$ are the samples taken from the set S. The constants τ_0, τ_u, τ_d are offsets, added to improve the numerical stability of the training. Notably, $B(x) = 0$ can be a set with small volume, thus it is highly unlikely that a single sample s will satisfy $B(s) = 0$. We thus relax this last condition and consider a belt $\mathcal{B}$ around $B(s) = 0$, namely $\mathcal{B} = |B(x)| \leq \beta$, which depends on the hyper-parameter β. Note that we must use continuously differentiable activations throughout, as we require the existence of Lie derivatives (cf. Eq. (2)), and thus cannot leverage simple ReLUs.

Enhanced Loss Functions The loss function in Eq. (4) experimentally yields possible drawbacks, which suggests a few ameliorations. Terms L_0 and L_u solely penalise samples with incorrect value of $B(x)$ without further providing a reward for samples with a correct value. The NN thus stops learning when the samples return correct values of $B(x)$ without further increasing the positivity of B over X_u or the negativity over X_0. As such, the training often returns a candidate $B(x)$ with values just below τ_0 in X_0 or above τ_u in X_u. These candidates are easily falsified, thus potentially leading to a large number of CEGIS iterations.

We improve the learning by adopting a (saturated) *Leaky* ReLU, hence rewarding samples that evaluate to a correct value of $B(x)$. Noting that

$$\text{LeakyReLU}(\alpha, x) = \text{ReLU}(x) - \alpha \, \text{ReLU}(-x), \tag{5}$$

where α is a small positive constant, we rewrite term L_0 as

$$L_0 = \frac{1}{N} \sum_{s_i \in X_0} \text{ReLU}(B(s_i) - \tau_0) - \alpha \cdot \text{satReLU}(-B(s_i) + \tau_0), \tag{6}$$

where satReLU is the saturated ReLU function[3]. The term L_u is similarly modified. The composite loss function works as follows. Incorrect samples account for the main contribution to the loss function, leading the NN to correct those first via the ReLU term in Eq. (6). At a second stage, the network finds a direction of improvement by following the *leaky* portion of the loss function. This is saturated to prevent the training from following only one of these directions, without improving the other loss terms.

Another possible drawback of the loss function in (4) derives from the term L_d: it solely accounts for a penalisation of the sample points within $\mathcal{B}$. To quickly and myopically improve the loss function, the training can generate a candidate BC for which no samples are within $\mathcal{B}$ - we experimentally find that this behaviour persists, regardless of the value of β. Similarly to L_0 and L_u, we reward the points within a belt fulfilling the BC condition: namely, we solely apply the satReLU function to reward samples s with a negative $\dot{B}(s)$, whilst not penalising values $\dot{B}(s) \geq 0$. The training is driven to include more samples in $\mathcal{B}$, guiding towards a negative $\dot{B}(s)$, and finally enhancing learning. The expression of L_d results in

$$L_d = -\frac{1}{N} \sum_{s \in \mathcal{B}} \text{satReLU}(-\dot{B}(s) + \tau_d). \tag{7}$$

---

[3] Let us define M to be an arbitrary upper bound, then $\text{satReLU}(x) = \min(\max(0, x), M)$.

Finally, we choose an asymmetric belt $\mathcal{B} = -\beta_1 \leq B(s) \leq \beta_2$, with $\beta_2 > \beta_1 > 0$ to both ensure a wider sample set and a stronger safety certificate.

Multi-layer Networks Polynomial activation functions generate interpretable barrier certificates with analytical expressions that are readily verifiable by an SMT solver. However, when considering polynomial networks, the use of multi-layer architectures quickly increases the order of the barrier function: a k-layer network with γ-th order activations returns a polynomial of $k\gamma$ degree. We have experienced that deep NN provide numerical robustness to our method, although the verification complexity increases with the order of the polynomial activation functions used and with the depth of the NN. As a consequence, our procedure leverages a deep architecture whilst maintaining a low-order polynomial by interchanging linear and polynomial activations over adjacent layers. We have observed that the use of linear activations, particularly in the output layer, positively affects the training: they provide robustness that is needed to the synthesis of BC (see Experimental results), without increasing the order of the network with new polynomial terms.

Learning in Separate Batches The structure of the conditions in (3) and the learning loss in (4) naturally suggests a separate approach to training. We then split the dataset S into three batches S_0, S_u and S_x, each including samples belonging to X_0, X_u and X, respectively. For training, we compute the loss function in a parallel fashion. Similarly, for the verifier, generated counter-examples are added to the relevant batch.

3.2 Certification of the Barrier Neural Network, or Falsification via Counter-examples

Every candidate BC function $B(x)$ which the learner generates requires to be certified by the verifier. Equivalently, in practice the SMT-based verifier aims at finding states that violate the barrier conditions in (3) over the continuous domain X. To this end, we express the *negation* of such requirements, and formulate a nonlinear constrained problem over real numbers, as

$$(x \in X_0 \wedge B(x) > 0) \vee (x \in X_u \wedge B(x) \leq 0) \vee (B(x) = 0 \wedge \dot{B}(x) \geq 0). \quad (8)$$

The verifier searches for solutions of the constraints in Eq. (8), which in general requires manipulating non-convex functions. This can be cumbersome and time-consuming, hence simple expressions of B can enhance the verification procedure. On the one hand, the soundness of our CEGIS procedure heavily relies on the correctness of SMT solving: an SMT solver never fails to assert the absence of solutions for (8). As a result, when it states that formula (8) is unsatisfiable, i.e. returns unsat, $B(x)$ is formally guaranteed to fulfil the BC conditions in Eq. (3). On the other hand, the CEGIS algorithm offers flexibility in the choice of the verifier, hence we implement and discuss two SMT solvers: dReal [13] and Z3 [11]. dReal is a δ-complete solver, namely the unsat decision is correct [12], whereas when a solution for (8) is found, this comes with a δ-error bound. The value of δ characterises the procedure precision. In our setting, it is acceptable to return spurious counter-examples: indeed, these are then used as additional samples and do not invalidate the sound outcomes of the procedure, but rather help synthesising a more robust barrier candidate. dReal is capable of handling non-polynomial terms, such as exponentials or trigonometric vector fields f for some of the models considered in Section 4. Z3 is a powerful, sound and complete SMT solver, namely its conclusions are provably correct both when it determines the validity of a BC candidate and when it provides counter-examples. The shortcoming of Z3 is that it is unable to handle non-polynomial formulae.

Prioritisation and Relaxation of Constraints The effectiveness of the CEGIS framework is underpinned by rapid exchanges between the learner and the verifier, as well as by quick NN training and SMT verification procedures. We have experienced that the bottleneck resides in the handling of the constraint $\eta_d = (B(x) = 0 \wedge \dot{B}(x) \geq 0)$ by the SMT solver, since the formula contains the high-order expression $\dot{B}(x)$ and because it is defined over the thin region of the state space implicitly characterised by $B(x) = 0$. As a consequence, we have prioritised constraints $\eta_0 = (x \in X_0 \wedge B(x) > 0)$ and $\eta_u = (x \in X_u \wedge B(x) \leq 0)$: that is, if either clauses is satisfied, i.e. a counter-example is found for at least one of them, the verifier omits testing η_d whilst the obtained counter-examples are passed to the learner. The constraint η_d is thus checked solely if η_0 and η_u are both deemed to be **unsat**. Whenever this occurs, and the verification of η_d times out, the solver searches for a solution of a relaxed constraint $(|B(x)| < \tau_v \wedge \dot{B}(x) \geq 0)$, similarly to the improved learning conditions discussed in Eq. (7). Whilst this constraint is arguably easier to solve in general, it may generate spurious counter-examples, namely a sample $\bar{x}$ that satisfy the relaxed constraint, but such that $B(\bar{x}) \neq 0$. The generation of these samples does not contradict the soundness of the procedure, and indeed improve the robustness of the next candidate BC – this of course comes with the cost of increasing the number of CEGIS iterations.

Increased Information from Counter-examples The verification task encompasses an SMT solver attempting to generate a counter-example, namely a (single) instance satisfying Eq. (8). However, a lone sample might not always provide insightful information for the learner to process. Naïvely asking the SMT solver to generate more than one counter-example can be in general expensive. Specifically, the verifier solves Eq. (8) to find a first counter-example $\bar{x}$; then, to find any additional sample, we include the statement $(x \neq \bar{x})$ and solve again for the resulting formula. We are interested in finding numerous points invalidating the BC conditions and feed them to the learner as a batch, or in increasing the information generated by the verifier by finding a sample that maximises the violation of the BC conditions. To this end, firstly we randomly generate a *cloud* of points around the generated counter-example: in view of the continuity of the candidate function B, samples around a counter-example are also likely to invalidate the BC conditions. Secondly, for the original counter-example, we compute the gradient of B (or of $\dot{B}$) and follow the direction that maximises the violation of the BC constraints. As such, we follow the B (resp. $\dot{B}$) maximisation when considering $x \in X_0$ (x s.t. $|B(x)| < \tau_v$), and vice versa when $x \in X_u$. This gradient computation is extremely fast as it exploits the neural architecture, and it provides more informative samples for further use by the learner.

Algorithm 1 Synthesis of Neural Barrier Certificate

---

function LEARNER(S, f)
  repeat
    $B(S) \leftarrow$ NN(S)
    $\dot{B}(S) \leftarrow \nabla B(S) \cdot f(S)$
    compute loss L, update NN
  until convergence
  return NN
end function

function VERIFIER(B, $\dot{B}$)
  encode conditions in (8)
  Cex or **unsat** $\leftarrow$ SMTcheck(B, $\dot{B}$)
  return Cex or **unsat**
end function

function CEGIS(f)
  initialise NN, S
  repeat
    NN $\leftarrow$ LEARNER(S, f)
    $B(x)$, $\dot{B}(x) \leftarrow$ Translate(NN, f)
    Cex or **unsat** $\leftarrow$ VERIFIER(B, $\dot{B}$)
    S $\leftarrow$ S $\cup$ Cex
  until unsat
  return $B(x)$, $\dot{B}(x)$
end function

---

4   Case Studies and Experimental Results

All experiments are performed on a laptop workstation with 8 GB RAM, running on Ubuntu 18.04. We demonstrate that the proposed method finds provably correct BCs on benchmarks from literature comprising both polynomial and non-polynomial dynamics: we compare our approach against the work [34], as this is the only work on sound synthesis of BCs with NNs to the best of our knowledge, and against the SOS optimisation software SOSTOOLS [18]. Beyond the benchmarks proposed in [34], we newly tackle a hybrid model as well as larger, (up to) 8-dimensional models, which push the boundaries of the verification engine and display a significant extension to the state of the art. To confirm the flexibility of our architecture, we employ SMT-solver dReal in the first four benchmarks, whereas we study the last four using Z3. In all the examples, we use a learning rate of 0.1 for the NN and the loss function in Section 3.1 with $\alpha = 10^{-4}$, $\tau_0 = \tau_u = \tau_d = 0.1$. The region in Eq. (7) is limited by $\beta_1 = 0.1$, whilst $\beta_2 = \infty$. Accordingly, the training over a large set $\mathcal{B}$ results in a candidate B with a negative derivative over this large region, which validity is more likely to be certified by the verifier. We set a verification parameter $\tau_v = 0.05$ (cf. Sec. 3.2), a timeout (later denoted as OOT) of 60 seconds and the precision for dReal to $\delta = 10^{-6}$. Table 1 summarises the outcomes. We emphasise that our approach supports any network depth and width. The presented results seek a tradeoff between speed (low order, small networks) and expressiveness (high order, larger networks): a different architecture may result in a slower or faster synthesis.

For the first four benchmarks, we compare our procedure, denoted as CEGIS, with the repeated results from [34], which however does not handle the hybrid model in the fifth benchmark. We have run the algorithm in [34] and reported the cumulative synthesis time under the 'Learn' column. However the verification is not included in the repeatability package, hence we report the results from [34], which are generated with much more powerful hardware. Due to this issue of lack of repeatability, we have not run [34] on the larger models. Compared to [34], the outcomes suggest that we obtain *much faster* synthesis and verification times, whilst requiring up to only 0.1% (see Obstacle Avoidance Problem) of the training data: [34] performs a uniform sampling of the space X, hence suffers especially in the 3-D case, where the learning runs *two orders of magnitude* faster. Evidently this gap in performance derives from the different synthesis procedure: it appears to be more advantageous to employ a smaller, randomly sampled initial dataset that is progressively augmented with counter-examples, rather than to uniformly sample the state space to then train the neural network.

Next, we have implemented the SOS optimisation problems in [10] within the software SOSTOOLS [18] to generate barrier candidates, which are polynomials up to order 4 (this is the maximum order of the polynomial candidates generated by our Learner). In a few instances we ought to conservatively approximate the expression of X_0 or X_u in order to encode them as SOS program - this makes their applicability less general. SOSTOOLS has successfully found BC candidates for five of the eight benchmarks, and they were generated consistently fast, in view of the convex structure of the underlying optimisation problem. However, recall that these techniques lack soundness (also due to numerical errors), which is instead a core asset of our approach. Consequently, we have passed them to the Z3 SMT solver, which should easily handle polynomial formulae: only one of them ('Hybrid Model') has been successfully verified; instead, the candidate for the 'Polynomial Model' has been invalidated (namely Z3 has found a counter-example for it), whereas the verification of the remaining BC candidates has run out of time. For the latter instances, we have experienced that SOSTOOLS generally returns numerically ill-conditioned expressions, namely candidates with coefficients of rather different magnitude, with many decimal digits: even after rounding, expressions with this structure are known to be hardly handled by SMT solvers [2,5], which results in long time needed to return an answer - this explains the experienced timeouts. These experiments suggest that the use of SOS programs within a CEGIS loop appears hardly attainable.

Notice that all the case studies are solved with a *small number* of iterations (up to 9) of the CEGIS loop: this feature, along with the limited runtimes, is promising towards tackling synthesis problems over larger models.

For the eight case studies, we report below the full expressions of the dynamics of the models, the spatial domain X (as a set of constrains), the set of initial conditions $X_0 \subset X$, and the unsafe set $X_u \subset X$. We add a detailed analysis of the CEGIS iterations involved in the synthesis of the corresponding BCs.

Benchmark	CEGIS (this work)				BC from [34]			SOS from [18]	
	Learn	Verify	Samples	Iters	Learn	Verify	Samples	Synth	Verify
Darboux	31.6	0.01	0.5 k	2	54.9	20.8	65 k	×	–
Exponential	15.9	0.07	1.5 k	2	234.0	11.3	65 k	×	–
Obstacle	55.5	1.83	2.0 k	9	3165.3	1003.3	2097 k	×	–
Polynomial	64.5	4.20	2.3 k	2	1731.0	635.3	65 k	8.10	×
Hybrid	0.58	2.01	0.5 k	1	–	–	–	12.30	0.11
4-d ODE	29.31	0.07	1 k	1	–	–	–	12.90	OOT
6-d ODE	89.52	1.61	1 k	3	–	–	–	16.60	OOT
8-d ODE	104.5	82.51	1 k	3	–	–	–	26.10	OOT

Table 1. Outcomes of the case studies: Cumulative time for Learning and Verification steps are given in seconds; 'Samples' indicates the size of input data for the Learner (in thousands); 'Iters' is the number of iterations of the CEGIS loop (which is specific to our work); × indicates a synthesis or verification failure; OOT denotes a verification timeout. The Hybrid and the three ODE Models are newly introduced in this work.

Darboux Model This 2-dimensional model is approached using polynomial BCs. Its analytical expression is

$$\begin{cases} \dot{x} = y + 2xy, \\ \dot{y} = -x + 2x^2 - y^2, \end{cases} \quad \text{with domains} \quad \begin{aligned} & X = \{-2 \le x, y \le 2\}, \\ & X_0 = \{0 \le x \le 1, 1 \le y \le 2\}, \\ & X_u = \{x + y^2 \le 0\}. \end{aligned}$$

The work [33] reports that methods based on linear matrix inequalities fail to verify this model using polynomial templates of degree 6. Our approach generates the BC shown in Fig. 2 (left) in approximately 30 seconds, roughly half as much as in [34], and using only 500 initial samples vs more than 65000. The initial and unsafe sets are depicted in green and red, respectively, whereas the level set $B(x) = 0$ is outlined in black. The BC is derived from a single-layer architecture of 10 nodes, with linear activations.

Exponential Model This model from [17] shows that our approach extends to non-polynomial systems encompassing exponential and trigonometric functions:

$$\begin{cases} \dot{x} = e^{-x} + y - 1, \\ \dot{y} = -\sin^2 x, \end{cases} \quad \text{with domains} \quad \begin{aligned} & X = \{-2 \le x, y \le 2\}, \\ & X_0 = \{(x + 0.5)^2 + (y - 0.5)^2 \le 0.16\}, \\ & X_u = \{(x - 0.7)^2 + (y + 0.7)^2 \le 0.09\}. \end{aligned}$$

Our algorithm provides a valid BC in 16 seconds, around 7% of the results in [34], again using solely 1500 initial samples. The BC, depicted in Fig.2 (centre), results from a single-layer neural architecture of 10 nodes, with polynomial ($\gamma = 3$) activation function.

Obstacle Avoidance Problem This 3-dimensional model, originally presented in [6], describes a robotic application: the control of the angular velocity of a

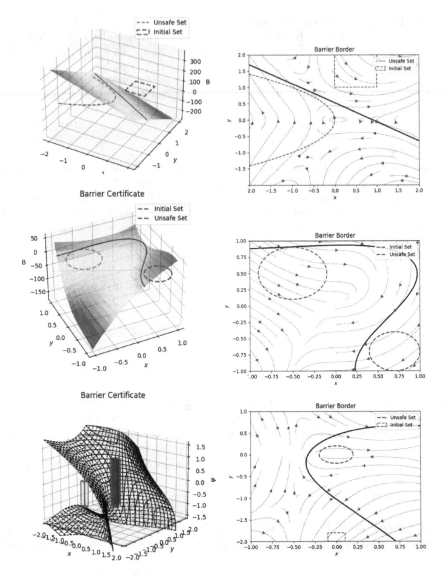

Fig. 2. The BC for the Darboux (top left), Exponential (middle left), and Obstacle Avoidance (the 3-D study, bottom left) models with corresponding vector fields (right column). Initial and unsafe sets are represented in green and red, respectively; the black line outlines the level curve $B(x) = 0$.

two-dimensional airplane, aimed at avoiding a still obstacle. The details are

$$\begin{cases} \dot{x} = v \sin \varphi, \\ \dot{y} = v \cos \varphi, \\ \dot{\varphi} = u, \quad \text{where} \quad u = -\sin \varphi + 3 \cdot \dfrac{x \sin \varphi + y \cos \varphi}{0.5 + x^2 + y^2}, \quad \text{with domains} \end{cases}$$

$$X = \{-2 \le x, y \le 2, -\pi/2 < \varphi < \pi/2\},$$
$$X_0 = \{-0.1 \le x \le 0.1, -2 \le y \le -1.8, -\pi/6 < \varphi < \pi/6\},$$
$$X_u = \{x^2 + y^2 \le 0.04\}.$$

The BC is obtained from a single-layer NN comprising 10 neurons, using ($\gamma = 3$) polynomial activations. Fig. 2 (right) plots the vector field on the plane $z = 0$. Our procedure takes 1% of the computational time in [34], providing a valid BC with 9 iteration starting from an initial dataset of 2000 samples.

Polynomial Model This model describes a polynomial system [22] and presents initial and unsafe sets with complex, non convex shapes [34], as follows:

$$\begin{cases} \dot{x} = y, \\ \dot{y} = -x + 1/3\,x^3 - y, \text{ with domains} \end{cases}$$

$$X = \{-3.5 \le x \le 2, -2 \le y \le 1\},$$
$$X_0 = \{(x - 1.5)^2 + y^2 \le 0.25 \lor (x \ge -1.8 \land x \le -1.2 \land y \ge -0.1 \land y \le 0.1)$$
$$\lor (x \ge -1.4 \land x \le -1.2 \land y \ge -0.5 \land y \le 0.1)\},$$
$$X_u = \{(x + 1)^2 + (y + 1)^2 \le 0.16 \lor (x \ge 0.4 \land x \le 0.6 \land y \ge 0.1 \land y \le 0.5)$$
$$\lor (x \ge 0.4 \land x \le 0.8 \land y \ge 0.1 \land y \le 0.3)\}.$$

SOS-based procedures [16,29], have required high-order polynomial templates, which has suggested the use of alternative activation functions. The BC, shown in Fig. 3, is generated using a 10-neuron, two-layer NN with polynomial ($\gamma = 3$) and tanh activations. Needing just around 1 min and only 2300 initial samples, the overall procedure is 30 times faster than that in [34].

Hybrid Model We challenge our procedure with a 2-dimensional hybrid model, which extends beyond the capability of the results in [34]. This hybrid framework partitions the set X into two non-overlapping subsets, X_1 and X_2. Each subset is associated to different model dynamics, respectively f_1 and f_2. In other words, the model trajectories evolve according to the f_1 dynamics when in X_1, and according to f_2 when in X_2.

$$f_1 = \begin{cases} \dot{x} = y, \\ \dot{y} = -x - 0.5x^3, \end{cases} \qquad f_2 = \begin{cases} \dot{x} = y, \\ \dot{y} = x - 0.25y^2, \end{cases}$$

with domain for $f_1 = \{(x, y) : x < 0\}$, domain for $f_2 = \{(x, y) : x \ge 0\}$, and sets

$$X = \{x^2 + y^2 \le 4\}, \qquad X_0 = \{(x + 1)^2 + (y + 1)^2 \le 0.25\},$$
$$X_u = \{(x - 1)^2 + (y - 1)^2 \le 0.25\}.$$

The structure of this model represents a non-trivial task for the verification engine, for which we employ the Z3 SMT solver. The learning phase has instead been quite fast. The BC (Fig.3) is obtained from a single-layer NN comprising 3 neurons, using polynomial activations with $\gamma = 2$, overall in less than 3 seconds, starting with an initial dataset of 500 samples.

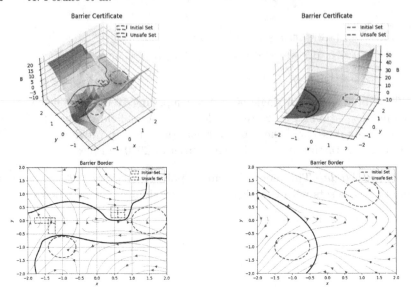

Fig. 3. The BC for the polynomial model (top left) and the hybrid model (top right) with the respective vector field (below).

Larger-dimensional Models We finally challenge our procedure with three high-order ODEs, respectively of order four, six and eight, to display the general applicability of our counter-example guided BC synthesis. We consider dynamical models described by the following differential equations:

$$x^{(4)} + 3980x^{(3)} + 4180x^{(2)} + 2400x^{(1)} + 576 = 0, \tag{9}$$

$$x^{(6)} + 800x^{(5)} + 2273x^{(4)} + 3980x^{(3)} + 4180x^{(2)} + 2400x^{(1)} + 576 = 0, \tag{10}$$

$$x^{(8)} + 20x^{(7)} + 170x^{(6)} + 800x^{(5)} + 2273x^{(4)}$$
$$+ 3980x^{(3)} + 4180x^{(2)} + 2400x^{(1)} + 576 = 0, \tag{11}$$

where we denote the i-th derivative of variable x by $x^{(i)}$. We translate the ODE into a state-space model with variables $x_1, \ldots, x_j$, where $j = \{4, 6, 8\}$, respectively. In all three instances, we select as spatial domain X an hyper-sphere centred at the origin of radius 4; an initial set X_0 as hyper-sphere[4] centred at $+\mathbf{1}^{[j]}$ of radius 0.25; an unsafe set X_u as an hyper-sphere centred at $-\mathbf{2}^{[j]}$ of radius 0.16. For the synthesis, we employ for all case studies a single-layer, 5-node architecture with polynomial ($\gamma = 1$) activation function. Whilst in particular the verification engine is challenged from the high dimensionality of the models, the CEGIS procedure returns a valid barrier certificate in up to 3 iterations and with very reasonable run times.

---

[4] We denote $\mathbf{1}^{[j]}$ the point of a j-dimensional state-space that has all its components equal to 1. For instance, $\mathbf{1}^{[3]}$ is the 3-dimensional point $[1, 1, 1]$. Similarly for $\mathbf{2}^{[j]}$.

Codebase Robustness The results in Table 1 are obtained setting the NN initialisation seed manually for repeatability. We now test the robustness of the overall algorithm by randomising the initialisation seed. We report in Table 2 the percentage of successful runs, the average time and iterations count, along with minimum and maximum values, over 50 runs. We set timeouts as a max running time of 10 minutes, or as 12 CEGIS loops. Notice that small architectures are highly susceptible to initialisations, which renders this test rather challenging. Compared to Table 1, we notice similar performances for the *Darboux*, *Exponential* and *Hybrid* models, vouching for the robustness of our approach. However, the performance decreases when tackling the most challenging models. Still, we highlight that the procedure can synthesise a valid BC very rapidly for every benchmark (notice the lower bounds of the computational times). This outcome suggests that a parallel approach - i.e. the procedure running on several networks simultaneously - may be suited to quickly synthesise candidates. Overall, the table shows a high degree of variance, possibly indicating the need for larger architectures to enhance robustness.

Benchmark	Success [%]	Iters	Avg Time
Darboux Model	84.0	4.76 [1, 12]	75.33 [15.00, 189.25]
Exponential Model	76.0	5.20 [1, 12]	9.50 [3.17, 21.59]
Obstacle Avoidance	28.0	9.88 [1, 11]	129.24 [16.17, 549.41]
Polynomial Model	8.0	5.56 [5, 9]	335.32 [230.86, 377.91]
Hybrid Model	84.0	4.20 [1, 12]	36.75 [0.43, 102.03]
4-d ODE Model	32.0	9.00 [1, 12]	362.14 [29.42, 681.41]
6-d ODE Model	40.0	8.60 [1, 12]	310.45 [30.65, 562.67]
8-d ODE Model	12.0	11.00 [2, 12]	495.23 [111.50, 698.93]

Table 2. Percentage of successful runs, average number of iterations and average computational times (in seconds) of the CEGIS procedure, over 50 runs. The square brackets contain the minimum and maximum values obtained.

5   Conclusions and Future Work

We have presented a new inductive, formal, automated technique to synthesise neural-based barrier certificates for polynomial and non-polynomial, continuous and hybrid dynamical models. Thanks to a number of architectural choices for the new procedure, our method requires less training data and thus displays faster learning, as well as quicker verification time, than state-of-the-art techniques.

Ongoing work is porting presented and related [5,2] theoretical results into a software tool [1]. Towards increased automation, future work includes the development of an automated selection of activation functions that are tailored to the dynamical models of interest.

References

1. Alessandro Abate, Daniele Ahmed, Alec Edwards, Mirco Giacobbe, and Andrea Peruffo. FOSSIL: A Software Tool for the Formal Synthesis of Lyapunov Functions and Barrier Certificates using Neural Networks. In *HSCC*. ACM, 2021.

2. Alessandro Abate, Daniele Ahmed, Mirco Giacobbe, and Andrea Peruffo. Formal Synthesis of Lyapunov Neural Networks. *IEEE Control Systems Letters*, 5(3):773–778, 2021.

3. Alessandro Abate, Cristina David, Pascal Kesseli, Daniel Kroening, and Elizabeth Polgreen. Counterexample Guided Inductive Synthesis Modulo Theories. In *Proceedings of CAV, LNCS 10981*, pages 270–288, 2018.

4. Alessandro Abate, Ashish Tiwari, and Shankar Sastry. Box Invariance in Biologically-inspired Dynamical Systems. *Automatica*, 45(7):1601–1610, 2009.

5. Daniele Ahmed, Andrea Peruffo, and Alessandro Abate. Automated and Sound Synthesis of Lyapunov Functions with SMT Solvers. In *TACAS (1)*, volume 12078 of *LNCS*, pages 97–114. Springer, 2020.

6. Andrew J Barry, Anirudha Majumdar, and Russ Tedrake. Safety Verification of Reactive Controllers for UAV Flight in Cluttered Environments using Barrier Certificates. In *2012 IEEE International Conference on Robotics and Automation*, pages 484–490. IEEE, 2012.

7. Urs Borrmann, Li Wang, Aaron D Ames, and Magnus Egerstedt. Control Barrier Certificates for Safe Swarm Behavior. *IFAC-PapersOnLine*, 48(27):68–73, 2015.

8. Dario Cattaruzza, Alessandro Abate, Peter Schrammel, and Daniel Kroening. Unbounded-Time Safety Verification of Guarded LTI Models with Inputs by Abstract Acceleration. *Journal of Automated Reasoning*, 2020.

9. Ya-Chien Chang, Nima Roohi, and Sicun Gao. Neural Lyapunov Control. In *NeurIPS*, pages 3240–3249, 2019.

10. Liyun Dai, Ting Gan, Bican Xia, and Naijun Zhan. Barrier Certificates Revisited. *Journal of Symbolic Computation*, 80:62–86, 2017.

11. Leonardo de Moura and Nikolaj Bjørner. Z3: An Efficient SMT Solver. In *TACAS*, volume 4963 of *LNCS*, pages 337–340. Springer, 2008.

12. Sicun Gao, Jeremy Avigad, and Edmund M Clarke. δ-complete Decision Procedures for Satisfiability over the Reals. In *International Joint Conference on Automated Reasoning*, pages 286–300. Springer, 2012.

13. Sicun Gao, Soonho Kong, and Edmund M Clarke. dReal: An SMT Solver for Nonlinear Theories over the Reals. In *International conference on automated deduction*, pages 208–214. Springer, 2013.

14. Hui Kong, Fei He, Xiaoyu Song, William NN Hung, and Ming Gu. Exponential-condition-based Barrier Certificate Generation for Safety Verification of Hybrid Systems. In *International Conference on Computer Aided Verification*, pages 242–257. Springer, 2013.

15. Daniel Kroening and Ofer Strichman. *Decision Procedures - An Algorithmic Point of View*. Springer Verlag, 2016.

16. Benoît Legat, Paulo Tabuada, and Raphaël M Jungers. Sum-of-Squares Methods for Controlled Invariant Sets with Applications to Model-predictive Control. *Nonlinear Analysis: Hybrid Systems*, 36:100858, 2020.

17. Jiang Liu, Naijun Zhan, Hengjun Zhao, and Liang Zou. Abstraction of Elementary Hybrid Systems by Variable Transformation. In *International Symposium on Formal Methods*, pages 360–377. Springer, 2015.

18. A. Papachristodoulou, J. Anderson, G. Valmorbida, S. Prajna, P. Seiler, and P. A. Parrilo. *SOSTOOLS: Sum of squares optimization toolbox for MATLAB.* http://arxiv.org/abs/1310.4716, 2013.
19. André Platzer and Edmund M Clarke. Computing Differential Invariants of Hybrid Systems as Fixedpoints. In *International Conference on Computer Aided Verification*, pages 176–189. Springer, 2008.
20. Stephen Prajna. Barrier Certificates for Nonlinear Model Validation. *Automatica*, 42(1):117–126, 2006.
21. Stephen Prajna and Ali Jadbabaie. Safety Verification of Hybrid Systems Using Barrier Certificates. In *International Workshop on Hybrid Systems: Computation and Control*, pages 477–492. Springer, 2004.
22. Stephen Prajna, Ali Jadbabaie, and George J Pappas. A Framework for Worst-case and Stochastic Safety Verification Using Barrier Certificates. *IEEE Transactions on Automatic Control*, 52(8):1415–1428, 2007.
23. Hadi Ravanbakhsh and Sriram Sankaranarayanan. Counter-example guided synthesis of control lyapunov functions for switched systems. In *IEEE Control and Decision Conference (CDC)*, pages 4232–4239, 2015.
24. Hadi Ravanbakhsh and Sriram Sankaranarayanan. Robust Controller Synthesis of Switched Systems Using Counterexample Guided Framework. In *ACM/IEEE Conference on Embedded Software (EMSOFT)*, pages 8:1–8:10, 2016.
25. Hadi Ravanbakhsh and Sriram Sankaranarayanan. Learning Control Lyapunov Functions from Counterexamples and Demonstrations. *Autonomous Robots*, pages 1–33, 2018.
26. Spencer M. Richards, Felix Berkenkamp, and Andreas Krause. The Lyapunov Neural Network: Adaptive Stability Certification for Safe Learning of Dynamical Systems. In *CoRL*, volume 87 of *Proceedings of Machine Learning Research*, pages 466–476. PMLR, 2018.
27. Sriram Sankaranarayanan, Xin Chen, and Erika Abraham. Lyapunov Function Synthesis using Handelman Representations. *IFAC Proceedings Volumes*, 46(23):576–581, 2013.
28. Shankar Sastry. *Nonlinear Systems: Analysis, Stability and Control.* Springer Verlag, 1999.
29. Christoffer Sloth, George J Pappas, and Rafael Wisniewski. Compositional Safety Analysis using Barrier Certificates. In *Proceedings of the 15th ACM international conference on Hybrid Systems: Computation and Control*, pages 15–24, 2012.
30. Andrew Sogokon, Khalil Ghorbal, Yong Kiam Tan, and André Platzer. Vector Barrier Certificates and Comparison Systems. In *International Symposium on Formal Methods*, pages 418–437. Springer, 2018.
31. Armando Solar-Lezama, Liviu Tancau, Rastislav Bodik, Sanjit Seshia, and Vijay Saraswat. Combinatorial sketching for finite programs. In *Proceedings of the 12th international conference on Architectural support for programming languages and operating systems*, pages 404–415, 2006.
32. Li Wang, Aaron D Ames, and Magnus Egerstedt. Safety Barrier Certificates for Collisions-free Multirobot Systems. *IEEE Transactions on Robotics*, 33(3):661–674, 2017.
33. Xia Zeng, Wang Lin, Zhengfeng Yang, Xin Chen, and Lilei Wang. Darboux-type Barrier Certificates for Safety Verification of Nonlinear Hybrid Systems. In *Proceedings of the 13th International Conference on Embedded Software*, pages 1–10, 2016.

34. Hengjun Zhao, Xia Zeng, Taolue Chen, and Zhiming Liu. Synthesizing Barrier Certificates Using Neural Networks. In *Proceedings of the 23rd International Conference on Hybrid Systems: Computation and Control*, HSCC '20, New York, NY, USA, 2020. Association for Computing Machinery.

Improving Neural Network Verification through Spurious Region Guided Refinement

Pengfei Yang[1,2], Renjue Li[1,2], Jianlin Li[1,2], Cheng-Chao Huang[3,4],
Jingyi Wang[5], Jun Sun[6], Bai Xue[1,2], and Lijun Zhang[1,2,3] (✉)

[1] SKLCS, Institute of Software, Chinese Academy of Sciences, Beijing, China
[2] University of Chinese Academy of Sciences, Beijing, China
[3] Institute of Intelligent Software, Guangzhou, China
[4] CAS Software Testing (Guangzhou) Co., Ltd., Guangzhou, China
[5] Zhejiang University NGICS Platform, Hangzhou, China
[6] Singapore Management University, Singapore, Singapore
zhanglj@ios.ac.cn

Abstract. We propose a spurious region guided refinement approach for robustness verification of deep neural networks. Our method starts with applying the DeepPoly abstract domain to analyze the network. If the robustness property cannot be verified, the result is inconclusive. Due to the over-approximation, the computed region in the abstraction may be *spurious* in the sense that it does not contain any true counterexample. Our goal is to identify such spurious regions and use them to guide the abstraction refinement. The core idea is to make use of the obtained constraints of the abstraction to infer new bounds for the neurons. This is achieved by linear programming techniques. With the new bounds, we iteratively apply DeepPoly, aiming to eliminate spurious regions. We have implemented our approach in a prototypical tool DeepSRGR. Experimental results show that a large amount of regions can be identified as spurious, and as a result, the precision of DeepPoly can be significantly improved. As a side contribution, we show that our approach can be applied to verify quantitative robustness properties.

1 Introduction

In the seminal work [34], deep neural networks (DNN) have been successfully applied in Go to play against expert humans. Afterwards, they have achieved exceptional performance in many other applications such as image, speech and audio recognition, self-driving cars, and malware detection. Despite the success of solving these problems, DNNs have also been shown to be often lack of robustness, and are vulnerable to adversarial samples [39]. Even for a well-trained DNN, a small (and even imperceptible) perturbation may fool the network. This is arguably one of the major obstacles when we deploy DNNs in safety-critical applications like self-driving cars [42], and medical systems [33].

It is thus important to guarantee the robustness of DNNs for safety-critical applications. In this work, we focus on (local) robustness, i.e., given an input and a manipulation region around the input (which is usually specified according to a certain

© The Author(s) 2021
J. F. Groote and K. G. Larsen (Eds.): TACAS 2021, LNCS 12651, pp. 389–408, 2021.
https://doi.org/10.1007/978-3-030-72016-2_21

norm), we verify that a given DNN never makes any mistake on any input in the region. The first work on DNN verification was published in [30], which focuses on DNNs with sigmoid activation functions with a partition-refinement approach. In 2017, Katz et al. [20] and Ehlers [10] independently implemented Reluplex and Planet, two SMT solvers to verify DNNs with the ReLU activation function on properties expressible with SMT constraints. Since 2018, abstract interpretation has been one of the most popular methods for DNN verification in the lead of AI^2 [13], and subsequent works like [36,37,23,1,35,28,24] have improved AI^2 in terms of efficiency, precision and more activation functions (like sigmoid and tanh) so that abstract interpretation based approach can be applied to DNNs of larger size and more complex structures.

Among the above methods, DeepPoly [37] is a most outstanding one regarding precision and scalability. DeepPoly is an abstract domain specially developed for DNN verification. It sufficiently considers the structures and the operators of a DNN, and it designs a polytope expression which not only fits for these structures and operators to control the loss of precision, but also works with a very small time overhead to achieve scalability. However, as an abstraction interpretation based method, it provides very little insight if it fails to verify the property. In this work, we propose a method to improve DeepPoly by eliminating spurious regions through abstraction refinement. A spurious region is a region computed using abstract semantics, conjuncted with the negation of the property to be verified. This region is spurious in the sense that if the property is satisfied, then this region, although not empty, does not contain any true counterexample which can be realized in the original program. In this case, we propose a refinement strategy to rule out the spurious region, i.e., to prove that this region does not contain any true counterexamples.

Our approach is based on DeepPoly and improves it by refinement of the spurious region through linear programming. The core idea is to intersect the abstraction constructed by abstract interpretation with the negation of the property to generate a spurious region, and perform linear programming on the constraints of the spurious region so that the bounds of the ReLU neurons whose behaviors are uncertain can be tightened. As a result, some of these neurons can be determined to be definitely activated or deactivated, which significantly improves the precision of the abstraction given by abstract interpretation. This procedure can be performed iteratively and the precision of the abstraction are gradually improved, so that we are likely to rule out this spurious region in some iteration. If we successfully rule out all the possible spurious regions through such an iterative refinement, the property is soundly verified. Our method is similar in spirit to counterexample guided abstraction refinement (CEGAR) [6], i.e., we apply abstract interpretation for abstraction and linear programming for refinement. A fundamental difference is that we use the constraints of the spurious region, instead of a concrete counterexample (which is challenging to construct in our setting), as the guidance of refinement.

The same spurious region guided refinement approach is also effective in quantitative robustness verification. Instead of requiring that all inputs in the region should be correctly classified, a certain probability of error in the region is allowed. Quantitative robustness is more realistic and general compared to the ordinary robustness, and a DNN verified against quantitative robustness is useful in practice as well. The spurious region guided refinement approach naturally fits for this setting, since a comparatively precise over-approximation of the spurious region implies a sound robustness confidence. To the best of our knowledge, for DNNs, this is the first work to verify quantitative robustness with strict soundness guarantee, which distinguishes our approach from the previous sampling based methods like [45,46,3].

In summary, our main contributions are as follows:

- We propose spurious region guided refinement to verify robustness properties of deep neural networks. This approach significantly improves the precision of Deep-Poly and it can verify more challenging properties than DeepPoly.
- We implement the algorithms as a prototype and run them on networks trained on popular datasets like MNIST and ACAS Xu. The experimental results show that our approach significantly improves the precision of DeepPoly in successfully verifying much stronger robustness properties (larger maximum radius) and determining the behaviors of a great proportion of uncertain ReLU neurons.
- We apply our approach to solve quantitative robustness verification problem with strict soundness guarantee. In the experiments, we observe that, comparing to using only DeepPoly, the bounds by our approach can be up to two orders of magnitudes better in the experiments.

Organisations of the paper. We provide preliminaries in Section 2. DeepPoly is recalled in Section 3. We present our overall verification framework and the algorithm in Section 4, and discuss quantitative robustness verification in Section 5. Section 6 evaluates our algorithms through experiments. Section 7 reviews related works and concludes the paper.

2   Preliminaries

In this section we recall some basic notions on deep neural networks, local robustness verification, and abstract interpretation. Given a vector $x \in \mathbb{R}^m$, we write x_i to denote its i-th entry for $1 \leq i \leq m$.

2.1   Robustness verification of deep neural networks

In this work, we focus on deep feedforward neural networks (DNNs), which can be represented as a function $f : \mathbb{R}^m \to \mathbb{R}^n$, mapping an input $x \in \mathbb{R}^m$ to its output $y = f(x) \in \mathbb{R}^n$. A DNN f often classifies an input x by obtaining the maximum dimension of the output, i.e., $\arg\max_{1 \leq i \leq n} f(x)_i$. We denote such a DNN by $C_f : \mathbb{R}^m \to C$ which is defined by $C_f(x) = \arg\max_{1 \leq i \leq n} f(x)_i$ where $C = \{1, \ldots, n\}$ is the set of classification classes.

A DNN has a sequence of layers, including an input layer at the beginning, followed by several hidden layers, and an output layer in the end. The output of a layer is the input of the next layer. Each layer contains multiple neurons, the number of which is known as the dimension of the layer. The DNN f is the composition of the transformations between layers. Typically an affine transformation followed by a non-linear activation function is performed. For an affine transformation $y = Ax + b$, if the matrix A is not sparse, we call such a layer fully connected. A DNN with only fully connected layers and activation functions is a fully connected neural network (FNN). In this work, we focus on the rectified linear unit (ReLU) activation function, defined as $\text{ReLU}(x) = \max(x, 0)$ for $x \in \mathbb{R}$. Typically, a DNN verification problem is defined as follows:

Definition 1. *Given a DNN $f : \mathbb{R}^m \to \mathbb{R}^n$, a set of inputs $X \subseteq \mathbb{R}^m$, and a property $P \subseteq \mathbb{R}^n$, we need to determine whether $f(X) := \{f(x) \mid x \in X\} \subseteq P$ holds.*

Local robustness describes the stability of the behaviour of a normal input under a perturbation. The range of input under this perturbation is the robustness region. For a DNN $C_f(x)$ which performs classification tasks, a robustness property typically states that C_f outputs the same class on the robustness region.

There are various ways to define a robustness region, and one of the most popular ways is to use the L_p norm. For $x \in \mathbb{R}^m$ and $1 \leq p < \infty$, we define the L_p norm of x to be $\|x\|_p = (\sum_{i=1}^m |x_i|^p)^{\frac{1}{p}}$, and its L_∞ norm $\|x\|_\infty = \max_{1 \leq i \leq m} |x_i|$. We write $\bar{B}_p(x, r) := \{x' \in \mathbb{R}^m \mid \|x - x'\|_p \leq r\}$ to represent a (closed) L_p ball for $x \in \mathbb{R}^m$ and $r > 0$, which is a neighbourhood of x as its robustness region. If we set $X = \bar{B}_p(x, r)$ and $P = \{y \in \mathbb{R}^n \mid \arg\max_i y_i = C_f(x)\}$ in Def. 1, it is exactly the robustness verification problem. Hereafter, we set $p = \infty$.

2.2   Abstract interpretation for DNN verification

Abstract interpretation [7] is a static analysis method and it is aimed to find an over-approximation of the semantics of programs and other complex systems so as to verify their correctness. Generally we have a function $f : \mathbb{R}^m \to \mathbb{R}^n$ representing the concrete program, a set $X \subseteq \mathbb{R}^m$ representing the property that the input of the program satisfies, and a set $P \subseteq \mathbb{R}^n$ representing the property to verify. The problem is to determine whether $f(X) \subseteq P$ holds. However, in many cases it is difficult to calculate $f(X)$ and to determine whether $f(X) \subseteq P$ holds. Abstract interpretation uses abstract domains and abstract transformations to over-approximate sets and functions so that an over-approximation of the output can be obtained efficiently.

Now we have a concrete domain $\mathcal{C}$, which includes X as one of its elements. To make computation efficient, we need an abstract domain $\mathcal{A}$ to abstract elements in the concrete domain. We assume that there is a partial order $\leq$ on $\mathcal{C}$ and $\mathcal{A}$, which in our settings is the subset relation $\subseteq$. We also have a concretization function $\gamma : \mathcal{A} \to \mathcal{C}$ which assigns an abstract element to its concrete semantics, and $\gamma(a)$ is the least upper bounds of the concrete elements that can be soundly abstracted by $a \in \mathcal{A}$. Naturally $a \in \mathcal{A}$ is a sound abstraction of $c \in \mathcal{C}$ if and only if $c \leq \gamma(a)$.

The design of an abstract domain is one of the most important problems in abstract interpretation because it determines the efficiency and precision. In practice, we use a certain type of constraints to represent the abstract elements in an abstract domain. Classical abstract domains for Euclidean spaces include Box, Zonotope [14,15], and Polyhedra [38].

Not only do we need abstract domains to over-approximate sets, but we are also required to adopt over-approximation to functions. Here we consider the lifting of the function $f : \mathbb{R}^m \to \mathbb{R}^n$ defined as $T_f(X) : \mathcal{P}(\mathbb{R}^m) \to \mathcal{P}(\mathbb{R}^n)$, $T_f(X) := f(X) =$

$\{f(x) \mid x \in X\}$. Now we have an abstract domain $\mathcal{A}_k$ for the k-dimension Euclidean space and the corresponding concretization γ. A function $T_f^\# : \mathcal{A}_m \rightarrow \mathcal{A}_n$ is a sound abstract transformer of T_f, if $T_f \circ \gamma \subseteq \gamma \circ T_f^\#$.

When we have a sound abstraction $X^\# \in \mathcal{A}$ of X and a sound abstract transformer $T_f^\#$, we can use the concretization of $T_f^\#(X^\#)$ to over-approximate $f(X)$ since we have $f(X) = T_f(X) \subseteq T_f(\gamma(X^\#)) \subseteq \gamma \circ T_f^\#(X^\#)$. If $\gamma \circ T_f^\#(X^\#) \subseteq P$, the property P is successfully verified. Obviously, verification through abstract interpretation is sound but not complete. Hereafter, we write $f^\#$ to represent $T_f^\#$ for simplicity.

AI^2 [13] first adopted abstract interpretation to verify DNNs, and many subsequent works like [36,37,23] focused on improving its efficiency and precision through, e.g., defining new abstract domains. As a deep neural network, the function $f : \mathbb{R}^m \rightarrow \mathbb{R}^n$ can be regarded as a composition $f = f_l \circ \cdots \circ f_1$ of its $l+1$ layers, where f_j performs the transformation between the j-th and the $(j+1)$-th layer, i.e., it can be an affine transformation, or a ReLU operation. If we choose Box, Zonotope, or Polyhedra as the abstract domain, then for linear transformations and the ReLU functions, their abstract transformers have been developed in [13]. After we abstract transformers $f_j^\#$ for these f_j, we can conduct abstract interpretation layer by layer as $f_l^\# \circ \cdots \circ f_1^\#(X^\#)$.

3   A Brief Introduction to DeepPoly

Our approach relies on the abstract domain DeepPoly [37], which is the state-of-the-art abstract domain for DNN verification. It defines the abstract transformers of multiple activation functions and layers used in DNNs. The core idea of DeepPoly is to give every variable an upper and a lower bound in the form of an affine expression using only variables that appear before it. It can express a polyhedron globally. Moreover, experimentally, it often has better precision than Box and Zonotope domains.

We denote the n-dimensional DeepPoly abstract domain with $\mathcal{A}_n$. Formally an abstract element $a \in \mathcal{A}_n$ is a tuple $(a^\leq, a^\geq, l, u)$, where $a^\leq$ and $a^\geq$ give the i-th variable x_i a lower bound and an upper bound, respectively, in the form of a linear combination of variables which appear before it, i.e. $\sum_{k=1}^{i-1} w_k x_k + w_0$, for $i = 1, \ldots, n$, and $l, u \in \mathbb{R}^n$ give the lower bound and upper bound of each variable, respectively. The concretization of a is defined as

$$\gamma(a) = \{x \in \mathbb{R}^n \mid a_i^\leq \leq x_i \leq a_i^\geq, \ i = 1, \ldots, n\}. \tag{1}$$

The abstract domain $\mathcal{A}_n$ also requests that its abstract elements a should satisfy the invariant $\gamma(a) \subseteq [l, u]$. This invariant helps construct efficient abstract transformers.

For an affine transformation $x_i = \sum_{k=1}^{i-1} w_k x_k + w_0$, we set

$$a_i^\leq = a_i^\geq = \sum_{k=1}^{i-1} w_k x_k + w_0.$$

By substituting the variables x_j appearing in $a_i^\leq$ with $a_j^\leq$ or $a_j^\geq$ according to its coefficient at most $i - 1$ times, we can obtain a sound lower bound in the form of linear

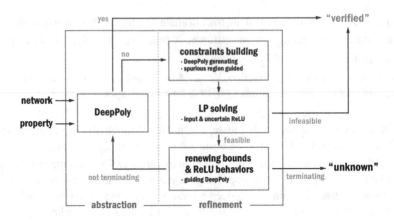

Fig. 1. Framework of spurious region guided refinement

combination on input variables only, and l_i can be computed immediately from the range of input variables. A similar procedure also works for computing u_i.

For a ReLU transformation $x_i = \mathrm{ReLU}(x_j)$, we consider two cases:

- If $l_j \geq 0$ or $u_j \leq 0$, this ReLU neuron is definitely *activated* or *deactivated*, respectively. In this case, this ReLU transformation actually performs an affine transformation, and thus its abstract transformer can be defined as above.
- If $l_j < 0$ and $u_j > 0$, the behavior of this ReLU neuron is *uncertain*, and we need to over-approximate this relation with a linear upper/lower bound. The best upper bound is $a_i^{\geq} = \frac{u_j(x_j - l_j)}{u_j - l_j}$. For the lower bound, there are multiple choices $a_i^{\leq} = \lambda x_j$ where $\lambda \in [0, 1]$. We choose $\lambda \in \{0, 1\}$ which minimizes the area of the constraints. Basically we have two abstraction modes here, corresponding to the two choices of λ.

Note that for a DNN with only ReLU as non-linear operators, over-approximation occurs only when there are uncertain ReLU neurons, which are over-approximated using a triangle. The key of improving the precision is thus to compute the bounds of the uncertain ReLU neurons as precisely as possible, and to determine the behaviors of the most uncertain ReLU neurons.

DeepPoly also supports activation functions which are monotonically increasing, convex on $(-\infty, 0]$ and concave on $[0, +\infty)$, like sigmoid and tanh, and it supports max pooling layers. Readers can refer to [37] for details.

4 Spurious Region Guided Refinement

We explain the main steps of our algorithm, as depicted in Fig. 1. For the input property and network, we first employ DeepPoly as the initial step to compute $f^{\#}(X^{\#})$. The concretization of $f^{\#}(X^{\#})$ is the conjunction of many linear inequities given in Eq. 1, and for the robustness property P, the negation $\neg P$ is the disjunction of several linear inequities $\neg P = \bigvee_{t \neq C_f(x)} (y_{C_f(x)} - y_t \leq 0)$.

1. We check whether $f^{\#}(X^{\#}) \cap^{\#} (y_{C_f(x)} - y_t \leq 0) = \bot$ holds for each t, which follows the same method as DeepPoly, i.e., we compute the lower bound of $y_{C_f(x)} - y_t$ and see whether it is larger than 0. In case of yes, it indicates that the label t cannot be classified, as it is dominated by $C_f(x)$. Otherwise, we have $f^{\#}(X^{\#}) \cap^{\#} \neg P \neq \bot$, we have the conjunction $\gamma(f^{\#}(X^{\#})) \wedge \neg P$ as a potential *spurious region*, which represents the intersection of the abstraction of the real semantics and the negation of the property to verify. We call such a region spurious because if the property is satisfied, then this region does not contain a true counterexample, i.e., a pair of input and output (x^*, y^*) such that $y^* = f(x^*)$ and y^* violates the property P. In this case, this region is spuriously constructed due to the abstraction of the real semantics, where the counterexamples cannot be realized, and thus we aim to rule out the spurious region.
2. If no potential spurious region is found, our algorithm safely returns yes.
3. Assume now that we have a the potential spurious region. The core idea is to use the constraints of the spurious region to refine this spurious region. Here a natural way to refine the spurious region is linear programming, since all the constraints here are linear inequities. If the linear programming is infeasible, it indicates that the region is spurious, and thus we can return an affirmative result. Otherwise, our refinement will tighten the bounds of variables involved in the DNN, especially the input variables and uncertain ReLU neurons, and these tightened bounds help further give a more precise abstraction.
4. As our approach is based on DeepPoly, similarly, we cannot guarantee completeness. We set a threshold N of the number of iterations as a simple termination condition. If the termination condition is not reached, we run DeepPoly again, and return to the first step.

Below we give an example, illustrating how refinement can help in robustness verification.

Example 1. Consider the network $f(x) = \text{ReLU}\left(\begin{pmatrix} 1 & -1 \\ 1 & 1 \end{pmatrix} x + \begin{pmatrix} 0 \\ 2.5 \end{pmatrix}\right)$ and the region $\bar{B}_{\infty}((0,0)^{\mathrm{T}}, 1)$. The robustness property P here is $y_2 - y_1 > 0$. We invoke first DeepPoly: the lower bound of $y_2 - y_1$ given by DeepPoly is -0.5. As a result, the robustness property cannot be verified directly. Fig. 2(a) shows details of the example.

We fail to verify the property in Example 1 because for the uncertain ReLU relation $y_1 = \text{ReLU}(x_3)$, the abstraction is imprecise, and the key to making the abstraction more precise here is to obtain as tight a bound as possible for x_3.

Example 2. We use the constraints in Fig. 2(a) and additionally the constraint $y_2 - y_1 \leq 0$ (i.e., $\neg P$) as the input of linear programming. Our aim is to obtain a tighter bound of the input neurons x_1 and x_2, as well as the uncertain ReLU neuron x_3, so the objective functions of the linear programming are $\min x_i$ and $\min -x_i$ for $i = 1, 2, 3$. All the three neurons have a tighter bound after the linear programming (see the red part in Fig. 2(b)). Fig. 2(b) shows the running of DeepPoly under these new bounds, where the input range and the abstraction of the uncertain ReLU neuron are both refined. Now the lower bound of $y_2 - y_1$ is 0.25, so DeepPoly successfully verifies the property.

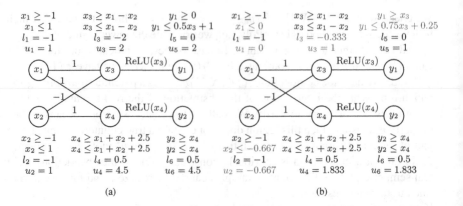

Fig. 2. Example 1 (left) and Example 2 (right): where the red parts are introduced through linear programming based refinement and the blue parts are introduced by a second run of DeepPoly.

4.1   Main algorithm

Alg. 1 presents our algorithm. First we run abstract interpretation to find the uncertain neurons and the spurious regions (Line 2–5). For each possible spurious region, we have a **while** loop which iteratively refines the abstraction. In each iteration we perform linear programming to renew the bounds of the input neurons and uncertain ReLU neurons; when we find that the bound of an uncertain ReLU neuron becomes definitely non-negative or non-positive, then the ReLU behavior of this neuron is renewed (Line 14–20). We use them to guide abstract interpretation in the next step (Line 21–22). Here in Line 22, we make sure that during the abstract interpretation, the abstraction of previous uncertain neurons (namely the uncertain neurons before the linear programming step in the same iteration) compulsorily follows the new bounds and new ReLU behaviors given by the current $C_{\geq 0}$, $C_{\leq 0}$, l, and u, where these bounds will not be renewed by abstract interpretation, and the concretization of Y is defined as

$$\gamma(Y) = \{x \mid \forall i.\ Y_i^{\leq} \leq x_i \leq Y_i^{\geq}\} \cap [l, u]. \tag{2}$$

The **while** loop ends when (i) either we find that the spurious region is infeasible (Line 11, 24) and we proceed to refine the next spurious region, with a label Verified True, (ii) or we reach the terminating condition and fail to rule out this spurious region, in which case we return UNKNOWN. If every **while** loop ends with the label Verified True, we successfully rule out all the spurious regions and return YES. An observation is that, if some spurious regions have been ruled out, we can add the constraints of their negation to make the current spurious region smaller so as to improve the precision (Line 9).

Here we discuss the soundness of Alg. 1. We focus on the **while** loop and claim that it has the following loop invariant:

Invariant 1 *The abstract element Y over-approximates the intersection of the semantics of f on $\bar{B}_\infty(x, r)$ and the spurious region, i.e., $f(\bar{B}_\infty(x, r)) \cap \mathrm{Spu} \subseteq \gamma(Y)$.*

Algorithm 1 Spurious region guided robustness verification

Input:
    DNN f, input x, radius r.
Output:
    Return "YES" if verified, or "UNKNOWN" otherwise.

1: **function** $\text{VERIFY}(f, x, r)$
2:     $Y_0 \leftarrow f^{\#}(\bar{B}_{\infty}(x, r))$ ▷ abstract interpretation with DeepPoly
3:     $V_u \leftarrow \{v \mid v \text{ was marked as uncertain in Line 2}\}$
4:     $A = \{t \mid Y_0 \cap^{\#} (y_{C_f(x)} - y_t \leq 0) \neq \bot\}$
5:     **if** $A = \emptyset$ **then return** YES   ▷ otherwise $A = \{t_1, \ldots, t_l\}$
6:     **for** $i \leftarrow 1$ to l **do**
7:         Verified $\leftarrow$ False, $V \leftarrow V_u, Y \leftarrow Y_0$ ▷ denote $Y = (Y^{\leq}, Y^{\geq}, l, u)$
8:         $C_{\geq 0} \leftarrow \emptyset, C_{\leq 0} \leftarrow \emptyset$ ▷ set of new activated/deactivated neurons
9:         Spu $\leftarrow (y_{C_f(x)} - y_{t_i} \leq 0) \wedge \bigwedge_{j=1}^{i-1}(y_{C_f(x)} - y_{t_j} \geq 0)$ ▷ spurious region
10:         **while** terminating condition not satisfied **do**
11:             **if** $Y \wedge$ Spu is infeasible **then**
12:                 Verified $\leftarrow$ True
13:                 **break**
14:             **for** $v \in V \cup V_0$ **do**   ▷ V_0: set of input neurons
15:                 $(l_v, u_v) \leftarrow \text{LP}(Y \wedge \text{Spu}, v)$
16:             **for** $v \in V$ **do**
17:                 **if** $l_v \geq 0$ **then**
18:                     $C_{\geq 0} \leftarrow C_{\geq 0} \cup \{v\}, V \leftarrow V \setminus \{v\}$
19:                 **else if** $u_v \leq 0$ **then**
20:                     $C_{\leq 0} \leftarrow C_{\leq 0} \cup \{v\}, V \leftarrow V \setminus \{v\}$
21:             $X \leftarrow \bigcap_{v \in V_0} \{l_v \leq v \leq u_v\}$
22:             $Y \leftarrow f^{\#}(X)$ according to $C_{\geq 0}, C_{\leq 0}, l$, and u
23:             $V \leftarrow \{v \mid v \text{ was marked as uncertain in Line 22}\} \setminus (C_{\geq 0} \cup C_{\leq 0})$
24:             **if** $Y \cap^{\#} (y_{C_f(x)} - y_{t_i} \leq 0) = \bot$ **then**
25:                 Verified $\leftarrow$ True
26:                 **break**
27:         **if** Verified $=$ False **then return** UNKNOWN
28:     **return** YES

The initialization of Y is $f^{\#}(\bar{B}_{\infty}(x, r))$ and it is naturally an over-approximation. The box X is obtained by linear programming on $Y \wedge$ Spu, and $f^{\#}(X)$ is calculated through abstract interpretation and the bounds given by linear programming on $Y \wedge$ Spu, and thus it remains an over-approximation. It is worth mentioning that, when we run DeepPoly in Line 22, we are using the bounds obtained by linear programming to guide DeepPoly, and this may violate the invariant $\gamma(a) \subseteq [l, u]$ mentioned in Sect. 3. Nonetheless, soundness still holds since the concretization of Y is newly defined in Eq. 2, where both items in the intersection over-approximate $f(\bar{B}_{\infty}(x, r)) \cap$ Spu. With Invarient 1, Alg. 1 returns YES if for any possible spurious region Spu, the over-approximation of $f(\bar{B}_{\infty}(x, r)) \cap$ Spu is infeasible, which implies the soundness of Alg. 1.

4.2 Iterative refinement of the spurious region

Here we present more theoretical insight on the iterative refinement of the spurious region. An iteration of the **while** loop in Alg. 1 can be represented as a function $\mathcal{L} : \mathcal{A} \rightarrow \mathcal{A}$, where $\mathcal{A}$ is the DeepPoly domain. An interesting observation is that, the abstract transformer $f^\#$ in the DeepPoly domain is not necessarily increasing, because different input ranges, even if they have inclusion relation, may lead to different choices of the abstraction mode of some uncertain ReLU neurons, which may violate the inclusion relation of abstraction. We have found such examples during our experiment, which is illustrated in the following example.

Example 3. Let $f(x) = \text{ReLU}(x)$ with input ranges $I_1 = [-2, 1]$ and $I_2 = [-2, 3]$. We have $f^\#(I_1) = \{(x_1, x_2)^{\mathrm{T}} \in \mathbb{R}^2 \mid -2 \leq x_1 \leq 1, \ x_2 \geq 0, \ x_2 \leq \frac{1}{3}x_1 + \frac{2}{3}\}$ and $f^\#(I_2) = \{(x_1, x_2)^{\mathrm{T}} \in \mathbb{R}^2 \mid -2 \leq x_1 \leq 3, \ x_2 \geq x_1, \ x_2 \leq \frac{3}{5}x_1 + \frac{6}{5}\}$. We observe $(1, 0)^{\mathrm{T}} \in f^\#(I_1)$ but $(1, 0)^{\mathrm{T}} \notin f^\#(I_2)$, which implies that the transformer $f^\#$ is not increasing.

This fact also implies that $\mathcal{L}$ is not necessarily increasing, which violates the condition of Kleene's Theorem on fixed point [4].

Now we turn to the analysis of the sequence $\{Y_k = \mathcal{L}^k(f^\#(\bar{B}_\infty(x, r)))\}_{k=1}^\infty$, where $\mathcal{L}^1 := \mathcal{L}$ and $\mathcal{L}^k := \mathcal{L} \circ \mathcal{L}^{k-1}$ for $k \geq 2$. First we have the following lemma showing that in our settings every decreasing chain S in the DeepPoly domain $\mathcal{A}$ has a meet $\bigcap^\# S \in \mathcal{A}$.

Lemma 1. *Let $\mathcal{A}_n$ be the n-dimensional DeepPoly domain and $\{a^{(k)}\} \subseteq \mathcal{A}_n$ a decreasing bounded sequence of non-empty abstract elements. If the coefficients in $a_i^{(k),\leq}$ and $a_i^{(k),\geq}$ are uniformly bounded, then there exists an abstract element $a^* \in \mathcal{A}_n$ s.t. $\gamma(a^*) = \bigcap_{k=1}^\infty \gamma(a^{(k)})$.*

Remark: The condition that the coefficients in $a_i^{(k),\leq}$ and $a_i^{(k),\geq}$ are uniformly bounded are naturally satisfied in our setting, since in a DNN the coefficients and bounds involved have only finitely many values. Readers can refer to [50] for a formal proof.

Lemma 1 implies that if our sequence $\{Y_k\}$ is decreasing, then the iterative refinement converges to an abstract element in DeepPoly, which is the greatest fixed point of $\mathcal{L}$ that is smaller than $f^\#(\bar{B}_\infty(x, r))$. A sufficient condition for $\{Y_k\}$ being decreasing is that during the abstract interpretation in every Y_k, every initial uncertain neuron maintains its abstraction mode, i.e. its corresponding λ does not change, before its ReLU behavior is determined. A weaker sufficient condition for convergence is that change in abstraction mode of uncertain neurons never happens after finitely many iterations.

If the abstraction mode of uncertain neurons changes infinitely often, generally the sequence $\{Y_k\}$ does not converge. In this case, we can consider its subsequence in which every Y_k is obtained with the same abstraction mode. It is easy to see that such a subsequence must be decreasing and thus have a meet, as it is an accumulative point of the sequence $\{Y_k\}$. Since there are only finitely many choices of abstraction modes, such a accumulative points exists in $\{Y_k\}$, and there are only finitely many accumulative points. We conclude these results in the following theorem which describes the convergence behavior of our iterative refinement of the spurious region:

Theorem 2. *There exists a subsequence $\{Y_{n_k}\}$ of $\{Y_k\}$ s.t. $\{Y_{n_k}\}$ is decreasing and thus has a meet $\bigcap^{\#}\{Y_{n_k}\}$. Moreover, the set*

$$\left\{ \bigcap{}^{\#}\{Y_{n_k}\} \mid \{Y_{n_k}\} \text{ is a decreasing subsequence of } \{Y_k\} \right\}$$

is finite, and it is a singleton if exact one abstraction mode of uncertain ReLU *neurons happens infinitely often.*

Proof. Since the abstraction modes of uncertain ReLU neurons have only finitely many choices, there must be one which happens infinitely often in the computation of the sequence $\{Y_k\}$, and we choose the subsequence $\{Y_{n_k}\}$ in which every item is computed through this abstraction mode. Obviously $\{Y_{n_k}\}$ is decreasing and thus has a meet.

For a decreasing subsequence $\{Y_{n_k}\}$, we can find its subsequnce in which the abstraction mode of uncertain ReLU neurons does not change, and they have the same meet. Since there are only finitely many choices of abstraction modes of uncertain ReLU neurons, such accumulative points of $\{Y_k\}$ also have finitely many values. If exact one abstraction mode of uncertain ReLU neurons happens infinitely often, obviously there is only one accumulative point in $\{Y_k\}$. □

4.3 Optimizations

In the implementation of our main algorithm, we propose the following optimizations to improve the precision of refinement.

Optimization 1: More precise constraints in linear programming. In Line 15 of Alg. 1, it is not the best choice to take the linear constraints in the abstract element Y into linear programming, because the abstraction of uncertain ReLU neurons in DeepPoly is not the best. Planet [10] has a component which gives a more precise linear approximation for uncertain ReLU relations, where it uses the linear constraints $y \leq \frac{u(x-l)}{u-l}$, $y \geq x$, $y \geq 0$ to over-approximate the relation $y = \text{ReLU}(x)$ with $x \in [l, u]$.

Optimization 2: Priority to work on small spurious regions. In Line 6 of Alg. 1, we determine the order of refining the spurious regions based on their sizes, i.e., a smaller region is chosen earlier. This is based on the intuition that Alg. 1 works effectively if the spurious region is small. After the small spurious regions are ruled out, the constraints of large spurious regions can be tightened with the conjunction $\bigwedge_{j=1}^{i-1}(y_{C_f(x)} - y_{t_j} \geq 0)$. It is difficult to strictly determine which spurious region is the smallest, and thus we refer to the lower bound of $y_{C_f(x)} - y_{t_i}$ given by DeepPoly, i.e., the larger this lower bound is, the smaller the spurious region is likely to be, and we perform the **for** loop in Line 6 of Alg. 1 in this order.

5   Quantitative Robustness Verification

In this section we recall the notion of quantitative robustness and show how to verify a quantitative robustness property of a DNN with spurious region guided refinement.

In practice, we may not need a strict condition of robustness to ensure that an input x is not an adversarial example. A notion of mutation testing is proposed in [44,43], which requires that an input x is normal if it has a low *label change rate* on its neighbourhood. They follow a statistical way to estimate the label change rate of an input, which motivates us to give a formal definition of the property showing a low label change rate, and to consider the verification problem for such a property. Below we recall the definition of *quantitative robustness* [27], where we have a parameter $0 < \eta \leq 1$ representing the confidence of robustness.

Definition 2. *Given a DNN $C_f : \mathbb{R}^m \to C$, an input $x \in \mathbb{R}^m$, $r > 0$, $0 < \eta \leq 1$, and a probability measure μ on $\bar{B}_\infty(x,r)$, f is η-robust at x, if*

$$\mu(\{x' \in \bar{B}_\infty(x,r) \mid C_f(x') = C_f(x)\}) \geq \eta.$$

Def. 2 has a tight association with label change rate, i.e., if x is η-robust, then the label change rate should be smaller than, or close to $1 - \eta$. Hereafter, we set μ to be the uniform distribution on $\bar{B}_\infty(x,r)$.

It is natural to adapt spurious region guided refinement to quantitative robustness verification. In Alg. 1, we do not return UNKNOWN when we cannot rule out a spurious region, but record the volume of the box X as an over-approximation of the Lebesgue measure of the spurious region. After we work on all the spurious regions, we calculate the sum of these volume, and obtain a sound robustness confidence. Here we do not calculate the volume of the spurious region because precise calculation of volume of a high-dimensional polytope remains open, and we do not choose to use randomized algorithms because it may not be sound.

We further improve the algorithm through the powerset technique [13]. Powerset technique is a classical and effective way to enhance the precision of abstract interpretation. We split the input region into several subsets, and run abstract interpretation on these subsets, In our quantitative robustness verification setting, powerset technique not only improves the precision, but also accelerates the algorithm in some situations: If the subsets have the same volume, and the percentage of the subsets on which we may fail to verify robustness is already smaller than $1 - \eta$, then we have successfully verified the η-robustness property.

6   Experimental Evaluation

We implement our approach as a prototype called DeepSRGR. The implementation is based on a re-implementation of the ReLU and the affine abstract transformers of DeepPoly in Python 3.7 and we amend it accordingly to implement Alg. 1. We use CVXPY [8] as our modeling language for convex optimization problems and CBC [18] as the LP solver. It is worth mentioning that we ignore the floating point error in our re-implementation of DeepPoly because sound linear programming currently does not scale in our experiments. In the terminating condition, we set $N = 5$. The two optimizations in Sect. 4.3 are adopted in all the experiments. All the experiments are conducted on a CentOS 7.7 server with 16 Intel Xeon Platinum 8153 @2.00GHz (16 cores) and 512G RAM, and they use 96 sub-processes concurrently at most. Readers can find all the source code and other experimental materials in https://iscasmc.ios.ac.cn/ToolDownload/?Tool=DeepSRGR.

Datasets. We use MNIST [22] and ACAS Xu [12,17] as the datasets in our experiments. MNIST contains 60 000 grayscale handwritten digits of the size 28×28. We can train DNNs to classify the images by the written digits on them. The ACAS Xu system is aimed to avoid airborne collisions for unmanned aircrafts and it uses an observation table to make decisions for the aircraft. In [19], the observation table is realized by training DNNs instead of storing it.

Networks. On MNIST, we trained seven fully connected networks of the size 6×20, 3×50, 3×100, 6×100, 6×200, 9×200, and 6×500, where $m \times n$ refers m hidden layers and n neurons in each hidden layer, and we name them from FNN2 to FNN8, respectively (we also have a small network FNN1 for testing). On ACAS Xu, we randomly choose three networks used in [20], all of the size 6×50.

6.1 Improvement in precision

First we compare DeepPoly and DeepSRGR in terms of their precision of robustness verification. We consider the following two indices: (i) the maximum radius that the two tools can verify, and (ii) the number of uncertain ReLU neurons whose behaviors can be further determined by DeepSRGR. For each network, we randomly choose three images from the MNIST dataset, and calculate their maximum radius that the two tools can verify through a binary search on the seven FNNs. In column *"# uncertin ReLU"* we record the number of the uncertain ReLU neurons when first applying DeepPoly, and also count how many of them are *renewed*, namely become definitely activated/deactivated in later iterations when applying DeepSRGR.

Table 1 shows the results. We can see from Table 1 that DeepSRGR can verify much stronger (i.e., larger maximum radius) robustness properties than DeepPoly. The average number of iterations for ruling out a spurious region is 2.875, and about half of the spurious regions can be ruled out within 2 iterations. DeepSRGR sometimes determines behaviors of a large proportion of uncertain ReLU neurons on large networks: Considering the last picture of the most challenging network FNN8, more than ninety percent ($92.6\% \approx \frac{1269}{1371}$) of the uncertain neurons are renewed. Improvement in precision evaluated in this experiment works for verification of both robustness and quantitative robustness, and this is why our method is effective in both tasks.

6.2 Robustness verification performance

In this setting, we randomly choose 50 samples from the MNIST dataset. We fix four radii, 0.037, 0.026, 0.021, and 0.015 for the four networks FNN4 – FNN7 respectively, and verify the robustness property with the corresponding radius on the 50 inputs. The radius chosen here is very challenging for the corresponding network.

Table 2 presents the results. As we can see, DeepSRGR can verify significantly more properties than DeepPoly. Linear programming in DeepSRGR takes a large amount of time in the experiment, and thus DeepSRGR is less efficient (a DeepPoly run takes no

| | Maximum radius | | # spurious | # uncertain ReLU | | % renewed | | # iterations | |
	DeepPoly	DeepSRGR	regions	Original	Renewed	MAX	AVG	MAX	GT
	0.034	0.047	6	51	38	74.5%	48.4%	5	17
FNN2	0.017	0.023	3	47	37	78.7%	51.8%	4	9
	0.017	0.023	1	34	25	73.5%	73.5%	4	4
	0.049	0.066	6	88	69	78.4%	60.9%	5	15
FNN3	0.025	0.033	7	94	85	90.4%	46.0%	5	18
	0.045	0.058	3	98	45	45.1%	27.2%	5	9
	0.045	0.060	6	180	102	56.7%	35.2%	5	19
FNN4	0.024	0.030	6	199	144	72.4%	36.5%	4	15
	0.035	0.046	2	155	103	66.5%	42.9%	5	7
	0.034	0.042	7	305	245	80.3%	37.8%	5	20
FNN5	0.016	0.019	5	315	204	64.8%	34.0%	4	14
	0.021	0.027	7	337	256	76.0%	34.9%	5	18
	0.022	0.026	7	683	271	39.7%	19.8%	4	18
FNN6	0.011	0.013	6	657	483	73.5%	36.7%	3	14
	0.021	0.025	8	723	169	23.4%	12.2%	5	21
	0.021	0.023	9	987	297	30.1%	10.0%	5	29
FNN7	0.010	0.011	5	877	648	73.9%	26.8%	3	11
	0.017	0.019	7	913	352	38.6%	24.3%	3	16
	0.037	0.044	9	1 504	976	64.9%	45.9%	5	36
FNN8	0.020	0.022	9	1 213	818	67.4%	33.3%	3	21
	0.033	0.040	9	1 371	1 269	92.6%	51.1%	5	37

Table 1. Maximum radius which can be verified by DeepPoly and DeepSRGR, and details of DeepSRGR running on its maximum radius, where in the number of renewed uncertain nuerons, we show the largest one among the spurious regions. MAX, AVG, and GT means the maximum, the average, and the grant total among the spurious regions, respectively. The indices of the three images are 414, 481, and 65 in the MNIST dataset.

more than 100 seconds on FNN7). Furthermore, we again run the 15 running examples which are not verified by DeepSRGR on FNN4, by resetting the maximum number of iterations to 20 and 50. We have the following observations:

- Two more properties (out of 15) are successfully verified when we change N to 20. No more properties can be verified even if we change N from 20 to 50.
- In this experiment, 13 more spurious regions are ruled out, six of which takes 6 iterations, one takes 7, two takes 8, and the other four takes 13, 22, 27, and 32 iterations, respectively. In these running examples, the average number of renewed ReLU behaviors is 102.8, and a large proportion are renewed in the last iteration (47.4% on average). Fig. 3 shows the detailed results.
- As for the 13 spurious regions which cannot be ruled out within 50 iterations, the average number of renewed ReLU behaviors is only 8.54, which is significantly lower than the average of the 13 spurious regions which are newly ruled out. In these running examples, changes in ReLU behaviors and ReLU abstraction modes do not happen after the 9th iteration, and the average number is 4.4.

Model	Size	Radius	# verified		Time (s)	
			DeepPoly	DeepSRGR	MAX	AVG
FNN4	3×100	0.037	14	35	3 384	781
FNN5	6×100	0.026	19	31	7 508	1 689
FNN6	6×200	0.021	14	25	23 157	6 178
FNN7	9×200	0.015	25	36	61 760	8 960

Table 2. The number that DeepPoly and DeepSRGR verifies among the 50 inputs, and the maximum/average running time of DeepSRGR.

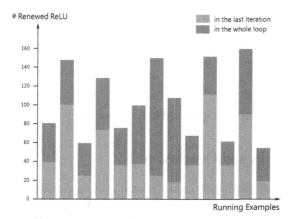

Fig. 3. Number of renewed ReLU behaviors in the spurious regions newly ruled out.

We observe that, by increasing the termination threshold N from 5 to 50, only two more properties out of 15 can be verified additionally. This suggests that our method can effectively identify these spurious regions which are relevant to verification of the property, in a small number of iterations.

6.3 Quantitative robustness verification on ACAS Xu networks

We evaluate DeepSRGR for quantitative robustness verification on ACAS Xu networks. We randomly choose five inputs, and compute the maximum robustness radius for each input on the three networks with DeepPoly through a binary search. In our experiment, the radius for a running example is the maximum robustness radius plus 0.02, 0.03, 0.04, 0.05, and 0.06. We use the powerset technique and the number of splits is 32. For DeepPoly, the robustness confidence it gives is the proportion of the splits on which DeepPoly verifies the property.

Fig. 4 shows the results. We can see that DeepSRGR gives significantly better over-approximation of $1 - \eta$ than DeepPoly. That is, in more than 90% running examples, our over-approximation is no more than one half of that given by DeepPoly, and in more than 75% of the cases, our over-approximation is even smaller than one tenth of that given by DeepPoly.

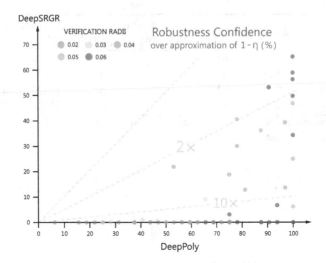

Fig. 4. Quantitative robustness verification using DeepPoly and DeepSRGR

7   Related Works and Conclusion

We have already discussed papers mostly related to our paper. Here we add some more new results. Marabou [21] has been developed as the next generation of Reluplex. Recently, verification approach based on abstraction of DNN models has been proposed in [11,2]. In addition, alternative approaches based on constraint-solving [26,29,5,25], layer-by-layer exhaustive search [16], global optimization [31,9,32], functional approximation [47], reduction to two-player games [48,49], and star set abstraction [41,40] have been proposed as well.

In this work, we propose a spurious region guided refinement approach for robustness and quantitative robustness verification of deep neural networks, where abstract interpretation calculates an abstraction, and linear programming performs refinement with the guidance of the spurious region. Our experimental results show that our tool can significantly improve the precision of DeepPoly, verify more robustness properties, and often provide a quantitative robustness with strict soundness guarantee.

Abstraction interpretation based framework is quite extensive to different DNN models, different properties, and incorporate different verification methods. As future work, we will investigate how to increase the precision further by using more precise linear over-approximation like [35].

Acknowledgement

This work has been partially supported by Key-Area Research and Development Program of Guangdong Province (Grant No. 2018B010107004), National Natural Science Foundation of China (Grant No. 61761136011, 61836005), Natural Science Foundation of Guangdong Province, China (Grant No. 2019A1515011689), and the Fundamental Research Funds for the Zhejiang University NGICS Platform.

References

1. Anderson, G., Pailoor, S., Dillig, I., Chaudhuri, S.: Optimization and abstraction: a synergistic approach for analyzing neural network robustness. In: McKinley, K.S., Fisher, K. (eds.) Proceedings of the 40th ACM SIGPLAN Conference on Programming Language Design and Implementation, PLDI 2019, Phoenix, AZ, USA, June 22-26, 2019. pp. 731–744. ACM (2019)
2. Ashok, P., Hashemi, V., Kretínský, J., Mohr, S.: Deepabstract: Neural network abstraction for accelerating verification. In: Hung, D.V., Sokolsky, O. (eds.) Automated Technology for Verification and Analysis - 18th International Symposium, ATVA 2020, Hanoi, Vietnam, October 19-23, 2020, Proceedings. Lecture Notes in Computer Science, vol. 12302, pp. 92–107. Springer (2020)
3. Baluta, T., Chua, Z.L., Meel, K.S., Saxena, P.: Scalable quantitative verification for deep neural networks. CoRR **abs/2002.06864** (2020), https://arxiv.org/abs/2002.06864
4. Baranga, A.: The contraction principle as a particular case of kleene's fixed point theorem. Discret. Math. **98**(1), 75–79 (1991)
5. Bunel, R., Lu, J., Turkaslan, I., Torr, P.H.S., Kohli, P., Kumar, M.P.: Branch and bound for piecewise linear neural network verification. J. Mach. Learn. Res. **21**, 42:1–42:39 (2020)
6. Clarke, E.M., Grumberg, O., Jha, S., Lu, Y., Veith, H.: Counterexample-guided abstraction refinement. In: Emerson, E.A., Sistla, A.P. (eds.) Computer Aided Verification, 12th International Conference, CAV 2000, Chicago, IL, USA, July 15-19, 2000, Proceedings. Lecture Notes in Computer Science, vol. 1855, pp. 154–169. Springer (2000)
7. Cousot, P., Cousot, R.: Abstract interpretation: A unified lattice model for static analysis of programs by construction or approximation of fixpoints. In: Fourth ACM Symposium on Principles of Programming Languages (POPL). pp. 238–252 (1977)
8. Diamond, S., Boyd, S.: CVXPY: A Python-embedded modeling language for convex optimization. Journal of Machine Learning Research **17**(83), 1–5 (2016)
9. Dutta, S., Jha, S., Sankaranarayanan, S., Tiwari, A.: Output range analysis for deep feedforward neural networks. In: Dutle, A., Muñoz, C.A., Narkawicz, A. (eds.) NASA Formal Methods - 10th International Symposium, NFM 2018, Newport News, VA, USA, April 17-19, 2018, Proceedings. Lecture Notes in Computer Science, vol. 10811, pp. 121–138. Springer (2018)
10. Ehlers, R.: Formal verification of piece-wise linear feed-forward neural networks. In: 15th International Symposium on Automated Technology for Verification and Analysis (ATVA2017). pp. 269–286 (2017)
11. Elboher, Y.Y., Gottschlich, J., Katz, G.: An abstraction-based framework for neural network verification. In: Lahiri, S.K., Wang, C. (eds.) Computer Aided Verification - 32nd International Conference, CAV 2020, Los Angeles, CA, USA, July 21-24, 2020, Proceedings, Part I. Lecture Notes in Computer Science, vol. 12224, pp. 43–65. Springer (2020)
12. von Essen, C., Giannakopoulou, D.: Analyzing the next generation airborne collision avoidance system. In: Ábrahám, E., Havelund, K. (eds.) Tools and Algorithms for the Construction and Analysis of Systems - 20th International Conference, TACAS 2014, Held as Part of the European Joint Conferences on Theory and Practice of Software, ETAPS 2014, Grenoble, France, April 5-13, 2014. Proceedings. Lecture Notes in Computer Science, vol. 8413, pp. 620–635. Springer (2014)
13. Gehr, T., Mirman, M., Drachsler-Cohen, D., Tsankov, P., Chaudhuri, S., Vechev, M.: AI^2: Safety and robustness certification of neural networks with abstract interpretation. In: 2018 IEEE Symposium on Security and Privacy (S&P 2018). pp. 948–963 (2018)
14. Ghorbal, K., Goubault, E., Putot, S.: The zonotope abstract domain taylor1+. In: International Conference on Computer Aided Verification. pp. 627–633. Springer (2009)

15. Ghorbal, K., Goubault, E., Putot, S.: A logical product approach to zonotope intersection. In: Touili, T., Cook, B., Jackson, P.B. (eds.) Computer Aided Verification, 22nd International Conference, CAV 2010, Edinburgh, UK, July 15-19, 2010. Proceedings. Lecture Notes in Computer Science, vol. 6174, pp. 212–226. Springer (2010)

16. Huang, X., Kwiatkowska, M., Wang, S., Wu, M.: Safety verification of deep neural networks. In: 29th International Conference on Computer Aided Verification (CAV2017). pp. 3–29 (2017)

17. Jeannin, J., Ghorbal, K., Kouskoulas, Y., Gardner, R., Schmidt, A., Zawadzki, E., Platzer, A.: Formal verification of ACAS x, an industrial airborne collision avoidance system. In: Girault, A., Guan, N. (eds.) 2015 International Conference on Embedded Software, EMSOFT 2015, Amsterdam, Netherlands, October 4-9, 2015. pp. 127–136. IEEE (2015)

18. johnjforrest, Vigerske, S., Santos, H.G., Ralphs, T., Hafer, L., Kristjansson, B., jpfasano, EdwinStraver, Lubin, M., rlougee, jpgoncal1, h-i gassmann, Saltzman, M.: coin-or/cbc: Version 2.10.5 (Mar 2020)

19. Julian, K.D., Kochenderfer, M.J., Owen, M.P.: Deep neural network compression for aircraft collision avoidance systems. CoRR **abs/1810.04240** (2018), http://arxiv.org/abs/1810.04240

20. Katz, G., Barrett, C.W., Dill, D.L., Julian, K., Kochenderfer, M.J.: Reluplex: An efficient SMT solver for verifying deep neural networks. In: 29th International Conference on Computer Aided Verification (CAV2017). pp. 97–117 (2017)

21. Katz, G., Huang, D.A., Ibeling, D., Julian, K., Lazarus, C., Lim, R., Shah, P., Thakoor, S., Wu, H., Zeljic, A., Dill, D.L., Kochenderfer, M.J., Barrett, C.W.: The marabou framework for verification and analysis of deep neural networks. In: Dillig, I., Tasiran, S. (eds.) Computer Aided Verification - 31st International Conference, CAV 2019, New York City, NY, USA, July 15-18, 2019, Proceedings, Part I. Lecture Notes in Computer Science, vol. 11561, pp. 443–452. Springer (2019)

22. Lécun, Y., Bottou, L., Bengio, Y., Haffner, P.: Gradient-based learning applied to document recognition. Proceedings of the IEEE **86**(11), 2278–2324 (1998)

23. Li, J., Liu, J., Yang, P., Chen, L., Huang, X., Zhang, L.: Analyzing deep neural networks with symbolic propagation: Towards higher precision and faster verification. In: Chang, B.E. (ed.) Static Analysis - 26th International Symposium, SAS 2019, Porto, Portugal, October 8-11, 2019, Proceedings. Lecture Notes in Computer Science, vol. 11822, pp. 296–319. Springer (2019)

24. Li, R., Li, J., Huang, C., Yang, P., Huang, X., Zhang, L., Xue, B., Hermanns, H.: Prodeep: a platform for robustness verification of deep neural networks. In: Devanbu, P., Cohen, M.B., Zimmermann, T. (eds.) ESEC/FSE '20: 28th ACM Joint European Software Engineering Conference and Symposium on the Foundations of Software Engineering, Virtual Event, USA, November 8-13, 2020. pp. 1630–1634. ACM (2020)

25. Lin, W., Yang, Z., Chen, X., Zhao, Q., Li, X., Liu, Z., He, J.: Robustness verification of classification deep neural networks via linear programming. In: IEEE Conference on Computer Vision and Pattern Recognition, CVPR 2019, Long Beach, CA, USA, June 16-20, 2019. pp. 11418–11427. Computer Vision Foundation / IEEE (2019)

26. Lomuscio, A., Maganti, L.: An approach to reachability analysis for feed-forward ReLU neural networks. In: KR2018 (2018)

27. Mangal, R., Nori, A.V., Orso, A.: Robustness of neural networks: A probabilistic and practical approach. CoRR **abs/1902.05983** (2019), http://arxiv.org/abs/1902.05983

28. Müller, C., Singh, G., Püschel, M., Vechev, M.T.: Neural network robustness verification on gpus. CoRR **abs/2007.10868** (2020), https://arxiv.org/abs/2007.10868

29. Narodytska, N., Kasiviswanathan, S.P., Ryzhyk, L., Sagiv, M., Walsh, T.: Verifying properties of binarized deep neural networks. In: McIlraith, S.A., Weinberger, K.Q. (eds.) Proceedings of the Thirty-Second AAAI Conference on Artificial Intelligence, (AAAI-18), the

30th innovative Applications of Artificial Intelligence (IAAI-18), and the 8th AAAI Symposium on Educational Advances in Artificial Intelligence (EAAI-18), New Orleans, Louisiana, USA, February 2-7, 2018. pp. 6615–6624. AAAI Press (2018)

30. Pulina, L., Tacchella, A.: An abstraction-refinement approach to verification of artificial neural networks. In: Computer Aided Verification, 22nd International Conference, CAV 2010, Edinburgh, UK, July 15-19, 2010. Proceedings. pp. 243–257 (2010)

31. Ruan, W., Huang, X., Kwiatkowska, M.: Reachability analysis of deep neural networks with provable guarantees. In: IJCAI2018. pp. 2651–2659 (2018)

32. Ruan, W., Wu, M., Sun, Y., Huang, X., Kroening, D., Kwiatkowska, M.: Global robustness evaluation of deep neural networks with provable guarantees for the hamming distance. In: Kraus, S. (ed.) Proceedings of the Twenty-Eighth International Joint Conference on Artificial Intelligence, IJCAI 2019, Macao, China, August 10-16, 2019. pp. 5944–5952. ijcai.org (2019)

33. Sheikhtaheri, A., Sadoughi, F., Dehaghi, Z.H.: Developing and using expert systems and neural networks in medicine: A review on benefits and challenges. J. Medical Syst. **38**(9), 110 (2014)

34. Silver, D., Huang, A., Maddison, C.J., Guez, A., Sifre, L., van den Driessche, G., Schrittwieser, J., Antonoglou, I., Panneershelvam, V., Lanctot, M., Dieleman, S., Grewe, D., Nham, J., Kalchbrenner, N., Sutskever, I., Lillicrap, T.P., Leach, M., Kavukcuoglu, K., Graepel, T., Hassabis, D.: Mastering the game of go with deep neural networks and tree search. Nature **529**(7587), 484–489 (2016)

35. Singh, G., Ganvir, R., Püschel, M., Vechev, M.T.: Beyond the single neuron convex barrier for neural network certification. In: Wallach, H.M., Larochelle, H., Beygelzimer, A., d'Alché-Buc, F., Fox, E.B., Garnett, R. (eds.) Advances in Neural Information Processing Systems 32: Annual Conference on Neural Information Processing Systems 2019, NeurIPS 2019, 8-14 December 2019, Vancouver, BC, Canada. pp. 15072–15083 (2019)

36. Singh, G., Gehr, T., Mirman, M., Püschel, M., Vechev, M.T.: Fast and effective robustness certification. In: Advances in Neural Information Processing Systems 31: Annual Conference on Neural Information Processing Systems 2018, NeurIPS 2018, 3-8 December 2018, Montréal, Canada. pp. 10825–10836 (2018)

37. Singh, G., Gehr, T., Püschel, M., Vechev, M.T.: An abstract domain for certifying neural networks. PACMPL **3**(POPL), 41:1–41:30 (2019)

38. Singh, G., Püschel, M., Vechev, M.T.: Fast polyhedra abstract domain. In: Castagna, G., Gordon, A.D. (eds.) Proceedings of the 44th ACM SIGPLAN Symposium on Principles of Programming Languages, POPL 2017, Paris, France, January 18-20, 2017. pp. 46–59. ACM (2017)

39. Szegedy, C., Zaremba, W., Sutskever, I., Bruna, J., Erhan, D., Goodfellow, I., Fergus, R.: Intriguing properties of neural networks. In: International Conference on Learning Representations (ICLR2014) (2014)

40. Tran, H., Bak, S., Xiang, W., Johnson, T.T.: Verification of deep convolutional neural networks using imagestars. In: Lahiri, S.K., Wang, C. (eds.) Computer Aided Verification - 32nd International Conference, CAV 2020, Los Angeles, CA, USA, July 21-24, 2020, Proceedings, Part I. Lecture Notes in Computer Science, vol. 12224, pp. 18–42. Springer (2020)

41. Tran, H., Lopez, D.M., Musau, P., Yang, X., Nguyen, L.V., Xiang, W., Johnson, T.T.: Star-based reachability analysis of deep neural networks. In: ter Beek, M.H., McIver, A., Oliveira, J.N. (eds.) Formal Methods - The Next 30 Years - Third World Congress, FM 2019, Porto, Portugal, October 7-11, 2019, Proceedings. Lecture Notes in Computer Science, vol. 11800, pp. 670–686. Springer (2019)

42. Urmson, C., Whittaker, W.: Self-driving cars and the urban challenge. IEEE Intell. Syst. **23**(2), 66–68 (2008)

43. Wang, J., Dong, G., Sun, J., Wang, X., Zhang, P.: Adversarial sample detection for deep neural network through model mutation testing. In: 2019 IEEE/ACM 41st International Conference on Software Engineering (ICSE). pp. 1245–1256. IEEE (2019)

44. Wang, J., Sun, J., Zhang, P., Wang, X.: Detecting adversarial samples for deep neural networks through mutation testing. CoRR **abs/1805.05010** (2018), http://arxiv.org/abs/1805.05010

45. Webb, S., Rainforth, T., Teh, Y.W., Kumar, M.P.: A statistical approach to assessing neural network robustness. In: 7th International Conference on Learning Representations, ICLR 2019, New Orleans, LA, USA, May 6-9, 2019. OpenReview.net (2019)

46. Weng, L., Chen, P., Nguyen, L.M., Squillante, M.S., Boopathy, A., Oseledets, I.V., Daniel, L.: PROVEN: verifying robustness of neural networks with a probabilistic approach. In: Chaudhuri, K., Salakhutdinov, R. (eds.) Proceedings of the 36th International Conference on Machine Learning, ICML 2019, 9-15 June 2019, Long Beach, California, USA. Proceedings of Machine Learning Research, vol. 97, pp. 6727–6736. PMLR (2019)

47. Weng, T.W., Zhang, H., Chen, H., Song, Z., Hsieh, C.J., Boning, D., Dhillon, I.S., Daniel, L.: Towards Fast Computation of Certified Robustness for ReLU Networks. In: ICML 2018 (Apr 2018)

48. Wicker, M., Huang, X., Kwiatkowska, M.: Feature-guided black-box safety testing of deep neural networks. In: Beyer, D., Huisman, M. (eds.) Tools and Algorithms for the Construction and Analysis of Systems - 24th International Conference, TACAS 2018, Held as Part of the European Joint Conferences on Theory and Practice of Software, ETAPS 2018, Thessaloniki, Greece, April 14-20, 2018, Proceedings, Part I. Lecture Notes in Computer Science, vol. 10805, pp. 408–426. Springer (2018)

49. Wu, M., Wicker, M., Ruan, W., Huang, X., Kwiatkowska, M.: A game-based approximate verification of deep neural networks with provable guarantees. Theor. Comput. Sci. **807**, 298–329 (2020)

50. Yang, P., Li, R., Li, J., Huang, C., Wang, J., Sun, J., Xue, B., Zhang, L.: Improving neural network verification through spurious region guided refinement. CoRR **abs/2010.07722** (2020), https://arxiv.org/abs/2010.07722

Analysis of Network Communication

Resilient Capacity-Aware Routing

Stefan Schmid[1], Nicolas Schnepf[2], and Jiří Srba[2](✉)[*]

[1] Faculty of Computer Science, University of Vienna, Vienna, Austria
[2] Department of Computer Science, Aalborg University, Aalborg, Denmark

Abstract. To ensure a high availability, communication networks provide resilient routing mechanisms that quickly change routes upon failures. However, a fundamental algorithmic question underlying such mechanisms is hardly understood: how to verify whether a given network reroutes flows along *feasible* paths, without violating capacity constraints, for up to k link failures? We chart the algorithmic complexity landscape of resilient routing under link failures, considering shortest path routing based on link weights as e.g. deployed in the ECMP protocol. We study two models: a *pessimistic* model where flows interfere in a worst-case manner along equal-cost shortest paths, and an *optimistic* model where flows are routed in a best-case manner, and we present a complete picture of the algorithmic complexities.We further propose a strategic search algorithm that checks only the critical failure scenarios while still providing correctness guarantees. Our experimental evaluation on a benchmark of Internet and datacenter topologies confirms an improved performance of our strategic search by several orders of magnitude.

1 Introduction

Routing and traffic engineering are most fundamental tasks in a communication network. Internet Service Providers (ISPs) today use several sophisticated strategies to efficiently provision their backbone network to serve intra-domain traffic. This is challenging as in addition to simply providing reachability, routing protocols should also account for capacity constraints: to meet quality-of-service guarantees, congestion must be avoided. Intra-domain routing protocols are usually based on shortest paths, and in particular the Equal-Cost-MultiPath (ECMP) protocol [24]. Flows are split at nodes where several outgoing links are on shortest paths to the destination, based on per-flow static hashing [7, 30]. In addition to default routing, most modern communication networks also provide support for *resilient routing*: upon the detection of a link failure, the network nodes quickly and collaboratively recompute the new shortest paths [21].

However, today, we still do not have a good understanding of the algorithmic complexity of shortest path routing subject to capacity constraints, especially under failures. In particular, in this paper we are interested in the basic question: "Given a capacitated network based on shortest path routing (defined by link weights), can the network tolerate up to k link failures without violating capacity constraints?" Surprisingly only little is known about the complexity aspects.

---

[*] srba@cs.aau.dk

© The Author(s) 2021
J. F. Groote and K. G. Larsen (Eds.): TACAS 2021, LNCS 12651, pp. 411–429, 2021.
https://doi.org/10.1007/978-3-030-72016-2_22

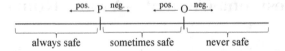

Fig. 1: Classification of possible network situations

	Pessimistic	Optimistic
Splittable	NL-complete	P-complete
Nonsplit.	NL-complete	NP-complete

(a) Without link failures ($k = 0$)

	Pessimistic	Optimistic
Splittable	co-NP-complete	co-NP-complete
Nonsplit.	co-NP-complete	Π_2^P-complete

(b) With link failures ($k \geq 0$)

Fig. 2: Summary of complexity results for capacity problems

Our Contributions. We provide a complete characterization of the algorithmic complexity landscape of resilient routing and introduce two basic models of how traffic is distributed across the multiple shortest paths. A **pessimistic (P)** one where flows add up in a worst-case manner; if a network is resilient in the pessimistic model, it is guaranteed that routing succeeds along *any* shortest path without overloading links. In the **optimistic (O)** model flows add up in a best-case manner; if a network is resilient in the optimistic model, it *may be* that the specific routing does not overload the links. The two models hence cover the two extremes in the spectrum and alternative routing schemes, e.g., (pseudo)random routing hence lies in between. Figure 1 illustrates the situations that can arise in a network: depending on the scenario, pessimistic (P) or optimistic (O), and whether the routing feasibility test is positive or negative, we can distinguish between three regimes. (1) If routing is feasible even in the pessimistic case, then flows can be safely forwarded by any routing policy without violating any capacity constraints. (2) If the pessimistic test is negative but positive in the optimistic case, then further considerations are required to ensure that flows use the feasible paths (e.g., a clever routing algorithm to find the suitable paths is needed). (3) If even the optimistic test is negative then no feasible routing solution exists; to be able to successfully route flows in this case, we need to change the network characteristics, e.g., to increase the link capacities.

We further distinguish between **splittable (S)** and **nonsplittable (N)** flows, and refer to the four possible problems by **PS, PN, ON,** and **OS**. Our main complexity results are summarized in Figure 2. We can see that without link failures (Figure 2a), the problems are solvable in polynomial time, except for the ON problem that becomes NP-complete. Moreover, the pessimistic variants of the problem can be solved even in nondeterministic logarithmic space, implying that they allow for efficient parallelization [33]. On the other hand, the optimistic splittable problem is hard for the class P. For the problems with link failures (Figure 2b) the complexity increases and the problems become co-NP-complete, apart from the ON problem that becomes more difficult to solve and is complete for the second level of the polynomial hierarchy [33].

The high computational complexity of the instances with link failures may indicate that a brute-force search algorithm exploring all failure scenarios is needed to verify whether routing is feasible. However, we present a more efficient solution, by defining a partial ordering on the possible failure scenarios with the property that for the pessimistic model, we only need to explore the minimum failure scenarios, and for the optimistic model, it is sufficient to explore the maximum failure scenarios. We present an efficient *strategic search* algorithm implementing these ideas, formally prove its correctness, and demonstrate the practical applicability of strategic search on a benchmark of Internet and data-center topologies. In particular, we find that our algorithm achieves up to several orders of magnitude runtime savings compared to the brute-force search.

Related Work. Efficient traffic routing has received much attention in the literature, and there also exist empirical studies on the efficiency of ECMP deployments, e.g., in Internet Service Provider Networks [17] or in datacenters [22]. A systematic algorithmic study of routing with ECMP is conducted by Chiesa et al. in [10]. The authors show that in the splittable-flow model [16], even approximating the optimal link-weight configuration for ECMP within any constant factor is computationally intractable. Before their work, it was only known that minimizing congestion is NP-hard (even to just provide "satisfactory" quality [2] and also under path cardinality constraints [5]) and cannot be approximated within a factor of 3/2 [19]. For specific topologies the authors further show that traffic engineering with ECMP remains suboptimal and computationally hard for hypercube networks. We significantly extend these insights into the algorithmic complexity of traffic engineering and introduce the concept of pessimistic and optimistic variants of routing feasibility and provide a complete characterization of the complexity of routing subject to *capacity constraints*, also in scenarios with *failures*. Accounting for failures is an important aspect in practice [13,31] but has not been studied rigorously in the literature before; to the best of our knowledge, so far there only exist heuristic solutions [18] with some notable exceptions such as Lancet [8] (which however does not account for congestion). We propose to distinguish between optimistic and pessimistic flow splitting; existing literature typically revolves around the optimistic scenario.

We note that while we focus on IP networks (and in particular shortest path routing and ECMP), there exist many interesting results on the verification and reachability testing in other types of networks and protocols, including BGP [4, 15], MPLS [25,38], OpenFlow [1] networks, or stateful networks [29,32,41]. While most existing literature focuses on verifying logical properties, such as reachability without considering capacity constraints, there also exist first works dealing with quantitative properties [20,26,29].

2 Network with Capacities and Demands

We shall now define the model of network with link capacities and flow demands and formally specify the four variants of the resilient routing problem. Let $\mathbb{N}$ be the set of natural numbers and $\mathbb{N}^0$ the set of nonnegative integers.

Definition 1 (Network with Capacities and Demands). *A Network with Capacities and Demands (NCD) is a triple $N = (V, C, D)$ where V is a finite set of nodes, $C : V \times V \mapsto \mathbb{N}^0$ is the capacity function for each network edge (capacity 0 implies the absence of a network link), and $D : V \times V \mapsto \mathbb{N}^0$ is the end-to-end flow demand between every pair of nodes such that $D(v, v) = 0$ for all $v \in V$ (demand 0 means that there is no flow).*

Let $N = (V, C, D)$ be an NCD. A *path* from v_1 to v_n where $v_1, v_n \in V$ is any nonempty sequence of nodes $v_1 v_2 \cdots v_n \in V^+$ such that $C(v_i, v_{i+1}) > 0$ for all i, $1 \leq i < n$. Let $s, t \in V$. By $Paths(s, t)$ we denote the set of all paths from s to t. Let $\pi \in Paths(s, t)$ be a path in N such that $\pi = v_1 v_2 \ldots v_n$. An *edge* is a pair of nodes $(v, v') \in V \times V$ such that $C(v, v') > 0$. We write $(v, v') \in \pi$ whenever $(v, v') = (v_i, v_{i+1})$ for some i, $1 \leq i < n$.

Routes in an NCD are traditionally determined by annotating the links with weights and employing shortest path routing (e.g. ECMP). In case of multiple shortest paths, traffic engineers select either one of the shortest paths or decide to split the flow among the different shortest paths for load-balancing purposes. When one or multiple links fail, the set of shortest paths may change and the routes need to be updated. The weight assignment is usually provided by the network operators and is primarily used for traffic engineering purposes.

Definition 2 (Weight Assignment). *Let $N = (V, C, D)$ be an NCD. A weight assignment on N is a function $W : V \times V \mapsto \mathbb{N} \cup \{\infty\}$ that assigns each link a positive weight where $C(v, v') = 0$ implies that $W(v, v') = \infty$ for all $v, v' \in V$.*

Assume now a fixed weight assignment for a given NCD $N = (V, C, D)$. Let $\pi = v_1 v_2 \cdots v_n \in V^+$ be a *path* from v_1 to v_n. The *weight* of the path π is denoted by $W(\pi)$ and defined by $W(\pi) = \sum_{i=1}^{n-1} W(v_i, v_{i+1})$. Let $s, t \in V$. The set of shortest paths from s to t is defined by $SPaths(s, t) = \{\pi \in Paths(s, t) \mid W(\pi) \neq \infty \text{ and } W(\pi) \leq W(\pi') \text{ for all } \pi' \in Paths(s, t)\}$. As the weights are positive, all shortest paths in the set $SPaths(s, t)$ are acyclic and hence the set is finite (though of possibly exponential size).

For a given NCD N and a set of failed links F, we can now define the NCD N^F where all links from F are removed.

Definition 3. *Let $N = (V, C, D)$ be an NCD with weight assignment W, and let $F \subseteq V \times V$ be a set of failed links. We define the pruned NCD $N^F = (V, C^F, D)$ with an updated weight assignment W^F by*

- *$C^F(v, v') = C(v, v')$ and $W^F(v, v') = W(v, v')$ if $(v, v') \notin F$, and*
- *$C^F(v, v') = 0$ and $W^F(v, v') = \infty$ if $(v, v') \in F$.*

By $Paths^F(s, t)$ and $SPaths^F(s, t)$ we denote the sets of the paths and shortest paths between s and t in the network $N^F = (V, C^F, D)$ with W^F.

We shall now define a flow assignment that for each nonempty flow demand between s and t and every failure scenario, determines the amount of traffic that should be routed through the shortest paths between s and t.

Definition 4 (Flow Assignment). *A flow assignment f in a capacity network $N = (V, C, D)$ with weight assignment W and with the set $F \subseteq V \times V$ of failed links is a family of functions $f_{s,t}^F :$ $SPaths^F(s,t) \mapsto [0,1]$ for all $s,t \in V$ where $D(s,t) > 0$ such that $\sum_{\pi \in SPaths^F(s,t)} f_{s,t}^F(\pi) = 1$. A flow assignment f is* nonsplittable *if $f_{s,t}^F(\pi) \in \{0,1\}$ for all $s,t \in V$ and all $\pi \in SPaths^F(s,t)$. Otherwise the flow assignment is* splittable.

The notation $[0,1]$ denotes the interval of all rational numbers between 0 and 1 and it determines how the load demand between the nodes s and t is split among the routing paths between the two nodes. A nonsplittable flow assignment assigns the value 1 to exactly one routing path between any two nodes s and t. If for a given failure scenario F there is no path between s and t for two nodes with $D(s,t) > 0$, then there is no flow assignment as the network is *disconnected*.

Definition 5. *An NCD $N = (V, C, D)$ is* connected *for the set of failed links $F \subseteq V \times V$ if $SPaths^F(s,t) \neq \emptyset$ for every $s,t \in V$ where $D(s,t) > 0$.*

For a connected NCD, we now define a feasible flow assignment that avoids congestion: the sum of portions of flow demands (determined by the flow assignment) that are routed through each link, may not exceed the link capacity.

Definition 6 (Feasible Flow Assignment). *Let $N = (V, C, D)$ be an NCD with weight assignment W. Let $F \subseteq V \times V$ be the set of failed links s.t. the network remains connected. A flow assignment f is* feasible *if every link $(v, v') \in V \times V$ with $C(v, v') > 0$ satisfies $\displaystyle\sum_{\substack{s,t \in V \\ \pi \in SPaths^F(s,t) \\ (v,v') \in \pi}} f_{s,t}^F(\pi) \cdot D(s,t) \leq C(v, v')$.*

We consider four different variants of the capacity problem.

Definition 7 (Pessimistic Splittable/Nonsplittable (PS/PN)). *Given an NCD N with a weight assignment and nonnegative integer k, is it the case that for* every *set F of failed links of cardinality at most k, the network remains connected and every splittable/nonsplittable flow assignment on N with the set F of failed links is feasible?*

Definition 8 (Optimistic Splittable/Nonsplittable (OS/ON)). *Given an NCD N with a weight assignment and a nonnegative integer k, is there a feasible splittable/nonsplittable flow assignment on N for* every *set of failed links F of cardinality at most k?*

A positive answer to the PN capacity problem implies positive answers to both PS and ON problems. A positive answer to either the PS or ON problem implies a positive answer to the OS problem. This is summarized in Figure 3 and it is easy to argue that the hierarchy is strict.

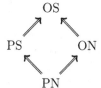

Fig. 3: Hierarchy

3   Analysis of Algorithmic Complexity

We now provide the arguments for the upper and lower bounds from Figure 2.

Algorithm 1 Computation of the shortest path graph function $spg^{s,t}$

Input: NCD $N = (V, C, D)$, weight assignment W and $s, t \in V$
Output: Shortest path graph function $spg^{s,t} : V \times V \to \{0, 1\}$
if $dist(s, t) = \infty$ then $spg^{s,t}(v, v') := 0$ for all $v, v' \in V$
else
    for $v, v' \in V$ do
        if $dist(s, t) = dist(s, v) + W(v, v') + dist(v', t)$ then $spg^{s,t}(v, v') := 1$
        else $spg^{s,t}(v, v') := 0$
  return $spg^{s,t}$

Complexity Upper Bounds. We present first a few useful observations. Because network connectivity can be checked independently for each source s and target t where $D(s, t) > 0$ by computing the maximum flow [14] between s and t, we obtain the following lemma.

Lemma 1. *Given an NCD $N = (V, C, D)$ and a nonnegative integer k, it is polynomial-time decidable if N remains connected for all sets of failed links $F \subseteq V \times V$ where $|F| \leq k$.*

Next, we present an algorithm that for an NCD $N = (V, C, D)$ with the weight assignment $W : V \times V \mapsto \mathbb{N} \cup \{\infty\}$ and a given pair of nodes $s, t \in V$ computes in polynomial time the function $spg^{s,t} : V \times V \to \{0, 1\}$ that assigns the value 1 to exactly all edges that appear on at least one shortest path (w.r.t. to the weight assignment W) between s and t. The edges that get assigned the value 1 hence form the shortest path subgraph between s and t. The algorithm uses the function $dist(v, v')$ that for every two nodes $v, v' \in V$ returns the length of the shortest path (again w.r.t. to the assignment W) from v to v' and if v and v' are not connected then it returns ∞. Such an all-pairs shortest path function can be precomputed in polynomial time using e.g. the Johnson's algorithms [27]. The function $spg^{s,t}$ is defined by Algorithm 1.

Lemma 2. *Let $N = (V, C, D)$ be an NCD with weight assignment W and $s, t \in V$. Algorithm 1 runs in polynomial time and the value of $spg^{s,t}(v, v')$ can be returned in nondeterministic logarithmic space. Moreover, there is an edge $(v, v') \in \pi$ for some $\pi \in SPaths(s, t)$ iff $spg^{s,t}(v, v') = 1$.*

We first present results for $k = 0$ (no link failures) and start by showing that the optimistic splittable variant of the capacity problem is decidable in polynomial time by reducing it to the feasibility of a linear program. Let $N = (V, C, D)$ be an NCD with weight assignment W and let $spg^{s,t}$ be precomputed for all pairs of s and t. We construct a linear program over the variables $x^{s,t}(v, v')$ for all $s, t, v, v' \in V$ where the variable $x^{s,t}(v, v')$ represents the percentage of the total demand $D(s, t)$ between s and t that is routed through the link (v, v'). In the equations below, we let s and t range over all nodes that satisfy $D(s, t) > 0$.

$$1 \geq x^{s,t}(v,v') \geq 0 \quad \text{for } s,t,v,v' \in V \tag{1}$$

$$\sum_{v \in V} x^{s,t}(s,v) \cdot spg^{s,t}(s,v) = 1 \quad \text{for } s,t \in V \tag{2}$$

$$\sum_{v \in V} x^{s,t}(v,t) \cdot spg^{s,t}(v,t) = 1 \quad \text{for } s,t \in V \tag{3}$$

$$\sum_{v' \in V} x^{s,t}(v',v) \cdot spg^{s,t}(v',v) =$$

$$\sum_{v' \in V} x^{s,t}(v,v') \cdot spg^{s,t}(v,v') \quad \text{for } s,t,v \in V, v \notin \{s,t\} \tag{4}$$

$$\sum_{s,t \in V} x^{s,t}(v,v') \cdot spg^{s,t}(v,v') \cdot D(s,t) \leq C(v,v') \quad \text{for } v,v' \in V \tag{5}$$

Equation 1 imposes that the flow portion on any link must be between 0 and 1. Equation 2 makes sure that portion of the demand $D(s,t)$ must be split along all outgoing links from s that belong to the shortest path graph. Similarly Equation 3 guarantees that the flows on incoming links to t in the shortest path graph deliver the total demand. Equation 4 is a flow preservation equation among all incoming and outgoing links (in the shortest path graph) connected to every node v. The first four equations define all possible splittings of the flow demands for all s and t such that $D(s,t) > 0$. Finally, Equation 5 checks that for every link in the network, the total sum of the flows for all s-t pairs does not exceed the link capacity. The size of the constructed system is quadratic in the number of nodes and its feasibility, that can be verified in polynomial time [39], corresponds to the existence of a solution for the OS problem.

Theorem 1. *The OS capacity problem without any link failures is decidable in polynomial time.*

If we now restrict the variables to nonnegative intergers, we get an instance of integer linear program where feasibility checking is NP-complete [39], and corresponds to the solution for the nonsplittable optimistic problem.

Theorem 2. *The ON capacity problem without any link failures is decidable in nondeterministic polynomial time.*

Next, we present a theorem stating that both the splittable and nonsplittable variants of the pessimistic capacity problem are decidable in polynomial time and in fact also in nondeterministic logarithmic space (the complexity class NL).

Theorem 3. *The PS and PN capacity problems without any link failures are decidable in nondeterministic logarithmic space.*

Proof. Let $N = (V,C,D)$ be a given NCD with a weight assignment W. Let us consider the shortest path graph represented by $spg^{s,t}$ as defined by Algorithm 1. Clearly, if the set $SPaths(s,t)$ for some $s,t \in V$ where $D(s,t) > 0$ is empty, the answer to both the splittable and nonsplittable problem is negative. Otherwise, for each pair $s, t \in V$ where $D(s, t) > 0$, the entire demand $D(s, t)$ can be routed (both in the splittable and nonsplittable case) through any edge (v, v') that satisfies $spg^{s,t}(v, v') = 1$. Hence we can check whether for every edge $(v, v') \in V \times V$ it holds

$$\sum_{\substack{s,t \in V \\ D(s,t)>0}} D(s, t) \cdot spg^{s,t}(v, v') \leq C(v, v') .$$

If this is the case, then the answer to both the splittable and the nonsplittable pessimistic problem is positive as there is no flow assignment that can exceed the capacity of any link. On the other hand, if for some link (v, v') the sum of all demands that can be possibly routed through (v, v') exceeds the link capacity, the answer to the problem (both splittable and nonsplittable) is negative. The algorithm can be implemented to run in nondeterministic logarithmic space. □

Let us now turn our attention to the four variants of the problem under the assumption that up to k links can fail (where k is part of the input to the decision problem). Given an NCD $N = (V, C, D)$ with a weight assignment W, we are asked to check, for all (exponentially many) failure scenarios $F \subseteq V \times V$ where $|F| \leq k$, whether the pruned NCD N^F with the weight assignment W^F (as defined in Definition 3) satisfies that the network N^F is connected and every flow assignment is feasible (in case of the pessimistic case) or there exists a feasible flow assignment (in case of the optimistic case). As these problems are decidable in polynomial time for PN, PS and OS, we can conclude that the variants of the problems with failures belong to the complexity class co-NP: for the negation of the problems we can guess the failure scenario F for which the problem does not have a solution—this can be verified in polynomial time by Theorems 1 and 3.

Theorem 4. *The PN, PS and OS problems with link failures are in co-NP.*

Finally, the same arguments can be used also for the optimistic nonsplittable problem with failures. However, as deciding the ON problem without failures is solvable only in nondeterministic polynomial time, the extra quantification of all failure scenarios means that the problem belongs to the class Π_2^P on the second level of the polynomial hierarchy [33]. This complexity class is believed to be computationally more difficult than the problems on the first level of the hierarchy (where the NP and co-NP problems belong to).

Theorem 5. *The ON problem with link failures is in the complexity class Π_2^P.*

Complexity Lower Bounds. We now prove the complexity lower bounds.

Theorem 6. *The OS capacity problem without any link failures is P-hard under NC-reducibility.*

Proof sketch. By NC-reduction from the P-complete maximum flow problem for directed acyclic graphs [35]: given a directed acyclic graph G with nonnegative edge capacities, two nodes s and t and a number m, is there a flow between s and t that preserves the capacity of all edges and has the volume of at least m? This problem can be rephrased as our OS problem by setting the demand $D(s,t) = m$ and defining a weight assignment so that every relevant edge in G is on some shortest path from s to t. This can be achieved by topologically sorting the nodes (in NC^2 [11,12]) and assigning the weights accordingly. □

Theorem 7. *The PS/PN problems without any link failures are NL-hard.*

Proof sketch. Follows from NL-hardness of reachability in digraphs [33]. □

Next, we show that the ON problem is NP-hard, even with no failures.

Theorem 8. *The ON capacity problem without any link failures is NP-hard, even for the case where all weights are equal to 1.*

Proof. By a polynomial-time reduction from the NP-complete problem CNF-SAT [33]. Let $\varphi = c_1 \wedge c_2 \wedge \ldots \wedge c_n$ be a CNF-SAT instance where every clause c_i, $1 \leq i \leq n$, is a disjunction of literals. A literal is either a variable $x_1, \ldots, x_k$ or its negation $\overline{x}_1, \ldots, \overline{x}_k$. If a literal $\ell_j \in \{x_j, \overline{x}_j\}$ appears in the disjunction for the clause c_i, we write $\ell_j \in c_i$. A formula φ is *satisfiable* if there is an assignment of the variables $x_1, \ldots, x_k$ to true or false, so that the formula φ is satisfied (evaluates to true under this assignment). For a given formula φ we now construct an NCD $N = (V, C, D)$ where

- $V = \{s_0, s_1, \ldots, s_k\} \cup \{x_1, \ldots, x_k\} \cup \{\overline{x}_1, \ldots, \overline{x}_k\} \cup \{c_i^s, c_i^e \mid 1 \leq i \leq n\}$,
- $C(s_{i-1}, x_i) = C(s_{i-1}, \overline{x}_i) = C(x_i, s_i) = C(\overline{x}_i, s_i) = n$ for all i, $1 \leq i \leq k$,
- $C(c_i^s, \ell_j) = C(s_j, c_i^e) = 1$ for all i, $1 \leq i \leq n$ and every literal $\ell_j \in \{x_j, \overline{x}_j\}$ such that $\ell_j \in c_i$,
- $D(s_0, s_k) = n$, and $D(c_i^s, c_i^e) = 1$ for all i, $1 \leq i \leq n$.

The capacities of edges and flow demands that are not mentioned above are all set to 0 and the weights of all edges are equal to 1. In Figure 4a we give an example of the reduction for a given satisfiable formula. As we consider the nonsplittable problem, the flow demand from s_0 to s_k means that the whole demand of n units must go through either the link (x_i, s_i) or $(\overline{x}_i, s_i)$, for every i. This corresponds to choosing an assignment of the variables to true or false. For every clause c_i we now have a unit flow from c_i^s to c_i^e that goes through the link (ℓ_j, s_j) for every literal ℓ_j appearing in the clause c_i. This is only possible if this link is not already occupied by the flow demand from s_0 to s_k; otherwise we exceed the capacity of the link. For each clause c_i we need to find at least one literal ℓ_j so that the flow can go through the edge (ℓ_j, s_j). As the capacity of the edge (ℓ_j, s_j) is n, it is possible to use this edge for all n clauses if necessary. We can observe that the capacity network can be constructed in polynomial time and we shall argue for the correctness of the reduction.

We can now observe that if φ is satisfiable, we can define a feasible flow assignment f by routing the flow demand of n between s_0 and s_k so that it does

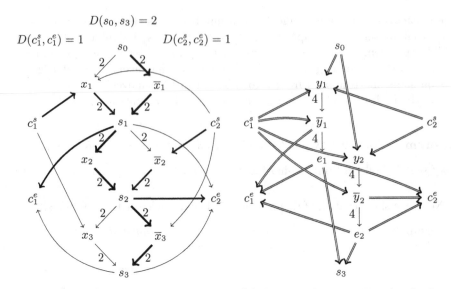

(a) NCD for the formula $(x_1 \lor x_3) \land (x_1 \lor \overline{x}_2 \lor \overline{x}_3)$. The capacity of unlabelled links is 1, otherwise 2; link weights are 1. Thick lines show a feasible nonsplittable flow assignment.

(b) Additional construction for the formula $\forall y_1, y_2.\ \exists x_1, x_2, x_3.\ (x_1 \lor x_3 \lor y_1 \lor \overline{y}_1 \lor \overline{y}_2) \land (x_1 \lor \overline{x}_2 \lor \overline{x}_3 \lor y_2)$. Capacity of all links is 4 and weight of links is 1. Double arrows are 2-unbreakable links.

(c) Definition of m-unbreakable link of capacity n with $m + 1$ intermediate nodes

Fig. 4: Reduction to ON capacity problem without/with failures

not use the links corresponding to the satisfying assignment for φ and then every clause in φ can be routed through the links corresponding to one of the satisfied literals. For the other direction where φ is not satisfieable, we notice that any routing of the flow demand between s_0 and s_k (corresponding to some truth assignment of φ) leaves at least one clause unsatisfied and it is then impossible to route the flow for such a clause without violating the capacity constraints. □

We now extend the reduction from Theorem 8 to the OS case with link failures and prove its hardness for the second level of the polynomial hierarchy.

Theorem 9. *The ON problem with link failures is Π_2^P-hard.*

Proof. By reduction from the validity of the quantified Boolean formula of the form $\forall y_1, y_2, \ldots, y_m.\ \exists x_1, x_2, \ldots, x_k.\ \varphi$ where $\varphi = c_1 \land c_2 \land \ldots \land c_n$ is a Boolean formula in CNF over the variables $y_1, \ldots, y_m, x_1, \ldots, x_k$. The validity problem of such quantified formula is Π_2^P-hard (see e.g. [33]). For a given quantified formula, we shall construct an instance of the ON problem such that the formula is valid if and only if the ON problem with up to m link failures (where m is the number of y-variables) has a positive answer. The reduction uses the construction from Theorem 8 where we described a reduction from the validity of the formula $\exists x_1, x_2, \ldots, x_k. \varphi$. The construction is further enhanced by introducing new nodes $y_j, \overline{y}_j, e_j$ and new edges of capacity $2n$ (where n is the number of clauses) such that $C(y_j, \overline{y}_j) = C(\overline{y}_j, e_j) = 2n$, for all i, $1 \leq j \leq m$.

Now for every clause c_i we add the so-called m-unbreakable edge of capacity n from c_i^s to y_j and from e_j to c_i^e for all $1 \leq i \leq n$ and $1 \leq j \leq m$. Moreover, whenever the literal y_j appears in the clause c_i, we also add an m-unbreakable edge from $\overline{y}_j$ to c_i^e and whenever the literal $\overline{y}_j$ appears in the clause c_i, we add m-unbreakable edge from c_i^s to $\overline{y}_j$. The construction of m-unbreakable edges (denoted by double arrows) is given in Figure 4c where the capacity of each link is set to n. Finally, for each j, $1 \leq j \leq m$, we add the unbreakable edges from s_1 to y_j and from e_j to s_k. The flow demands in the newly constructed network are identical to those from the proof of Theorem 8 and the weights of all newly added edges are set to 1 and we set the weight of the two links s_0 to x_1 and s_0 to $\overline{x}_1$ to 6. The reduction can be clearly done in polynomial time. Figure 4b demonstrates an extension of the construction from Figure 4a with additional nodes and links that complete the reduction. Observe, that even in case of m link failures, the unbreakable links that consist of $m + 1$ edge disjoint paths are still capable of carrying all the necessary flow traffic.

We shall now argue that if the formula $\forall y_1, y_2, \ldots, y_m. \exists x_1, x_2, \ldots, x_k. \varphi$ is valid then the constructed instance of the ON problem with up to m link failures has a solution. We notice that any subset of up to m failed links either breaks exactly one of the newly added edges $(y_j, \overline{y}_j)$ and $(\overline{y}_j, e_j)$ for all j, $1 \leq j \leq m$, in which case this determines a valid truth assignment for the y-variables and as in the previous proof, the flow from s_0 to s_k can now be routed so that for each clause there is at least one satisfied literal. Otherwise, there is a variable y_j such that both of the edges $(y_j, \overline{y}_j)$ and $(\overline{y}_j, e_j)$ are present and all flow demands can now be routed through these two edges (that have sufficient capacity for this) by using the m-unbreakable edges. The opposite direction where the formula is not valid means that there is a truth assignment to the y-variables so that irrelevant of the assignment for x-variables there is at least one clause that is not satisfied. We simply fail the edges that correspond to such a y-variables assigment and the same arguments as in the previous proof imply that there is not any feasible flow assignment for this failure scenario. $\square$

Theorem 10. *The PN, PS and OS problems with link failures are co-NP-hard.*

Proof sketch. By reduction from the NP-complete *shortest path most vital edges* problem (SP-MVE) [3,36]. The input to SP-MVE is a directed graph $G = (V, E)$ with positive edge weights, two nodes $s, t \in V$ and two positive numbers k and

---

Algorithm 2 Brute-force search

1: **Input:** NCD $N = (V, C, D)$ with weigth assignment W, a number $k \geq 0$ and type
   of the capacity problem $\tau \in \{\text{PS}, \text{PN}, \text{ON}, \text{OS}\}$
2: **Output:** *true* if the answer to the τ-problem is positive, else *false*
3: **for all** $F \subseteq V \times V$ s.t. $|F| \leq k$ and $C(v, v') > 0$ for all $(v, v') \in F$ **do**
4:     construct network N^F and weight assignment W^F by Definition 3
5:     **switch** τ **do**
6:         **case** OS: use Theorem 1 on N^F and W^F (without failed links)
7:         **case** ON: use Theorem 2 on N^F and W^F (without failed links)
8:         **case** PS/PN: use Theorem 3 on N^F and W^F (without failed links)
9:     **if** the answer to the τ-problem on N^F and W^F is negative **then return** *false*
10: **endfor**
11: **return** *true*

H. The question is whether there exist at most k edges in E such that their removal creates a graph with the length of the shortest path between s and t being at least H. We reduce the SP-MVE to the negation of the PN/PS in order to demonstrate co-NP-hardness.

We modify the G by inserting a new edge between s and t of weight H and capacity 1, while setting the capacity 2 for all other edges in G. If the SP-MVE problem has a solution $F \subseteq E$ where $|F| \leq k$, then the added edge (s, t) becomes one of the shortest paths between s and t under the failure scenario F and a flow demand of size 2 between s and t can be routed through this edge, violating the capacity constraints. If the SP-MVE problem does not have a solution, then after the removal of at most k links, the length of the shortest path between s and t remains strictly less than H and any flow assignment along the shortest paths is feasible. We hence conclude that PN/PS problems are co-NP-hard. A small modification of the construction is needed for hardness of the OS problem. $\square$

4   A Fast Strategic Search Algorithm

In order to solve the PS, PN, ON and OS problems, we can enumerate all failure scenarios for up to k failed links (omitting the links with zero capacity), construct the pruned network for each such failure scenario and then apply our algorithms in Theorems 1, 2 and 3. This brute-force search approach is formalized in Algorithm 2 and its worst-case running time is exponential.

Our complexity results indicate that the exponential behavior of any algorithm solving a co-NP-hard (or even Π_2^P-hard) problem is unavoidable (unless P=NP). However, in practice many concrete instances can be solved fast if more refined search algorithms are used. To demonstrate this, we present a novel strategic search algorithm for verifying the feasibility of shortest path routing under failures. At the heart of our algorithm lies the idea to reduce the number of explored failure scenarios by skipping the "uninteresting" ones. Let us fix an NCD $N = (V, C, D)$ with the weight assignment W. We define a relation $\prec$ on failure scenarios such that $F \prec F'$ iff for all flow demands we preserve in F' at least one of the shortest paths that are present under the failure scenario F.

Definition 9. *Let $F, F' \in V \times V$. We say that F preceeds F', written $F \prec F'$, if $SPaths^F(s,t) \supseteq SPaths^{F'}(s,t)$ and $SPaths^F(s,t) \cap SPaths^{F'}(s,t) \neq \emptyset$ for all $s,t \in V$ where $D(s,t) > 0$.*

We first show that if $F \prec F'$ and the failure scenario F has a feasible routing solution for the pessimistic problem, then F' also has a solution. Thus instead of exploring all possible failure scenarios like in the brute-force algorithm, it is sufficient to explore only failure scenarios that are minimal w.r.t. $\prec$ relation.

Lemma 3. *Let $F, F' \in V \times V$ where $F \prec F'$. A positive answer to the PS/PN problem for the network N^F with weight assignment W^F implies a positive answer to the PS/PN problem for the network $N^{F'}$ with weight assignment $W^{F'}$.*

For the optimistic scenario, the implication is valid in the opposite direction: it is sufficient to explore only the maximum failure scenarios w.r.t. $\prec$.

Lemma 4. *Let $F, F' \in V \times V$ where $F \prec F'$. A positive answer to the OS/ON problem for the network $N^{F'}$ with weight assignment $W^{F'}$ implies a positive answer to the OS/ON problem for the network N^F with weight assignment W^F.*

Hence for the pessimistic scenario, the idea of strategic search is to ignore failure scenarios that remove only some of the shortest paths but preserve at least one of such shortest paths. For the optimistic scenario, we on the other hand explore only the maximal failure scenarios where removing one additional link causes the removal of all shortest paths for at least one source and destination.

In our algorithm, we use the notation $spg_F^{s,t}$ for the shortest path graph as defined in Algorithm 1 for the input graph N^F with weight assignment W^F. The function $min\_cuts(spg_F^{s,t}, s, t)$ returns the set of all minimum cuts separating the nodes s and t (sets of edges that disconnect the source node s from the target node t in the shortest-path graph $spg_F^{s,t}$). This function can be computed e.g. using the Provan and Shier algorithm [34], assuming that each edge has a unit weight and hence minimizing the number of edges in the minimum cut. There can be several incomparable minimum cuts (with the same number of edges) and by $mincut\_size(spg_F^{s,t}, s, t)$ we denote the number of edges in each the minimum cuts from the set $min\_cuts(spg_F^{s,t}, s, t)$.

Algorithm 3 now presents our fast search strategy, called *strategic search*. The input to the algorithm is the same as for the brute-force search. The algorithm initializes the *pending* set of failure scenarios to be explored to the empty failure scenario and it remembers the set of *passed* failure scenarios that were already verified. In the main while loop, a failure scenario F is removed from the *pending* set and depending on the type τ of the problem, we either directly verify the scenario F in the case of the pessimistic problems, or we call the function *MaxFailureCheck(F)* that instead verifies all maximal failure scenarios F' such that $F \prec F'$. The correctness of Algorithm 3 is formally stated as follows.

Theorem 11. *Algorithm 3 terminates and returns true iff the answer to the τ-problem is positive.*

Algorithm 3 Strategic search

1: **Input:** NCD $N = (V, C, D)$ with weigth assignment W, a number $k \geq 0$ and type of capacity problem $\tau \in \{PS, PN, ON, OS\}$
2: **Output:** *true* if the answer to the τ-problem is positive, else *false*
3: $pending := \{\emptyset\}$ * initialize the pending set with the empty failure scenario *\\
4: $passed := \emptyset$ * already processed failure scenarios *\\
5: **while** $pending \neq \emptyset$ **do**
6:    let $F \in pending$; $pending := pending \setminus \{F\}$
7:    **switch** τ **do**
8:       **case** $\tau \in \{PS, PN\}$: Build N^F and W^F by Definition 3, use Theorem 3
9:          **if** the answer to the τ-problem was negative **then return** *false*
10:      **case** $\tau \in \{OS, ON\}$: **call** *MaxFailureCheck(F)*
11:    $passed := passed \cup \{F\}$
12:    **for** $s, t \in V$ such that $D(s, t) > 0$ **do**
13:       **if** $|F| + mincut\_size(spg_F^{s,t}, s, t) \leq k$ **then**
14:          $succ := \{F \cup C \mid C \in min\_cuts(spg_F^{s,t}, s, t), F \cup C \notin (pending \cup passed)\}$
15:          $pending := pending \cup succ$
16: **endwhile**
17: **return** *true*
18:
19: **procedure** *MaxFailureCheck(F)*   * to be run only for the optimistic cases *\\
20: **for** $s, t \in V$ such that $D(s, t) > 0$ **do**
21:    **for** $C \in min\_cuts(spg_F^{s,t}, s, t)$ **do**
22:       **for all** $C' \subset C$ such that $|F \cup C'| = \min(k, |F \cup C| - 1)$ **do**
23:          **if** $F \cup C' \notin passed$ **then**
24:             construct $N^{F \cup C'}$ and $W^{F \cup C'}$ by Definition 3
25:             **switch** τ **do**
26:                **case** $\tau = OS$: use Theorem 1 and **if** negative **then return** *false*
27:                **case** $\tau = ON$: use Theorem 2 and **if** negative **then return** *false*
28:             $passed := passed \cup \{F \cup C'\}$
29:       **endfor**
30:    **endfor**
31: **endfor**

---

5   Experiments

To evaluate the practical performance of our strategic search algorithms, we conducted experiments on various wide-area and datacenter network topologies. The reproducibility package with our Python implementation can be found at [37].

We study the algorithms' performance on a range of network topologies, and consider both sparse and irregular wide-area networks (using the Internet Topology Zoo [28] data set) as well as dense and regular datacenter topologies (namely fat-tree [9], BCube [23], and Xpander [40]). To model demands, for each topology, we consider certain nodes to serve as core nodes which have significant pairwise demands. Overall, we created 24,388 problem instances for our experimental benchmark, out of which we were able to solve 23,934 instances

Topology	Problem	B.iter	B.time	S.iter	S.time	Speedup
BCube	ON	105	79.5	1	1.7	47.1
BCube	OS	2081	348.2	768	125.1	2.8
BCube	PS/PN	5051	170.0	1	0.1	4684.0
Fat-tree	ON	105	59.4	1	1.2	47.6
Fat-tree	OS	41	2.0	1	0.2	8.5
Fat-tree	PS/PN	43745	562.6	1	0.1	66976.3
Xpander	ON	254	407.3	1	3.0	137.7
Xpander	OS	170	124.1	1	1.6	78.0
Xpander	PS/PN	-	>7200.0	1	5.4	>1340.6
Topology Zoo	ON	127	59.6	8	4.6	12.9
Topology Zoo	OS	596	35.3	46	2.6	13.4
Topology Zoo	PS/PN	86	4.3	2	0.1	82.7

Fig. 5: Median results, time in seconds (**B**: brute-force search, **S**: strategic search)

within a 2-hour timeout. In our evaluation, we filter out the trivial instances where the runtime is less than 0.1 second for both the brute-force and strategic search (as some of the instances e.g. contain a disconnected flow demand already without any failed links). The benchmark contains a mixture of both positive and negative instances for each problem for increasing number k of failed links.

Table 5 shows the median times for each series of experiments for the different scenarios. All experiments for each topology and given problem instance are sorted by the speedup ratio, i.e. B.time divided by S.time; we display the result for the experiment in the middle of each table. Clearly, our strategic search algorithm always outperforms the brute-force one by a significant factor in all the scenarios. We also report on the number of iterations (B.iter and S.iter) of the two algorithms, showing the number of failure scenarios to be explored.

Let us first discuss the pessimistic scenarios in more detail. Figure 6 shows a cactus plot [6] for the wide-area network setting (on the left) and for the data-center setting (on the right). We note that y-axis in the figure is logarithmic. For example, to solve the 1500th fastest instances in the wide-area network (left), the brute-force algorithm uses more than 100 seconds, while the strategic algorithm solves the problem in less than a second; this corresponds to a speedup of more than two orders of magnitude. For more difficult instances, the difference in runtime continues to grow exponentially, and becomes several orders of magnitude. For datacenter networks (right), the difference is even larger. The latter can be explained by the fact that datacenters provide a higher path diversity and multiple shortest paths between source and target nodes and hence more opportunities for a clever skipping of "uninteresting instances". As the pessimistic problems we aim to solve are co-NP-hard, there are necessarily some hard instances also for our strategic search; this is demonstrated by the S-shaped curve showing a significantly increased runtime for the most difficult instances.

We next discuss the optimistic scenarios, including the experiments both for splittable and nonsplittable cases. Figure 7 shows a cactus plot for the wide-area

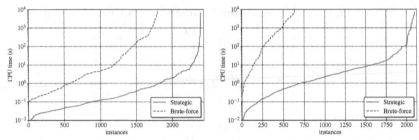

Fig. 6: Pessimistic scenario. Left: wide-area networks, right: datacenter networks

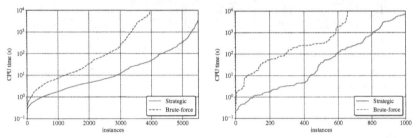

Fig. 7: Optimistic scenario. Left: wide-area networks, right: datacenter networks

network setting (on the left) and for the datacenter setting (on the right). Again, our strategic algorithm significantly outperforms the baseline in both scenarios. Interestingly, in the optimistic scenario, the relative performance benefit is larger for wide-area networks as the optimistic strategic search explores all the maximum failure scenarios and there are significantly more of such scenarios in the highly connected datacenter topologies. Hence, while for datacenters (right) the strategic search maintains about one order of magnitude better performance, the performance for the wide-area networks improves exponentially.

6   Conclusion

We presented a comprehensive study of the algorithmic complexity of verifying feasible routes under failures without violating capacity constraints, covering both optimistic and pessimistic, as well as splittable and nonsplittable scenarios. We further presented algorithms, based on strategic failure scenario enumerations, which we proved efficient in realistic scenarios. While our paper charts the complete landscape, there remain several interesting avenues for future research like further scalability improvements and a parallelization of the algorithm.

Acknowledgements. Research supported by the Vienna Science and Technology Fund (WWTF) project ICT19-045 and by the DFF project QASNET.

References

1. Carolyn Jane Anderson, Nate Foster, Arjun Guha, Jean-Baptiste Jeannin, Dexter Kozen, Cole Schlesinger, and David Walker. Netkat: Semantic foundations for networks. *Acm sigplan notices*, 49(1):113–126, 2014.
2. Ron Banner and Ariel Orda. Multipath routing algorithms for congestion minimization. In *IEEE/ACM Transactions on Networking (TON)*, volume 15, pages 92–122, 02 2005.
3. Cristina Bazgan, André Nichterlein, and Rolf Niedermeier. A refined complexity analysis of finding the most vital edges for undirected shortest paths. In Vangelis Th. Paschos and Peter Widmayer, editors, *International Conference on Algorithms and Complexity*, volume 9079 of *LNCS*, pages 47–60. Springer, 2015.
4. Ryan Beckett, Ratul Mahajan, Todd Millstein, Jitendra Padhye, and David Walker. Don't mind the gap: Bridging network-wide objectives and device-level configurations. In *Proceedings of the 2016 ACM SIGCOMM Conference*, pages 328–341, 2016.
5. Y. Bi, C. W. Tan, and A. Tang. Network utility maximization with path cardinality constraints,. In *Proceedings of the 35th Annual IEEE International Conference on Computer Communications (IEEE INFOCOM 2016)*, 2016.
6. Martin Nyx Brain, James H. Davenport, and Alberto Griggio. Benchmarking solvers, SAT-style. In *Proceedings of the 2nd International Workshop on Satisfiability Checking and Symbolic Computation co-located with the 42nd International Symposium on Symbolic and Algebraic Computation (ISSAC'17)*, volume 1974 of *CEUR*, pages 1–15. CEUR-WS.org, 2017.
7. Zhiruo Cao, Zheng Wang, and Ellen Zegura. Performance of hashing-based schemes for internet load balancing. In *Proceedings of IEEE INFOCOM 2000.*, volume 1, pages 332–341. IEEE, 2000.
8. Yiyang Chang, Chuan Jiang, Ashish Chandra, Sanjay Rao, and Mohit Tawarmalani. Lancet: Better network resilience by designing for pruned. *SIGMETRICS Perform. Eval. Rev.*, 48(1):53–54, July 2020.
9. Charles E. Leiserson. Fat-trees: Universal networks for hardware-efficient supercomputing. volume 34, pages 892–901, 1985.
10. M. Chiesa, G. Kindler, and M. Schapira. Traffic engineering with equal-cost-multipath: An algorithmic perspective,. In *IEEE/ACM Transactions on Networking, vol. 25, no. 2, pp. 779-792*, 2017.
11. Stephen A. Cook. A taxonomy of problems with fast parallel algorithms. *Information and Control*, 64(1):2 – 22, 1985.
12. Eliezer Dekel, David Nassimi, and Sartaj Sahni. Parallel matrix and graph algorithms. *SIAM Journal on Computing*, 10(4):657–675, 1981.
13. Camil Demetrescu, Mikkel Thorup, Rezaul Chowdhury, and Vijaya Ramachandran. Oracles for distances avoiding a failed node or link. *SIAM J. Comput.*, 37:1299–1318, 01 2008.
14. Jack Edmonds and Richard M. Karp. Theoretical improvements in algorithmic efficiency for network flow problems. 19(2):248–264, 1972.
15. Ahmed El-Hassany, Petar Tsankov, Laurent Vanbever, and Martin Vechev. Network-wide configuration synthesis. In *International Conference on Computer Aided Verification*, pages 261–281. Springer, 2017.
16. Bernard Fortz. Internet traffic engineering by optimizing OSPF weights. In *in Proc. IEEE INFOCOM*, pages 519–528, 2000.

17. Bernard Fortz, Jennifer Rexford, and Mikkel Thorup. Traffic engineering with traditional IP routing protocols. *IEEE Comm. Magazine*, 40(10):118–124, 2002.
18. Bernard Fortz and Mikkel Thorup. Optimizing OSPF/IS-IS weights in a changing world. *IEEE Journal on Selected Areas in Communications (JSAC)*, 20(4):756–767, 2002.
19. Bernard Fortz and Mikkel Thorup. Increasing internet capacity using local search. *Computational Optimization and Applications*, 29(1):13–48, 2004.
20. Nate Foster, Dexter Kozen, Konstantinos Mamouras, Mark Reitblatt, and Alexandra Silva. Probabilistic NetKAT. In Peter Thiemann, editor, *Programming Languages and Systems (ESOP'16)*, volume 9632 of *LNCS*, pages 282–309. Springer, 2016.
21. Pierre Francois, Clarence Filsfils, John Evans, and Olivier Bonaventure. Achieving sub-second igp convergence in large IP networks. *ACM SIGCOMM Computer Communication Review*, 35(3):35–44, 2005.
22. Albert Greenberg, James R Hamilton, Navendu Jain, Srikanth Kandula, Changhoon Kim, Parantap Lahiri, David A Maltz, Parveen Patel, and Sudipta Sengupta. Vl2: a scalable and flexible data center network. In *Proceedings of the ACM SIGCOMM 2009 conference on Data communication*, pages 51–62, 2009.
23. Chuanxiong Guo, Guohan Lu, Dan Li, Haitao Wu, Xuan Zhang, Yunfeng Shi, Chen Tian, Yongguang Zhang, Songwu Lu, and Guohan Lv. Bcube: A high performance, server-centric network architecture for modular data centers. In *ACM SIGCOMM*. Association for Computing Machinery, Inc., August 2009.
24. Christian Hopps et al. Analysis of an equal-cost multi-path algorithm. Technical report, RFC 2992, November, 2000.
25. Jesper Stenbjerg Jensen, Troels Beck Krøgh, Jonas Sand Madsen, Stefan Schmid, Jiří Srba, and Marc Tom Thorgersen. P-Rex: Fast verification of MPLS networks with multiple link failures. In *Proc. 14th International Conference on emerging Networking EXperiments and Technologies (CoNEXT)*, pages 217–227, 2018.
26. P.G. Jensen, D. Kristiansen, S. Schmid, M.K. Schou, B.C. Schrenk, and J. Srba. Aalwines: A fast and quantitative what-if analysis tool for mpls networks. In *Proceedings of the 16th International Conference on Emerging Networking EXperiments and Technologies (CoNEXT'20)*, pages 474–481. ACM, 2020.
27. Donald B. Johnson. Efficient algorithms for shortest paths in sparse networks. *Journal of ACM*, 24(1):1–13, 1977.
28. Simon Knight, Hung Nguyen, Nickolas Falkner, Rhys Bowden, and Matthew Roughan. The internet topology Zoo. *Selected Areas in Communications, IEEE Journal on*, 29:1765 – 1775, 11 2011.
29. Kim G. Larsen, Stefan Schmid, and Bingtian Xue. WNetKAT: A weighted SDN programming and verification language. In *Proc. 20th International Conference on Principles of Distributed Systems (OPODIS)*, 2016.
30. John Moy et al. OSPF version 2. 1998.
31. Sebastian Orlowski and Michal Pioro. Complexity of column generation in network design with path-based survivability mechanism. *Networks*, 59:132 – 147, 01 2012.
32. Aurojit Panda, Ori Lahav, Katerina Argyraki, Mooly Sagiv, and Scott Shenker. Verifying reachability in networks with mutable datapaths. In *14th USENIX Symposium on Networked Systems Design and Implementation (NSDI'17)*, pages 699–718, 2017.
33. Christos M. Papadimitriou. *Computational complexity*. Addison-Wesley, Reading, Massachusetts, 1994.
34. J. S. Provan and D. R. Shier. A paradigm for listing (s, t)-cuts in graphs. *Algorithmica*, 15(4):351–372, apr 1996.

35. V. Ramachandran. The complexity of minimum cut and maximum flow problems in an acyclic network. 17(4):387–392, 1987.
36. Baruch Schieber, Amotz Bar-Noy, and Samir Khuller. The complexity of finding most vital arcs and nodes. Technical report, USA, 1995.
37. S. Schmid, N. Schnepf, and J. Srba. Reproducibility Package for TACAS'21 Paper Resilient Capacity-Aware Routing, January 2021. https://doi.org/10.5281/zenodo.4421365.
38. S. Schmid and J. Srba. Polynomial-time what-if analysis for prefix-manipulating MPLS networks. In *Proc. IEEE INFOCOM*, pages 1799–1807. IEEE, 2018.
39. Alexander Schrijver. *Theory of Linear and Integer Programming*. John Wiley & Sons, Inc., USA, 1986.
40. A. Valadarsky, G. Shahaf, M. Dinitz, and M. Schapira. Xpander: Towards optimal-performance datacenters. In *CoNEXT*, pages 205–219. ACM, 2016.
41. Yaron Velner, Kalev Alpernas, Aurojit Panda, Alexander Rabinovich, Mooly Sagiv, Scott Shenker, and Sharon Shoham. Some complexity results for stateful network verification. In *Proc. of TACAS'16*, pages 811–830. Springer, 2016.

Network Traffic Classification by Program Synthesis

Lei Shi[1]✉, Yahui Li[2], Boon Thau Loo[1], and Rajeev Alur[1]

[1] University of Pennsylvania, Philadelphia PA 19104, USA
{shilei,boonloo,alur}@seas.upenn.edu
[2] Tsinghua University, Beijing, China
li-yh15@mails.tsinghua.edu.cn

Abstract. Writing classification rules to identify interesting network traffic is a time-consuming and error-prone task. Learning-based classification systems automatically extract such rules from positive and negative traffic examples. However, due to limitations in the representation of network traffic and the learning strategy, these systems lack both expressiveness to cover a range of applications and interpretability in fully describing the traffic's structure at the session layer. This paper presents Sharingan system, which uses program synthesis techniques to generate network classification programs at the session layer. Sharingan accepts raw network traces as inputs and reports potential patterns of the target traffic in NetQRE, a domain specific language designed for specifying session-layer quantitative properties. We develop a range of novel optimizations that reduce the synthesis time for large and complex tasks to a matter of minutes. Our experiments show that Sharingan is able to correctly identify patterns from a diverse set of network traces and generates explainable outputs, while achieving accuracy comparable to state-of-the-art learning-based systems.

Keywords: Program synthesis · Network traffic analysis · Supervised learning.

1 Introduction

Network monitoring systems are essential for network infrastructure management. These systems require classification of network traffic at their core. Today, network operators and equipment vendors write classification programs or patterns upfront in order to differentiate target flows such as attacks or undesired application traffic from normal ones. The process of writing these classification programs often requires deep operator insights, can be error prone, and is not easy to extend to handle new scenarios.

There have been a number of recent attempts at automated generation of classifiers for malicious traffic using machine learning[16,38,5,12] and data mining[6,28,34,39,19] techniques. These classifiers have not gained much traction in production systems, in part due to unavoidable false positive reports and the

J. F. Groote and K. G. Larsen (Eds.): TACAS 2021, LNCS 12651, pp. 430–448, 2021.
https://doi.org/10.1007/978-3-030-72016-2_23

gap between the learning output and explainable operational insights[31]. The challenges call for a more expressive, interpretable and maintainable learning-based classification system.

To be specific, such challenges first come from the extra difficulties learning-based systems face in network applications compared to traditional use cases such as recommendation systems, spam mail filtering or OCR [31]. Misclassifications in network systems have tangible cost such as the need for operators to manually verify potential false reports. Due to the diverse nature and large data volumes of networks in production environments, entirely avoiding these costly mistakes by one training stage is unlikely. Therefore explainability and maintainability plays a core role in a usable learning system.

Properly representing network traffic and learnt patterns is another major difficulty. As a data point for classification purposes, a network trace is a sequence of packets of varying lengths listed in increasing timestamp order. Existing approaches frequently compress it into a regular expression or a feature vector for input. Such compression will eliminate session-layer details and intermediate states in network protocols, making it hard to learn application-layer protocols or multi-stage transactions. These representations also require laborious task-specific feature engineering to get effective learning results, which undermines the systems' advantages of automation. It can also be hard to interpret the learning results to understand the intent and structure of the traffic, due to the blackbox model of many machine-learning approaches and the lack of expressiveness in the inputs and outputs to these learning systems.

To address the above limitations, we introduce Sharingan, which uses program synthesis techniques to auto-generate network classification programs from labeled examples of network traffic traces. Sharingan aims to bridge the gap between learning systems and operator insights, by identifying properties of the traffic that can help inform the network operators on its nature, and provide a basis for automated generation of the classification rules. Sharingan does not aim to outperform state-of-the-art learning systems in accuracy, but rather match their accuracy, while generating output that is more explainable and easier to maintain.

To achieve these goals, we adopt techniques from *syntax guided program synthesis* [1] to generate a NetQRE [37] program that distinguishes the positive and negative examples. NetQRE, which stands for Network *Quantitative Regular Expressions*, enables quantitative queries for network traffic, based on flow-level regular pattern matching. Given an input network trace, a NetQRE program generates a numerical value that quantifies the matching of the trace with the described pattern. The classification is done by comparing the synthesized program's output for each example with a learnt threshold T. Positive examples fall above T. The synthesized NetQRE program serves the role of network classifier, identifying flows which match the program specifications.

Sharingan has the following key advantages over prior approaches, which either rely on keyword and regular expression generation [6,28,34,39,19] or statistical traffic analysis [16,38,5,12].

Requires minimal feature engineering: NetQRE [37] is an expressive language, and allows succinct description of a wide range of tasks ranging from detecting security attacks to enforcing application-layer network management policies. Sharingan can synthesize any network task on raw traffic expressible as a NetQRE program, without any additional feature engineering. This is an improvement over systems based on manually extracted feature vectors. Also, one outstanding feature of search-based program synthesis is that the only a priori knowledge it needs is information about the language itself. No task-specific heuristics are required.

Efficient implementation: The NetQRE program synthesized by Sharingan can be compiled, as has been shown in prior work [37], to efficient low-level implementations that can be integrated into routers and other network devices. On the other hand, traditional statistical classifiers are not directly usable or executable in network filtering systems.

Easy to decipher and edit: Finally, Sharingan generates NetQRE programs that can be read and edited. Since they are generic executable programs with high expressiveness, the patterns in the program reveal the stateful protocol structure that is used for the classification, which blackbox statistical models, packet-level regular expressions and feature vectors have difficulty describing. The programs are also amenable to calibration by a network operator, for example, to mix in local policies or debug.

The key technical challenge in design and implementation of Sharingan is the computationally demanding problem of finding a NetQRE expression that is able to separate positive network traffic examples from the negative ones. This search problem is an instance of the *syntax-guided synthesis*. While this problem has received a lot of attention in recent years, no existing tools and techniques can solve the instances of interest in our context due to the unique semantics of NetQRE programs, the complexity of the expressions to be synthesized and the scale of the data set of network traffic examples used in training. To address this challenge, we devised two novel techniques for optimizing the search – *partial execution* and *merge search*, which effectively achieve orders of magnitude reduction in synthesis time. We summarize our key contributions:

Synthesis-based classification architecture. We propose the methodology of reducing a network traffic classification problem to a synthesis from examples instance.

Efficient synthesis algorithm We devise two efficient algorithms: *partial execution* and *merge search*, which efficiently explore the program space and enable learning from very large data sets. Independent of our network traffic classification use cases, these algorithms advance the state-of-the-art in program synthesis.

Implementation and evaluation. We have implemented Sharingan and evaluated it for a rich set of metrics using the CICIDS2017 [25,7] intrusion detection benchmark database. Sharingan is able to synthesize a large range of network classification programs in a matter of minutes with accuracy comparable to state-of-the-art systems. Moreover, the generated NetQRE program is easy to interpret, tune, and can be compiled into configurations usable by existing network monitoring systems.

2 Overview

Sharingan's workflow is largely similar to a statistical supervised learning system, although the underlying mechanism is different. Sharingan takes labeled positive and negative network traces as input and outputs a classifier that can classify any new incoming trace. To preserve most of the information from input data and minimize the need for feature engineering, Sharingan considers three kinds of properties in a network trace: (1) all available packet-level header fields, (2) position information of each packet within the sequence, and (3) time information associated with each packet.

Specifically, Sharingan represents a network trace as a stream of feature vectors: $S = v_0, v_1, v_2, \ldots$. Each vector represents a packet. Vectors are listed in timestamp order. Contents of the vector are parsed field values of that packet. For example, we can define

$v[0] = ip.src$, $v[1] = tcp.sport$, $v[2] = ip.dst, \ldots$

Depending on the information available, different sets of fields can be used to represent a packet. By default, we extract all header fields at the TCP/IP level. To make use of the timestamp information, we also append time interval since the previous packet in the same flow to a packet's feature vector. Feature selection is not necessary for Sharingan.

The output classifier is a NetQRE program p that takes in a stream of feature vectors. Instead of giving a probability score that the data point is positive, it outputs an integer that quantifies the matching of the stream and the pattern. The program includes a learnt threshold T. Sharingan aims to ensure that p's outputs for positive and negative traces fall on different sides of the threshold T. Comparing p's output for a data point with T generates a label. It is possible to translate p and T into executable rules using a compilation step.

Given the above usage model, a network operator can use Sharingan to generate a NetQRE program trained to distinguish normal and suspected abnormal traffic generated from unsupervised learning systems. The synthesized programs themselves, as we will later show, form the basis for deciphering each unknown trace. Consequently, traces whose patterns look interesting can be subjected to a detailed manual analysis by the network operator. Moreover, the generated NetQRE programs can be further refined and compiled into filtering system's rules.

3 Background on NetQRE

NetQRE [37] is a high-level declarative language for querying network traffic. Streams of tokenized packets are matched against regular expressions and aggregated by multiple types of quantitative aggregators. The NetQRE language is defined by the BNF grammar in Listing 1.1.

```
<classifier>::= <program> > <value>                    |  _
<program> ::= <group-by>              <pred> ::= <pred> && <pred>
<group-by> ::= (<group-by>)<op>|<              | <pred> || <pred>
    feats>                                     | [<feat> == <value>]
          | <qre>                              | [<feat> >= <value>]
<qre> ::= (<qre> <qre>)<op>                     | [<feat> <= <value>]
       | (<qre>)*<op>                          | [<feat> -> <prefix>]
       | <unit>                  <feats> ::= <feat>
<unit> ::= /<re>/                            | <feats>, <feat>
<re> ::= <re> <re>              <feat>  ::= 0 | 1 | 2 | ......
      | (<re>)*                 <op>    ::= max | min | sum
      | <pred>
```

Listing 1.1: NetQRE Grammar

As an example, if we want to find out if any single source is sending more than 100 TCP packets, the following classifier based on a NetQRE program describes the desired classifier:

```
( ( / [ip.type = TCP] / )*sum )max|ip.src_ip > 100
```

At the top level, there are two parts of the classifier. A processing program on the left that maps a network trace to an output number, and a threshold against which this value is compared on the right. They together form the classifier. Inputs fall into different classes based on the results of the comparison.

Group-by expression (<group-by>) splits the trace into sub-flows based on the value of the specified field (source IP address in this example):

```
( ............ )max|ip.src_ip
```

Packets sharing the same value in the field will be assigned to the same sub-flow. Sub-flows are processed individually, and the outputs of which are aggregated according to the aggregation operator (<op>) (maximum in this example).

In each sub-flow, we want to count the number of TCP packets. This can be broken down into three operations: (1) specifying a pattern that a single packet is a TCP packet, (2) specifying that this pattern repeats arbitrary number of times, and (3) adding 1 to a counter each time this pattern is matched.

(1) is achieved by a *plain regular expression* involving *predicates*. A predicate describes properties of a packet that can match or mismatch one packet in the trace. Four types of properties frequently used in networks can be described:

1. It equals a value. For example: [tcp.syn == 1]
2. It is not less than a value. For example: [ip.len >= 200]
3. It is not greater a value. For example: [tcp.seq <= 15]
4. It matches a prefix. For example: [ip.src_ip -> 192.168]

Predicates combined by concatenation and Kleene-star form a plain regular expression, which matches a network trace considered as a string of packets.

A *unit expression* indicates that a plain regular expression should be viewed as atomic for quantitative aggregation (in this case a single TCP packet):

```
/ [ip.type = TCP] /
```

It either matches a substring of the trace and outputs the value 1, or does not match.

To achieve (2) and (3), we need a construct to both connect the regular patterns to match the entire flow and also aggregate outputs bottom up from units at the same time. We call it *quantitative regular expression* (`<qre>`). In this example, we use the iteration operator:

```
( / [ip.type = TCP] / )*sum
```

It matches exactly like the Kleene-star operator, and at the same time, for each repetition of the sub-pattern, the sub-expression's output is aggregated by the aggregation operator. In this case, the sum is taken, which acts as a counter for the number of TCP packets. The aggregation result for this expression will in turn be returned as an output for higher-level aggregations.

The language also supports the concatenation operator:

```
(<qre> <qre>)<op>
```

which works analogous to concatenation for regular matching. It aggregates the quantity by applying the `<op>` on the outputs of two sub-expressions that match the prefix and suffix.

In addition to this core language, there is a specialization for the synthesis purpose. We observe that comparing a field with values that do not appear in any of the given examples is expensive but will not produce any meaningful information. Therefore we use the relative position in the examples' value space instead of a specific value, for example, 50% instead of 3 in value space $\{1, 3, 12, 15\}$.

4   Synthesis Algorithm

Given a set of positive and negative examples E_p and E_n, respectively, the goal of our synthesis algorithm is to derive a NetQRE program p_f and a threshold T that differentiates E_p apart from E_n. We start with notations to be used in this section:

Notation. p and q denote individual programs, and P and Q denote sets of programs. $p_1 \rightarrow p_2$ denotes it is possible to mutate p_1 following production rules in NetQRE's grammar to get p_2. The relation $\rightarrow$ is transitive. We assume the starting symbol is always `<program>`.

$p(x)$ denotes program p's output on input x, where x is a sequence of packets and $p(x)$ is a numerical value. If p is an incomplete program, i.e., if p contains some non-terminals, then $p(x) = \{q(x) \,|\, p \rightarrow q\}$ is a set of numerical values, containing x's output through all possible programs p can mutate into. We define $p(x).max$ to be the maximum value in this set. Similarly, $p(x).min$ is the minimum value.

The synthesis goal can be formally defined as: $\forall e \in E_p, p_f(e) > T$ and $\forall e \in E_n, p_f(e) < T$.

4.1   Overview

Our design needs to address two key challenges. First, NetQRE's rich grammar allows a large possible program space and many possible thresholds for search. Second, the need to check each possible program against a large data set collected from network monitoring tasks poses scalability challenge to the synthesis.

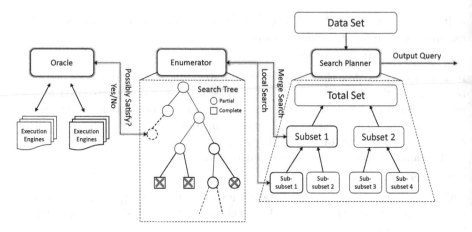

Fig. 1: Synthesizer Overview

We propose two techniques for addressing these challenges: *partial execution* (Section 4.2) and *merge search* (Section 4.3). Figure 1 shows an overview of the synthesizer.

The top-level component is the *search planner*, that assigns search tasks over subsets of the entire training data to the enumerator in a divide-and-conquer manner. Each such task is a search-based synthesis instance, where the *enumerator* enumerates all possible programs starting from s_0, expanded using the productions in NetQRE grammar, until one that can distinguish the assigned subset of E_p and E_n is found.

The *enumerator* optimizes for the first challenge by querying the distributed *oracle* about each partial program's feasibility and doing pruning early. The *oracle* evaluates partial programs using *partial execution*. The *search planner* optimizes for the second challenge by merging search results from subsets of the large training data, so as to save unnecessary checking, which we call the *merge search* strategy.

We next explain each technique in detail in the rest of this section.

4.2   Partial Execution

A *partial program* is an incomplete program with non-terminals. Similar to prior work making overestimation on regular expressions and imperative languages for early pruning in the search process [14,29,30], we want to evaluate a partial NetQRE program for the feasibility of all possible completions of it, so as to decide early if any of them can serve as a proper classifier for E_p and E_n.

This process includes three main steps: (1) finding an equivalent completion $\hat{p}$ of a partial program p so that evaluating $\hat{p}$ on any input x is equivalent to evaluating the combination of all possible completions of p on x, (2) efficiently evaluating $\hat{p}(x)$, (3) deciding whether to discard p based on the evaluation result.

Equivalent Completion: Recall that we define $p(x)$ of a partial program p to be the union of all $q(x)$ such that $p \to q$. Since we mainly care about outputs of positive and negative examples on different sides of a threshold, the essential information is the upper and lower bounds for $p(x)$. Therefore, the criterion for finding an equivalent completion is the bounds of $\hat{p}(x)$ should include $p(x)$ for any input x.

Many non-terminals have a straightforward equivalent completion. We replace (1) any uncertain numerical value with the largest or smallest possible value depending on the context, (2) any unknown predicate with *unknown*, (3) any unknown regular expression with _* and (4) any unknown quantitative regular expression with (/_ _*/)*sum. We skip the formal proof of correctness of this approach. Intuitively, the first two include all possible values at the position, and the latter two include all possible matching and aggregation strategies for a trace.

There are some non-terminals that do not have an equivalent completion, such as <group-by> and <op>. While doing enumeration, we put a complexity penalty over these non-terminals if they are not expanded, therefore encouraging earlier expansion of them so that partial execution is possible.

Computing Ambiguity: Notice that regular patterns naturally allow multiple matching strategies if a character(packet) in the input can match more than one predicate in the program, which is why we can estimate a set of NetQRE programs by one equivalent completion $\hat{p}$. The goal and also the major challenge in evaluating $\hat{p}(x)$ on arbitrary input x is to compute the quantitative outputs from all valid matching strategies, which can grow exponentially with the input trace's length.

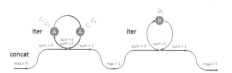
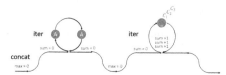

Fig. 2: Illustration of an unambiguous program. Predicate A matches packet C's while predicate B matches packet D.

Fig. 3: Illustration of the first 3 steps of strategy one when predicate B is not yet explored.

To solve the problem of too many matching strategies, we use an approximation: merging "close" matching strategies. Two strategies are defined to be "close" if at some step of their matching process (1) they have matched the same number of packets in the trace and (2) the last predicate they have matched is exactly the same. We explore all matching strategies simultaneously and do a merging whenever two strategies can be identified to be close. Notice that each matching strategy maintains a distinct copy of aggregation states for every <qre> expression. States for a same expression as well as the final results are merged into one interval.

As an example, Figure 2,3,4,5 illustrates the evaluation process of a partial program during the search for the following pattern with CCCCD as input:

```
( ( /AA/ )*sum ( /B/ )*sum )max
```

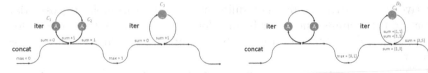

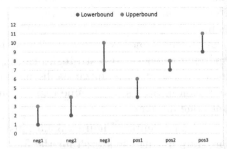

Fig. 4: Illustration of the first 3 steps of strategy two

Fig. 5: Illustration of the last 2 steps of merged strategy one & two

By the properties of interval arithmetic and regular expressions, it can be proven that the approximation result strictly contains the true output range. Or more formally, $\hat{p}(x).min \leq p(x).min \leq p(x).max \leq \hat{p}(x).max$.

Intuitively, the proposed evaluation scheme works well because we only care about the boundary of outputs, which are represented by intervals as the abstract data type. We implement the execution and approximation process by the Data Transducer model proposed by [2], which consumes a small constant memory and linear time to the input trace's length given a specific program.

Make Decision: To make a decision regarding a partial program p, let q be a complete program and assume there is only one pair of examples e_p and e_n. For q to accept e_p and e_n, there must be a threshold T such that $q(e_n).max < T < q(e_p).min$. Therefore, given a pair of examples e_p and e_n, a program q is correct if and only if $q(e_n).max < q(e_p).min$. When this holds, any value between $q(e_n).max$ and $q(e_p).min$ can be used as the threshold.

Lemma 1: There exists a correct program q such that $p \rightarrow q$ only if $\hat{p}(e_n).min < \hat{p}(e_p).max$

Lemma 2: If $\hat{p}(e_n).max < \hat{p}(e_p).min$ then any program q such that $p \rightarrow q$ is correct.

From Lemma 1, we can decide if p must be rejected. From Lemma 2, we can decide if p must be accepted. These criteria can be extended to more than 1 pair of examples. We will not give formal proof to the lemmas. Figures 6 and 7 show two intuitive examples for explanations of the decision making process. (but do not necessarily represent properties of real data sets). Each vertical bar represents the output range of the corresponding data point produced by the program under investigation.

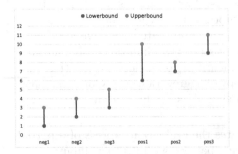

Fig. 6: A correct program found. No negative output can ever be greater than any positive output. 5.5 can be used as a threshold

Fig. 7: A bad program. pos 1 can never be greater than neg 3.

4.3   Merge Search

In the rest of this subsection, we describe three heuristics for scaling up synthesis to large data sets, namely *divide and conquer, simulated annealing,* and *parallel processing.* We call the combination of these the *merge search* technique.

Divide and Conquer. Enumerating and verifying programs on large data sets is expensive. Our core strategy to improve performance is to learn patterns on small subsets and merge them into a global pattern with low overhead.

It is based on two observations: First, the pattern of the entire data set is usually shaped by a few extreme data points. Looking at these extreme data points locally is enough to figure out critical properties of the global pattern. Second, conflicts in local patterns are mostly describing different aspects of a same target rather than fundamental differences, thus can be resolved by simple merge operations such as disjunction, truncation or concatenation.

This divide and conquer strategy is captured in the following algorithm:

```
def d&c(dataset)
    if dataset.size > threshold
        subsetL,subsetR = split(dataset)
        candidateL = d&c(subsetL)
        candidateR = d&c(subsetR)
        return merge(dataset, candidateL, candidateR)
    else
        return synthesize(dataset, s0)
```

The "split" step corresponds to evenly splitting positive and negative examples. Then sub-patterns are synthesized on smaller subsets. The conquer, or "merge" step requires synthesizing the pattern again on the combined dataset. But sub-patterns are reused in two ways to speedup this search.

First, if we see a sub-pattern as an AST, then its low-level sub-trees up to certain depth threshold are added to the syntax as a new production option for the corresponding non-terminal at the sub-tree's root. They can then serve as shortcuts for likely building blocks. Second, the sub-patterns' skeletons left after removing these sub-trees are used as seeds for higher-level searches, which serve as shortcuts for likely overall structures. Both are given complexity rewards to encourage the reuse.

In practice, many search results can be directly reused from cached results generated from previous tasks on similar subsets. This optimization can further reduce the synthesis time.

Simulated Annealing When searching for local patterns at lower levels, we require the Enumerator to find not 1 but t candidate patterns for each subset. Such searches are fast for smaller data sets and can cover a wider range of possible patterns. As the search goes to higher levels for larger data sets, we discard the least accurate local patterns and also reduce t. The search will focus on refining the currently optimal global pattern. This idea is based on traditional simulated annealing algorithms and helps to improve the synthesizer's performance in many cases.

Parallelization. Most steps in the synthesis process are inherently parallelizable. They include (1) doing synthesis on different subsets of data, (2) exploring different programs in the enumeration, (3) verifying different programs found so far, (4) executing a program on different data points during the verification.

We focus less on optimizing (1) and (2) since they are not the performance bottlenecks. We instead focus on parallelizing (3) and (4) over multiple cores. In our implementation, using 5 machines with 32 cores each, we devote one thread each to run task (1) and (2) on one machine, 64 threads on the same machine to run task (3), and 512 threads distributed over the remaining four machines to run task (4). The distributed version is approximately two orders of magnitude faster than the single-threaded version for complex tasks. Given more computing power, a proportional speedup can be expected.

5   Evaluation

We implemented Sharingan in 10K lines of C++ code. Our experiments are carried out in a cluster of five machines directly connected by Ethernet cables, each with 32 Intel(R) Xeon(R) E5-2450 CPUs. The frequency for each core is 2.10GHz. Arrangements of tasks are explained in the last part of Sec 4.3. We will evaluate the minimal feature engineering(5.1), accuracy(5.2), interpretability and editability(5.3), efficient implementation(5.4), and synthesis algorithm efficiency(5.5) aspects of Sharingan in order.

5.1   Data Preparation

We utilize eight types of attacks from the CICIDS2017 database[25,7], a public repository of benign and attack traffic used for evaluating intrusion detection systems. They cover a wide range of attack traffic including botnets, Denial of service (DoS), port scanning, and password cracking.

The data is labelled per flow by an attack type or "Benign". We learn each type of attack against benign traffic separately. To use as much data as possible, for each attack type, we use 1500 positive (attack) flows and 10000 negative (benign) flows for training, and another distinct data set of similar size for testing.

The main benefit of Sharingan in this step is the *minimal need* for feature engineering. We simply use all header fields of TCP and IP, and the inter-packet arrival time between adjacent packets in the same flow as features. In total, there are 19 features per packet and $N \times 19$ features per trace of length N.

In contrast, other state-of-the-art systems rely on a carefully designed feature extraction step to work well. For example, the feature vectors included in CICIDS2017 database contain 84 features extracted by the CICFlowMeter [9,13] tool for each flow, characterizing performance metrics of the entire flow such as duration, mean forward packet length, min activation time, etc. Kitsune [16] extracts bandwidth information over the past short periods as packet-level features. DECANTeR [6] uses HTTP-level properties such as constant header fields, language, amount of outgoing information, etc. as flow-level features.

5.2   Learning Accuracy

We next validate Sharingan's learning accuracy using the following evaluation methodology. For each individual attack type, we use the training data (attack and normal traffic) as input to Sharingan to learn a NetQRE program. The NetQRE program is then validated on the corresponding testing set for accuracy. The output of Sharingan includes a NetQRE program that maps a network trace to an integer output and a recommended range for the threshold. By modifying the threshold, true positive rate (TP) and false positive rate (FP) can be adjusted, as we will later explain in Section 5.3. We use AUC (Area under Curve) - ROC (Receiver Operating Characteristics) metric, which is a standard statistical measure of classification performance.

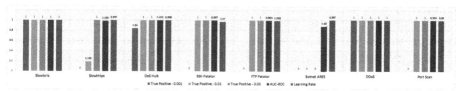

Fig. 8: Sharingan's true positive rate under low false positive rate, AUC-ROC and learning rate for 8 attacks in CICIDS2017 (higher is better)

Figure 8 contains results for eight types of attacks. Apart from AUC-ROC values, we also show the true positive rates when false positive rate is adjusted to 3 different levels: 0.001, 0.01, and 0.03. Given that noise is common in most network traffic, the last metric shown in Figure 8 is the highest achievable learning rate.

Overall, we observe that Sharingan performs well across a range of attacks with accuracy numbers on par with prior state-of-the-art systems such as Kitsune, which has an average AUC-ROC value of 0.924 on nine types of IoT-based attacks, and DECANTeR, which has an average detection rate of 97.7% and a false positive rate of 0.9% on HTTP-based malware. In six out of eight attacks, Sharingan achieves above 0.994 of AUC-ROC and 100% of true positive rate at 1% false positive rate. The major exception is Botnet ARES, which consists of a mix of malicious attack vectors. Handling such multi-vector attacks is an avenue for our future work.

5.3   Post-processing and Interpretation

One of the benefits of Sharingan is that it generates an actual classification program that can be further adapted and tuned by a network operator. The program itself is also close to the stateful nature of session-layer protocols and attacks, and thus is readable and provides a basis for the operator to understand the attack cause. We briefly illustrate these capabilities in this section.

FP-TP Tradeoff Network operators need to occasionally tune a classifier's sensitivity to false positives and true positives. Sharingan generates a NetQRE program with a threshold T. This threshold can be adjusted to vary the false

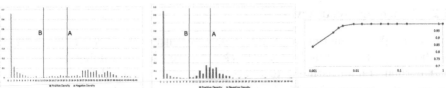

Fig. 9: Output distribution of training set(DoS Hulk)

Fig. 10: Output distribution of test set(DoS Hulk)

Fig. 11: ROC Curve, logarithmic scale(DoS Hulk)

positive and true positive rate. Figures 9 and 10 show the output distribution from positive and negative examples in the DoS Hulk attack. A denotes the largest negative output and B denotes the smallest positive output. When $A > B$, there is some unavoidable error. We can slide the threshold T from B to A and obtain an ROC curve for the test data, as illustrated in Figure 11.

Interpretation We describe a learnt NetQRE program to demonstrate how a network operator can interpret the classifiers. [3] The NetQRE program synthesized by Sharingan for DDoS task above is:

```
( ( /_* A _* B _*/ )*sum /_* C _*/ )sum > 4
Where
A = [ip.src_ip->[0%,50%]]        B = [tcp.rst==1]
C = [time_since_last_pkt<=50%]
```

DDoS is a flood attack from a botnet of machines to exhaust memory resources on the victim server. The detected pattern consists of packets that start with source IP in a certain range, followed by a packet with the reset bit set to 1, and then a packet with a short time interval from its predecessor. Finally, the program considers the flow a match if the patterns show up with a total count of over 4.

The range of source IP addresses specified in the pattern possibly contains botnet IP addresses. Attack flows are often reset when the load cannot be handled or the flows' states cannot be recognized, which indicates the attack is successfully launched. Packets with short intervals further support a flood attack. Unique properties of DDoS attack are indeed captured by this program!

Refinement by Human Knowledge Finally, an advantage of generating a program for classification is that it enables the operator to augment the generated NetQRE program with domain knowledge before deployment. For example, in the DDoS case, if they know that the victim service is purely based on TCP, they can append [ip.type = TCP] to all predicates. Alternatively, if they know that the victim service is designed for 1000 requests per second, they can explicitly replace the arrival time interval with $1ms$. The modified program then is:

```
( ( /_* A _* B _*/ )*sum /_* C _*/ )sum > 4
Where
```

---

[3] A full list of learnt NetQRE programs can be found in our tech report https://arxiv.org/abs/2010.06135.

```
A = [ip.type = TCP]&&[ip.src_ip->[0%,50%]]
B = [ip.type = TCP]&&[tcp.rst==1]
C = [ip.type = TCP]&&[time_since_last_pkt<=1ms]
```

5.4   Deployment Scenarios

We now describe three ways for network operators to deploy the output of Sharingan: (1) taking action hinted by the interpretation; (2) directly executing the NetQRE program as a monitoring system; and (3) translating the NetQRE program to rules in other monitoring systems.

Revisiting the DDoS example in Section 5.3, in the first case, the operator may refine the source IP part to find out the accurate range of attacker machines and block them.

If the NetQRE program itself is to be used as a monitoring system, its runtime system can be directly deployed on any general purpose machine. Prior work [37] has shown that NetQRE generates performance that is comparable to optimized low-level implementations. Moreover, these programs can be easily compiled into other formats acceptable to existing monitoring systems.

5.5   Program Synthesis Performance

Synthesis time: In our final experiment, the performance of Sharingan is measured, in terms of time needed for program synthesis.

Figure 12 shows the program complexity (Y-axis) and synthesis (learning) time (in minutes). Not surprisingly, complex programs require more time to synthesize. We further observe that Sharingan is able to synthesize complex programs with at least 20-30 terms, mostly within minutes to an hour, which is practical for many real-world use cases and can be further reduced through parallelism over more machines. As a comparison, Kitsune reports training times between 8 minutes and 52 minutes on individual attacks [16], and DECANTeR reports training times between 5 hours and 10 hours on individual users' data [6].

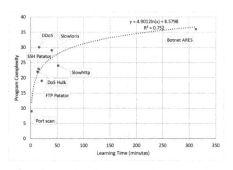

Fig. 12: Time-complexity relation

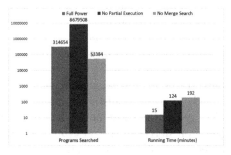

Fig. 13: Impact of optimizations on synthesis performance

Effectiveness of Optimizations.   We explore the effectiveness of the individual optimization strategies described in Section 4. In Figure 13, we compare the synthesis time and the number of programs searched for a fully optimized Sharingan against results from disabling each optimization. SSH Patator is used as the demonstrating example since it is moderately complex.

We observe that disabling partial execution optimization makes both metrics significantly worse. Being able to prune early can indeed greatly reduce time wasted on unnecessary exploration and checking. By disabling merge search, although the number of programs searched decreases, the total synthesis time increases given the overhead of having to check each program against the entire data set. The synthesis cannot finish within reasonable time if both are disabled.

In summary, all optimization strategies are effective to speed up the synthesis process. A synthesis task that is otherwise impossible to finish within practical time can now be done in less than 15 minutes.

6   Related Work

Auto-Generation of Network Configurations. Broadly speaking, network traffic classification rule is a type of network configuration. There are other lines of research that aim at the automatic generation of different categories of network configurations. EasyACL [15] aims at synthesis of access control lists(ACL) from natural language descriptions. NetGen [24], NetComplete [10] and Genesis [32] synthesize data plane routing configurations based on SMT solvers given policy specifications. NetEgg [36] instead takes examples provided by user to generate routing configurations in an interactive way. Sharingan focuses on network traffic classification and has a different target from them.

Other Learning-based Systems. Apart from competing systems we explicitly compared to above, there are other learning-based systems under different settings from Sharingan.

Unsupervised learning systems are useful for recognizing outliers and other types of "abnormal" flows [17,38,35], most notably in intrusion detection systems. Its ability to differentiate unknown types of traffic from the known cannot be replaced by Sharingan. Sharingan can augment unsupervised learning systems by reducing the effort required for analyzing the reported traces.

Learning systems using state machine[18] or regular expressions for payload strings[34] as models both share the advantage of requiring minimal feature engineering. The former generates less succinct models compared to Sharingan and is typically used for verification of network protocols. The latter learns patterns at individual packet level rather than session level.

There are state-of-the-art point solutions focusing on specific scenarios rather than general-purpose network traffic classification. For example, PrivateEye focuses on detecting privacy breaches in the cloud[4]. RFDIDS solves intrusion detection challenges unique to power systems[26].

Syntax-Guided Synthesis. Sharingan builds on a large body of work on syntax-guided synthesis [11,21,23,20,22,29,27]. However, synthesis techniques proposed in this paper go beyond the state of the art, and have the potential to be applied to other applications of program synthesis.

Partial execution share similarity to the overestimation idea in [14] (see also follow-ups [29,30,33]), where the system learns plain regular expressions and overestimates the feasibility of a non-terminal with a Kleene-star. But no prior work proposed an overestimation algorithm for quantitative stream query languages similar to NetQRE. Nor do they consider the specification format for a classifier program with unknown numerical thresholds.

[3] proposed a divide-and-conquer strategy similar to merge search for optimizing program synthesis. It is focused on standard SyGuS tasks based on logical constraints and uses decision tree to combine sub-patterns instead of trying to merge them into one compact program. Merge search proposed in this work is not specific to Sharingan, and can be used in other synthesis tasks to allow the handling of large data sets.

Finally, there is no prior work that solely uses program synthesis to perform accurate real-world large-scale classification. The closest work concerns simple low-accuracy programs synthesized as weak learners [8], and requires a separate SVM to assemble them into a classifier.

7 Conclusion

This paper presents Sharingan, which develops syntax-guided synthesis techniques to automatically generate NetQRE programs for classifying session-layer network traffic. Sharingan can be used for generating network monitoring queries or signatures for intrusion detection systems from labeled traces. Our results demonstrate three key value propositions for Sharingan, namely minimal feature engineering, efficient implementation, and interpretability as well as editability. While achieving accuracy comparable to state-of-the-art statistical and signature-based learning systems, Sharingan is significantly more usable and requires synthesis time practical for real-world tasks. [4]

Acknowledgements

We thank the anonymous reviewers for their feedback. This research was supported in part by NSF grant CCF 1763514, CNS 1513679, and Accountable Protocol Customization under the ONR TPCP program with grant number N00014-18-1-2618.

References

1. Rajeev Alur, Rastislav Bodik, Garvit Juniwal, Milo MK Martin, Mukund Raghothaman, Sanjit A Seshia, Rishabh Singh, Armando Solar-Lezama, Emina Torlak, and Abhishek Udupa. Syntax-guided synthesis. In *2013 Formal Methods in Computer-Aided Design*, pages 1–8. IEEE, 2013.

---

[4] Sharingan's code is publicly available at https://github.com/SleepyToDeath/NetQRE.

2. Rajeev Alur, Konstantinos Mamouras, and Caleb Stanford. Modular quantitative monitoring. *Proceedings of the ACM on Programming Languages*, 3(POPL):50, 2019.

3. Rajeev Alur, Arjun Radhakrishna, and Abhishek Udupa. Scaling enumerative program synthesis via divide and conquer. In *International Conference on Tools and Algorithms for the Construction and Analysis of Systems*, pages 319–336. Springer, 2017.

4. Behnaz Arzani, Selim Ciraci, Stefan Saroiu, Alec Wolman, Jack Stokes, Geoff Outhred, and Lechao Diwu. Privateeye: Scalable and privacy-preserving compromise detection in the cloud. In *17th {USENIX} Symposium on Networked Systems Design and Implementation ({NSDI} 20)*, pages 797–815, 2020.

5. Przemysław Bereziński, Bartosz Jasiul, and Marcin Szpyrka. An entropy-based network anomaly detection method. *Entropy*, 17(4):2367–2408, 2015.

6. Riccardo Bortolameotti, Thijs van Ede, Marco Caselli, Maarten H Everts, Pieter Hartel, Rick Hofstede, Willem Jonker, and Andreas Peter. Decanter: Detection of anomalous outbound http traffic by passive application fingerprinting. In *Proceedings of the 33rd Annual Computer Security Applications Conference*, pages 373–386, 2017.

7. Canadian Institute for Cybersecurity. Ids 2017 — datasets — research — canadian institute for cybersecurity — unb, 2020. [Online; accessed 15-October-2019].

8. Alvin Cheung, Armando Solar-Lezama, and Samuel Madden. Using program synthesis for social recommendations. *arXiv preprint arXiv:1208.2925*, 2012.

9. Gerard Draper-Gil, Arash Habibi Lashkari, Mohammad Saiful Islam Mamun, and Ali A Ghorbani. Characterization of encrypted and vpn traffic using time-related. In *Proceedings of the 2nd international conference on information systems security and privacy (ICISSP)*, pages 407–414, 2016.

10. Ahmed El-Hassany, Petar Tsankov, Laurent Vanbever, and Martin Vechev. Netcomplete: Practical network-wide configuration synthesis with autocompletion. In *15th {USENIX} Symposium on Networked Systems Design and Implementation ({NSDI} 18)*, pages 579–594, 2018.

11. Sumit Gulwani. Automating string processing in spreadsheets using input-output examples. *ACM Sigplan Notices*, 46(1):317–330, 2011.

12. Donghwoon Kwon, Hyunjoo Kim, Jinoh Kim, Sang C Suh, Ikkyun Kim, and Kuinam J Kim. A survey of deep learning-based network anomaly detection. *Cluster Computing*, pages 1–13, 2017.

13. Arash Habibi Lashkari, Gerard Draper-Gil, Mohammad Saiful Islam Mamun, and Ali A Ghorbani. Characterization of tor traffic using time based features. In *ICISSP*, pages 253–262, 2017.

14. Mina Lee, Sunbeom So, and Hakjoo Oh. Synthesizing regular expressions from examples for introductory automata assignments. In *ACM SIGPLAN Notices*, volume 52, pages 70–80. ACM, 2016.

15. Xiao Liu, Brett Holden, and Dinghao Wu. Automated synthesis of access control lists. In *2017 International Conference on Software Security and Assurance (ICSSA)*, pages 104–109. IEEE, 2017.

16. Yisroel Mirsky, Tomer Doitshman, Yuval Elovici, and Asaf Shabtai. Kitsune: an ensemble of autoencoders for online network intrusion detection. *arXiv preprint arXiv:1802.09089*, 2018.

17. Preeti Mishra, Vijay Varadharajan, Uday Tupakula, and Emmanuel S Pilli. A detailed investigation and analysis of using machine learning techniques for intrusion detection. *IEEE Communications Surveys & Tutorials*, 21(1):686–728, 2018.

18. Soo-Jin Moon, Jeffrey Helt, Yifei Yuan, Yves Bieri, Sujata Banerjee, Vyas Sekar, Wenfei Wu, Mihalis Yannakakis, and Ying Zhang. Alembic: automated model inference for stateful network functions. In *16th USENIX Symposium on Networked Systems Design and Implementation (NSDI 19)*, pages 699–718, 2019.
19. James Newsome, Brad Karp, and Dawn Song. Polygraph: Automatically generating signatures for polymorphic worms. In *2005 IEEE Symposium on Security and Privacy (S&P'05)*, pages 226–241. IEEE, 2005.
20. Peter-Michael Osera and Steve Zdancewic. Type-and-example-directed program synthesis. *ACM SIGPLAN Notices*, 50(6):619–630, 2015.
21. Emilio Parisotto, Abdel-rahman Mohamed, Rishabh Singh, Lihong Li, Dengyong Zhou, and Pushmeet Kohli. Neuro-symbolic program synthesis. *arXiv preprint arXiv:1611.01855*, 2016.
22. Nadia Polikarpova, Ivan Kuraj, and Armando Solar-Lezama. Program synthesis from polymorphic refinement types. *ACM SIGPLAN Notices*, 51(6):522–538, 2016.
23. Oleksandr Polozov and Sumit Gulwani. Flashmeta: a framework for inductive program synthesis. In *ACM SIGPLAN Notices*, volume 50, pages 107–126. ACM, 2015.
24. Shambwaditya Saha, Santhosh Prabhu, and P Madhusudan. Netgen: Synthesizing data-plane configurations for network policies. In *Proceedings of the 1st ACM SIGCOMM Symposium on Software Defined Networking Research*, pages 1–6, 2015.
25. Iman Sharafaldin, Arash Habibi Lashkari, and Ali A Ghorbani. Toward generating a new intrusion detection dataset and intrusion traffic characterization. In *ICISSP*, pages 108–116, 2018.
26. Tohid Shekari, Christian Bayens, Morris Cohen, Lukas Graber, and Raheem Beyah. Rfdids: Radio frequency-based distributed intrusion detection system for the power grid. In *NDSS*, 2019.
27. Xujie Si, Yuan Yang, Hanjun Dai, Mayur Naik, and Le Song. Learning a metasolver for syntax-guided program synthesis. In *International Conference on Learning Representations*, 2018.
28. Sumeet Singh, Cristian Estan, George Varghese, and Stefan Savage. Automated worm fingerprinting. In *OSDI*, volume 4, pages 4–4, 2004.
29. Sunbeom So and Hakjoo Oh. Synthesizing imperative programs from examples guided by static analysis. In *International Static Analysis Symposium*, pages 364–381. Springer, 2017.
30. Sunbeom So and Hakjoo Oh. Synthesizing pattern programs from examples. In *IJCAI*, pages 1618–1624, 2018.
31. Robin Sommer and Vern Paxson. Outside the closed world: On using machine learning for network intrusion detection. In *2010 IEEE symposium on security and privacy*, pages 305–316. IEEE, 2010.
32. Kausik Subramanian, Loris D'Antoni, and Aditya Akella. Genesis: Synthesizing forwarding tables in multi-tenant networks. In *Proceedings of the 44th ACM SIGPLAN Symposium on Principles of Programming Languages*, pages 572–585, 2017.
33. Chenglong Wang, Alvin Cheung, and Rastislav Bodik. Synthesizing highly expressive sql queries from input-output examples. In *ACM SIGPLAN Notices*, volume 52, pages 452–466. ACM, 2017.
34. Yu Wang, Yang Xiang, Wanlei Zhou, and Shunzheng Yu. Generating regular expression signatures for network traffic classification in trusted network management. *Journal of Network and Computer Applications*, 35(3):992–1000, 2012.
35. Guowu Xie, Marios Iliofotou, Ram Keralapura, Michalis Faloutsos, and Antonio Nucci. Subflow: Towards practical flow-level traffic classification. In *2012 Proceedings IEEE INFOCOM*, pages 2541–2545. IEEE, 2012.

36. Yifei Yuan, Rajeev Alur, and Boon Thau Loo. Netegg: Programming network policies by examples. In *Proceedings of the 13th ACM Workshop on Hot Topics in Networks*, pages 1–7, 2014.

37. Yifei Yuan, Dong Lin, Ankit Mishra, Sajal Marwaha, Rajeev Alur, and Boon Thau Loo. Qantitative network monitoring with NetQRE. In *SIGCOMM*, 2017.

38. Jun Zhang, Xiao Chen, Yang Xiang, Wanlei Zhou, and Jie Wu. Robust network traffic classification. *IEEE/ACM Transactions on Networking (TON)*, 23(4):1257–1270, 2015.

39. Zhuo Zhang, Zhibin Zhang, Patrick PC Lee, Yunjie Liu, and Gaogang Xie. Toward unsupervised protocol feature word extraction. *IEEE Journal on Selected Areas in Communications*, 32(10):1894–1906, 2014.

General Decidability Results for Asynchronous Shared-Memory Programs: Higher-Order and Beyond ⋆

Rupak Majumdar, Ramanathan S. Thinniyam ✉, and Georg Zetzsche

Max Planck Institute for Software Systems (MPI-SWS), Kaiserslautern, Germany
{rupak,thinniyam,georg}@mpi-sws.org

Abstract. The model of asynchronous programming arises in many contexts, from low-level systems software to high-level web programming. We take a language-theoretic perspective and show general decidability and undecidability results for asynchronous programs that capture all known results as well as show decidability of new and important classes. As a main consequence, we show decidability of safety, termination and boundedness verification for *higher-order* asynchronous programs—such as OCaml programs using Lwt—and undecidability of liveness verification already for order-2 asynchronous programs. We show that under mild assumptions, surprisingly, safety and termination verification of asynchronous programs with handlers from a language class are decidable *iff* emptiness is decidable for the underlying language class. Moreover, we show that configuration reachability and liveness (fair termination) verification are equivalent, and decidability of these problems implies decidability of the well-known "equal-letters" problem on languages. Our results close the decidability frontier for asynchronous programs.

Keywords: Higher-order asynchronous programs · Decidability

1 Introduction

Asynchronous programming is a common way to manage concurrent requests in a system. In this style of programming, rather than waiting for a time-consuming operation to complete, the programmer can make *asynchronous* procedure calls which are stored in a *task buffer* pending later execution. Each asynchronous procedure, or *handler*, is a sequential program. When run, it can change the *global shared state* of the program, make internal synchronous procedure calls, and post further instances of handlers to the task buffer. A scheduler repeatedly and non-deterministically picks pending handler instances from the task buffer and executes their code *atomically* to completion. Asynchronous programs appear in many domains, such as operating system kernel code, web programming,

---

⋆ This research was sponsored in part by the Deutsche Forschungsgemeinschaft project 389792660 TRR 248–CPEC and by the European Research Council under the Grant Agreement 610150 (ERC Synergy Grant ImPACT).

J. F. Groote and K. G. Larsen (Eds.): TACAS 2021, LNCS 12651, pp. 449–467, 2021.
https://doi.org/10.1007/978-3-030-72016-2_24

or user applications on mobile platforms. This style of programming is supported natively or through libraries for most programming environments. The interleaving of different handlers hides latencies of long-running operations: the program can process a different handler while waiting for an external operation to finish. However, asynchronous scheduling of tasks introduces non-determinism in the system, making it difficult to reason about correctness.

An asynchronous program is *finite-data* if all program variables range over finite domains. Finite-data programs are still infinite state transition systems: the task buffer can contain an unbounded number of pending instances and the sequential machine implementing an individual handler can have unboundedly large state (e.g., if the handler is given as a recursive program, the stack can grow unboundedly). Nevertheless, verification problems for finite-data programs have been shown to be decidable for several kinds of handlers [12,30,20,6]. Several algorithmic approaches have been studied, which tailor to (i) the kinds of permitted handler programs and (ii) the properties that are checked.

State of the art We briefly survey the existing approaches and what is known about the decidability frontier. The *Parikh approach* applies to (first-order) recursive handler programs. Here, the decision problems for asynchronous programs are reduced to decision problems over Petri nets [12]. The key insight is that since handlers are executed atomically, the order in which a handler posts tasks to the buffer is irrelevant. Therefore, instead of considering the sequential order of posted tasks along an execution, one can equivalently consider its Parikh image. Thus, when handlers are given as pushdown systems, the behaviors of an asynchronous program can be represented by a (polynomial sized) Petri net. Using the Parikh approach, safety (formulated as reachability of a global state), termination (whether all executions terminate), and boundedness (whether there is an a priori upper bound on the task buffer) are all decidable for asynchronous programs with recursive handlers, by reduction to corresponding problems on Petri nets [30,12]. Configuration reachability (reachability of a specific global state and task buffer configuration), fair termination (termination under a fair scheduler), and fair non-starvation (every pending handler instance is eventually executed) are also decidable, by separate ad hoc reductions to Petri net reachability [12]. A "reverse reduction" shows that Petri nets can be simulated by polynomial-sized asynchronous programs (already with finite-data handlers).

In the *downclosure approach*, one replaces each handler with a finite-data program that is equivalent up to "losing" handlers in the task buffer. Of course, this requires that one can compute equivalent finite-data programs for given handler programs. This has been applied to checking safety for recursive handler programs [3]. Finally, a bespoke *rank-based approach* has been applied to checking safety when handlers can perform restricted higher-order recursion [6].

Contribution Instead of studying individual kinds of handler programs, we consider asynchronous programs in a general language-theoretic framework. The class of handler programs is given as a language class $\mathcal{C}$: An asynchronous program over a language class $\mathcal{C}$ is one where each handler defines a language from $\mathcal{C}$ over the alphabet of handler names, as well as a transformer over the global state. This view leads to general results: we can obtain simple characterizations of which classes of handler programs permit decidability. For example, we do not need the technical assumptions of computability of equivalent finite-data programs from the Parikh and the downclosure approach.

Our first result shows that, under a mild language-theoretic assumption, safety and termination are decidable if and only if the underlying language class $\mathcal{C}$ has decidable emptiness problem.[1] Similarly, we show that boundedness is decidable iff *finiteness* is decidable for the language class $\mathcal{C}$. These results are the best possible: decidability of emptiness (resp., finiteness) is a requirement for safety and termination verification already for verifying the safety or termination (resp., boundedness) of one *sequential* handler call. As corollaries, we get new decidability results for all these problems for asynchronous programs over *higher-order recursion schemes*, which form the language-theoretic basis for programming in higher-order functional languages such as OCaml [21,28], as well as other language classes (lossy channel languages, Petri net languages, etc.).

Second, we show that configuration reachability, fair termination, and fair starvation are mutually reducible; thus, decidability of any one of them implies decidability of all of them. We also show decidability of these problems implies the decidability of a well-known combinatorial problem on languages: given a language over the alphabet $\{a, b\}$, decide if it contains a word with an equal number of as and bs. Viewed contrapositively, we conclude that all these decision problems are undecidable already for asynchronous programs over order-2 pushdown languages, since the equal-letters problem is undecidable for this class.

Together, our results "close" the decidability frontier for asynchronous programs, by demonstrating reducibilities between decision problems heretofore studied separately and connecting decision problems on asynchronous programs with decision problems on the underlying language classes of their handlers.

While our algorithms do not assume that downclosures are effectively computable, we use downclosures to prove their correctness. We show that safety, termination, and boundedness problems are invariant under taking downclosures of runs; this corresponds to taking downclosures of the languages of handlers.

The observation that safety, termination, and boundedness depend only on the downclosure suggests a possible route to implementation. If there is an effective procedure to compute the downclosure for class $\mathcal{C}$, then a direct verification algorithm would replace all handlers by their (regular) downclosures, and invoke existing decision procedures for this case. Thus, we get a direct algorithm based on downclosure constructions for higher order recursion schemes, using the string of celebrated recent results on effectively computing the downclosure of *word schemes* [33,15,7].

We find our general decidability result for asynchronous programs to be surprising. Already for regular languages, the complexity of safety verification jumps

---

[1] The "mild language-theoretic assumption" is that the class of languages forms an effective full trio: it is closed under intersections with regular languages, homomorphisms, and inverse homomorphisms. Many language classes studied in formal language theory and verification satisfy these conditions.

from NL (NFA emptiness) to EXPSPACE (Petri net coverability): asynchronous programs are far more expressive than individual handler languages. It is therefore surprising that safety and termination verification remains decidable whenever it is decidable for individual handler languages.

Full proofs of our results are available here [25].

2   Preliminaries

Basic Definitions We assume familiarity with basic definitions of automata theory (see, e.g., [18,31]). The projection of word w onto some alphabet Σ', written $\mathrm{Proj}_{\Sigma'}(w)$, is the word obtained by erasing from w each symbol which does not belong to Σ'. For a language L, define $\mathrm{Proj}_{\Sigma'}(L) = \{\mathrm{Proj}_{\Sigma'}(w) \mid w \in L\}$. The *subword* order $\sqsubseteq$ on Σ^* is defined as $w \sqsubseteq w'$ for $w, w' \in \Sigma^*$ if w can be obtained from w' by deleting some letters from w'. For example, $abba \sqsubseteq bababa$ but $abba \not\sqsubseteq baaba$. The *downclosure* $\downarrow w$ with respect to the subword order of a word $w \in \Sigma^*$ is defined as $\downarrow w := \{w' \in \Sigma^* \mid w' \sqsubseteq w\}$. The downclosure $\downarrow L$ of a language $L \subseteq \Sigma^*$ is given by $\downarrow L := \{w' \in \Sigma^* \mid \exists w \in L \colon w' \sqsubseteq w\}$. Recall that the downclosure $\downarrow L$ of any language L is a regular language [17].

A *multiset* $\mathbf{m} \colon \Sigma \to \mathbb{N}$ over Σ maps each symbol of Σ to a natural number. Let $\mathrm{M}[\Sigma]$ be the set of all multisets over Σ. We treat sets as a special case of multisets where each element is mapped onto 0 or 1. As an example, we write $\mathbf{m} = [\![a, a, c]\!]$ for the multiset $\mathbf{m} \in \mathrm{M}[\{a, b, c, d\}]$ such that $\mathbf{m}(a) = 2$, $\mathbf{m}(b) = \mathbf{m}(d) = 0$, and $\mathbf{m}(c) = 1$. We also write $|\mathbf{m}| = \sum_{\sigma \in \Sigma} \mathbf{m}(\sigma)$.

Given two multisets $\mathbf{m}, \mathbf{m}' \in \mathrm{M}[\Sigma]$ we define the multiset $\mathbf{m} \oplus \mathbf{m}' \in \mathrm{M}[\Sigma]$ for which, for all $a \in \Sigma$, we have $(\mathbf{m} \oplus \mathbf{m}')(a) = \mathbf{m}(a) + \mathbf{m}'(a)$. We also define the natural order $\preceq$ on $\mathrm{M}[\Sigma]$ as follows: $\mathbf{m} \preceq \mathbf{m}'$ iff there exists $\mathbf{m}^{\Delta} \in \mathrm{M}[\Sigma]$ such that $\mathbf{m} \oplus \mathbf{m}^{\Delta} = \mathbf{m}'$. We also define $\mathbf{m}' \ominus \mathbf{m}$ for $\mathbf{m} \preceq \mathbf{m}'$ analogously: for all $a \in \Sigma$, we have $(\mathbf{m} \ominus \mathbf{m}')(a) = \mathbf{m}(a) - \mathbf{m}'(a)$. For $\Sigma \subseteq \Sigma'$ we regard $\mathbf{m} \in \mathrm{M}[\Sigma]$ as a multiset of $\mathrm{M}[\Sigma']$ where undefined values are sent to 0.

Language Classes and Full Trios A *language class* is a collection of languages, together with some finite representation. Examples are the regular (e.g. represented by finite automata) or the context-free languages (e.g. represented by pushdown automata or PDA). A relatively weak and reasonable assumption on a language class is that it is a *full trio*, that is, it is closed under each of the following operations: taking intersection with a regular language, taking homomorphic images, and taking inverse homomorphic images. Equivalently, a language class is a full trio iff it is closed under *rational transductions* [5].

We assume that all full trios $\mathcal{C}$ considered in this paper are *effective*: Given a language L from $\mathcal{C}$, a regular language R, and a homomorphism h, we can compute a representation of the languages $L \cap R$, $h(L)$, and $h^{-1}(L)$ in $\mathcal{C}$.

Many classes of languages studied in formal language theory form effective full trios. Examples include the regular and the context-free languages [18], the indexed languages [2,10], the languages of higher-order pushdown automata [26], higher-order recursion schemes (HORS) [16,9], Petri nets [14,19], and lossy channel systems (see Section 4.1). (While HORS are usually viewed as representing a tree or collection of trees, one can also view them as representing a word language, as we explain in Section 5.)

Informally, a language class defined by non-deterministic devices with a finite-state control that allows ε-transitions and imposes no restriction between input letter and performed configuration changes (such as non-deterministic pushdown automata) is always a full trio: The three operations above can be realized by simple modifications of the finite-state control. The deterministic context-free languages are a class that is *not* a full trio.

Asynchronous Programs: A Language-Theoretic View We use a language-theoretic model for asynchronous shared-memory programs.

Definition 1. *Let C be an (effective) full trio. An* asynchronous program *(AP)* over C is a tuple $\mathfrak{P} = (D, \Sigma, (L_c)_{c \in \mathfrak{C}}, d_0, \mathbf{m}_0)$, where D is a finite set of global states, Σ is an alphabet of handler names, $(L_c)_{c \in \mathfrak{C}}$ is a family of languages from C, one for each $c \in \mathfrak{C}$ where $\mathfrak{C} = D \times \Sigma \times D$ is the set of contexts, $d_0 \in D$ is the initial state, and $\mathbf{m}_0 \in \mathbb{M}[\Sigma]$ is a multiset of initial pending handler instances.

A configuration $(d, \mathbf{m}) \in D \times \mathbb{M}[\Sigma]$ *of $\mathfrak{P}$ consists of a global state d and a multiset $\mathbf{m}$ of pending handler instances. For a configuration c, we write $c.d$ and $c.\mathbf{m}$ for the global state and the multiset in the configuration respectively. The* initial configuration c_0 *of $\mathfrak{P}$ is given by $c_0.d = d_0$ and $c_0.\mathbf{m} = \mathbf{m}_0$. The semantics of $\mathfrak{P}$ is given as a labeled transition system over the set of configurations, with the transition relation $\xrightarrow{\sigma} \subseteq (D \times \mathbb{M}[\Sigma]) \times (D \times \mathbb{M}[\Sigma])$ given by*

$$(d, \mathbf{m} \oplus [\![\sigma]\!]) \xrightarrow{\sigma} (d', \mathbf{m} \oplus \mathbf{m}') \quad iff \quad \exists w \in L_{d\sigma d'} : \mathsf{Parikh}(w) = \mathbf{m}'$$

We use $\to^*$ for the reflexive transitive closure of the transition relation. A configuration c is said to be reachable *in $\mathfrak{P}$ if $(d_0, \mathbf{m}_0) \to^* c$.*

Intuitively, the set Σ of handler names specifies a finite set of procedures that can be invoked asynchronously. The shared state takes values in D. When a handler is called asynchronously, it gets added to a bag of pending handler calls (the multiset $\mathbf{m}$ in a configuration). The language $L_{d\sigma d'}$ captures the effect of executing an instance of σ starting from the global state d, such that on termination, the global state is d'. Each word $w \in L_{d\sigma d'}$ captures a possible sequence of handlers posted during the execution.

Suppose the current configuration is $(d, \mathbf{m})$. A non-deterministic scheduler picks one of the outstanding handlers $\sigma \in \mathbf{m}$ and executes it. Executing σ corresponds to picking one of the languages $L_{d\sigma d'}$ and some word $w \in L_{d\sigma d'}$. Upon execution of σ, the new configuration has global state d' and the new bag of pending calls is obtained by taking $\mathbf{m}$, removing an instance of σ from it, and adding the Parikh image of w to it. This reflects the current set of pending handler calls—the old ones (minus an instance of σ) together with the new ones added by executing σ. Note that a handler is executed atomically; thus, we atomically update the global state and the effect of executing the handler.

Let us see some examples of asynchronous programs. It is convenient to present these examples in a programming language syntax, and to allow each

```
1  global var turn = ref 0 and x = ref 0;
2  let rec s1 () = if * then begin post a; s1(); post b end
3  let rec s2 () = if * then begin post a; s2(); post b end else post b
4  let a () = if !turn = 0 then begin turn := 1; x := !x + 1 end else post a
5  let b () = if !turn = 1 then begin turn := 0; x := !x - 1 end else post b
6
7  let s3 () = post s3; post s3
8
9  global var t = ref 0;
10 let c () = if !t = 0 then t := 1 else post c
11 let d () = if !t = 1 then t := 2 else post d
12 let f () = if !t = 2 then t := 0 else post f
13
14 let cc x = post c; x
15 let dd x = post d; x
16 let ff x = post f; x
17 let id x = x
18 let h g y = cc (g (dd y))
19 let rec produce g x = if * then produce (h g) (ff x) else g x
20 let s4 () = produce id ()
```

Fig. 1. Examples of asynchronous programs

handler to have *internal actions* that perform local tests and updates to the global state. As we describe informally below, and formally in the full version, when $\mathcal{C}$ is a full trio, internal actions can be "compiled away" by taking an intersection with a regular language of internal actions and projecting the internal actions away. Thus, we use our simpler model throughout.

Examples Figure 1 shows some simple examples of asynchronous programs in an OCaml-like syntax. Consider first the asynchronous program in lines 1–5. The alphabet of handlers is s1, s2, a, and b. The global states correspond to possible valuations to the global variables turn and x; assuming turn is a Boolean and x takes values in $\mathbb{N}$, we have that $D = \{0, 1\} \times \{0, 1, \omega\}$, where ω abstracts all values other than $\{0, 1\}$. Since s1 and s2 do not touch any variables, for $d, d' \in D$, we have $L_{d,\text{s1},d} = \{a^n b^n \mid n \geq 0\}$, $L_{d,\text{s2},d} = \{a^n b^{n+1} \mid n \geq 0\}$, and $L_{d,\text{s1},d'} = L_{d,\text{s2},d'} = \emptyset$ if $d' \neq d$.

For the languages corresponding to a and b, we use syntactic sugar in the form of *internal actions*; these are local tests and updates to the global state. For our example, we have, e.g., $L_{(0,0),\text{a},(1,1)} = \{\varepsilon\}$, $L_{(1,x),\text{a},(1,x)} = \{a\}$ for all values of x, and similarly for b. The meaning is that, starting from a global state $(0, 0)$, executing the handler will lead to the global state $(1, 1)$ and no handlers will be posted, whereas starting from a global state in which turn is 1, executing the handler will keep the global state unchanged but post an instance of a. Note that all the languages are context-free.

Consider an execution of the program from the initial configuration $((0, 0), [\![\text{s1}]\!])$. The execution of s1 puts n as and n bs into the bag, for some $n \geq 0$. The global variable turn is used to ensure that the handlers a and b alternately update x. When turn is 0, the handler for a increments x and sets turn to 1, otherwise it re-posts itself for a future execution. Likewise, when turn is 1, the handler for b decrements x and sets turn back to 0, otherwise it re-posts itself for a future execution. As a result, the variable x never grows beyond 1. Thus, the program satisfies the *safety* property that no execution sets x to ω.

It is possible that the execution goes on forever: for example, if s1 posts an a and a b, and thereafter only b is chosen by the scheduler. This is not an "interesting" infinite execution as it is not fair to the pending a. In the case of a fair scheduler, which eventually always picks an instance of every pending task, the program terminates: eventually all the as and bs are consumed when they are scheduled in alternation. However, if instead we started with [[s2]], the program will not terminate even under a fair scheduler: the last remaining b will not be paired and will keep executing and re-posting itself forever.

Now consider the execution of s3. It has an infinite fair run, where the scheduler picks an instance of s3 at each step. However, the number of pending instances grows without bound. We shall study the *boundedness problem*, which checks if the bag can become unbounded along some run. We also study a stronger notion of fair termination, called *fair non-starvation*, which asks that every *instance* of a posted handler is executed under any fair scheduler. The execution of s3 is indeed fair, but there can be a specific instance of s3 that is never picked: we say s3 can *starve* an instance.

The program in lines 9–20 is *higher-order* (produce and h take functions as arguments). The language of s4 is the set $\{c^n d^n f^n \mid n \geq 0\}$, that is, it posts an equal number of cs, ds, and fs. It is an indexed language; we shall see (Section 5) how this and other higher-order programs can be represented using higher-order recursion schemes (HORS). Note the OCaml types of produce : $(o \to o) \to o \to o$ and h : $(o \to o) \to o \to o$ are higher-order.

The program is similar to the first: the handlers c, d, and f execute in "round robin" fashion using the global state t to find their turns. Again, we use internal actions to update the global state for readability. We ask the same decision questions as before: does the program ever reach a specific global state and does the program have an infinite (fair) run? We shall see later that safety and termination questions remain decidable, whereas fair termination does not.

3   Decision Problems on Asynchronous Programs

We now describe decision problems on runs of asynchronous programs.

Runs, preruns, and downclosures A *prerun* of an AP $\mathfrak{P} = (D, \Sigma, (L_c)_{c \in \mathfrak{C}}, d_0, \mathbf{m}_0)$ is a finite or infinite sequence $\rho = (e_0, \mathbf{n}_0), \sigma_1, (e_1, \mathbf{n}_1), \sigma_2, \ldots$ of alternating elements of tuples $(e_i, \mathbf{n}_i) \in D \times \mathbb{M}[\Sigma]$ and symbols $\sigma_i \in \Sigma$. The set of preruns of $\mathfrak{P}$ will be denoted $\mathsf{Preruns}(\mathfrak{P})$. Note that if two asynchronous programs $\mathfrak{P}$ and $\mathfrak{P}'$ have the same D and Σ, then $\mathsf{Preruns}(\mathfrak{P}) = \mathsf{Preruns}(\mathfrak{P}')$. The *length*, denoted $|\rho|$, of a finite prerun ρ is the number of configurations in ρ. The ith configuration of a prerun ρ will be denoted $\rho(i)$.

We define an order $\trianglelefteq$ on preruns as follows: For preruns $\rho = (e_0, \mathbf{n}_0), \sigma_1, (e_1, \mathbf{n}_1), \sigma_2, \ldots$ and $\rho' = (e_0', \mathbf{n}_0'), \sigma_1', (e_1', \mathbf{n}_1'), \sigma_2', \ldots$, we define $\rho \trianglelefteq \rho'$ if $|\rho| = |\rho'|$ and $e_i = e_i', \sigma_i = \sigma_i'$ and $\mathbf{n}_i \preceq \mathbf{n}_i'$ for each $i \geq 0$. The *downclosure* $\downarrow R$ of a set R of preruns of $\mathfrak{P}$ is defined as $\downarrow R = \{\rho \in \mathsf{Preruns}(\mathfrak{P}) \mid \exists \rho' \in R. \rho \trianglelefteq \rho'\}$.

A *run* of an AP $\mathfrak{P} = (D, \Sigma, (L_c)_{c \in \mathfrak{C}}, d_0, \mathbf{m}_0)$ is a prerun $\rho = (d_0, \mathbf{m}_0), \sigma_1, (d_1, \mathbf{m}_1), \sigma_2, \ldots$ starting with the initial configuration $(d_0, \mathbf{m}_0)$, where for each $i \geq 0$, we have $(d_i, \mathbf{m}_i) \xrightarrow{\sigma_{i+1}} (d_{i+1}, \mathbf{m}_{i+1})$. The set of runs of $\mathfrak{P}$ is denoted $\mathsf{Runs}(\mathfrak{P})$ and $\downarrow\mathsf{Runs}(\mathfrak{P})$ is its downclosure with respect to $\trianglelefteq$.

An infinite run $c_0 \xrightarrow{\sigma_0} c_1 \xrightarrow{\sigma_1} \ldots$ is *fair* if for all $i \geq 0$, if $\sigma \in c_i.\mathbf{m}$ then there is some $j \geq i$ such that $c_j \xrightarrow{\sigma} c_{j+1}$. That is, whenever an instance of a handler is posted, some instance of the handler is executed later. Fairness does not preclude that a specific instance of a handler is never executed. An infinite fair run *starves* handler σ if there exists an index $J \geq 0$ such that for each $j \geq J$, we have (i) $c_j.\mathbf{m}(\sigma) \geq 1$ and (ii) whenever $c_j \xrightarrow{\sigma} c_{j+1}$, we have $c_j.\mathbf{m}(\sigma) \geq 2$. In this case, even if the run is fair, a specific instance of σ may never be executed.

Now we give the definitions of the various decision problems.

Definition 2 (Properties of finite runs). *The* **Safety (Global state reachability)** *problem asks, given an asynchronous program $\mathfrak{P}$ and a global state $d_f \in D$, is there a reachable configuration c such that $c.d = d_f$? If so, d_f is said to be* reachable *(in $\mathfrak{P}$) and* unreachable *otherwise. The* **Boundedness (of the task buffer)** *problem asks, given an asynchronous program $\mathfrak{P}$, is there an $N \in \mathbb{N}$ such that for every reachable configuration c, we have $|c.\mathbf{m}| \leq N$? If so, the asynchronous program $\mathfrak{P}$ is* bounded; *otherwise it is* unbounded. *The* **Configuration reachability** *problem asks, given an asynchronous program $\mathfrak{P}$ and a configuration c, is c reachable?*

Definition 3 (Properties of infinite runs). *All the following problems take as input an asynchronous program $\mathfrak{P}$. The* **Termination** *problem asks if all runs of $\mathfrak{P}$ are finite. The* **Fair Non-termination** *problem asks if $\mathfrak{P}$ has some fair infinite run. The* **Fair Starvation** *problem asks if $\mathfrak{P}$ has some fair run that starves some handler.*

Our main result in this section shows that many properties of an asynchronous program $\mathfrak{P}$ only depend on the downclosure $\downarrow\mathsf{Runs}(\mathfrak{P})$ of the set $\mathsf{Runs}(\mathfrak{P})$ of runs of the program $\mathfrak{P}$. The proof is by induction on the length of runs. For any AP $\mathfrak{P} = (D, \Sigma, (L_c)_{c \in \mathfrak{C}}, d_0, \mathbf{m}_0)$, we define the AP $\downarrow\mathfrak{P} = (D, \Sigma, (\downarrow L_c)_{c \in \mathfrak{C}}, d_0, \mathbf{m}_0)$, where $\downarrow L_c$ is the downclosure of the language L_c under the subword order.

Proposition 1. *Let $\mathfrak{P} = (D, \Sigma, (L_c)_{c \in \mathfrak{C}}, d_0, \mathbf{m}_0)$ be an asynchronous program. Then $\downarrow\mathsf{Runs}(\downarrow\mathfrak{P}) = \downarrow\mathsf{Runs}(\mathfrak{P})$. In particular, the following holds. (1) For every $d \in D$, $\mathfrak{P}$ can reach d if and only if $\downarrow\mathfrak{P}$ can reach d. (2) $\mathfrak{P}$ is terminating if and only if $\downarrow\mathfrak{P}$ is terminating. (3) $\mathfrak{P}$ is bounded if and only if $\downarrow\mathfrak{P}$ is bounded.*

Intuitively, safety, termination, and boundedness is preserved when the multiset of pending handler instances is "lossy": posted handlers can get lost. This corresponds to these handlers never being scheduled by the scheduler. However, if a run demonstrates reachability of a global state, or non-termination, or unboundedness, in the lossy version, it corresponds also to a run in the original problem (and conversely). In contrast, simple examples show that configuration reachability, fair termination, and fair non-starvation properties are not preserved under downclosures.

4 General Decidability Results

In this section, we characterize those full trios $\mathcal{C}$ for which particular problems for asynchronous programs over $\mathcal{C}$ are decidable. Our decision procedures will use the following theorem, summarizing the results from [12], as a subprocedure.

Theorem 1 ([12]). *Safety, boundedness, configuration reachability, termination, fair non-termination, and fair non-starvation are decidable for asynchronous programs over regular languages.*

4.1 Safety and termination

Our first main result concerns the problems of safety and termination.

Theorem 2. *Let $\mathcal{C}$ be a full trio. The following are equivalent:*

(i) Safety is decidable for asynchronous programs over $\mathcal{C}$.
(ii) Termination is decidable for asynchronous programs over $\mathcal{C}$.
(iii) Emptiness is decidable for $\mathcal{C}$.

We begin with "(i)$\Rightarrow$(iii)". Let $K \subseteq \Sigma^*$ be given. We construct $\mathfrak{P} = (D, \Sigma, (L_c)_{c \in \mathfrak{C}}, d_0, \mathbf{m}_0)$ such that $\mathbf{m}_0 = [\![\sigma]\!]$, $D = \{d_0, d_1\}$, $L_{d_0, \sigma, d_1} = K$ and $L_c = \emptyset$ for $c \neq (d_0, \sigma, d_1)$. We see that $\mathfrak{P}$ can reach d_1 iff K is non-empty. Next we show "(ii)$\Rightarrow$(iii)". Consider the alphabet $\Gamma = (\Sigma \cup \{\varepsilon\}) \times \{0, 1\}$ and the homomorphisms $g \colon \Gamma^* \to \Sigma^*$ and $h \colon \Gamma^* \to \{\sigma\}^*$, where for $x \in \Sigma \cup \{\varepsilon\}$, we have $g((x, i)) = x$ for $i \in \{0, 1\}$, $h((x, 1)) = \sigma$, and $h((x, 0)) = \varepsilon$. If $R \subseteq \Gamma^*$ is the regular set of words in which exactly one position belongs to the subalphabet $(\Sigma \cup \{\varepsilon\}) \times \{1\}$, then the language $K' := h(g^{-1}(K) \cap R)$ belongs to $\mathcal{C}$. Note that K' is $\emptyset$ or $\{\sigma\}$, depending on whether K is empty or not. We construct $\mathfrak{P} = (D, \Sigma, (L_c)_{c \in \mathfrak{C}}, d_0, \mathbf{m}_0)$ with $D = \{d_0\}$, $\mathbf{m}_0 = [\![\sigma]\!]$, $L_{d_0, \sigma, d_0} = K'$ and all languages $L_c = \emptyset$ for $c \neq (d_0, \sigma, d_0)$. Then $\mathfrak{P}$ is terminating iff K is empty.

To prove "(iii)$\Rightarrow$(i)", we design an algorithm deciding safety assuming decidability of emptiness. Given asynchronous program $\mathfrak{P}$ and state d as input, the algorithm consists of two semi-decision procedures: one which searches for a run of $\mathfrak{P}$ reaching the state d, and the second which enumerates regular overapproximations $\mathfrak{P}'$ of $\mathfrak{P}$ and checks the safety of $\mathfrak{P}'$ using Theorem 1. Each $\mathfrak{P}'$ consists of a regular language A_c overapproximating L_c for each context c of $\mathfrak{P}$. We use decidability of emptiness to check that $L_c \cap (\Sigma^* \setminus A_c) = \emptyset$ to ensure that $\mathfrak{P}'$ is indeed an overapproximation.

The algorithm clearly gives a correct answer if it terminates. Hence, we only have to argue that it always does terminate. Of course, if d is reachable, the first semi-decision procedure will terminate. In the other case, termination is due to the regularity of downclosures: if d is not reachable in $\mathfrak{P}$, then Proposition 1 tells us that $\downarrow\mathfrak{P}$ cannot reach d either. But $\downarrow\mathfrak{P}$ is an asynchronous program over regular languages; this means there exists a safe regular overapproximation and the second semi-decision procedure terminates.

Like the algorithm for safety, the algorithm for termination consists of two semi-decision procedures. By standard well-quasi-ordering arguments, an infinite run of an asynchronous program $\mathfrak{P}$ is witnessed by a finite self-covering run. The first semi-decision procedure enumerates finite self-covering runs (trying to show non-termination). The second procedure enumerates regular asynchronous programs $\mathfrak{P}'$ that overapproximate $\mathfrak{P}$. As before, to check termination of $\mathfrak{P}'$, it applies the procedure from Theorem 1. Clearly, the algorithm's answer is always correct. Moreover, it gives an answer for every input. If $\mathfrak{P}$ does not terminate, it will find a self-covering sequence. If $\mathfrak{P}$ does terminate, then Proposition 1 tells us that $\downarrow\mathfrak{P}$ is a terminating finite-state overapproximation. This implies that the second procedure will terminate in that case.

Let us point out a particular example. The class $\mathcal{L}$ of languages of lossy channel systems is defined like the class of languages of WSTS with upward-closed sets of accepting configurations as in [13], except that we only consider lossy channel systems [1] instead of arbitrary Well-Structured Transition Systems (WSTS). Then $\mathcal{L}$ forms a full trio with decidable emptiness. Although downclosures of lossy channel languages are not effectively computable (an easy consequence of [27]), our algorithm employs Theorem 2 to decide safety and termination.

4.2   Boundedness

Theorem 3. *Let $\mathcal{C}$ be a full trio. The following are equivalent:*

    (i) Boundedness is decidable for asynchronous programs over $\mathcal{C}$.
    (ii) Finiteness is decidable for $\mathcal{C}$.

Clearly, the construction for "(i)$\Rightarrow$(iii)" of Theorem 2 also works for "(i)$\Rightarrow$(ii)": $\mathfrak{P}$ is unbounded iff K is infinite.

For the converse, we first note that if finiteness is decidable for $\mathcal{C}$ then so is emptiness. Given $L \subseteq \Sigma^*$ from $\mathcal{C}$, consider the homomorphism $h\colon (\Sigma \cup \{\lambda\})^* \to \Sigma^*$ with $h(\mathsf{a}) = \mathsf{a}$ for every $\mathsf{a} \in \Sigma$ and $h(\lambda) = \varepsilon$. Then $h^{-1}(L)$ belongs to $\mathcal{C}$ and $h^{-1}(L)$ is finite if and only if L is empty: in the inverse homomorphism, λ can be arbitrarily inserted in any word. By Theorem 2, this implies that we can also decide safety. As a consequence of considering only full trios, it is easy to see that the problem of *context reachability* reduces to safety: a context $\hat{c} = (\hat{d}, \hat{\sigma}, \hat{d}') \in \mathfrak{C}$ is *reachable in* $\mathfrak{P}$ if there is a reachable configuration $(\hat{d}, \mathbf{m})$ in $\mathfrak{P}$ with $\mathbf{m}(\hat{\sigma}) \geq 1$.

We now explain our algorithm for deciding boundedness of a given aysnchronous program $\mathfrak{P} = (D, \Sigma, (L_c)_{c\in\mathfrak{C}}, d_0, \mathbf{m}_0)$. For every context c, we first check if L_c is infinite (feasible by assumption). This paritions the set of contexts of $\mathfrak{P}$ into sets I and F which are the contexts for which the corresponding language L_c is infinite and finite respectively. If any context in I is reachable, then $\mathfrak{P}$ is unbounded. Otherwise, all the reachable contexts have a finite language. For every finite language L_c for some $c \in F$, we explicitly find all the members of L_c. This is possible because any finite set A can be checked with L_c for equality. $L_c \subseteq A$ can be checked by testing whether $L_c \cap (\Sigma^* \setminus A) = \emptyset$ and $L_c \cap (\Sigma^* \setminus A)$ effectively belongs to $\mathcal{C}$. On the other hand, checking $A \subseteq L_c$ just means checking whether $L_c \cap \{w\} \neq \emptyset$ for each $w \in A$, which can be done the same way. We can now construct asynchronous program $\mathfrak{P}'$ which replaces all languages for contexts in I by $\emptyset$ and replaces those corresponding to F by the explicit description. Clearly $\mathfrak{P}'$ is bounded iff $\mathfrak{P}$ is bounded (since no contexts from I are reachable) and the former can be decided by Theorem 1.

We observe that boundedness is strictly harder than safety or termination: There are full trios for which emptiness is decidable, but finiteness is undecidable, such as the languages of reset vector addition systems [11] (see [32] for a definition of the language class) and languages of lossy channel systems.

4.3 Configuration reachability and liveness properties

Theorems 2 and 3 completely characterize for which full trios safety, termination, and boundedness are decidable. We turn to configuration reachability, fair termination, and fair starvation. We suspect that it is unlikely that there is a simple characterization of those language classes for which the latter problems are decidable. However, we show that they are decidable for a limited range of infinite-state systems. To this end, we prove that decidability of any of these problems implies decidability of the others as well, and also implies the decidability of a simple combinatorial problem that is known to be undecidable for many expressive classes of languages.

Let $Z \subseteq \{a, b\}^*$ be the language $Z = \{w \in \{a, b\}^* \mid |w|_a = |w|_b\}$. The Z-*intersection problem* for a language class $\mathcal{C}$ asks, given a language $K \subseteq \{a, b\}^*$ from $\mathcal{C}$, whether $K \cap Z \neq \emptyset$. Informally, Z is the language of all words with an equal number of as and bs and the Z-intersection problem asks if there is a word in K with an equal number of as and bs.

Theorem 4. *Let $\mathcal{C}$ be a full trio. The following statements are equivalent:*

(i) Configuration reachability is decidable for asynchronous programs over $\mathcal{C}$.
(ii) Fair termination is decidable for asynchronous programs over $\mathcal{C}$.
(iii) Fair starvation is decidable for asynchronous programs over $\mathcal{C}$.

Moreover, if decidability holds, then Z-intersection is decidable for $\mathcal{C}$.

We prove Theorem 4 by providing reductions among the three problems and showing that Z-intersection reduces to configuration reachability. We use diagrams similar to automata to describe asynchronous programs. Here, circles represent global states of the program and we draw an edge $\overset{\sigma | L}{d \longrightarrow d'}$ in case we have $L_{d,\sigma,d'} = L$ in our asynchronous program $\mathfrak{P}$. Furthermore, we have $L_{d,\sigma,d'} = \emptyset$ whenever there is no edge that specifies otherwise. To simplify notation, we draw an edge $d \overset{w|L}{\longrightarrow} d'$ in an asynchronous program for a word $w \in \Sigma^*$, $w = \sigma_1 \ldots \sigma_n$ with $\sigma_1, \ldots, \sigma_n \in \Sigma$, to symbolize a sequence of states

which removes $[\![\sigma_1, \ldots, \sigma_n]\!]$ from the task buffer and posts a multiset of handlers specified by L.

Proof of "(ii)⇒(i)" Given an asynchronous program $\mathfrak{P} = (D, \Sigma, (L_c)_{c \in \mathcal{C}}, d_0, \mathbf{m}_0)$ and a configuration $(d_f, \mathbf{m}_f) \in D \times \mathbb{M}[\Sigma]$, we construct asynchronous program $\mathfrak{P}'$ as follows. Let $\mathbf{z}$ be a fresh letter and let $\mathbf{m}_f = [\![\sigma_1, \ldots, \sigma_n]\!]$. We obtain $\mathfrak{P}'$ from $\mathfrak{P}$ by adding a new state d'_f and including the following edges:

$$\underbrace{(d_f)}\xrightarrow{z\sigma_1 \cdots \sigma_n | \{z\}} \underbrace{(d'_f)}\circlearrowleft z | \{z\}$$

Starting from $(d_0, \mathbf{m}_0 \oplus [\![\mathbf{z}]\!])$, the program $\mathfrak{P}'$ has a fair infinite run iff $(d_f, \mathbf{m}_f)$ is reachable in $\mathfrak{P}$. The 'if' direction is obvious. Conversely, $\mathbf{z}$ has to be executed in any fair run ρ of $\mathfrak{P}'$ which implies that d'_f is reached by $\mathfrak{P}'$ in ρ. Since only $\mathbf{z}$ can be executed at d'_f in ρ, this means that the multiset is exactly $\mathbf{m}_f$ when d_f is reached during ρ. Clearly this initial segment of ρ corresponds to a run of $\mathfrak{P}$ which reaches the target configuration.

Proof of "(iii)⇒(ii)" We construct $\mathfrak{P}' = (D, \Sigma', (L'_c)_{c \in \mathcal{C}'}, d_0, \mathbf{m}'_0)$ given $\mathfrak{P} = (D, \Sigma, (L_c)_{c \in \mathcal{C}}, d_0, \mathbf{m}_0)$ over $\mathcal{C}$ as follows. Let $\Sigma' = \Sigma \cup \{\mathbf{s}\}$, where $\mathbf{s}$ is a fresh handler. Replace each edge

$$\underbrace{(d)}\xrightarrow{\sigma | L} \underbrace{(d')} \quad \text{by} \quad \underbrace{(d)}\xrightarrow{\sigma | L \cup Ls} \underbrace{(d')}\circlearrowleft s | \varepsilon$$

at every state $d \in D$. Moreover, we set $\mathbf{m}'_0 = \mathbf{m}_0 \oplus [\![\mathbf{s}, \mathbf{s}]\!]$. Then $\mathfrak{P}'$ has an infinite fair run that starves some handler if and only if $\mathfrak{P}$ has an infinite fair run. From an infinite fair run ρ of $\mathfrak{P}$, we obtain an infinite fair run of $\mathfrak{P}'$ which starves $\mathbf{s}$, by producing $\mathbf{s}$ while simulating ρ and consuming it in the loop. Conversely, from an infinite fair run ρ' of $\mathfrak{P}'$ which starves some τ, we obtain an infinite fair run ρ of $\mathfrak{P}$ by omitting all productions and consumptions of $\mathbf{s}$ and removing two extra instances of $\mathbf{s}$ from all configurations.

Proof of "(i)⇒(iii)" From $\mathfrak{P} = (D, \Sigma, (L_c)_{c \in \mathcal{C}}, d_0, \mathbf{m}_0)$ over $\mathcal{C}$, for each subset $\Gamma \subseteq \Sigma$ and $\tau \in \Sigma$, we construct an asynchronous program $\mathfrak{P}_{\Gamma, \tau} = (D', \Sigma', (L_c)_{c \in \mathcal{C}'}, d'_0, \mathbf{m}'_0)$ over $\mathcal{C}$ such that a particular configuration is reachable in $\mathfrak{P}_{\Gamma, \tau}$ if and only if $\mathfrak{P}$ has a fair infinite run $\rho_{\Gamma, \tau}$, where Γ is the set of handlers that is executed infinitely often in $\rho_{\Gamma, \tau}$ and $\rho_{\Gamma, \tau}$ starves τ. Since there are only finitely many choices for Γ and τ, decidability of configuration reachability implies decidability of fair starvation. The idea is that run $\rho_{\Gamma, \tau}$ exists if and only if there exists a run

$$(d_0, \mathbf{m}_0) \xrightarrow{\sigma_1} \cdots \xrightarrow{\sigma_n} (d_n, \mathbf{m}_n) = (e_0, \mathbf{n}_0) \xrightarrow{\gamma_1} (e_1, \mathbf{n}_1) \xrightarrow{\gamma_2} \cdots \xrightarrow{\gamma_k} (e_k, \mathbf{n}_k), \quad (1)$$

where $\bigcup_{i=1}^{k} \{\gamma_i\} = \Gamma$, for each $1 \leq i \leq k$ $\mathbf{n}_i \in \mathbb{M}[\Gamma]$, $\mathbf{m}_n \preceq \mathbf{n}_k$, and for each $i \in \{1, \ldots, k\}$ with $\gamma_i = \tau$, we have $\mathbf{n}_{i-1}(\tau) \geq 2$. In such a run, we call $(d_0, \mathbf{m}_0) \xrightarrow{\sigma_1} \cdots \xrightarrow{\sigma_n} (d_n, \mathbf{m}_n)$ its *first phase* and $(e_0, \mathbf{n}_0) \xrightarrow{\gamma_1} \cdots \xrightarrow{\gamma_k} (e_k, \mathbf{n}_k)$ its *second phase*.

Let us explain how $\mathfrak{P}_{\Gamma, \tau}$ reflects the existence of a run as in Eq. (1). The set Σ' of handlers of $\mathfrak{P}_{\Gamma, \tau}$ includes Σ, $\bar{\Sigma}$ and $\hat{\Sigma}$, where $\bar{\Sigma} = \{\bar{\sigma} \mid \sigma \in \Sigma\}$ and $\hat{\Sigma} = \{\hat{\sigma} \mid \sigma \in \Sigma\}$ are disjoint copies of Σ. This means, a multiset $\mathbb{M}[\Sigma']$ contains multisets $\mathbf{m}' = \mathbf{m} \oplus \bar{\mathbf{m}} \oplus \hat{\mathbf{m}}$ with $\mathbf{m} \in \mathbb{M}[\Sigma]$, $\bar{\mathbf{m}} \in \mathbb{M}[\bar{\Sigma}]$, and $\hat{\mathbf{m}} \in \mathbb{M}[\hat{\Sigma}]$. A run of $\mathfrak{P}_{\Gamma, \tau}$ simulates the two phases of ρ. While simulating the first phase, $\mathfrak{P}_{\Gamma, \tau}$ keeps two copies of the task buffer, $\mathbf{m}$ and $\bar{\mathbf{m}}$. The copying is easily accomplished by a homomorphism with $\sigma \mapsto \sigma\bar{\sigma}$ for each $\sigma \in \Sigma$. At some point, $\mathfrak{P}_{\Gamma,\tau}$ switches into simulating the second phase. There, $\bar{\mathbf{m}}$ remains unchanged, so that it stores the value of $\mathbf{m}_n$ in Eq. (1) and can be used in the end to make sure that $\mathbf{m}_n \preceq \mathbf{n}_k$.

Hence, in the second phase, $\mathfrak{P}_{\Gamma,\tau}$ works, like $\mathfrak{P}$, only with Σ. However, whenever a handler $\sigma \in \Sigma$ is executed, it also produces a task $\hat{\sigma}$. These handlers are used at the end to make sure that every $\gamma \in \Gamma$ has been executed at least once in the second phase. Also, whenever τ is executed, $\mathfrak{P}_{\Gamma,\tau}$ checks that at least two instances of τ are present in the task buffer, thereby ensuring that τ is starved.

In the end, a distinguished final state allows $\mathfrak{P}_{\Gamma,\tau}$ to execute handlers in Γ and $\bar{\Gamma}$ simultaneously to make sure that $\mathbf{m}_n \preceq \mathbf{n}_k$. In its final state, $\mathfrak{P}_{\Gamma,\tau}$ can execute handlers $\hat{\gamma} \in \hat{\Gamma}$ and $\gamma \in \Gamma$ (without creating new handlers). In the final configuration, there can be no $\hat{\sigma}$ with $\sigma \in \Sigma \setminus \Gamma$, and there has to be exactly one $\hat{\gamma}$ for each $\gamma \in \Gamma$. This guarantees that (i) each handler in Γ is executed at least once during the second phase, (ii) every handler executed in the second phase is from Γ, and (iii) $\mathbf{m}_n$ contains only handlers from Γ (because handlers from $\bar{\Sigma}$ cannot be executed in the second phase).

Decidability of Z-intersection To complete the proof of Theorem 4, we reduce Z-intersection to configuration reachability. Given $K \subseteq \{\mathsf{a},\mathsf{b}\}^*$ from $\mathcal{C}$, we construct the asynchronous program $\mathfrak{P} = (D, \Sigma, (L_c)_{c \in \mathcal{C}}, d_0, \mathbf{m}_0)$ over $\mathcal{C}$ where $D = \{d_0, 0, 1\}$, $\Sigma = \{\mathsf{a},\mathsf{b},\mathsf{c}\}$, by including the following edges:

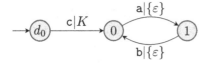

The initial task buffer is $\mathbf{m}_0 = [\![\mathsf{c}]\!]$. Then clearly, the configuration $(0, [\![]\!])$ is reachable in $\mathfrak{P}$ if and only if $K \cap Z \neq \emptyset$.

Theorem 4 is useful in the contrapositive to show undecidability. For example, one can show undecidability of Z-intersection for languages of lossy channel systems (see Section 4.1): One expresses reachability in a non-lossy FIFO system by making sure that the numbers of enqueue- and dequeue-operations match. Thus, for asynchronous programs over lossy channel systems, the problems of Theorem 4 are undecidable. We also use Theorem 4 in Section 5 to conclude undecidability for higher-order asynchronous programs, already at order 2.

5   Higher-Order Asynchronous Programs

We apply our general decidability results to asynchronous programs over (deterministic) higher-order recursion schemes (HORS). Kobayashi [21] has shown how higher-order functional programs can be modeled using HORS. In his setting, a program contains instructions that access certain resources. For Kobayashi, the path language of the HORS is the set of possible sequences of instructions. For us, the input program contains **post** instructions and we translate higher-order programs with **post** instructions into a HORS whose path language is used as the language of handlers.

We recall some definitions from [21]. The set of *types* is defined by the grammar $A := o \mid A \to A$. The *order* $\mathrm{ord}(A)$ of a type A is inductively defined as $\mathrm{ord}(o) = 0$ and $\mathrm{ord}(A \to B) := \max(\mathrm{ord}(A) + 1, \mathrm{ord}(B))$. The *arity* of a type is inductively defined by $\mathrm{arity}(o) = 0$ and $\mathrm{arity}(A \to B) = \mathrm{arity}(B) + 1$. We assume a countably infinite set Var of typed variables $x : A$. For a set Θ of typed symbols, the set $\tilde{\Theta}$ of *terms* generated from Θ is the least set which contains Θ such that whenever $s : A \to B$ and $t : A$ belong to $\tilde{\Theta}$, then also $s\,t : B$ belongs to $\tilde{\Theta}$. By convention the type $o \to \ldots (o \to (o \to o))$ is written $o \to \ldots \to o \to o$ and the term $((t_1 t_2) t_3 \cdots) t_n$ is written $t_1 t_2 \cdots t_n$. We write $\bar{x}$ for a sequence $(x_1, x_2, \ldots, x_n)$ of variables.

A higher-order recursion scheme (HORS) is a tuple $\mathscr{S} = (\Sigma, \mathcal{N}, \mathcal{R}, S)$ where Σ is a set of typed *terminal* symbols of types of order 0 or 1, $\mathcal{N}$ is a set of typed *non-terminal* symbols (disjoint from terminal symbols), $S : o$ is the start non-terminal symbol and $\mathcal{R}$ is a set of rewrite rules $F x_1 x_2 \cdots x_n \twoheadrightarrow t$ where $F : A_1 \to \cdots \to A_n \to o$ is a non-terminal in $\mathcal{N}$, $x_i : A_i$ for all i are variables and $t : o$ is a term generated from $\Sigma \cup \mathcal{N} \cup$ Var. The order of a HORS is the maximum order of a non-terminal symbol. We define a rewrite relation $\twoheadrightarrow$ on terms over $\Sigma \cup \mathcal{N}$ as follows: $F \bar{a} \twoheadrightarrow t[\bar{x}/\bar{a}]$ if $F \bar{x} \twoheadrightarrow t \in \mathcal{R}$, and if $t \twoheadrightarrow t'$ then $ts \twoheadrightarrow t's$ and $st \twoheadrightarrow st'$. The reflexive, transitive closure of $\twoheadrightarrow$ is denoted $\twoheadrightarrow^*$. A *sentential form* t of $\mathscr{S}$ is a term over $\Sigma \cup \mathcal{N}$ such that $S \twoheadrightarrow^* t$.

If N is the maximum arity of a symbol in Σ, then a (possibly infinite) tree over Σ is a partial function tr from $\{0, 1, \ldots, N-1\}^*$ to Σ that fulfills the following conditions: $\varepsilon \in \mathrm{dom}(tr)$, $\mathrm{dom}(tr)$ is closed under prefixes, and if $tr(w) = a$ and $\mathrm{arity}(a) = k$ then $\{j \mid wj \in \mathrm{dom}(tr)\} = \{0, 1, \ldots, k-1\}$.

A *deterministic* HORS is one where there is exactly one rule of the form $F x_1 x_2 \cdots x_n \to t$ for every non-terminal F. Following [21], we show how a deterministic HORS can be used to represent a higher-order pushdown language arising from a higher-order functional program.

Sentential forms can be seen as ranked trees over $\Sigma \cup \mathcal{N} \cup$ Var. A sequence Π over $\{0, 1, \ldots, n-1\}$ is a *path* of tr if every finite prefix of $\Pi \in \mathrm{dom}(tr)$. The set of paths in a tree tr will be denoted $\mathsf{Paths}(tr)$. Note that we are only interested in finite paths in our context. Associated with any path $\Pi = n_1, n_2, \ldots, n_k$ is the word $w_\Pi = tr(n_1) tr(n_1 n_2) \cdots tr(n_1 n_2 \cdots n_k)$. Let $\Sigma_1 := \{a \in \Sigma \mid \mathrm{arity}(a) = 1\}$. The *path language* $\mathcal{L}_\mathsf{p}(\mathscr{S})$ of a deterministic HORS $\mathscr{S}$ is defined as $\{\mathrm{Proj}_{\Sigma_1}(w_\Pi) \mid \Pi \in \mathsf{Paths}(\mathcal{T}_\mathscr{S})\}$. The *tree language* $\mathcal{L}_\mathsf{t}(\mathscr{S})$ associated with a HORS is the set of finite trees over Σ generated by $\mathscr{S}$.

The deterministic HORS corresponding to the higher-order function **s3** from Figure 1 is given by $\mathscr{S} = (\Sigma, \mathcal{N}, \mathcal{R}, S)$, where

$$\Sigma = \{\mathsf{br} : o \to o \to o, \mathsf{c}, \mathsf{d}, \mathsf{f} : o \to o, \mathsf{e} : o\}$$

$$\mathcal{N} = \{S : o, F : (o \to o) \to o \to o, H : (o \to o) \to o \to o, I : o \to o\}$$

$$\mathcal{R} = \{S \twoheadrightarrow F\,I\,\mathsf{e}, I\,x \twoheadrightarrow x, F\,G\,x \twoheadrightarrow \mathsf{br}(F\,(H\,G)\,(\mathsf{f}x))\,(G\,x),$$
$$H\,G\,x \twoheadrightarrow \mathsf{c}(G(\mathsf{d}x))\}$$

The path language $\mathcal{L}_p(\mathscr{S}) = \{c^n d^n f^n \mid n \geq 0\}$. To see this, apply the reduction rules to get the value tree $\mathcal{T}_{\mathscr{S}}$ shown on the right:

$S \twoheadrightarrow F\ I\ \mathsf{e} \twoheadrightarrow \mathsf{br}\ (F\ (HI)\ (\mathsf{fe}))\ (I\mathsf{e})$

$\twoheadrightarrow \mathsf{br}\ (F\ (HI)\ (\mathsf{fe}))\ \mathsf{e}$

$\twoheadrightarrow \mathsf{br}\ (\mathsf{br}\ (F\ (H^2 I)\ (\mathsf{f}^2 \mathsf{e}))\ (HI)(\mathsf{fe}))\ \mathsf{e}$

$\twoheadrightarrow \mathsf{br}\ (\mathsf{br}\ (F\ (H^2 I)\ (\mathsf{f}^2 \mathsf{e}))\ \mathsf{c}(I(\mathsf{dfe}))\ \mathsf{e}$

$\twoheadrightarrow \mathsf{br}\ (\mathsf{br}\ (F\ (H^2 I)\ (\mathsf{f}^2 \mathsf{e}))\ \mathsf{cdfe})\ \mathsf{e}$

$\twoheadrightarrow \cdots$

A HORS $\mathscr{S}$ is called a *word scheme* if it has exactly one nullary terminal symbol e and all other terminal symbols $\tilde{\Sigma}$ are of arity one. The *word language* $\mathcal{L}_w(\mathscr{S}) \subseteq \tilde{\Sigma}^*$ defined by $\mathscr{S}$ is $\mathcal{L}_w(\mathscr{S}) = \{a_1 a_2 \cdots a_n \mid (a_1(a_2 \cdots (a_n(\mathsf{e})) \cdots)) \in \mathcal{L}_t(\mathscr{S})\}$. We denote by $\mathcal{H}$ the class of languages $\mathcal{L}_w(\mathscr{S})$ that occur as the word language of a higher-order recursion scheme $\mathscr{S}$. Note that path languages and languages of word schemes are both word languages over the set $\tilde{\Sigma}$ of unary symbols considered as letters. They are connected by the following proposition.[2]

Proposition 2. *For every order-n HORS $\mathscr{S} = (\Sigma, \mathcal{N}, S, \mathcal{R})$ there exists an order-n word scheme $\mathscr{S}' = (\Sigma', \mathcal{N}', S', \mathcal{R}')$ such that $\mathcal{L}_p(\mathscr{S}) = \mathcal{L}_w(\mathscr{S}')$.*

A consequence of [21] and Prop. 2 is that the "post" language of higher-order functional programs can be modeled as the language of a word scheme. Hence, we define an *asynchronous program over* HORS as an asynchronous program over the language class $\mathcal{H}$ and we can use the following results on word schemes.

Theorem 5. HORS *and word schemes form effective full trios [7]. Emptiness [23] and finiteness [29] of order-n word schemes are $(n-1)$-EXPTIME-complete.*

Now Theorems 2 and 3, together with Proposition 2 imply the decidability results in Corollary 1. The undecidability result is a consequence of Theorem 4 and the undecidability of the Z-intersection problem for indexed languages or equivalently, order-2 pushdown automata as shown in [33]. Order-2 pushdown automata can be effectively turned into order-2 OI grammars [10], which in turn can be translated into order-2 word schemes [9]. See also [22, Theorem 4].

Corollary 1. *For asynchronous programs over* HORS: *(1) Safety, termination, and boundedness are decidable. (2) Configuration reachability, fair termination, and fair starvation are undecidable already at order-2.*

A Direct Algorithm We say that *downclosures are computable* for a language class $\mathcal{C}$ if for a given description of a language L in $\mathcal{C}$, one can compute an automaton for the regular language $\downarrow L$. From Proposition 1 and Theorem 1,

---

[2] The models of HORS (used in model checking higher order programs [21]) and word schemes (used in language-theoretic exploration of downclosures [15,7]) are somewhat different. Thus, we show an explicit reduction between the two formalisms.

if one can compute downclosures for a language class, then one can avoid the enumerative approaches of Section 4 and get a "direct algorithm." The algorithm replaces each handler by its downclosure and then invokes the decision procedure summarized in Theorem 1. The direct algorithm for asynchronous programs over HORS relies on the recent breakthrough results on computing downclosures.

Theorem 6 ([33,15,7]). *Downclosures are effectively computable for* $\mathcal{H}$.

Unfortunately, current techniques for computing downclosures do not yet provide a complexity upper bound as we describe below. In [33], it was shown that in a full trio, downclosures are computable if and only if the *diagonal problem* for $\mathcal{C}$ is decidable. The latter asks, given a language $L \subseteq \Sigma^*$, whether for every $k \in \mathbb{N}$, there is a word $w \in L$ with $|w|_\sigma \geq k$ for every $\sigma \in \Sigma$. The diagonal problem was then shown to be decidable for higher-order pushdown automata [15] and then for word schemes [7]. The algorithm from [33] to compute downclosures using an oracle for the diagonal problem employs enumeration to compute a downclosure automaton, thus we have hidden the enumeration into the downclosure computation. We conjecture that downclosures can be computed in elementary time for word schemes of fixed order. This would imply an elementary time procedure for asynchronous programs over HORS of fixed order.

For handlers over context-free languages, given as PDAs, Ganty and Majumdar [12] show an EXPSPACE upper bound for safety, termination, and boundedness. Their algorithm constructs for each handler a polynomial-size Petri net with certain guarantees (forming so-called *adequate family of Petri nets*) that accepts a Parikh equivalent language. These Petri nets are then used to construct a larger Petri net, polynomial in the size of the asynchronous program and the adequate family of Petri nets, in which safety, termination, or boundedness can be phrased as a query decidable in EXPSPACE.

A natural question is whether a downclosure-based algorithm matches the same complexity. We can replace the Parikh-equivalent Petri nets of [12] with Petri nets recognizing the downclosure of a language. It is an easy consequence of Proposition 1 that the resulting Petri nets can be used in place of the adequate families of Petri nets in the procedures for safety, termination, and boundedness of [12]. Unfortunately, a finite automaton for $\downarrow L$ may require exponentially many states in the PDA [4], so a naive approach gives a 2EXPSPACE algorithm.

In the full version of this paper, we show that that for each context-free language L, one can construct in polynomial time a 1-bounded Petri net accepting $\downarrow L$. (Recall that a 1-bounded Petri net if every reachable marking has at most one token in each place.) When used in the construction of [12], this matches the EXPSPACE upper bound for safety, termination, and boundedness verification.

As a byproduct, we get a simple direct construction of a finite automaton for $\downarrow L$ when L is given as a PDA. This is of independent interest because earlier constructions of $\downarrow L$ always start from a context-free grammar and produce (necessarily!) exponentially large NFAs [24,8,4]. The key observation is that the downclosure of the language of a PDA can be represented, after some simple modifications, as the language accepted by the PDA with a *bounded* stack.

References

1. Abdulla, P.A., Bouajjani, A., Jonsson, B.: On-the-fly analysis of systems with unbounded, lossy FIFO channels. In: Proceedings of the 10th International Conference on Computer Aided Verification (CAV 1998). pp. 305–318 (1998). https://doi.org/10.1007/BFb0028754

2. Aho, A.V.: Indexed grammars - an extension of context-free grammars. J. ACM **15**(4), 647–671 (1968). https://doi.org/10.1145/321479.321488

3. Atig, M.F., Bouajjani, A., Qadeer, S.: Context-bounded analysis for concurrent programs with dynamic creation of threads. In: Proceedings of TACAS 2009. pp. 107–123 (2009)

4. Bachmeier, G., Luttenberger, M., Schlund, M.: Finite automata for the sub- and superword closure of CFLs: Descriptional and computational complexity. In: Proceedings of LATA 2015. pp. 473–485 (2015)

5. Berstel, J.: Transductions and context-free languages. Teubner-Verlag (1979)

6. Chadha, R., Viswanathan, M.: Decidability results for well-structured transition systems with auxiliary storage. In: CONCUR '07: Proc. 18th Int. Conf. on Concurrency Theory. LNCS, vol. 4703, pp. 136–150. Springer (2007)

7. Clemente, L., Parys, P., Salvati, S., Walukiewicz, I.: The diagonal problem for higher-order recursion schemes is decidable. In: Proceedings of the 31st Annual ACM/IEEE Symposium on Logic in Computer Science, LICS '16, New York, NY, USA, July 5-8, 2016. pp. 96–105. ACM (2016). https://doi.org/10.1145/2933575.2934527

8. Courcelle, B.: On constructing obstruction sets of words. Bulletin of the EATCS **44**, 178–186 (1991)

9. Damm, W.: The IO-and OI-hierarchies. Theoretical Computer Science **20**(2), 95–207 (1982)

10. Damm, W., Goerdt, A.: An automata-theoretical characterization of the OI-hierarchy. Information and Control **71**(1), 1–32 (1986)

11. Dufourd, C., Finkel, A., Schnoebelen, P.: Reset nets between decidability and undecidability. In: Proceedings of ICALP 1998. pp. 103–115 (1998)

12. Ganty, P., Majumdar, R.: Algorithmic verification of asynchronous programs. ACM Transactions on Programming Languages and Systems (TOPLAS) **34**(1), 6 (2012)

13. Geeraerts, G., Raskin, J., Begin, L.V.: Well-structured languages. Acta Inf. **44**(3-4), 249–288 (2007). https://doi.org/10.1007/s00236-007-0050-3

14. Greibach, S.A.: Remarks on blind and partially blind one-way multi-counter machines. Theoretical Computer Science **7**(3), 311 – 324 (1978). https://doi.org/10.1016/0304-3975(78)90020-8

15. Hague, M., Kochems, J., Ong, C.L.: Unboundedness and downward closures of higher-order pushdown automata. In: POPL 2016: Principles of Programming Languages. pp. 151–163. ACM (2016)

16. Hague, M., Murawski, A.S., Ong, C.L., Serre, O.: Collapsible pushdown automata and recursion schemes. In: Proceedings of the Twenty-Third Annual IEEE Symposium on Logic in Computer Science, LICS 2008, 24-27 June 2008, Pittsburgh, PA, USA. pp. 452–461 (2008). https://doi.org/10.1109/LICS.2008.34

17. Haines, L.H.: On free monoids partially ordered by embedding. Journal of Combinatorial Theory **6**(1), 94–98 (1969)

18. Hopcroft, J.E., Motwani, R., Ullman, J.D.: Introduction to automata theory, languages, and computation, 3rd Edition. Pearson international edition, Addison-Wesley (2007)

19. Jantzen, M.: On the hierarchy of Petri net languages. RAIRO - Theoretical Informatics and Applications - Informatique Théorique et Applications **13**(1), 19–30 (1979), http://www.numdam.org/item?id=ITA_1979__13_1_19_0

20. Jhala, R., Majumdar, R.: Interprocedural analysis of asynchronous programs. In: POPL '07: Proc. 34th ACM SIGACT-SIGPLAN Symp. on Principles of Programming Languages. pp. 339–350. ACM Press (2007)

21. Kobayashi, N.: Types and higher-order recursion schemes for verification of higher-order programs. In: Proceedings of the 36th ACM SIGPLAN-SIGACT Symposium on Principles of Programming Languages, POPL 2009, Savannah, GA, USA, January 21-23, 2009. pp. 416–428 (2009). https://doi.org/10.1145/1480881.1480933

22. Kobayashi, N.: Inclusion between the frontier language of a non-deterministic recursive program scheme and the Dyck language is undecidable. Theoretical Computer Science **777**, 409–416 (2019)

23. Kobayashi, N., Ong, C.L.: Complexity of model checking recursion schemes for fragments of the modal mu-calculus. Logical Methods in Computer Science **7**(4) (2011)

24. van Leeuwen, J.: Effective constructions in well-partially-ordered free monoids. Discrete Mathematics **21**(3), 237–252 (1978). https://doi.org/10.1016/0012-365X(78)90156-5

25. Majumdar, R., Thinniyam, R.S., Zetzsche, G.: General decidability results for asynchronous shared-memory programs: Higher-order and beyond (2021), http://arxiv.org/abs/2101.08611

26. Maslov, A.: The hierarchy of indexed languages of an arbitrary level. Doklady Akademii Nauk **217**(5), 1013–1016 (1974)

27. Mayr, R.: Undecidable problems in unreliable computations. Theoretical Computer Science **297**(1-3), 337–354 (2003)

28. Ong, L.: Higher-order model checking: An overview. In: 30th Annual ACM/IEEE Symposium on Logic in Computer Science, LICS 2015, Kyoto, Japan, July 6-10, 2015. pp. 1–15 (2015). https://doi.org/10.1109/LICS.2015.9

29. Parys, P.: The complexity of the diagonal problem for recursion schemes. In: Proceedings of FSTTCS 2017. Leibniz International Proceedings in Informatics (LIPIcs), vol. 93, pp. 45:1–45:14 (2018)

30. Sen, K., Viswanathan, M.: Model checking multithreaded programs with asynchronous atomic methods. In: CAV '06: Proc. 18th Int. Conf. on Computer Aided Verification. LNCS, vol. 4144, pp. 300–314. Springer (2006)

31. Sipser, M.: Introduction to the theory of computation. PWS Publishing Company (1997)

32. Thinniyam, R.S., Zetzsche, G.: Regular separability and intersection emptiness are independent problems. In: Proceedings of FSTTCS 2019. Leibniz International Proceedings in Informatics (LIPIcs), vol. 150, pp. 51:1–51:15. Schloss Dagstuhl–Leibniz-Zentrum fuer Informatik, Dagstuhl, Germany (2019). https://doi.org/10.4230/LIPIcs.FSTTCS.2019.51

33. Zetzsche, G.: An approach to computing downward closures. In: ICALP 2015. vol. 9135, pp. 440–451. Springer (2015), the undecidability of Z intersection is shown in the full version: http://arxiv.org/abs/1503.01068

Author Index

Printed in the United States
by Baker & Taylor Publisher Services